HANDBOOK OF PERSONOLOGY
AND PSYCHOPATHOLOGY

HANDBOOK OF PERSONOLOGY AND PSYCHOPATHOLOGY

Edited by

Stephen Strack

WILEY

John Wiley & Sons, Inc.

This book is printed on acid-free paper. ∞

Published by John Wiley & Sons, Inc., Hoboken, New Jersey.
Published simultaneously in Canada.

This publication is designed to provide accurate and authoritative information in regard to the subject
matter covered. It is sold with the understanding that the publisher is not engaged in rendering professional
services. If legal, accounting, medical, psychological, or any other expert assistance is required, the services
of a competent professional person should be sought.

Designations used by companies to distinguish their products are often claimed as trademarks. In all
instances where John Wiley & Sons, Inc. is aware of a claim, the product names appear in initial capital or
all capital letters. Readers, however, should contact the appropriate companies for more complete
information regarding trademarks and registration.

For general information on our other products and services please contact our Customer Care
Department within the United States at (800) 762-2974, outside the United States at (317) 572-3993 or
fax (317) 572-4002.

Wiley also publishes its books in a variety of electronic formats. Some content that appears in print may
not be available in electronic books. For more information about Wiley products, visit our web site at
www.wiley.com.

Library of Congress Cataloging-in-Publication Data:

Handbook of personology and psychopathology / edited by Stephen Strack.
    p.   cm.
  Festschrift for Theodore Millon.
  Includes bibliographical references and index.
  ISBN 0-471-45907-0 (cloth)
  1. Personality disorders. 2. Personality. 3. Personality assessment. 4. Psychology,
Pathological. 5. Mental illness—Classification. 6. Millon, Theodore. I. Strack, Stephen. II.
Millon, Theodore.
  RC554.H366   2005
  616.85′81—dc22   2004042237

Printed in the United States of America.

10 9 8 7 6 5 4 3 2 1

This volume comprises essays written in honor of
Theodore Millon
Architect of, and advocate for, a comprehensive,
integrated science of personology and psychopathology
With admiration and gratitude from his students,
colleagues, and friends

"A lerer iz vi a boym vos trogt gute frukht"
(A teacher is like a tree that bears good fruit)

Contents —————————————————————————————

Part V   Treatment Issues

Part VI   Future Perspective

Preface

Recorded history informs us that as long as human beings have had free time to contemplate matters beyond those of basic survival, they have been acutely interested in understanding the nature of their own behavior. Early writers from Greece, for example, were impressed by numerous redundancies among people of the same and different cultures, but they also noted specific abnormalities as well as systematic differences between groups and individuals. In trying to grasp the nature of these similarities, differences, and abnormalities, early personologists (e.g., Heraclitus, Socrates, Hippocrates, Aristotle, Galen) created theories that explained human behavior as a function of ethereal manipulation, social pressures, personal choices, and physical characteristics such as the quantity of fluids or "humors" in the body (Durant, 1939; Hergenhahn, 1992; Russell, 1945).

Progress in understanding human behavior from a scientific perspective took a giant leap forward following Darwin's (1859) work on the evolution of species. Although Darwin did not elaborate on the origin of group and individual differences at the phenotypic level, his contemporaries and followers (e.g., Galton, Helmholtz, Wundt, James) helped create the fledgling science of psychology from philosophy as the study of human behavior. In the late nineteenth and early twentieth centuries, scientific and technological advances helped psychologists develop complex explanations for behavior as stemming from a mixture of evolutionary, biological, social, and personal variables (Goodwin, 1998; Koch & Leary, 1992).

Based on his training in neurology, clinical observations of neurotic patients, and appreciation of Darwinian theory, Sigmund Freud (1895/1966, 1915/1957) sought to develop a comprehensive model of normal and abnormal human behavior based on neurological evolution. Although many aspects of Freud's neurobiological model did not take hold among his contemporaries, his method of understanding behavior from a psychodynamic perspective did, and later spawned rival paradigms that viewed behavior as stemming from social, familial, interpersonal, cognitive, and learning factors (e.g., Freud, 1923/1961; Goodwin, 1998; Hergenhahn, 1992).

Like Darwin, Freud provided ideas that allowed people from many disciplines to discuss human behavior from a completely new viewpoint. Freud could explain normal as well as abnormal behavior, and he could treat people with a variety of ailments using his psychoanalytic methods. However, his ideas seemed to explain some behaviors better than others; he lacked a comprehensive taxonomy; and he discouraged experimental validation.

The study of human behavior went in many directions after Freud. Gordon Allport (1937) and Henry Murray (1938) developed a science of personology that was independent of abnormal behavior. Psychiatry continued to be influenced by psychodynamic thinkers like Fenichel (1945) and Reich (1949) but never lost its focus on taxonomy and the biological observations of those such as Kraepelin (1904), Bleuler (1924), Kretschmer (1925), and Jaspers (1948).

World War II shifted the heart of science to the United States and to theories that could explain behavior from sociocultural and interpersonal perspectives (e.g., Horney, Fromm, Sullivan). Another consequence of WW II was the proliferation of nonmedically trained mental health practitioners, particularly clinical psychologists, who helped shape the future of mental health theory and treatment.

By the last quarter of the twentieth century, students of human behavior could pick from dozens of theories that explained various forms of normal and abnormal functioning from intrapsychic, biological, behavioral, interpersonal, phenomenological, and sociocultural perspectives (Hall & Lindzey, 1979). Too often these theories focused on specific phenomena or global aspects of functioning, normal or abnormal behavior, and either etiology or treatment of dysfunction. In many ways, the person got lost in an effort to explain behavioral details or outside shaping forces.

Renewed interest in the interface between normal and abnormal behavior, personology and psychopathology was ushered in by the atheoretical and multiaxial format of the third edition of the *Diagnostic and Statistical Manual of Mental Disorders* (*DSM-III;* American Psychiatric Association, 1980). For the first time, psychiatric pathology was separated from specific etiology (e.g., psychodynamics) as well as from personality, medical illness, and psychosocial stressors. Mental health practitioners were asked to consider the pathology they were treating from whatever vantage point they felt was appropriate, and in the context of the whole person.

Just as Darwin and Freud had galvanized the attention of scientists from many walks of life and created a flurry of new ideas and research, *DSM-III* radically changed the way behavioral scientists conducted themselves in the clinic and laboratory. They started examining the interface between normal and abnormal behavior, questioned the need for separate theories that focused on symptoms outside the scope of personality or health beyond the scope of pathology, and helped people begin to see the similarities in theories that previously seemed different. The hope of integrating ideas about the nature of human development, personality functioning, psychopathology, and treatment is again pushing through. People from different disciplines and schools of thought are now working toward a comprehensive, biopsychosocial understanding of normal and abnormal behavior that can encompass, or be compatible with, the many perspectives that have shown promise in the past, including biological, psychodynamic, sociocultural, and interpersonal (Strack & Lorr, 1994).

At the beginning of the twenty-first century, the study of personology and psychopathology has moved beyond the confines of the *DSM* (Livesley, 2001). The *DSM* model does not offer an empirically based taxonomy, and it has kept its categorical distinction between normality and pathology in the face of scientific evidence that argues against this. But just as contemporary personologists have moved away from atheoretical, dualistic conceptions of human behavior, they no longer expect a single model of behavior to encompass the vast array of human features, both normal and abnormal. There is greater tolerance for, and interest in, dimensional conceptualizations of personality and psychopathology that have empirical backing, as well as models that predict and demonstrate discontinuity in some behaviors and disorders.

A welcome addition to contemporary thinking is the idea of integration without the need for procrustean solutions to areas of disagreement (Livesley, 1995, 2001; Millon, 1990). This is perhaps best represented in the realm of psychotherapy. Psychological observers were aware of the similarities between different therapeutic modalities as early as the 1930s (e.g., Rosenzweig, 1936), but until proponents of various schools could boast empirical validation during the past several years, there did not seem to be enough common ground for practitioners to admit the obvious. Of course, integrating commonalities at a theoretical level is not as easy as noting conceptual similarities (Gold, 1996).

Among active theorists, perhaps none is more exemplary of the current effort to bring together knowledge of normal and abnormal human development than Theodore Millon. As early as 1969 (Millon, 1969/1983) he was advocating for the integration of various perspectives on personality and psychopathology in the interest of understanding personality disorders. His goal was to move beyond then current conceptions of behavior that focused on specific aspects of human functioning without reference to the whole person, to create a theory-driven system for understanding human behavior at the personologic level that would draw on the best ideas from psychology and adjacent disciplines. His thinking was based on the idea that "persons" are the only organically integrated system in the psychological domain, evolved through the millennia and inherently created as natural entities rather than culture-bound and experience-derived gestalts (Millon, 1999, 2003).

Coining the term *psychosynergy* for his effort, Millon (1999) has labored for over 35 years to resynthesize and integrate science, theory, classification, assessment, and therapy so that we will have a coherent system for understanding how people develop and live their lives, that is, think, feel, behave, love, work, relate, become ill, and get well.

This *Handbook* was conceived and developed by its contributors as an overview of the science of personology and psychopathology in recognition of the central—indeed seminal—role played by Theodore Millon in shaping the field as it exists today. A *Festschrift*, the volume is divided into six parts that reflect Millon's blueprint for a clinical science: First, conceptual issues (Part I) are reviewed that help define the boundaries of theoretical models (Part II) designed to provide coherent, empirically supportable propositions that can then lead to coherent taxonomies and classification systems (Part III). The value of assessment methods (Part IV) can be gauged based on how well they operationalize the theory-derived classification systems that precede them. In Part V, there is a review of therapeutic techniques that were derived from coherent theories and taxonomies and integrated with appropriate assessment methods. Finally, in Part VI, there is a review of future perspectives.

In preparing their chapters, authors were asked to write for the growing number of mental health clinicians, researchers, and students who want to know about current directions in the field of personology and psychopathology, but who may be unfamiliar with some concepts and methods. In addition to providing an overview of their particular area of expertise, authors were asked to stretch themselves to help bridge existing gaps and to suggest avenues for future inquiry.

Theodore Millon's (2003) dream of an integrated clinical science is far-reaching and ambitious, but it is not complete. The process of synthesis and integration must continue in order to yield the end result that he envisions: a multidisciplinary system founded on the universal laws of nature that coordinates psychological theory, a derivable taxonomic classification, a series of operational assessment tools, and a flexible yet integrated group of remediation techniques.

Until the last quarter of the twentieth century, traditional boundaries kept most researchers and clinicians within academic or applied frameworks, within the scope of normality or pathology, focusing on limited aspects of human behavior. Because of progress in defining the basic structures of personality and psychopathology, we are now seeing cross-fertilization and a willingness to expand existing models and methods across traditional lines. The current scene is marked by enthusiasm and hope for a better grasp of how all people function as personologic entities. The chapters that follow provide ample food for thought. This book both informs readers of the array of ideas and findings in the area of personology and psychopathology and inspires new opinions and avenues for inquiry.

Stephen Strack

Los Angeles, CA
June 2004

REFERENCES

Allport, G. (1937). *Personality: A psychological interpretation.* New York: Henry Holt.

American Psychiatric Association. (1980). *Diagnostic and statistical manual of mental disorders* (3rd ed.). Washington, DC: Author.

Bleuler, E. (1924). *Textbook of psychiatry.* New York: Macmillan.

Darwin, C. R. (1859). *On the origin of species by means of natural selection.* London: Murray.

Durant, W. (1939). *The story of civilization: Part II. The life of Greece.* New York: Simon & Schuster.

Fenichel, O. (1945). *The psychoanalytic theory of neurosis.* New York: Norton.

Freud, S. (1957). Instincts and their vicissitudes. In J. Strachey (Ed. & Trans.), *The standard edition of the complete psychological works of Sigmund Freud* (Vol. 14, pp. 117–140). London: Hogarth Press. (Original work published 1915)

Freud, S. (1961). The ego and the id. In J. Strachey (Ed. & Trans.), *The standard edition of the complete psychological works of Sigmund Freud* (Vol. 19, pp. 1–66). London: Hogarth Press. (Original work published 1923)

Freud, S. (1966). Project for a scientific psychology. In J. Strachey (Ed. & Trans.), *The standard edition of the complete psychological works of Sigmund Freud* (Vol. 1, pp. 281–397). London: Hogarth Press. (Original work published 1895)

Gold, J. (1996). *Key concepts in psychotherapy integration.* New York: Plenum Press.

Goodwin, C. J. (1998). *A history of modern psychology.* New York: Wiley.

Hall, C. S., & Lindzey, G. (1979). *Theories of personality* (3rd ed.). New York: Wiley.

Hergenhahn, B. R. (1992). *An introduction to the history of psychology* (2nd ed.). Belmont, CA: Wadsworth.

Jaspers, K. (1948). *General psychopathology.* London: Oxford University Press.

Koch, S., & Leary, D. E. (Eds.). (1992). *A century of psychology as science.* Washington, DC: American Psychological Association.

Kraepelin, E. (1904). *Lectures on clinical psychiatry.* New York: Wood.

Kretschmer, E. (1925). *Physique and character.* New York: Harcourt Brace.

Livesley, W. J. (Ed.). (1995). *The DSM-IV personality disorders.* New York: Guilford Press.

Livesley, W. J. (Ed.). (2001). *Handbook of personality disorders.* New York: Guilford Press.

Millon, T. (1983). *Modern psychopathology.* Prospect Heights, IL: Waveland Press. (Original work published 1969)

Millon, T. (1990). *Toward a new personology: An evolutionary model.* New York: Wiley.

Millon, T. (1999). Reflections on psychosynergy: A model for integrating science, theory, classification, assessment, and therapy. *Journal of Personality Assessment, 72,* 437–456.

Millon, T. (2003). It's time to rework the blueprints: Building a science for clinical psychology. *American Psychologist, 58,* 949–961.

Murray, H. A. (1938). *Explorations in personality.* New York: Oxford University Press.

Reich, W. (1949). *Character analysis* (3rd ed.). New York: Farrar, Straus and Giroux.

Rosenzweig, S. (1936). Some implicit common factors in diverse methods of psychotherapy. *American Journal of Orthopsychiatry, 6,* 412–415.

Russell, B. (1945). *A history of Western philosophy.* New York: Simon & Schuster.

Strack, S., & Lorr, M. (Eds.). (1994). *Differentiating normal and abnormal personality.* New York: Springer.

Contributors

Michael H. Antoni, PhD
Department of Psychology
University of Miami
Coral Gables, Florida

Aaron T. Beck, MD
Department of Psychiatry
University of Pennsylvania
Philadelphia, Pennsylvania

Judith Beck, PhD
Beck Institute
Bala Cynwyd, Pennsylvania

Lorna Smith Benjamin, PhD
Department of Psychology
University of Utah
Salt Lake City, Utah

David P. Bernstein, PhD
Department of Psychology
Fordham University
Bronx, New York

Ronald Blackburn, MA, MSc, PhD,
CPsychol, FBPsS
Department of Clinical Psychology
University of Liverpool
Liverpool
United Kingdom

Roger K. Blashfield, PhD
Department of Psychology
Auburn University
Auburn, Alabama

Neil Bockian, PhD
Illinois School of Professional Psychology
Chicago, Illinois

Robert F. Bornstein, PhD
Department of Psychology
Gettysburg College
Gettysburg, Pennsylvania

Rebekah Bradley, PhD
Psychological Center
Emory University
Atlanta, Georgia

Paul T. Costa Jr., PhD
National Institute on Aging
Baltimore, Maryland

Jan Derksen, PhD
Department of Clinical Psychology
University of Nijmegen
Nijmegen
The Netherlands

Darwin Dorr, PhD
Department of Psychology
Wichita State University
Wichita, Kansas

George S. Everly Jr., PhD
Loyola College–Maryland
Johns Hopkins University
Baltimore, Maryland

Elizabeth H. Flanagan, PhD
Department of Psychology
Yale University
New Haven, Connecticut

Jerry Gold, PhD, ABPP
Derner Institute of Advanced
    Psychological Studies
Adelphi University
Garden City, New York

Adolf Grünbaum, PhD
Andrew Mellon Professor of Philosophy of
    Science
University of Pittsburgh
Pittsburgh, Pennsylvania

Clyde Hendrick, PhD
Department of Psychology
Texas Tech University
Lubbock, Texas

Leonard M. Horowitz, PhD
Department of Psychology
Stanford University
Stanford, California

Aubrey Immelman, PhD
Department of Psychology
St. John's University
Collegeville, Minnesota

Kerry L. Jang, MD
Department of Psychiatry
University of British Columbia
Vancouver, British Columbia
Canada

Otto F. Kernberg, MD
Personality Disorders Institute
Weill Cornell Medical College
White Plains, New York

Robert L. Leahy, PhD
American Institute for Cognitive Therapy
New York, New York

W. John Livesley, MD, PhD
Department of Psychiatry
University of British Columbia
Vancouver, British Columbia
Canada

**Jeffrey J. Magnavita, PhD, ABPP,
    FAPA**
Glastonbury Medical Arts Center
Glastonbury, Connecticut

Robert R. McCrae, PhD
National Institute on Aging
Baltimore, Maryland

Theodore Millon, PhD, DSc
Institute for Advanced Studies in
    Personology and Psychopathology
Coral Gables, Florida

Joel Paris, MD
Department of Psychiatry
McGill University
Montreal, Quebec
Canada

Aaron L. Pincus, PhD
Department of Psychology
Pennsylvania State University
University Park, Pennsylvania

Melvin Sabshin, MD
Emeritus Professor
University of Illinois
Chicago, Illinois

Marshall L. Silverstein, PhD
Department of Psychology
Long Island University
Brookville, New York

Erik Simonsen, MD
Institute of Personality Theory and
    Psychopathology
Roskilde
Denmark

Hedwig Sloore, PhD
Department of Personality and Social
    Psychology
Free University of Brussels
Brussels
Belgium

Stephen Strack, PhD
Psychology Service
U.S. Department of Veterans Affairs
Los Angeles, California

Irving B. Weiner, PhD
Department of Psychiatry and Behavioral
    Medicine
University of South Florida
Tampa, Florida

Drew Westen, PhD
Departments of Psychology and Psychiatry
    and Behavioral Sciences
Emory University
Atlanta, Georgia

Kelly R. Wilson, MA
Department of Psychology
Stanford University
Stanford, California

PART I

Conceptual Issues

Chapter 1 ──────────────────────────────

EVOLUTION AS A FOUNDATION FOR PSYCHOLOGICAL THEORIES

CLYDE HENDRICK

Charles Darwin's (1859) *Origin of Species* was published a few years before the emergence of psychology as a scientific discipline. One would expect that the theory of evolution would have had a major impact on shaping psychology. Clearly, there was some impact, but the history of evolutionary thinking in psychology is very complex, even convoluted, and a definitive history has not been written. Until recently, the major impact of evolution on psychology was through the genetic/heredity route, although there were also some influences on behavioral theories in psychology developed during the past century.

One reason for the complexity of the story of evolution in psychology is the complexity of the story of evolution in biology. Evolution by natural selection had no proximal explanatory mechanism for about 50 years, until the concept of the gene was well established. The mix of genes and natural selection was supposed to provide a "grand synthesis" for biology. However, to a considerable extent, the study of genetics has remained a discipline separate from other facets of evolutionary biology, especially behavioral biology. That same separation is manifest in psychology. To a considerable extent, behavioral genetics is a discipline apart from the more recent development of evolutionary psychology.

This chapter chronicles and remains faithful to the complexity of the main areas of contact between evolution and psychology. The first section provides a brief history of some of the connections between evolution and psychology since Darwin. Before tackling evolution and modern psychology, it is useful to examine evolutionary biology briefly, the task of the second major section. We will see that the reigning paradigm for a quarter-century did try to trace a direct sequence from controlling gene all the way to complex social behavior. There were many theoretical arguments in evolutionary biology. Two issues are surveyed to give the flavor of the controversies: the unit of selection and the evolution of sex. As we will see, evolutionary biology is in a continuing state of conceptual flux.

Against this background, current work in evolution and psychology is described under the two broad categories in which such work is done: behavioral genetics and evolutionary psychology. Behavioral genetics will not make sense to most people without a minimal understanding of basic genetics. Thus, a tutorial section, "Molecular Genetics and Evolution," precedes the section on behavioral genetics.

EVOLUTION AND PSYCHOLOGY: A BRIEF HISTORY

One line of thinking views evolution as permeating psychology from its beginning. Another view is that the major impact of evolutionary thinking is quite recent, occurring perhaps only 25 years or so ago.

In favor of the first view, Kimble and Wertheimer (1998) named Darwin as one of the top 20 psychologists of all time. Masterson (1998) referred to Darwin as the "father of evolutionary psychology," noting a chapter on instinct in *Origins*. Further, Darwin's *Expressions of Emotions in Man and Animals* (1872) clearly is of psychological interest, as is *The Descent of Man, and Selection in Relation to Sex* (1871/1981). An interesting volume on evolutionary thought in the United States, edited by Persons (1950), included an extensive chapter by E. G. Boring (1950). As Boring noted, Galton's (1869) volume on the inheritance of genius stimulated an interest in individual differences and, indirectly, psychological testing. Although Germany had the most influence on the creation of experimental psychology in the United States, people such as William James and John Dewey were tremendously influenced by Darwin. In fact, Boring claimed that evolution permeated the development of functional psychology and pragmatism. Evolution also influenced the development of comparative psychology. The notion of evolution of mind became common currency, a theme strongly echoed in somewhat modern form by Kantor (1935).

Other interesting sources on the relations between psychology and evolution include Gruber (1998), Alexander (1992), and Glickman (1992). A fascinating article by Dewsbury (2002) described the "Chicago Five," eminent psychologists trained under Karl Lashley at the University of Chicago from 1929 to1935: Norman Maier, Theodore Schneirla, Frank Beach, Donald Hebb, and Krechevsky (later David Krech). Dewsbury discussed nine guiding principles loosely held by the Chicago Five. Almost all of the principles have an evolutionary halo. The two most explicit are numbers 4 and 8:

> 4. Understanding the evolution of mind and behavior in general and its emergent characteristics in particular, is important to psychology.
> 8. Behavioral development is an epigenetic process resulting from the continuous, dynamic interaction of genes, environment, and organisms. (pp. 25, 28)

The notion of epigenesis is a contentious issue in some areas of evolutionary biology (see Markos, 2002, for a history of the concept of epigenesis). The current strong emphasis on molecular biology tends to deify "the gene." Biologists who work with whole organisms, especially developmental biologists, are more likely to lean toward an epigenetic approach.

The second view of evolution in psychology is that the influence of evolutionary thinking had little impact until E. O. Wilson's (1975) *Sociobiology*. This controversial volume soon stimulated a huge literature (e.g., see Crawford, 1989; Crawford & Anderson, 1989; Crawford, Smith, & Krebs, 1987).

Despite the richness of literature noted above for the first view, my own impressionistic view is that after the onset of Watson's behaviorism early in the twentieth century, psychology had a long dry spell of environmentalism, with the charge led primarily by several decades of learning theory. To test such impressions, I consulted the PsychINFO database for citation counts of several terms. The term "evolutionary theory" appeared in the database 638 times (as of February 5, 2003). From the beginning in 1887 through 1980, evolutionary theory appeared only 77 times. The pace picked up from 1981 to 1990 (132 times). From 1991 to February 2003, the term appeared 428 times. Clearly, the interest in evolutionary theory has grown strongly in psychological literature, particularly over the past dozen years.

Other terms give a fuller picture. Psychologists were very interested in genetics; this term appeared 15,860 times. "Evolution" appeared 18,614 times, but the number doesn't mean much because evolution is also used generically for change of any kind. Psychologists were relatively interested in sociobiology; the term appeared 735 times, more than for evolutionary theory. It seems clear that evolution is of rapidly growing interest in many areas of psychology and will increasingly affect psychological theorizing. In fact, it already has; the term "evolutionary psychology" appears to have been coined only in the 1980s (e.g., Tooby, 1988).

There are many ways that evolutionary concepts may affect psychological theorizing. In fact, there will undoubtedly be much fragmentation in conceptual approaches over the next several years. Why? Because the various disciplines that form evolutionary biology are in fractious disagreement, ranging from the role of the gene to the place of the ecological habitat in evolution. Before focusing on psychology, it will be useful to make a modest excursion into biology.

EVOLUTIONARY BIOLOGY: A BRIEF EXCURSION

The Reigning Paradigm

As is famously known, Darwin had no mechanism to explain how natural selection led to species formation and change over time. He was unaware of Mendel's experiments, and it was well into the twentieth century before genetics was joined with natural selection. During the 1930s, several volumes were published connecting genetics to Darwinian evolution, culminating in Dobzhansky's (1937) *Genetics and The Origin of Species,* the defining volume of what was named the neo-Darwinian synthesis (Fisher, 1991). During the 1950s, molecular biology developed strongly, beginning with the discovery of the double helix form of the genome (Watson & Crick, 1953). Molecular biology gradually became a dominant intellectual force in the study of evolution. For biologists who viewed everything about an organism as under genetic control, evolution could be simply defined as relative change in gene frequency within a population over time. The processes for genetic change include gene mutation, genetic drift, migration of organisms across populations, and natural selection (construed as differential reproduction). Natural selection is by far the most important process for evolutionary change, according to most evolutionary biologists. Differential reproduction goes hand in hand with better adaptations in the environment in which selection occurs.

During the 1960s, a spate of theorizing about behavior and evolution (especially social behavior) occurred, stimulated by Hamilton's (1964a, 1964b) pair of articles on the genetical evolution of social behavior. His concept of inclusive fitness allowed limited altruism toward genetic relatives, in addition to one's own children. These relatives also carry some portion of one's genes. So, genes may be propagated both by direct descendants and indirectly by other genetic relatives.

Following Hamilton's papers, a flood of writing on social behavior occurred. Some of the more important work included the parental investment model (Trivers, 1972), evolution of reciprocal altruism (Trivers, 1971), parent-offspring conflict (e.g., Alexander, 1974), evolution of deception strategies (Alexander, 1974; Trivers, 1971), and the evolution of sexuality (Symons, 1979). This sequence of thought that traces a linear trend from the controlling gene to social behavior might be called the "hard-line" approach to the evolution of social behavior. Loosely construed, this approach is the "standard model" for behavioral evolution. This hard-line approach is, by and large, the set of assumptions for what became evolutionary psychology.

There have always been dissents from and questions about the standard model of organismic evolution. Two illustrations (from many possible ones) are discussed briefly: the unit of selection and the issue of why sexual reproduction evolved.

What Is the Unit of Selection?

The unit of selection is a time-honored debate in biology, a debate that is far from closure. For most of the era since Darwin, biologists considered the group, or perhaps the species, as the unit for which evolution selected. One main reason for this assumption was the existence of sexual reproduction. In a sense, sex is costly to the individual because only 50% of the genes are passed on. So sex must be for the benefit of the species, or group, because it speeds up the evolutionary process, presumably leading to ever better adaptations. An extreme version of group selection views a set of behaviors as benefiting the group (altruism) without any benefit to the individual (e.g., see Wynne-Edwards, 1962). After a few years, group selection theory was severely criticized. Although most biologists would allow for some kinds of group or kin selection, they were not viewed as important forces in evolution (e.g., Ridley, 1996).

In a very influential book, Williams (1966) argued for the individual organism as the basic unit of selection, with the gene as the underlying basis for that selection. The "unit" organism is basically selfish, although altruistic behavior is recognized. Much ink has been spilled over how evolution produces altruism out of the selfish organism. Dawkins (1976) skirted this issue by claiming the "selfish gene" as the basic unit of selection. Dawkins received much criticism for his view (see Stove, 1992, for a particularly pungent critique). It soon became clear, however, that Dawkins was using "gene" as an abstract concept to designate the unit that replicates. Dawkins (1982) made clear that any part of a chromosome, large or small, could serve as a replicator. The concept of replicator in turn spawned its own literature (e.g., see Richards, 2002). A good review is given by Godfrey-Smith (2000).

Waller (1999) proposed a more extreme version of Dawkins's idea. Waller argued that the gene is not the unit of selection. Rather, the part of the genome concerned with reproduction is the basic unit of selection. It is assumed that these sexual reproduction genes (SRGs) are carried by the most successful members of a breeding group. Variation in genetic diversity provides SRGs the best prospects for future replication. The individual organism counts for nothing in this approach:

> Proportionate transfers of parental genetic material have no relevance whatsoever. The fundamental effect of sexual reproduction is the perpetuation of SRGs. Individuals are puppets, not puppeteers. (p. 9)

One might suppose that SRGs are well-defined molecular units on a chromosome. Kimura (1983) developed a neutral theory of molecular evolution that argued that at the molecular level changes are random and more or less cancel out. Positive Darwinian selection must operate at a higher level, presumably at the organismic level. Neutral theory generated an explosion of literature. Current thinking appears to be that there can be non-neutral molecular evolution, but its nature is far from clear (e.g., Golding, 1994).

Among biologists, one can note a trend toward broader thinking, even as molecular biology continues to make great strides. Harold (2001), a cell biologist, tried to mediate between the extremes of molecularism and holism inherent in evolutionary and ecological biology. That mediating link is the cell. In a pithy chapter title, Harold (p. 99) made the important point that "it takes a cell to make a cell," suggesting that the minimal unit that makes sense as life is the cell.

Even a hard-line biologist such as Maynard Smith (1998) has softened his original position. He argued that we need to consider both developmental genetics and the holistic tradition of self-organization with the complex behavior patterns that can emerge from dynamical systems. We must "pay attention to dynamical processes as well as to genetic control" (p. 2). Still more extreme, Avital and Jablonka (2000) argued that selection at the level of genes is not sufficient to account for behavior. Evolutionary explanations must take into account the transmission of learning across generations. Thus, the authors argue for a behavioral inheritance system as an addendum to Darwinism evolution.

The question of the unit of selection has not yet been answered. D. S. Wilson (2001) titled his review of L. Keller's (1999) edited volume on levels of selection "Evolutionary Biology: Struggling to Escape Exclusively Individual Selection." Many other volumes have been written on the issue of selection during the past two decades, with no resolution in sight. The concept of the gene has become equally nebulous. In an edited volume, Beurton, Falk, and Rheinberger (2000) presented many varied conceptions of the gene, so many, in fact, that Griffiths (2002) titled his review of the volume "Lost: One Gene Concept. Reward to Finder." We must conclude that currently there is no consensus on what the unit of selection might be, and there is confusion about the nature of "the gene." This lack of closure should be kept in mind when we examine possible contributions of evolution to psychological theory.

Evolution of Sex

When Williams (1966) and others settled on the individual as the unit of selection, sexual reproduction immediately became a problem. Why? In the backhanded language of biologists, sex is "expensive," relative to asexual reproduction (e.g., Lewis, 1987). First, as noted previously, a sexual individual can pass on only 50% of its genetic material to its offspring. Second, the mixing of two gametes may easily lead to bad outcomes. Third, finding a suitable mate, reproducing, and caring for the young is very effortful. If genes are truly selfish, one would expect asexual reproduction to be more common.

A large literature was soon generated attempting to account for why sexual reproduction evolved. Williams (1975) presented several possible models; Maynard Smith (1978) also described a diverse set of models. No single model fully satisfied theorists (e.g., see Ghiselin, 1988), and by the 1990s, 20 different theories had been proposed to account for the evolution of sex (Fehr, 2001).

Three concepts are crucial in conceptualizing sex: genetic recombination, reproduction of offspring (or replication), and gender (Stearns, 1987). Recombination is not an automatic part of reproduction. "The production of offspring can occur sexually or asexually, with or without recombination" (Stearns, 1987, p. 16). For species with differing genders, gender "is the principal consequence of a history of sexual selection" (p. 17).

Sexual reproduction is viewed as an important adaptation by biologists. But exactly what its adaptive significance is no one can yet say. "No one has yet given a convincing, single-generation, micro-evolutionary and experimental demonstration of the advantages of sex, which must nevertheless exist" (Stearns, 1987, pp. 26–27). Space precludes discussion of the many advantages theorized for sex. However, for each advantage, a disadvantage can be proposed. Some excellent readings are included in edited volumes by Abramson and Pinkerton (1995), Michod and Levin (1988), and Stearns (1987). One interesting theory of sex evolution, the parasite hypothesis, is explored in fascinating detail by the science writer Matt Ridley (e.g., 1993a, 1993b).

Despite the fact that biologists cannot yet explain why sex is an evolved adaptation, many writers nevertheless focus on reproduction as the overwhelming fact of life. For example, "Reproduction is the sole goal for which human beings are designed; everything else is a means to that end" (Ridley, 1993b, p. 4). Although not usually so boldly stated, this assumption is one major cornerstone of the new discipline of evolutionary psychology (e.g., Buss, 1999; Kenrick & Trost, 1989; Kirkpatrick, 1998).

We should tread carefully in accepting this assumption as fact. We should remember the "costs" of sexual reproduction. Taking the classic view of genes as relatively discrete units, the major cost of mating is that only half of our remaining genes will be passed on in each succeeding generation. Assuming mating as a random process over generations, in only 25 human generations (about 500 years) only 0.5^{25} of our genes would remain in our descendants, a very small fraction indeed! The notion of "genetic immortality" through one's genes is a cultural myth (e.g., Hendrick, 2002). On the other hand, if we were bacteria, undergoing cell division every 20 minutes, we would soon have (assuming no mutations) 2^{25} copies of ourselves, or about 33 million genetic replicas. If we lust for genetic immortality, asexual reproduction is clearly the way to go. The notion of selfish genes and related ideas of replicators need serious rethinking. There is nothing wrong with some anthropomorphism: It can stimulate new ideas. But when we project such thinking to the molecular level, we are easily led astray, especially when such thinking is projected back to the everyday level of human life.

As these two excursions on units of selection and the evolution of sexuality make clear, evolutionary biology is in a state of continuous theoretical ferment and change. That is good for biology; disciplines must grow and change or become moribund. Such continuous change, however, can become a problem for a borrowing discipline such as psychology. To not fixate at a certain level of conceptual development in biology, psychologists must stay abreast of the ongoing changes in biological knowledge. To do so is extremely difficult, and the process may transform psychology into something other than what it is now. Whether such transformation is good or bad is ultimately a question of values.

EVOLUTIONARY IDEAS AND MODERN PSYCHOLOGY

I noted previously that genetics appeared in the PsychINFO database over 15,000 times. Clearly, psychology has historically had a keen interest in genetics, inheritance, and the like over the past century. Most of this interest has little to do with evolution per se; rather, the interest stems from possible heritability of behavioral patterns such as criminality, retardation, and mental illness.

The section that follows provides an overview of genetics and evolution; the second section deals with behavioral genetics; and the third section gives an overview of evolutionary psychology.

Molecular Genetics and Evolution

According to E. F. Keller (2000), the terms "genetics" and "gene" were coined in 1906 and 1909, respectively. At first, the gene was only a hypothetical entity, but by the

1930s it had become a material, fixed entity in the minds of most biologists. People, including scientists, tend to attribute powerful, even magical properties to unseen entities, relative to mundane, everyday visible reality. So it was with the gene. In time, the gene became the sole basis for heredity, and even the unfolding of life itself, from the fertilized egg to mature organism. The discovery of the double helix of DNA in 1953 finally gave material proof of the gene's reality, and the gene became the foundation concept for biology. However, the very success of molecular biology during the second half of the twentieth century gradually undermined the solid materiality of the discrete gene. The gene became a lot more complicated with respect to its structure, and in its relation to evolution.

Classic work in evolution distinguished between the concept of a genotype (the underlying genetic structure specified by gene pairs across chromosomal loci) and phenotype (the phenomenal manifestation of genotype and environmental influences in the actual organism). According to Schuster (2003):

> The success and efficiency of Darwinian evolution is based on a dichotomy of genotype and phenotype: The former is the object under variation; whereas, the latter constitutes the target of selection. (p. 163)

Further, "Genotype-phenotype relations are highly complex and hence variation and selection are uncorrelated" (p. 163). This presumed lack of correlation has allowed molecular biologists to focus primarily on genetic structure and function, and evolutionary psychologists to focus primarily on presumed mechanisms of behavioral evolution.

However, as hinted above, the discrete gene has morphed into a more complicated system. First, not all genes code, but genes that do code (i.e., DNA) mostly code for amino acids; amino acids in turn create proteins, some of which serve as enzymes that provide feedback and repair of DNA sequences that keep the process going in a complex, circular fashion. Ultimately, the entire cell is involved in the maintenance of genetic structure and function. Perhaps Harold (2001) was correct; perhaps the cell must be taken as the primary conceptual unit for the study of molecular evolutionary processes, a proposition with which E. F. Keller (2000) agreed.

Darwin was mostly interested in biological change. Perhaps even more remarkable than change is the stability of a phenotype over long periods. What accounts for such stability, and how much instability is needed for evolutionary processes to work? Instability (or mutability) itself appears to be genetically regulated. Stability and mutability are both equally at the mercy of enzymatic processes. This delicate balance itself is under cellular regulation, and that balance can change in response to changes in the cellular environment (Radman, 1999).

This kind of thinking is far removed from the idea of the gene as a stable molecule, subject only to occasional mutations. This cellular complexity better fits the pattern of nonlinear dynamical systems (Crutchfield & Schuster, 2003), a conceptual approach increasingly evident in biology. Further, given the idea of neutral evolution noted previously (Kimura, 1983), it is clear that most genetic change does not result in any direct phenotype change (i.e., the two are relatively independent). Genotypes vary constantly, usually in small ways, yet the phenotype remains true to type over long periods.

An interesting demonstration of genotype/phenotype independence was reported by Papadopoulos et al. (1999) across 10,000 generations of the bacterium *E. coli:*

> As has often been suggested, but not previously shown by experiment, the rates of phenotypic and genomic change were discordant, both across replicate populations and over time within a population. (p. 3807)

Genomic change was ongoing and relatively continuous, whereas phenotypic attributes (e.g., cell size) evolved much more slowly and in a discontinuous fashion. Another comparable experiment (Elena, Cooper, & Lenski, 1996), using 3,000 generations of *E. coli,* found that evolution of increased cell size followed an abrupt step function during the first 1,500 generations, after which size remained stable for the next 1,500 generations. Apparently, many small genetic changes accumulate over generations until such change hits a critical point, resulting in a sudden, nonlinear shift in some feature of the phenotype. On a large scale, this kind of species change might account for the (then) controversial concept of punctuated equilibria in species evolution proposed by Gould and Eldredge (1977). A later summary review (Gould & Eldredge, 1993) indicated that punctuated equilibrium is now widely accepted.

E. F. Keller (2000) suggested that, given the dynamic conjunction of stability and mutagenesis, living beings may have evolved second-order mechanisms to ensure their continued evolvability. If so, mutagenesis itself would have been positively selected (Radman, 1999; Radman, Matic, & Taddei, 1999). Evolvability is a dramatic concept (an excellent brief overview is provided by West-Eberhard, 1998). In fact, Keller declared evolvability as "molecular biology's challenge to neo-Darwinism" (p. 36). Other theorists agree (e.g., Gerhart & Kirschner, 1997; Kirschner & Gerhart, 1998; Shapiro, 1999). One interesting consequence of evolvability is that the concept "strongly implies the operation of selection on levels higher than the gene, and higher even than the individual organism" (Keller, 2000, p. 38). Natural selection may not be about reproduction per se, but about reproduction only insofar as it contributes to species evolvability. This notion is, of course, very contentious for the current received view of evolution.

Ironically, the term "evolvability" may have been first coined by Dawkins (1989), the scholar who had previously argued for the selfish gene as the basic unit of selection. Dawkins's shift in conception occurred because of an interest he developed in computer programs that can evolve into new programs. This field of study became known as "artificial life," a field invented by Langton (e.g., 1997).

Artificial life concerns the question of how closely evolution can be simulated, and with what degree of realism. In one sense, this is pretend biology, but it has led to fields of important new scholarship. For example, Franklin (1995) wrote a large book on "artificial minds." Kauffman (1993) inquired as to the origins of order in the natural world. He explored the concept of self-organization and how that concept might bear on selection processes in evolution. These areas (and others) point toward the ultimate question of whether there can be a universal biology of pure organization, independent of the material world (Moreno, Etxeberria, & Umerez, 1994). However, there are real-world implications of such thinking. The concept of genetic algorithms (Holland, 1995) was developed to help understand complex adaptive systems. One branch, genetic programming, has led to computer programs sophisticated enough to discover patentable inventions (Koza, Keane, & Streeter, 2003). These fascinating areas cannot be pursued further here for lack of space.

Ideas such as evolvability led E. F. Keller (2000) to conclude that "by now, we have abandoned the hope of finding in the molecular structure of particulate genes an adequate explanation for the stability of biological organization across generations" (p. 40). She might have also added that the current neo-Darwinism synthesis will therefore undergo dramatic revision as well.

Keller's statement implies that the concept of gene as a distinct, material unit of heredity is no longer viable. As new ideas of hereditary units develop, they will undoubtedly strongly affect the area we turn to next: behavioral genetics.

Behavioral Genetics

"Behavioral genetics aims to identify genetic and environmental influences underlying individual differences in behavior" (Segal & MacDonald, 1998, p. 165). This succinct definition captures the essence of behavioral genetics as traditionally conceived. Perhaps this area is best known for the calculation of heritability coefficients (Fuller, 1987), but more recent developments include linking a heritable behavior to a relevant genetic locus on a chromosome and more intensive study of the environment, particularly genotype-environment interactions.

Disciplinary Considerations

Behavioral genetics is interdisciplinary. However, it appears to be increasingly dominated by psychology. The recent massive volume *Behavioral Genetics in the Postgenomic Era,* published by the American Psychological Association (Plomin, DeFries, Craig, & McGuffin, 2003) suggests that the discipline of psychology is firmly stamping its imprint on behavioral genetics. Psychiatry is also getting involved, as witnessed by the recent volume *Molecular Genetics and the Human Personality,* published by the American Psychiatric Association (Benjamin, Ebstein, & Belmaker, 2002).

This disciplinary emphasis by psychology is reflected in newsletters of the American Psychological Association. For example, a recent article in *Monitor on Psychology* (Azar, 2002b) touted the search for genes to explain our personalities. The same issue announced the formation of a Working Group on Genetics Research Issues, created by the Board of Scientific Affairs of the APA (Azar, 2002a). This eminent group of six scientists provided a brief initial report (Hewitt et al., 2003) with the promise to post a final report and recommendations on the APA Web site. More broadly, over 120 professional societies created the National Coalition for Health Professional Education in Genetics to define the core competencies needed by health professionals in dealing with the genetics of health and disease (see Patenaude, Guttmacher, & Collins, 2002, for an overview). These core competencies include many skills and knowledge that most psychologists do not currently have. The Working Group of the APA was very clear that genetics must be incorporated into the graduate training curriculum if psychologists are to be competitive in areas of genetics as diverse as clinical services, research, ethical expertise, and public policy work (Patenaude et al., 2002). In truth, the postgenomic era will create many new services and niches for professional practice in numerous disciplines. The need to compete to get "our share" of the business is very real. The slight sense of urgency to get psychologists trained, at least minimally, in genetics is also real and probably warranted.

Finding Genetics in Behavior

In one sense, behavioral genetics rests on a very thin thread. Roughly 99.9% of human DNA sequence is identical across all humans, leaving only 0.1% of the genes to vary (Plomin et al., 2003). But from that tiny percentage derives all the wondrous individual differences that constantly absorb human attention. A powerful discipline has emerged from this focus on individual differences. Most areas of psychology focus on the "universals," or a search for normative laws of behavior that hold generally. In such a general focus, individual differences are a nuisance, or "error variance."

Behavioral genetics treats variation as the norm. This perspective on individual differences views attributes as normally distributed and continuous. Thus, rarity (e.g., mental retardation or genius) is simply the extremes of a normal distribution. This approach is quantitative, relying on dimensional analyses rather than categorization. Traditionally, this quantitative approach attempted to partition behavioral variation into genetic and environmental components. Heritability can be a tricky concept. Technically, for a given attribute, heritability is the ratio of genotypic variation to phenotypic variation within a population. The complementary concept is environmentality, the ratio of environmental variation to phenotypic variation (Sternberg & Grigorenko, 1999). Thus, heritability is the proportion of individual difference in a population that is inherited. As a statistical concept it says nothing about an individual. The concept is also relative to the phenotypic variation in the population. If phenotypic variation increases, the heritability ratio decreases; if phenotypic variation decreases, the heritability ratio increases. Seven myths about heritability and education are engagingly discussed by Sternberg and Grigorenko. The eminent geneticist Richard Lewontin (e.g., 1987) has also taken some interesting swipes at the misinterpretations of heritability. There are many ways of estimating heritability and related concepts (e.g., see Carey, 2003, for an excellent, but somewhat advanced introduction).

According to Plomin et al. (2003), there are two worlds of genetics: the quantitative approach of behavioral genetics and traditional molecular genetics. According to these authors, molecular genetics (similar to most areas of psychology) took a species-universal perspective in a search for universal genetic laws. Thus, the two approaches drifted apart early in the twentieth century. These two approaches to genetics are beginning to come together, as exemplified in the Plomin et al. volume: "The future of behavioral genetic research lies in identifying specific genes responsible for heritability" (p. 11). Further, "For behavioral genetics, the most important next step is the identification of the DNA sequences that make us different from each other" (p. 12). This future approach might be called "molecular genomics." This general approach to finding out how genes work is gaining the label of "functional genomics." Applied to the behavioral level, Plomin et al. dub it "behavioral genomics" (p. 13).

Applications of Behavioral Genetics

Several substantive areas are represented in the Plomin et al. (2003) volume. Cognitive abilities and disabilities receive much attention (eight chapters). Psychopharmacology is also prominent (three chapters). Personality (three chapters) and psychopathology (four chapters) share about one-third of the volume. The section on psychopathology includes chapters on hyperactivity disorder, schizophrenia, affective disorders, and dementias. Additional pathologies are discussed in a review article (Plomin & McGuffin, 2003).

It appears that research and publications on the genetics of abilities and personality are about equal in volume. As noted previously, the "other" APA volume is devoted to a broad array of personality topics and genetics. Other recent examples include heritability of subjective well-being and dominance in chimpanzees (Weiss, King, & Enns, 2002) and a 42-page query as to what we can learn about personality from animal research (Gosling, 2001).

Millon (1990) noted the resurgence in personology beginning in the 1980s. Thus, it makes sense that evolution (genetic and behavioral) would be linked to the study of personality. In fact, Millon was a pioneer in this interface with the 1990 publication of his classic *Toward a New Personology: An Evolutionary Model*. This volume was followed by numerous chapters applying his model of evolution to various facets of personality. Some examples include "normality" (Millon, 1991), normal and abnormal personality (Millon & Davis, 1994), personality disorders (Millon & Davis, 1996), and attributes of personality (Millon, 2002).

Millon's (2002) theory "seeks to generate the principles, mechanisms, and typologies of personality through formal processes of deduction" (p. 5). His general approach is an analogue to Darwin's attempt to explain the origin of species, but specialized to derivation of the origins of "the structure and style of personalities that have previously been generated on the basis of clinical observation alone" (p. 5). Millon's deductive base begins with four foundational concepts: existence, adaptation, replication, and abstraction. Three of these concepts entail universal polarities: existence (pleasure and pain), adaptation (passivity and activity), and replication (self and other), The fourth, abstraction, applies primarily to the human level.

From this deductive foundation, a massive attempt has been made to classify personality disorders and their modes of therapy (Millon & Davis, 1996). Millon's general approach should be compared to evolutionary theorizing by Buss (e.g., 1991) on personality as an evolved set of mental mechanisms. Millon's systematic application of evolutionary principles to psychotherapy might also be contrasted with approaches described in an eclectic edited volume by Gilbert and Bailey (2000), *Genes on the Couch.*

Millon's evolutionary theory has been used as a vast organizing device to collate disparate areas in personality, psychopathology, and psychotherapy. That is one powerful function of a good theory. As noted in a previous quote, this organization was based on previously generated clinical observations. To date, that is a weakness of the theory. Many theories can be fitted to a given field of data. It is the ability to foresee and predict new findings that makes a great theory. Thus, the next big push for the theory should be, in my opinion, the generation of strong novel predictions that can be confirmed.

It should be noted that this vast effort to link evolution to personality is only one of Ted Millon's many contributions to personology.

All Is Not Quite Well in Paradise

The hope of the new behavioral genomics is that we will soon be able to map ever increasing polygenic complexity onto complex behavioral attributes, especially that complex omnibus called "personality." It is a grand vision. However, even Plomin et al. (2003) noted in passing "the slower-than-expected progress to date in finding genes associated with behavior" (p. 13). Given that the human genome has been fully sequenced, why would progress be slow? There are several reasons.

First, consider the concept of evolvability discussed earlier. Kirschner and Gerhart (1998) analyzed evolvability at the molecular, cellular, and developmental levels. Several processes are discussed that may aid in second-order evolvability. Linkage, as one example, refers to the dependence of one process on another. When linkage is weak, dependence is weak. According to Kirschner and Gerhart, "Weak is a characteristic of information transfer (regulatory) pathways, e.g., signal transduction, neural relays, or transcriptional control circuits" (p. 8421). Weak linkage means that variation and selection can occur downline, far removed from direct gene control. To the extent that neural processes are weakly linked, one can immediately intuit the tremendous difficulty of mapping genes onto complex behavior.

An example of this complexity is given by Ezzell (2003). Cloned animals do not yield identical animals. Cloned pigs showed much behavioral variability, about the same as did normal pigs. In a herd of cloned cattle, the usual social hierarchy still developed. The genes are identical, but behavior is widely variable. Mapping genes onto behavior is impossible in this case. Such difficulties are reinforced by the growing literature on developmental plasticity (West-Eberhard, 2003), developmental instability (Polak, 2003), and cellular evolution and embryology (Gerhart & Kirschner, 1997).

Other problems come from the environmental direction. The environment includes not only the external physical world, but also the complexities of the body as it develops and changes over time. Some examples include "developmental-behavioral initiation of evolutionary change" (Gottlieb, 2002), evidence showing that environmental influences routinely affect gene activation (Gottlieb, 1998), biocultural orchestration of developmental plasticity (Li, 2003), the interactivity of genes and environment in the developmental process (Turkheimer, 1998, 2000), and the coming recognition that the genome is "fluid" (Ho, 1997).

The concept of shared and nonshared environments was developed to help account for the many differences between children in the same family (Plomin & Daniels, 1987). In strong critiques, Turkheimer (2000; Turkheimer & Waldron, 2000) found that objectively defined nonshared environmental variables do not account for much variability. Why? According to Turkheimer (2000, p. 163), the answer is "because of the unsystematic effects of all environmental events, compounded by the equally unsystematic processes that expose us to environmental events in the first place." Space does not permit more detailed exploration of this fascinating topic. Only time will tell whether behavioral genetics can truly become behavioral genomics.

Evolutionary Psychology

"Behavioral genetics and evolutionary psychology remind us of ships passing in the night" (Segal & MacDonald, 1998, p. 159). Scarr (1995) called attention to the fact that evolutionary psychology focuses on the *typical* in the search for general evolutionary laws of behavior, in contrast to behavioral genetics' focus on variation and individual differences. Fuller (1987) noted that behavioral genetics and sociobiology have almost nothing to do with each other. All three of these papers called for an integration of the two areas. However, the fact that behavioral genetics and evolutionary psychology appear to be two very different conceptual paradigms will make true integration exceedingly difficult.

What Is Evolutionary Psychology?

This question is not easy to answer. In a volume entitled *Sense and Nonsense,* Laland and Brown (2002) titled an early section "A Guide for the Bewildered" (p. 8) and noted, "In truth, there are many ways of using evolutionary theory to study human behaviour and there is much disagreement within the field as to the best way to do it" (p. 9). If anything, the history of the field is even more complicated. One line of descent traces back to animal ethology in the 1950s (a photo of ducklings following Konrad Lorenz must be in every introductory psychology text). An early contributor to ethology (Tinbergen, 1963) described four kinds of scientific questions one can pose: (1) proximate causes of behavior, (2) the unfolding development of an individual, (3) the function of a behavior and its evolutionary advantage, and (4) the evolutionary history of a trait, including comparisons across species. The early ethologists focused on proximate mechanisms, a question quite different from asking about the evolutionary function of a behavior.

Different approaches to answering the four questions emerged over the past 50 years, leading to somewhat different research disciplines with much disagreement among them. Animal sociobiology developed around the work of biologists such as Hamilton, Trivers, Symons, and Maynard Smith, discussed earlier. It remained for E. O. Wilson (1975) to synthesize this work and coin the term "sociobiology." Applied to animals, this research tradition was not controversial. In review, some key concepts of animal sociobiology are the gene (the unit of selection), kin selection and inclusive fitness, reciprocal altruism, and parent-offspring conflict, among others. This research tradition is still pursued by evolutionary biologists and is sometimes referred to as behavioral ecology (Laland & Brown, 2002).

E. O. Wilson's (1975) inclusion of a chapter on humans made his book very famous, and controversial. Human sociobiology has had a contentious history, but space precludes recounting that history. For our purposes, human sociobiology diverged into two streams: human behavioral ecology and evolutionary psychology (other emerging areas include memetics and gene-culture coevolution, but they are not discussed in this chapter). Behavioral ecologists and evolutionary psychologists often strongly disagree with each other. To an untutored eye, these fights often appear to be over how best to split hairs! Home disciplines matter: Behavioral ecology is the preserve of biological anthropologists primarily, whereas evolutionary psychology stems primarily from academic psychology.

Human behavioral ecology is interested in the adaptive nature of human behavior under its current conditions insofar as that behavior maximizes reproductive success (for an excellent overview, see the volume by Cronk, Chagnon, & Irons, 2000). This approach is broad in its nature because environmental effects on behavior lead to different behavioral strategies that, in the large, create different cultures. In a sense, behavioral ecology is most interested in human behavioral differences (providing an analogue to behavioral genetics) and how such differences are adaptive responses to the different environments in which people live. The assumption is that people optimize their behavioral strategies, and much labor is invested in mathematical models of optimization.

The most general criticism of behavioral ecology is that it studies the current function of behavior, rather than any true evolutionary processes. One illustration of the subtle nature of the criticism will suffice. Ecology studies the adaptiveness of behavior. But is that the same as an adaptation? Evolutionary psychologists would say no. According to Laland and Brown (2002):

> An *adaptation* is a character favoured by natural selection for its effectiveness in a particular role; that is, it has an evolutionary history of selection. To be labeled as *adaptive,* a character has to function currently to increase reproductive success. (p. 132)

Behavioral ecology views humans as evolved for *adaptability* for many different environments. Specific adaptations are less important; further, it is often difficult to say whether or not a given trait is an evolved adaptation.

Evolutionary psychologists take a different approach and have harshly criticized behavioral ecology. They do strongly believe in adaptations as the root concept of Darwinian evolution (e.g., Symons, 1990). As Symons noted, Darwinism is a type of historical explanation, and what it explains is the "origin and maintenance of *adaptations*" (p. 435). Tooby and Cosmides (1990) also strongly subscribe to this view in an article entitled "The Past Explains the Present" (p. 375). Evolutionary psychologists also believe that behavior itself cannot be selected directly; rather, evolution selects underlying psychological mechanisms (e.g., Cosmides & Tooby, 1987; Symons, 1987). The notion of psychological mechanism is perhaps the key concept of evolutionary psychology. Such mechanisms serve as *the* intervening variable between evolution and output behaviors. This approach implies a modular approach to mind, rather than mind as a general-purpose information processor. This approach also assumes that the mental mechanisms provide a proximate level of explanation and thereby "[gives] rich insight into the present and past selective pressures" (Cosmides & Tooby, 1987, p. 283).

A further key notion is that our current form evolved and was fixed during the Pleistocene era. "Our species spent over 99% of its evolutionary history as hunter-gatherers in Pleistocene environments" (Cosmides & Tooby, 1987, p. 280). One implication is that in the current era we are out of step with our "environment of evolutionary adaptedness." Explanation using this approach involves a complex set of six steps (Tooby & Cosmides,

1989). Suffice it to say here that these six steps require strong inference as to the adaptive problems that had to be solved in the Pleistocene era and perhaps a uniformity of the adaptive problems across all human groups in all habitats.

Evolutionary psychology perhaps arrived at full credibility through the publication of a respected book, *The Adapted Mind* (Barkow, Cosmides, & Tooby, 1992). Since then, theoretical contributions have exploded. For example, Buss (1995) proposed evolutionary psychology as a new paradigm for the psychological sciences. A substantial handbook (Crawford & Krebs, 1998), an interesting volume by Hardcastle (1999), and several annual review articles (e.g., Caporael, 2001; Jones, 1999; Siegert & Ward, 2002) were published. An introductory psychology text follows an evolutionary approach (Gaulin & McBurney, 2001), although a review (Denniston, Waring, & Buskist, 2003) suggests that this approach may not yet be quite ready for prime time. A surprising number of upper-level texts have been written (e.g., Badcock, 2000; Buss, 1999; Cartwright, 2000; Palmer & Palmer, 2002). The volumes are reasonably consistent with each other. For example, Buss (1999) has good chapters on the history and definition of the field, three chapters on sexual strategies, and chapters on parenting, kinship, cooperation, aggression, gender conflict, and status/dominance. Many specialty volumes have been edited. Examples include volumes on cognition (Heyes & Huber, 2000), intelligence (Sternberg & Kaufman, 2002), and mind (Cummins & Allen, 1998). The literature is so vast that one is almost forced to conclude that evolutionary psychology has emerged as a new discipline.

Critiques of Evolutionary Psychology

In a manner similar to human sociobiology, evolutionary psychology arouses passions and argumentation. The intramural fights between behavioral ecology and evolutionary psychology have been noted. There are also criticisms from other quarters, mostly over conceptual issues, but some empirical findings have been disputed as well. One volume (Rose & Rose, 2000) was subtitled "Arguments against Evolutionary Psychology." Other writers are equally pessimistic about the possibilities for evolutionary psychology. One chapter began: "If it were the purpose of this chapter to say what is actually known about the evolution of human cognition, we could stop at the end of this sentence" (Lewontin, 1990, p. 229; also see Lewontin, 1998). In support of Lewontin's (1998) critique of adaptation, Lloyd (1999), an eminent philosopher of biology, is severely critical of Cosmides and Tooby: "Cosmides and Tooby's interpretations arise from misguided and simplistic understandings of evolutionary biology" (p. 211). Panksepp and Panksepp (2000) discussed "the seven sins of evolutionary psychology" (p. 108). Recent evolutionary interpretations of rape are chastised by de Waal (2002). The concept of "environment of evolutionary adaptedness" has been severely criticized (Foley, 1995). The concept does appear to involve an infinite regress: Today we are adapted to the Pleistocene era; Pleistocene inhabitants were adapted to a previous era, and so on. The concept needs a more rigorous logical analysis.

The concept of a "psychological mechanism" also needs closer scrutiny. In a careful analysis of the general concept of mechanism, Machamer, Darden, and Craver (2000) gave a clear definition: "Mechanisms are entities and activities organized such that they are productive of regular changes from start or set-up to finish or termination conditions" (p. 3). The notion of a psychological mechanism must always contain a metaphorical element because the material entity component of the mechanism is missing. For example, "mental modules" is clearly metaphorical; no physical modules are clipped somewhere in the brain. As I noted in a critique (Hendrick, 1995) of the use of mental mechanism by Buss (1995), there is at best a very loose analogy between a mind mechanism and a clearly defined mechanistic function of a bodily organ. Lacking that material substrate to hang the mental mechanism on, such mechanisms cannot pass the test posed by Machamer et al. (2000) that a mechanism must be "productive of regular changes from start or set-up to finish" (p. 3). Clearly, the mental mechanisms of evolutionary psychology are metaphors. In fairness, however, psychology deals heavily in metaphors; the material substrate for most of our major concepts cannot be defined.

CONCLUSIONS

To what extent is the theory of evolution a foundation for psychological science? As we have seen, there are many versions of evolutionary theory, and there are an even larger number of psychological sciences. So the question has no simple answer. My own conjectures are something as follows. First, behavioral genetics and evolutionary psychology will remain far apart for the foreseeable future. Second, behavioral genetics will outstrip evolutionary psychology in growth and appeal for the next decade or so. Why? Primarily because of the growth of employment opportunities for psychologists in a variety of genetics-related areas. This prediction holds, however, *only* if psychology doctoral programs strongly incorporate training in genetics into doctoral training.

I am pessimistic that behavioral genetics will ever progress to the point of complex behavioral predictions from complicated polygenic configurations of genes. If the concept of evolvability proves valid, genetic predictions will have to become cellular systems' predictions. So far as we can see now, predictive equations will be highly nonlinear. But perhaps detailed predictability is not needed. If behavioral genetics progresses to allow a much stronger handle than we have now on mental illness, retardation, and similar deficits, perhaps that will be progress enough.

Third, I do not believe that evolutionary psychology will survive in its current form. E. F. Keller's (2000) quip about molecular biology's challenge to the neo-Darwinian synthesis suggests that another synthesis is in the offing. If so, that change will necessarily impact evolutionary psychology. In fact, the discipline is under assault from many directions. The leading theorists have made a strong set of Popperian conjectures, and they are being subjected to an equally strong set of refutations.

Thus, change is inevitable, but the exact directions are difficult to predict. One promising new approach meshes dynamical systems theory with evolutionary psychology (Kenrick, 2001; Kenrick, Li, & Butner, 2003; Kenrick et al., 2002). Other promising approaches will undoubtedly emerge. It is unlikely that the discipline will become extinct! Individuals such as Cosmides, Buss, Kenrick, and Tooby have theorized boldly and courageously. They were a powerful stimulus to the growth of the discipline. They have also been punished for their boldness. But it does not matter if they were wrong on specific points. Out of the matrix of strong conjectures and refutations a stronger and more rounded theory will emerge. Indeed, perhaps in a couple of generations, Scarr's (1995) appeal for the joining of genetics with evolutionary psychology may occur. At that point, evolution will become the foundation for psychology. Indeed, if this joining occurs, psychology will *become* evolutionary psychology.

REFERENCES

Abramson, P. R., & Pinkerton, S. D. (Eds.). (1995). *Sexual nature and sexual culture.* Chicago: University of Chicago Press.

Alexander, R. D. (1974). The evolution of social behavior. *Annual Review of Ecology and Systematics, 5,* 325–383.

Alexander, R. D. (1992). Genes, consciousness, and behavior theory. In S. Koch & D. E. Leary (Eds.), *A century of psychology as science* (pp. 783–802). Washington, DC: American Psychological Association.

Avital, E., & Jablonka, E. (2000). *Animal traditions: Behavioral inheritance in evolution.* Cambridge, England: Cambridge University Press.

Azar, B. (2002a). APA forms working group on genetics research issues. *Monitor on Psychology, 33*(8), 45.

Azar, B. (2002b). Searching for genes that explain our personalities. *Monitor on Psychology, 33*(8), 44–46.

Badcock, C. (2000). *Evolutionary psychology: A critical introduction.* Malden, MA: Blackwell.

Barkow, J. H., Cosmides, L., & Tooby, J. (Eds.). (1992). *The adapted mind: Evolutionary psychology and the generation of culture.* New York: Oxford University Press.

Benjamin, J., Ebstein, R. P., & Belmaker, R. H. (Eds.). (2002). *Molecular genetics and the human personality.* Washington, DC: American Psychiatric Press.

Beurton, P. J., Falk, R., & Rheinberger, H.-J. (Eds.). (2000). *The concept of the gene in development and evolution: Historical and epistemological perspectives.* Cambridge, England: Cambridge University Press.

Boring, E. G. (1950). The influence of evolutionary thought upon American psychological thought. In S. Persons (Ed.), *Evolutionary thought in America* (pp. 268–298). New Haven, CT: Yale University Press.

Buss, D. M. (1991). Evolutionary personality psychology. *Annual Review of Psychology, 42,* 459–491.

Buss, D. M. (1995). Evolutionary psychology: A new paradigm for psychological science. *Psychological Inquiry, 6,* 1–30.

Buss, D. M. (1999). *Evolutionary psychology: The new science of the mind.* Boston: Allyn & Bacon.

Caporael, L. R. (2001). Evolutionary psychology: Toward a unifying theory and a hybrid science. *Annual Review of Psychology, 52,* 607–628.

Carey, G. (2003). *Human genetics for the social sciences.* Thousand Oaks, CA: Sage.

Cartwright, J. (2000). *Evolution and human behavior: Darwinian perspectives on human nature.* Cambridge, MA: MIT Press.

Cosmides, L., & Tooby, J. (1987). From evolution to behavior: Evolutionary psychology as the missing link. In J. Dupre (Ed.), *The latest on the best: Essays on evolution and optimality* (pp. 277–306). Cambridge, MA: MIT Press.

Crawford, C. B. (1989). The theory of evolution: Of what value to psychology? *Journal of Comparative Psychology, 103,* 4–22.

Crawford, C. B., & Anderson, J. L. (1989). Sociobiology: An environmentalist discipline? *American Psychologist, 44,* 1449–1459.

Crawford, C. B., & Krebs, D. L. (Eds.). (1998). *Handbook of evolutionary psychology: Ideas, issues, and applications.* Mahwah, NJ: Erlbaum.

Crawford, C. B., Smith, M., & Krebs, D. L. (Eds.). (1987). *Sociobiology and psychology: Ideas, issues and applications.* Hillsdale, NJ: Erlbaum.

Cronk, L., Chagnon, N., & Irons, W. (Eds.). (2000). *Adaptation and human behavior: An anthropological perspective.* New York: Aldine de Gruyter.

Crutchfield, J. P., & Schuster, P. (2003). Preface: Dynamics of evolutionary processes. In J. P. Crutchfield & P. Schuster (Eds.), *Evolutionary dynamics: Exploring the interplay of selection, accident, neutrality, and function* (pp. xiii–xxxiv). New York: Oxford University Press.

Cummins, D. D., & Allen, C. (Eds.). (1998). *The evolution of mind.* New York: Oxford University Press.

Darwin, C. (1859). *The origin of species.* New York: Modern Library.

Darwin, C. (1872). *The expressions of emotions in man and animals.* Chicago: University of Chicago Press.

Darwin, C. (1981). *The descent of man, and selection in relation to sex.* Princeton, NJ: Princeton University Press. (Original work published 1871)

Dawkins, R. (1976). *The selfish gene* New York: Oxford University Press.

Dawkins, R. (1982). *The extended phenotype: The gene as unit of selection.* San Francisco: Freeman.

Dawkins, R. (1989). The evolution of evolvability. In C. G. Langton (Ed.), *Artificial life: The proceedings of an interdisciplinary workshop on the synthesis and simulation of living systems* (pp. 201–220). New York: Addison-Wesley.

Denniston, J. C., Waring, D. A., & Buskist, W. F. (2003). Charles Darwin teaches introductory psychology [Review of the book *Psychology: An evolutionary approach*]. *Contemporary Psychology: APA Review of Books, 48,* 238–241.

de Waal, F. B. M. (2002). Evolutionary psychology: The wheat and the chaff. *Current Directions in Psychological Science, 11,* 187–191.

Dewsbury, D. A. (2002). THE CHICAGO FIVE: A family group of integrative psychobiologists. *History of Psychology, 5,* 16–37.

Dobzhansky, T. G. (1937). *Genetics and the origin of species.* New York: Columbia University Press.

Elena, S. F., Cooper, V. S., & Lenski, R. E. (1996). Punctuated evolution caused by selection of rare beneficial mutations. *Science, 272,* 1802–1804.

Ezzell, C. (2003). Ma's eyes, not her ways. *Scientific American, 288*(4), 30.

Fehr, C. (2001). The evolution of sex: Domains and explanatory pluralism. *Biology and Philosophy, 16,* 145–170.

Fisher, A. (1991). A new synthesis comes of age. *Mosaic, 22*(1), 2–17.

Foley, R. (1995). The adaptive legacy of human evolution: A search for the environment of evolutionary adaptedness. *Evolutionary Anthropology, 4*(6), 194–203.

Franklin, S. (1995). *Artificial minds.* Cambridge, MA: MIT Press.

Fuller, J. L. (1987). What can genes do? In C. B. Crawford, M. Smith, & D. L. Krebs (Eds.), *Sociobiology and psychology: Ideas, issues and applications* (pp. 147–174). Hillsdale, NJ: Erlbaum.

Galton, F. (1869). *Hereditary genius: An inquiry into its laws and consequences.* London: Macmillan.

Gaulin, S. J. C., & McBurney, D. H. (2001). *Psychology: An evolutionary approach.* Upper Saddle River, NJ: Prentice-Hall.

Gerhart, J., & Kirschner, M. (1997). *Cells, embryos, and evolution.* Malden, MA: Blackwell Science.

Ghiselin, M. T. (1988). The evolution of sex: A history of competing points of view. In R. E. Michod & B. R. Levin (Eds.), *The evolution of sex: An examination of current ideas* (pp. 7–23). Sunderland, MA: Sinauer.

Gilbert, P., & Bailey, K. G. (Eds.). (2000). *Genes on the couch: Explorations in evolutionary psychotherapy.* Philadelphia: Taylor & Francis.

Glickman, S. E. (1992). Some thoughts on the evolution of comparative psychology. In S. Koch & D. E. Leary (Eds.), *A century of psychology as science* (pp. 738–782). Washington, DC: American Psychological Association.

Godfrey-Smith, P. (2000). The replicator in retrospect. *Biology and Philosophy, 15,* 403–423.

Golding, B. (Ed.). (1994). *Non-neutral evolution: Theories and molecular data* New York: Chapman & Hall.

Gosling, S. D. (2001). From mice to men: What can we learn about personality from animal research? *Psychological Bulletin, 127,* 45–86.

Gottlieb, G. (1998). Normally occurring environmental and behavioral influences on gene activity: From central dogma to probabilistic epigenesis. *Psychological Review, 105,* 792–802.

Gottlieb, G. (2002). Developmental-behavioral initiation of evolutionary change. *Psychological Review, 109,* 211–218.

Gould, S. J., & Eldredge, N. (1977). Punctuated equilibria: The tempo and mode of evolution reconsidered. *Paleobiology, 3,* 115–151.

Gould, S. J., & Eldredge, N. (1993). Punctuated equilibrium comes of age. *Nature, 366,* 223–227.

Griffiths, P. E. (2002). Lost: One gene concept: Reward to finder. *Biology and Philosophy, 17,* 271–283.

Gruber, H. E. (1998). Diverse relations between psychology and evolutionary thought. In R. W. Rieber & K. D. Salzinger (Eds.), *Psychology: Theoretical-historical perspectives* (2nd ed., pp. 227–252). Washington, DC: American Psychological Association.

Hamilton, W. D. (1964a). The genetical evolution of social behavior: I. *Journal of Theoretical Biology, 7,* 1–16.

Hamilton, W. D. (1964b). The genetical evolution of social behavior: II. *Journal of Theoretical Biology, 7,* 17–52.

Hardcastle, V. G. (Ed.). (1999). *Where biology meets psychology: Philosophical essays.* Cambridge, MA: MIT Press.

Harold, F. M. (2001). *The way of the cell: Molecules, organisms and the order of life.* New York: Oxford University Press.

Hendrick, C. (1995). Evolutionary psychology and models of explanation. *Psychological Inquiry, 6,* 47–49.

Hendrick, C. (2002). A new age of prevention? *Journal of Social and Personal Relationships, 19,* 621–627.

Hewitt, J., DeFries, J., Wehner, J., Flint, J., Heath, A., & Moffitt, T. (2003). BSA Working Group on genetics research. *Psychological Science Agenda, 16*(1), 8–9.

Heyes, C., & Huber, L. (Eds.). (2000). *The evolution of cognition.* Cambridge, MA: MIT Press.

Ho, M. W. (1997). [Review of the book *The thread of life: The story of genes and genetic engineering*]. *Heredity, 78,* 223.

Holland, J. H. (1995). *Hidden order: How adaptation builds complexity.* Reading, MA: Addison-Wesley.

Jones, D. (1999). Evolutionary psychology. *Annual Review of Anthropology, 28,* 553–575.

Kantor, J. R. (1935). Evolution of mind. *Psychological Review, 42,* 455–465.

Kauffman, S. A. (1993). *The origins of order: Self-organization and selection in evolution.* New York: Oxford University Press.

Keller, E. F. (2000). *The century of the gene.* Cambridge, MA: Harvard University Press.

Keller, L. (Ed.). (1999). *Levels of selection in evolution.* Princeton, NJ: Princeton University Press.

Kenrick, D. T. (2001). Evolutionary psychology, cognitive science, and dynamical systems: Building an integrative paradigm. *Current Directions in Psychological Science, 10*(1), 13–17.

Kenrick, D. T., Li, N. P., & Butner, J. (2003). Dynamical evolutionary psychology: Individual decision rules and emergent social norms. *Psychological Review, 110,* 3–28.

Kenrick, D. T., Maner, J. K., Butner, J., Li, N. P., Becker, D. V., & Schaller, M. (2002). Dynamical evolutionary psychology: Mapping the domains of the new interactionist paradigm. *Personality and Social Psychology Review, 6,* 347–356.

Kenrick, D. T., & Trost, M. R. (1989). A reproductive exchange model of heterosexual relationships: Putting proximate economics in ultimate perspective. In C. Hendrick (Ed.), *Close relationships* (pp. 92–118). Newbury Park, CA: Sage.

Kimble, G. A., & Wertheimer, M. (Eds.). (1998). *Portraits of pioneers in psychology: Vol. 3.* Washington, DC: American Psychological Association/Erlbaum.

Kimura, M. (1983). *The neutral theory of molecular evolution.* New York: Cambridge University Press.

Kirkpatrick, L. A. (1998). Evolution, pair-bonding, and reproductive strategies: A reconceptualization of adult attachment. In J. A. Simpson & W. S. Rholes (Eds.), *Attachment theory and close relationships* (pp. 353–393). New York: Guilford Press.

Kirschner, M., & Gerhart, J. (1998). Evolvability. *Proceedings of the National Academy of Sciences, USA, 95,* 8420–8427.

Koza, J. R., Keane, M. A., & Streeter, M. J. (2003). Evolving inventions. *Scientific American, 228*(2), 52–59.

Laland, K. N., & Brown, G. R. (2002). *Sense and nonsense: Evolutionary perspectives on human behavior.* Oxford, England: Oxford University Press.

Langton, C. G. (Ed.). (1997). *Artificial life: An overview.* Cambridge, MA: MIT Press.

Lewis, W. M., Jr. (1987). The cost of sex. In S. C. Stearns (Ed.), *The evolution of sex and its consequences* (pp. 33–57). Boston: Birkhauser.

Lewontin, R. C. (1987). The irrelevance of heritability. *Science for the People, 19*(6), 23, 32.

Lewontin, R. C. (1990). The evolution of cognition. In D. N. Osherson & E. E. Smith (Eds.), *Thinking: An invitation to cognitive science* (Vol. 3, pp. 229–246). Cambridge, MA: MIT Press.

Lewontin, R. C. (1998). The evolution of cognition: Questions we will never answer. In D. Scarborough & S. Sternberg (Eds.), *Methods, models, and conceptual issues: An invitation to cognitive science* (Vol. 4, pp. 107–132). Cambridge, MA: MIT Press.

Li, S.-C. (2003). Biocultural orchestration of developmental plasticity across levels: The interplay of biology and culture in shaping the mind and behavior across the life span. *Psychological Bulletin, 129,* 171–194.

Lloyd, E. A. (1999). Evolutionary psychology: The burden of proof. *Biology and Philosophy, 14,* 211–233.

Machamer, P., Darden, L., & Craver, C. F. (2000). Thinking about mechanisms. *Philosophy of Science, 67,* 1–25.

Markos, A. (2002). *Readers of the book of life: Contextualizing developmental evolutionary biology.* New York: Oxford University Press.

Masterson, R. B. (1998). Charles Darwin: Father of evolutionary psychology. In G. A. Kimble & M. Wertheimer (Eds.), *Portraits of pioneers in psychology* (Vol. 3, pp. 17–29). Washington, DC: American Psychological Association/Erlbaum.

Maynard Smith, J. (1978). *The evolution of sex.* New York: Cambridge University Press.

Maynard Smith, J. (1998). *Shaping life: Genes, embryos and evolution.* New Haven, CT: Yale University Press.

Michod, R. E., & Levin, B. R. (Eds.). (1988). *The evolution of sex: An examination of current ideas.* Sunderland, MA: Sinauer.

Millon, T. (1990). *Toward a new personology: An evolutionary model.* New York: Wiley.

Millon, T. (1991). Normality: What may we learn from evolutionary theory? In D. Offer & M. Sabshin (Eds.), *The diversity of normal behavior: Further contributions to normatology* (pp. 356–404). New York: Basic Books.

Millon, T. (2002). Evolution: A generative source for conceptualizing the attributes of personality. In I. B. Weiner (Series Ed.) & T. Millon & M. J. Lerner (Vol. Eds.), *Handbook of psychology: Vol. 5. Personality and social psychology* (pp. 3–30). Hoboken, NJ: Wiley.

Millon, T., & Davis, R. D. (1994). Millon's evolutionary model of normal and abnormal personality: Theory and measures. In S. Strack & M. Lorr (Eds.), *Differentiating normal and abnormal personality* (pp. 79–113). New York: Springer.

Millon, T., & Davis, R. D. (1996). An evolutionary theory of personality disorders. In J. F. Clarkin & M. F. Lenzenweger (Eds.), *Major theories of personality disorder* (pp. 221–346). New York: Guilford Press.

Moreno, A., Etxeberria, A., & Umerez, J. (1994). Universality without matter. In R. A. Brooks & P. Maes (Eds.), *Artificial life. IV: Proceedings of the fourth international workshop on the synthesis and simulation of living systems* (pp. 406–410). Cambridge, MA: MIT Press.

Palmer, J. A., & Palmer, L. K. (2002). *Evolutionary psychology: The ultimate origins of human behavior.* Boston: Allyn & Bacon.

Panksepp, J., & Panksepp, J. B. (2000). The seven sins of evolutionary psychology. *Evolution and Cognition, 6,* 108–131.

Papadopoulos, D., Schneider, D., Meier-Eiss, J., Arber, W., Lenski, R. E., & Blot, M. (1999). Genomic evolution during a 10,000-generation experiment with bacteria. *Proceedings of the National Academy of Sciences, USA, 96,* 3807–3812.

Patenaude, A. F., Guttmacher, A. E., & Collins, F. S. (2002). Genetic testing and psychology: New roles, new responsibilities. *American Psychologist, 57,* 271–282.

Persons, S. (Ed.). (1950). *Evolutionary thought in America.* New Haven, CT: Yale University Press.

Plomin, R., & Daniels, D. (1987). Why are children in the same family so different from one another? *Behavioral and Brain Sciences, 10,* 1–60.

Plomin, R., DeFries, J. C., Craig, I. W., & McGuffin, P. (2003). Behavioral genetics. In R. Plomin, J. C. DeFries, I. W. Craig, & P. McGuffin (Eds.), *Behavioral genetics in the postgenomic era* (pp. 3–15). Washington, DC: American Psychological Association.

Plomin, R., DeFries, J. C., Craig, I. W., & McGuffin, P. (Eds.). (2003). *Behavioral genetics in the postgenomic era.* Washington, DC: American Psychological Association.

Plomin, R., & McGuffin, P. (2003). Psychopathology in the postgenomic era. *Annual Review of Psychology, 54,* 205–228.

Polak, M. (Ed.). (2003). *Developmental instability: Causes and consequences.* New York: Oxford University Press.

Radman, M. (1999). Enzymes of evolutionary change. *Nature, 401,* 866–867, 869.

Radman, M., Matic, I., & Taddei, F. (1999). Evolution of evolvability. In L. H. Caporale (Ed.), *Molecular strategies in biological evolution* (pp. 146–155). New York: New York Academy of Sciences.

Richards, R. (2002). What can philosophy contribute to biology? *Quarterly Review of Biology, 77,* 169–173.

Ridley, M. (1993a). *The red queen: Sex and the evolution of human nature.* New York: Penguin.

Ridley, M. (1993b). Is sex good for anything? *New Scientist, 140*(1902), 36–40.

Ridley, M. (1996). *Evolution* (2nd ed.). Cambridge, MA: Blackwell Scientific.

Rose, H., & Rose, S. (Eds.). (2000). *Alas, poor Darwin: Arguments against evolutionary psychology.* New York: Harmony Books.

Scarr, S. (1995). Psychology will be truly evolutionary when behavior genetics is included. *Psychological Inquiry, 6,* 68–71.

Schuster, P. (2003). Molecular insights into evolution of phenotypes. In J. P. Crutchfield & P. Schuster (Eds.), *Evolutionary dynamics: Exploring the interplay of selection, accident, neutrality, and function* (pp. 163–215). New York: Oxford University Press.

Segal, N. L., & MacDonald, K. B. (1998). Behavioral genetics and evolutionary psychology: Unified perspective on personality research. *Human Biology, 70,* 159–184.

Shapiro, J. A. (1999). Genome system architecture and natural genetic engineering in evolution. In L. H. Caporale (Ed.), *Molecular strategies in biological evolution* (pp. 23–35). New York: New York Academy of Sciences.

Siegert, R. J., & Ward, T. (2002). Evolutionary psychology: Origins and criticisms. *Australian Psychologist, 37,* 20–29.

Stearns, S. C. (Ed.). (1987a). *The evolution of sex and its consequences.* Boston: Birkhauser.

Stearns, S. C. (1987b). Why sex evolved and the differences it makes. In S. C. Stearns (Ed.), *The evolution of sex and its consequences* (pp. 15–31). Boston: Birkhauser.

Sternberg, R. J., & Grigorenko, E. L. (1999). Myths in psychology and education regarding the gene-environment debate. *Teachers College Record, 100,* 536–553.

Sternberg, R. J., & Kaufman, J. C. (2002). *The evolution of intelligence.* Mahwah, NJ: Erlbaum.

Stove, D. (1992). The demons and Dr. Dawkins. *American Scholar, 61*(1), 67–78.

Symons, D. (1979). *Evolution of human sexuality.* New York: Oxford University Press.

Symons, D. (1987). If we're all Darwinians, what's all the fuss about? In C. B. Crawford, M. Smith, & D. L. Krebs (Eds.), *Sociobiology and psychology: Ideas, issues and applications* (pp. 121–146). Hillsdale, NJ: Erlbaum.

Symons, D. (1990). Adaptiveness and adaptation. *Ethology and Sociobiology, 11,* 427–444.

Tinbergen, N. (1963). On aims and methods of ethology. *Zeitschrift fur Tierpsychologie, 20,* 410–433.

Tooby, J. (1988). The emergence of evolutionary psychology. In D. Pines (Ed.), *Emerging syntheses in science* (pp. 67–75). Redwood City, CA: Addison-Wesley.

Tooby, J., & Cosmides, L. (1989). Evolutionary psychology and the generation of culture: Part I. *Ethology and Sociobiology, 10,* 29–49.

Tooby, J., & Cosmides, L. (1990). The past explains the present: Emotional adaptations and the structure of ancestral environments. *Ethology and Sociobiology, 11,* 375–424.

Trivers, R. L. (1971). The evolution of reciprocalaltruism. *Quarterly Review of Biology, 46,* 35–57.

Trivers, R. L. (1972). Parental investment and sexual selection. In B. Campbell (Ed.), *Sexual selection and the descent of man, 1871–1971* (pp. 136–179). Chicago: Aldine.

Turkheimer, E. (1998). Heritability and explanation. *Psychological Review, 105,* 782–791.

Turkheimer, E. (2000). Three laws of behavioral genetics and what they mean. *Current Directions in Psychological Science, 9,* 160–164.

Turkheimer, E., & Waldron, M. (2000). Nonshared environment: A theoretical, methodological, and quantitative review. *Psychological Bulletin, 126,* 78–108.

Waller, M. J. C. (1999). Group selection and the selfish gene: The units-of-selection problem revisited. In J. M. G. van der Dennen, D. Smillie, & D. R. Wilson (Eds.), *The Darwinian heritage and sociobiology* (pp. 3–45). Westport, CT: Praeger.

Watson, J. D., & Crick, F. (1953). A structure for deoxyribose nucleic acid. *Nature, 171,* 737–738.

Weiss, A., King, J. E., & Enns, R. M. (2002). Subjective well-being is heritable and genetically correlated with dominance in chimpanzees [*Pan troglodytes*]. *Journal of Personality and Social Psychology, 83,* 1141–1149.

West-Eberhard, M. J. (1998). Evolution in the light of developmental and cell biology, and vice versa. *Proceedings of the National Academy of Sciences, USA, 95,* 8417–8419.

West-Eberhard, M. J. (2003). *Developmental plasticity and evolution.* New York: Oxford University Press.

Williams, G. C. (1966). *Adaptation and natural selection: A critique of some current evolutionary thought.* Princeton, NJ: Princeton University Press.

Williams, G. C. (1975). *Sex and evolution.* Princeton, NJ: Princeton University Press.

Wilson, D. S. (2001). Evolutionary biology: Struggling to escape exclusively individual selection. *Quarterly Review of Biology, 76,* 199–205.

Wilson, E. O. (1975). *Sociobiology: The new synthesis.* Cambridge, MA: Harvard University Press.

Wynne-Edwards, V. C. (1962). *Animal dispersion in relation to social behavior.* Edinburgh, UK: Oliver & Boyd.

Chapter 2

NATURE AND NURTURE IN PERSONALITY DISORDERS

JOEL PARIS

Controversy about the relative importance of nature and nurture in human behavior has raged for generations, and the struggle is far from over. In the academic world, departments of psychology are still divided into competing biological and psychosocial camps. Similar divisions can be seen in the clinical world (Paris, 1999). Most psychiatrists subscribe to a biomedical model that emphasizes nature. Psychotherapists with a traditionally analytic perspective tend to emphasize nurture, since they focus attention on the impact of childhood experiences. Cognitive therapists fall somewhere in the middle.

The nature-nurture problem has aroused strong emotions (Pinker, 2002). Biological theories have come to dominate medicine, while exciting new research in psychology (e.g., LeDoux, 2002) is rooted in neurophysiology and neurochemistry. No one denies that human traits are shaped by evolution. Why should the mind be an exception?

Even so, genetic-biological theories of human behavior have aroused resistance. An emphasis on nature can seem reductionistic and determinist, while a focus on nurture may be seen as humanistic and hopeful. Some opposition has come from clinicians who fear that genetic theories deny patients the capacity to change (Paris, 1999, 2000b). Psychoanalysts (Hale, 1995) and behaviorists (Skinner, 1957), although they disagree about many things, both subscribe to theories in which psychopathology is seen as a product of life experience. In psychiatry, critics of contemporary practice (e.g., Luhrmann, 2000) have expressed concern that physicians who base interventions exclusively on biology lose empathy for the suffering of patients.

Intellectual issues also underlie opposition to theories in which human behavior is shaped by nature. Many have been concerned about the political and ideological implications of biological models (Pinker, 2002). In particular, Marxist biologists (e.g., Lewontin, Rose, & Kamin, 1985) have opposed the concept of a fixed human nature. Tenacious opposition to genetic or biological explanations of behavior has also come from sociologists and anthropologists who espouse various forms of cultural relativism (Degler, 1991). Finally, developmental psychology has been dominated by an almost exclusive focus on environmental factors (Harris, 1998).

In recent years, the Zeitgeist has been changing, and the pendulum has swung away from nurture and toward nature. Recent advances in behavioral genetics (Plomin, DeFries, McClearn, & Rutter, 2001) conclusively show that biology is a major determinant of individual differences in human psychology, and future research may discover links to molecular genetics (Rutter & Plomin, 1997). These advances have been noted by the general public. Patients today are as likely to attribute their difficulties to chemical imbalances as to childhood traumas.

Two conceptual problems have delayed resolution of the nature-nurture problem. First, it is easier to think in a linear than in a multivariate, nonlinear fashion. Considering the multitude of interactions among biological, psychological, and social factors, keeping such complexities in mind takes some effort. Even sophisticated researchers sometimes fall into the trap of confusing correlation with causation. For example, all research that correlates parental behaviors with child outcomes, but fails to control for genetic factors, is potentially flawed (Harris, 1998).

A second problem derives from a failure to consider psychological phenomena from a systems perspective. Applying general systems theory (Sameroff, 1995), we can take the biological roots of behavior into account without being reductionistic. While mental processes ultimately derive from neurochemical and neurophysiological processes, they have emergent properties that cannot be explained at other levels of analysis.

These principles can usefully be applied to the understanding of personality disorders. Multivariate approaches and systems theory illuminate complex forms of psychopathology, in which genetic-biological, experiential-psychological, and social factors all play a role. Applying nonlinear models to personality disorder would be consistent with general theories of developmental psychopathology (Rutter & Plomin, 1997).

The stress-diathesis model (Monroe & Simons, 1991) is a general model for conceptualizing the causes of psychopathology. Research has shown that every category of mental disorder is associated with genetic vulnerabilities (Paris, 1999). This is not to say that genes *cause* disorders. Rather, genetic factors are associated with temperamental and trait variations, and traits can be maladaptive under specific environmental conditions. Thus, there is no absolute causal relationship between diatheses and disorders. Vulnerabilities may never become apparent unless uncovered and unleashed by stressors. An individual can be predisposed and never fall ill. For example, only half of identical twins in which one has schizophrenia are concordant (Meehl, 1990).

This model also helps us understand how adverse life events contribute to the development of psychopathology. Diatheses and stressors have an interactive relationship that involves feedback loops. Genetic variability influences the way individuals respond to their environment, while environmental factors determine whether genes are expressed. Finally, the stress-diathesis model helps explain why adverse life events, by themselves, do not consistently lead to pathological sequelae. Most children are resilient to all but the most severe and consistent adversities (Rutter & Maughan, 1997). Trauma, neglect, and dysfunctional families have their greatest effects on children who are temperamentally vulnerable (Paris, 2000b).

PERSONALITY TRAITS AND PERSONALITY DISORDERS

The stress-diathesis model is particularly useful for explaining the origin of personality disorders (Paris, 2003). Underlying predispositions or diatheses are expressed as traits. Personality trait dimensions describe individual differences that are fully compatible with normality. But trait profiles determine what type of disorder can develop in any individual.

Personality disorders, personality traits, and temperament have a hierarchical nested relationship (Rutter, 1987). Temperament, that is, behavioral dispositions present at birth, largely reflects the genetic factors in development. Personality traits, individual differences in behavior that remain stable over time and context, are actually an amalgam of temperament and life experience. Personality disorders describe dysfunctional outcomes that can occur when traits are amplified and used in rigid and maladaptive ways.

These relationships can be best understood by going beyond individual categories and considering the three clusters of disorder on Axis II of the *Diagnostic and Statistical Manual of Mental Disorders,* fourth edition (*DSM-IV;* American Psychiatric Association, 2000). While personality disorders will undoubtedly be reclassified once we understand them better (Paris, 2000a), the existing Axis II clusters broadly correspond to trait dimensions. In Cluster A, all three categories fall into the schizophrenic spectrum (Paris, 2003; Siever & Davis, 1991), suggesting a common diathesis. In Cluster B, trait impulsivity constitutes a diathesis for disorders (Siever & Davis, 1991; Zanarini, 1993). Trait anxiety is associated with Cluster C disorders (Kagan, 1994; Paris, 1997).

The Axis II clusters parallel the broadest dimensions of psychopathology. Thus, we can consider that Cluster A corresponds to a cognitive dimension, while Clusters B and C correspond, respectively, to externalizing and internalizing dimensions. These dimensions (externalizing and internalizing) account for most psychological symptoms in children (Achenbach & McConaughy, 1997) and for most of the variance in adults, as shown in factor analytic studies of psychiatric diagnoses (Krueger, 1999).

There is no clear separation between personality traits and disorders (Cloninger, Svrakic, & Przybeck, 1993; Costa & Widiger, 2001; Livesley, Jank, Jackson, & Vernon, 1993; Millon & Davis, 1995; Paris, 2003; Siever & Davis, 1991). While everyone has a personality profile, the cutoff point for defining disorders is fuzzy. Traits seem to be more fundamental: Genetic, neuropsychological, and biological markers are usually related to traits but not to disorders (Livesley, 2003; Livesley & Jang, 2000). It is interesting that this principle is broadly applicable to all forms of psychopathology, including Axis I disorders (Kendell & Jablensky, 2003).

Applying *DSM* criteria, epidemiological studies (Samuels et al., 2002; Weissman, 1993) have estimated that at least 10% of the general population have a personality disorder. But this figure can be no more precise than the arbitrary cutoff point between traits and disorders. It could be higher (or, more likely, lower) depending on how much dysfunction is required for a diagnosis.

In *DSM-IV* (American Psychiatric Association, 2000), overall diagnosis of a personality disorder requires an enduring pattern of inner experience and behavior that deviates markedly from the expectations of the individual's culture, affecting cognition, affectivity, interpersonal functioning, and impulse control. The pattern must be inflexible and pervasive across a broad range of personal and social situations; lead to clinically significant distress or impairment in social, occupational, or other important areas of functioning; be stable and of long duration; and have an onset that can be traced back at least to adolescence or early adulthood.

Each of these criteria requires an informed clinical judgment. Personality disorder diagnosis is likely to be most reliable when pathology is severe and least reliable when it is not. Only three categories of personality disorder (schizotypal, antisocial, and borderline) have a large empirical literature, and these are also the most useful Axis II diagnoses. There has been very little research on other Cluster B disorders and hardly any on the categories in Cluster C. Moreover, many patients meet the overall criteria in *DSM-IV* for a personality disorder but do not fall into any specific category. They can be classified only as "personality disorder, not otherwise specified" (NOS; about a third of all cases fall into this group; Loranger, Sartori, Andreoli, & Berger, 1994).

In general, categorical diagnosis is useful when cases are truly prototypical. For example, when we describe a patient as a typical case of borderline personality disorder, crucial information is communicated in a compact fashion, pointing to a characteristic outcome and a characteristic treatment response (Paris, 2003).

We need to learn more about the etiology and pathogenesis of personality disorders before we can properly define and categorize them. The current categories are not well-defined phenotypes (Jang, Vernon, & Livesley, 2001), and meaningful diagnosis should ultimately be based on biological findings (Paris 2000a). This is another reason the Axis II clusters may be more valid than individual disorders: They correspond to broad dimensions of psychopathology (cognitive, impulsive, and anxious-affective) that cut across Axis I and Axis II of the *DSM* classification (Krueger, 1999; Paris, 2003; Siever & Davis, 1991). One of the most prominent difficulties with the existing categories is that they overlap, with most patients earning more than one diagnosis (e.g., Pfohl, Coryell, Zimmerman, & Stangl, 1986). Yet many (albeit not all) of these overlaps occur within clusters, again suggesting that the clusters reflect underlying dimensions.

GENES, ENVIRONMENT, AND PERSONALITY TRAITS

Personality traits are heritable, with genetic factors accounting for nearly half of the variance (Plomin, DeFries, et al., 2001). However, single genes are not associated with single traits; rather, the heritable component of personality probably emerges from complex and interactive polygenetic mechanisms associated with variations in multiple alleles. While associations between personality traits and genetic variations might be expected to be measurable as quantitative trait loci, this line of investigation has thus far been disappointing. Promising earlier reports (e.g., Lesch et al., 1996) have not generally been replicated (e.g., Gelertner, Kranzler, & Lacobelle, 1998).

The existence of a genetic component in personality implies that traits could be linked to biological markers. These relationships have also been obscure, with the strongest finding being a consistent relationship between low levels of central serotonin activity and impulsivity (Mann, 1998). Again, the problem lies in the lack of a precise phenotype. Livesley (2003) has suggested that genes and biological markers are more likely to correlate with narrowly defined traits than broader traits such as the "Big Five."

In behavioral genetic research, the other half of the variance in personality differences derives from the "unshared" environment (Plomin, Asbury, & Dunn, 2001; Plomin, DeFries, et al., 2001). Thus, most environmental influences on traits do not derive from being raised in the same family. This finding has been the subject of much controversy because it contradicts classical ideas in developmental and clinical psychology, which focus on parenting as the primary factor shaping personality development (Harris, 1998).

There are several possible reasons that unshared, but not shared, environmental factors influence traits (Plomin, Asbury, et al., 2001). First, a child's temperament affects the response of other people in his or her environment. In a large-scale study of adolescents (Reiss, Hetherington, & Plomin, 2000), using a combination of twin and family methods, multivariate analyses indicated that the temperament of the child was the underlying factor driving differential parenting and behavioral outcomes.

Second, even when the environment is similar for siblings growing up in the same family, each will perceive it differently and respond with different behavioral patterns. Again, it could be that temperamental differences make environmental influences unshared.

A third explanation is that the most important environmental factors affecting personality could be extrafamilial. Every child has shaping experiences with peers, with teachers, or with community leaders (Rutter & Maughan, 1997). Harris (1998) has proposed that peer groups could be more crucial than parents for personality development.

Whatever the ultimate explanation, these findings have profound implications for developmental psychopathology. Harris (1998) suggests that almost all the literature claiming to establish links between childhood experiences and personality has to be questioned and that temperament and traits are latent variables affecting how the environment is perceived and how it affects development. In a telling example of this principle, Plomin and Bergeman (1991) found that behavioral genetic studies of standard measures of life experience, past and present, all demonstrated a heritable component that reflects underlying personality traits.

GENETIC FACTORS IN PERSONALITY DISORDERS

Once we accept the principle that personality disorders are amplified traits, it is logical to expect these conditions to show levels of heritability similar to those behavioral genetic studies have shown for traits. This expectation has now been confirmed. Torgersen et al. (2000) located a large sample of twins in Norway in which one proband met criteria for at least one categorical Axis II diagnosis (including all except the antisocial category). All personality disorders had heritabilities resembling those observed for traits (i.e., close to half the variance). Although the findings cannot be considered quantitatively precise (due to small sample size), they were consistent.

Thus, the heritability coefficient for personality disorders as a whole was .60 (.37 for Cluster A, .60 for Cluster B, and .62 for Cluster C). The lower heritability for Cluster A may seem paradoxical, given the relationship of these disorders to schizophrenia, but it could have been an artifact of a sample in which the base rates of these traits were relatively high, reducing the heritability coefficient.

Although there were no antisocial patients in this cohort, other lines of research (Cadoret, Yates, Troughton, Woodworth, & Stewart, 1995; Cloninger, Sigvardsson, Bohman, & von Knorring, 1982) have suggested heritable factors in that disorder. Notably, in two disorders (the borderline and narcissistic categories) that have aroused the interests of psychoanalysts and have not traditionally been considered to be heritable, genetic factors accounted for about two-thirds of the variance.

Genetic factors influencing traits and disorders have also been supported by the findings of family history studies that have examined spectra of disorders on both Axis I and Axis II. Thus, first-degree relatives of patients with disorders in the A cluster have pathology in the schizophrenic spectrum (Siever & Davis, 1991), patients in the B cluster tend to have relatives with other impulsive disorders (Zanarini, 1993), and patients in the C cluster have first-degree relatives with anxiety disorders (Paris, 1997).

All these findings are best accounted for by a stress-diathesis model. The genetic factors in personality disorders are the same as those determining underlying traits. Given that trait dimensions underlie all forms of psychopathology, it also makes sense for patients with Axis II disorders to have wide-ranging Axis I comorbidity associated with personality pathology.

As already noted, the findings of behavioral genetic research justify a search for biological markers associated with personality disorders. In addition to neurotransmitter activity, suggestive findings have emerged from neurophysiological and neuropsychological research. The most consistent results demonstrate functional abnormalities in prefrontal cortex associated with traits of impulsive aggression. Raine, Lencz, and Bilhul (2000) reported decreases in the mass of frontal gray matter in subjects with antisocial personality. Patients with antisocial and borderline personality demonstrate deficits in executive function as measured by the Wisconsin Card Sorting Test (O'Leary, 2000). Traits associated with Cluster B disorders, most particularly impulsive aggression, are associated with ab-normal responses to neurobiological challenge tests (Coccaro et al., 1989).

PSYCHOLOGICAL FACTORS IN PERSONALITY DISORDERS

Half the variance in personality disorders is environmental: The problem is to determine where it comes from. Traditionally, it was believed that their origins lie in early child-hood, most probably from adverse events associated with defective parenting (Paris, 2000b). This idea seemed to be supported by the defining features of personality disor-ders, which include an early onset and a chronic course. However, disorders that begin early in life and go on to chronicity generally have strong genetic factors in their etiology (Childs & Scriver, 1986; Paris, 2003).

Nonetheless, a large body of evidence supports the concept that childhood adversities do constitute risk factors for personality disorders. In particular, research on borderline personality disorder has documented that histories of sexual abuse, physical abuse, and gross neglect are common (Paris, 1994; Zanarini, 2000). The problem in interpreting these findings is causality. Thus, it has been consistently shown that the impact of psy-chosocial adversities is very different in clinical and community samples. Community surveys of the impact of childhood sexual abuse (Browne & Finkelhor, 1986; Rind & Tro-mofovitch, 1997), as well as of physical abuse (Malinovsky-Rummell & Hansen, 1993), show that only a minority of children exposed to these adversities suffer measurable se-quelae. Trait profiles associated with genetic vulnerabilities may determine whether life experiences lead to psychopathology. Again, adversity would have its greatest effect in a vulnerable subpopulation, so that nature and nurture would have an interactive influence on personality development.

Finally, it is worth remembering that single traumatic events are rarely, by themselves, associated with pathological sequelae, while continuously adverse circumstances lead to cumulative effects (Rutter, 1989). Thus, we cannot understand the impact of childhood trauma outside a longitudinal and developmental context.

One of the main problems with personality disorder research that has examined child-hood risk factors is the use of retrospective methodologies. Reports of life experiences oc-curring many years in the past tend to be colored by recall bias, that is, the tendency for individuals with symptoms in the present to remember more adversities in the past (Robins, Schoenberg, & Holmes, 1985). Again, to address this problem, we need longitudinal data.

A famous follow-back study of children with conduct disorder (Robins, 1966) found that the strongest predictor of adult antisocial personality among conduct-disordered chil-dren was parental psychopathy (usually in the father). This association has also been sup-ported by other researchers (Farrington, 1998). Similarly, first-degree relatives of patients with borderline personality disorder have increased levels of impulsive spectrum disorders (Links, Steiner, & Huxley, 1988; Zanarini, 1993). The precise mechanism of these rela-tionships is unclear (it could involve inheritance, modeling, or pathological parenting). To separate the effects of personality traits common between parents and children from the effects of family dysfunction, research designs are needed in which temperament is con-trolled for. An ongoing study (Dionne, Tremblay, Boivin, Laplante, & Perusse, 2003) has been prospectively following large cohorts of monozygotic and dizygotic twins beginning in early childhood, but results will not be available for some time.

Community studies can be more informative than clinical populations in determining the risk factors for psychopathology. One large-scale prospective longitudinal project, the Albany-Saratoga study, has confirmed a relationship between childhood adversity and personality disorders. In a cohort of children followed into young adulthood, Johnson, Cohen, Brown, Smailes, and Bernstein (1999) observed that early adversities, including neglect, physical abuse, and sexual abuse, were significantly associated with a higher number of personality disorder symptoms. This study is unique, although it had the limitation that the researchers had to use a continuous variable (number of symptoms) to measure outcome, since too few subjects in this study had a diagnosable personality disorder. Another limitation is that the design of the Albany-Saratoga study lacked data on temperamental factors in early childhood that would have preceded environmental adversities.

SOCIAL FACTORS IN PERSONALITY DISORDERS

The role of social factors on personality disorders has been relatively neglected. Yet, like any other form of mental illness, Axis II pathology develops in a sociocultural context. In particular, we might expect to see cross-cultural differences in personality disorders when there is a dysfunction between individual traits and social expectations (Paris, 1996).

While the broader dimensions of personality are similar in different societies (McCrae & Costa, 1999), this may not be so for personality disorders. The categories described by *DSM-IV* (American Psychiatric Association, 2000) or by the *International Classification of Diseases* (ICD-10; World Health Organization, 1992) can be identified in clinical settings around the world (Loranger et al., 1994), but we lack good epidemiological data to measure cross-cultural differences in community prevalence.

Mental disorders can present with different symptoms in different cultures, with some categories of illness being seen only in specific social settings (Murphy, 1982). These principles should apply to personality disorders, which reflect behaviors and feelings highly sensitive to culture. If disorders are pathological amplifications of normal traits that demonstrate some degree of sociocultural variation, personality disorders could present with different symptoms in different social contexts, and some categories might even be culture-bound.

Answering these questions requires transcultural epidemiological research. The largest community surveys, such as the Epidemiological Catchment Area Study (Robins & Regier, 1991) and the National Comorbidity Survey (Kessler et al., 1994), have examined only antisocial personality disorder (with behavioral symptoms that are readily measured). The upcoming International Comorbidity Study will make use of a previously validated instrument, the International Personality Disorder Examination (Loranger et al., 1994), to determine the prevalence of borderline personality disorder.

The strongest evidence for sociocultural factors in personality disorders has come from cohort effects (changes in prevalence over short time periods). Antisocial personality, as well as other impulsive spectrum disorders, has become more common in adolescents and young adults, both in North America and Europe, since World War II (Rutter & Smith, 1999).

Cross-cultural studies have also supported the importance of social factors in antisocial personality disorder. This category is less prevalent in traditional societies such as Taiwan (Hwu, Yeh, & Change, 1989) and Japan (Sato & Takeichi, 1993) but shows a similar prevalence to North American and European levels in Korea (Lee, Kovac, & Rhee, 1987). East Asian cultures that have a low prevalence of antisocial personality have cultural and family structures that tend to be protective against antisocial behavior, in that they support high levels of cohesion. These families are a veritable mirror image of the risk factors for the disorder described by Robins (1966): Fathers are strong and authoritative, expectations of children are high, and family loyalty is prized. These structures, as well as high social cohesion outside the family, would contain individuals whose temperament might otherwise make them vulnerable to impulsive actions. In the same way, the effects of family and social structure on antisocial personality seen in Western societies would affect only individuals who also have an impulsive temperament.

Theodore Millon (1987, 1993, 2000) was the first writer to suggest the existence of cohort effects on the prevalence of borderline personality disorder. Expanding on Millon's ideas, Paris (1996, 2004) pointed out parallel increases in the prevalence of parasuicide and completed suicide (Bland, Dyck, Newman, & Orn, 1998), as well as the finding that a third of youth suicides can be diagnosed with borderline personality disorder (Lesage, Boyer, Grunberg, Morisette, Vanier, et al., 1994).

Millon (1987) also suggested a mechanism accounting for an increase of prevalence for borderline personality: the breakdown of traditional structures guiding the development of adolescents and young adults. In general, traditional societies have high social cohesion, fixed social roles, and intergenerational continuity, while modern societies have lower social cohesion, fluid social roles, and decreased continuity between generations (Lerner, 1958).

Borderline personality disorder may be an example of a condition whose prevalence changes with time and circumstance because it is "socially sensitive" (Paris, 2003, 2004). Many socially sensitive disorders (e.g., substance abuse, eating disorders, antisocial personality, borderline personality) have externalizing symptoms and impulsive traits that are particularly responsive to social context, contained by structure and limits, and amplified by their absence.

Applying a stress-diathesis model, these effects would be seen only in individuals who also have the biological and psychological risk factors for borderline personality. In a similar formulation, Linehan (1993) suggested that borderline patients are vulnerable because of emotional dysregulation and that decreases in social support, interfering with the buffering of affective intensity, amplify this trait.

A parallel conjecture could be made concerning narcissistic personality disorder (Paris, 2003). Although we have no good community studies of the prevalence of narcissistic personality disorder, some clinicians (e.g., Kohut, 1977) have thought that more cases are presenting for treatment. If this is so, we might hypothesize that heritable narcissistic traits are normally channeled into fruitful ambition by strong family and social structures but that under conditions of rapid social change, the same traits can become dysfunctional.

Avoidant personality disorder could be another example of the interaction between nature and nurture. Kagan (1994) has described a temperamental syndrome of "behavioral inhibition" in infants that increases the risk for anxious spectrum disorders in adolescence and that can be amplified by overprotective parenting. Similarly, avoidant personality disorder might not be seen in a traditional society, where anxious traits are buffered by family and community structures, while in modern society, anxious traits are more likely to be disabling, pervasive, and to lead to overt disorders (Paris, 1997).

NATURE, NURTURE, AND THE ETIOLOGY OF PERSONALITY DISORDERS

While both genetic-temperamental factors and psychosocial factors are necessary conditions for the development of personality disorders, neither is sufficient. A good environment may stabilize a vulnerable temperament. In the same way, the effects of adversity are greatest in individuals who are predisposed to psychopathology. Only a combination of risks, that is, a two-hit or multiple-hit mechanism, can account for the development of personality disorders. While the cumulative effects of multiple risk factors determine whether psychopathology develops, the specific disorder that ultimately emerges depends on temperament.

The cumulative effect of multiple risk factors is amplified by gene-environment interactions. Abnormal temperament is associated with a greater sensitivity to environmental risk factors, while individuals with problematic temperaments also experience more adversities during development (Rutter & Maughan, 1997). Children with difficult temperaments elicit responses from others that tend to amplify their most problematic characteristics, creating a positive feedback loop.

The more affected children are by adverse experiences, the more their traits become amplified. The more traits are amplified, the more likely children are to experience further adversities.

EARLY ONSET, COURSE, AND OUTCOME IN PERSONALITY DISORDERS

Well before the development of diagnosable disorders, children may express their vulnerability through early behavioral disturbances. Children at the age of 3 with unusually high levels of aggression and irritability have been shown to be at risk for antisocial personality disorder in early adulthood (Caspi, Moffitt, Newman, & Silva, 1996). When conduct symptoms begin earlier in childhood and are more severe, antisocial personality is likely to develop in adulthood (Zoccolillo, Pickles, Quinton, & Rutter, 1992). However, environmental factors are equally important, and conduct disorder is one of the few diagnoses in psychiatry with a large shared environmental component (Cadoret et al., 1995).

Similarly, infants with unusual shyness and reactivity (behavioral inhibition) may be at risk for anxiety disorders (Kagan, 1994) and for anxious cluster personality disorders as adults (Paris, 1998). Although we do not have as much data on Cluster C disorders, there is some evidence (Head, Baker, & Williamson, 1991) that the environment also plays a role in their etiology.

Typical cases of personality disorder can often be identified in adolescents (Kernberg, Weiner, & Bardenstein, 2000). While specific categories are not necessarily stable over time, personality disorders do not usually remit, but shift within the boundaries of Axis II clusters (Bernstein, Cohen, Skodol, Bezirganian, & Book, 1993). Most young adults with personality disorders can be expected to go on to a chronic course.

Cluster B disorders tend to burn out by middle age (Paris, 2003). In contrast, disorders in Clusters A and C show little improvement over time (Seivewright, Tyrer, & Johnson, 2002). These differences reflect the trait dimensions behind personality disorders: Impulsivity is a trait that normally levels out over time, while cognitive abnormalities and social anxiety do not.

NATURE AND NURTURE IN TREATMENT

The stress-diathesis model of personality disorders has a number of important clinical implications. We must avoid applying purely nature-based or nurture-based perspectives to treatment.

A nature-based perspective would tend to support providing biological treatment for patients with personality disorders. But the efficacy of drugs has to be proved in clinical trials. Currently, severe personality disorders are often seen by psychiatrists who prescribe pharmacotherapy. In the borderline category, patients are often prescribed as many as four to five drugs (Zanarini, Frankenburg, Khera, & Bleichmar, 2001). Yet the value of pharmacotherapy in this group is not well substantiated. While a number of drugs have been used (Soloff, 2000), the best that can be said for them is that they "take the edge off" symptoms such as impulsivity (Paris, 2003). Notably, all agents were originally developed for other conditions: neuroleptics for schizophrenia, antidepressants for depression, and mood stabilizers for bipolar disorder. When we understand the unique pathophysiology associated with personality traits and disorders, we may be in a better position to develop more specific and more useful drugs.

An exclusively nurture-based perspective would tend to justify making psychotherapy the primary form of treatment for personality disorders. Again, the efficacy of such treatment must be demonstrated in clinical trials. In practice, patients with personality disorders are relatively unresponsive to standard forms of psychotherapy, as compared to patients with Axis I disorders without Axis II comorbidity (Shea, Pilkonis, & Beckham, 1990).

There are three possible explanations for the resistance of patients with personality disorders to therapy. First, maladaptive behavioral patterns have been established in childhood and reinforced during adult life. Second, underlying traits are genetically influenced and relatively fixed in adult life. Third, the sequence of interactions between genes and environment that leads to personality disorders may itself produce biological changes. All of these mechanisms may play a role.

Traditionally, patients with personality disorders were seen as having long-term problems that require long-term psychotherapy, based on psychodynamic principles. The problem is that such approaches have not been consistently tested. There is some evidence that these methods can be useful in selected patients with borderline personality (Bateman & Fonagy, 1999; Stevenson & Meares, 1992), but these findings may or may not be generalizable to most patients.

Cognitive approaches to personality disorders (Beck & Freeman, 1990) are overtly based on a stress-diathesis model. While only a few cognitive-behavioral therapy approaches have been systematically tested on patients, the best researched method, dialectical behavior therapy (DBT) for borderline personality (Linehan, 1993), has demonstrated value for reducing impulsive behavior in this population. Positive results have been established within one year, although DBT has not been examined for its long-term efficacy.

When we understand personality disorders better, we will develop integrated and evidence-based treatments based on both nature and nurture. Clinicians of the future will have access to biological interventions that target symptoms more specifically and will prescribe targeted forms of psychotherapy.

CONCLUSIONS

Almost everyone who attempts to deal with the nature-nurture problem has come to the conclusion that both are important. Unfortunately, this principle is often paid only lip service. Those who favor nature give just a little room for nurture and vice versa.

This scenario has played itself out for mental disorders in general and for personality disorders in particular. The pendulum of theory has swung back and forth over the years.

Ultimately, the problem is conceptual. Our minds are programmed for linear ideas and simple attributions. It is difficult to think interactively and multidimensionally, even if we need to do so. Complex models have come to dominate medicine and abnormal psychology. They will generate clinical guidelines for the management of our most chronic and difficult patients.

REFERENCES

Achenbach, T. M., & McConaughy, S. H. (1997). *Empirically based assessment of child and adolescent psychopathology: Practical applications* (2nd ed.). Thousand Oaks, CA: Sage.

American Psychiatric Association. (2000). *Diagnostic and statistical manual of mental disorders* (4th ed., text revision). Washington, DC: Author.

Bateman, A., & Fonagy, P. (1999). Effectiveness of partial hospitalization in the treatment of borderline personality disorder: A randomized controlled trial. *American Journal of Psychiatry, 156,* 1563–1569.

Beck, A. T., Freeman, A., & Associates. (1990). *Cognitive therapy of personality disorders.* New York: Guilford Press.

Bernstein, D. P., Cohen, P., Skodol, A., Bezirganian, S., & Book, J. S. (1993). Prevalence and stability of the *DSM-III* personality disorders in a community-based survey of adolescents. *American Journal of Psychiatry, 150,* 1237–1243.

Bland, R. C., Dyck, R. J., Newman, S. C., & Orn, H. (1998). Attempted suicide in Edmonton. In A. A. Leenaars, S. Wenckstern, I. Sakinofsky, R. J., Dyck, M. J. Kral, R. C. Bland (Eds.), *Suicide in Canada* (pp. 136–150). Toronto: University of Toronto Press.

Browne, A., & Finkelhor, D. (1986). Impact of child sexual abuse: A review of the literature. *Psychological Bulletin, 99,* 66–77.

Cadoret, R. J., Yates, W. R., Troughton, E., Woodworth, G., & Stewart, M. A. (1995). Genetic environmental interaction in the genesis of aggressivity and conduct disorders. *Archives of General Psychiatry, 52,* 916–924.

Caspi, A., Moffitt, T. E., Newman, D. L., & Silva, P. A. (1996). Behavioral observations at age three predict adult psychiatric disorders: Longitudinal evidence from a birth cohort. *Archives of General Psychiatry, 53,* 1033–1039.

Childs, B., & Scriver, C. R. (1986). Age at onset and causes of disease. *Perspectives in Biology and Medicine, 29,* 437–460.

Cloninger, C. R., Sigvardsson, S., Bohman, M., & von Knorring, A. L. (1982). Predisposition to petty criminality in Swedish adoptees: II. Cross-fostering analysis of gene-environment interactions. *Archives of General Psychiatry, 39,* 1242–1247.

Cloninger, C. R., Svrakic, D. M., & Przybeck, T. R. (1993). A psychobiological model of temperament and character. *Archives of General Psychiatry, 50,* 975–990.

Coccaro, E. F., Siever, L. J., Klar, H. M., Maurer, G., Cochrane, K., Cooper, T. B., et al. (1989). Serotonergic studies in patients with affective and personality disorders. *Archives of General Psychiatry, 46,* 587–599.

Costa, P. T., & Widiger, T. A. (Eds.). (2002). *Personality disorders and the Five-Factor Model of Personality* (2nd ed.). Washington, DC: American Psychological Association.

Degler, C. N. (1991). *In search of human nature: The decline and revival of Darwinism in American social thought.* New York: Oxford University Press.

Dionne, G., Tremblay, R., Boivin, M., Laplante, D., & Perusse, D. (2003). Physical aggression and expressive vocabulary in 19-month-old twins. *Developmental Psychology, 39,* 261–273.

Farrington, D. P. (1998). Youth crime and antisocial behavior. In A. Campbell & S. Muncer (Eds.), *The social child* (pp. 353–392). Hove, England: Psychology Press.

Gelertner, J., Kranzler, H., & Lacobelle, J. (1998). Population studies of polymorphisms at loci of neuropsychiatric interest (tryptophan hydroxylase, TPH), dopamine transporter protein (SLC6A3), D3 dopamine receptor (DRD3), apolipoprotein E (APOE), mu opioid receptor (OPRM1), and ciliary neurotrophic factor (CNTF). *Genomics, 52,* 289–297.

Hale, R. (1995). *The rise and crisis of psychoanalysis in the United States.* New York: Oxford University Press.

Harris, J. R. (1998). *The nurture assumption.* New York: Free Press.

Head, S. B., Baker, J. D., & Williamson, D. A. (1991). Family environment characteristics and dependent personality disorder. *Journal of Personality Disorders, 5,* 256–263.

Hwu, H. G., Yeh, E. K., & Change, L. Y. (1989). Prevalence of psychiatric disorders in Taiwan defined by the Chinese Diagnostic Interview Schedule. *Acta Psychiatrica Scandinavica, 79,* 136–147.

Jang, K., Vernon, P. A., & Livesley, W. J. (2001). Behavioural genetic perspectives on personality function. *Canadian Journal of Psychiatry, 46,* 234–244.

Johnson, J. G., Cohen, P., Brown, J., Smailes, E. M., & Bernstein, D. P. (1999). Childhood maltreatment increases risk for personality disorders during early adulthood. *Archives of General Psychiatry, 56,* 600–606.

Kagan, J. (1994). *Galen's prophecy.* New York: Basic Books.

Kendell, R., & Jablensky, A. (2003). Distinguishing between the validity and utility of psychiatric diagnoses. *American Journal of Psychiatry, 160,* 4–12.

Kernberg, P. F., Weiner, A. S., & Bardenstein, K. K. (2000). *Personality disorders in children and adolescents.* New York: Basic Books.

Kessler, R. C., McGonagle, K. A., Nelson, C. B., Hughes, M., Eshelman, S., Wittchen, H. U., et al. (1994). Lifetime and 12-month prevalence of *DSM-III-R* psychiatric disorders in the United States. *Archives of General Psychiatry, 51,* 8–14.

Kohut, H. (1977). *The restoration of the self.* New York: International Universities Press.

Krueger, R. F. (1999). The structure of common mental disorders. *Archives of General Psychiatry, 56,* 921–926.

LeDoux, J. E. (2002). *The synaptic self: How our brains become who we are.* New York: Viking.

Lee, K. C., Kovac, Y. S., & Rhee, H. (1987). The national epidemiological study of mental disorders in Korea. *Journal of Korean Medical Science, 2,* 19–34.

Lerner, D. (1958). *The passing of traditional society.* New York: Free Press.

Lesage, A. D., Boyer, R., Grunberg, F., Morisette, R., Vanier, C., Morrisette, R., et al. (1994). Suicide and mental disorders: A case control study of young men. *American Journal of Psychiatry, 151,* 1063–1068.

Lesch, K. P., Bengel, D., Heils, A., Sabol, S. Z., Greenberg, B. D., Petri, S., et al. (1996). Association of anxiety-related traits with a polymorphism in the serotonin transporter gene regulatory region. *Science, 274,* 1527–1531.

Lewontin, R. C., Rose, S., & Kamin, L. J. (1985). *Not in our genes: Biology, ideology and human nature.* New York: Pantheon.

Linehan, M. M. (1993). *Cognitive behavioral therapy of borderline personality disorder.* New York: Guilford Press.

Links, P. S., Steiner, B., & Huxley, G. (1988). The occurrence of borderline personality disorder in the families of borderline patients. *Journal of Personality Disorders, 2,* 14–20.

Livesley, W. J. (2003). *Personality disorders: A practical approach.* New York: Guilford Press.

Livesley, W. J., & Jang, K. L. (2000). Toward an empirically based classification of personality disorder. *Journal of Personality Disorders, 14,* 137–151.

Livesley, W. J., Jang, K. L., Jackson, D. N., & Vernon, P. A. (1993). Genetic and environmental contributions to dimensions of personality disorders. *American Journal of Psychiatry, 150,* 1826–1831.

Loranger, A. W., Sartori, N., Andreoli, A., & Berger, P. (1994). The International Personality Disorder Examination. *Archives of General Psychiatry, 51,* 215–224.

Luhrmann, T. M. (2000). *Of two minds: The growing disorder in American psychiatry.* New York: Knopf.

Malinovsky-Rummell, R., & Hansen, D. J. (1993). Long-term consequences of physical abuse. *Psychological Bulletin, 114,* 68–79.

Mann, J. J. (1998). The neurobiology of suicide. *Nature Medicine, 4,* 425–430.

McCrae, R. R., & Costa, P. T. (1999). A five-factor theory of personality. In L. A. Pervin & O. P. John (Eds.), *Handbook of personality: Theory and research* (2nd ed., pp. 139–153). New York: Guilford Press.

Meehl, P. E. (1990). Toward an integrated theory of schizotaxa, schizotypy, and schizophrenia. *Journal of Personality Disorders, 4,* 1–99.

Millon, T. (2000). *Personality disorders in modern life.* New York: Wiley.

Millon, T. (1987). On the genesis and prevalence of borderline personality disorder: A social learning thesis. *Journal of Personality Disorders, 1,* 354–372.

Millon, T. (1993). Borderline personality disorder: A psychosocial epidemic. In J. Paris (Ed.), *Borderline personality disorder: Etiology and treatment* (pp. 197–210). Washington, DC: American Psychiatric Press.

Millon, T. (2000). Sociocultural conceptions of the borderline personality. *Psychiatric Clinics of North America, 23,* 123–136.

Millon, T., & Davis, R. D. (1995). *Personality disorders:* DSM-IV *and beyond.* New York: Wiley.

Monroe, S. M., & Simons, A. D. (1991). Diathesis-stress theories in the context of life stress research. *Psychological Bulletin, 110,* 406–425.

Murphy, H. B. M. (1982). *Comparative psychiatry.* New York: Springer.

O'Leary, K. M. (2000). Neuropsychological testing results. *Psychiatric Clinics North America, 423,* 1–60.

Paris, J. (1994). *Borderline personality disorder: A multidimensional approach.* Washington, DC: American Psychiatric Press.

Paris, J. (1996). *Social factors in the personality disorders.* Cambridge, UK: Cambridge University Press.

Paris, J. (1997). Childhood trauma as an etiological factor in the personality disorders. *Journal of Personality Disorders, 11,* 34–49.

Paris, J. (1998). Anxious traits, anxious attachment, and anxious cluster personality disorders. *Harvard Review of Psychiatry, 6,* 142–148.

Paris, J. (1999). *Nature and nurture in psychiatry.* Washington, DC: American Psychiatric Press.

Paris, J. (2000a). The classification of personality disorders should be rooted in biology. *Journal of Personality Disorders, 14,* 127–136.

Paris, J. (2000b). *Myths of childhood.* Philadelphia: Brunner/Mazel.

Paris, J. (2003). *Personality disorders over time.* Washington, DC: American Psychiatric Press.

Paris, J. (2004). Sociocultural factors in the management of personality disorders. In T. Magnavita (Ed.), *Treatment of personality disorders* (pp. 135–147). Hoboken, NJ: Wiley.

Pfohl, B., Coryell, W., Zimmerman, M., & Stangl, D. (1986). *DSM-III* personality disorders: Diagnostic overlap and internal consistency of individual *DSM-III* criteria. *Comprehensive Psychiatry, 27,* 21–34.

Pinker, S. (2002). *The blank slate.* New York: Viking.

Plomin, R., Asbury, K., & Dunn, J. (2001). Why are children in the same family so different? Nonshared environment a decade later. *Canadian Journal of Psychiatry, 46,* 225–233.

Plomin, R., & Bergeman, C. S. (1991). The nature of nurture: Genetic influence on "environmental" measures. *Behavioral and Brain Sciences, 14,* 373–427.

Plomin, R., DeFries, J. C., McClearn, G. E., & Rutter, M. (2001). *Behavioral genetics* (4th ed.). New York: Freeman.

Raine, A., Lencz, T., & Bilhul, S. (2000). Reduced prefrontal gray matter and reduced autonomic activity in antisocial personality disorder. *Archives of General Psychiatry, 37,* 119–127.

Reiss, D., Hetherington, E. M., & Plomin, R. (2000). *The relationship code.* Cambridge, MA: Harvard University Press.

Rind, B., & Tromofovitch, P. (1997). A meta-analytic review of findings from national samples on psychological correlates of child sexual abuse. *Journal of Sex Research, 34,* 237–255.

Robins, L. N. (1966). *Deviant children grown up.* Baltimore: Williams & Wilkins.

Robins, L. N., & Regier, D. A. (Eds.). (1991). *Psychiatric disorders in America.* New York: Free Press.

Robins, L. N., Schoenberg, S. P., & Holmes, S. J. (1985). Early home environment and retrospective recall: A test for concordance between siblings with and without psychiatric disorders. *American Journal of Orthopsychiatry, 55,* 27–41.

Rutter, M. (1987). Temperament, personality, and personality development. *British Journal of Psychiatry, 150,* 443–448.

Rutter, M. (1989). Pathways from childhood to adult life. *Journal of Child Psychology and Psychiatry, 30,* 23–51.

Rutter, M., & Maughan, B. (1997). Psychosocial adversities in psychopathology. *Journal of Personality Disorders, 11,* 19–33.

Rutter, M., & Plomin, R. (1997). Opportunities for psychiatry from genetic findings. *British Journal of Psychiatry, 171,* 209–219.

Rutter, M., & Smith, D. J. (1995). *Psychosocial problems in young people.* Cambridge, UK: Cambridge University Press.

Sameroff, A. J. (1995). General systems theories and developmental psychopathology. In D. Cicchetti & D. J. Cohen (Eds.), *Developmental psychopathology: Theory and methods* (pp. 659–699). New York: Wiley.

Samuels, J., Eaton, W. W., Bienvenu, J., Clayton, P., Brown, H., Costa, P. T., et al. (2002). Prevalence and correlates of personality disorders in a community sample. *British Journal of Psychiatry, 180,* 536–542.

Sato, T., & Takeichi, M. (1993). Lifetime prevalence of specific psychiatric disorders in a general medicine clinic. *General Hospital Psychiatry, 15,* 224–233.

Seivewright, H., Tyrer, P., & Johnson, T. (2002). Change in personality status in neurotic disorders. *Lancet, 359,* 2253–2254.

Shea, M. T., Pilkonis, P. A., & Beckham, E. (1990). Personality disorders and treatment outcome in the NIMH Treatment of Depression Collaborative Research Program. *American Journal of Psychiatry, 147,* 711–718.

Siever, L. J., & Davis, K. L. (1991). A psychobiological perspective on the personality disorders. *American Journal of Psychiatry, 148,* 1647–1658.

Skinner, B. F. (1957). *Verbal behavior.* Englewood Cliffs, NJ: Prentice-Hall.

Soloff, P. (2000). Psychopharmacological treatment of borderline personality disorder. *Psychiatric Clinics of North America, 23,* 169–192.

Stevenson, J., & Meares, R. (1992). An outcome study of psychotherapy for patients with borderline personality disorder. *American Journal of Psychiatry, 149,* 358–362.

Torgersen, S., Lygren, S., Oien, P. A., Skre, I., Onstad, S., Edvardsen, J., et al. (2000). A twin study of personality disorders. *Comprehensive Psychiatry, 41,* 416–425.

Weissman, M. M. (1993). The epidemiology of personality disorders: A 1990 update. *Journal of Personality Disorders, 7*(Suppl.), 44–62.

World Health Organization. (1992). *International classification of diseases* (10th ed.). Geneva, Switzerland: Author.

Zanarini, M. C. (1993). Borderline personality as an impulse spectrum disorder. In J. Paris (Ed.), *Borderline personality disorder: Etiology and treatment* (pp. 67–86). Washington, DC: American Psychiatric Press.

Zanarini, M. C. (2000). Childhood experiences associated with the development of borderline personality disorder. *Psychiatric Clinics North America, 23,* 89–101.

Zanarini, M. C., Frankenburg, F. R., Khera, G. S., & Bleichmar, J. (2001). Treatment histories of borderline inpatients. *Comprehensive Psychiatry, 42,* 144–150.

Zoccolillo, M., Pickles, A., Quinton, D., & Rutter, M. (1992). The outcome of childhood conduct disorder: Implications for defining adult personality disorder and conduct disorder. *Psychological Medicine, 22,* 971–986.

Chapter 3

IDENTITY DIFFUSION IN SEVERE PERSONALITY DISORDERS

OTTO F. KERNBERG

A FEW DEFINITIONS

To begin, I shall refer to temperament and character as crucial aspects of personality. Temperament refers to the constitutionally given and largely genetically determined, inborn disposition to particular reactions to environmental stimuli, particularly to the intensity, rhythm, and thresholds of affective responses. I consider affective responses, particularly under conditions of peak affect states, crucial determinants of the organization of the personality. Inborn thresholds regarding the activation of both positive, pleasurable, rewarding, and negative, painful, aggressive affects represent, I believe, the most important bridge between biological and psychological determinants of the personality (Kernberg, 1994). Temperament also includes inborn dispositions to cognitive organization and to motor behavior, such as, the hormonal-, particularly testosterone-derived differences in cognitive functions and aspects of gender role identity that differentiate male and female behavior patterns. Regarding the etiology of personality disorders, however, the affective aspects of temperament appear as of fundamental importance.

In addition to temperament, character is another major component of personality. Character refers to the particular dynamic organization of behavior patterns of each individual that reflect the overall degree and level of organization of such patterns. While academic psychology differentiates character from personality, the clinically relevant terminology of character pathology, character neurosis, and neurotic character refer to the same conditions, also referred to as personality trait and personality pattern disturbances in earlier *DSM* classifications, and to the personality disorders in *DSM-III* and *DSM-IV*. From a psychoanalytic perspective, I propose that character refers to the behavioral manifestations of ego identity, while the subjective aspects of ego identity, that is, the integration of the self-concept and of the concept of significant others are the intrapsychic structures that determine the dynamic organization of character. Character also includes all the behavioral aspects of what in psychoanalytic terminology is called ego functions and ego structures.

From a psychoanalytic viewpoint, the personality is codetermined by temperament and character, but also by an additional intrapsychic structure, the superego. The integration of value systems, the moral and ethical dimension of the personality—from a psychoanalytic viewpoint, the integration of the various layers of the superego—are an important component of the total personality. Personality itself, then, may be considered the dynamic integration of all behavior patterns derived from temperament, character, and internalized value systems (Kernberg, 1976, 1980). In addition, the dynamic unconscious or the id constitutes the dominant, and potentially conflictive, motivational system of the personality. The extent to which sublimatory integration of id impulses into ego and superego functions has taken place reflects the normally adaptive potential of the personality.

The normal personality is characterized by an integrated concept of the self and an integrated concept of significant others. These structural characteristics, jointly called ego identity (Erikson, 1956; Jacobson, 1964) are reflected in an internal sense and an external appearance of self-coherence and are a fundamental precondition for normal self-esteem, self-enjoyment, and zest for life. An integrated view of one's self assures the capacity for a realization of one's desires, capacities, and long-range commitments. An integrated view of significant others guarantees the capacity for an appropriate evaluation of others, empathy, and an emotional investment in others that implies a capacity for mature dependency while maintaining a consistent sense of autonomy as well.

IDENTITY AND OBJECT RELATIONS THEORY

At the Personality Disorders Institute of the Department of Psychiatry of the Weill Cornell Medical College, we have studied the psychopathology, clinical diagnosis and psychotherapeutic treatment of identity diffusion on the basis of the application of contemporary psychoanalytic object relations theory. I have applied this theory to the understanding of the development of normal and pathological identity, and, in the process, defined and explored further the characteristics of identity diffusion (Kernberg, 1976, 1984, 1992).

In essence, the basic assumption of contemporary object relations theory is that all internalizations of relationships with significant others, from the beginning of life on, have different characteristics under the conditions of peak affect interactions and low affect interactions. Under conditions of low affect activation, reality-oriented, perception controlled cognitive learning takes place, influenced by temperamental dispositions, that is, the affective, cognitive and motor reactivity of the infant, leading to differentiated, gradually evolving definitions of self and others. These definitions start out from the perception of bodily functions, the position of the self in space and time, and the permanent characteristics of others. As these perceptions are integrated and become more complex, interactions with them are cognitively registered, evaluated, and working models of them established. Inborn capacities to differentiate self from nonself, and the capacity for cross-modal transfer of sensorial experience play an important part in the construction of the model of self and the surrounding world.

In contrast, under conditions of peak affect activation—be they of an extremely positive, pleasurable or an extremely negative, painful mode, specific internalizations take place framed by the dyadic nature of the interaction between the baby and the caretaking person, leading to the setting up of specific affective memory structures with powerful motivational implications. These structures are constituted, essentially, by a representation of self interacting with a representation of significant other under the dominance of a peak affect state. The importance of these affective memory structures lies in their constituting the basis of the primary psychic motivational system, in the direction of efforts to approach, maintain, or increase the conditions that generate peak positive affect states, and to decrease, avoid, and escape from conditions of peak negative affect states.

Positive affect states involve the sensuous gratification of the satisfied baby at the breast, erotic stimulation of the skin, the disposition to euphoric "in tune" interactions with mother; peak negative affective states involve situations of intense physical pain, hunger, or painful stimuli that trigger intense reactions of rage, fear, or disgust, and may motivate general irritability and hypersensitivity to frustration and pain. Object relations theory assumes that these positive and negative affective memories are built up separately in the early internalization of these experiences and, later on, are actively split or dissociated from each other in an effort to maintain an ideal domain of experience of the relation between self and others, and to escape from the frightening experiences of negative affect states. Negative affect states tend to be projected, to evolve into the fear of "bad" external objects, while positive affect states evolve into the memory of a relationship with "ideal" objects. This development evolves into two major, mutually split domains of early psychic experience, an idealized and a persecutory or paranoid one, idealized in the sense of a segment of purely positive representations of self and other, and persecutory in the sense of a segment of purely negative representations of other and threatened representation of self. This early split experience protects the idealized experiences from "contamination" with bad ones, until a higher degree of tolerance of pain and more realistic assessment of external reality under painful conditions evolves.

This early stage of development of psychic representations of self and other, with primary motivational implications—move toward pleasure and away from pain—eventually evolves toward the integration of these two peak affect determined segments, an integration facilitated by the development of cognitive capacities and ongoing learning regarding realistic aspects of self and others interacting under circumstances of low affect activation. The normal predominance of the idealized experiences leads to a tolerance of integrating the paranoid ones, while neutralizing them in the process. In simple terms, the child recognizes that it has both "good" and "bad" aspects, and so does mother and the significant others of the immediate family circle, while the good aspects predominate sufficiently to tolerate an integrated view of self and others.

This state of development, referred to by Kleinian authors (Klein, 1940; Segal, 1964) as the shift from the paranoid-schizoid to the depressive position, and by ego psychological authors as the shift into object constancy, presumably takes place somewhere between the end of the first year of life and the end of the third year of life. Here Margaret Mahler's (Mahler, 1972a, 1972b) research on separation-individuation is relevant, pointing to the gradual nature of this integration over the first three years of life. At the same time, however, in the light of contemporary infant research, Margaret Mahler's notion of an initial autistic phase of development followed by a symbiotic phase of development seem contradicted by the nature of the evidence. Rather than reflecting a symbiotic stage of development, what seems relevant are "symbiotic" moments of fantasized fusion between self representation and object representation under peak affect conditions, momentary fusions that are counteracted by the inborn capacity to differentiate self from nonself, and the real and fantasized intervention of "third excluded others," particularly the representation of father disrupting the states of momentary symbiotic unity between infant and mother. Here mother's capacity to represent a "third excluded other" becomes important: French authors have stressed the importance of the image of the father in the mother's mind.

Peter Fonagy's (Fonagy & Target, 2003) referral to the findings regarding mother's capacity to "mark" the infant's affect that she congruently reflects to the infant points to a related process: mother's contingent (accurate) mirroring the infant's affect, while marked (differentiated) signaling that she does not share it while still empathizing with it, contributes to the infant's assimilating his own affect while marking the boundary between self and other. Under normal conditions, then, an integrated sense of self ("good and bad"), surrounded by integrated representations of significant others ("good and bad"), that are also differentiated among each other in terms of their gender characteristics as well as their status/role characteristics, jointly determine normal identity.

The concept of ego identity originally formulated by Erikson included in its definition the integration of the concept of the self; an object relations approach expands this definition with the corresponding integration of the concepts of significant others. In contrast, when this developmental stage of normal identity integration is not reached, the earlier developmental stage of dissociation or splitting between an idealized and a persecutory segment of experience persists. Under these conditions, multiple, nonintegrated representations of self split into an idealized and persecutory segment, and multiple representations of significant others split along similar lines, jointly constituting the syndrome of identity diffusion. One might argue that, in so far as Erikson considered the confirmation of the self by the representations of significant others as an aspect of normal identity, he already stressed the relevance of that relationship between the self concept and the concept of significant others, but he did not as yet conceive of the intimate connection between the integration or lack of it on the part of the concepts of self and the parallel achievement or failure in the corresponding concepts of others. It was the work of Edith Jacobson (1954) in the United States, powerfully influencing Margaret Mahler's conceptualizations, and the work of Ronald Fairbairn (1954) in Great Britain, who pointed to the dyadic nature of the development of early internalizations and created the basis for the contemporary psychoanalytic object relations theory.

This formulation of the internalization of dyadic units under the impact of peak affect states has significant implications for the psychoanalytic theory of drives, for the understanding of the etiology of identity diffusion, and for the psychoanalytic psychotherapy of severe personality disorders or borderline personality organization. Regarding the psychoanalytic theory of drives, this formulation supports the proposal I have formulated in recent years, that affects are the primary motivational system, and that Freud's dual drive theory of libido and aggression corresponds, respectively, to the hierarchically supraordinate integration of positive and negative affect states. The integration of affects determines the functions of the drives, and the drives, in turn, are manifest in each concrete instance in the activation of an affect state that links a certain representation of self with a certain representation of object. These include the wishful and frightening erotic fantasies of highly desired and potentially forbidden relationships between self and others, as well as highly threatening and potentially disorganizing fantasies of aggressive relationships.

ETIOLOGY OF IDENTITY DIFFUSION

In short, the major proposed hypothesis regarding the etiological factors determining severe personality disorders or borderline personality organization is that, starting from a temperamental predisposition to the predominance of negative affect and impulsivity or lack of effortful control, the development of disorganized attachment, exposure to physical or sexual trauma, abandonment, or chronic family chaos predispose the individual to the abnormal fixation at the early stage of development that predates the integration of normal identity: a general split persists between idealized and persecutory internalized experiences under the dominance of corresponding negative and positive peak affect states. Clinically, this state of affairs is represented by the syndrome of identity diffusion, with its lack of integration of the concept of the self and the lack of integration of the concepts of significant others. The question still remains, what other temperamental, psychodynamic, or psychosocial factors may then influence the development of the specific constellations of pathological character traits that differentiate the various constellations of severe personality disorder from each other, a subject that remains to be explored. The fact that much of the relevant research involves borderline personality disorder points to the need to carry out such studies involving other severe personality disorders.

From a clinical standpoint, the syndrome of identity diffusion explains the dominant characteristics of borderline personality organization. The predominance of primitive dissociation or splitting of the idealized segment of experience from the paranoid one is naturally reinforced by primitive defensive operations intimately connected with splitting mechanisms, such as, projective identification, denial, primitive idealization, devaluation, omnipotence and omnipotent control. All these defensive mechanisms contribute to distorting interpersonal interactions and create chronic disturbances in interpersonal relations, thus reinforcing the lack of self reflectiveness and of "mentalization" in a broad sense, decreasing the capacity to assess other people's behavior and motivation in depth, particularly, of course, under the impact of intense affect activation. The lack of integration of the concept of the self interferes with a comprehensive integration of one's past and present into a capacity to predict one's future behavior, and decreases the capacity for commitment to professional goals, personal interests, work and social functions, and intimate relationships.

The lack of integration of the concept of significant others interferes with the capacity of realistic assessment of others, with selecting partners harmonious with the individual's actual expectations, and with investment in others. All sexual excitement involves a discrete aggressive component (Kernberg, 1995). The predominance of negative affect dispositions leads to an infiltration of the disposition for sexual intimacy with excessive aggressive components, determining, at best, an exaggerated and chaotic persistence of polymorphous perverse infantile features as part of the individual's sexual repertoire, and, at worst, a primary inhibition of the capacity for sensual responsiveness and erotic enjoyment. Under these latter circumstances, severely negative affects eliminate the very capacity for erotic response, clinically reflected in the severe types of sexual inhibition that are to be found in the most severe personality disorders.

The lack of integration of the concept of self and of significant others also interferes with the internalization of the early layers of internalized value systems, leading particularly to an exaggerated quality of the idealization of positive values and the ego ideal, and to a persecutory quality of the internalized, prohibitive aspects of the primitive superego. These developments lead, in turn, to a predominance of splitting mechanisms at the level of internalized value systems or superego functions, with excessive projection of internalized prohibitions, while the excessive, idealized demand for perfection further interferes with the integration of a normal superego. Under these conditions, antisocial behavior may emerge as an important aspect of severe personality disorders, particularly in the syndrome of malignant narcissism, and in the most severe type of personality disorder, namely, the antisocial personality proper, which evinces most severe identity diffusion as well (Kernberg, 1984, 1992). In general, normal superego formation is a consequence of identity integration, and, in turn, protects normal identity. Severe superego disorganization, in contrast, worsens the effects of identity diffusion.

The treatment of personality disorders depends, in great part, on their severity, reflected in the syndrome of identity diffusion. The presence or absence of identity diffusion can be elicited clinically in initial diagnostic interviews focused on the structural characteristics of personality disorders. The dimensional aspects—greater or lesser degrees of identity diffusion—still require further research. From a clinical standpoint, the extent to which ordinary social tact is still maintained or lost is the dominant indicator of the severity of the syndrome. The diagnosis of identity diffusion or of normal identity, in short, acquires fundamental importance in the clinical assessment of patients with personality disorders.

THE CLINICAL ASSESSMENT OF IDENTITY

At the Personality Disorders Institute at Cornell we have developed a particular mental status examination designated "structural interviewing," geared to the differential diagnosis of personality disorders. In essence, this interview, that ordinarily takes up to one and one half-hours of exploration, consists of various steps of inquiry into the patient's functioning. The first step evaluates all the patient's symptoms, including physical, emotional, interpersonal and generally psychosocial aspects of malfunctioning, inappropriate affect experience and display, inappropriate behavior, inordinate difficulties in assessing self and others in interactions and in negotiating ordinary psychosocial situations. This inquiry into symptoms is pursued until a full differential diagnosis of prominent symptoms and characterological difficulties has been achieved.

The second step of this interview explores the patient's present life situation, including his or her adaptation to work or a profession, the patient's love life and sexual experiences, the family of origin, the patient's friendships, interests, creative pursuits, leisure activities, and social life in general. It also explores the patient's relation to society and culture, particularly ideological and religious interests, and his or her relationship to sports, arts, and hobbies. In short, we attempt to obtain as full a picture as possible of the patient's present life situation and interactions, raising questions whenever any aspect of the patient's present life situation seems obscure, contradictory, or problematic. This inquiry complements the earlier step of exploration of symptoms and, at the same time, makes it possible to compare the patient's assessment of his or her life situation and potential challenges and problems with the patient's interaction with the diagnostician as this exploration proceeds. At this point, we obtain an early assessment of pathological character traits, be they predominantly inhibitory, reaction formations, or contradictory and conflictual behavior patterns.

A third step of this structural interview consists in raising the question of the personality assessment by the patient of the two or three most important persons in his or her present life, followed by the assessment of his or her description of himself or herself as a unique, differentiated individual. The leading questions here are: "Could you now describe to me the personality of the most important persons in your present life that you have mentioned, so that I can acquire a live picture of them?" "And now, could you also describe yourself, your own personality, as it is unique or different from anybody else, so that I can acquire a live picture of it?"

As the fourth step of this interview, and only in cases with significant disturbances in the manifestations of their behavior, affects, thought content, or formal aspects of verbal communication during the interview, the diagnostician raises, tactfully, questions about that aspect of the patient's behavior, affect, thought content, or verbal communication that has appeared as particularly curious, strange, inappropriate, or out of the ordinary, warranting such attention. The diagnostician communicates to the patient that a certain aspect of his or her communication has appeared puzzling or strange to the diagnostician, and raises the question, whether the patient can see that, and what his or her explanation would be for the behavior that puzzles the diagnostician.

Such a tactful confrontation will permit the patient with good reality testing to be aware of what it is in himself or herself that has created a particular reaction of the interviewer, and provide him or her with an explanation that reduces the strangeness or puzzling aspect of that behavior. This response, in other words, indicates good reality testing. If, to the contrary, such inquiry leads to an increased confusion, disorganization, or abnormal behavior in the interaction with the diagnostician, reality testing is presumably lost. The maintenance of reality testing is an essential aspect of the personality disorders, who may have lost the subtle aspects of tactfulness in social interactions, but maintained good reality testing under ordinary social circumstances. Loss of reality testing presumably indicates an atypical psychotic disorder or an organic mental disorder: that finding would lead to further exploration of such behavior, affect, or thought in terms of a standard mental status examination. In any case, a clear loss of reality testing indicates that an active psychotic or organic mental disorder is present, and that the primary diagnosis of a personality disorder cannot be established at this time.

Otherwise, with reality testing maintained, the interview would permit the diagnosis of a personality disorder, the predominant constellation of pathological character traits, and its severity in terms of the presence or absence of the syndrome of identity diffusion. The capacity to provide an integrated view of significant others and of self indicates normal identity. Good interpersonal functioning, that does not even raise the question of any strange or puzzling aspect of the present interaction would not warrant the exploration of reality testing. Patients with borderline personality organization, who present identity diffusion, also typically evince behaviors reflecting primitive defensive operations in the interaction with the diagnostician. These findings are less crucial than the diagnosis of the identity diffusion, but they certainly reinforce that diagnostic conclusion.

While this method of clinical interviewing has proven enormously useful in the clinical setting, it does not lend itself, unmodified, for empirical research. A group of researchers at our Institute is presently transforming this structural interview into a semi-structured interview, geared to permit the assessment of personality disorders by way of an instrument (Structured Interview for Personality Organization [STIPO]; Clarkin, Caligor, Stern, & Kernberg, 2003) geared to empirical research. The clinical usefulness of the structural interview, however, may be illustrated by typical findings in various characterological constellations.

To begin, in the case of adolescents, structural interviewing makes it possible to differentiate adolescent identity crises from identity diffusion. In the case of identity crises, the adolescent may present with a sense of confusion about the attitude of significant others toward himself, and puzzlement about their attitude that does not correspond to his self-assessment. Asked to describe the personality of significant others, however, particularly from his immediate family, their description is precise and in depth. By the same token, while describing a state of confusion about his relationships with others, the description of his own personality also conveys an appropriate, integrated view, even including such confusion about his relationships that corresponds to the impression that the adolescent gives to the interviewer. In addition, adolescents with identity crisis but without identity diffusion usually show a normal set of internalized ethical values, interests, and ideals, commensurate with their social and cultural background. It is remarkable that, even if such adolescents are involved in intense struggles around dependence and independence, autonomy and rebelliousness with their environment, they have a clear sense of these issues and their conflictual nature, and their description of significant others with whom they enter in conflict continues to be realistic and cognizant of the complexity of the interactions.

To the contrary, in the case of identity diffusion, the descriptions of the most important persons in his or her life on the part of an adolescent with borderline personality organization are vague and chaotic, and so is his or her description of the self, in addition to the emergence of significant discrepancies in the description of the adolescent's present psychosocial interactions, on the one hand, and the interaction with the interviewer, on the other. It is also typical for severe identity diffusion in adolescence that there exists a breakdown in the normal development of ideals and aspirations. The adolescent with identity diffusion may display a severe lack of internalized value systems, or a chaotic and contradictory attitude toward such value systems.

In contrast to the diagnostic value of exploring identity and internalized value systems, other aspects of the mental status examination are less important in the case of adolescents. Thus, particularly, the dominance of primitive defensive operations is less important than it would be in adult patients. The reason is that, with a reactivation of oedipal conflicts, and conflicts about sexuality in general, primitive defensive operations may emerge, particularly in the area of conflicts with the parents. Severe conflicts with intimate members of the family are diagnostically much less important than they would be later on. Chaotic experiences in the sexual realm, manifestations of polymorphous perverse infantile sexuality, rather extreme oscillations between inhibited, puritanical attitudes and impulsive sexual behavior also are not necessarily indicative of identity diffusion at this time.

The nature of adolescent school failure also includes a broad spectrum of diagnostic possibilities and does not reflect directly the syndrome of identity diffusion: depressive reactions, attention-deficit-hyperactivity disorder, physical, sexual or emotional abuse, significant inhibitions of many origins, the characteristic pattern of narcissistic personalities of being the best student in some courses and the worst in others, and generalized breakdown in the functioning at school as a reflection of identity diffusion have to be differentiated from each other. The capacity to fall in love and to maintain a stable love relation, in general, is related to normal identity, but some adolescents may be delayed in their capacity to establish sexual intimacy out of inhibition, and the absence of that capacity is not necessarily diagnostic. Sexual promiscuity, on the other hand, may or may not reflect identity diffusion in adolescence. Significant changes in mood and emotional lability are also less important in the diagnosis of identity diffusion in adolescence than in adults. Finally, the relationship of an adolescent with his or her particular psychosocial group may provide important clues to both identity and superego developments. The capacity for a harmonious participation in group structures needs to be differentiated from the blind adherence to an isolated social subgroup, and from the incapacity to function outside the protective structure of such a group. Chronic social isolation, in contrast to the capacity to adjust to group situations also may point to significant character pathology. The relationship to groups permits us to clarify the potential presence of a negative identity.

The most typical manifestations of the syndrome of identity diffusion, that is, a clear lack of integration of the concept of self and of the concept of significant others can be found in patients with borderline personality disorder, and, to a somewhat lesser degree, in patients with histrionic or infantile personality disorder. In contrast, in the case of the narcissistic personality disorder, what is most characteristic is the presence of an apparently integrated, but pathological, grandiose self, contrasting sharply with a severe incapacity to develop an integrated view of significant others: the lack of the capacity for grasping the personality of significant others is most dramatically illustrated in the narcissistic personality disorder. An opposite situation may emerge in patients with schizoid personality disorders, where a lack of integration of the concept of the self may be matched by very subtle observations of significant others. In the case of schizotypal personality, in contrast, both the concept of self and the concept of significant others are severely fragmented, similar to the case of the borderline personality disorders. It is interesting to observe that in the rare cases of multiple personalities, a careful evaluation of the personality structure of the alters reflects the mutually split off fragmentation of the patient's self concept, while a similar lack of integration of the concept of significant others permeates all the alters of the patient's personality.

THE TREATMENT OF IDENTITY DIFFUSION

The transference focused psychotherapy (TFP) that we have developed over the past twenty-five years at the Personality Disorders Institute at the Weill Cornell University Medical College is specifically geared to resolve the identity diffusion of patients with borderline personality organization (Clarkin, Yeomans, & Kernberg, 1999; Kernberg, 1984; Koenigsberg et al., 2000; Yeomans, 1992). It is the central objective of the corresponding treatment strategies. Transference focused psychotherapy is a specialized form of psychoanalytic or psychodynamic psychotherapy, that has been manualized. The efficacy of this manualized treatment has been empirically confirmed and further empirical studies of it are under way (Clarkin et al., 2001). This treatment can be characterized by its defined techniques, strategies, and tactics. The techniques are, in essence, those of standard psychoanalysis, modified quantitatively for these patients, including interpretation, transference analysis, and technical neutrality. Transference focused psychotherapy requires a minimum of two sessions per week and is carried out in "face to face" sessions. The patient receives instructions for carrying out a modified form of free association, and the therapist's interventions are limited to psychoanalytic techniques, as mentioned before, and avoids supportive technical interventions to facilitate full and in depth analysis of the transference.

The tactical principles of the treatment include rules and procedures that apply in each session, the consideration of particular priorities of interventions, and management of complications in the treatment. These tactics involve, first of all, special modes of contract setting geared to protecting, at all times, the patient's life, the lives of others, the continuity of the treatment, and, above all, the maintenance of the treatment frame. This frame usually is severely tested by regressive transference developments. In addition, tactics involve a series of priorities of interventions in the light of frequent complications in the treatment, including severe suicidal behavior, threats to the continuity of the treatment, severe acting out in and outside the sessions, patients' mendacity, blocking of treatment development by severe narcissistic resistances, and defensive trivialization of the content of the hours.

Particular tactics are geared to deal with the manifestation of extreme aggression in the hours, the management of affect storms, psychopathic transferences, paranoid micropsychotic episodes, chronic sado-masochistic acting out, and the threat to the treatment by drug or alcohol abuse, eating disorders, and other psychopathologies frequently complicating severe personality disorders. Treatment tactics also involve the application of general psychoanalytic techniques as mentioned before, such as the dynamic, economic, and structural considerations regarding when, how, and what to focus upon and in what order to intervene interpretively in each session. The severity of the fragmentation of the communicative process, the dominance of nonverbal communication and intense counter-transference activations are other aspects of typical treatment developments that are included in setting these tactical principles for technical interventions in each hour.

The overall strategy consists of the focus on the diagnosis and resolution of identity diffusion. This strategic objective guides the nature of transference interpretations from the beginning of the treatment, throughout its entire duration. This strategy is expressed in three successive steps of interpretive interventions: first, the clarification, at each point of each session, of the now dominant, primitive, fantasized, enacted or acted out interpersonal relationship emerging in the session, and the affect expressing it in the transference. A second step is the clarification of the representation of self and the representation of the other in the activation of this object relation in the transference, and of the dominant affect state framing the relationship between self and object representations at that point. In addition, as part of this second step, the therapist interprets consistently the interchange between representation of self and representation of object that is characteristic for the primitive transference developments of borderline patients, a result of their primitive defensive operations, particularly projective identification. The third step is the interpretive integration of mutually split off internalized object relations activated in the transference, so that the idealized object relationships and their corresponding split off, paranoid counterparts are brought together in the therapist's interpretive comments, thus leading to an integration of the concept of self and the integration of the concept of significant others.

The fact that the dominant object relations are clarified in step one, and then, in step two, systematically analyzed throughout time, including their frequent role reversals, facilitates the patient's growing capacity to accept his or her unconscious identifications with mutually split off self and object representations, thus also facilitating that third step of integrative interpretive interventions.

Step one of this procedure evolves, practically, from the first session of treatment on, and constitutes a consistent effort throughout the entire treatment. Step two requires extensive work over many weeks and even months, before a situation evolves that permits the therapist to move into the interpretive stance of step three. The entire cycle of this movement, therefore, may at first last for many months, only to repeat itself as part of the working through of the same transference predispositions, in cycles that gradually reduce their length to weeks, and, eventually, days. Toward the termination of the treatment, the entire cycle of interventions—the three steps—might be condensed within the same hour.

As a result of this strategy and the gradual integration of the concept of self and of significant others, there also evolves a gradual integration, modulation, and cognitive complexity of affect states, together with a greater capacity of the patient to reduce affective impulsivity, and a deepening of his or her object relations in the context of the consistent increase in the capacity for self reflectiveness that evolves as a major consequence of this strategic approach. The manual published by our Institute describing transference focused psychotherapy explains in detail and illustrates clinically this entire treatment approach (Clarkin et al., 1999).

CONCLUSION

Identity diffusion is a defining characteristic of those with severe personality disorders that results in disturbances of affect regulation as well as the ability to accurately assess, interpret, and judge the meaning of important interpersonal and intrapersonal events. In this essay I describe the etiology of identity diffusion, as well as its assessment and treatment using a structured interview and manualized treatment protocol developed at the Personality Disorders Institute at Cornell University.

REFERENCES

Clarkin, J. F., Caligor, E., Stern, B., & Kernberg, O. F. (2003). *Structured interview of personality organization* (STIPO). Unpublished manuscript.

Clarkin, J. F., Foelsch, P. A., Levy, K. N., Hull, J. W., Delaney, J. C., & Kernberg, O. F. (2001). The development of a psychodynamic treatment for patients with borderline personality disorder: A preliminary study of behavioral change. *Journal of Personality Disorders, 15*(6), 487–495.

Clarkin, J. F., Yeomans, F. E., & Kernberg, O. F. (1999). *Psychotherapy for borderline personality.* New York: Wiley.

Erikson, E. H. (1956). The problem of ego identity. *Journal of the American Psychoanalytic Association, 4,* 56–121.

Fairbairn, W. R. D. (1954). *An object-relations theory of the personality.* New York: Basic Books.

Fonagy, P., & Target, M. (2003). *Psychoanalytic: Perspectives on developmental psychopathology.* London: Routledge.

Jacobson, E. (1954). The self and the object world. *Psychoanalytic Study of the Child, 9,* 75–127.

Jacobson, E. (1964). *The self and object world.* New York: International Universities Press.

Kernberg, O. F. (1976). *Object relations theory and clinical psychoanalysis.* New York: Aronson.

Kernberg, O. F. (1980). *Internal world and external reality: Object relations theory applied.* New York: Aronson.

Kernberg, O. F. (1984). *Severe personality disorders: Psychotherapeutic strategies.* New Haven, CT: Yale University Press.

Kernberg, O. F. (1992). *Aggression in personality disorders and perversions.* New Haven, CT: Yale University Press.

Kernberg, O. F. (1994). Aggression, trauma, and hatred in the treatment of borderline patients. In I. Share (Ed.), *Borderline personality disorder: The psychiatric clinics of North America* (pp. 701–714). Philadelphia: Saunders.

Kernberg, O. F. (1995). *Love relations: Normality and pathology.* New Haven, CT: Yale University Press.

Klein, M. (1940). Mourning and its relation to man-depressive states. In *Contributions to psychoanalysis, 1921–1945* (pp. 311–338). London: Hogarth Press.

Koenigsberg, H. W., Kernberg, O. F., Stone, M. H., Appelbaum, A. H., Yeomans, F. E., & Diamond, D. (2000). *Borderline patients: Extending the limits of treatability.* New York: Basic Books.

Mahler, M. S. (1972a). On the first three subphases of the separation-individuation process. *International Journal of Psycho-Analysis, 53,* 333–338.

Mahler, M. S. (1972b). Rapprochement subphases of separation-individuation process. *Psychoanalytic Quarterly, 41,* 487–506.

Segal, H. (1964). *Introduction to the work of Melanie Klein.* New York: Basic Books.

Yeomans, F. E. (1992). *Treating the borderline patient: A contract based approach.* New York: Basic Books.

Chapter 4

A LANGUAGE AND METHODOLOGY FOR STUDYING THE HIERARCHIES IN THE DSMS

ROGER K. BLASHFIELD AND ELIZABETH H. FLANAGAN

The *Diagnostic and Statistical Manual of Mental Disorders* (*DSM*) has undergone six revisions in the past 60 years (*DSM-I*, 1952; *DSM-II*, 1968; *DSM-III*, 1980; *DSM-III-R*, 1987; *DSM-IV*, 1994; *DSM-IV-TR*, 2000). The primary goal of these revisions has been to create better definitions of diagnostic categories. As a result of this aim, over time, diagnostic categories have gone from being defined by prose paragraphs (in *DSM-I* and *DSM-II*) to lists of diagnostic criteria (after *DSM-III*). An aspect of the *DSM* that has often been ignored by researchers is that these diagnostic categories are also arranged into a hierarchy (for an exception, see Phillips, Price, Greenberg, & Rasmussen, 2003). This lack of focus on the hierarchy of the *DSM* is problematic because, to create a classification system that is useful to the clinicians who diagnose and treat people with mental disorders, it is important to understand the relationship between diagnostic categories in the *DSM* as well as how these categories are organized in clinicians' minds.

DSM HIERARCHICAL ORGANIZATION OF MENTAL DISORDERS

The hierarchical nature of the *DSM* is implied by the list of diagnostic category names that appear near the start of each edition. For example, pages 2 to 7 of the *DSM-I* (American Psychiatric Association, 1952) listed all of the diagnoses appearing in that edition. The hierarchical organization on these pages was denoted by the outline format of these categories so that the category names form a hierarchy. At the highest level, this hierarchical arrangement starts (from top down) with a binary subdivision of mental disorders into organic disorders versus nonorganic disorders. Interestingly, mental retardation was listed as a minor exception to this binary starting level because, presumably, mental retardation was viewed as a mixture of organic and psychological factors. In the *DSM-I*, these three starting categories were defined as:

I. Disorders caused by or associated with impairment of brain tissue function.

II. Mental deficiency.

III. Disorders of psychogenic origin or without clearly defined physical cause or structural change of the brain.

These three major groups were further divided into second-level categories. For example, superordinate group III ("Disorders of psychogenic origin . . .") was subdivided into:

A. Psychotic disorders.
B. Physiologic autonomic and visceral disorders.
C. Psychoneurotic disorders.
D. Personality disorders.
E. Transient situational personality disorders.

Notice that these categories are organized essentially along a severity continuum from psychosis (most severe) to transient situational disorders (least severe). Each of these secondary categories was further subdivided. For instance, part of the classification of personality disorders in the *DSM-I* had the following hierarchical structure:

III. Disorders of psychogenic origin.
   D. Personality disorders.
      1. Personality pattern disturbance.
         a. Inadequate personality.
         b. Schizoid personality.
         c. Cyclothymic personality.
         d. Paranoid personality.
      2. Personality trait disturbance.
         a. Emotionally unstable personality.
         b. Passive-aggressive personality.
         c. Compulsive personality.
         d. Personality trait disturbance, other.
      3. Etc., etc., etc., etc.

The hierarchical organization of mental disorder categories was not unique to the *DSM-I*. On pages 13 to 26 of the *DSM-IV-TR* (2000), the most recent version of the *DSM*, is a listing of all diagnostic categories that are recognized in this edition. The highest level of this hierarchical system is represented by names, which are set off by double lines above and below (for an example, see Table 4.1). There are 17 categories at this highest level, in contrast to the relative simplicity of the three superordinate categories in the *DSM-I*. Examples of the names in the *DSM-IV-TR* superordinate categories are:

• Disorders usually first diagnosed in infancy, childhood and adolescence.
• Delirium, dementia and amnestic and other cognitive disorders.
• Mental disorders due to a general medical condition not elsewhere classified.
• Factitious disorders.
• Dissociative disorders.
• Sexual and gender identity disorders.

Table 4.1   Example of Hierarchical Diagnosis in *DSM-IV-TR*

<hr>

Sexual and Gender Identity Disorders

Sexual Dysfunctions

The following specifiers apply to all primary sexual dysfunctions:
Lifelong type/Acquired type
General type/Situational type
Due to psychological factors/Due to combined factors

Sexual Desire Disorders

302.71 Hypoactive sexual desire disorder
302.79 Sexual aversion disorder

Sexual Arousal Disorders

302.72 Female sexual arousal disorder
302.72 Male erectile disorder

Orgasmic Disorders

302.73 Female orgasmic disorder
302.74 Male orgasmic disorder
302.75 Premature ejaculation

Sexual Pain Disorders

302.76 Dyspareunia (Not due to a general medical condition)
306.51 Vaginismus (Not due to a general medical condition)

Sexual Dysfunction Due to a General Medical Condition

625.8   Female hypoactive sexual desire due to...[Indicate the general medical condition]
608.89 Male hypoactive sexual desire disorder due to...[Indicate the general medical condition]
607.84 Male erectile disorder due to...[Indicate the general medical condition]
625.0   Female dyspareunia due to...[Indicate the general medical condition]
608.89 Male dyspareunia due to...[Indicate the general medical condition]
625.8   Other female sexual dysfunction due to...[Indicate the general medical condition]
608.89 Other male sexual dysfunction due to...[Indicate the general medical condition]
___.__ Substance-induced sexual dysfunction (refer to Substance-Related Disorders for
          substance-specific codes) *Specify if:* With impaired desire/With impaired arousal/
          With impaired orgasm/with sexual pain *Specify if:* With onset during intoxication
302.70 Sexual dysfunction NOS

Paraphilias

302.4   Exhibitionism
302.81 Fetishism
302.89 Frotteurism
302.2   Pedophilia *Specify if:* Sexually attracted to males/Sexually attracted to females/Sexually
          attracted to both *Specify if:* Limited to incest *Specify if:* Exclusive type/Nonexclusive
          type
302.83 Sexual masochism
302.84 Sexual sadism
302.3   Transvestic fetishism *Specify if:* With gender dysphoria
302.82 Voyeurism
302.9   Paraphilia NOS

Table 4.1   *(Continued)*

Gender Identity Disorders

302.xx Gender identity disorder

.6 in children

.85 in adolescents and adults *Specify if:* Sexually attracted to males/Sexually attracted to females/Sexually attracted to both/Sexually attracted to neither

302.6 Gender identity disorder NOS

302.9 Sexual disorder NOS

Note: Compiled from *DSM-IV-TR* (American Psychiatric Association, 2000; pp. 22–23).

Source: Reprinted with permission from the *Diagnostic and Statistical Manual of Mental Disorders, Fourth Edition,* Text Revision copyright 2000, American Psychiatric Association.

- Eating disorders.
- Sleep disorders.

These highest level categories are then subdivided into second-level categories denoted in the *DSM-IV-TR* in uppercase, boldface letters (e.g., **SEXUAL DYSFUNCTIONS**). The third level of categories is represented in boldface, but appears in lowercase letters (e.g., **Sexual Desire Disorders**). The fourth level lists the names in roman type, with the first letter of each word capitalized and preceded by a full ICD code number (e.g., Hypoactive Sexual Desire Disorder). The fifth level contains names that are indented, often start with a preposition (e.g., a subdivision of Gender Identity Disorder is "in children"), and have abbreviated ICD code numbers. The sixth level contains subdivisions that appear as "specifiers" that are written in roman type (e.g., a specifier for Gender Identity Disorder is "sexually attracted to males"). The fourth level of names in this hierarchical system is considered to be the diagnostic level (i.e., the level on which clinicians generally make diagnoses), as most of these categories are defined using diagnostic criteria in the body of the *DSM-IV-TR*. Most categories at other levels are not defined using diagnostic criteria.

One aspect of the psychiatric classification system that varies across diagnoses is the logic of the subdivisions of the categories. For instance, the **Sexual Arousal Disorders** are divided based on gender. **Dyssomnias** are divided based on the symptoms of the sleep problem (e.g., insomnia, hypersomnia). Gender Identity Disorder is divided based on age (i.e., "in children" versus "in adolescents or adults"). In the childhood disorders, the subdivisions of **MENTAL RETARDATION,** like the severity continuum in the *DSM-I* organization of "psychogenic" disorders, are organized along a dimension of severity from "mild" to "profound." The subdivision of other disorders appears to be nominal. **LEARNING DISORDERS** is divided into Reading Disorder, Mathematics Disorder, Disorder of Written Expression, and Learning Disorder NOS, paralleling the main skills learned in school (i.e., "reading, 'riting and 'rithmetic").

GOALS OF THIS CHAPTER

Little attention has been paid to the structure and implications of this hierarchical system. There were work groups responsible for determining the disorders included in each of the higher order categories of the *DSM* as well as the definitions of the disorders; however, no work group was dedicated to determining the overall structure of the psychiatric classification system. Arguably, the overall structure of the *DSM* was monitored by the parent committee on nomenclature. However, given the complicated political forces that faced the parent committee, a separate work group charged with the responsibility of determining the organization of the *DSM* and checking the output from the other work groups for consistency with this organization would have been a better solution.

There are two primary goals of this chapter. The first goal is to provide a vocabulary for discussing hierarchical systems. With a common language, researchers can start discussing the implications of a hierarchical system and work toward building a more meaningful and useful diagnostic system. To achieve this first goal, we discuss three metaphors for studying hierarchical systems: set theoretical notions of hierarchies from biological classification, shallow hierarchies focused on the basic level studied by cognitive psychologists, and complex hierarchies determined by anthropologists studying folk taxonomies. We discuss the role and implications of hierarchies in these models and analyze the *DSM* in accordance with these models.

The second goal of this chapter is to suggest a methodology, based in folk taxonomic theory, for studying the hierarchy of the *DSM*. Anthropologists have been studying hierarchical classification systems for the past 40 years. These anthropologists have a rich and generative folk taxonomic theory about the structure and implications of these systems. Recently, cognitive psychologists have used this theory to study the hierarchical structure of people's conceptions of plants and animals (e.g., Medin, Lynch, Coley, & Atran, 1997). There is great potential for this methodology to be a feasible measure of clinicians' thinking about mental disorders and the hierarchical structure of clinicians' taxonomies. In this chapter, we present preliminary data showing the application of this method to clinicians' taxonomies of mental disorders.

Our hope is that, with a common language and methodology, researchers will be able to discuss the relationship between diagnostic categories and the hierarchical structure that underlies all recent classification systems of psychopathology. It is only by understanding the implications of the structure of our diagnostic classification system that we will be able to develop a valid and useful classification system of psychopathology.

HIERARCHY IN BIOLOGICAL CLASSIFICATION

When attempting to clarify conceptual issues associated with psychiatric classification, some writers have used other areas of scientific classification. For instance, Paul Meehl (1995) made reference to biological classification in his lecture when receiving the American Psychological Association Award for Distinguished Professional Contribution to Knowledge:

> Biological taxa are defined with words that biologists choose, relying on the relevant morphological, physiological, ecological, and ethological facts. We admire Linneaus, the creator of modern taxonomy, for discerning the remarkable truth—a "deep structure" fact, as Chomsky might say—that a bat doesn't sort with the chickadee and the whale doesn't sort with the pickerel, but both are properly sorted with the grizzly bear; whereas Pliny the Elder had it the other way around.
>
>   It must be obvious that I am not a scientific fictionist but a scientific realist. I see classification as an enterprise that aims to carve nature at its joints (Plato), identifying categories of entities that are in some sense (not metaphysical "essentialist") nonarbitrary, not man-made. The verbal definition of them once we have scientific insight is, of course, man-made, a truism that does not prove anything about ontology or epistemology. There

are gophers, there are chipmunks, but there are no gophmunks. Those two species would be there whether any human being noticed them or christened them. (pp. 267–268)

Meehl's (1995) metaphorical references to biological classification as a means of elucidating our ideas about psychiatric classification seem reasonable. Biologists have focused on the issues of classification for over three centuries. In the past 20 years, the topic of classification in the biological sciences has experienced a resurgence of interest with the development of competing theories about classification (Hull, 1988).

Definitions of Categories

Buck and Hull (1966), who studied set theory classification in biology, suggested that there are two major ways to define categories. In the *extensional* definition, a name is defined by listing its members. An extensional definition of borderline personality disorder, for instance, would contain the names of all people who have that disorder. Although the number of members for a mental disorder category is finite, the number is usually so large as to be uncountable. Thus, this type of definition is not useful for mental disorder categories.

The other type of definition for categories is *intensional* (Buck & Hull, 1966). In an intensional definition, a taxon is defined by listing the characteristics that are needed for an entity to be a member of that category. Biologists (e.g., Beckner, 1959) recognize two broad types of intensional definitions: *monothetic* and *polythetic*. A monothetic definition lists the characteristics that an entity *must have* to be considered a member of the category. If the entity does not have all characteristics, it is not considered a member of the category. The first two versions of the *Diagnostic and Statistical Manual of Mental Disorders, DSM-I* (1952) and *DSM-II* (1968), had monothetic definitions. Specifically, categories were defined by a prose definition that indicated the important features that were necessary for a person to have the disorder. For instance, in the *DSM-I* (1952), the definition for someone with schizoid personality was as follows:

> Inherent traits in such personalities are (1) avoidance of close relations with others, (2) inability to express direct hostility or even ordinary aggressive feelings, and (3) autistic thinking. These qualities result early in coldness, aloofness, emotional detachment, fearfulness, avoidance of competition, and daydream revolving around the need for omnipotence. As children, they are usually quiet, shy, obedient, sensitive, and retiring. At puberty, they frequently become more withdrawn, then manifesting the aggregate of personality traits known as introversion, namely, quietness, seclusiveness, "shut-in-ness," and unsociability, often with eccentricity. (p. 35)

In this definition, the characteristics that a person with schizoid personality must possess are indicated. These qualities are described over time as well as how certain deficits (e.g., inability to express hostility) turn into particular characteristics. Having these characteristics is necessary to have schizoid personality. Similarly, having these characteristics is enough to qualify someone for having the disorder. Either a person possesses these characteristics, thereby having a schizoid personality, or he or she does not have these characteristics, thereby not having a schizoid personality. There is no discussion of what to do if a person possesses some characteristics of this disorder but not others. Last, with this definition, all people with schizoid personality will look alike and have these features; therefore, all people who have schizoid personality are similarly good members of the category.

In *polythetic* definitions, all characteristics listed are not necessary, but some subsets of the characteristics are jointly sufficient. Although even Aristotle realized that requiring monothetic definitions for all taxa would not be practical, no formal discussion of polythetic definitions appeared in the literature until Beckner (1959). According to Beckner, a category has a polythetic definition if:

1. Each member of the category possesses a large (but unspecified) number of the total number of defining characteristics of the category.
2. Each defining characteristic is possessed by a large number of members of the category.
3. No property is possessed by every member of the category (adapted from Mayr, 1969).

Starting with the *DSM-III* (1980), polythetic definitions have been used to define many mental disorder categories. For instance, to be diagnosed with borderline personality disorder according to the *DSM-IV* (1994), a person must demonstrate at least five of the following nine features:

1. Frantic efforts to avoid abandonment.
2. Unstable interpersonal relationships.
3. Identity disturbance.
4. Self-damaging impulsivity.
5. Recurrent suicidal gestures.
6. Affective instability due to a marked reactivity of mood.
7. Chronic feelings of emptiness.
8. Inappropriate, intense anger.
9. Transient, stress-related paranoid ideation.

With this kind of definition, there is considerable heterogeneity among category members (i.e., people with borderline personality disorder). In fact, there are 126 different ways (regardless of order) for a patient to display five of the nine features. Thus, it is quite possible that two people with borderline personality disorder will have only one feature in common.

An issue associated with intensional definitions of categories is choosing the characteristics that will be used in these definitions. Frake (1972) used the concept of *contrast set* to denote which characteristics were important to include in an intensional definition. A contrast set refers to the set of categories from which a particular category must be distinguished when it is defined. In biological classification, a contrast set consists of all categories occurring immediately below a common node in the hierarchy. For instance, the contrast set for the species *Felis catus* includes other species that are members of the genus *Felis* (the higher order category that includes *Felis catus*). Because all members of the genus *Felis* share the feature "having fur," this characteristic is not listed as a defining feature of *Felis catus*. Instead, the features for *Felis catus* are the characteristics that differentiate it from other categories that are included in the higher order category *Felis*.

In psychiatric classification, the contrast set is often listed as "differential diagnoses," or other diagnoses that the clinician should consider when diagnosing a person with a disorder. Unlike biological classification, however, the contrast sets of psychiatric classification do not follow the hierarchical structure of the system (i.e., the contrast categories are not all part of the same higher order category). For instance, the differential diagnosis list for borderline personality disorder includes *mood disorders, personality change due to a general medical condition,* the V code *identity problem,* and the other 12 personality disorders, most of which are in a different personality disorder cluster than is borderline. According to the principles of biological classification and Frake's (1972) notion of contrast sets, the most useful way to differentiate borderline from other mental disorder categories is to have the "differential diagnoses" all be part of the same higher order category. Also, to be most useful, the definition of borderline and the definitions for the other mental disorders in the same higher order category should be based on what features *differentiate* between the disorders. Features that they share in common should be listed as defining the higher order category (e.g., defining the superordinate category of personality disorders).

Hierarchical Structure in Biological Classification

In 1954, a logician named John Gregg published a monograph entitled *The Language of Taxonomy.* In this monograph, Gregg discussed the hierarchical structure of biological classification using principles from set theory. In Gregg's perspective, there are three levels of names in a standard biological classification:

N1 names—the names of individual organisms (e.g., "Mittens").

N2 names—the names of individual categories (e.g., *Felis catus* or *Acinonyx jubatus*).

N3 names—the names of ranks (e.g., species, genus, family).

Gregg stated that three relationships can exist among the types of names. The first relationship is *membership.* This relationship can occur between any two names that are one type (of name) apart. For instance, "Mittens" (an N1 name) is a member of the category *Felis catus* (an N2 name). The category *Felis catus* (an N2 name) is a member of the rank named species (an N3 name). Similarly, the Glenn Close character in the movie *Fatal Attraction* is a member of the category borderline personality disorder (an N2 name). There is no relationship between N2 and N3 names in the *DSM* because there are no names for the ranks (i.e., there are no names analogous to genus, species, or family).

In fact, a primary difference between psychiatric and biological hierarchical structure is that there are no names for the ranks in psychiatric classification. In addition, the number of ranks varies considerably depending on the higher order category. For instance, the higher order category Anxiety Disorders has no intermediate categories between the parent category (Anxiety Disorders) and the diagnostic categories. Under the higher order category Sexual and Gender Identity Disorders, however, there are two levels of intermediate categories between the parent category and the diagnoses. For instance, the diagnostic category hypoactive sexual desire disorder is included in the intermediate category Sexual Desire Disorders, which is included in the higher level intermediate category Sexual Dysfunctions, which is included in the parent category Sexual and Gender Identity Disorders. Psychiatric classification needs to have names for the ranks so that the number of ranks is consistent across disorders and the hierarchical level of the diagnostic category is clear from the rank. This type of consistency will improve communication among clinicians and clinicians' conceptualizations of patients.

A second relationship that can exist among the three types of names is the relationship of *inclusion.* Inclusion is a relation that can occur only among N2 (i.e., category) names.

The family-level category *Felidae* "includes" the genus *Felis* as well as the species *Felis catus, Panthera tigris,* and *Acinonyx*. The relationship of inclusion occurs between two names of the different ranks when all members of the included category are also members of the higher ranked category. Thus, the species *Felis catus* is included in the family *Felidae* because all organisms that are members of *Felis catus* are also members of *Felidae*. Similarly, Personality Disorders includes the categories schizotypal, avoidant, histrionic, dependent, and so on. All people who are members of these categories are also members of the category Personality Disorders.

A third relationship that can exist among names is *hierarchy*. In his monograph, Gregg (1954) proposed a complex, formal definition of hierarchy in terms of the relationships among N2 (category) names. In essence, Gregg's definition of hierarchy stipulates that categories at lower ranks have fewer members than categories at higher ranks; that there are successively fewer categories as the hierarchy moves upward; and that all categories of the same rank are mutually exclusive. The structure of the *DSM* somewhat follows Gregg's definition of hierarchy. Categories at lower ranks (i.e., schizoid personality disorder) have fewer members than categories at higher ranks (i.e., personality disorders). There are more categories at the lower, diagnostic level than at higher levels of the *DSM* hierarchy. For example, there are 17 superordinate categories in the *DSM-IV-TR,* but there are over 200 categories with diagnostic criteria (fourth-level categories). The issue of whether all categories of the same rank are mutually exclusive is problematic.

This last point is quite important. Whether categories are *mutually exclusive* is problematic in psychiatric classification on two levels. First, in biological classification, being mutually exclusive means that, if a particular animal is a member of one category, then that animal cannot also be a member of another category. For instance, the housecat Mittens is a member of *Felis catus*. The property of being mutually exclusive prohibits Mittens from also being a member of the category *Panthera leo* (lion). In contrast, voluminous data on psychiatric comorbidity show that patients often receive more than one diagnosis, especially for the personality disorders (Blashfield, McElroy, Pfohl, & Blum, 1994; McGlashan et al., 2000).

The second problem with mutual exclusivity in psychiatric classification is that there is much overlap in the criteria for diagnostic categories. As we indicated in the discussion of contrast sets (Frake, 1972), to be most useful, the defining features of categories should represent what differentiates categories from each other. This lack of feature overlap is also important for creating categories that are mutually exclusive. For example, paranoid ideation is a symptom of schizotypal personality disorder, paranoid personality disorder, borderline personality disorder, paranoid schizophrenia, schizoaffective disorder, delusional disorder, brief psychotic disorder, shared psychotic disorder, psychotic disorder due to a medical condition, substance-induced psychotic disorder, and psychotic disorder NOS. Because "paranoid ideation" is a feature of all of those categories, these categories are not mutually exclusive. Moreover, this collection of categories (i.e., borderline personality disorder + delusional disorder + schizoaffective disorder) does not create a useful contrast set that a clinician can use when making a diagnosis.

A last important feature of hierarchical systems from the perspective of biological classification is that the categories should be *exhaustive* (Bailey, 1994). This property requires that categories exist at all of the required ranks so that any individual organism can be identified in terms of these categories. Therefore, if a paleontologist discovers the skeleton of a cat that is sufficiently different from any other known species of cats, then a new taxonomic category can be created. This new taxonomic category is also included in a genus, a family, and so on. Psychiatric classification is exhaustive as a result of the "not otherwise specified" (NOS) categories. These categories are "wastebasket" categories with no defining features so that atypical patient presentations can be fit into a diagnostic category. These categories also fit into higher order categories (e.g., personality disorder NOS is included in the higher order category Personality Disorders).

THE FAILURE OF THE MODEL OF BIOLOGICAL CLASSIFICATION FOR THE CLASSIFICATION OF PSYCHOPATHOLOGY

We have discussed several differences between biological classification and psychiatric classification. The lack of mutually exclusive categories is the most obvious reason the model of biological classification does not fit psychiatric classification. In biological classification, if categories are not mutually exclusive, then the inclusion relation among categories is violated and the hierarchical nesting of categories makes little sense. In psychiatric classification, there is extensive overlap in category membership, even across wide branches of the hierarchical tree (e.g., patients with avoidant personality disorder are often very similar to patients with the subtype of anxiety disorder known as social phobia). Notice also that, although clinicians know that an important issue in diagnosis of avoidant personality disorder is its differentiation from social phobia, these two disorders are not included under the same superordinate category.

Another way of emphasizing the almost total lack of separation among categories in psychiatric classification when these categories are viewed as sets is to examine the list of differential diagnoses for specific categories. As was shown previously, the list of differential diagnoses for most categories is quite lengthy and is not restricted to categories that fall in the same section of the hierarchical structure of the classification.

A second major difference between the set theory model of biological classification and psychiatric classification is the lack of names for ranks associated with psychiatric classification. Concepts like species, genus, family, order, and so on have no obvious parallels. The only plausible parallel is between the concept of "species" and the concept of "disease." This parallel would make sense if all of the categories at the lowest level in psychiatric classification were viewed as representing specific diseases. To most casual users of a classification of psychopathology, this would mean that there should be evidence for separate etiologies associated with these disease-rank categories. Although one might view this possibility as theoretically desirable, clearly the disease status of most forms of psychopathology is still questionable. The preceding analysis introduces a second reason why there is a parallel between disease and species: Both have extensive histories of controversial attempts to define them. In effect, the definitions of these concepts have been subject to metadiscussions about which theoretical approach to biological or psychiatric classification is most fruitful and should have dominance.

The final comment about the differences between the set theoretical model of biological classification and psychiatric classification is that, if diagnostic categories are not mutually exclusive sets, this fact calls into question many of the standard research designs about psychopathology. For instance, a common design to test the diagnostic specificity of a new therapeutic drug is to sample patients with two or three different diagnoses and compare the outcomes of the patients while on this drug. This simple one-way ANOVA design assumes that the diagnoses represent nonoverlapping sets of patients. Patients are randomly sampled from these sets, often with the requirement that these patients must meet the criteria for only one of the diagnoses. If the diagnostic categories do not represent separate sets of patients, then the appropriateness of this research design needs to be rethought.

HIERARCHICAL STRUCTURE AND BASIC-LEVEL CATEGORIES

We discussed hierarchies of categories according to the set theoretical approach of biological classification. Hierarchies of categories have also been discussed by cognitive psychologists. Rosch (1978) described hierarchies of categories as the "vertical dimension": "the level of inclusiveness of the category—the dimension along which the terms collie, dog, mammal, animal, and living thing vary" (p. 30). In contrast, "The horizontal dimension concerns the segmentation of categories at the same level of inclusiveness—the dimension on which dog, cat, car, bus, chair, and sofa vary" (p. 30).

The vertical dimension is based on the notion that not all levels of inclusiveness of categories are equally useful (Rosch, 1978). In particular, the *basic level* is the level of inclusiveness at which the feature structure in the category mirrors the correlation structure of the features in the real world. Categories more inclusive than the basic-level categories are called *superordinate categories,* and categories less inclusive than the basic level are called *subordinate categories.* For instance, consider the features four legs, flat top surface, and used for eating. A basic-level name for this group of features might be "table," a superordinate name might be "furniture," and a subordinate category might be "kitchen table."

Across different domains (e.g., objects, events, person categories), basic, superordinate, and subordinate categories have similar features. The basic level of category usually has a short name, which is familiar to most people, is learned earliest by children, and is given most quickly and most often in the presence of the category (Murphy, 2002). Superordinate and subordinate categories are more difficult to learn. Children do not seem to know the meaning of either level right away, and people avoid naming individual objects on these levels.

Also, there are similarities across domains in the structure of these various categories. Superordinate categories (e.g., "furniture") tend to have few features in common, and the features that members do share tend to be abstract and functional (Murphy, 2002). For instance, "entertainment center" and "sofa" are both kinds of furniture, but they have few similar features except for the abstract feature "is in one's house" and the functional feature "is used for daily living." Subordinate categories (e.g., "kitchen table"), on the other hand, share many of the features of the basic-level category and generally have the same functions as the basic-level category, although more specific details are included in the subordinate category that allow them to be more informative to a user. Despite this added information, people tend to name categories on the basic level unless the information given by the subordinate level is particularly relevant.

Determining the basic level is an empirical question, and defining it has aroused debate. Rosch (1978) argued that the basic level maximizes *cue validity* and *category resemblance.* Cue validity is determined by the frequency that a feature x is a predictor of a given category y. The validity of a cue x as a predictor of category y increases or decreases as a function of the number of times that x and y are associated in the real world. In the previous example, "having four legs" is a better predictor of the basic-level category "table" than it is of "furniture" because "having four legs" is more often associated with tables in the real world than with furniture. Thus, Rosch argued that cue validity is maximized on the basic level. Contrary to Rosch, Murphy (1982) argued that the superordinate level has the highest cue validity because a superordinate category includes basic-level categories and the cue validity of a category can never be lower than the category it includes. Thus, cue validity alone cannot account for the basic level.

Rosch (1978) also argued that the basic-level categories maximize category resemblance, the weighted sum of all the common features in a category minus the sum of all of the distinctive features. Distinctive features include those features that belong to only some members of the category in addition to features belonging to other categories. For instance, members of the basic-level category "table" share many features in common and do not have many features that belong to other categories. In the superordinate category "furniture," however, members share fewer common attributes, and there are many atypical items (e.g., "entertainment center") that have features that are not shared by the rest of members. On the other hand, members of the subordinate category "kitchen table" all have common attributes, but there is also much overlap in the features of that category and the features of other categories (e.g., kitchen tables are quite similar to dining room tables and coffee tables). In essence, category resemblance is the conditional probability of possessing a feature given category membership. This probability is roughly the opposite of the probability for the cue validity measure and is therefore subject to a similar criticism raised by Murphy (1982): Category resemblance is highest at the subordinate level because more specific categories have less variability in their features.

In response to the difficulties with Rosch's definition, Jones (1983) proposed that the basic level can be predicted by computing the *category-feature collocation,* which is the product of cue and category validity measures. Corter and Gluck (1992) argued that this measure is inadequate and proposed the measure *category utility,* which combines base rate information about the category, the category validity of the category's features, and the base rate of each of the category's features. One problem with all of these methods is deciding which features should be included in the analysis (Murphy, 1982; Murphy & Medin, 1985).

As an explanation of the basic-level phenomenon, Murphy and Brownell (1985) argued that the basic level is preferred because it is the most differentiated; basic-level categories are associated with large amounts of information (i.e., have high *informativeness*) and also are quite different from other categories at the same level (i.e., have high *distinctiveness*). Subordinate categories are informative (in fact, are often more informative than basic-level categories), but they are not very distinct. In contrast, superordinate categories are quite distinct but not very informative. Rosch (1978) argued that the basic-level phenomenon occurs because of the need for cognitive economy. In theory, all categories should be as informative as possible. Informativeness is greatest at the most subordinate level; however, most humans cannot simply memorize categories at the subordinate level because there are too many of them. In fact, the human conceptual system works better with a few fairly informative concepts than with a large number of highly informative concepts. Thus, the principle of distinctiveness serves to limit the number of concepts. Despite the controversy over how to explain the basic level (e.g., is it due to cue validity, category validity, category-feature collocation, or category utility), the occurrence of basic-level categories is quite robust and they appear consistently in all types of classifications.

Cantor, Smith, French, and Mezzich (1980) conducted the only study to date that measured the basic-level categories in psychopathology. Using categories from the *DSM-II* (1968), Cantor et al., asked subjects to list the features that characterize the prototypical patient for one higher level category (functional psychosis), two middle-level categories (schizophrenia and affective disorder), and six lower level categories (paranoid schizophrenia, schizoaffective disorder, chronic undifferentiated schizophrenia, manic depressive disorder-depressed, manic depressive disorder-manic, and involutional melancholia). Across the categories, there were many features given by only one clinician, a considerable number of features given by 2 to 4 clinicians, and very few features given by all 13 clinicians. In addition, clinicians gave many features not listed in the *DSM-II*.

In Rosch, Mervis, Grey, Johnson, and Boyes-Braem's (1976) studies of objects, they defined the basic level as the hierarchical level at which there was a large change in the number of features listed as compared with a superordinate category and not many more features listed at the subordinate level. When examining the number of features clinicians listed at each hierarchical level, Cantor et al. (1980) found that the largest change in the number of features listed generally occurred when moving from the highest level to the middle level (i.e., the diagnostic level) of the hierarchy, and that many more features were not listed at the lower level of the hierarchy compared with the middle level. In fact, for the subordinate categories of schizophrenia, clinicians listed the same number of or fewer features for the subordinate categories as for schizophrenia. The one exception to this pattern was a larger change in the number of features listed going from the diagnostic category affective disorder to the subordinate category manic depressive disorder-manic (nine features were added) than from the superordinate category functional psychosis to the diagnostic category affective disorder (eight features were added).

Cantor et al. (1980) also found that the categories at the middle level (i.e., diagnostic level) of the hierarchy were most distinctive. The feature lists for schizophrenia and affective disorders shared only 1 feature in common, whereas the disorders on the lowest level of the hierarchy (e.g., involutional melancholia) shared on average 6.3 features with other disorders that were subtypes of the same diagnostic category. Similarly, the middle-level categories had an average of 15.5 distinctive features (features appearing only for that category), while the lower level categories had an average of 11.6 distinctive features in comparison with other disorders that were subtypes of the same diagnostic category.

The Basic Level and the Classification of Psychopathology

After the publication of the Cantor et al. (1980) paper, interest in the relationship between the prototype model and psychopathology burgeoned. Researchers investigated the extent to which psychodiagnostic categories were heterogeneous (Clarkin, Widiger, Frances, Hurt, & Gilmore, 1983; Widiger, Sanderson, & Warner, 1986) and fit the family resemblance hypothesis (Blashfield, Sprock, Haymaker, & Hodgin, 1989; Horowitz, Post, French, Wallis, & Siegelman, 1981; Horowitz, Wright, Lowenstein, & Parad, 1981; Livesley, 1985a, 1985b, 1986; McElroy, Davis, & Blashfield, 1989). Considerable effort was also expended trying to determine which cases were prototypes for disorders. Surprisingly, it was quite difficult to find prototypes for some disorders. Also, patients with more features of a category were not always considered to be more prototypic of the category (Blashfield, Sprock, Pinkston, & Hodgin, 1985).

Cantor et al. (1980) suggested that the polythetic definitions used in the *DSM* are consistent with the idea of "family resemblances," which is central to the prototype model. This association of the prototype model with polythetic definitions, however, is not correct. In particular, what Wittgenstein (1953) meant by the concept of family resemblances is not the same as a polythetic definition. For Wittgenstein, family resemblance is based on the idea that subsets of category members share some characteristics. Other entities not belonging to that category can also have those characteristics. There can also be category members that do not share many of the important characteristics. Polythetic definitions make no comments about the last two points (i.e., members of other categories or atypical members of the categories).

In contrast, Beckner (1959) argued that a category has a polythetic definition if (1) each member is similar to other members because all members possess an unspecified but large amount of the total number of defining characteristics, (2) each characteristic is possessed by many members of the category, and (3) no property is possessed by every member of the category. The "Chinese menu" style of polythetic definition (in which an entity fits into a category because it has several defining features of the category) does fit Beckner's meaning of a polythetic definition, but Beckner's meaning is broader than merely having several defining features. This style of polythetic definition assumes that all features are linearly related and combine in an equally weighted manner. Beckner's definition does not make any assumptions about the relationship between the features or the manner in which they combine.

Thus, the prototype model and polythetic definitions of categories should not be equated, although they often have been (e.g., Cantor et al., 1980; Clarkin et al., 1983; Widiger & Frances, 1985; Widiger et al., 1986). One possible source of this confusion could be the phonetic similarity of the words "prototype" and "polythetic." Another likely reason is that, when the *DSM* switched from monothetic to polythetic definitions, from *DSM-II* (1968) to *DSM-III* (1980), writers at the time (see list above) stated that the *DSM* was based on a prototype model. However, no edition of the *DSM* has explicitly specified what classificatory model was being used.

Another reason for thinking that the *DSM-III* (1980) does not fit the prototype model is that a major goal of the prototype model is to describe how humans use concepts. The creators of the *DSM-III* did not view their goal as representing how clinicians use concepts. The authors were trying to create the best scientific classification system possible at the time, with an emphasis on definitions that described the symptoms of patients.

With the publication of the *DSM-IV* in the early 1990s, interest in the prototype model died out. The makers of the *DSM-IV* made no attempt to specify the type of classification system (e.g., set theoretical, prototype) they were creating, and the *DSM* moved away from any attempt to structure psychiatric classification around the way clinicians think about mental disorders. Instead, the goal of the *DSM-IV* became increasingly essentialist: to "carve nature at its joints" (Meehl, 1995), thereby creating a classification that was empirically valid. Interest in dimensional models of psychopathology sprang up, especially in the personality disorders, in response to the extensive comorbidity or diagnostic overlap among mental disorder categories (e.g., Blashfield et al., 1994; McGlashan et al., 2000). Thus, dissatisfaction with the classical view of categories did not lead to exploration of other categorical models, but to speculations about using radically different approaches to measuring and describing psychopathology (Costa & Widiger, 1994, 2002).

Prototype theory focuses on the structure of categories (e.g., heterogeneity, family resemblances) and about how people use these categories (e.g., typicality effects). Related research by cognitive psychologists has focused on the organization of heterogeneous categories into hierarchies (e.g., Cantor et al., 1980; Rosch et al., 1976), but this research has been considerably less extensive than the research on category structure. In addition, the cognitive research on hierarchies has focused on defining and understanding the basic-level categories. Superordinate and subordinate categories are defined and understood in relation to these basic-level categories. In general, these hierarchies are shallow (one superordinate rank, a basic-level rank, and a single subordinate rank), and most of the research has focused on these three-level hierarchies. Because the *DSM-IV* (1994) has more than three levels (up to six levels in some higher order categories, such as the sexual disorders), it is questionable how research on three-level hierarchies would apply to understanding the *DSM*. Thus, other models of hierarchical structures might be more helpful for studying the *DSM*.

FOLK TAXONOMIC MODEL

A generative theoretical framework for studying hierarchies is folk taxonomic theory. Folk taxonomy has little, if anything, to say about the definitions of categories. The focus of this theory is almost entirely on how categories are organized into hierarchies. In other papers, we have extensively discussed the applicability of folk taxonomic theory to psychopathology (Flanagan & Blashfield, 2000, 2002). In this chapter, our goal is only to outline an approach to folk taxonomic theory that describes a methodology for studying the hierarchical structure of the *DSM*.

Anthropologists have studied native, non-Western folk taxonomies of plants and animals for the past century. From this extensive research, Berlin (1992) developed a theory about the structure of these folk taxonomies. He argued that these taxonomies are surprisingly consistent across cultures and domains, and that the taxonomies have an underlying simple structure.

Folk taxonomies often have five levels. At the highest level is *kingdom*. This level determines the domain in question (e.g., plants, animals, mental disorders). Underneath the kingdom level is the *life-form* level. There are usually four to five life-form categories in a hierarchy. These life-form categories often correspond to broad differences between categories. For instance, for the Aguaruna people in Peru, plants are divided at the life-form level into trees, vines, shrubs, and palms (Berlin, 1976). The heart of folk taxonomies is the *generic* categories. These are the categories that reflect visible discontinuities in the world and that just "cry out to be named" (Berlin, 1992). Generic categories are usually familiar to all members of the community, are learned first by children, are reliably identified, and have short, pithy names. In plant folk taxonomies, examples of generic categories are "oak," "maple," "elm," and "spruce." Culturally important generic categories are divided into *specific*-level categories such as "Dutch elm" and *varietal*-level categories such as "white Dutch elm."

In the realm of mental disorders, a likely generic-level category is the diagnosis of major depressive disorder. Major depression is a disorder that is familiar to most clinicians; most clinicians in training have had some experience with this disorder, clinicians are fairly reliable in diagnosing this disorder, and the name for the category is abbreviated as MDD. Because this disorder is culturally important, it is subdivided into the specific-level category "recurrent major depression" and the varietal-level category "recurrent major depressive disorder, with psychotic features and postpartum onset." Then, based on the current structure of the *DSM-IV*, major depressive disorder is included in the life-form-level category affective disorders and the kingdom-level category mental disorders.

Note, in the above example, that all the mental disorder names we gave were categories in the *DSM-IV*. Another important aspect of folk taxonomies is that they differ markedly from the scientific taxonomy (Berlin, 1992). Usually, they have fewer levels (three to five), fewer superordinate categories (four to five), and the entire taxonomy has only about 500 categories. Most likely, the relative simplicity of these taxonomies stems from the need for cognitive economy: A person needs to be able to effectively remember these folk taxonomies so that he or she can use them. Thus, what folk taxonomies of psychopathology would actually look like is an empirical question, and it is likely that they will not look like the *DSM-IV*.

Methods for Studying Folk Taxonomies

Medin et al. (1997) published an article in which they examined the taxonomies used by three different groups of tree experts: (1) landscapers who made decisions about trees to plant and/or keep in various building projects, (2) maintenance workers who trimmed and worked on trees, and (3) taxonomists (forestry professors). All three samples of experts lived in the Chicago area of northern Illinois, and the trees chosen as stimuli were trees found in that area of the United States. Medin et al. asked the subjects to place 48 tree species into groups that "go together by nature." Subjects made successively larger groups until they indicated that no further grouping was logical. Then the original groupings were restored and subjects divided the groups into smaller and smaller groups. Justifications for the groupings were requested at all levels. The results of these groupings were compared with the accepted scientific classification of trees.

Medin et al. (1997) found certain regularities in the results from these three different types of tree experts. First, they found that all of the experts formed hierarchical arrangements of categories that had from three to six levels. Second, the forestry professors generated the hierarchical structures that had the greatest similarity to accepted scientific classification of these trees. Third, the greatest similarity across types of experts in the sortings occurred at the basic level represented by the initial sorting of the trees. Subjects' taxonomies varied more at the successively larger or successively smaller groupings than at the initial sorting.

Flanagan's (2003) recent dissertation utilized a similar methodology to look at how clinical psychologists viewed the classification of mental disorders. In her study, clinicians were given 67 index cards on which were written the names of *DSM-IV* diagnoses. These diagnoses came from a layperson's guide to the *DSM* titled *Am I Okay?* written by Allen Frances and Michael First (1998). Both of these individuals had central roles in the creation of the *DSM-IV:* First was the text editor and Frances was the chairperson. Thus, the 67 categories listed by Frances and First seemed like reasonable choices of mental disorder diagnoses that all mental health professionals should know. After being given the 67 diagnoses, clinicians were asked to discard the diagnoses with which they did not have personal, clinical experience. Then they were asked to put the diagnoses into groups that had "similar treatments, that feel the same to you as a clinician." They were asked to not think about the *DSM* when making these judgments but instead to consider their personal experience with mental disorders. After making the groups of diagnoses, clinicians were asked to name the categories. Then they were asked to make larger groups of diagnoses and to name those groups. Clinicians were asked to make larger and larger groups of diagnoses until they indicated that no further grouping seemed natural. Then the clinicians were asked to make smaller and smaller groups until they indicated that no further division seemed natural.

Figures 4.1 and 4.2 show hierarchical taxonomies made by two clinicians (see Appendix for key to diagnostic codes). Visually, these two hierarchical arrangements of mental disorder categories have different structures. For instance, clinician 1 (see Figure 4.1) generated a solution that had four hierarchical levels, whereas clinician 2 (see Figure 4.2) made a taxonomy with three hierarchical levels. Also, within their taxonomies, clinicians did not create the same higher order categories. Clinician 1 grouped her diagnoses into four superordinate categories ("need cognitive structure," "normal," "might or might not be able to connect," "relationship struggles of power and control"), whereas clinician 2 grouped her diagnoses into three higher order categories ("behavioral treatments," "therapy is insight/growth oriented so focus on relationship," and "biochemical disorders"). In

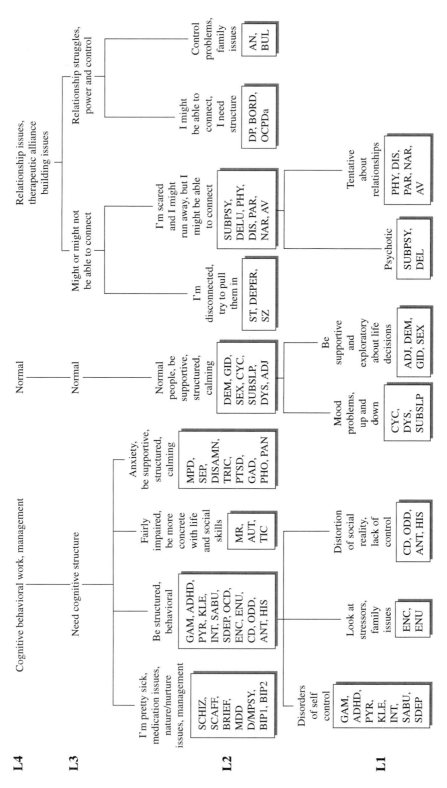

Figure 4.1 Taxonomy of Clinician #1 (42-Year-Old Caucasian Female with 20 Years of Experience, Eclectic Orientation, Who Consults the *DSM* "Whenever I have to turn in an Insurance Form")

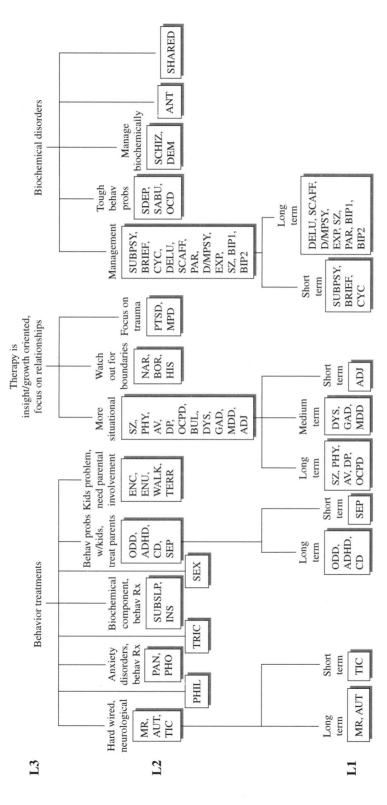

Figure 4.2 Taxonomy of Clinician #2 (45-Year-Old Caucasian Female with 18 Years of Clinical Experience, Who Consults the *DSM* Once Every Two Weeks)

addition to the superficial differences, the clinicians used many different aspects of being a clinician to make their higher order categories. Clinician 1 described the severity of the disorders ("normal"), her therapeutic technique ("need cognitive structure"), her relationship with the patients ("might or might not be able to connect"), and the primary issues of those patients ("relationship struggles with power and control"). Clinician 2 described her actions in therapy ("behavioral treatments," "therapy is insight/growth oriented so focus on relationships") as well as her view of the etiology of the disorders ("biochemical disorder"). Thus, there did not appear to be a consensus as to the rationale for the higher order categories. Indeed, the categories could be based on severity, therapeutic relationship, therapeutic technique, symptoms, or etiology. Another interesting aspect of these taxonomies is that neither clinician grouped disorders based on the *DSM* organization. Nor did either clinician use the *DSM* higher order category names.

The currently accepted classification of psychopathology (the *DSM-IV*) would predict that the generic category of major depression would be grouped into the life-form-level category affective disorders and the kingdom-level category mental disorders. These results were not supported by our data. There was no consensus across clinicians as to the grouping of generic-level categories into life-forms. Also, the superordinate category affective disorders did not appear in clinician taxonomies. Instead, there appeared to be little consensus in clinician folk taxonomies.

CONCLUSIONS

In this chapter, we outlined three approaches to understanding the structure of categories and how these categories are organized into hierarchies: the set theoretical model from biological classification, the basic-level issue studied by cognitive psychologists, and the folk taxonomic model investigated by anthropologists. The set theoretical model of biological classification is not a good fit for the structure of the *DSM* given that the diagnostic categories are not mutually exclusive and the contrast sets specified in the *DSM-IV* are not restricted to diagnoses within the same node of the hierarchy. Viewing psychopathology in terms of a prototype approach does have its uses, but authors of the *DSM-III-R* and *DSM-IV* paid relatively little attention to empirical studies that used clinicians as subjects. Finally, we outlined the principles of folk taxonomic theory and how it offers a language as well as a methodology for studying hierarchy and hierarchical systems. This generative theory and methodology could be quite powerful in understanding the taxonomies of psychopathology and how clinicians use these taxonomies.

As mentioned, the previous revisions of the *DSM* focused on the definitions of individual mental disorder categories; the organization of those categories into hierarchies is an area that has hardly been addressed. Because of this lack of attention, the *DSM* has become ungainly. First, the earliest version of the *DSM* had only two major and one minor category at the highest level of this system. The most recent substantive revision of the *DSM* (i.e., the *DSM-IV,* 1994) has 17 higher level categories. Second, the number of levels in the *DSM* varies widely depending on the superordinate category, whereas most natural hierarchies have a similar number of levels across superordinate categories. The anxiety disorders have no intermediate-level categories between the diagnostic level and the superordinate category anxiety disorders, whereas the sexual disorders have several intermediate categories between the diagnostic level and the superordinate level. Third, the divisions of diagnostic-level categories are not based on any sort of logic. Within the superordinate category disorders first diagnosed in childhood, divisions of the diagnosis mental retardation are based on a severity continuum (e.g., mild, moderate, severe), whereas the divisions of learning disorders are nominal and based on types of learning problems (e.g., reading, writing, arithmetic).

In this chapter, we have raised more questions than provided answers. In general, the issue of the organization of mental disorder categories into hierarchies has been ignored (for an exception, see Phillips et al., 2003). Researchers who have discussed this issue often confuse, for instance, polythetic definitions with a prototype model. Indeed, becoming muddled is easy. With these issues, the more one thinks about them, the less clear they become. The data are messy, and often the patterns are not robust. Classification is not a topic to which many people choose to devote their careers. Most of the present classification research discusses patterns of patient presentation rather than the global issues or how clinicians use the diagnostic categories. However, to develop a valid classification system, it is important to think about the overall structure of the arrangement of mental disorders, how people use hierarchical arrangements, and the implications of this structure for theories about psychopathology.

APPENDIX

Key for diagnostic codes in figures

ADHD	= Attention deficit-hyperactivity disorder		D/MPSY	= Depression or mania with psychotic features
ADJ	= Adjustment disorder		DP	= Dependent
AN	= Anorexia nervosa		DYS	= Dysthymia
ANT	= Antisocial		ENC	= Encopresis
AUT	= Autistic or "pervasive developmental disorder"		ENU	= Enuresis
			EXP	= Intermittent explosive disorder
AV	= Avoidant		GAD	= Generalized anxiety disorder
BIP1	= Bipolar I		GAM	= Pathological gambling
BIP2	= Bipolar II		GID	= Gender identity disorder
BOR	= Borderline		HIS	= Histrionic
BRIEF	= Brief psychotic disorder		INS	= Primary insomnia
BUL	= Bulimia nervosa		KLE	= Kleptomania
CD	= Conduct disorder		MDD	= Major depressive disorder
CYC	= Cyclothymic		MPD	= Dissociative identity disorder
DELU	= Delusion disorder		MR	= Mental retardation
DEM	= Dementia		NAR	= Narcissistic
DEPER	= Depersonalization disorder		NIG	= Nightmare disorder
DIS	= Focus on fear of disease (hypochondriasis, body dysmorphic disorder)		OCD	= Obsessive-compulsive disorder
			OCPD	= Obsessive-compulsive personality disorder
DISAMN	= Dissociative amnesia		ODD	= Oppositional defiant disorder

PAN	= Panic disorder	SEP	= Separation anxiety disorder
PAR	= Paranoid	SEX	= Sexual dysfunction
PHIL	= Paraphilias	SHARED	= Shared psychotic disorder
PHO	= Phobias	ST	= Schizotypal
PHY	= Focus on physical symptoms (somatization disorder, conversion disorder, pain disorder)	SUBPSY	= Substance-induced psychotic disorder
		SUBSLP	= Substance-induced sleep disorder
PTSD	= Posttraumatic stress disorder	SZ	= Schizoid
PYR	= Pyromania	TERR	= Sleep terror disorder
SABU	= Substance abuse	TIC	= Tic disorder
SCAFF	= Schizoaffective disorder	TRIC	= Trichotillomania
SCHIZ	= Schizophrenia	WALK	= Sleepwalking disorder
SDEP	= Substance dependence		

REFERENCES

American Psychiatric Association. (1952). *Diagnostic and statistical manual of mental disorders.* Washington, DC: Author.

American Psychiatric Association. (1968). *Diagnostic and statistical manual of mental disorders* (2nd ed.). Washington, DC: Author.

American Psychiatric Association. (1980). *Diagnostic and statistical manual of mental disorders* (3rd ed.). Washington, DC: Author.

American Psychiatric Association. (1987). *Diagnostic and statistical manual of mental disorders* (3rd ed., rev.). Washington, DC: Author.

American Psychiatric Association. (1994). *Diagnostic and statistical manual of mental disorders* (4th ed.). Washington, DC: Author.

American Psychiatric Association. (2000). *Diagnostic and statistical manual of mental disorders* (4th ed., text rev.). Washington, DC: Author.

Bailey, K. D. (1994). *Typologies and taxonomies: An introduction to classification techniques.* Thousand Oaks, CA: Sage.

Beckner, M. (1959). *The biological way of thought.* New York: Columbia University Press.

Berlin, B. (1976). *Ethnobiological classification.* In E. Rosch & B. B. Lloyd (Eds.), *Cognition and categorization.* Hillsdale, NJ: Erlbaum.

Berlin, B. (1992). *Ethnobiological classification.* Princeton, NJ: Princeton University.

Blashfield, R. K., McElroy, R. A., Pfohl, B., & Blum, N. (1994). Comorbidity and the prototype model. *Clinical Psychology: Science and Practice, 1,* 96–99.

Blashfield, R. K., Sprock, J., Haymaker, D., & Hodgin, J. (1989). The family resemblance hypothesis applied to psychiatric classification. *Journal of Nervous and Mental Diseases, 177,* 492–497.

Blashfield, R. K., Sprock, J., Pinkston, K., & Hodgin, J. (1985). Exemplar prototypes of personality disorder diagnosis. *Comprehensive Psychiatry, 26,* 11–21.

Buck, R. C., & Hull, D. L. (1966). The logical structure of the Linnean hierarchy. *Systematic Zoology, 15,* 97–111.

Cantor, N., Smith, E. E., French, R. D., & Mezzich, J. (1980). Psychiatric diagnosis as a prototype categorization. *Journal of Abnormal Psychology, 89*(2), 181–193.

Clarkin, J. F., Widiger, T. A., Frances, A., Hurt, S. W., & Gilmore, M. (1983). Prototypic - typology and the borderline personality disorder. *Journal of Abnormal Psychology, 92,* 263–275.

Corter, J. E., & Gluck, M. A. (1992). Explaining basic categories: Feature predictability and information. *Psychological Bulletin, 111,* 291–303.

Costa, P. T., & Widiger, T. A. (Eds.). (1994). *Personality disorders and the Five-Factor Model of Personality.* Washington, DC: American Psychological Association.

Costa, P. T., & Widiger, T. A. (Eds.). (2002). *Personality disorders and the Five-Factor Model of Personality* (2nd ed.). Washington, DC: American Psychological Association.

Flanagan, E. H. (2003). *Novice and expert psychologists' natural taxonomies of mental disorders.* Unpublished doctoral dissertation, Auburn University, Auburn, AL.

Flanagan, E. H., & Blashfield, R. K. (2000). Essentialism and a folk-taxonomic approach to the classification of psychopathology. *Philosophy, Psychiatry, and Psychology, 7,* 183–190.

Flanagan, E. H., & Blashfield, R. K. (2002). Psychiatric classification through the lens of ethnobiology. In L. E. Beutler & M. L. Malik (Ed.), *Rethinking the DSM: A psychological perspective* (pp. 121–148). Washington, DC: American Psychological Association.

Frake, C. O. (1972). The ethnographic study of cognitive systems. In J. A. Fishman (Ed.), *Readings in the sociology of language.* The Hague, The Netherlands: Mouton.

Frances, A., & First, M. B. (1998). *Am I okay?: A layman's guide to the psychiatrist's bible.* New York: Simon & Schuster.

Gregg, J. R. (1954). *The language of taxonomy.* New York: Columbia University Press.

Horowitz, L. M., Post, D. L., French, R. S., Wallis, K. D., & Siegelman, E. Y. (1981). The prototype as a construct in abnormal psychology: 2. Clarifying disagreement in psychiatric judgments. *Journal of Abnormal Psychology, 90,* 575–585.

Horowitz, L. M., Wright, J. C., Lowenstein, E., & Parad, H. W. (1981). The prototype construct in abnormal psychology: 1. A method for deriving prototypes. *Journal of Abnormal Psychology, 90,* 568–574.

Hull, D. L. (1988). *Science as a process.* Chicago: University of Chicago Press.

Jones, G. V. (1983). Identifying basic categories. *Psychological Bulletin, 94,* 423–428.

Livesley, W. J. (1985a). Classification of personality disorders: I. The choice of category concepts. *Canadian Journal of Psychiatry, 30,* 353–358.

Livesley, W. J. (1985b). Classification of personality disorders: II. The problem of diagnostic criteria. *Canadian Journal of Psychiatry, 30,* 359–362.

Livesley, W. J. (1986). Trait and behavioral prototypes of personality disorder. *American Journal of Psychiatry, 143,* 728–732.

Mayr, E. (1969). *Principles of systematic zoology.* New York: McGraw-Hill.

McElroy, R. A., Davis, R. T., & Blashfield, R. K. (1989). Variations of the family resemblance hypothesis as applied to personality disorders. *Comprehensive Psychiatry, 30,* 449–456.

McGlashan, T. H., Grilo, C. M., Skodol, A. E., Gunderson, J. G., Shea, M. T., Morey, L. C., et al. (2000). The Collaborative Longitudinal Personality Disorders study: Baseline Axis I/II and II/II diagnostic co-occurrence. *Acta Psychiatrica Scandinavica, 102,* 256–264.

Medin, D. L., Lynch, E. B., Coley, J. D., & Atran, S. (1997). Categorization and reasoning among tree experts: Do all roads lead to Rome? *Cognitive Psychology, 32,* 49–96.

Meehl, P. E. (1995). Bootstrap taxometrics: Solving the classification problem in psychopathology. *American Psychologist, 50,* 266–275.

Murphy, G. L. (1982). Cue validity and levels of categorization. *Psychological Bulletin, 91,* 174–177.

Murphy, G. L. (2002). *The big book of concepts.* Cambridge, MA: MIT Press.

Murphy, G. L., & Brownell, H. H. (1985). Category differentiation in object recognition: Typicality constraints on the basic category advantage. *Journal of Experimental Psychology: Learning, Memory, and Cognition, 11,* 70–84.

Murphy, G. L., & Medin, D. L. (1985). The role of theories in conceptual coherence. *Psychological Review, 92,* 289–316.

Phillips, K. A., Price, L. H., Greenberg, B. D., & Rasmussen, S. A. (2003). Should the *DSM* diagnostic groupings be changed? In K. A. Phillips, M. B. First, & H. A. Pincus (Eds.), *Advancing DSM: Dilemmas in psychiatric diagnosis* (pp. 57–84). Washington, DC: American Psychiatric Association.

Rosch, E. (1978). Principles of categorization. In E. Rosch & B. B. Lloyd (Eds.), *Cognition and categorization* (pp. 27–48). Hillsdale, NJ: Erlbaum.

Rosch, E., Mervis, C., Grey, W., Johnson, D., & Boyes-Braem, P. (1976). Basic objects in natural categories. *Cognitive Psychology, 8,* 382–439.

Widiger, T. A., & Frances, A. (1985). The *DSM-III* personality disorders: Perspectives from psychology. *Archives of General Psychiatry, 42,* 615–623.

Widiger, T. A., Sanderson, C., & Warner, L. (1986). The MMPI, prototypal topology, and borderline personality disorder. *Journal of Personality Assessment, 50,* 540–553.

Wittgenstein, L. (1953). *Philosophical investigations.* New York: Macmillan.

Chapter 5

CRITIQUE OF PSYCHOANALYSIS

ADOLF GRÜNBAUM

It is indeed a great pleasure to contribute a chapter to this *Handbook* honoring the work of my old friend Ted Millon, whom I have known since the 1950s, when we were both on the faculty of Lehigh University, where I taught philosophy with emphasis on the philosophy of science.

Classical long-term psychoanalytic treatment has fallen on hard times in the United States. But the membership of Division 39 of the American Psychological Association (APA), which is concerned with psychoanalytic psychology, is quite active, and so-called psychoanalytically oriented psychotherapy of shorter duration still needs to be reckoned with in this country. Indeed, I venture to claim that some key Freudian notions remain quite influential in psychotherapeutic practice, though sometimes unbeknown to both the practitioners and their patients.

In my essay "Critique of Psychoanalysis," which first appeared in the 2002 *Freud Encyclopedia* (edited by Edward Erwin), I have distilled from my writings a systematic critique of the fundamental hypotheses of the psychoanalytic enterprise, both theoretical and therapeutic, employing a philosophy of science perspective.

INTRODUCTION

The most basic ideas of psychoanalytic theory were initially enunciated in Josef Breuer and Sigmund Freud's "Preliminary Communication" of 1893, which introduced their *Studies on Hysteria.* But the first published use of the word "psychoanalysis" occurred in Freud's 1896 French paper on "Heredity and the Aetiology of the Neuroses" (p. 151). Therein Freud designated Breuer's method of clinical investigation as "a new method of psycho-analysis." Breuer used hypnosis to revive and articulate a patient's unhappy memory of a supposedly *repressed* traumatic experience. The *repression* of that painful experience had occasioned the first appearance of a particular hysterical symptom, such as a phobic aversion to drinking water. Thus, Freud's mentor also induced the release of the suppressed emotional distress originally felt from the trauma. Thereby Breuer's method provided a catharsis for the patient.

The cathartic *lifting* of the repression yielded relief from the particular hysterical symptom. Breuer and Freud believed that they could therefore hypothesize that the *repression,* coupled with affective suppression, was the crucial cause for the development of the patient's psychoneurosis (1893, pp. 6–7, 29–30).

Having reasoned in this way, they concluded in Freud's words:

> Thus one and the same procedure served simultaneously the purposes of [causally] investigating and of getting rid of the ailment; and this unusual conjunction was later retained in psycho-analysis. (1924, p. 194)

In a 1924 historical retrospect, Freud acknowledged the pioneering role of Breuer's cathartic method:

> The cathartic method was the immediate precursor of psychoanalysis; and, in spite of every extension of experience and of every modification of theory, is still contained within it as its nucleus. (p. 194)

Yet Freud was careful to highlight the contribution he made himself after the termination of his collaboration with Breuer. Referring to himself in the third person, he tells us:

> Freud devoted himself to the further perfection of the instrument left over to him by his elder collaborator. The technical novelties which he introduced and the discoveries he made changed the cathartic method into psycho-analysis. (1924, p. 195)

These extensive elaborations have earned Freud the mantle of being the *father* of psychoanalysis.

By now, the psychoanalytic enterprise has completed its first century. Thus, the time has come to take thorough *critical* stock of its past performance qua theory of human nature and therapy, as well as to have a look at its prospects. Here I can do so only in broad strokes.

It is important to distinguish between the validity of Freud's work qua *psychoanalytic* theoretician, and the merits of his earlier work, which would have done someone else proud as the achievement of a lifetime. Mark Solms has edited and translated a forthcoming four-volume series, *The Complete Neuroscientific Works of Sigmund Freud* (London: Karnac). One focus of these writings is the neurological representation of mental functioning; another is Freud's discovery of the essential morphological and physiological unity of the nerve cell and fiber. They also contain contributions to basic neuroscience such as the histology of the nerve cell, neuronal function, and neurophysiology. As a clinical neurologist, Freud wrote a major monograph on aphasia (Solms & Saling, 1990). As Solms points out in his preview *An Introduction to the Neuro-Scientific Works of Sigmund Freud* (unpublished), Freud wrote major papers on cerebral palsy that earned him the status of a world authority. More generally, he was a distinguished pediatric neurologist in the field of the movement disorders of childhood. Furthermore, Freud was one of the founders of neuropsychopharmacology. For instance, he did scientific work on the properties of cocaine that benefited perhaps from his own use of that drug. Alas, that intake may well also account for some of the abandon featured by the more bizarre and grandiose of his psychoanalytic forays.

As Solms has remarked (private conversation), it is an irony of history that Freud, the psychoanalyst who postulated the ubiquity of bisexuality in humans, started out by deeming himself a *failure* for having had to conclude that eels are indeed bisexual. In a quest to learn how they reproduce, one of Freud's teachers of histology and anatomy assigned him the task of finding the hitherto elusive testicles of the eel as early as 1877, when he was 21 years old. After having dissected a lobular organ in about 400 specimens in Trieste, Freud found that this organ apparently had the properties of an ovary no less than those of a testicle. Being unable to decide whether he had found the ever elusive testicles, Freud inferred that he had failed, as he reported in a rueful 1877 paper.

In 1880, he published a (free) translation of some of J. S. Mill's philosophical writings (Stephan, 1989, pp. 85–86). Yet he was often disdainful of philosophy (Assoun, 1995), despite clearly being indebted to the Viennese philosopher Franz Brentano, from whom he had taken several courses: The marks of Brentano's (1995) quondam representationalist and intentionalist account of the mental are clearly discernible in Freud's conception of ideation. And the arguments for the existence of God championed by the quondam Roman Catholic priest Brentano further solidified the thoroughgoing atheism of Freud, the "godless Jew" (Gay, 1987, pp. 3–4).

HISTORY AND LOGICAL RELATIONS OF THE "DYNAMIC" AND "COGNITIVE"

Species of the Unconscious

Freud was the creator of the full-blown theory of psychoanalysis, but even well-educated people often don't know that he was certainly *not at all* the first to postulate the existence of *some kinds or other of unconscious mental processes.* A number of thinkers did so earlier to explain conscious thought and overt behavior for which they could find no other explanation (1915a, p. 166). As we recall from Plato's dialogue *The Meno,* that philosopher was concerned to understand how an ignorant slave boy could have arrived at geometric truths under mere questioning by an interlocutor with reference to a diagram. Plato argued that the slave boy had not acquired such geometric knowledge during his life. Instead, he explained, the boy was tapping prenatal but *unconsciously stored* knowledge, and restoring it to his conscious memory.

At the turn of the eighteenth century, Leibniz gave psychological arguments for the occurrence of *subthreshold* sensory perceptions and for the existence of unconscious mental contents or motives that manifest themselves in our behavior (Ellenberger, 1970, p. 312). Moreover, Leibniz (1981, p. 107) pointed out that when the contents of some forgotten experiences subsequently emerge in our consciousness, we may *misidentify* them as *new* experiences, rather than recognize them as having been unconsciously stored in our memory. As Leibniz put it:

> It once happened that a man thought that he had written original verses, and was then found to have read them word for word, long before, in some ancient poet. . . . I think that dreams often revive former thoughts for us in this way. (p. 107)

Rosemarie Sand (personal communication, March 1, 1996) has pointed out that Leibniz's notion anticipates, to some extent, Freud's dictum that *"The interpretation of dreams is the royal road to a knowledge of the unconscious activities of the mind"* (1900, p. 608).

Before Freud was born, Hermann von Helmholtz discovered the phenomenon of "unconscious inference" as being present in sensory perception (Ellenberger, 1970, p. 313). For example, we often unconsciously infer the *constancy* of the *physical* size of nearby objects that move away from us when we have *other* distance cues, although their *visual* images decrease in size. Similarly, there can be unconsciously inferred constancy of brightness and color under changing conditions of illumination when the light source remains visible. Such unconscious *inferential compensation* for visual discrepancies also occurs when we transform our *non*-Euclidean (hyperbolic) binocular *visual* space into the "seen" Euclidean physical space (Grünbaum, 1973, pp. 154–157).

Historically, it is more significant that Freud also had other precursors who anticipated some of his key ideas with impressive *specificity.* As he himself acknowledged

(1914, pp. 15–16), Arthur Schopenhauer and Friedrich Nietzsche had speculatively propounded major psychoanalytic doctrines that he himself reportedly developed independently from his clinical observations only thereafter. Indeed, a new German book by the Swiss psychologist Marcel Zentner (1995) traces the foundations of psychoanalysis to the philosophy of Schopenhauer.

Preparatory to my critical assessment of the psychoanalytic enterprise, let me emphasize the existence of major differences between the unconscious processes hypothesized by current cognitive psychology, on the one hand, and the unconscious contents of the mind claimed by psychoanalytic psychology, on the other (Eagle, 1987). These differences will show that the existence of the *cognitive* unconscious clearly fails to support, and even may cast doubt on, the existence of Freud's *psychoanalytic* unconscious. His so-called *dynamic* unconscious is the supposed repository of repressed forbidden wishes of a sexual or aggressive nature, whose reentry or initial entry into consciousness is prevented by the defensive operations of the ego. Though socially unacceptable, these instinctual desires are so imperious and peremptory that they recklessly seek immediate gratification, independently of the constraints of external reality.

Indeed, according to Freud (1900, pp. 566–567), we would not even have developed the skills needed to engage in cognitive activities if it had been possible to gratify our instinctual needs without reliance on these cognitive skills. Thus, as Eagle (1987, p. 162) has pointed out:

> Freud did not seem to take seriously the possibility that cognition and thought could be inherently programmed to reflect reality and could have their own structure and development—an assumption basic to cognitive psychology.

After World War II, the psychoanalyst Heinz Hartmann was driven, by facts of biological maturation discovered *non*psychoanalytically, to acknowledge in his so-called ego psychology that such functions as cognition, memory, and thinking can develop autonomously by innate genetic programming, and independently of instinctual drive gratification (Eagle, 1993, pp. 374–376).

In the cognitive unconscious, there is great rationality in the ubiquitous computational and associative problem-solving processes required by memory, perception, judgment, and attention. By contrast, as Freud emphasized, the wish content of the dynamic unconscious makes it operate in a highly illogical way.

There is a further major difference between the two species of unconscious (Eagle, 1987, pp. 161–165): The dynamic unconscious acquires its content largely from the unwitting repression of ideas in the form they originally had in consciousness. By contrast, in the generation of the processes in the cognitive unconscious, neither the expulsion of ideas and memories from consciousness nor the censorious denial of entry to them plays any role at all. Having populated the dynamic unconscious by means of repressions, Freud reasoned that the use of his new technique of free association could *lift* these repressions of instinctual wishes, and could thereby bring the repressed ideas back to consciousness *unchanged.* But in the case of the cognitive unconscious, we typically cannot bring to phenomenal consciousness the intellectual processes that are presumed to occur in it, although we can describe them theoretically.

For example, even if my life depended on it, I simply could not bring into my phenomenal conscious experience the elaborate scanning or search process by which I rapidly come up with the name of the Russian czarina's confidante Rasputin when I am asked for it. Helmholtz's various processes of "unconscious inference" illustrate the same point. By glossing over the stated major differences between the two species of unconscious, some psychoanalysts have claimed their compatibility within the same genus without ado (Shevrin et al., 1992, pp. 340–341). But Eagle (1987, pp. 166–186) has articulated the extensive modifications required in the Freudian notion of the dynamic unconscious if it is to be made compatible with the cognitive one.

More important, some Freudian apologists have overlooked that, even after the two different species of the genus "unconscious" are thus made logically *compatible,* the dynamic unconscious as such cannot derive any *credibility* from the presumed existence of the cognitive unconscious. Nonetheless, faced with mounting attacks on their theory and therapy, some psychoanalysts have made just that fallacious claim. Thus, the Chicago analyst Michael Franz Basch (1994, p. 1) reasoned in vain that because neurophysiological evidence supports the hypothesis of a *generic* unconscious, "psychoanalytic theory has passed the [epistemological] test with flying colors." On the contrary, we must bear in mind that evidence for the cognitive unconscious does not, as such, also furnish support for the dynamic unconscious as such.

HAS PSYCHOANALYTIC THEORY BECOME A STAPLE OF WESTERN CULTURE?

In appraising psychoanalysis, we must also beware of yet another logical blunder that has recently become fashionable: the bizarre argument recently given by a number of American philosophers (e.g., Nagel, 1994), that the supposed pervasive influence of Freudian ideas in Western culture vouches for the validity of the psychoanalytic enterprise. This argument is demonstrably untenable (Grünbaum, 1994).

Even its premise that Freudian theory has become part of the intellectual ethos and folklore of Western culture cannot be taken at face value. As the great Swiss scholar Henri Ellenberger (1970, pp. 547–549) has stressed in his monumental historical work, *The Discovery of the Unconscious,* the prevalence of vulgarized *pseudo*-Freudian concepts makes it very difficult to determine reliably the extent to which *genuine* psychoanalytic hypotheses have actually become influential in our culture at large. For example, *any* slip of the tongue or other bungled action (parapraxis) is typically yet incorrectly called a "Freudian slip."

But Freud himself has called attention to the existence of a very large class of lapses or slips whose psychological motivation is simply *transparent* to the person who commits them or to others (1916–1917, p. 40). And he added commendably that neither he nor his followers deserve any credit for the motivational explanations of such perspicuous slips (p. 47). In this vein, a psychoanalyst friend of mine provided me with the following example of a *pseudo*-Freudian slip that would, however, be wrongly yet widely called "Freudian": A man who is at a crowded party in a stiflingly hot room starts to go outdoors to cool off but is confronted by the exciting view of a woman's décolleté bosom and says to her: "Excuse me, I have to get a *breast* of *flesh* air." Many otherwise educated people would erroneously classify this slip as Freudian for two *wrong* reasons: first, *merely* because it is motivated, rather than a purely mechanical *lapsus linguae,* and, second, because its theme is sexual.

Yet what is required for a slip or so-called parapraxis to qualify as *Freudian* is that it be motivationally *opaque* rather than transparent, precisely because its psychological motive is repressed (1916–1917, p. 41). As the father of psychoanalysis declared unambiguously (1901, p. 239): If psychoanalysis is to provide an explanation of a parapraxis, "we must not be aware in ourselves of any motive for it. We must rather be tempted to explain it by 'inattentiveness,' or to put it down to 'chance.'" And Freud characterized the pertinent explanatory unconscious causes of slips as "motives of unpleasure." Thus, when a young man forgot the Latin word *aliquis* in a quotation from Virgil, Freud diagnosed its interfering cause as the man's distressing unconscious fear that his girlfriend had become pregnant by him (1901, p. 9). *If* that latent fear was actually the motive of the slip, it was surely *not apparent* to anyone.

Once it is clear what is *meant* by a bona fide Freudian slip, we need to ask whether there *actually exist* any such slips at all, that is, slips that *appear* to be psychologically *unmotivated* but are actually caused by repressed, unpleasant ideas. It is very important to appreciate how difficult it is to provide cogent evidence for such causation. K. Schüttauf, J. Bredenkamp, and E. K. Specht (1997) claim to have produced just such evidence. They note that, according to psychoanalytic etiologic theory, obsessive-compulsive neurosis is attributable to an unconscious conflict whose repressed component features anal-erotic and sadistic wishes, which are presumably activated by regression. Then they reason that when such conflict-laden material is to be verbalized by obsessive-compulsive neurotics, Freudian theory expects a higher incidence of misspeakings (slips of the tongue) among them than among normal subjects. And these researchers report that all of their findings bore out that expectation.

This investigation by Schüttauf, Bredenkamp, and Specht differs from Bröder's (1995) strategy, which was designed to inquire into "the possible influence of unconscious information-processing on the frequency of specific speech-errors in an experimental setting." Thus, Bröder and Bredenkamp (1996) claim to have produced experimental support for the "weaker Freudian thesis" of verbal slip generation by unconscious, rather than repressed, thoughts: "Priming words that remain unconscious induce misspeaking errors with higher probability than consciously registered ones."

As for the soundness of the design of Schüttauf, Bredenkamp, and Specht, Hans Eysenck (Rosemarie Sand, personal communication, March 1, 1996) raised several objections: (1) "As the author [Schüttauf] himself acknowledges, this is not an experiment, as ordinarily understood; it is a simple correlational study . . . correlation cannot be interpreted as causation, which he unfortunately attempts to do." (2) The members of the experimental group were severely neurotic, while the control group were normals. But "the proper control group would have been severely [disturbed] neurotics suffering from a different form of neurosis than that of obsessive compulsive behaviour." (3) "Freudian theory posits a causal relationship between the anal stage of development and obsessive compulsive neurosis; the author does not even try to document this hypothetical relationship." (4) "Obsessive-compulsive neurotics suffer from fear of dirt and contamination, so that on those grounds alone they would be likely to react differentially to stimuli suggesting such contamination. . . . It is truly commonsensical to say that people whose neurosis consists of feelings of dirt will react differentially to verbal presentations of words related to dirt."

Naturally, I sympathize with Schüttauf and his coworkers in their avowed effort (sec. 4) to escape my criticism (Grünbaum, 1984, pp. 202–205) of an earlier purported experimental confirmation of Freud's theory of slips by Motley (1980). I had complained that the independent variable Motley manipulated in his speech-error experiments did *not* involve *unconscious* antecedents—but only conscious ones. As Schüttauf, Bredenkamp, and Specht tell us, precisely to escape my criticism of Motley, they relied on Freud's etiology of obsessive-compulsive neurosis to infer that subjects who exhibit the symptoms of that neurosis fulfill the requirement of harboring repressions of anal-sadistic wishes. Thus, *only* on that etiologic assumption does their use of compulsive subjects *and* their manipulation of words pertaining to anal-sadistic themata warrant their expectation of a higher incidence of verbal slips in this group than among normals.

Surely one could not reasonably expect the authors themselves to have carried out empirical tests of the etiology on which their entire investigation is *crucially predicated.* Nonetheless, Eysenck's demand for such evidence is entirely appropriate: Without independent *supporting* evidence for that etiology, their test is definitely not a test of Freud's theory of slips of the tongue, let alone—as they conclude—a confirmation of it.

Thus, as long as good empirical support for the Freudian scenario is unavailable, we actually don't know whether any bona fide Freudian slips exist at all. Just this lack of evidence serves to undermine Nagel's thesis that cultural influence is a criterion of validity. After all, if we have no cogent evidence for the existence of genuinely Freudian slips, then Freud's theory of bungled actions (parapraxes) might well be false. And if so, it would not contribute one iota to its validity even if our entire culture unanimously believed in it and made extensive explanatory use of it: When an ill-supported theory is used to provide explanations, they run the grave risk of being bogus, and its purported insights may well be *pseudo*-insights.

A second example supporting my rejection of Nagel's cultural criterion is furnished by the work of the celebrated art historian Meyer Schapiro of Columbia University. Schapiro saw himself as greatly influenced by Freud in his accounts of the work of such painters as Paul Cézanne, who died in 1906 (Solomon, 1994). Of course, Schapiro never actually put Cézanne on the psychoanalytic couch. But he subjected artists indirectly "to his own [brand of speculative] couch treatment" (Solomon, 1994). In his best-known essay, Schapiro "turns the Frenchman into a case history." Indeed, a recent tribute to Schapiro's transformation of scholarship in art history (Solomon, 1994) says that his "accomplishment was to shake off the dust and open the field to a style of speculation and intellectual bravura that drew . . . most notably [on] psychoanalysis" (p. 24). Reportedly, "his insights into . . . the apples of Cézanne" (p. 24) make the point that Cézanne's "depictions of apples contain [in Schapiro's words] 'a latent erotic sense.' " But if apples are held to symbolize sex unconsciously for Cézanne or anyone else, why doesn't *anything else* that resembles apples in *some* respect (e.g., being quasi-spherical) do likewise? Yet we learn that Schapiro's 1968 publication "The Apples of Cézanne" is "his best known essay" (p. 25). Alas, if Schapiro's claim that Cézanne was "unwillingly chaste" is to be a psychoanalytic insight gleaned from his art, rather than a documented biographical fact, Schapiro's psychodiagnosis is an instance of what Freud himself deplored as " 'Wild' Psycho-Analysis" (1910, pp. 221–227). In any case, *pace* Nagel, such art historical invocation of Freud, however influential, does nothing, I claim, to enhance the *credibility* of psychoanalysis.

For centuries, even as far back as in New Testament narratives, both physical disease and insanity have been attributed to demonic possession in Christendom, no less than among primitive peoples. That demon theory has been used, for example, to explain deafness, blindness, and fever as well as such psychopathological conditions as epilepsy, somnambulism, and hysteria. Our contemporary medical term "epilepsy" comes from the Greek word *epilepsis* ("seizure") and reflects etymologically the notion of being seized by a demon. Because exorcism is designed to drive out the devil, it is the supposed *therapy* for demonic possession. In the Roman Catholic exorcist ritual, which has been endorsed by the present pope and by John Cardinal O'Connor of New York, the existence of death is blamed on Satan. And that ritual also survives in baptism as well as in blessing persons and consecrating houses.

How does the strength of the cultural influence of such religious beliefs and practices compare to that of Freud's teachings? Though Freud characterized his type of psychotherapy as *"primus inter pares"* (1933, p. 157), he conceded sorrowfully: "I do not think our [psychoanalytic] cures can compete with those of Lourdes. There are so many more people who believe in the miracles of the Blessed Virgin than in the existence of the unconscious" (p. 152). Clearly, the psychoanalytic and theological notions of etiology and of therapy clash, and their comparative cultural influence cannot cogently decide between them. But, if it *could,* psychoanalysis would be the loser! This alone, I claim, is a reductio ad absurdum of the thesis that the validity of the psychoanalytic enterprise is assured by its wide cultural influence.

Nor can Nagel buttress that thesis by the dubious, vague declaration that psychoanalysis is an "extension" of common sense. As I have shown elsewhere (Grünbaum, forthcoming), the term "extension" is hopelessly unable to bear the weight required by his thesis if actual psychoanalytic theory is to square with it. What, for example is *commonsensical* about the standard psychoanalytic etiologic explanation of male diffidence and social anxiety by repressed adult *"castration* anxiety" (Fenichel, 1945, p. 520), or of a like explanation of a male driver's stopping at a *green* traffic light as if it were red (Brenner, 1982, pp. 182–183)? Common sense rightly treats such explanations incredulously as bizarre, and rightly so: As I have shown (Grünbaum, 1997), these etiologic explanations rest on quicksand, even if we were to grant Freud's Oedipal scenario that all adult males unconsciously dread castration by their father for having lusted after their mother.

CRITIQUE OF FREUDIAN AND POST-FREUDIAN PSYCHOANALYSIS

Let me now turn to my critique of the core of Freud's original psychoanalytic theory and to a verdict on its fundamental modifications by two major post-Freudian sets of hypotheses, called self psychology and object relations theory.

The pillars of the avowed "cornerstone" of Freud's theoretical edifice comprise several major theses: (1) Distressing mental states induce the operation of a psychic mechanism of repression, which consists in the banishment from consciousness of *unpleasurable* psychic states (1915b, p. 147); (2) once repression is operative (more or less fully), it not only banishes such negatively charged ideas from consciousness, but plays a *further* crucial multiple causal role: It is *causally necessary* for the pathogens of neuroses, the production of our dreams, and the generation of our various sorts of slips (bungled actions); and (3) the "method of free association" can identify and lift (undo) the patient's repressions; by doing so, it can identify the pathogens of the neuroses, and the generators of our dreams, as well as the causes of our motivationally opaque slips; moreover, by lifting the pathogenic repressions, free association functions therapeutically, rather than only investigatively.

Freud provided two sorts of arguments for his cardinal etiologic doctrine that repressions are the pathogens of the neuroses: His earlier one, which goes back to his original collaboration with Josef Breuer, relies on purported *therapeutic successes* from lifting repressions; the later one, designed to show that the pathogenic repressions are sexual, is drawn from presumed reenactments ("transferences") of infantile episodes in the adult patient's interactions with the analyst during psychoanalytic treatment.

It will be expositorily expeditious to deal with Freud's earlier etiologic argument below, and to appraise the subsequent one, which goes back to his "Dora" case history of 1905, after that. But also for expository reasons, it behooves us to devote an introduction to his account of the actuation of the hypothesized mechanism of repression by "motives of unpleasure."

Negative Affect and Forgetting

As Freud told us, "The theory of repression is the cornerstone on which the whole structure of psycho-analysis rests. It is the most essential part of it" (1914, p. 16). The *process* of repression, which consists in the banishment of ideas from consciousness or in denying them entry into it, is itself presumed to be unconscious (1915b, p. 147). In Freud's view, our neurotic symptoms, the manifest contents of our dreams, and the slips we commit are each constructed as "compromises between the demands of a repressed impulse and the resistances of a censoring force in the ego" (1925, p. 45; and 1916–1917, p. 301). By being only such compromises, rather than fulfillments of the instinctual impulses, these products of the unconscious afford only *substitutive* gratifications or outlets. For brevity, one can say, therefore, that Freud has offered a unifying "compromise model" of neuroses, dreams, and parapraxes.

But what, in the first place, is the *motive* or cause that initiates and sustains the operation of the unconscious mechanism of repression *before* it produces its own later effects? Apparently, Freud assumes *axiomatically* that distressing mental states, such as forbidden wishes, trauma, disgust, anxiety, anger, shame, hate, guilt, and sadness—all of which are *unpleasurable*—almost always actuate, and then fuel, *forgetting* to the point of repression. Thus, repression regulates pleasure and unpleasure by defending our consciousness against various sorts of *negative affect*. Indeed, Freud claimed perennially that repression is the paragon among our *defense* mechanisms (Thomä & Kächele, 1987, pp. 107–111). As Freud put it dogmatically: "The tendency to forget what is disagreeable seems to me to be a quite universal one" (1901, p. 144), and "The recollection of distressing impressions and the occurrence of distressing thoughts are opposed by a resistance" (p. 146).

Freud tries to disarm an important objection to his thesis that "distressing memories succumb especially easily to motivated forgetting" (1901, p. 147, italics added). He says:

> The assumption that a defensive trend of this kind exists cannot be objected to on the ground that one often enough finds it impossible, on the contrary, to get rid of distressing memories that pursue one, and to banish distressing affective impulses like remorse and the pangs of conscience. For we are not asserting that this defensive trend is able to put itself into effect *in every case*.

He acknowledges as "also a true fact" that "distressing things are particularly hard to forget" (1916–1917, pp. 76–77).

For instance, we know from Charles Darwin's autobiography that his father had developed a remarkably retentive memory for painful experiences (cited in Grünbaum, 1994), and that a half century after Giuseppe Verdi was humiliatingly denied admission to the Milan Music Conservatory, he recalled it indignantly (Walker, 1962, pp. 8–9). Freud himself told us as an adult (1900, p. 216) that he "can remember very clearly," from age 7 or 8, how his father rebuked him for having relieved himself in the presence of his parents in their bedroom. In a frightful blow to Freud's ego, his father said: "The boy will come to nothing."

But Freud's attempt here to uphold his thesis of motivated forgetting is *evasive* and *unavailing:* Because some painful mental states are vividly remembered while others are forgotten or even repressed, I claim that *factors different from their painfulness determine whether they are remembered or forgotten.* For example, personality dispositions or situational variables may in fact be causally relevant. To the great detriment of his theory, Freud never came to grips with the *unfavorable* bearing of this key fact about the mnemic effects of painfulness on the tenability of the following pillar of his theory of repression:

When painful or forbidden experiences are forgotten, the forgetting is tantamount to their repression *due to their negative affect,* and thereby produces neurotic symptoms or other compromise formations. Thomas Gilovich, a professor of psychology at Cornell University, is now doing valuable work on the conditions under which painful experiences are *remembered* and on those *other* conditions under which they are forgotten.

The numerous and familiar occurrences of vivid and even obsessive recall of negative experiences pose a fundamental *statistical* and explanatory challenge to Freud that neither he nor his followers have ever met. We must ask (Grünbaum, 1994): Just what is the *ratio* of the forgetting of distressing experiences to their recall, and what *other* factors determine that ratio? Freud gave no statistical evidence for assuming that forgetting them is the *rule* and remembering them is the exception. Yet, as we can see, his theory of repression is devastatingly undermined from the outset if forgettings of negative experiences do not greatly outnumber rememberings statistically. After all, if forgetting is not the rule, then what *other* reason does Freud offer for supposing that when distressing experiences are actually forgotten, these forgettings are instances of genuine repression due to affective displeasure? And if he has no such other reason, then, a fortiori, he has no basis at all for his pivotal etiologic scenario that forbidden or aversive states of mind are usually repressed and thereby cause compromise formations.

Astonishingly, Freud thinks he can parry this basic statistical and explanatory challenge by an evasive dictum, as follows: "Mental life is the arena and battle-ground for mutually opposing purposes [of forgetting and remembering] (1916–1917, p. 76) . . . ; there is room for both. It is only a question . . . of what effects are produced by the one and the other" (p. 77). Indeed, just that question cries out for an answer from Freud if he is to make his case. Instead, he cavalierly left it to dangle epistemologically in limbo.

The Epistemological Liabilities of the Psychoanalytic Method of Free Association

Another basic difficulty, which besets all three major branches of the theory of repression alike, lies in the epistemological defects of Freud's so-called fundamental rule of free association, the supposed microscope and X-ray tomograph of the human mind. This rule enjoins the patient to tell the analyst without reservation whatever comes to mind. Thus, it serves as the fundamental method of clinical investigation. We are told that by using this technique to unlock the floodgates of the unconscious, Freud was able to show that neuroses, dreams, and slips are caused by repressed motives. Just as in Breuer's cathartic use of hypnosis, it is a cardinal thesis of Freud's entire psychoanalytic enterprise that his method of free association has a twofold major capability, which is both investigative and therapeutic: (1) It can *identify* the unconscious causes of human thoughts and behavior, both abnormal and normal, and (2) by overcoming resistances and lifting repressions, it can remove the unconscious pathogens of neuroses and thus provide therapy for an important class of mental disorders.

But on what grounds did Freud assert that free association has the stunning investigative capability to be *causally probative* for etiologic research in psychopathology? Is it not too good to be true that one can put a psychologically disturbed person on the couch and fathom the etiology of her or his affliction by free association? As compared to fathoming the causation of major somatic diseases, that seems almost miraculous, *if at all true.* Freud tells us very clearly (1900, p. 528) that his argument for his investigative tribute to free association as a means of uncovering the causation of neuroses is, at bottom, a *therapeutic* one going back to the cathartic method of treating hysteria. Let me state and articulate his argument.

One of Freud's justifications for the use of free association as a *causally probative* method of dream investigation leading to the identification of the repressed dream thoughts, he tells us (1900, p. 528), is that it "is identical with the procedure [of free association] by which we resolve hysterical symptoms; and there the correctness of our method [of free association] is warranted by the coincident emergence and disappearance of the symptoms." But, as I have pointed out elsewhere (Grünbaum, 1993, pp. 25–26), his original German text here contains a confusing slip of the pen. As we know, the patient's symptoms hardly first emerge simultaneously with their therapeutic dissipation. Yet, Strachey translated Freud correctly as having spoken of "the coincident emergence and disappearance of the symptoms." It would seem that Freud means to speak of the *resolution* (German: *Auflösung*), rather than of the emergence (*Auftauchen*), of the symptoms as coinciding with their therapeutic dissipation. Now, for Freud, the "resolution of a symptom," in turn, consists of using free association to uncover the repressed pathogen that enters into the compromise formation that is held to constitute the symptom. This much, then, is the statement of Freud's appeal to therapeutic success to vouch for the "correctness of our method" of free association as causally probative for etiologic research in psychopathology.

To articulate the argument adequately, however, we must still clarify Freud's original basis for claiming that (unsuccessful) repression is indeed the pathogen of neurosis. Only then will he have made his case for claiming that free association is etiologically probative because it is uniquely capable of uncovering repressions. The pertinent argument is offered in Breuer and Freud's "Preliminary Communication" (1893, pp. 6–7). There they wrote:

> For we found, to our great surprise at first, that each individual hysterical symptom immediately and permanently disappeared when we had succeeded in bringing clearly to light the memory of the event by which it was provoked and in arousing its accompanying affect, and when the patient had described that event in the greatest possible detail and had put the affect into words. Recollection without affect almost invariably produces no result. The psychical process which originally took place must be repeated as vividly as possible; it must be brought back to its status nascendi and then given verbal utterance.

Breuer and Freud make an important comment on their construal of this therapeutic finding:

> It is plausible to suppose that it is a question here of unconscious suggestion: the patient expects to be relieved of his sufferings by this procedure, and it is this expectation, and not the verbal utterance, which is the operative factor. This, however, is not so. (p. 7)

And their avowed reason is that, in 1881, that is, in the "'pre-suggestion' era," the cathartic method was used to remove *separately* distinct symptoms, "which sprang from separate causes" such that any one symptom disappeared only after the cathartic ("abreactive") lifting of a *particular* repression. But Breuer and Freud do not tell us why the likelihood of placebo effect should be deemed to be lower when several symptoms are wiped out seriatim than in the case of getting rid of only one symptom. Thus, as I have pointed out elsewhere (Grünbaum, 1993, p. 238), to discredit the hypothesis of placebo effect, it would have been essential to have comparisons with treatment outcome from a suitable control group whose repressions are *not* lifted. If that control group were to fare equally well, treatment gains from psychoanalysis would then be placebo effects after all.

In sum, Breuer and Freud inferred that the therapeutic removal of neurotic symptoms was produced by the cathartic lifting of the patient's previously ongoing repression of the pertinent traumatic memory, not by the therapist's suggestion or some other placebo factor (see Grünbaum, 1993, pp. 69–107 for a very detailed analysis of the placebo concept). We can codify this claim as follows:

> T. Therapeutic Hypothesis: Lifting repressions of traumatic memories cathartically is *causally relevant* to the disappearance of neuroses.

As we saw, Breuer and Freud (1893, p. 6) reported the immediate and permanent disappearance of each hysterical symptom after they cathartically lifted the repression of the memory of the trauma that occasioned the given symptom. They adduce this "evidence" to draw an epoch-making inductive *etiologic* inference, which postulates "a causal relation between the determining [repression of the memory of the] psychical trauma and the hysterical phenomenon" (p. 6). Citing the old scholastic dictum "*Cessante causa cessat effectus*" (When the cause ceases, its effect ceases), they invoke its contrapositive (p. 7), which states that as long as the effect (symptom) persists, so does its cause (the repressed memory of the psychical trauma). And they declare just that to be the pattern of the pathogenic action of the repressed psychical trauma. This trauma, we learn, is *not* a mere *precipitating* cause. Such a mere "*agent provocateur*" just releases the symptom, "which thereafter leads an independent existence." Instead, "the [repressed] memory of the trauma . . . acts like a foreign body which long after its entry must continue to be regarded as an agent that is still at work" (p. 6).

The upshot of their account is that their observations of positive therapeutic outcome on the abreactive lifting of repressions, which they interpret in the sense of their therapeutic hypothesis, spelled a paramount etiologic moral as follows:

> E. Etiologic Hypothesis: An ongoing repression accompanied by affective suppression is causally necessary for the initial pathogenesis *and* persistence of a neurosis.

(This formulation of the foundational etiology of psychoanalysis supersedes the one I gave at the suggestion of Carl Hempel and Morris Eagle [in Grünbaum, 1984, p. 181, last paragraph]. The revised formulation here is faithful to Breuer and Freud's reference to "accompanying affect" [p. 6] apropos of the traumatic events whose repression occasioned the symptoms.)

Clearly, this etiologic hypothesis *E* permits the *valid deduction* of the therapeutic finding reported by Breuer and Freud as codified in their therapeutic hypothesis *T*: The cathartic lifting of the repressions of traumatic memories of events that occasion symptoms engendered the disappearance of the symptoms. And, as they told us explicitly (1893, p. 6), this therapeutic finding is their "evidence" for their cardinal etiologic hypothesis *E*.

But I maintain that this inductive argument is vitiated by what I like to call the "fallacy of crude hypothetico-deductive (H-D) pseudo-confirmation." Thus, note that the remedial action of aspirin consumption for tension headaches does not lend H-D support to the outlandish etiologic hypothesis that a hematolytic aspirin *deficiency* is a causal sine qua non for having tension headaches, although such remedial action is validly deducible from that bizarre hypothesis. Twenty-five years ago, Wesley Salmon called attention to the fallacy of inductive causal inference from mere valid H-D deducibility by giving an example in which a deductively valid pseudo-explanation of a man's avoiding pregnancy can readily give rise to an H-D pseudo-confirmation of the addle-brained attribution of his nonpregnancy to his consumption of birth control pills. Salmon (1971, p. 34) states the fatuous pseudo-explanation:

John Jones avoided becoming pregnant during the past year, for he had taken his wife's birth control pills regularly, and every man who regularly takes birth control pills avoids pregnancy.

Plainly, this deducibility of John Jones's recent failure to become pregnant from the stated premises does not lend any credence at all to the zany hypothesis that this absence of pregnancy is *causally attributable* to his consumption of birth control pills. Yet it is even true that any men who consume such pills *in fact* never do become pregnant. Patently, as Salmon notes, the fly in the ointment is that men just do not become pregnant, whether they take birth control pills or not.

His example shows that neither the empirical truth of the deductively inferred conclusion and of the pertinent initial condition concerning Jones nor the deductive validity of the inference can provide bona fide confirmation of the causal hypothesis that male consumption of birth control pills prevents male pregnancy: That hypothesis would first have to meet other epistemic requirements, which it manifestly cannot do.

Crude H-D confirmationism is a paradise of spurious causal inferences, as illustrated by Breuer and Freud's unsound etiologic inference. Thus, psychoanalytic narratives are replete with the belief that a hypothesized etiologic scenario embedded in a psychoanalytic narrative of an analysand's affliction is *made credible* merely because the postulated etiology then permits the logical deduction or probabilistic inference of the neurotic symptoms to be explained.

Yet some apologists offer a facile excuse for the fallacious H-D confirmation of a causal hypothesis. We are told that the hypothesis is warranted by an "Inference to the Best Explanation" (1965, pp. 88–95). But in a careful new study, Wesley Salmon (2001, p. 79) has argued that "the characterization of nondemonstrative inference as inference to the best explanation serves to muddy the waters . . . by fostering confusion" between two sorts of why-questions that Hempel had distinguished: *explanation*-seeking questions as to why something is the case, and *confirmation*-seeking why-questions as to why a hypothesis is *credible*. Thus, a hypothesis that is pseudo-confirmed by some data cannot be warranted qua being "the only [explanatory] game in town." Alas, "best explanation"—sanction was claimed for psychoanalytic etiologies to explain and treat the destructive behavior of sociopaths *to no avail* for years (cf. Cleckley, 1988, pp. 238–239, 438–439).

I can now demonstrate the multiple failure of Freud's therapeutic argument for the etiologic probativeness of free association in psychopathology, no matter how revealing the associative contents may otherwise be in regard to the patient's psychological preoccupations and personality dispositions. Let us take our bearings and first encapsulate the structure of his therapeutic argument.

First, Freud inferred that the therapeutic disappearance of the neurotic symptoms is *causally attributable* to the cathartic lifting of repressions *by means of the method of free association*. Relying on this key therapeutic hypothesis, he then drew two further major theoretical inferences: (1) The seeming removal of the neurosis by means of cathartically *lifting* repressions is good inductive evidence for postulating that repressions accompanied by affective suppression are themselves *causally necessary* for the very existence of a neurosis (1893, pp. 6–7), and (2) granted that such repressions are thus the essential causes of neurosis, *and* that the method of free association is uniquely capable of uncovering these repressions, this method is uniquely competent *to identify the causes* or pathogens of the neuroses. (Having convinced himself of the causal probativeness of the method of free association on therapeutic grounds in the case of those neuroses he believed to be successfully treatable, Freud also felt justified in deeming the method reliable as a means of unearthing the etiologies of those other neuroses—the so-called narcissistic ones, such as paranoia—that he considered psychoanalytically *untreatable.*)

But the argument fails for the following several reasons. In the first place, the durable therapeutic success on which it was predicated did not materialize (Borch-Jacobsen, 1996), as Freud was driven to admit both early and very late in his career (1925, p. 27; 1937, pp. 23, 216–253). But even insofar as there was transitory therapeutic gain, we saw that Freud *failed* to rule out a rival hypothesis that undermines his attribution of such gain to the lifting of repressions by free association: the ominous hypothesis of placebo effect, which asserts that treatment ingredients *other than* insight into the patient's repression—such as the mobilization of the patient's hope by the therapist—are responsible for any resulting improvement (Grünbaum, 1993, chap. 3). Nor have other analysts ruled out the placebo hypothesis during the past century. A case in point is a 45-page study "On the Efficacy of Psychoanalysis" (Bachrach, Galatzer, Skolnikoff, & Waldron, 1991), published in the official *Journal of the American Psychoanalytic Association.* Another is the account of analytic treatment process by Vaughan and Roose (1995).

Last, but not least, the repression etiology is evidentially ill founded, as we saw earlier and will see further in the next section. It is unavailing to the purported *etiologic* probativeness of free associations that they may lift repressions, because Freud failed to show that the latter are pathogenic. In sum, Freud's argument has forfeited its premises.

Freud's Etiologic Transference Argument

Now let us consider Freud's argument for his cardinal thesis that *sexual* repressions in particular are the pathogens of all neuroses, an argument he deemed "decisive." Drawing on my earlier writings (Grünbaum, 1990, pp. 565–567; 1993, pp. 152–158), we shall now find that this argument is without merit.

According to Freud's theory of transference, the patient *transfers* onto his or her psychoanalyst feelings and thoughts that originally pertained to important figures in his or her earlier life. In this important sense, the fantasies woven around the psychoanalyst by the analysand, and quite generally the latter's conduct toward his or her doctor, are hypothesized to be *thematically recapitulatory* of childhood episodes. And by thus being recapitulatory, the patient's behavior during treatment can be said to exhibit a thematic kinship to such very early episodes. Therefore, when the analyst interprets these supposed reenactments, the ensuing interpretations are called "transference interpretations."

Freud and his followers have traditionally drawn the following highly questionable causal inference: Precisely in virtue of being thematically recapitulated in the patient-doctor interaction, the hypothesized earlier scenario in the patient's life can cogently be held to have originally been a *pathogenic* factor in the patient's affliction. For example, in his case history of the "Rat-Man," Freud (1909) infers that a certain emotional conflict had originally been the precipitating cause of the patient's inability to work, merely because this conflict had been thematically reenacted in a fantasy the "Rat-Man" had woven around Freud during treatment.

Thus, in the context of Freud's transference interpretations, the thematic reenactment is claimed to show that the early scenario had originally been *pathogenic.* According to this etiologic conclusion, the patient's thematic reenactment in the treatment setting is also asserted to be *pathogenically* recapitulatory by being pathogenic in the adult patient's here and now, rather than only thematically recapitulatory. Freud (1914, p. 12) extols this dubious etiologic transference argument in his *History of the Psycho-Analytic Movement,* claiming that it furnishes the most unshakable proof for his sexual etiology of all the neuroses:

The fact of the emergence of the transference in its crudely sexual form, whether affectionate or hostile, in every treatment of a neurosis, although this is neither desired nor induced by either doctor or patient, has always seemed to me the most irrefragable proof [original German: "unerschütterlichste Beweis"] that the source of the driving forces of neurosis lies in sexual life [sexual repressions]. This argument has never received anything approaching the degree of attention that it merits, for if it had, investigations in this field would leave no other conclusion open. As far as I am concerned, this argument has remained the decisive one, over and above the more specific findings of analytic work.

On the contrary, the patient's thematically recapitulatory behavior toward his or her doctor *does not show* that it is also *pathogenically* recapitulatory. How, for example, does the reenactment, during treatment, of a patient's early conflict show at all that the original conflict had been pathogenic in the first place? Quite generally, how do transference phenomena focusing on the analyst show that a presumed current replica of a past event is *pathogenic* in the here and now?

Therefore, I submit, the purportedly "irrefragable proof" of which Freud spoke deserves more attention *not* because its appreciation "would leave no other conclusion open," as he would have it; instead, I contend that the "Rat-Man" case and other such case histories show how baffling it is that Freud deemed the etiologic transference argument cogent *at all,* let alone unshakably so.

Marshall Edelson (1984, p. 150) has offered a rebuttal to my denial of the cogency of the etiologic transference argument:

> In fact, in psychoanalysis the pathogen is not merely a remote event, or a series of such events, the effect of which lives on. The pathogen reappears in all its virulence, with increasing frankness and explicitness, in the transference—in a new edition, a new version, a reemergence, a repetition of the past pathogenic events or factors.

And Edelson elaborates (p. 151):

> The pathogen together with its pathological effects are, therefore, under the investigator's eye, so to speak, in the psychoanalytic situation, and demonstrating the causal relation between them in that situation, by experimental or quasi-experimental methods, surely provides support, even if indirect, for the hypothesis that in the past the same kind of pathogenic factors were necessary to bring about the same kind of effects.

But how does the psychoanalyst demonstrate, within the confines of his or her clinical setting, that the supposed *current* replica of the remote, early event is *presently* the virulent *cause* of the patient's neurosis, let alone that the original pathogen is replicated at all in the transference? Having fallaciously identified a conflict as a pathogen because it reappears in the transference, many Freudians conclude that pathogens must reappear in the transference. And in this way, they beg the key question I have just asked. How, for example, did Freud show that the "Rat-Man's" marriage conflict depicted in that patient's transference fantasy was the *current* cause of his *ongoing death obsessions*? Neither Edelson's book nor his 1986 paper offers a better answer. Thus, in the latter, he declares:

> The psychoanalyst claims that current mental representations of particular past events or fantasies are constitutive (i.e., *current* operative) causes of current behavior, and then goes on to claim that therefore past actual events or fantasies are etiological causes of the analysand's symptoms.

And Edelson concludes:

> Transference phenomena are . . . nonquestion-begging evidence for . . . inferences about causally efficacious psychological entities existing or occurring in the here and now. (p. 110)

In sum, despite Edelson's best efforts, the etiologic transference argument on which both Freud and he rely is ill founded: (1) They employ epistemically circular reasoning when inferring the occurrence of infantile episodes from the adult patient's reports and then claiming that these early episodes are thematically recapitulated in the adult analysand's conduct toward the analyst; (2) they beg the *etiologic* question by inferring that, qua being thematically recapitulated, the infantile episodes had been pathogenic at the outset; and (3) they reason that the adult patient's thematic reenactment is *pathogenically* recapitulatory such that the current replica of the infantile episodes is pathogenic in the here and now.

Freud went on to build on the quicksand of his etiologic transference argument. It inspired two of his further fundamental tenets: first, the *investigative* thesis that the psychoanalytic dissection of the patient's behavior toward the analyst can reliably identify the *original pathogens* of his or her long-term neurosis; second, the cardinal therapeutic doctrine that the working through of the analysand's so-called transference neurosis is the key to overcoming his or her perennial problems.

Free Association as a Method of Dream Interpretation

Yet, as we learn from Freud's opening pages on his method of dream interpretation, he *extrapolated* the presumed causally probative role of free associations from being only a method of etiologic inquiry aimed at therapy, to serving likewise as an avenue for finding the purported *unconscious* causes of dreams (1900, pp. 100–101; p. 528). And in the same breath, he reports that when patients told him about their dreams while associating freely to their symptoms, he extrapolated his compromise model from neurotic symptoms to manifest dream contents. A year later, he carried out the same twofold extrapolation to include slips or bungled actions.

But what do free associations tell us about our dreams? Whatever the manifest content of dreams, they are *purportedly wish-fulfilling* in at least two logically distinct specific ways: For every dream D, there exists at least one normally unconscious infantile wish W such that (1) W is the motivational cause of D, and (2) the manifest content of D graphically displays, more or less disguisedly, the state of affairs desired by W. As Freud opined (1925, p. 44): "When the latent dream-thoughts that are revealed by the analysis [via free association] of a dream are examined, one of them is found to stand out from among the rest . . . the isolated thought is found to be a wishful impulse." But Freud manipulated the free associations to yield a distinguished wish motive (Glymour, 1983).

Quite independently of Freud's abortive therapeutic argument for the causal probativeness of free association, he offered his analysis of his 1895 "Specimen Irma Dream" as a *non*therapeutic argument for the method of free association as a cogent means of identifying hypothesized hidden, forbidden wishes as the motives of our dreams. But in my detailed critique of that unjustly celebrated analysis (Grünbaum, 1984, pp. 216–239), I have argued that Freud's account is, alas, no more than a piece of false advertising: (1) It does not deliver at all the promised vindication of the probativeness of free association; (2) it does nothing toward warranting his foolhardy dogma that *all* dreams are wish-fulfilling in his stated sense; (3) it does not even pretend that his alleged "Specimen Dream" is evidence for his compromise model of manifest-dream content; and (4) the inveterate and continuing celebration of Freud's analysis of his "Irma Dream" in the psychoanalytic literature as the paragon of dream interpretation is completely unwarranted, because it is mere salesmanship.

Alas, Freud's 1895 neurobiological wish-fulfillment theory of dreaming was irremediably flawed from the outset (Grünbaum, forthcoming). Furthermore, he astonishingly did not heed a patent epistemological consequence of having abandoned his 1895 *Project*'s neurological energy model of *wish-driven* dreaming: By precisely that abandonment, he himself had *forfeited* his initial biological *rationale* for claiming that at least all "normal" dreams are wish fulfilling. A fortiori, this forfeiture left him without any kind of energy-based warrant for then *universalizing* the doctrine of wish fulfillment on the psychological level to extend to *any* sort of dream. Yet, unencumbered by the total absence of any such warrant, the *universalized* doctrine, now formulated in psychological terms, rose like a Phoenix from the ashes of Freud's defunct energy model.

Once he had clearly *chained* himself gratuitously to the universal wish monopoly of dream generation, his interpretations of dreams were constrained to reconcile *wish-contravening* dreams with the decreed universality of wish fulfillment. Such reconciliation demanded imperiously that all other parts and details of his dream theory be obligingly *tailored* to the governing wish dogma so as to sustain it. Yet Freud artfully obscured this *dynamic* of theorizing, while begging the methodological question (1900, p. 135). Wish-contravening dreams include anxiety dreams, nightmares, and the "counter-wish dreams" (p. 157). As an example of the latter, Freud reports a trial attorney's dream that he had lost all of his court cases (p. 152).

Freud's initial 1900 statement of his dual wish fulfillment in dreams had been: "*Thus, its content was the fulfilment of a wish and its motive was a wish*" (p. 119). But the sense in which dreams are wish fulfilling *overall* is purportedly *threefold* rather than only twofold: One motivating cause is the universal *preconscious* wish to sleep, which purportedly provides a generic causal explanation of dreaming *as such* and, in turn, makes dreaming the guardian of sleep (pp. 234, 680); another is the individualized *repressed* infantile wish, which is activated by the day's residue and explains the *particular* manifest *content* of a given dream; furthermore, as already noted, that manifest content of the dream graphically displays, more or less disguisedly, the state of affairs desired by the unconscious wish. The disguise is supposedly effected by the defensive operation of the "dream-*distortion*" of the content of forbidden unconscious wishes.

But this theorized distortion of the hypothesized latent content must not be identified with the very familiar *phenomenological bizarreness* of the manifest dream content! That bizarreness stands in contrast to the stable configurations of ordinary waking experiences. By achieving a compromise with the *repressed* wishes, the postulated distortion makes "plausible that even dreams with a distressing content are to be construed as wish fulfillments" (Freud, 1900, p. 159). Accordingly, Freud concedes: "The fact that dreams really have a secret meaning which represents the fulfillment of a wish must be proved afresh in each particular case by analysis" (p. 146).

But in a 1993 book (Grünbaum, 1993, chap. 10; and in Grünbaum, forthcoming), I have argued that this dream theory of universal wish fulfillment should be presumed to be false at its core rather than just ill founded.

More conservatively, the psychoanalysts Jacob Arlow and Charles Brenner (1964) claimed, for reasons of their own, "A dream is not simply the visually or auditorily hallucinated fulfillment of a childhood wish" (Arlow & Brenner, 1988, p. 7). And they countenanced a range of dream motives *other than* wishes, such as anxiety, though ultimately still rooted in childhood (p. 8).

But this modification did not remedy the fundamental epistemological defect in the claim that the method of free association can reliably identify dream motives. Undaunted, Arlow and Brenner (1988, p. 8) declare: "The theory and technique of dream analysis [by free association] in no way differs from the way one would analyze . . . a neurotic symptom, . . . a parapraxis, . . . or any other object of [psycho]analytic scrutiny." By the same token, these analysts insouciantly announce: "Dreams are, in fact, compromise-formations like any others" (pp. 7–8). Yet this ontological conclusion is predicated on the ill-founded epistemological thesis that free associations reliably identify repressions to be the causes of symptoms, dreams, and slips.

Careful studies have shown that the so-called free associations are not free but are strongly influenced by the psychoanalyst's subtle promptings to the patient (Grünbaum, 1984, pp. 211–212). And recent memory research has shown further how patients and others can be induced to generate *pseudo*-memories, which are false but deemed veridical by the patients themselves (Goleman, 1994).

As a corollary of the latter epistemological defects of the method of free association, it appears that such associations *cannot* reliably vouch for the *contents* of presumed past repressions that are lifted by them. Thus, the products of such associations cannot justify the following repeated claim of the later (post-1923) Freud: The mere painfulness or unpleasurableness of an experience is *not itself* the prime motive for its repression; instead, its negativity must involve the conscious emergence of an instinctual desire recognized by the superego as illicit or dangerous (1933, pp. 57, 89, 91, 94; 1937, p. 227; 1940, pp. 184–187).

But because Freud had also stressed the well-nigh universal tendency to *forget* negative experiences per se, his later view of the dynamics of repression disappointingly leaves dangling theoretically (1) the relation of forgetting to repression, and (2) why some forgettings, no less than repressions, supposedly cannot be undone without the use of the controlled method of free association. In James Strachey's *Standard Edition* (1901, p. 301), the general index lists two subcategories, among others, under "Forgetting": (1) "motivated by avoidance of unpleasure" and (2) "motivated by repression." But alas, Freud himself leaves us in a total quandary whether these two categories of Strachey's represent a distinction without a difference.

The Explanatory *Pseudo*-Unification Generated by Freud's Compromise Model of Neuroses, Dreams, and Slips

My indictment of the compromise model, if correct, spells an important lesson, I claim, for both philosophical ontology and the theory of scientific explanation. Advocates of psychoanalysis have proclaimed it to be an explanatory virtue of their theory that its compromise model gives a *unifying* account of such prima facie disparate domains of phenomena as neuroses, dreams, and slips, and indeed that the theory of repression also illuminates infantile sexuality and the four stages hypothesized in Freud's theory of psychosexual development. In fact, some philosophers of science, such as Michael Friedman, have hailed explanatory unification as one of the great achievements and desiderata of the scientific enterprise. Thus, one need only think of the beautiful way in which Newton's theory of mechanics and gravitation served all at once to explain the motions of a pendulum on earth and of binary stars above by putting both terrestrial and celestial mechanics under a single theoretical umbrella.

Yet, in other contexts, unification can be a vice rather than a virtue. Thales of Miletus, though rightly seeking a rationalistic, rather than mythopoetic, picture of the world, taught that everything is made of water. And other philosophical monists have enunciated their own unifying ontologies. But the Russian chemist Dmitry Mendeleyev might have said to Thales across the millennia in the words of Hamlet: "There are more things in heaven and earth, Horatio, than are dreamt of in your philosophy" (Shakespeare, *Hamlet,* Act I, Scene V).

As I have argued, the same moral applies to Freud: By invoking the alleged causal cogency of the method of free association as a warrant for his compromise model, he generated a *pseudo*-unification of neurotic behavior with dreaming and the bungling of actions. This dubious unification was effected by conceiving of the *normal* activities of dreaming and occasionally bungling actions as *mini*-neurotic symptoms, of a piece with *abnormal* mentation in neuroses and even psychoses. To emphasize this monistic psychopathologizing of normalcy, Freud pointedly entitled his magnum opus on slips *The Psychopathology of Everyday Life* (1901). To this I can only say in metaphorical theological language: "Let no man put together what God has kept asunder," a gibe that was used by Wolfgang Pauli, I believe, against Einstein's unified field theory.

The "Hermeneutic" Reconstruction of Psychoanalysis

The French philosopher Paul Ricoeur (1970, p. 358), faced with quite different criticisms of psychoanalysis from philosophers of science during the 1950s and 1960s (Von Eckardt, 1985, pp. 356–364), hailed the *failure* of Freud's theory to qualify as an empirical science by the received standards as the basis for "a counter-attack" against those who deplore this failure. In concert with the so-called hermeneutic German philosophers Karl Jaspers and Jürgen Habermas, Ricoeur believed that victory can be snatched from the jaws of the *scientific failings* of Freud's theory by abjuring his scientific aspirations as misguided. Claiming that Freud himself had "scientistically" misunderstood his own theoretical achievement, some hermeneuts misconstrue it as a semantic accomplishment by trading on the multiply ambiguous word "meaning" (Grünbaum, 1984, 1990, 1993, pp. 109–166). In Freud's theory, an overt symptom manifests one or more underlying unconscious causes and gives evidence for its cause(s), so that the "sense" or "meaning" of the symptom is constituted by its latent motivational cause(s). But this notion of "meaning" is different from the one appropriate to the context of *communication,* in which *linguistic* symbols acquire *semantic* meaning by being used deliberately to designate their referents. Clearly, the relation of being a manifestation, which the symptom bears to its cause, differs from the semantic relation of designation, which a linguistic symbol bears to its object.

The well-known academic psychoanalyst Marshall Edelson (1988, pp. 246–249) is in full agreement with this account and elaborates it lucidly:

> For psychoanalysis, the *meaning* of a mental phenomenon is a set of unconscious psychological or intentional states (specific wishes or impulses, specific fears aroused by these wishes, and thoughts or images which might remind the subject of these wishes and fears). The mental phenomenon substitutes for this set of states. That is, these states would have been present in consciousness, instead of the mental phenomenon requiring interpretation, had they not encountered, at the time of origin of the mental phenomenon or repeatedly since then, obstacles to their access to consciousness. If the mental phenomenon has been a relatively enduring structure, and these obstacles to consciousness are removed, the mental phenomenon disappears as these previously unconscious states achieve access to consciousness.

That the mental phenomenon substitutes for these states is a manifestation of a causal sequence (pp. 247–248). And drawing on Freud's compromise model of symptoms in which symptoms are held to provide *substitutive* outlets or gratifications, Edelson continues:

> Suppose the question is: "Why does the analysand fear the snake so?" Suppose the answer to that questions is: "A snake stands for, or symbolizes, a penis." It is easy to see that by itself this is no answer at all; for one thing, it leads immediately to the question: "Why does the analysand fear a penis so?" The question is about an inexplicable [unexplained] mental phenomenon (i.e., "fearing the snake so") and its answer depends on an entire causal explanation. . . . "A snake stands for, or symbolizes, a penis" makes sense as an answer only if it is understood as shorthand for a causal explanation. . . . Correspondingly, "the child stands for, or symbolizes, the boss" is not a satisfactory answer (it does not even sound right) to the question, "Why does this father beat his child?" (p. 249)

For my part, in this context I would wish to forestall a semantic misconstrual of the perniciously ambiguous term "symbol" by saying: In virtue of the similarity of shape, the snake *causally* evokes the unconscious image of a feared penis; thereby the snake itself becomes a dreaded object.

Speaking of Freud's writings, Edelson (1988, p. 247) says illuminatingly:

> Certain passages (occasional rather than preponderant) allude, often metaphorically, to symbolizing activities in human life. I think it could be argued that these indicate an effort on Freud's part to clarify by analogy aspects of the subject matter he is studying, including in some instances aspects of the clinical activity of the psychoanalyst—while at the same time perhaps he paid too little attention to disanalogies—rather than indicate any abandonment on his part of the [*causally*] explanatory objectives he so clearly pursues. There is no more reason to suppose that just because Freud refers to language, symbols, representations, and symbolic activity (part of his subject matter), he has rejected, or should have rejected, canons of scientific method and reasoning, than to suppose that just because Chomsky studies language (his subject matter), his theory of linguistics cannot be a theory belonging to natural science and that he cannot be seeking causal explanations in formulating it.

The "hermeneutic" reconstruction of psychoanalysis slides illicitly from one of two familiar senses of "meaning" encountered in ordinary discourse to another. When a pediatrician says that a child's spots on the skin "*mean* measles," the "meaning" of the symptom is constituted by one of its *causes,* much as in the Freudian case. Yet, the analyst Anthony Storr (1986, p. 260), when speaking of Freud's "making sense" of a patient's symptoms, conflates the fathoming of the *etiologic* "sense" or "meaning" of a symptom with the activity of making *semantic* sense of a text (Grünbaum, 1986, p. 280), declaring astonishingly: "Freud was a man of genius whose expertise lay in semantics." And Ricoeur erroneously credits Freud's theory of repression with having provided, *malgré lui,* a veritable "semantics of desire."

Achim Stephan (1989, pp. 144–149) takes issue with some of my views (Grünbaum, 1990, 1993, chap. 4). (Quotations from Stephan below are my English translations of his German text.) He does not endorse Ricoeur's "semantics of desire" (p. 123). But he objects to my claim that "In Freud's theory, an overt symptom manifests one or more underlying unconscious causes and gives evidence for its cause(s), so that the 'sense' or 'meaning' of the symptom is constituted by its latent motivational cause(s)" (p. 146, item [3]).

As Stephan recognizes (1989, p. 27), Freud (1913, pp. 176–178) avowedly "overstepped" common usage when he generalized the term "language" to designate not only the verbal expression of thought but also gestures "and every other method . . . by which mental activity can be expressed" (p. 176). And Freud declared that "the interpretation of dreams [as a cognitive activity] is completely analogous to the decipherment of an ancient pictographic script such as Egyptian hieroglyphs" (p. 177). But surely this common challenge of *problem solving* does not license the assimilation of the *psychoanalytic* meaning of manifest dream content to the *semantic* meaning of spoken or written language (Grünbaum, 1993, p. 115).

Stephan does countenance (1989, p. 148) my emphasis on the distinction between the relation of manifestation, which the symptom bears to its cause, and the semantic relation of designation, which a linguistic symbol bears to its object. Yet, his principal objection to my view of the psychoanalytic "sense" of symptoms as being causal manifestations of unconscious ideation is that I assign "exclusively nonsemantic significance" to them by *denying* that they also have "semiotic" significance like linguistic symbols (pp. 148–149). He grants that Freud did not construe the sense or meaning of symptoms as one of semantic reference to their causes. Yet according to Stephan's own reconstruction of Freud's conception, "He did assume that the manifest phenomena [symptoms] semantically stand for the same thing as the (repressed) ideas for which they substitute"; that is, "they stand semantically for what the repressed (verbal) ideas stand (or rather would stand, if they were expressed verbally)" (p. 149).

Searle (1990, pp. 161–167) has noted illuminatingly (p. 175) that, unlike many mental states, language is *not intrinsically* "intentional" in Brentano's directed sense; instead, the intentionality (aboutness) of language is *extrinsically imposed* on it by deliberately "decreeing" it to function referentially. Searle (pp. 5, 160, 177) points out that the mental states of some animals and of "pre-linguistic" very young children do have intrinsic intentionality but *no* linguistic referentiality.

I maintain that Stephan's fundamental hermeneuticist error was to slide illicitly from the *intrinsic, non*semantic intentionality of (many, but *not* all) mental states to the *imposed,* semantic sort possessed by language. Moreover, *some* of the neurotic symptoms of concern to psychoanalysts, such as diffuse depression and manic, undirected elation even *lack* Brentano intentionality.

Finally, the aboutness (contents) of Freud's repressed conative states is avowedly different from the intentionality (contents) of their psychic manifestations in symptoms. But Stephan erroneously insists that they are the same.

Yet some version of a hermeneutic reconstruction of the psychoanalytic enterprise has been embraced with alacrity by a considerable number of analysts no less than by professors in humanities departments of universities. Its psychoanalytic adherents see it as buying absolution for their theory and therapy from the criteria of validation mandatory for causal hypotheses in the empirical sciences, although psychoanalysis is replete with just such hypotheses. This form of escape from accountability also augurs ill for the future of psychoanalysis, because the methods of the hermeneuts have not spawned a single new important hypothesis. Instead, their reconstruction is a negativistic ideological battle cry whose disavowal of Freud's scientific aspirations presages the death of his legacy from sheer sterility, at least among those who demand the validation of theories by cogent evidence.

Post-Freudian Psychoanalysis

But what have been the contemporary *post*-Freudian developments insofar as they still qualify as psychoanalytic in content rather than only in name? And have they advanced the debate by being on firmer epistemological ground than Freud's original major hypotheses (Grünbaum, 1984, chap. 7)? Most recently, the noted clinical psychologist and philosopher of psychology Morris Eagle (1993) has given a comprehensive and insightful answer to this question on which we can draw.

Eagle (1993, p. 374) begins with a caveat:

> It is not at all clear that there is a uniform body of thought analogous to the main corpus of Freudian theory that can be called contemporary psychoanalytic theory. In the last 40 or 50 years there have been three major theoretical developments in psychoanalysis: ego psychology, object relations theory, and self-psychology. If contemporary psychoanalytic theory is anything, it is one of these three or some combination, integrative or otherwise, of the three.

Eagle makes no mention of Lacan's version of psychoanalysis, presumably because he does not take it seriously, as Lacanians have avowedly forsaken the need to validate their doctrines by familiar canons of evidence, not to mention Lacan's willful, irresponsible obscurity and notorious cruelty to patients (Green, 1995).

Previously, we had occasion to note that Heinz Hartmann's ego psychology departed from Freud's instinctual anchorage of the cognitive functions. But, more important, both Heinz Kohut's self psychology and the object relations theory of Otto Kernberg and the British school more fundamentally reject Freud's compromise model of psychopathology. Indeed, self psychology has repudiated virtually every one of Freud's major tenets (Eagle, 1993, p. 388). Thus, Kohut supplants Freud's conflict model of psychopathology, which is based on the repression of internal sexual and aggressive wishes, by a psychology of self-defects and faulty function caused by hypothesized *environmental events* going back to the first two years of infancy. Relatedly, Kohut (1984) denies, contra Freud, that insight is curative, designating instead the analyst's empathic understanding as the operative therapeutic agent. Again, the object relations theorists deny that the etiology of pathology lies in Freudian (Oedipal) conflicts and traumas involving sex and aggression, claiming instead that the quality of maternal caring is the crucial factor.

Yet these two post-Freudian schools not only diverge from Freud but also disagree with each other. Thus, the orthodox psychoanalysts Arlow and Brenner speak ruefully of "the differences among all these theories, so apparent to every observer" (1964, p. 9), hoping wistfully that refined honing of the psychoanalytic method of free association will yield a common body of data, which "would in the end resolve the conflict among competing theories" (p. 11). But their hope is utopian, if only because of the severe probative limitations of the method of free association. How, for example, could a method of putting adults on the couch possibly have the epistemological resources to resolve the three-way clash among the Freudian and two post-Freudian schools in regard to the *infantile* etiologies of psychopathology? Otto Kernberg's (1993) account of the "Convergences and Divergences in Contemporary Psychoanalytic Technique" does not solve that problem. And, as other psychoanalysts themselves have documented, there are several clear signs that the future of the sundry clinical and theoretical enterprises that label themselves "psychoanalytic" is now increasingly in jeopardy. For example, the pool of patients seeking (full-term) psychoanalytic treatment in the United States has been steadily shrinking, and academic psychoanalysts are becoming an endangered species in American medical schools (Reiser, 1989). No wonder that the subtitle of the 1988 book *Psychoanalysis* by the well-known analyst Marshall Edelson is *A Theory in Crisis*.

But what about the evidential merits of the two post-Freudian developments that are usually designated as "*contemporary* psychoanalysis"? Do they constitute an *advance* over Freud? The answer turns largely, though not entirely, on whether there is *better evidential support* for them than for Freud's classical edifice. But Eagle (1993, p. 404) argues that the verdict is clearly negative:

The different variants of so-called contemporary psychoanalytic theory . . . are on no firmer epistemological ground than the central formulations and claims of Freudian theory. . . . There is no evidence that contemporary psychoanalytic theories have remedied the epistemological and methodological difficulties that are associated with Freudian theory.

What Are the Future Prospects of Psychoanalysis?

Finally, what are the prospects for the future of psychoanalysis in the twenty-first century? In their 1988 paper on that topic, the psychoanalysts Arlow and Brenner reached the following sanguine conclusion about both its past and its future:

> Of some things about the future of psychoanalysis we can be certain. Fortunately, they are the most important issues as well. Psychoanalysis will continue to furnish the most comprehensive and illuminating insight into the human psyche. It will continue to stimulate research and understanding in many areas of human endeavor. In addition to being the best kind of treatment for many cases, it will remain, as it has been, the fundamental base for almost all methods that try to alleviate human mental suffering by psychological means. (p. 13)

By contrast, a dismal verdict is offered by the distinguished American psychologist and psychoanalyst Paul E. Meehl (1995). Because one of my main arguments figures in it, let me mention that apropos of my critiques of Freud's theories of transference and of obsessional neurosis ("Rat-Man"), I demonstrated the *fallaciousness* of inferring a *causal* connection between mental states from a mere "meaning" or thematic connection between them. Meehl refers to the latter kind of shared thematic content as "the existence of a theme":

> His [Grünbaum's] core objection, the epistemological difficulty of inferring a causal influence from the existence of a theme (assuming the latter can be statistically demonstrated), is the biggest single methodological problem that we [psychoanalysts] face. If that problem cannot be solved, we will have another century in which psychoanalysis can be accepted or rejected, mostly as a matter of personal taste. Should that happen, I predict it will be slowly but surely abandoned, both as a mode of helping and as a theory of the mind [reference omitted]. (p. 1021)

Returning to Arlow and Brenner (1988), I hope I have shown that, in regard to the past 100 years, their rosy partisan account is very largely ill founded, if only because the lauded comprehensiveness of the core theory of repression is only a *pseudo*-unification, as I have argued. Among Arlow and Brenner's glowingly optimistic statements about the future, just one is plausible: the expectation of a continuing heuristic role for psychoanalysis. Such a function does *not* require the correctness of its current theories at all. As an example of the heuristic role, one need only think of the issues I raised apropos of Freud's dubious account of the relation of affect to forgetting and remembering. These issues range well beyond the concerns of psychoanalysis. As the Harvard psychoanalyst and schizophrenia researcher Philip Holzman (1994, p. 190) sees it: "This view of the heuristic role of psychoanalysis, even in the face of its poor science, is beginning to be appreciated only now." Holzman (private communication) mentions three areas of inquiry as illustrations: (1) the plasticity and reconstructive role of memory as against photographic reproducibility of the past, (2) the general role of affect in cognition, and (3) the relevance of temperament (e.g., shyness) in character development, as currently investigated by Jerome Kagan at Harvard.

CONCLUSION

Since the psychoanalytic enterprise is now in its second century, it behooves us to take thorough stock of its past performance qua theory of human nature and therapy, as well as to assess its prospects. In this essay, I have offered such a critical appraisal from a philosophy of science perspective.

REFERENCES

Arlow, J., & Brenner, C. (1964). *Psychoanalytic concepts and the structural theory.* New York: International Universities Press.

Arlow, J., & Brenner, C. (1988). The future of psychoanalysis. *Psychoanalytic Quarterly, 57,* 1–14.

Assoun, P. (1995). *Freud, la philosophie, et les philosophes.* Paris: Presses Universitaires de France.

Bachrach, H., Galatzer, L. R., Skolnikoff, A., & Waldron, S. J. (1991). On the efficacy of psychoanalysis. *Journal of the American Psychoanalytic Association, 39,* 871–916.

Basch, M. (1994). Psychoanalysis, science and epistemology. *Bulletin of the [Chicago] Institute for Psychoanalysis, 4*(2), 1, 8–9.

Borch-Jacobsen, M. (1996). *Remembering Anna O: 100 years of psychoanalytic mystification.* New York: Routledge.

Brenner, C. (1982). *The mind in conflict.* New York: International Universities Press.

Brentano, B. (1995). *Psychology from an empirical standpoint.* New York: Routledge & Kegan Paul.

Breuer, J., & Freud, S. (1893). On the psychical mechanism of hysterical phenomena: Preliminary communication. In J. Strachey (Ed. & Trans.), *The standard edition of the complete psychological works of Sigmund Freud* (Vol. 2, pp. 1–17). London: Hogarth Press.

Bröder, A. (1995). *Unbewusstes semantisches priming laborinduzierter sprechfehler (Unconscious semantic priming of laboratory-induced slips of the tongue).* Bonn, Germany: University of Bonn. *"Diplomarbeit"* in psychology.

Bröder, A., & Bredenkamp, J. (1996). SLIP-Technik, prozessdissoziationsmodell und multinomiale modellierrung: Neue werkzeuge zum experimentellen nachweis "Freudscher versprecher" (Slip-technique, process-dissociation-model and multinomial modeling: New methods for the experimental confirmation of Freudian slips of the tongue)*Zeitschrift für Experimentelle Psychologie, 43,* 175–202.

Cleckley, H. (1988). *The mask of sanity* (5th ed.). Augusta, GA: Emily S. Cleckley.

Eagle, M. (1987). The psychoanalytic and the cognitive unconscious. In R. Stern (Ed.), *Theories of the unconscious and theories of the self* (pp. 155–189). Hillsdale, NJ: Analytic Press.

Eagle, M. (1993). The dynamics of theory change in psychoanalysis. In J. Earman, A. I. Janis, G. J. Massey, & N. Rescher (Eds.), *Philosophical problems of the internal and external worlds: Essays on the philosophy of Adolf Grünbaum* (pp. 373–408). Pittsburgh, PA: University of Pittsburgh Press.

Edelson, M. (1984). *Hypothesis and evidence in psychoanalysis.* Chicago: University of Chicago Press.

Edelson, M. (1986). Causal explanation in science and in psychoanalysis. *Psychoanalytic Study of the Child, 41*, 89–127.

Edelson, M. (1988). *Psychoanalysis: A theory in crisis.* Chicago: University of Chicago Press.

Ellenberger, H. (1970). *The discovery of the unconscious.* New York: Basic Books.

Fenichel, O. (1945). *The psychoanalytic theory of neurosis.* New York: Norton.

Freud, S. (1893). On the psychical mechanism of hysterical phenomena. In J. Strachey (Ed. & Trans.), *The standard edition of the works of Sigmund Freud* (Vol. 3, pp. 27–39). London: Hogarth Press.

Freud, S. (1895). Project for a scientific psychology. In J. Strachey (Ed. & Trans.), *The standard edition of the works of Sigmund Freud* (Vol. 1, pp. 283–343). London: Hogarth Press.

Freud, S. (1896). Heredity and the aetiology of the neuroses. In J. Strachey (Ed. & Trans.), *The standard edition of the works of Sigmund Freud* (Vol. 3, pp. 143–156). London: Hogarth Press.

Freud, S. (1900). The interpretation of dreams. In J. Strachey (Ed. & Trans.), *The standard edition of the works of Sigmund Freud* (Vol. 4–5, pp. 1–621). London: Hogarth Press.

Freud, S. (1900). Specimen Irma dream. In J. Strachey (Ed. & Trans.), *The standard edition of the works of Sigmund Freud* (Vol. 4, pp. 96–121). London: Hogarth Press.

Freud, S. (1901). The psychopathology of everyday life. In J. Strachey (Ed. & Trans.), *The standard edition of the works of Sigmund Freud* (Vol. 6, pp. 1–279). London: Hogarth Press.

Freud, S. (1905). Fragment of an analysis of a case of hysteria. In J. Strachey (Ed. & Trans.), *The standard edition of the works of Sigmund Freud* (Vol. 7, pp. 249–254). London: Hogarth Press.

Freud, S. (1909). Notes upon a case of obsessional neurosis. In J. Strachey (Ed. & Trans.), *The standard edition of the works of Sigmund Freud* (Vol. 10, pp. 155–318). London: Hogarth Press.

Freud, S. (1910). "Wild" psycho-analysis. In J. Strachey (Ed. & Trans.), *The standard edition of the works of Sigmund Freud* (Vol. 11, pp. 219–230). London: Hogarth Press.

Freud, S. (1913). The claims of psycho-analysis to scientific interest. In J. Strachey (Ed. & Trans.), *The standard edition of the works of Sigmund Freud* (Vol. 13, pp. 165–190). London: Hogarth Press.

Freud, S. (1914). On the history of the psycho-analytic movement. In J. Strachey (Ed. & Trans.), *The standard edition of the works of Sigmund Freud* (Vol. 14, pp. 7–66). London: Hogarth Press.

Freud, S. (1915a). The unconscious. In J. Strachey (Ed. & Trans.), *The standard edition of the works of Sigmund Freud* (Vol. 14, pp. 166–215). London: Hogarth Press.

Freud, S. (1915b). Repression. In J. Strachey (Ed. & Trans.), *The standard edition of the works of Sigmund Freud* (Vol. 14, pp. 146–158). London: Hogarth Press.

Freud, S. (1916–1917). Introductory lectures on psycho-analysis. In J. Strachey (Ed. & Trans.), *The standard edition of the works of Sigmund Freud* (Vol. 15–16, pp. 9–496). London: Hogarth Press.

Freud, S. (1924). A short account of psychoanalysis. In J. Strachey (Ed. & Trans.), *The standard edition of the works of Sigmund Freud* (Vol. 19, pp. 191–209). London: Hogarth Press.

Freud, S. (1925). An autobiographical study. In J. Strachey (Ed. & Trans.), *The standard edition of the works of Sigmund Freud* (Vol. 20, pp. 7–74). London: Hogarth Press.

Freud, S. (1933). New introductory lectures on psychoanalysis. In J. Strachey (Ed. & Trans.), *The standard edition of the works of Sigmund Freud* (Vol. 22, pp. 5–185). London: Hogarth Press.

Freud, S. (1937). Analysis terminable and interminable. In J. Strachey (Ed. & Trans.), *The standard edition of the works of Sigmund Freud* (Vol. 23, pp. 209–253). London: Hogarth Press.

Freud, S. (1940). An outline of psycho-analysis. In J. Strachey (Ed. & Trans.), *The standard edition of the works of Sigmund Freud* (Vol. 23, pp. 139–207). London: Hogarth Press.

Gay, P. (1987). *A Godless Jew: Freud, atheism, and the making of psychoanalysis.* New Haven, CT: Yale University Press.

Glymour, C. (1983). The theory of your dreams. In R. S. Cohen & L. Laudan (Eds.), *Physics, philosophy, and psychoanalysis: Essays in honor of Adolf Grünbaum* (pp. 57–71). Boston: Reidel.

Goleman, D. (1994, May 31). Miscoding is seen as the root of false memories. *New York Times,* Sec. C, pp. C1, C8.

Green, A. (1995). Against Lacanism. *Journal of European Psychoanalysis,* 169–185.

Grünbaum, A. (1973). *Philosophical problems of space and time* (2nd ed., Boston Studies in the Philosophy of Science, Vol. 12). Dordrecht, The Netherlands: Reidel.

Grünbaum, A. (1984). *The foundations of psychoanalysis: A philosophical critique.* Berkeley: University of California Press.

Grünbaum, A. (1986, June). Author's response to 40 reviewers: Is Freud's theory well-founded? *Behavioral and Brain Sciences, 9*(2), 266–284.

Grünbaum, A. (1990, September). "Meaning" connections and causal connections in the human sciences: The poverty of hermeneutic philosophy. *Journal of the American Psychoanalytic Association, 38*(3), 559–577.

Grünbaum, A. (1993). *Validation in the clinical theory of psychoanalysis: A study in the philosophy of psychoanalysis.* Madison, CT: International Universities Press.

Grünbaum, A. (1994, August 11). Freud's permanent revolution: An exchange, a response to Thomas Nagel. *New York Review of Books, 41*(14), 54–55.

Grünbaum, A. (1997). Is the concept of "psychic reality" a theoretical advance? *Psychoanalysis and Contemporary Thought, 20*(2), 245–267.

Grünbaum, A. (Forthcoming). Critique of Freud's neurobiological and psychoanalytic dream theories. In A. Grünbaum (Ed.), *Philosophy of science in action* (Vol. 2). New York: Oxford University Press.

Harman, G. (1965). Inference to the best explanation. *Philosophical Review, 74,* 88–95.

Holzman, P. (1994, July). Hilgard on psychoanalysis as science. *Psychological Science, 5*(4), 190–191.

Kernberg, O. F. (1993). Convergences and divergences in contemporary psychoanalytic technique. *International Journal of Psychoanalysis, 74,* 659–673.

Kohut, H. (1984). *How does analysis cure?* Chicago: University of Chicago Press.

Leibniz, G. (1981). *New essays on human understanding* (P. Remnant & J. Bennett, Trans.). Cambridge, England: Cambridge University Press. (Original work published 1705)

Meehl, P. E. (1995). Commentary: Psychoanalysis as science. *Journal of the American Psychoanalytic Association, 43*(4), 1015–1021.

Motley, M. (1980). Verification of "Freudian slips" and semantic prearticulatory editing via laboratory-induced spoonerisms. In V. Fromkin (Ed.), *Errors in linguistic performance: Slips of the tongue, ear, pen, and hand* (pp. 133–147). New York: Academic Press.

Nagel, T. (1994, May 12). Freud's permanent revolution. *New York Review of Books, 41*(9), 34–38.

Reiser, M. (1989). The future of psychoanalysis in academic psychiatry: Plain talk. *Psychoanalytic Quarterly, 58,* 158–209.

Ricoeur, P. (1970). *Freud and philosophy.* New Haven, CT: Yale University Press.

Salmon, W. (1971). *Statistical explanation and statistical relevance.* Pittsburgh, PA: University of Pittsburgh Press.

Salmon, W. (2001). Explanation and confirmation: A Bayesian critique of inference to the best explanation. In G. Hon & S. S. Rackover (Eds.), *Explanation: Theoretical approaches and applications* (pp. 61–91). Dordrecht, The Netherlands: Kluwer Press.

Schapiro, M. (1968). The apples of Cézanne. *Art News Annual, 34,* 34–53.

Schüttauf, K., Bredenkamp, J., & Specht, E. K. (1997). Induzierte "Freudsche versprecher" und zwangsneurotischer konflikt (Induced "Freudian slips of the tongue" and obsessive-compulsive conflict). *Sprache und Kognition, 16,* 3–13.

Searle, J. (1990). *Intentionality.* New York: Cambridge University Press.

Shevrin, H., William, W. J., Marshall, R. E., Hertel, R. K., Bond, J. A., & Brakel, L. A. (1992). Event-related potential indicators of the dynamic unconscious. *Consciousness and Cognition, 1,* 340–366.

Solms, M. (2002). An introduction to the neuroscientific works of Sigmund Freud. In G. Van De Vijver & F. Geerardyn (Eds.), *The pre-psychoanalytic writings of Sigmund Freud* (pp. 25–26). London: Karnac Books.

Solms, M. (Ed. & Trans.). (Forthcoming). *The complete neuroscientific works of Sigmund Freud.* London: Karnac Books.

Solms, M., & Saling, M. (Eds. & Trans.). (1990). *A moment of transition: Two neuroscientific articles by Sigmund Freud.* New York: Karnac Books.

Solomon, D. (1994, August 14). Meyer Schapiro. *New York Times Magazine,* 22–25.

Stephan, A. (1989). *Sinn als bedeutung: Bedeutungstheoretische untersuchungen zur psychoanalyse Sigmund Freud's* [Sense as meaning: Meaning-theoretic researches concerning Sigmund Freud's psychoanalytic theory]. Berlin, Germany: Walter de Gruyter.

Storr, A. (1986). Human understanding and scientific validation. *Behavioral and Brain Sciences, 9,* 259–260.

Thomä, H., & Kächele, H. (1987). *Psychoanalytic practice* (Vol. 1). Berlin, Germany: Springer-Verlag.

Vaughan, S., & Roose, S. (1995). The analytic process: Clinical and research definitions. *International Journal of Psycho-Analysis, 76,* 343–356.

Von Eckardt, B. (1985). Adolf Grünbaum: Psychoanalytic epistemology. In J. Reppen (Ed.), *Beyond Freud: A study of modern psychoanalytic theorists* (pp. 353–403). Hillsdale, NJ: Analytic Press.

Walker, F. (1962). *The man Verdi.* New York: Alfred A. Knopf.

Zentner, M. (1995). *Die flucht ins vergessen: Die anfänge der psychoanalyse Freud's bei Schopenhauer* [Escape into forgetting: The beginnings of Freudian psychoanalysis in the work of Schopenhauer]. Darmstadt: Wissenschaftliche Buchgessellschaft.

PART II

Theoretical Models, Topics, and Issues

Chapter 6

GENETIC CONTRIBUTIONS TO PERSONALITY STRUCTURE

W. JOHN LIVESLEY AND KERRY L. JANG

The study of personality seeks to address two basic problems: the characterization of enduring qualities that give rise to regularities and consistencies in behavior, and how these qualities are organized to achieve an integrated structure and coherent functioning at the overall level of the person. Although these themes are pursued in different ways according to theoretical perspective, for many approaches the exploration of these themes involves the search for the universal aspects of personality—aspects of personality structure and functioning that are common elements of human nature. Much of the significance of Theodore Millon's contributions lies in the persistent pursuit of basic organizing principles that account for the constellations characterizing normal and disordered personality. Millon finds these universals in basic polarities that give rise to coherent patterns of characteristics and behavior. In a similar vein, traditional trait theorists find universals in broad dispositions that are present in all individuals but to different degrees.

The trait approach has been primarily concerned with identifying the basic dimensions of personality required to provide a systematic account of individual differences. Trait theories assume that personality is hierarchically organized: lower order traits are assumed to covary, giving rise to the higher order traits that are the traditional focus of research. The organization of personality has largely been understood as a function of the relationships, or patterns of covariation, among traits. Thus, the objective of trait theory is largely taxonomic (Goldberg, 1990). Consistent individual differences are explained by a few general dispositions, such as neuroticism and extraversion, and personality structure is described by the way subordinate traits are related to these broader dispositions. The proponents of trait theory are enthusiastic about the progress that has been achieved in delineating the hierarchical structure of traits and the consistency with which a structure involving five broad domains is identified by studies using different measures and samples and the extent to which the structure is robust across cultures.

This chapter explores the ways genetically informed studies may contribute to resolving problems that remain in identifying the fundamental elements of personality and in delineating a universal trait taxonomy and examines the genetic basis for the hierarchical structure of personality traits. We begin by highlighting unresolved issues in the phenotypic structure of personality.

PHENOTYPIC STRUCTURE OF PERSONALITY

Despite agreement among trait theorists that personality is hierarchically organized and enthusiasm for the five-factor structure, there are several unresolved problems regarding the trait structure of personality. Confusions remain regarding the number and, perhaps more important, the content of higher order domains (Almagor, Tellegen, & Waller, 1995; Zuckerman, 1991, 1994, 1999; Zuckerman, Kulhman, Joireman, Teta, & Kraft, 1993), and about the nature of the relationship between lower order and higher order traits within the hierarchy of personality descriptors.

Disputes about the number of major domains underlying personality have abated recently without clear resolution. Eysenck (1991, 1992) argued that three factors were sufficient to account for individual differences. He maintained that because the five domains differ in abstractness they could be accommodated within his three-factor model of Psychoticism, Extraversion, and Neuroticism. In contrast, Almagor et al. (1995) concluded that a seven-factor model provides a better representation of lexical descriptions of personality.

Even more problematic for the acceptance of a universal structure are problems with the definition of domains and lack of agreement on the lower order traits that specify each domain. Consider, for example the cluster of traits labeled impulsive-sensation seeking. For Zuckerman (1991, 1994), these traits define a separate higher order factor that resembles Eysenck's psychoticism and Tellegen's (1985) constraint. In contrast, the five-factor model of Costa and McCrae (1992) assigns impulsivity and sensation seeking to separate domains. Impulsiveness is considered a facet of neuroticism, and sensation seeking is considered a facet of extraversion. This means that the definitions of major constructs such as neuroticism and extraversion differ across models.

Similar disagreements occur with other domains. For example, according to Costa and McCrae (1995), conscientiousness is a single factor defined by competence, order, dutifulness, achievement striving, self-discipline, and deliberateness. Paunonen and Jackson (1996), however, question the homogeneity of conscientiousness, citing evidence that the domain consists of three separate but overlapping dimensions: methodical and orderly, dependable and reliable, and ambitious and driven to succeed. They conclude that the overlap among these three facets may not be high enough to justify their aggregation in an overall measure of conscientiousness.

Such definitional problems reveal basic uncertainties about the taxonomy of personality traits and compromise claims that the five-factor model provides a basic assessment framework. The persistence of problems suggests that typical phenotypic and psychometric analyses used to describe trait structure may not be sufficient to resolve questions of domain definition (Livesley, Jang, & Vernon, 2003). Such analyses rely on constructs that are by their nature fuzzy and imprecise, as illustrated by the confusion about the components of extraversion (Depue & Collins, 1999; Watson & Clark, 1997). Conceptions of extraversion include sociability or affiliation (agreeableness, affiliation, gregariousness, social closeness, social recognition, and warmth), agency (achievement, ambitiousness, ascendancy, assertion, endurance, persistence, social dominance, and surgency), activation (active, activity level, energy level, liveliness, and talkativeness), impulsive-sensation seeking (adventurousness, boldness, boredom susceptibility, excitement seeking, impulsivity, monotony avoidance, novelty seeking, risk taking, sensation seeking, thrill and adventure seeking, unorderly, and unreliability), positive emotions (cheerful, elated, enthusiastic, exuberant, jovial, merry, and positive affect), and optimism (Depue & Collins, 1999). Given this range of content, it is not surprising that studies of phenotypic structure yield somewhat inconsistent findings. Not only do the lower order traits defining extraversion differ across models, but the definition of each lower order trait may also differ, and the meaning of some facet traits often merge with the meaning of other facets of the same domain and facets of other domains. This imprecision, which is probably a consequence of using natural language concepts to describe complex behaviors, contributes to the considerable variability in personality phenotypes.

Faced with this fuzziness, personality research has used a variety of psychometric procedures to foster the reliability and validity of trait measures and analytic strategies to describe trait covariation. Nevertheless, minor variations in measures and samples influence the number and contents of factors, and many decisions about methodology and analytic strategies have an arbitrary component. This suggests the need for more objective criteria to supplement those traditionally used to guide decisions on the number of higher order domains and the location of lower order or basic traits within domains, and to define a systematic set of lower order traits. An etiological perspective, as opposed to a purely descriptive approach, in which traits and behaviors, including test items, are grouped according to a shared etiology at each level of the trait hierarchy, is one potential way to begin to resolve these issues.

GENETIC BASIS FOR TRAIT STRUCTURE

The potential of behavioral genetics to provide an informed perspective on personality structure stems from the consistent finding that personality traits have a substantial heritable component and that genetic factors contribute to trait covariance.

The Heritablity of Personality Traits

The evidence from twin studies indicates that genetic influences account for approximately 40% and 60% of the variance for virtually all personality traits and that the remaining variance is explained by nonshared environmental effects (Bouchard, 1999; Loehlin & Nicholls, 1976; Plomin, Chipeur, & Loehlin, 1990). For example, Loehlin (1992), examining the heritability of multiple personality scales organized according to the five-factor framework, obtained estimates of about 40% heritability for each domain. Subsequent twin studies using the Neuroticism Extraversion and Openness to Experience-Personality Inventory-Revised yielded heritability estimates of 41% for neuroticism, 53% for extraversion, 41% for agreeableness, and 40% for conscientiousness (Jang, Livesley, Vernon, & Jackson, 1996; see also Bergeman et al., 1993; Jang, McCrae, Angleitner, Riemann, & Livesley, 1998). With openness to experience, nonadditive genetic effects accounted for 61% of the variance.

It appears that all self-report measures of personality are heritable (Plomin & Caspi, 1999). The putative distinction between temperament traits (the heritable component of personality) and character traits (the environmentally influenced component) is not supported by evidence from genetically informed studies. Traits such as openness to experience that have been designated characterological are as heritable as so-called temperament traits. In addition, molecular genetic studies report allelic associations between traits, such as cooperativeness and self-directedness, that have been designated characterological and the 5-HTTLPR allele (Hamer, Greenberg, Sabol, & Murphy, 1999).

Although most heritability studies have used self-report measures, the few studies that have used alternative methods of measurement have yielded similar results (Heath, Neale, Kessler, Eaves, & Kendler, 1992; Riemann, Angleitner, & Strelau, 1997). Riemann and colleagues, for example, evaluated the heritability of the five factors using self-report questionnaires with peer ratings. Heritability estimates based on self-report were similar to those reported by other studies. The peer ratings were also heritable, although estimates were lower than those obtained from self-reports. Multivariate genetic analyses showed that the same genetic factors contributed to self-report and peer ratings.

Given that all personality traits have a substantial heritable component, evidence that a given trait is heritable provides relatively little information (Turkheimer, 1998). The value of evidence of heritability in clarifying personality structure is also limited by the fact that heritability explains only the variation in a single trait. Information on heritability does, however, provide the foundation for understanding the etiology of personality: The ubiquity of these findings suggests that personality structure is founded on an underlying genetic architecture. The major significance of behavioral genetic studies for identifying the basic components of personality and trait structure lies in multivariate genetic analyses that provide the basis for understanding the origins of personality structure by decomposing trait covariation into genetic and environmental components.

Trait Covariation

Trait theory describes personality in terms of covarying traits. Similarly, classifications of personality disorder assume that these conditions may be defined in terms of clusters of traits. An important question for theories of personality structure and its development is why personality traits consistently sort themselves into the traditional patterns of normal theories and psychiatric classifications and the relative contributions of genes and environment to trait covariation. Multivariate genetic analyses shed light on this question.

The degree to which two traits have common genetic and environmental influences is indexed by genetic (r_G) and environmental correlation coefficients (r_E). The calculation of the genetic correlation is similar to estimating the heritability of a single variable. A higher within-pair correlation for monozygotic (MZ) twins than dizygotic (DZ) twins suggests the presence of genetic influences because the greater similarity is directly attributable to the twofold increase in genetic similarity in MZ as compared to DZ twins. In the multivariate case, a common genetic influence is suggested when the MZ cross-correlation (the correlation between one twin's score on one of the variables and the other twin's score on the other variable) exceeds the DZ cross-correlation. Genetic and environmental correlations may be interpreted as any other correlation coefficient and subjected to further statistical procedures, such as factor analysis (Crawford & DeFries, 1978).

A critical issue for understanding the etiological structure of personality and for the use of multivariate genetic analyses to clarify personality structure is the degree to which the phenotypic organization of traits reflects an underlying biological structure as opposed to the influence of environmental factors. The evidence indicates that the phenotypic structure of traits closely resembles the underlying genetic architecture and, to a lesser degree, environmental structure (Livesley, Jang, & Vernon, 1998; Loehlin, 1987). These conclusions are based on comparisons of the factors extracted from matrices of phenotypic, genetic, and environmental correlations computed among traits constituting a given model or measure.

The approach is illustrated by Loehlin's (1987) analysis of the etiological structure of scales from the California Psychological Inventory (CPI; Gough, 1989). Three matrices were computed from data obtained from samples of MZ and DZ twins to represent the covariance among traits due to genetic, shared environmental, and nonshared environmental factors. Factor analysis of the matrix of genetic covariances yielded four factors representing Neuroticism, Extraversion, Openness, and Conscientiousness (few items related to the fifth factor, Agreeableness, are included in the CPI; see McCrae, Costa, & Piedmont, 1993). Analysis of shared environmental effects, which make relatively little contribution to the variance of personality traits, yielded two factors: family problems and masculinity/femininity. The former is not an aspect of personality per se, and the latter is probably an artifact of the exclusive use of same-sex twins (Loehlin, 1987). The important finding was that analysis of nonshared environmental effects yielded three factors that resembled Neuroticism, Extraversion, and Conscientiousness. Thus, the structure of nonshared environmental influences largely mirrored genetic influences.

Livesley et al. (1998) reported similar congruence of genetic and phenotypic factor structures underlying traits delineating personality disorder (assessed using the Dimensional Assessment of Personality Pathology [DAPP; Livesley & Jackson, in press]) across a group of personality-disordered patients and two general population groups: a sample of volunteers and a volunteer twin sample. Matrices of phenotypic correlations were computed separately for the three samples and matrices of genetic and environmental correlations were computed for the twin sample. These were compared with the phenotypic structures derived from all three samples. All matrices were examined in separate principal components analyses. Phenotypic structure was similar across all samples.

Four factors were extracted from all five matrices. The first factor, Emotional Dysregulation, representing unstable and reactive affects and interpersonal problems, resembled neuroticism as measured by the NEO-PI-R (Costa & McCrae, 1992; Schroeder, Wormworth, & Livesley, 1992) and the Eysenck Personality Questionnaire (EPQ; Jang & Livesley, 1999) and the *DSM-IV* diagnosis of borderline personality disorder. The second factor, Dissocial Behavior, which was negatively correlated with NEO-PI-R agreeableness, described antisocial traits. The factor resembled the *DSM-IV* antisocial personality disorder, Eysenck's psychoticism, and Zuckerman's impulsive-sensation seeking. The third factor, Inhibition, was defined by intimacy problems and restricted expression of inner experiences and feelings. The factor correlated negatively with NEO-PI-R and EPQ extraversion and resembled the *DSM-IV* avoidant and schizoid personality disorders. The fourth factor, Compulsivity, clearly resembled NEO-PI-R conscientiousness and *DSM-IV* obsessive-compulsive personality disorder. Congruency coefficients computed between the genetic and phenotypic factors on Emotional Dysregulation, Dissocial, Inhibition, and Compulsivity were .97, .97, .98, and .95, respectively. The congruence between factors extracted from the phenotypic and nonshared environmental matrices were also high: .99, .96, .99, and .96, respectively.

This method was also applied to domains of the five-factor model assessed by Costa and McCrae's (1992) NEO-PI-R scale. Jang, Livesley, Angleitner, Riemann, and Vernon (2002) estimated the genetic and environmental correlations between all 30 of the NEO-PI-R facet scales in two independent samples of twins recruited in Germany and Canada. Factor analysis of these matrices yielded five factors that were clearly recognizable as Neuroticism, Extraversion, Openness to Experience, Agreeableness, and Conscientiousness. The correlation between the five genetic factors and the five normative factor structure was high at .83, .72, .92, .88, and .70. This correspondence between the genetic and observed factor structure of the NEO-PI-R suggests that all of the constituent parts of each broad domain share a common genetic basis.

These findings clearly indicate that the phenotypic structure of personality closely resembles the underlying genetic architecture, and that this observation is consistent across different measures. This congruence also applies to personality disorder—an observation that is especially interesting given the general lack of correspondence between genotype and phenotype for most mental disorders (Merikangas, 2002). It appears that the genetics of personality disorder traits resembles that of normal personality more closely than other mental disorders—further evidence in support of a dimensional representation of these disorders. It is also interesting that the structure of environmental effects is similar to the genetic structure, a finding that is consistent across a range of studies (Plomin, DeFries, & McClearn, 1990). This suggests that genetic factors are largely responsible for the patterns of trait covariation observed in phenotypic analyses of trait structure and that environmental factors operate largely to consolidate this structure. Consequently, the trait constellations described by major theories may represent the unfolding of a genetic blueprint rather than the product of a developmental process influenced by genetic and environmental factors.

Genetic factors may, however, have a more important effect on trait structure than environmental effects because the resemblance of the structure of nonshared environmental effects to the observed structure of traits may be an artifact (McCrae et al., 2001). McCrae and colleagues suggested that the similarity between the structure of nonshared environmental effects and genetic structure may arise because nonshared effects are usually estimated as a residual term that may include systematic bias due to the effects of implicit personality theory. These effects on personality judgments were demonstrated by Passini and Norman (1966) by asking students to rate the personalities of complete strangers and individuals well-known to them. Similar structures were obtained regardless of the person rated. This finding raises the possibility that trait structure is merely a reflection of effects of semantic biases on person perceptions (Shweder, 1975). The ratings of strangers reflect such biases because they cannot be influenced by knowledge of unfamiliar individuals' true personalities. This bias may also influence self-reports and ratings of well-known individuals. If this is the case, part of the covariance among traits may arise from systematic biases in person perception, producing correlated errors in individual judgments. In which case, similarities in structure between genetic covariance and nonshared environmental covariance could reflect the biasing effects of implicit personality theory on the latter.

In a test for this possibility, McCrae and colleagues (2001) decomposed estimates of nonshared environmental covariances into effects due to implicit personality theory bias and true nonshared effects. This was achieved by supplementing self-report twin data with cross-observer correlations on the NEO-PI-R. This permitted the computation of two matrices of nonshared environmental covariance. When these matrices were examined by factor analysis, only the matrix derived from estimates of covariance due to implicit personality theory bias yielded the typical five-factor structure. Congruence coefficients with normative structure were .81, .45, .81, .89, and .85 for Neuroticism, Extraversion, Openness, Agreeableness, and Conscientiousness, respectively. Analysis of the matrix that was free from systematic bias with targeted rotations to the normative NEO-PI-R factors produced low congruence coefficients at .53, .68, .22, .61, and .80 for Neuroticism, Extraversion, Openness, Agreeableness, and Conscientiousness, respectively. Subsequent factor analysis of this matrix yielded two factors. One resembled Conscientiousness with salient loading of the facets Activity, Order, Dutifulness, Achievement Striving, Self-Discipline, and (low) Impulsiveness. The other was defined by the facets Warmth, Gregariousness, Positive Emotions, Openness to Feelings, Altruism, and Tender-Mindedness.

Implications for the Development of Trait Theory

Evidence that the four or five factors consistently identified in analyses of personality phenotypes reflect the underlying genetic architecture of personality suggests that these domains represent fundamental distinctions in the way behavior is organized at a biological level. If this conclusion is correct, it forms the basis for developing a model of trait structure based on biological foundations in which etiological considerations would supplement psychometric and analytic considerations when defining the number and content of domains. Identification of higher order factors from matrices of genetic covariances suggests the occurrence of general genetic factors that influence all lower order traits forming a given domain. This finding implies that domains could be defined as traits sharing a common etiology. Questions about the definition of domains, such as the issue of whether traits composing impulsive-sensation seeking are components of neuroticism, extraversion, or psychoticism, could be resolved by genetic studies of the etiological relationships between these traits and the specific traits defining other domains. Such an approach provides a systematic way to refine current trait taxonomies and a relatively objective criterion to resolve definitional disputes. In the case of impulsive-sensation seeking, the evidence from twin studies suggests that these traits are part of the domain referred to variously as psychoticism and dissocial behavior (Livesley et al., 1998).

The suggestion that trait clusters are defined etiologically does not imply that lower order traits are influenced only by genetic factors that are shared with other traits defining the cluster or domain. The evidence suggests that these traits have an additional, specific genetic component. This is the issue considered next.

THE PERSONALITY HIERARCHY RECONSIDERED

Typically, higher order domains emerge from factor analytic studies of a large number of lower order traits. Although these factors are essentially statistical entities, trait theories assume that they reflect basic psychological and, in some cases, biological entities. They also appear to assume that these entities are the primary dimensions of personality: Research effort has largely focused on the higher order domains with comparative neglect of lower order traits. This leaves the status of the lower order traits unclear. Are they merely facets or subcomponents of higher order traits or distinct entities with their own etiology?

Lower Order Traits

The designation of lower order traits as "facet traits" implies that they are conceptualized as components of the broader domains. Behavioral genetic perspectives have tended to adopt this assumption. Because the higher order traits are heritable, there has been a tendency until recently to assume that the genetic contribution to personality largely operates at the higher order level. Lower order traits are assumed to be heritable because of their association with higher order traits (Loehlin, 1992). That is, the subtraits defining a domain derive their genetic underpinning from the same genetic factor. Recent research showing that most subtraits have a unique heritable component questions this assumption (Jang et al., 1998; Livesley et al., 1998).

Jang and colleagues (1998) estimated the heritability of the 30 NEO-PI-R facet traits after all genetic influence due to the higher order traits was removed from each using a regression technique. Substantial residual heritability was found for each trait that accounted for between 25% (competence) and 65% (dutifulness) of the variance in each trait. Livesley and colleagues (1998) reported similar findings for personality disorder traits.

The occurrence of specific genetic influences on subtraits has important implications for conceptualizing trait structure. These specific sources of genetic variance suggest that subtraits are not derivative structures but etiologically distinct entities. The emphasis of trait theory on global dispositions, such as extraversion and neuroticism, may have been misplaced or, at least, needs to be supplemented with greater attention to the significance of subtraits and their contribution to trait structure. Thus far, little attention has been paid to conceptualizing their relationship to higher order structures or to developing methods to identify them. Most trait theories, including the five-factor model, have relied on rational analysis to identify subtraits presumably because they were considered merely subcomponents of a higher order domain and hence reflected largely arbitrary distinctions. Given consistent evidence of specific genetic influences, greater attention needs to be given to identifying and defining these fundamental building blocks of personality. An etiological approach suggests that just as domains may be defined as clusters of traits sharing a common genetic influence, subtraits may be defined as clusters of behaviors (or test items) sharing the same specific genetic influence. This definition offers a criterion to refine the item content of a scale to foster convergent and discriminant validity.

Having demonstrated that the lower order traits are not merely subcomponents of the higher order domains but have a distinct genetic component besides a common component shared with other traits forming the same domain, we are left with intriguing questions about how the common and specific genetic components are organized to form the coherent constellations of traits described by trait theories and about the nature or status of the higher order constructs. Do the common genetic factors give rise to phenotypic structures or mechanisms with a distinct biological and psychological basis, as assumed by most trait models? With this model, the common genetic component underlying a domain is assumed to have an indirect effect on subtraits via this higher order structure. Or, do the common genetic entities have a direct influence on the expression of specific components and the resulting trait? This is a critical issue for trait models of personality.

Evaluating Models of Genetic Influence

These different models of genetic influence on personality traits may be explored using a model-fitting approach (Neale & Cardon, 1992). The *common pathway model* is structurally similar to the model of exploratory factor analysis used to specify the phenotypic structure of traits. It postulates a single latent variable (higher order trait) that mediates the covariation among a set of variables (lower order traits) that also have their own genetic and environmental basis. As shown in Figure 6.1, the covariation in a set of variables is hypothesized to be mediated by a single superordinate latent phenotypic variable (P), such as a higher order trait, which is influenced by a single additive genetic (A_1, $h_{j,k}$), one shared (C_1; $c_{j,k}$) and one nonshared environmental factor (E_1, $e_{j,k}$). Genetic (A'_k, a'_k) and environmental effects (C'_k, c'_k and E'_k, e'_k) specific to each variable are also specified. As applied to each domain of the five-factor model, the model postulates a single latent factor that mediates the influence of genetic and environmental effects on each lower order trait. Thus, a latent variable of neuroticism is hypothesized that mediates the influence of genetic and environmental influences on each of the six facets of Anxiety, Hostility, Depression, Self-consciousness, Impulsivity, and Vulnerability.

In contrast to this model, the *independent pathway model* specifies direct links between one or more genetic and environmental influences to each lower order trait. In Figure 6.2, the subscript j identifies the common factor and k identifies the variable and direct links ($h_{j,k}$, $c_{j,k}$, $e_{j,k}$) are shown from one or more additive genetic, shared and nonshared environmental influences common to all the variables (denoted A_j, E_j, respectively). Like

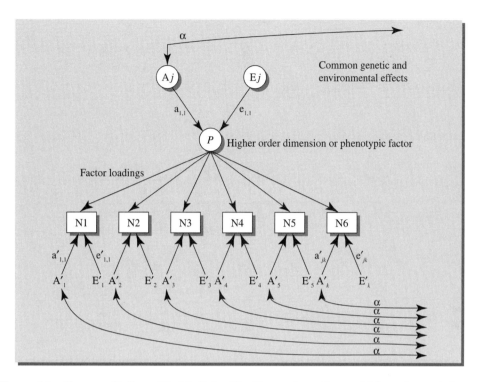

Figure 6.1   Common Pathway Model. *Note:* **The figure shows the model for only one twin and only some paths are marked in this figure for clarity; α = 1.0 for MZ/.50 for DZ twin; A, E = Common additive genetic and nonshared environmental factors; A′, E′ = Variable specific additive genetic and nonshared environmental factors; N1 = Anxiety; N2 = Hostility; N3 = Depression; N4 = Self-consciousness; N5 = Impulsivity; N6 = Vulnerability.** (*Source:* **From "Genetic and Environmental Influences on the Covariance of Facets Defining the Domains of the Five-Factor Model of Personality," by K. L. Jang, W. J. Livesley, A. Angleitner, R. Riemann, and P. A. Vernon, 2002,** *Personality and Individual Differences, 33,* **pp. 83–101. Reprinted with permission.**

the common pathways model, unique genetic and environmental influences are also specified for each lower order trait (A'_k, a'_k, and E'_k, e'_k, respectively).

It should be noted that both models are consistent with the findings discussed earlier that subtraits are influenced by common and specific genetic factors. The models are tested by examining the extent to which they fit the data derived from twin studies. If the common pathways model is found to provide the best fit, the implication is that the hierarchical structure of personality arises from the effects of higher order factors that have a genetic and environmental basis. The task is then to explain how this entity differs from lower order or facet traits and the role it plays in the formation of the hierarchy. If the independent pathways model provides the best fit, the implication is that the higher order constructs of phenotypic analyses reflect the pleiotropic action of genes shared by all subtraits forming that domain rather than the effects of a phenotypic entity. In this case, the task is to explicate the mechanisms that lead to trait clusters. Besides the value of the models in evaluating personality structure, the approach also provides information on the

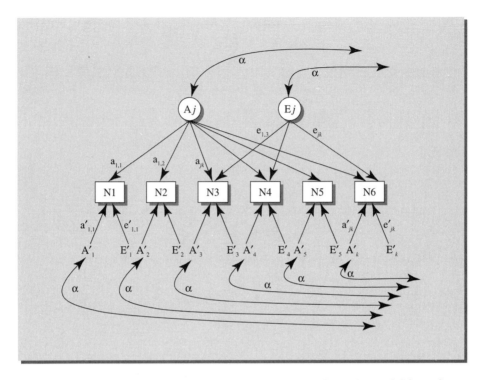

Figure 6.2   Independent Pathways Model. *Note:* **The figure shows the model for only one twin and only some are paths marked in this figure for clarity;** α = 1.0 for MZ/.50 for DZ **twin; A, E = Common additive genetic and nonshared environmental factors; A′, E′ = Variable specific additive genetic and nonshared environmental factors; N1 = Anxiety; N2 = Hostility; N3 = Depression; N4 = Self-consciousness; N5 = Impulsivity; N6 = Vulnerability.** (*Source:* **From "Genetic and Environmental Influences on the Covariance of Facets Defining the Domains of the Five-Factor Model of Personality," by K. L. Jang, W. J. Livesley, A. Angleitner, R. Riemann, and P. A. Vernon, 2002,** *Personality and Individual Differences, 33,* **pp. 83–101. Reprinted with permission.**

magnitude of genetic and environmental influences unique to each facet. This provides the basis for determining which facets should be grouped together within the taxonomy.

Jang and colleagues (2002) used this approach to evaluate the structure of the five-factor model assessed with the NEO-PI-R (see Table 6.1). Common and independent pathways models were applied to two samples of twins: a sample of 253 identical and 207 fraternal twin pairs from Canada and 526 identical and 269 fraternal pairs from Germany. An independent pathways model specifying two additive genetic factors and two non-shared environmental factors provided the best fit in each domain in both sets of twins.

In the case of Neuroticism, the Angry Hostility facet marked the first genetic factor, and the second factor influenced all facets except Angry Hostility and Impulsivity. With Extraversion, the most salient component of the first genetic factor was Gregariousness in both samples. All facets except Gregariousness and Excitement Seeking loaded on the second factor. Although this factor appeared similar in the two samples, in the Canadian sample the factor emphasized Warmth and Positive Emotions, whereas in the German sample it emphasized Assertiveness and Activity. The first general genetic factor contributing to the Openness to Experience domain was defined by the Fantasy, Aesthetics,

Table 6.1 Multivariate Genetic Analysis of Two Cross-National Samples

Proportions of the Total Variance Accounted for by Each Genetic and Environmental Factor (Independent Pathways Model) of the NEO-PI-R Neuroticism Facets on a Sample of German and a Sample of Canadian Twins and Proportions of the Total Variance Accounted for by Each Genetic and Environmental Parameter

| | Variance Accounted by Each Parameter | | | | | |
| | A | | E | | | |
Facet Scale	1	2	1	2	A′	E′
Canadian Sample						
Anxiety	.59	.19	.38	.14	.23	.48
Hostility	1.00	.00	.15	.08	.00	.78
Depression	.46	.42	.62	.12	.12	.26
Self-consciousness	.40	.28	.32	.10	.31	.58
Impulsivity	.34	.00	1.00	.00	.66	.00
Vulnerability	.48	.35	.30	.08	.17	.61

$x^2 = 152.30$, $p = .05$, df = 125, RMSEA = .025, 90% UL = .042, AIC = −97.70

German Sample						
Anxiety	.46	.25	.15	.38	.28	.47
Hostility	1.00	.00	1.00	.00	.00	.00
Depression	.47	.43	.21	.40	.10	.39
Self-consciousness	.26	.41	.09	.23	.34	.68
Impulsivity	.15	.00	.06	.00	.85	.94
Vulnerability	.42	.40	.19	.43	.18	.38

$x^2 = 137.76$, $p = .22$, df = 126, RMSEA = .011, 90% UL = .027, AIC = −114.24

Parameter Estimates (Independent Pathways Model) of the NEO-PI-R Extraversion Facets on a Sample of German and a Sample of Canadian Twins and Proportions of the Total Variance Accounted for by Each Genetic and Environmental Parameter

| | Variance Accounted by Each Parameter | | | | | |
| | A | | E | | | |
Facet Scale	1	2	1	2	A′	E′
Canadian Sample						
Warmth	.32	.50	1.00	.00	.18	.00
Gregariousness	1.00	.00	.19	.05	.00	.76
Assertiveness	.22	.30	.00	.26	.48	.74
Activity	.16	.36	.00	.61	.47	.39
Excitement seeking	.32	.00	.09	.00	.68	.91
Positive emotions	.29	.49	.20	.10	.23	.70

$x^2 = 170.92$, $p = .01$, df = 128, RMSEA = .033, 90% UL = .048, AIC = −85.08

German Sample						
Warmth	.46	.20	.98	.02	.34	.00
Gregariousness	1.00	.00	.12	.14	.00	.74
Assertiveness	.18	.46	.01	.31	.37	.68
Activity	.07	.47	.01	.32	.45	.67
Excitement seeking	.30	.00	.00	.21	.70	.79
Positive emotions	.34	.32	.18	.16	.34	.66

$x^2 = 221.87$, $p = .00$, df = 125, RMSEA = .043, 90% UL = .056, AIC = −28.13

(continued)

Table 6.1   *(Continued)*

Parameter Estimates (Independent Pathways Model) of the NEO-PI-R Openness Facets on a Sample of German and a Sample of Canadian Twins and Proportions of the Total Variance Accounted for by Each Genetic and Environmental Parameter

| Facet Scale | Variance Accounted by Each Parameter | | | | | |
| | A | | E | | | |
	1	2	1	2	A′	E′
Canadian Sample						
Fantasy	.47	.00	.47	.04	.53	.49
Aesthetics	.79	.00	.00	1.00	.21	.00
Feelings	.48	.00	.07	.15	.52	.78
Actions	.37	.43	.03	.03	.20	.94
Ideas	.50	.06	.04	.14	.44	.82
Values	.19	.30	.07	.00	.51	.93

$x^2 = 138.79$, $p = .21$, df = 126, RMSEA = .018, 90% UL = .038, AIC = −113.21

Facet Scale						
German Sample						
Fantasy	.42	.07	.24	.07	.51	.69
Aesthetics	.56	.08	.00	1.00	.37	.00
Feelings	.66	.07	.26	.22	.27	.52
Actions	.00	1.00	.06	.04	.00	.91
Ideas	.18	.27	.01	.13	.55	.86
Values	.11	.31	.02	.00	.59	.98

$x^2 = 153.72$, $p = .04$, df = 125, RMSEA = .025, 90% UL = .037, AIC = −96.28

Parameter Estimates (Independent Pathways Model) of the NEO-PI-R Agreeableness Facets on a Sample of German and a Sample of Canadian Twins and Proportions of the Total Variance Accounted for by Each Genetic and Environmental Parameter

| Facet Scale | Variance Accounted by Each Parameter | | | | | |
| | A | | E | | | |
	1	2	1	2	A′	E′
Canadian Sample						
Trust	1.00	.00	.03	.12	.00	.85
Straightforwardness	.16	.84	.00	.42	.00	.58
Altruism	.36	.11	.11	.33	.54	.56
Compliance	.17	.25	.03	.36	.58	.61
Modesty	.00	.40	.04	.16	.60	.80
Tender-mindedness	.20	.23	1.00	.00	.56	.00

$x^2 = 138.80$, $p = .22$, df = 127, RMSEA = .020, 90% UL = .039, AIC = −115.20

Facet Scale						
German Sample						
Trust	.38	.00	.24	.03	.62	.73
Straightforwardness	.09	.32	.00	.29	.59	.71
Altruism	.72	.15	.25	.14	.13	.61
Compliance	.41	.20	.06	.22	.39	.73
Modesty	.00	1.00	.04	.29	.00	.67
Tender-mindedness	.23	.19	.17	.03	.58	.80

$x^2 = 184.83$, $p = .00$, df = 129, RMSEA = .043, 90% UL = .056, AIC = −73.17

Table 6.1   *(Continued)*

Parameter Estimates (Independent Pathways Model) of the NEO-PI-R Conscientiousness Facets on a Sample of German and a Sample of Canadian Twins and Proportions of the Total Variance Accounted for by Each Genetic and Environmental Parameter

| | Variance Accounted by Each Parameter | | | | | |
| | A | | E | | | |
Facet Scale	1	2	1	2	A′	E′
Canadian Sample						
Competence	.36	.20	.81	.19	.44	.00
Order	.32	.25	.00	.31	.43	.69
Dutifulness	.52	.20	.03	.32	.28	.65
Achievement striving	.26	.34	.11	.22	.41	.66
Self-discipline	.17	.66	.04	.67	.17	.29
Deliberation	1.00	.00	.07	.19	.00	.74

$$x^2 = 153.42, p = .04, df = 124, RMSEA = .030, 90\% \ UL = .046, AIC = -94.58$$

German Sample						
Competence	.12	.71	.00	.33	.18	.67
Order	.53	.17	.01	.30	.31	.68
Dutifulness	.68	.08	.01	.33	.25	.66
Achievement striving	.20	.37	.00	.40	.43	.60
Self-discipline	.55	.20	.00	.61	.25	.39
Deliberation	.67	.00	.00	.76	.33	.24

$$x^2 = 182.41, p = .00, df = 125, RMSEA = .035, 90\% \ UL = .046, AIC = -67.59$$

Note: All parameters are significant at $p < .05$; RMSEA 90% UL = 90% upper confidence interval for RMSEA estimate; A = common additive genetic effects; E = common nonshared environmental factors; A′ = facet-specific additive genetic effects; E′ = facet-specific nonshared environmental effects.

Table adapted from "Genetic and Environmental Influences on the Covariance of Facets Defining the Domains of the Five-Factor Model of Personality," by K. L. Jang, W. J. Livesley, A. Angleitner, R. Riemann, and P. A. Vernon, 2002, *Personality and Individual Differences, 33*, pp. 83–101.

Reproduced with permission from Elsevier Publishing.

and Feelings facets, whereas the Actions, Ideas, and Values facets defined the second factor. With the Agreeableness domain, slightly greater differences were observed across the two samples. In the German sample, the first genetic factor was defined by high loadings on Trust, Altruism, and Compliance. In the Canadian sample, Compliance did not have such a high loading. The second genetic factor was described by Straightforwardness and Modesty in the Canadian sample. In the German sample, Modest had a much higher loading than other facets. Finally, even greater differences were observed across samples for the Conscientiousness domain. In the German sample, the facets Order, Dutifulness, and Self-Discipline characterized the first genetic factor, and Competence and Achievement Striving defined the second. In the Canadian sample, the first factor was defined by Deliberation and Dutifulness, whereas the second factor emphasized Self-Discipline.

The significant feature of this study for understanding personality structure is the failure of the common pathways model. The study also suggests that the higher order domains are not as genetically homogeneous as once thought. Instead, the genetic architecture of each domain is complex; each is influenced by two general genetic dimensions that directly affect most facet traits forming the domain, and multiple genetic dimensions that have a specific influence on a given facet. The phenotypic coherence of each domain is not explained by a higher order trait, such as neuroticism or extraversion, as assumed by trait theory, but by the overlapping effects of the general genetic dimensions that directly affect facet traits. The implication is that the enduring or fundamental components of personality sought by trait theory are to be found at the more specific level of the facet trait rather than at the level of broad dispositions. Earlier, it was proposed that domains be defined as clusters of facet traits that share the same genetic etiology. Similarly, facet traits may be defined as genetically homogeneous units: clusters of items that share the same specific genetic etiology.

In light of these proposals, the term *facet trait,* which implies that they are subsidiary to the higher order domains, seems inappropriate; a term such as *basic trait* seems more pertinent given that they appear to constitute the biological building blocks of personality. The greater significance placed on basic traits by a behavioral genetic perspective and the failure of the one-factor common pathways genetic model creates uncertainty about the conceptual standing of the higher order traits. These are probably best considered labels describing clusters of covarying traits. That is, they are heuristic devices that describe pleiotropic effects and the common influence of environmental factors of clusters of basic traits and the summative effects of specific traits that are useful for some purposes, such as global predictions and descriptions of broad tendencies, rather than distinct entities with an underlying biological structure.

CONCLUSIONS

The results of behavioral genetic analyses of genetic and environmental influences on personality sheds new light on the structure of personality traits and the factors responsible for trait covariation. They also demonstrate that behavioral genetic methods are potentially a powerful tool in elucidating basic questions about the enduring qualities that constitute personality and the way they are organized.

The evidence that genetic factors are responsible for the specific traits that form personality and the organization of these traits into clusters does not imply that environmental influences are unimportant. To the contrary, behavioral genetic studies consistently show that environmental factors, especially nonshared effects, are responsible for approximately as much variance as genetic factors. The nature of this influence and the mechanisms involved have, however, proved elusive. The findings discussed suggest that these effects are likely to operate at the level of specific traits rather than more generally, where they are likely to influence the extent and form of expression of these traits (Livesley, 2003).

The model emerging from this work suggests that personality is influenced by a relatively large number of genetic dimensions that have specific effects. Some directly influence multiple traits, whereas others are highly specific, influencing a single trait. Within this framework, emphasis is placed on the lower order traits as the primary units of personality structure and primary pathways of genetic influence—a conclusion that contrasts with the traditional emphasis of trait theory on broad dispositions as the primary focus of description and explanation. From this perspective, higher order constructs, such as neuroticism and extraversion, are merely labels for describing the pleiotropic action of genes rather than entities with a distinct psychological and genetic basis. It is also apparent that the integrated and coherent nature of personality functioning is not merely the result of connections and functional links forming within the personality system during development, but is also the emergent product of the direct effects on common genetic mechanisms on the expression of the individual traits delineating a given domain.

REFERENCES

Almagor, M., Tellegen, A., & Waller, N. G. (1995). The Big Seven Model: A cross-cultural replication and further exploration of the basic dimensions of natural language trait descriptors. *Journal of Personality and Social Psychology, 69,* 300–307.

Bergeman, C. S., Chipeur, H. M., Plomin, R., Pederson, N. L., McClearn, G. E., Nesselroade, J. R., et al. (1993). Genetic and environmental effects on openness to experience, agreeableness, and conscientiousness: An adoption/twin study. *Journal of Personality, 61,* 159–179.

Bouchard, T. J. (1999). Genes, environment, and personality. In S. J. Ceci & W. M. Williams (Eds.), *The nature-nurture debate: The essential readings in developmental psychology* (pp. 97–103). Malden, MA: Blackwell.

Costa, P. T., & McCrae, R. R. (1992). *Revised NEO Personality Inventory (NEO-PI-R) and the NEO Five-Factor Inventory (NEO-FFI) professional manual.* Odessa, FL: Psychological Assessment Resources.

Costa, P. T., & McCrae, R. R. (1995). Domains and facets: Hierarchical personality assessment using the Revised NEO Personality Inventory. *Journal of Personality Assessment, 64,* 21–50.

Crawford, C. B., & DeFries, J. C. (1978). Factor analysis of genetic and environmental correlation matrices. *Multivariate Behavioral Research, 13,* 297–318.

Depue, R. A., & Collins, P. F. (1999). Neurobiology of the structure of personality: Dopamine, facilitation of incentive motivation, and extraversion. *Behavioral and Brain Sciences, 22,* 491–569.

Eysenck, H. J. (1991). Dimensions of personality: 16, 5 or 3? Criteria for a taxonomic paradigm. *Personality and Individual Differences, 12,* 773–790.

Eysenck, H. J. (1992). Four ways five factors are *not* basic. *Personality and Individual Differences, 13,* 667–673.

Goldberg, L. R. (1990). An alternative "description of personality": The big-five factor structure. *Journal of Personality and Social Psychology, 59,* 1216–1229.

Gough, H. G. (1989). The California Psychological Inventory. In C. S. Newmark (Ed.), *Major psychological assessment instruments* (Vol. 2., pp. 67–98). Needham Heights, MA: Allyn & Bacon.

Hamer, D. H., Greenberg, B. D., Sabol, S. Z., & Murphy, D. L. (1999). Role of serotonin transporter gene in temperament and character. *Journal of Personality Disorders, 13,* 312–328.

Heath, A. C., Neale, M. C., Kessler, R. C., Eaves, L. J., & Kendler, K. S. (1992). Evidence for genetic influences on personality from self-reports and informant ratings. *Journal of Personality and Social Psychology, 63,* 85–96.

Jang, K. L., & Livesley, W. J. (1999). Why do measures of normal and disordered personality correlate? A study of genetic comorbidity. *Journal of Personality Disorders, 13,* 10–17.

Jang, K. L., Livesley, W. J., Angleitner, A., Riemann, R., & Livesley, W. J. (2002). Genetic and environmetal influences on the covariance of facets defining the domains of the five-factor model of personality. *Personality and Individual Differences, 33,* 83–101.

Jang, K. L., Livesley, W. J., Vernon, P. A., & Jackson, D. N. (1996). Heritability of personality disorder traits: A twin study. *Acta Psychiatrica Scandinavica, 94,* 438–444.

Jang, K. L., McCrae, R. R., Angleitner, A., Riemann, R., & Livesley, W. J. (1998). Heritability of facet-level traits in a cross-cultural twin study: Support for a hierarchical model of personality. *Journal of Personality and Social Psychology, 74,* 1556–1565.

Livesley, W. J. (2003). *Practical management of personality disorder.* New York: Guilford Press.

Livesley, W. J., & Jackson, D. N. (in press). *Manual for the dimensional assessment of personality pathology.* Port Huron, MI: Sigma Press.

Livesley, W. J., Jang, K. L., & Vernon, P. A. (1998). The phenotypic and genetic architecture of traits delineating personality disorder. *Archives of General Psychiatry, 55,* 941–948.

Livesley, W. J., Jang, K. L., & Vernon, P. A. (2003). The genetic basis of personality structure. In T. Millon & M. J. Lerner (Eds.), *Handbook of psychology* (Vol. 5, pp. 59–83). New York: Wiley.

Loehlin, J. C. (1987). Heredity, environment, and the structure of the California Psychological Inventory. *Multivariate Behavioral Research, 22,* 137–148.

Loehlin, J. C. (1992). *Genes and environment in personality development.* Newbury Park, CA: Sage.

Loehlin, J. C., & Nicholls, R. C. (1976). *Heredity, environment, and personality.* Austin: University of Texas Press.

McCrae, R. R., Costa, P. T., & Piedmont, R. L. (1993). Folk concepts, natural language, and psychological constructs: The California Psychological Inventory and the Five-Factor Model. *Journal of Personality, 61,* 1–26.

McCrae, R. R., Jang, K. L., Livesley, W. J., Riemann, R., & Angleitner, A. (2001). Sources of structure: Genetic, environmental, and artifactual influences on the covariation of personality traits. *Journal of Personality, 69*(4), 511–535.

Merikangas, K. R. (2002). Implications of genetic epidemiology for classification. In J. E. Helzer & J. J. Hudziak (Eds.), *Defining psychopathology in the 21st century* (pp. 195–209). Washington, DC: American Psychiatric Press.

Neale, M. C., & Cardon, L. R. (1992). *Methodology for genetic studies of twins and families.* Dordrecht, The Netherlands: Kluwer Academic Press.

Passini, F. T., & Norman, W. T. (1966). A universal conception of personality structure? *Journal of Personality and Social Psychology, 4,* 44–49.

Paunonen, S. V., & Jackson, D. N. (1996). The Jackson Personality Inventory and the Five-Factor Model of Personality. *Journal of Research in Personality, 30,* 42–59.

Plomin, R., & Caspi, A. (1999). Behavioral genetics and personality. In L. A. Pervin & O. P. John (Eds.), *Handbook of personality* (2nd ed., pp. 221–276). New York: Guilford Press.

Plomin, R., Chipeur, H. M., & Loehlin, J. C. (1990). Behavior genetics and personality. In L. A. Pervin (Ed.), *Handbook of personality: Theory and research* (pp. 225–243). New York: Guilford Press.

Plomin, R., DeFries, J. C., & McClearn, G. E. (1990). *Behavioral genetics: A primer* (2nd ed.). New York: Freeman.

Riemann, R., Angleitner, A., & Strelau, J. (1997). Genetic and environmental influences on personality: A twin study. *Journal of Personality, 65,* 449–476.

Schroeder, M. L., Wormworth, J. A., & Livesley, W. J. (1992). Dimensions of personality disorder and their relationships to the big five dimensions of personality. *Psychological Assessment: A Journal of Consulting and Clinical Psychology, 4,* 47–53.

Shweder, R. A. (1975). How relevant is an individual difference theory of personality? *Journal of Personality, 43,* 455–484.

Tellegen, A. (1985). Structures of mood and personality and their relevance to assessing anxiety with an emphasis on self-report. In A. H. Tuma & J. D. Maser (Eds.), *Anxiety and the anxiety disorders* (pp. 681–706). Hillsdale, NJ: Erlbaum.

Turkheimer, E. (1998). Heritability and biological explanation. *Psychological Review, 105,* 782–791.

Watson, D., & Clark, L. A. (1997). Extraversion and its positive emotional core. In R. Hogan & J. A. Johnson (Eds.), *Handbook of personality psychology* (pp. 767–793). San Diego, CA: Academic Press.

Zuckerman, M. (1991). *Psychobiology of personality.* Cambridge, England: Cambridge University Press.

Zuckerman, M. (1994). An alternative Five-Factor Model for Personality. In C. F. Halverson Jr. & G. A. Kohnstamm (Eds.), *The developing structure of temperament and personality from infancy to adulthood* (pp. 53–68). Hillsdale, NJ: Erlbaum.

Zuckerman, M. (1999). Incentive motivation. *Personality and Social Psychology, 65,* 757–768.

Zuckerman, M., Kuhlman, D. M., Joireman, J., Teta, P., & Kraft, M. (1993). A comparison of three structural models of personality: The big three, the big five, and the alternative five. *Journal of Personality and Social Psychology, 65,* 757–768.

Chapter 7

THE INTERPERSONAL NEXUS OF PERSONALITY DISORDERS

AARON L. PINCUS

Personality disorders continue to be perplexing clinical phenomena to define, classify, diagnose, and effectively treat. Although conceptions of abnormal personalities have existed since the earliest clinical nosologies of the twentieth century (Abraham, 1921/1927; Kraepelin, 1907; Reich, 1933/1949; Schneider, 1923/1950), the publication of the third edition of the *Diagnostic and Statistical Manual of Mental Disorders* (*DSM-III;* American Psychiatric Association, 1980) was a landmark event for the clinical science of personality disorder. *DSM-III* provided a separate diagnostic axis (Axis II) on which personality disorders were to be evaluated and also introduced the contemporary categories of avoidant, borderline, dependent, and narcissistic personality disorder to the official nomenclature. From 1980 through the end of the century, *DSM-III* Axis II and its subsequent revisions (*DSM-III-R,* APA, 1987; *DSM-IV,* APA, 1994; *DSM-IV-TR,* APA, 2000) stimulated an enormous increase in psychological theory and empirical research on the nature, classification, and treatment of personality disorders. While the work stimulated by the *DSM* Axis II categories of personality disorder is invaluable to clinical science, it appears that the benefits of the approach have now been all but exhausted and the study of personality disorders has entered the post *DSM-III/DSM-IV* era (Livesley, 2001).

In recent years, a number of leading personality disorder investigators have published increasingly explicit and critical assessments of the *DSM* system of classifying and diagnosing personality disorders based on psychometric, theoretical, and clinical grounds (Bornstein, 1997, 2003; Clark, Livesley, & Morey, 1997; Cloninger, 2000; Endler & Kocovski, 2002; Livesley, 2001; Millon, 2000; Parker et al., 2002; Westen & Arkowitz-Westen, 1998; Westen & Shedler, 2000; Widiger, 2000). For example, Cloninger declared:

> Our current official classification of personality disorders is fundamentally flawed by its assumption that personality disorder is composed of multiple discrete categorical disorders. The current list of clusters and categories are highly redundant and overlapping. Systematic diagnosis of so many categories is not feasible in clinical practice and unjustifiable in psychometric research. Predictive power of categorical diagnoses is weak and inconsistent. (pp. 106–107)

Similarly, Livesley (2001) stated:

> Despite the progress of the last 20 years, problems with the *DSM* model are all too obvious. The approach has limited clinical utility. Diagnostic overlap is a major problem, and there

is limited evidence that current categories predict response to treatment. In sum, the construct validity of the system has yet to be established. Problems are equally apparent from a research perspective. *DSM* diagnoses are too broad and heterogeneous to use in investigations of biological and psychological mechanisms, forcing investigators to use alternative constructs and measures. (pp. 6–7)

Finally and perhaps most directly, Westen and Shedler (2000) asserted:

> The increasing consensus among personality disorder researchers is that Axis II does not rest on a firm enough foundation. We may do well to rebuild it from the basement up rather than trying to plug the leaks or replace the roof. (p. 110)

In light of such assessments, the current chapter extends a contemporary integrative interpersonal approach to personality (Pincus, in press; Pincus & Ansell, 2003) to the conceptualization of personality disorder. The emerging framework attempts to address the needs of both the personologist and the diagnostician in the post *DSM* era.

TWO TRENDS IN PERSONALITY DISORDER CLASSIFICATION

A review of the recent literature on personality disorder classification reveals two trends that can be referred to as "causal-theoretical approaches" and "practical-empirical approaches." Although not mutually exclusive in terms of group membership or concerns, the two approaches do have several contrasting emphases that are outlined in Table 7.1. Causal-theoretical approaches tend to emphasize theory, open concepts, the nature of pathology, and the definition of personality disorder and view classification in the context of explanation. In contrast, practical-empirical approaches tend to emphasize methods, operational definitions, phenomenology, and the description of individual differences in personality disorder and view classification in the context of the practical task of diagnosis.

Theory versus Method

Theoretical models of personality disorder usually propose and prioritize fundamental principles that underlie the integrated functioning of the whole person, which is assumed to then organize the contents and functional relationships among domains of personality. All such theories have normative and pathological implications. Clarkin and Lenzenweger (1996) and Millon, Meagher, and Grossman (2001) identified the major

Table 7.1   Emphases of Two Trends in Personality Disorder Classification

Causal-Theoretical Approaches	Practical-Empirical Approaches
Theory	Method
Open concepts	Operational definitions
Pathology	Phenomenology
Definition	Diagnosis
Explanation	Description
Based on theory	Based on empirical data
Based on empirical data	Based on theory
Accept, ignore, or revise *DSM* system	Revise *DSM* system

theoretical approaches to personality disorder as cognitive theories, interpersonal theories, intrapsychic (psychodynamic) theories, evolutionary theories, and neurobiological theories. Millon et al. suggested that a limitation of most theoretical approaches to personality disorder is their typical allegiance to one domain of personality (e.g., cognition) as central, while casting all other domains as peripheral or derivative.

Methodologically driven models of personality disorder do not make a priori theoretical commitments and thus are free to address any domain (or even several domains) of personality. In such approaches, investigators make no a priori assumptions about what dimensions/domains might emerge. Millon et al. (2001) cautioned that purely methods-based approaches to personality disorder typically provide retrospective rationales for findings, and "structure and sufficiency are thus offered in compensation for lack of a compelling theory" (p. 47).

Open Concepts versus Operational Definitions

These two emphases mark the endpoints of an epistemological continuum of conceptual breadth versus conceptual specificity (Millon, 1987). Open concepts are more abstract and hypothetical, reflecting the nature of personality constructs as less rigidly organized than many constructs in the hard sciences. That is, in the field of personology, we have few one-to-one relationships among personality, behavior, experience, and development, and we have many more feedback, feedforward, stochastic, and transactional processes involving indeterminate or inferential intervening concepts. As suitable as open concepts are to personology, Millon et al. (2001) noted that conceptualizing personality disorder strictly in terms of open concepts runs the risk of growing so circuitous in references as to become tautological and imply no links to anything observable. This undermines the scientific contribution of theory by rendering it both untestable and inapplicable to clinical diagnosis (Millon, 1991).

Operational definitions seek to anchor personality disorder directly in the empirical world of observation, linking each personological attribute to an indicator in a one-to-one fashion. The goal is to reduce inference and maximize the relationship between attribute and method of measurement. In clinical assessment, operational definitions allow for diagnostic indicators to be directly translatable into assessment guidelines that maximize precision (reliability); however, such approaches can be deficient in scope (validity) if they are based on any single methodological procedure (e.g., factor analysis).

Pathology, Definition, and Explanation versus Phenomenology, Diagnosis, and Description

These concepts are all related to whether one views classification of psychopathology as mainly in the service of the practical task of clinical identification or mainly in the service of understanding the nature of normality and abnormality. A set of diagnostic criteria can be interpreted as defining what is meant by the disorder or as providing a set of fallible indicators for determining when the disorder is present (Widiger & Trull, 1991). The 10 specific *DSM-IV* personality disorder criteria sets really serve the latter function as the manual provides a definition of personality disorder distinct from them, but the definition is not systematically and specifically used in making *DSM* diagnoses. Widiger (1991) suggested that *DSM* criteria sets tend to describe the phenomenology of individual differences in personality disorder rather than fundamentally describing the pathology of personality disorders in relation to normality. Similarly, Parker et al. (2002) suggested that *DSM-IV* criteria sets mix and confuse indicators of personality dysfunction (which could serve to define and explain personality disorder) with descriptors of personality style (which serve to distinguish and portray individual differences in personality disorder phenomenology).

Theoretical versus Empirical Basis

Given how divergent the priorities of the causal-theoretical and practical-empirical approaches can appear to be, I am sometimes confused by the fact that in most of the literature from both sets of approaches one can find statements endorsing both theory and empiricism as the required basis for classification of personality disorders. Of the nine requirements for an empirically based classification provided by Livesley (2001), he included, "The classification should be based on empirical evidence" and "The classification should be theory based" (p. 30). He noted that current classification is at odds with empirical data, yet he also suggested that no currently existing theory of personality disorder is yet adequate to provide the necessary basis for classification. Lenzenweger and Clarkin (1996) seem, at times, to confuse the goals of the causal-theoretical and practical-empirical approaches. Many of their critical issues for *theories* of personality disorder are strongly tied to, and some even derived from, practical-empirical issues (e.g., the types of populations used in personality disorder research, categorical versus dimensional diagnostic systems, structure of the *DSM* multiaxial system).

In reality, I don't think there's a true distinction here, as few in the field view either source of information as truly distinct and sufficient. However, I do think that more integration of theory and method is clearly necessary. When one reviews critiques of personality disorder research (e.g., Bornstein, 2003; Lenzenweger & Clarkin, 1996), there is often little to inform theory development. When one reviews theory, there is often little connection with the issues debated in the practical-empirical approaches.

The *DSM* System

Current major theories of personality disorder vary in terms of their assessment of *DSM* Axis II. Benjamin's (1996a, 1996b) interpersonal theory based on Structural Analysis of Social Behavior (SASB) and Beck's cognitive theory (Beck & Freedman, 1990; Pretzer & Beck, 1996) both generally accept the *DSM* classification. Contemporary psychodynamic theories (e.g., Kernberg, 1984, 1996; McWilliams, 1994) and neurobiological theories (e.g., Depue, 1996; Paris, 2000) tend to ignore *DSM* classification in favor of current or future alternatives. Millon's (1990) evolutionary theory tends to parallel the *DSM* (Millon & Davis, 1996), although he is clear about *DSM*'s limitations (Millon, 2000). Almost all of the recent practical-empirical literature concludes that the *DSM* system needs revision, although suggestions differ in terms of whether to focus revisions on the structure of the *DSM* (e.g., Axis I versus Axis II distinctions, categorical versus dimensional versus prototypal classification) or to focus revisions on the nature and scope of diagnostic criteria, or both.

TOWARD A NEW CLASSIFICATION OF PERSONALITY DISORDERS

There are several recent proposals for revising the classification and diagnosis of personality disorders. Westen and Shedler (2000) endorsed the use of a prototype matching procedure based on empirically derived clinical descriptors and diagnostic categories. Widiger

(2000) endorsed the use of a purely dimensional model with empirically derived cut-off scores. Several investigators have suggested that classification should be based on biology/neurobiology (Depue, 1996; Paris, 2000; Silk, 1997). Millon (2000) recommended the *DSM* criteria sets be increased in scope and uniformity of coverage of necessary domains of personality, and that *DSM* categories be considered as psychological prototypes with many subtypes (see also Millon, 1996). Bornstein (2003) suggested revision of *DSM* criteria via behaviorally referenced criterion validation based on experimental manipulation of personality disorder processes that produce measurable behavioral change.

Two-Step Diagnostic Approaches

Several substantively divergent alternatives actually converge in proposing a two-step diagnostic process that distinguishes *definition* of personality disorder pathology (Step 1) from *description* of individual differences in personality disorder phenomenology (Step 2).[1] I believe that explicitly decoupling definition of personality disorder and description of individual differences in phenomenological expression is the most promising approach to optimizing classification for both the personologist and the diagnostician. In general, it appears that causal-theoretical approaches may best inform Step 1 and practical-empirical approaches may best inform Step 2. Some examples of two-step diagnostic approaches are noted below.

In Kernberg's (1984, 1996) structural diagnosis of personality organization, maturational level of object-relations *defines* three levels of personality organization (neurotic, borderline, psychotic) with increasing levels of pathological severity. This is then combined with character type, which *describes* unique constellations of defenses, needs, and expectancies that give rise to individual differences in the expression of normal and pathological personality organization.

DSM-IV also took a step in this direction by providing general criteria for personality disorder (Step 1) in a format similar to criteria sets for specific Axis II categories (Step 2). According to the manual, a personality disorder involves clinically significant distress or impairment due to an enduring, inflexible, and pervasive pattern of inner experience and behavior that deviates markedly from cultural expectations as manifested in two or more areas: cognition, affectivity, interpersonal functioning, and impulse control. However, these criteria are not systematically incorporated into clinical diagnostic practice, no empirical research has evaluated them, and theoretical linkages among criteria are not provided.

Cloninger (2000) proposed that the defining features of personality disorder (Step 1) be based on low levels of the character dimensions of the Temperament and Character Inventory (TCI; Cloninger, Przybeck, Svrakic, & Wetzel, 1994). Low levels of Self-directedness are reflected in irresponsibility, purposelessness, helplessness, poor self-acceptance, and impulsivity. Low levels of Cooperativeness are reflected in intolerance, narcissism, hostility, revengefulness, and opportunism. Low levels of Affective Stability are reflected in anxiousness, irritability, envy, hatefulness, and bitterness. Low levels of Self-transcendence are reflected in an unstable self-image, an erratic worldview, magical thinking, emptiness, and aesthetic insensitivity. Individual differences in personality disorder phenomenology (Step 2) are then based on variation in combinations and levels of the TCI temperament dimensions of Harm Avoidance, Novelty Seeking, and Reward Dependence.

---

[1] In the current chapter, I focus more on Step 1 than on Step 2. For a full exposition, see Pincus (in press).

An even larger set of defining features (Step 1) is provided by Parker et al. (2002), including disagreeableness, inability to care for others, lack of cooperation, causes discomfort to others, ineffectiveness, lack of empathy, failure to form and maintain interpersonal relationships, failure to learn from experience, impulsivity, inflexibility, maladaptability, immorality, extremes of optimism, self-defeating behaviors, low self-directedness, lack of humor, and tenuous stability under stress. While many of these features clearly fit clinical experiences with personality disordered patients, it's unclear how to distinguish many of these features from the assessment of lower order traits of personality disorder, such as those reflected in Clark's Schedule for Nonadaptive and Adaptive Personality (SNAP; Clark, 1993) and Livesley's Dimensional Assessment of Personality Pathology (DAPP; Livesley & Jackson, in press), both of which would be most suited to describing individual differences in personality disorder phenomenology (Step 2).

In contrast to the large number of specific features detailed by Parker et al. (2002) that appear more suitable to Step 2, Livesley (1998, 2001) proposed that review of the clinical literature on personality disorders reveals two major features of dysfunction that can be used to elegantly and parsimoniously define personality disorder (Step 1). He suggested that personality disorder could be clinically defined by *chronic interpersonal dysfunction* and *problems with self or identity.* The former is characterized by pervasive abnormalities in social functioning, including failure to develop adaptive relational functioning, impairments in cooperative and prosocial relational capacity, and instability and poor integration of mental representations of others and relationships. Such deficits often give rise to interpersonal relationships marred by deleterious vicious circles (Millon, 1996), self-fulfilling prophecies (Carson, 1982), and maladaptive transaction cycles (Kiesler, 1991). Self/identity problems are characterized by unstable and poorly integrated mental representations of self and others reflected in the subjective experience of chronic emptiness, contradictory self-perceptions, contradictory behavior that cannot be integrated in an emotionally meaningful way, and shallow, flat, impoverished perceptions of others. Difficulties maintaining self-cohesion, goal-directedness, and a sense of well-being and vitality are common (Kohut & Wolf, 1978). Finally, personality disordered individuals' cognitive schemas, core beliefs, expectancies, and thoughts about the self are dysfunctional, distressing, or both.

Switching briefly to Step 2, the task of describing individual differences in personality disorder phenomenology, a number of potential specific descriptive systems could be employed (see Table 7.2). The most common models for describing individual differences in personality and personality disorder are dimensional trait models, which have several advantages, including their inherent continuity with normal functioning. Even the SNAP and DAPP personality disorder trait dimensions exhibit continuous distributions across normal and clinical populations. Examples of categorical systems proposed for describing individual differences in personality disorder phenomenology include prototype matching (Westen & Shedler, 2000), specific cognitive schemas (Pretzer & Beck, 1996; Young, 1990), constellations of defense mechanisms (McWilliams, 1994; Vaillant & McCullough, 1998), and broad classes of evolutionary adaptations (Millon, 1990; Millon & Davis, 1996).

AN OVERVIEW OF THE NEXUS OF PERSONALITY DISORDERS

I believe Livesley's (1998, 2001) distillation of the core clinical features of personality disorder, that is, *chronic interpersonal dysfunction* and *problems with self and identity,* provides an excellent starting point for a definition of personality disorder. However, Livesley (2001) lamented that no theory of personality disorder currently exists to link

Table 7.2   Some Systems to Describe Individual Differences in Personality Disorder Phenomenology

Dimensional Systems

- Personality Trait Dimensions
  Interpersonal Circumplex (IPC)
  Eysenck's 3-Factor Model (P-E-N)
  Five-Factor Model (FFM)
- Personality Disorder Trait Dimensions
  Schedule for Nonadaptive and Adaptive Personality (SNAP)
  Dimensional Assessment of Personality Pathology (DAPP)
- Temperament Dimensions
  Temperament and Character Inventory (TCI)
- Livesley's Convergent Dimensions
- Emotional Dysregulation, Dissocial Behavior, Inhibitedness, Compulsivity

Categorical Systems

- Prototype matching
- Specific cognitive schemas
- Constellations of defense mechanisms
- Broad classes of evolutionary adaptations

this definition of personality disorder to an empirically based classification system. In terms of the trends discussed in the present chapter, a new classification of personality disorders requires a scheme that can coordinate the definitional strengths of causal-theoretical approaches and the descriptive strengths of practical-empirical approaches. My view is that the interpersonal theory of personality (e.g., Benjamin, 2003; Carson, 1969; Kiesler, 1983; Leary, 1957; McLemore & Benjamin, 1979; Pincus, 1994, in press; Pincus & Ansell, 2003; Sullivan, 1953a, 1953b; Wiggins & Trapnell, 1996) is in a unique position to provide a *nexus* between the two sets of approaches because it provides a basis for the definition of personality disorder (for Step 1) and empirically based models and methods for describing personality disorder phenomenology (for Step 2). An overview of the interpersonal nexus of personality disorders is presented in Figure 7.1. The current chapter focuses more on the interpersonal definition of personality disorder than on the interpersonal description of personality disorder phenomenology.

The interpersonal nexus of personality disorders can enhance the explanatory implications of Livesley's core defining features of personality disorder through the application of contemporary integrative interpersonal theory (Pincus, in press; Pincus & Ansell, 2003) that emphasizes the "interpersonal situation" as an integrative theoretical concept. To fully satisfy the theoretical and personological needs of definition, the interpersonal nexus must also articulate the motivational and developmental factors influencing disordered self-concepts and maladaptive patterns of relating to others, and account for the fluctuating severity of personality disorder symptomology. What makes this a true nexus is that the interpersonal theory of personality also has a long and reciprocally influential history with research programs that have culminated in well-validated, empirically derived models and methods to describe interpersonal behavior (Pincus, 1994). Thus, the interpersonal nexus of personality disorders also includes multiple methods to assess the fundamental interpersonal dimensions of Agency and Communion (Wiggins, 1991) and

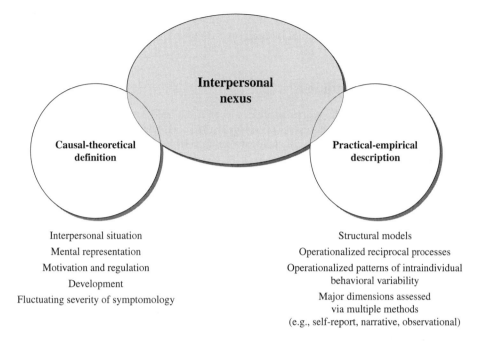

Figure 7.1   **Interpersonal Theory Provides a Nexus to Coordinate Definition and Description of Personality Disorders**

associated circumplex structural models (Benjamin, 1974; Wiggins, 1996), operational definitions of reciprocal interpersonal processes (Benjamin, 1996b), and operational definitions of intraindividual variability in interpersonal behavior (Moskowitz & Zuroff, 2004). In addition, the descriptive models and methods are based on personality dimensions that are continuous with normal and disordered functioning. Utilizing the entire scope of the interpersonal nexus of personality disorders allows for coordination of the causal-theoretical definition of personality disorder with the practical-empirical description of personality disorder phenomenology needed for efficient and clinically useful classification and diagnosis.

Derivative versus Integrative Theories

In their critique of personality disorder theories, Millon et al. (2001) suggested that current theories tend to be aligned with one psychological domain and consider other domains either derivative or peripheral. In most reviews of personality disorder theory, authors list cognitive, interpersonal, psychodynamic, evolutionary, and neurobiological theories as separate and distinct categories. However, just like *DSM* Axis II categories of personality disorders, these theoretical approaches to personality disorder really have a number of shared characteristics, making their distinctions fuzzy. Pincus and Ansell (2003) argued that interpersonal theory was integrative rather than derivative. For example, contemporary integrative interpersonal theory would not suggest that cognitive functioning is somehow derivative of or peripheral to relational experience. It simply asserts that when we look at a domain of personality such as cognition, our best bet may be to look at it in relation to interpersonal functioning. Thus, in their contemporary account, the interpersonal approach is also a nexus for bringing together elements across the theoretical spectrum. All theories of personality disorder address interpersonal functioning, and interpersonal theory can serve as an integrative framework via consideration of the "interpersonal situation."

The Interpersonal Situation

> I had come to feel over the years that there was an acute need for a discipline that was determined to study not the individual organism or the social heritage, but the interpersonal situations through which persons manifest mental health or mental disorder. (Sullivan, 1953b, p. 18)

> Personality is the relatively enduring pattern of recurrent interpersonal situations which characterize a human life. (Sullivan, 1953b, pp. 110–111)

Pincus and Ansell (2003) began their contemporary treatment of interpersonal theory by revisiting the Sullivanian concept of the "interpersonal situation." They noted that the most basic implication of Sullivan's interpersonal situation was that the expression of personality (and the study of its nature) focuses on phenomena involving more than one person; that is, some form of relating is occurring. Sullivan's (1953a, 1953b) interpersonal theory suggested that individuals express "integrating tendencies" that bring them together in mutual pursuit of both satisfactions (generally a large class of biologically grounded needs) and security (i.e., felt self-esteem and anxiety-free functioning). These integrating tendencies develop into increasingly complex patterns, or dynamisms, of interpersonal experience. From infancy through six developmental epochs these dynamisms are encoded and elaborated in memory via age-appropriate learning. Interpersonal learning of social behaviors and self-concept is based on an anxiety gradient associated with interpersonal situations. All interpersonal situations range from rewarding (highly secure) through various degrees of anxiety and ending in a class of situations associated with such severe anxiety that they are dissociated from experience. The interpersonal situation underlies genesis, development, maintenance, and mutability of personality through the continuous patterning and repatterning of interpersonal experience in relation to the vicissitudes of satisfactions, security, and esteem. Over time, this gives rise to lasting conceptions of self and other (Sullivan's "personifications") as well as to enduring patterns of interpersonal relating.

Individual variation in learning occurs due to the interaction between the developing person's level of cognitive maturation (i.e., Sullivan's prototaxic, parataxic, and syntaxic modes of experience) and the characteristics of the interpersonal situations encountered. Interpersonal experience is understood differently depending on the developing person's grasp of cause-and-effect logic and the use of consensual symbols such as language. This affects how one makes sense of the qualities of significant others (including their "reflected appraisals" of the developing person), as well as the ultimate outcomes of interpersonal situations characterizing a human life. Pincus and Ansell (2003) summarized Sullivan's concept of the interpersonal situation as

> the experience of a pattern of relating self with other associated with varying levels of anxiety (or security) in which learning takes place that influences the development of self-concept and social behavior. (p. 210)

This is a very fundamental human experience which can serve as a point for pantheoretical integration. Notably, *maladaptive* relational strategies and *dysfunctional* conceptions of self and others developed over the course of a lifetime of interpersonal situations converge nicely with the two core features of personality disorder proposed by Livesley: *chronic interpersonal dysfunction* and *problems with self or identity*. Thus, interpersonal situations also can be seen as central to the genesis, development, maintenance, and mutability of personality disorder.

Interpersonal Situations Occur Between People and Within the Mind

Pincus and Ansell (2003) noted that because Sullivan's (1953a, 1953b) interpersonal theory of psychiatry was a response to Freud's strong emphasis on drive-based intrapsychic aspects of personality and clearly discarded the drives as sources of personality structuralization, a common misinterpretation of the term "interpersonal" is to assume it refers to a limited class of phenomena that can be observed only in the immediate interaction between two proximal people. Review of Sullivan's body of work clearly reveals that this dichotomous conception of the interpersonal and the intrapsychic as two sets of distinct phenomena—one residing between people and one residing within a person—is an incorrect interpretation (Mitchell, 1988; Pincus & Ansell, 2003). From his emphasis on the interpersonal sources of the self-concept to his conceptions of personifications and parataxic distortions, Sullivan clearly viewed the interpersonal situation as equally likely to be found within the mind of the person as it is to be found in the observable interactions between two people. In fact, Sullivan (1964) defined psychiatry as the "study of the phenomena that occur in configurations made up of two or more people, all but one of whom may be more or less completely illusory" (p. 33). In Pincus and Ansell's contemporary integrative interpersonal theory:

> The term *interpersonal* is meant to convey a sense of primacy, a set of fundamental phenomena important for personality development, structuralization, function, and pathology. It is not a geographic indicator of locale: It is not meant to generate a dichotomy between what is inside the person and what is outside the person. (p. 212)

This quote makes it clear that interpersonal functioning occurs not only between people, but also inside people via the capacity for mental representation of self and others (e.g., Blatt, Auerbach, & Levy, 1997). It also allows the contemporary interpersonal perspective to incorporate important pantheoretical representational constructs such as cognitive interpersonal schemas, internalized object relations, and internal working models. Contemporary interpersonal theory does suggest that the most important personological phenomena are relational in nature, but it does not suggest that such phenomena are limited to contemporaneous, observable behavior. Interpersonal situations as defined by Pincus and Ansell (2003) occur both between proximal interactants and within the minds of those interactants. They occur in perceptions of contemporaneous events, memories of past experiences (however accurate or distorted), and fantasies of future experiences. The ability to address both internal experiences and external relationships is necessary for a theory of personality disorder, as Livesley's two core defining features both have representational and proximal relational implications. Both internal and external interpersonal situations continuously influence an individual's learned relational strategies and conception of self/identity.

Parataxic Distortions

Sullivan (1953a) proposed the concept of "parataxic distortion" to describe the mediation of proximal relational behavior by internal subjective interpersonal situations, and suggested that these occur when, beside the interpersonal situation as defined within the awareness of the speaker, there is a concomitant interpersonal situation quite different as to its principal integrating tendencies, of which the speaker is more or less completely unaware. (p. 92)

The effects of parataxic distortions on interpersonal relations can occur in several forms, including chronic distortions of new interpersonal experiences (input); generation of rigid, extreme, and/or chronically nonnormative interpersonal behavior (output); and dominance of internal interpersonal situations and other affect or self-regulation goals leading to the disconnection of interpersonal input and output.

Normal and pathological personalities may be differentiated by their enduring tendencies to organize interpersonal experience in particular ways, leading to integrated or disturbed interpersonal relations. Pincus (in press) proposed that healthy interpersonal relations are promoted by the capacity to organize and elaborate incoming interpersonal input in generally undistorted ways, allowing for the mutual needs of self and other to be met. That is, the proximal interpersonal field and the internal interpersonal field are relatively consistent (i.e., free of parataxic distortion). Maladaptive interpersonal functioning is promoted when the proximal interpersonal field is encoded in distorted or biased ways, leading to behavior (output) that disrupts interpersonal relations due to conflicting or disconnected relational goals. In the psychotherapy context, this can be identified by difficulties developing a therapeutic alliance. Such therapeutic experiences are common in the early phase of treatment of personality disorders.

Motivation and Development

An interpersonal theory of personality disorder must also account for which situations are most influential, how their influence is manifest, and how interpersonal situations contribute to personality development across the life span. I propose that two necessary conditions be present for interpersonal situations to significantly impact personality development (i.e., the development of enduring patterns of interpersonal relating and relatively stable conceptions of self/identity). First, a "catalyst of internalization" (Pincus & Ansell, 2003) must be present (see Table 7.3). That is, a developmentally salient motive must be activated, achieved, or frustrated; or, an organismic trauma must impinge on the person. Second, the experience must involve what I refer to as regulatory metagoals. Finally, I propose that the process by which interpersonal situations promote enduring influences on personality development is through the internalization and mental representation of reciprocal

Table 7.3   Some Possible Catalysts of Internalization

Developmental Achievements	Traumatic Learning
Attachment	Early loss of attachment figure
Security	Childhood illness or injury
Separation/Individuation	Physical abuse
Positive affects	Sexual abuse
Gender identity	Emotional abuse
Resolution of Oedipal issues	Parental neglect
Self-esteem	
Self-confirmation	
Mastery of unresolved conflicts	
Identity formation	

interpersonal patterns in relationships that are associated with particular motives and regulatory goals.

Catalysts of Internalization

Pincus and Ansell (2003) proposed, "Reciprocal interpersonal patterns develop in concert with emerging motives that take developmental priority" (p. 223). These developmentally emergent motives may begin with the formation of early attachment bonds and felt security; but later, separation-individuation, the experience of self-esteem and positive affects, development of gender identity, and resolution of Oedipal issues may become priorities. Later still, adult identity formation and its confirmation from the social world, as well as mastery of continuing unresolved conflicts, may take precedence. In addition to the achievement of emerging developmental goals, influential interpersonal patterns are associated with traumatic learning, stemming from the need to cope with impinging events such as early loss of an attachment figure, childhood illness or injury, and physical or sexual abuse. The consequences of internalizing such experiences are an individual's consistently sought-after relational patterns and his or her typical strategies for achieving them. These become the basis for the recurrent interpersonal situations that characterize a human life. If we are to understand the relational strategies individuals employ when such developmental motives or traumas are reactivated, we must learn what interpersonal behaviors and patterns were associated with achievement or frustration of particular developmental milestones or were required to cope with a trauma in the first place.

Identifying the developmental and traumatic catalysts for internalization of reciprocal interpersonal patterns allows for greater understanding of current behavior. For example, in terms of achieving adult attachment relationships, some individuals have developed hostile strategies such as verbally or physically fighting in order to elicit some form of interpersonal connection, whereas others have developed submissive strategies such as avoiding conflict and deferring to the wishes of the other in order to be liked and elicit gratitude. While interpersonal theory asserts that internal interpersonal situations can mediate the perception and encoding of new input, the overt behavior of the other is influential, particularly as it activates a person's expectancies, wishes, fears, and so on that are associated with important motives or traumas. This will significantly influence individuals' covert experience. Along with unfortunate traumatic experiences, the most important motives of individuals are those associated with the central achievements of personality development that have been identified across the theoretical spectrum.

Regulatory Metagoals

Pincus (in press) proposed an additional level of interpersonal learning that takes place concurrently with the association of particular patterns of interpersonal relating to the specific goals associated with emerging developmental achievements and coping with trauma. The second condition necessary for internalization of interpersonal experience is the association of the interpersonal situation with one or more of three superordinate regulatory functions or metagoals: field regulation, emotion regulation, and self-regulation. The concept of regulation has become almost ubiquitous in psychological theory, particularly in the domain of human development. Most theories of personality emphasize the importance of developing mechanisms for emotion regulation and self-regulation. Interpersonal theory is unique in its added emphasis on field regulation, that is, the processes by which the behavior of self and other transactionally influence each other (Mitchell, 1988; Sullivan, 1948; Wiggins & Trobst, 1999). This has led to operational definitions of reciprocal interpersonal processes to describe the patterning of mutual influence of self and other within the interpersonal field. Consistent with their integrative efforts, Pincus and Ansell (2003) argued that the same patterns of influence that occur in the proximal interactions of two people also occur in the internal interpersonal field of mental representations. Field regulation thus provides a third regulatory metagoal, complementing the important functions of emotion regulation and self-regulation. Emerging developmental motives and the coping demands of traumas listed in Table 7.3 all have significant implications for emotion regulation, self-regulation, and field regulation. This further contributes to the generalization of interpersonal learning to new interpersonal situations by providing a small number of superordinate psychological triggers to activate internal interpersonal situations.

The importance of distinguishing these three regulatory metagoals is most directly related to understanding the shifting priorities that may be associated with interpersonal behavior. At any given time, the most prominent metagoal may be proximal field regulation. However, interpersonal behavior may also be associated with self-regulation, such as derogation of others to promote one's self-esteem, or emotion regulation, such as the use of sexual availability in order to feel more emotionally secure and stable. In such instances, interpersonal behavior may play a central role, even if the priority is not explicitly field regulation. Interpersonal behavior enacted in the service of regulating the self or emotion may reduce the contingencies associated with the behavior of the other person. This is another pathway to parataxic distortion and, as will be discussed shortly, also helps to account for the fluctuating symptomology of personality disorders.

Internalization of Interpersonal Experience

Interpersonal situations are most likely to be internalized, and thus have an enduring influence on personality, when they are linked with activation, achievement, or frustration of developmentally significant motives or with organismic traumas. These catalysts of internalization are both associated with regulatory metagoals. Benjamin (1996b, 2003) has suggested three forms of internalization (or interpersonal copy processes) that give rise to enduring relational patterns and regulatory strategies. *Identification* is defined as behaving toward others in ways an important other behaved toward the self. *Recapitulation* is defined as reacting to others as if an internalized other is present and still in control. Finally, *introjection* is defined as treating the self as you have been treated by important others. Thus, an interpersonal situation can be composed of a proximal interpersonal field in which overt behavior serves important communicative and regulatory functions, as well as an internal interpersonal field that gives rise to enduring individual differences in covert experience through the elaboration of interpersonal input.

AN INTERPERSONAL APPROACH TO THE DEFINITION OF PERSONALITY DISORDER

The elaboration of interpersonal input may be healthy or disordered depending on the developmental history of interpersonal situations characterizing an individual's life. In normative social environments, reasonably accurate interpretations of interpersonal input from others may lead to adaptive relationship-enhancing behaviors (output) and a positive, stable self-image; serious distortions of interpersonal input may lead to both *chronic interpersonal dysfunction* and *problems with self or identity*.

For example, if an individual feels too enmeshed in a current relationship and experiences the motive to individuate self from other, achieving this may serve self-, emotion, and field regulatory metagoals. Depending on their developmental history, different people will likely experience the enmeshment in different ways (e.g., as a hostile threat, as being controlled, or perhaps simply as a relationship that needs some recalibration) and employ interpersonal strategies that have been successful in achieving individuation under similar conditions in the past. Some individuals will have internalized adaptive forms of self-differentiation, such as asserting their opinions and needs in an affiliative manner, and others will have internalized more disordered forms of differentiation, such as walling-off, neglecting, abandoning, or even attacking the other. The overt behavior of the other is most influential as it activates a person's expectancies, needs, and fears associated with core motivations and regulatory metagoals, thus influencing his or her covert experience of the relationship.

Pincus (in press) proposed that the key element distinguishing the normal and disordered personality involves the capacity to enter into new proximal interpersonal situations without parataxic distortion. In other words, the larger the range of proximal interpersonal situations that can be entered in which the person exhibits anxiety-free functioning (little need for emotion regulation) and maintains self-esteem (little need for self-regulation), the more adaptive the personality. When this is the case, there is no need to activate mediating internal interpersonal situations and the person can focus on the proximal situation, encode incoming interpersonal input without distortion, respond in adaptive ways that facilitate interpersonal relations (i.e., meet the agentic and communal needs of self and other), and establish complementary patterns of reciprocal behavior (Kiesler, 1983) by fully participating in the proximal interpersonal field. The individual's current behavior will exhibit relatively strong contingency with the proximal behavior of the other and the normative contextual press of the situation. Adaptive interpersonal functioning is promoted by relatively trauma-free development in a culturally normative facilitating environment that has allowed the person to achieve most developmental milestones in normative ways, leading to full capacity to encode and elaborate incoming interpersonal input without bias from competing psychological needs.

In contrast, when the individual develops in a traumatic or nonnormative environment, significant nonnormative interpersonal learning around basic motives such as attachment, individuation, gender identity, and so on may be internalized and associated with difficulties with self-regulation, emotion regulation, and field regulation. In contrast to the healthy personality, personality disorder is reflected in a large range of proximal interpersonal situations that elicit anxiety (activating emotion-regulation strategies), threaten self-esteem (activating self-regulation strategies), and elicit dysfunctional behaviors (nonnormative field-regulation strategies). When this is the case, internal interpersonal situations are activated and the individual is prone to exhibit various forms of parataxic distortion as his or her interpersonal learning history dictates. Thus, the perception of the proximal interpersonal situation is mediated by internal experience, incoming interpersonal input is distorted, behavioral responses (output) disrupt interpersonal relations (i.e., fail to meet the agentic and communal needs of self and other), and relationships tend toward maladaptive patterns of reciprocal behavior. The individual's current behavior will exhibit relatively weak contingency with the proximal behavior of the other.

Fluctuating Severity of Personality Disorder Symptomology

It is important for personologists to avoid confusing the stability of personality (e.g., Roberts & DelVecchio, 2000) with the (presumed) stability of personality disorder symptomology. I have been treating personality disordered patients and supervising their treatment for more than 13 years. Clearly, these patients do not walk around like robots emitting the same behaviors over and over again regardless of the situation (or interpersonal situation). As noted by Livesley (2001), many personality disorders exhibit fluctuating courses of acute symptomatic states, crises of all sorts, and overall level of functioning. Many personality disordered patients can be perfectly appropriate with clinic staff, waiters and waitresses, and others they encounter in daily living situations. Some can maintain employment or even attend university and complete advanced degrees. There is considerable evidence that personality disorder symptomology fluctuates, and that is good news for psychotherapists. If it were otherwise, there would be little sense in treating clients with personality disorder. Therapeutic strategies for personality disorder take advantage of stable periods and work toward containment and reestablishing more adaptive functioning during times of dysregulation.

The interpersonal approach developed here accounts for this fluctuating severity in terms of interpersonal learning associated with developmentally salient motives and regulatory metagoals. That is, while symptoms of personality disordered patients fluctuate and they exhibit transient capacity for adaptive functioning, when it becomes necessary for them to regulate their sense of self (e.g., cohesion, esteem, identity), their emotions, or the behavior of others, this is when we often see an increase in severity of symptomology. This is because such regulatory metagoals are likely to be associated with core motives and the internalized patterns of relating associated with their achievement or frustration. When such metagoals and motives are evoked or thwarted, activation of internalized relations that guide perception of new input and expression of interpersonal behavior dominate the individual's functioning (i.e., parataxic distortion). In healthy personalities, only a small number of interpersonal situations require significant regulatory effort, but in personality disordered individuals, many more interpersonal situations appear to elicit anxiety and self-esteem threat.

A Preliminary Interpersonal Definition of Personality Disorder

Below I provide the elements for a preliminary contemporary interpersonal definition of personality disorder that elaborates on the core clinical features of *chronic interpersonal dysfunction* and *problems with self or identity*. In doing so, this chapter accomplishes only half of the classification task. The elements provide a causal-theoretical definition of personality disorder for Step 1 of a two-step diagnostic process that can be coordinated with practical-empirical approaches to description of individual differences in personality disorder phenomenology through the structural models, operational definitions, and empirical methods of the interpersonal tradition. While space precludes elaborating on Step 2 here, Table 7.4 briefly provides interested readers with basic models, concepts, and some key references.

Personality disorder can be defined by the following:

A. In a large range of situations, the individual exhibits strongly internalized relational patterns associated with (i) activation, achievement, or frustration of salient developmental motives; (ii) traumatic learning; and (iii) regulatory metagoals. These internalized patterns pervade the self-concept and perception of others (via schemas, self-talk, imagery, object relations, internal working models, etc.) leading to parataxic distortions that:

1. Interfere with accurate encoding of new interpersonal experiences (input).

2. Generate inflexible, extreme, and/or nonnormative interpersonal behavior leading to vicious circles, self-fulfilling prophecies, and maladaptive transaction cycles (output).

Table 7.4   Foundations for the Interpersonal Description of Individual Differences in Personality Disorder Phenomenology

- Structural models
  Interpersonal Circumplex (IPC; Kiesler, 1996; Wiggins, 1996)
  Structural Analysis of Social Behavior (SASB; Benjamin, 1974, 1996b)
- Reciprocal Interpersonal Processes (Benjamin, 1996a; Kiesler, 1983)
  Complementarity, opposition, similarity, antithesis, introjection
- Intraindividual variability in interpersonal behavior
  Flux, pulse, spin (Moskowitz & Zuroff, 2004)
- Assessing agency and communion

Self-Report

Interpersonal Adjective Scales (IAS; Wiggins, 1995)
Inventory of Interpersonal Problems (IIP-C; Alden, Wiggins, & Pincus, 1990)
Intrex Questionnaires (Benjamin, 1974, 2000)
Circumplex Scales of Interpersonal Values (CSIV; Locke, 2000)
Social Behavior Inventory (SBI; Moskowitz, 1994)

Observational Coding

SASB Observational Coding System (Benjamin & Cushing, 2000)
Checklist of Interpersonal Transactions (CLOIT-R; Kiesler, Goldston, & Schmidt, 1991)
Checklist of Psychotherapy Transactions (CLOPT-R; Kiesler, Goldston, & Schmidt, 1991)

Narrative Coding

Life Stories and Narratives (McAdams, 1993)
Free Descriptions of Self and Others (Heck & Pincus, 2001)

3. Reduce the contingency between the individual's behavior (output) and the behavior of others (input) or the normative situational press (input).

B. Such disturbances typically develop in a toxic social environment at odds with normative developmental experiences, leading to identification, recapitulation, and introjection of maladaptive self-, emotion-, and field-regulatory strategies that generate self-defeating and nonnormative interpersonal behavior.

C. Lack of insight is common and may be due to distortion of interpersonal input, dominance of internal field-regulation goals, or preoccupation with self-regulation or emotion-regulation metagoals.

Lack of insight is one of the most challenging aspects of treating personality disorders. Such patients are notoriously unaware of their impact on others or the consequences of their behavior for themselves. The underlying causes of poor insight are the various forms of impairment brought about by parataxic distortions. First, distorted input leads to behaviors that make sense to the personality disordered individual, but not to others. Second, the priority metagoal may be to regulate the behavior of an internalized other rather than regulation of an actual other in the proximal interpersonal field (e.g., to receive positive reflected appraisals from internalized others for "acting like them": identification). Third, the priority metagoal may be regulation of the self or regulation of emotion rather than regulation of an other in the proximal interpersonal field. While self- and emotion-regulation strategies can be largely interpersonal in nature, they typically reduce the contingencies associated with interpersonal input and output.

CONCLUSIONS

The interpersonal nexus of personality disorders coordinates this causal-theoretical *definition* of pathology with a practical-empirical *description* of individual differences in phenomenology of disorder (see also Pincus, in press). This approach can form the foundation of a new classification system that meets the needs of the personologist and the diagnostician in the post-*DSM-III/IV* era.

REFERENCES

Abraham, K. (1927). *Selected papers in psychoanalysis.* London: Hogarth Press. (Original work published 1921)

Alden, L. E., Wiggins, J. S., & Pincus, A. L. (1990). Construction of circumplex scales for the Inventory of Interpersonal Problems. *Journal of Personality Assessment, 55,* 521–536.

American Psychiatric Association. (1980). *Diagnostic and statistical manual of mental disorders* (3rd ed.). Washington, DC: Author.

American Psychiatric Association. (1987). *Diagnostic and statistical manual of mental disorders* (3rd ed., rev.). Washington, DC: Author.

American Psychiatric Association. (1994). *Diagnostic and statistical manual of mental disorders* (4th ed.). Washington, DC: Author.

American Psychiatric Association. (2000). *Diagnostic and statistical manual of mental disorders* (4th ed., text rev.). Washington, DC: Author.

Beck, A. T., Freeman, A., & Associates. (1990). *Cognitive therapy of personality disorders.* New York: Guilford Press.

Benjamin, L. S. (1974). Structural analysis of social behavior. *Psychological Review, 81,* 392–425.

Benjamin, L. S. (1996a). *Interpersonal diagnosis and treatment of personality disorders* (2nd ed.). New York: Guilford Press.

Benjamin, L. S. (1996b). An interpersonal theory of personality disorders. In J. F. Clarkin & M. F. Lenzenweger (Eds.), *Major theories of personality disorder* (pp. 141–220). New York: Guilford Press.

Benjamin, L. S. (2000). *Intrex user's manual and software.* Salt Lake City: University of Utah.

Benjamin, L. S. (2003). *Interpersonal reconstructive therapy.* New York: Guilford Press.

Benjamin, L. S., & Cushing, G. (2000). *Manual for coding social interactions in terms of structural analysis of social behavior.* Salt Lake City: University of Utah.

Blatt, S. J., Auerbach, J. S., & Levy, K. N. (1997). Mental representations in personality development, psychopathology, and the therapeutic process. *Review of General Psychology, 1,* 351–374.

Bornstein, R. F. (1997). Dependent personality disorder in the *DSM-IV* and beyond. *Clinical Psychology: Science and Practice, 4,* 175–187.

Bornstein, R. F. (2003). Behaviorally referenced experimentation and symptom validation: A paradigm for 21st-century personality disorder research. *Journal of Personality Disorders, 17,* 1–18.

Carson, R. C. (1969). *Interaction concepts of personality.* Chicago: Aldine.

Carson, R. C. (1982). Self-fulfilling prophecy, maladaptive behavior, and psychotherapy. In J. C. Anchin & D. J. Kielser (Eds.), *Handbook of interpersonal psychotherapy* (pp. 64–77). New York: Pergamon Press.

Clark, L. A. (1993). *Manual for the schedule for nonadaptive and adaptive personality.* Minneapolis: University of Minnesota Press.

Clark, L. A., Livesley, W. J., & Morey, L. (1997). Personality disorder assessment: The challenge of construct validity. *Journal of Personality Disorders, 11,* 205–231.

Clarkin, J. F., & Lenzenweger, M. F. (1996). *Major theories of personality disorder.* New York: Guilford Press.

Cloninger, C. R. (2000). A practical way to diagnose personality disorder: A proposal. *Journal of Personality Disorders, 14,* 99–108.

Cloninger, C. R., Przybeck, T. R., Svrakic, D., & Wetzel, R. D. (1994). *The Temperament and Character Inventory (TCI): A guide to its development and use.* St. Louis, MO: Washington University, Center for Psychobiology of Personality.

Depue, R. A. (1996). A neurobiological framework for the structure of personality and emotion: Implications for personality disorders. In J. F. Clarkin & M. F. Lenzenweger (Eds.), *Major theories of personality disorder* (pp. 347–390). New York: Guilford Press.

Endler, N. S., & Kocovski, N. L. (2002). Personality disorders at the crossroads. *Journal of Personality Disorders, 16,* 487–502.

Heck, S. A., & Pincus, A. L. (2001). Agency and communion in the structure of parental representations. *Journal of Personality Assessment, 76,* 180–184.

Kernberg, O. F. (1984). *Severe personality disorders: Psychotherapeutic strategies.* New Haven, CT: Yale University Press.

Kernberg, O. F. (1996). A psychoanalytic theory of personality disorders. In J. F. Clarkin & M. F. Lenzenweger (Eds.), *Major theories of personality disorder* (pp. 106–140). New York: Guilford Press.

Kiesler, D. J. (1983). The 1982 interpersonal circle: A taxonomy for complementarity in human transactions. *Psychological Review, 90,* 185–214.

Kiesler, D. J. (1991). Interpersonal methods of assessment and diagnosis. In C. R. Snyder & D. R. Forsyth (Eds.), *Handbook of social and clinical psychology* (pp. 438–468). New York: Guilford Press.

Kiesler, D. J. (1996). *Contemporary interpersonal theory and research: Personality, psychopathology, and psychotherapy.* New York: Wiley.

Kiesler, D. J., Goldston, C. S., & Schmidt, J. A. (1991). *Manual for the Check List of Interpersonal Transactions–Revised (CLOIT-R) and the Check List of Psychotherapy Transactions–Revised (CLOPT-R).* Richmond: Virginia Commonwealth University.

Kohut, H., & Wolf, E. S. (1978). The disorders of the self and their treatment: An outline. *International Journal of Psycho-Analysis, 59,* 413–425.

Kraepelin, E. (1907). *Clinical psychiatry.* New York: Macmillan.

Leary, T. (1957). *Interpersonal diagnosis of personality.* New York: Ronald Press.

Lenzenweger, M. F., & Clarkin, J. F. (1996). The personality disorders: History, classification, and research issues. In J. F. Clarkin & M. F. Lenzenweger (Eds.), *Major theories of personality disorder* (pp. 1–35). New York: Guilford Press.

Livesley, W. J. (1998). Suggestions for a framework for an empirically based classification of personality disorder. *Canadian Journal of Psychiatry, 43,* 137–147.

Livesley, W. J. (2001). Conceptual and taxonomic issues. In J. Livesley (Ed.), *Handbook of personality disorders* (pp. 3–38). New York: Guilford Press.

Livesley, W. J., & Jackson, D. N. (in press). *Manual for the dimensional assessment of personality pathology–basic questionnaire (DAPP).* Port Huron, NI: Sigma Press.

Locke, K. D. (2000). Circumplex scales of interpersonal values: Reliability, validity, and applicability to interpersonal problems and personality disorders. *Journal of Personality Assessment, 75,* 249–267.

McAdams, D. P. (1993). *The stories we live by: Personal myths and the making of the self.* New York: Morrow.

McLemore, C. W., & Benjamin, L. S. (1979). Whatever happened to interpersonal diagnosis? *American Psychologist, 34,* 17–34.

McWilliams, N. (1994). *Psychoanalytic diagnosis.* New York: Guilford Press.

Millon, T. (1987). On the nature of taxonomy in psychopathology. In C. Last & M. Hersen (Eds.), *Issues in diagnostic research* (pp. 3–85). New York: Plenum Press.

Millon, T. (1990). *Toward a new personology: An evolutionary model.* New York: Wiley.

Millon, T. (1991). Classification in psychopathology: Rationale, alternatives, and standards. *Journal of Abnormal Psychology, 100,* 245–261.

Millon, T. (1996). *Disorders of personality:* DSM-IV *and beyond* (2nd ed.). New York: Wiley.

Millon, T. (2000). Reflections on the future of *DSM* Axis II. *Journal of Personality Disorders, 14,* 30–41.

Millon, T., & Davis, R. D. (1996). An evolutionary theory of personality disorders. In J. F. Clarkin & M. F. Lenzenweger (Eds.), *Major theories of personality disorder* (pp. 221–346). New York: Guilford Press.

Millon, T., Meagher, S. E., & Grossman, S. D. (2001). Theoretical perspectives. In W. J. Livesley (Ed.), *Handbook of personality disorders* (pp. 39–59). New York: Guilford Press.

Mitchell, S. A. (1988). The intrapsychic and the interpersonal: Different theories, different domains, or historical artifacts? *Psychoanalytic Inquiry, 8,* 472–496.

Moskowitz, D. S. (1994). Cross-situational generality and the interpersonal circumplex. *Journal of Personality and Social Psychology, 66,* 921–933.

Moskowitz, D. S., & Zuroff, D. C. (2004). Flux, pulse, and spin: Dynamic additions to the personality lexicon. *Journal of Personality and Social Psychology, 86,* 880–893.

Paris, J. (2000). The classification of personality disorders should be rooted in biology. *Journal of Personality Disorders, 14,* 127–136.

Parker, G., Both, L., Olley, A., Hadzi-Pavlovic, D., Irvine, P., & Jacobs, G. (2002). Defining personality disordered functioning. *Journal of Personality Disorders, 16,* 503–522.

Pincus, A. L. (1994). The interpersonal circumplex and the interpersonal theory: Perspectives on personality and its pathology. In S. Strack & M. Lorr (Eds.), *Differentiating normal and abnormal personality* (pp. 114–136). New York: Springer.

Pincus, A. L. (in press). A contemporary integrative interpersonal theory of personality disorders. In J. F. Clarkin & M. F. Lenzenweger (Eds.), *Major theories of personality disorder* (2nd ed.). New York: Guilford Press.

Pincus, A. L., & Ansell, E. B. (2003). Interpersonal theory of personality. In T. Millon & M. J. Lerner (Eds.), *Personality and social psychology* (pp. 209–229). Vol. 5 in I. B. Weiner (Editor-in-Chief), *Handbook of Psychology.* New York: Wiley.

Pretzer, J. L., & Beck, A. T. (1996). A cognitive theory of personality disorders. In J. F. Clarkin & M. F. Lenzenweger (Eds.), *Major theories of personality disorder* (pp. 36–105). New York: Guilford Press.

Reich, W. (1949). *Character analysis* (3rd ed.). New York: Farrar, Straus and Giroux. (Original work published 1933)

Roberts, B. W., & DelVecchio, W. F. (2000). The rank order consistency of personality traits from childhood to old age: A quantitative review of longitudinal studies. *Psychological Bulletin, 126,* 3–25.

Schneider, K. (1950). *Psychopathic personalities.* London: Cassell. (Original work published 1923)

Silk, K. R. (1997). *Biology of personality disorders.* Washington, DC: American Psychiatric Press.

Sullivan, H. S. (1948). The meaning of anxiety in psychiatry and life. *Psychiatry, 11,* 1–13.

Sullivan, H. S. (1953a). *Conceptions of modern psychiatry.* New York: Norton.

Sullivan, H. S. (1953b). *The interpersonal theory of psychiatry.* New York: Norton.

Sullivan, H. S. (1964). *The fusion of psychiatry and social science*. New York: Norton.

Vaillant, G. E., & McCullough, L. (1998). The role of ego mechanisms of defense in the diagnosis of personality disorders. In J. W. Barron (Ed.), *Making diagnosis meaningful* (pp. 139–158). Washington, DC: American Psychological Association.

Westen, D., & Arkowitz-Westen, L. (1998). Limitations of Axis II in diagnosing personality pathology in clinical practice. *American Journal of Psychiatry, 155,* 1767–1771.

Westen, D., & Shedler, J. (2000). A prototype matching approach to diagnosing personality disorders: Toward *DSM-V. Journal of Personality Disorders, 14,* 109–126.

Widiger, T. A. (1991). Definition, diagnosis, and differentiation. *Journal of Personality Disorders, 5,* 42–51.

Widiger, T. A. (2000). Personality disorders in the 21st-century. *Journal of Personality Disorders, 14,* 3–16.

Widiger, T. A., & Trull, T. J. (1991). Diagnosis and clinical assessment. *Annual Review of Psychology, 42,* 109–133.

Wiggins, J. S. (1991). Agency and communion as conceptual coordinates for the understanding and measurement of interpersonal behavior. In W. Grove & D. Cicchetti (Eds.), *Thinking clearly about psychology: Essays in honor of Paul E. Meehl* (Vol. 2, pp. 89–113). Minneapolis: University of Minnesota Press.

Wiggins, J. S. (1995). *Interpersonal adjective scales: Professional manual.* Odessa, FL: Psychological Assessment Resources.

Wiggins, J. S. (1996). An informal history of the interpersonal circumplex tradition. *Journal of Personality Assessment, 66,* 217–233.

Wiggins, J. S., & Trapnell, P. D. (1996). A dyadic interactional perspective on the five-factor model. In J. S. Wiggins (Ed.), *The Five-Factor Model of Personality: Theoretical perspectives* (pp. 88–162). New York: Guilford Press.

Wiggins, J. S., & Trobst, K. K. (1999). The fields of interpersonal behavior. In L. Pervin & O. P. John (Eds.), *Handbook of personality theory and research* (2nd ed., pp. 653–670). New York: Guilford Press.

Young, J. (1990). *Cognitive therapy for personality disorders: A schema-focused approach.* Sarasota, FL: Professional Resource Exchange.

Chapter 8

SYSTEMS THEORY FOUNDATIONS OF PERSONALITY, PSYCHOPATHOLOGY, AND PSYCHOTHERAPY

JEFFREY J. MAGNAVITA

For a holistic study of personality, we need logical tools adequate for dealing with the structure of wholes. We need, in fact, a new type of logic of holistic systems, which would be the counterpart of the conventional logic of relations. This is a large order and a task for the future (Angyal, 1982, p. 45).

Alfred Adler (1968) wrote: "Our whole attitude toward our fellow man is dependent upon our understanding him; an implicit necessity for understanding him therefore is a fundamental of the social relationship" (p. 4). We are driven to understand the complexity and chaos of human functioning, adaptation, and expression—no mean feat. More specifically, in the scope of understanding human functioning, the conceptualization of personality "disorders" or personality dysfunction (Magnavita, 2002) is a major challenge to theorists, clinicians, and researchers. We are entering a new phase in the field as we begin the second century of contemporary personology and psychopathology and the treatment of these dysfunctioning systems. Much has been accomplished during the past century, but we are still in our infancy in our conceptualization and treatment of personality dysfunction. Theory is critical to the development of the field, and we are moving toward a stage previously described as "unification" (Magnavita, 2004c). In this chapter, the basic elements of a component systems model (CSM) of personality dysfunction and a personality-guided relational approach based on major advances in the application of systems and other nonlinear models are presented. It is beyond the scope of this chapter to present my evolving unified model. Readers may refer to the chapter on this topic in the *Handbook of Personality Disorders: Theory and Practice* (Magnavita, 2004c) and the volume *Personality-Guided Relational Therapy: A Component System Model* (Magnavita, in press). This chapter highlights the central role that systemic modeling plays in the conceptualization of a unified or holistic model. Following presentation of the historical developments that presaged this model, I discuss the major components systems and briefly review the necessary models for the development of a unified paradigm.

THE SEARCH FOR A UNIFIED OR HOLISTIC MODEL OF HUMAN FUNCTIONING

The search for unification of knowledge has been a recent preoccupation with some scientists (Wilson, 1998) and grand theorists (Wilber, 2000a). Unification can also have a less grand purpose: to unite clinical science so that theorists, practitioners, and researchers have a common base with which to understand the complex embedded nature of structures and processes of human functioning from the intrapsychic-biological level of analysis to the socialcultural level. In this section, we will focus on the important interrelationships of subdisciplines of clinical science and some of the vital elements necessary for unification.

Personality Theory, Psychopathology, and Psychotherapy

Virtually since the fields of psychology and psychiatry entered modernity in the late nineteenth century with the development of scientific psychology, descriptive psychiatry, and the emergence of the field of psychotherapy, many have considered that the ultimate attainment in the field would be a unified or holistic model of human behavior. Freud (1966) was the first modern-day theorist to offer a comprehensive metapsychology, but there were limitations in that psychoanalysis and the derivatives of his followers primarily focused on the intrapsychic system and later on Sullivan's (1953) work in the interpersonal domain. Many important elements of a unified model were missing. By and large, the environmental, familial, cultural, and evolutionary factors were not articulated.

More than 50 years ago, Angyal (1941, 1982) articulated many important aspects required for a holistic or unified model. His conceptual range was compelling, especially given the era in which he generated his theory. Going back even farther, one of the interesting aspects of the early pre-Freudian evolution of clinical sciences is that the three overlapping sciences of personology, psychopathology, and psychotherapy were often isolated from one another. Freud's psychoanalytic metapsychology offered the first grand attempt at unifying these important domains, conceptualizing how personality unfolds and how psychopathology is expressed, as well as a psychotherapeutic approach to treating neurotic (clinical syndromes) and character pathologies (personality disorders). Clearly, clinical science needs to have a system that unifies these three domains; otherwise, scientific progress suffers from fractionalization, and treatment methods become a hodgepodge of uncoordinated efforts. Millon (1990) a comment: "And what better sphere is there within the psychological sciences to undertake such synthesis than within the subject matter of personology" (p. 12).

In the following section, some of the major theoreticians and pioneering figures central to the evolution of a unified model are introduced, although it is beyond the scope of this chapter to present a comprehensive review of all those who have influenced this movement. A few of the most influential systemic and unified theorists and those presaging a contemporary unified model are highlighted.

What Is Necessary for Unification?

A unified science of human functioning is equivalent in its enormity and importance to the recently achieved mapping of the human genome. Our task is even larger: the identification of the major and minor components of the personality system, as well as the processes that interconnect them. Many of the major domains, such as neurobiological, cognitive-affective, attachment patterns, interpersonal configurations, and family structures, have been identified, but their subcomponents or subsystems require further elaboration. Neuroscientists, psychologists, and others are actively pursuing one relevant aspect of unification under the guise of attempting to crack the conundrum of "consciousness." The number of volumes devoted to modeling the mind-brain using knowledge gleaned from brain research is staggering. Scientists and theorists are combining this knowledge gleaned from the new tools of neuroscience such as PET scans and combining these findings with insights from developmental psychology, interpersonal theory, and other bodies of knowledge in a creative interdisciplinary and remarkable way. Each author believes that he or she has derived a model that will explain how our brain can give rise to consciousness and the self. These are crucial exercises and useful models, but they don't necessarily carry over directly to the clinical and social sciences, although they are beginning to shed light on what we have been doing in many forms of psychotherapy. In his call for a unified theory, which he refers to as the "second revolution" in psychological science, Staats (1983) wrote:

> A word should also be said about the characteristics that in general we can expect early unified theory to have. Such theory will not be couched in the mathematical purity of axiomatic theories of the physical sciences that have served as the philosophy of science models for psychology and other social sciences. Unified theory in psychology will have to be hierarchical and systemic, but in a less formal sense. The derivations of the bridging theories between the levels in the unified theory have to be consistent always with the basic principles and previous derivations. But these theoretical structures will not be stated in formal logic and mathematics. The material to be handled is too complex.
>
> . . . It should be realized that any general, unified theory in its early development will not be detailed throughout its range of extension. It is very clear to me that no one person, during one professional lifetime, will be able to span the range and confusion of knowledge of contemporary psychology in constructing a unified theory, and do it in homogeneous detail throughout. (p. 328)

A Practical Challenge

The search for unification is an important goal of the clinical and social sciences. It is particularly important for practitioners who in their clinical practices face the treatment of personality dysfunction, especially the severe expressions and the complex clinical syndromes that are more often co-occurring. Treating these personality disorders or dysfunctions and their complex clinical syndromes remains one of the many challenges of modern clinical sciences warranting a major focus of resources. The costs of these disorders to the individual, family, and society is staggering (Magnavita, 2004a).

As stated, three crucial related disciplines must be included in any utilitarian unified model. To be effective, a unified model must relate the "three sisters"—personality theory, developmental psychopathology, and psychotherapy. A theory of personality must explain how both functional and dysfunctional personality organizations develop and the forces that make them function and dysfunction. We must also be able to identify what constitutes mental health (Vaillant, 2003). A related theory of psychopathology must logically derive from personality theory and explain how dysfunctioning personality systems express themselves in various manners of interpersonal dysfunction and symptom complexes. Finally, a theory of psychotherapy should articulate how these personality systems can be altered by using methods and techniques of human change processes (Mahoney,

1991). Most therapists develop their own unified or holistic model, which they use to guide their work. Angyal (1982) commented:

> After some years of experience every therapist evolves a conception of what is going on in his patients and between his patients and himself, even if this conception remains unformulated or is, in part, a "borrowed Bible." I believe it is to the advantage of our work to formulate a theory of treatment as explicitly as possible, even though it must be kept flexible. The holistic approach postulates that man is to be understood not in terms of specific functions or traits, but in terms of the broad system principles which organize these traits into a hierarchy of systems and subsystems. (p. 203)

Identifying these unifying principles is extremely important for clinical practice, as well as efforts at prevention (Shonkoff & Phillips, 2000), a major concern of developmental psychopathologists and other developmental specialists.

In addition, neuroscientific findings should support these theoretical underpinnings. For example, in the field of trauma there is accruing evidence that severe or chronic trauma reduces the size of the hippocampus, which is the region of the brain that influences emotional processing. Finally, innovative ways of testing the veracity of dynamic modeling need to be developed to verify component systems and their interrelationships (Gottman, Murray, Swanson, Tyson, & Swanson, 2002).

Historical Developments of a Unified Model of Personality and Psychopathology

It is helpful to explore some of the historical trends that have stimulated and set the stage for a contemporary unification movement. The interest in unification began almost with the birth of modern psychology in the late nineteenth century. Freud (1966) was probably the most cogent and influential of the early unifiers in his presentation of psychoanalytic theory but his vision was more focused on the intrapsychic system. Later he did expand his interest to broader sociocultural forces. In this section a brief review of some of the important historical and theoretical influences are presented. Some of the figures interested in unification are well known to psychologists and others less so.

Early Origins

William James in his *Principles of Psychology* (1890) understood that the search for a unified model would take advances in our understanding of many of the component systems and processes related to human functioning, so although he mused about this, he realized that many significant developments needed to be achieved first. Personality and unification are points of convergence, and the term *personology* was yet to be coined by Murray (1938). However, even before James's publication of *Principles,* others less well known to American psychology have identified the study of personality as a worthy scientific discipline, as well as calling for holism (Lombardo & Foschi, 2003).

Ribot (1885), a nineteenth-century French scientific psychologist, believed that the study of personality "was undoubtedly one of the most important themes of French research" (Lombardo & Foschi, 2003, p. 128). According to these authors, another influential French psychologist, Taine (1870), wrote a lengthy chapter on the study of personality in his volume. They summarized Taine's definition of personality as: "the feeling of *moi,* which represents the person in its wholeness, as an integrated aggregate, not a mere sum of parts, of psychological events (ideas, images, feelings), detached from physiological ones" (Lombardo & Foschi, 2003, p. 126). "Thus the path was cleared for the componential model of personality as a metahistorical object of knowledge, which was assimilated by American philosophic and scientific culture" (p. 124). This struggle to define the domain of scientific personality and to establish the need to do so holistically was certainly prescient. Gardner Murphy (1947) also laid out the importance of the biosocial field and the holism of interconnected levels. He wrote: "If all the man and all of the culture—its geographic, economic, institutional patterns—are held in view at once, personality study becomes a biosocial, not only biological investigation" (p. 6). However, the breakthrough paradigm necessary for unification, *general system theory,* which is discussed shortly, and many other key paradigms, such as the biopsychosocial model, the rediscovery of trauma theory, and the diathesis-stress model, had not yet been achieved. Furthermore, many of the component subsystems of personality, such as the attachment system, intrapsychic system, interpersonal-dyadic system, triadic system, and ecological system had not yet been clearly articulated through clinical observation and empirical validation. Before determining how these models help explain the dynamical forces and their cascade of interrelationships among domains, much had to be achieved by workers in many disciplines.

Later Theoretical Developments

In researching the more recent evolution of this movement toward unification, I found it interesting that this current stage of psychotherapy-personality-psychopathology was presaged by a number of forward-thinking theoreticians and clinicians of the mid-twentieth century. Sometimes in reading the work of our predecessors who have struggled with these problems, we can have a tremendous sense of resonance that seems to reduce the span of 50 to 100 years, when these individuals struggling with their conceptualizations and observations wrote down their thoughts.

One virtually unknown to contemporary psychologists is the clinical theorist Andras Angyal. His theorizing during the era of ascendancy of the psychoanalytic model, considered by many to be the most complete metapsychology of the twentieth century (Magnavita, 2003), is even more remarkable. In his volume *Neurosis and Treatment: A Holistic Theory,* Angyal (1982) wrote:

> The basic tenet of the holistic approach is that personality is an organized whole and not a mere aggregate of discrete parts. Its functioning does not derive from the functioning of its parts; rather the parts must be viewed in light of the organizational principles governing the whole. (p. xvi)

Reading this volume, after the publication of *Theories of Personality: Contemporary Approaches to the Science of Personality* (Magnavita, 2002) and the *Handbook of Personality Disorders: Theory and Practice* (2003), was exciting and affirming of my own journey toward unification. Angyal and other contemporary theorists, such as Millon (1990), have described personality as a complex multidomain system that cannot be isolated into parts without a loss of conceptual clarity. Personality is not a static or fixed unit or a machine that responds only to learning paradigms without the necessity of consciousness or free will, but rather, as we discuss later, is an "emergent" phenomenon of multiple interrelated domain systems.

It is difficult to determine whether Angyal was aware of the development of general system theory, as he does not cite any work in his bibliography. It is unclear whether he developed his very similar thoughts independently. I will leave this uncertainty for the historians of psychology.

A New Era for Unification—von Bertalanffy's General System Theory

Emerging in the mid-twentieth century, an innovative wave of thinking heralded in a new paradigm, which changed the nature of scientific modeling in many fields. System theory emerged in the post-World War II milieu when computers were beginning to be developed, cognitive sciences were emerging from behaviorism, and the mechanistic, reductionistic models of science were challenged by a new approach that highlighted the importance of processes and principles that organize and set the parameters for how complex systems function (von Bertalanffy, 1968). These innovative ways of understanding complex phenomenon were applied to biological and social sciences. In the clinical sciences, individuals such as Gregory Bateson (1972), Murray Bowen (1978), and many others began to apply these principles to understanding and treating families. Bateson's early work focused on understanding family communication and process in families with schizophrenic members.

Gottman et al. (2002) wrote of this remarkable advance:

> When we analyze the metaphors of general systems theory as applied to the study of couples, we are at first struck by the advances in thought created by these ideas over and above a psychology that focused only on the individual. Previously unquestioned was the idea that some kind of order regarding human behavior, and marriage as well, would emerge from the study of personality traits. . . . The general systems theories of marriage focused instead on interaction and communication. This change in thinking was a major breakthrough in the study of marriage because it focused not on the individuals, but on the temporal patterns they create when they are together, much as one focuses on the harmonies of a jazz quartet. (p. 165)

General system theory was never applied directly to the study of personality although it remained a sidebar in many theoretical systems. The theorist who first directly applied a systemic paradigm to personality was Angyal; his paradigm is briefly reviewed in the following section.

Angyal's Systemic Paradigm for Personality

Angyal (1941), to my knowledge, published the only volume truly devoted to a systemic presentation of personality. His thinking on the topic in many ways bears remarkable similarities to Millon's, as well as my own modeling (Magnavita, 2002). Angyal, however, was at a disadvantage in that systemic thinking with its various subsequent incarnations had not taken hold as it has today, and, as stated, many of the component subsystems of the personality biopsychosocial sphere had not yet been articulated. The study of personology needed to be expanded beyond the individual or intrapsychic to encompass broader domains. Angyal wrote an incisive passage that is contemporaneous even more than 60 years after its publication in his volume, Foundations for a Science of Personality

> Personality can be regarded as a hierarchy of systems. In the larger personality organization the significant positions are occupied by constituents which themselves are also systems; the constituents of the secondary system may also be systems; and so on. Thus,

personality may be considered as a hierarchy with the total personality organization at the top; below it follow the subsystems of first order, second order, third order, and so on. When one studies the connections in such a hierarchy from the dynamic point of view, it is useful to distinguish the dynamics within a given subsystem and between systems of different orders. (Angyal, 1941, pp. 286–287)

Angyal's notions about psychopathological adaptations clearly emerge from the personality configuration and are not independent entities that are unanchored to their personality moorings. He termed the expression of psychopathology "bionegativity," which he described: "*Bionegativity may be defined as a personality constellation in which one or more part processes disrupt the total functioning of the organism*" (1941, p. 329). His conception of bionegativity, he believed, was integrative:

> Neither the personality as such nor any of its part processes in themselves can be called bionegative; these terms refer to their relationship. Even in the most sweeping personality disorders, the total personality tends to behave according to its inherent tendencies, although their expressions are distorted in consequence of severe bionegativity in any personality organization, e.g., a damage or lack of some part function which is essential for their total function, as in the case of brain injuries. (pp. 58–59)

He relied on the concept of *trauma* as being central to symptom formation, which is the result of "system action" (Angyal, 1941, p. 335). He basically allowed for symptomatic expression to occur as a result of (1) direct response by the system to trauma, (2) "planful organismic reactions and attempts to repair the damage caused by the traumatic agent," and (3) the reaction to the trauma causing further trauma (p. 336). In other words, trauma can guide the personality system to different pathways: Trauma can cause dysfunction as in a shell-shocked soldier; trauma can result in a person's avoiding further trauma, as in the case of a person who avoids a partner who has been abusive; and trauma can in severe or chronic sexual abuse lead to an increasing spiral of dysfunctional adaptation by increasingly using a maladaptive response that disallows future corrective experiences.

Toward a Unified Paradigm

Angyal (1941) proposed the basic framework for a unification paradigm and perspicaciously hinted at chaos theory, yet to be developed:

> Of the total process of life a *unified system of factors* can be separated by abstraction. However, not every moment of the life process is organized into that system. The life process in its concrete form also contains factors alien to the system, or "random" from the point of the system. The biological total process results from the interaction of system-determined (self-governed, autonomous) factors and factors which are alien to the system (governed from outside the system, heteronomous). (pp. 93–94)

The Importance of the Cultural Subsystem

The cultural contribution to personality was also emphasized in Angyal's (1941) theory, usually the domain of anthropology, sociology, and social psychology. He believed that the cultural subsystem consisted of cultural patterns that influence behavior patterns, or "memes," as we discuss later. "Culture can be defined as an organized body of behavior patterns which is transmitted by social inheritance, that is, by tradition, and which is characteristic of a given culture or people" (p. 187). Further, he wrote: "The factor of acculturalization makes a person out of a human organism. The term personality derives from the Latin *persona:* an individual carrying out a role" (p. 199). The connotation is slightly different from the usual one of mask (Magnavita, 2002). Others have emphasized the importance of the cultural and social system—most noteworthy of these, Erik Erickson (1950) in his volume *Childhood and Society* and the anthropologist, Edward Sapir (Mandelbaum, 1963), who also believed that sociocultural and personality phenomenon are only artificially separated. It is interesting that before his premature death, Sullivan collaborated with Sapir about the cultural contributions he was articulating in his interpersonal theory. Sapir wrote: "But we do maintain that such differences of analysis are merely imposed by the nature of the interest of the observer and are not inherent in the phenomenon themselves" (p. 546). However, what is remarkable is that most personality theorists still conceived of personality as the processes within the individual, although this would change dramatically with Sullivan's (1953) interpersonal model and Bowen's (1978) triadic model.

Arthur Staats (1983) was also a proponent of unification. In his volume *Psychology's Crisis of Disunity: Philosophy and Method for a Unified Science,* he wrote:

> The optimistic message in the present work, nevertheless, is that what psychology has achieved in its 100 or so years of self-conscious striving does provide the raw materials for making the leap to the status of a unified science. I believe psychology is ready for the revolution to the unified state that must inevitably occur, for there is now a deep tension in psychology produced by its disorganization. (p. vi)

Millon's Evolutionary-Based Model of Interrelated Domains and Psychosynergy or Personality-Guided Therapy

Millon's model of personality-psychopathology-psychotherapy is the culmination of his evolving system based on evolutionary principles and an ecological perspective (Millon, 1990). He views personology as the major intersection of psychological domains and worthy of developing grand systems that tie this search to the natural and physical sciences (p. 11). Millon's theoretical model is probably the most encompassing system that has been developed to date, representing a major achievement in the field (Magnavita, 2002). Millon's evolutionary-based domain model is also probably best conceptually framed as a "unified" model to which he has strived, in his efforts toward theoretical breadth and integration. His thinking and conceptual efforts have been toward synthesis:

> The intersection between the study of "psychopathology" and the study of "personality" is one of these spheres of significant intellectual activity and clinical responsibility. Theoretical formulations that bridge this intersection would represent a major and valued conceptual step, but to limit efforts to this junction alone will lead to overlooking the solid footings necessary for fundamental progress, and which are provided increasingly by more mature sciences (e.g., psychics and evolutionary biology). (p. 7)

The current evolution of Millon's (1999) theoretical synthesis has been in his advancing the importance of personality-guided psychotherapy in clinical practice, as well as his efforts toward instrumentation. In many ways, this parallels many of the key elements of psychoanalytic metapsychology wherein symptom expressions are best understood in the context of characterologic organization. This conceptual advance has spawned an interest in applying this metatheory to many contemporary clinical challenges and populations, and a series of personality-guided volumes are beginning to be published by leading clinicians.

In many ways, Millon has been responsible for the resurgence in the study of personality and for its move toward center stage as a vital aspect of scientific psychology.

CURRENT ESSENTIAL CONCEPTUAL SYSTEMS FOR UNIFICATION

Over the course of the past century, many important models have been developed, which when interwoven, can provide us with the basic conceptual schema and dynamic relationships of the entire personality sphere or total ecological system of human functioning, adaptation, and evolution. Millon (2003) likened this to a "tapestry." These models include: (1) biopsychosocial model, (2) diathesis-stress model, (3) trauma theory, and (4) chaos and complexity theory. Each of these is briefly reviewed.

Biopsychosocial Model

As Anchin (2003) offered, "the biopsychosocial model, as a systemic perspective of the patient, synthesizes, in one fell swoop, the enormous structural complexity of the individual, and the contextual nature of human processes" (p. 5). Engel (1980) proposed the biopsychosocial model, the first widely incorporated unifying paradigm. The biopsychosocial model identified the various levels or substrates of the human system but failed to attempt to illustrate how these subsystems are interrelated and what processes organize them. Combining the biopsychosocial paradigm with a systemic model makes a stronger amalgam out of both.

Diathesis-Stress Model

The diathesis-stress model is an essential construct for a unified systemic model. The model, developed by Monroe and Simons (1991), explains how each dynamic subsystem has a certain genetically predisposed or psychologically predisposed vulnerable point. When a certain threshold of stress or disequilibria is generated in any component system, a perturbation in larger system or subsystem functioning can occur—what Angyal termed (1941) the "bionegativity." Each individual has certain tolerance for stress, as well as each of the four systems of the personality sphere, which are discussed shortly (see Figure 8.1). Chaos and complexity theory can help us understand how this diathesis-stress regulatory function occurs; when a particular domain of the personality sphere is impacted, homeostasis is disrupted, and either single or multiple domain systems can be disrupted.

Trauma Theory

Trauma theory is essential, as Angyal (1941) and others have underscored, to understanding the impact and functioning of various events or experiences that are disorganizing to various systems of the personality sphere (Herman, 1992). Trauma is in effect the point of strain on the personality system and a well-documented pathway to personality dysfunction (Magnavita, 2004a). The disruptive influence of trauma can occur at an individual level such as in child abuse, at a family level, with sickness or loss, or at a societal level as occurred with the downing of the World Trade Center on September 11, 2001. It can also occur at an international level as in a world war. Trauma in essence is action, and the diathesis is the system or vulnerable subsystem that is destabilized often resulting in

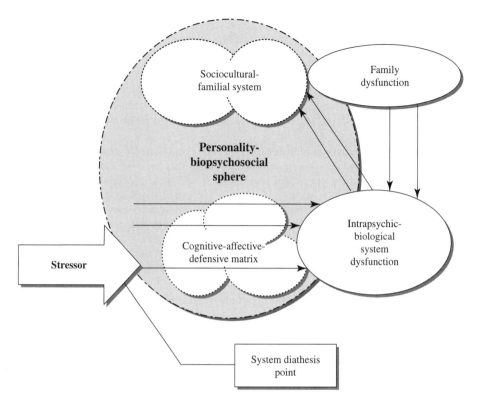

Figure 8. 1   The Impact of Stress-Trauma on the Personality Biopsychosocial Sphere and the Multidirectional Expression of Dysfunction

disorganization or symptom outbreaks. For example, an individual with cognitive-perceptual domain vulnerability might develop a psychotic reaction whereas an individual with an attachment insufficiency and impulse regulatory vulnerability might become violent under the same stressor.

Chaos and Complexity Theory

Chaos, along with its most recent derivation, complexity theory, is a fairly recent development that offers a unique way in which to view the functioning of complex systems (Gleick, 1987). Gleick wrote about those systems years before he published his volume on chaos:

> In the intervening twenty years, physicists, mathematicians, biologists, and astronomers have created an alternative set of ideas. Simple systems give rise to complex behavior. Complex systems give rise to simple behavior. And most important, the laws of complexity hold universally, caring not at all for the details of a system's constituent atoms. (p. 304)

Chaos theory is a nonlinear theory, which postulates that within chaos, there exists a self-organizing capacity that will reorder the system after it is punctuated by perturbations and that even within chaotic systems, there is order. The example often given for nonlinear systems is that of the butterfly that flaps its wings in China creating a hurricane in the tropics: Small perturbations in systems can have a cascading effect on the entire system. The processes in systems are best described as nonlinear. For example, an individual may be functioning effectively as stressors increase in his or her life, but at a certain threshold a nonlinear function may ensue, such as a major breakdown. This is the proverbial straw that broke the camel's back; it wasn't the 1,000 pounds but the additional straw. Chamberlain and Butz (1998) edited a volume titled *Clinical Chaos: A Therapist's Guide to Non-Linear Dynamics and Therapeutic Change,* in which they explore the interface among existing psychological theories and chaos theory. Anchin (2003) explored the usefulness of a cybernetic system, which is characterized by complexity as a key paradigm of a holistic model:

> The patient, then, is a system in his or her own right, constituted by simultaneously interacting subsystems, and inescapably intertwined with other systems comprising the social environment. At a more macrolevel of analysis, each of these "individual systems" can also be viewed as subsystem components of the broader system of, e.g., the family, with multiple family systems in turn construable as respective subsystems in its own right, and the point at which a given system can be considered to be just one subsystem component of a broader system, is arbitrary; where one draws boundaries differentiating "subsystem" from "systems" is highly contingent on one's judgment relative to the analytic and/or applied purposes at hand. (p. 337)

Chaos theory emerged in part from the study of fractal patterns, which were described by Mandlebrot (1997) as:

> Random fluctuations and irregularities in ostensibly chaotic states may come to form not only complicated rhythms and patterns, but also demonstrate both recurrences and replicated designs . . . here, the same shapes emerge from fluctuations time and time again, taking form sequentially on smaller and smaller scales. (p. 31)

Again, Gleick (1987) summarized:

> Nature forms patterns. Some are orderly in space but disorderly in time, others are orderly in time but disorderly in space. Some patterns are fractal, exhibiting structures self-similar in scale. Others give rise to steady states or oscillating ones. Pattern formation has become a branch of physics and of materials science, allowing scientists to model the aggregation of particles into clusters, the fractured spread of electric discharges, and the growth of crystals in ice and metal allows. The dynamics seem so basic—shapes changing in space and time— yet only now are the tools available to understand them. (p. 308)

All psychotherapy entails complex forms of pattern recognition. Fractals are seen in almost every important domain of the personality sphere. Various theorists, researchers, and clinicians have identified and termed these processes that lead to embedded structures such as core issues, cognitive schema, early maladaptive schema, relational schema, repetition compulsion, reenactment, self-defeating personality patterns, projective process, kindling, brain lock, and so forth. Seasoned therapists know that most roads lead to core issues and that within all patterns of behavior and expression, a fractal of the enduring problem can be viewed. Might these constructs and tools of systemic, chaos, and complexity theorists change the paradigms for viewing personality dysfunction?

An Additional Requirement toward Unification—Reducing Interdisciplinary Boundaries

A major impediment to developing a unified model is the traditional interdisciplinary boundaries that artificially separate scientific fields. Millon (2003) emphasizes the importance for psychology to draw from other scientific disciplines and emphasized this in his award speech. Award for Distinguished Professional Contributions to Applied Research (APA, 2003). As Sternberg and Grigorenko (2001) suggest, we need "multiparadigmatic, multidisciplinary, and integrated study of psychological phenomenon through converging operations" (p. 1069). Using multiple perspectives is a crucial aspect of unification, which includes the communication among various disciplines such as anthropology, developmental psychopathology, psychology, psychobiology, and so forth. We hope to soon be able to gather together a cross-disciplinary group of leading theorists, researchers, and clinicians to address the challenge of unification. Gardner Murphy (1947) emphasized the importance of multiple perspectives for personology many years ago:

> The data to be used in such an enterprise are of every conceivable sort: experimental, biographical, clinical; gleanings from anthropology and sociological field studies; oddments from general biology and general sociology, as well as general psychology; educational experience; artistic perception of meanings; impressions of an individual observer of an individual subject; tables of statistical findings from large groups. (p. 14)

ELEMENTS OF A UNIFIED COMPONENTS SYSTEM MODEL

In a recent volume, *Personality-Guided Relational Therapy: A Component System Model* (Magnavita, in press), the foundation for a unified model of psychotherapy is presented. This model uses many of the component systems that have been identified and verified clinically and empirically over the past century as being critical in the development of personality and their states of dysfunction. It emphasizes the dynamical processes and characteristics that shape complex systems.

We can divide the personality system into various related and interrelated processes and component systems, which are the basic building blocks of the personality system. *Personality system* is defined as the elements of the total ecological system that shape and maintain human personality functioning in either adaptive or maladaptive process, which is termed the *personality-biopsychosocial sphere*.

ORGANIZATIONAL LEVELS OF THE PERSONALITY SYSTEM REPRESENTING THE TOTAL ECOLOGY OF THE PERSONALITY SYSTEM

Within each of these major systems are nested structure-process components, whereby the intrapsychic is the most microscopic and the sociocultural-family the most macroscopic, each level being subsumed by the other in what Bronfenbrenner (1969) described as "nested Russian dolls" in his landmark volume, *The Ecology of Developmental Process: Experiments by Nature and Design*. Germain (1991) wrote:

> Ecology is the science that studies the relations between organisms and their environments. . . . It facilitates our taking a holistic view of people and environments as a unit in which neither can be fully understood except in the context of its relationship to the other. That relationship is characterized by continuous reciprocal exchanges, or transactions, in which people and environments influence, shape, and sometimes change each other. (pp. 15–16)

The Four Major Systems of the Personality Sphere

The personality-biopsychosocial sphere can be divided into four major interrelated systems, among which we can draw boundaries for heuristic purposes. These conceptualizations represent various levels of dynamical systems based on models developed over the past century by leading theorists from various orientations (Magnavita, 1997, 2000). They can be depicted as fluid triangular configurations and their subcomponent processes as follows: (1) intrapsychic-biological triangle (affective/cognitive-defensive-anxiety matrix), (2) interpersonal-dyadic triangle (early relational matrix-current relational matrix-expected relational matrix), (3) relational-triadic configuration (2 person + *n* system), and (4) sociocultural-familial triangle (individual personality system-culture-family; Magnavita, 2004c). These four systems are depicted along with the theoretical models necessary for unification in Figure 8.2.

Intrapsychic-Biological Triangle/System

The *intrapsychic-biological domain system* has been the major focus of twentieth-century clinical scientists and psychotherapists. This system includes the processes that occur in the individual matrix of the personality system. The main domain is the cognitive-affective experience-defensive matrix. In this system, we are concerned with conscious and unconscious process, affective-anxiety regulation, defensive functioning, representations of self and others, cognitive schemata, attachment schema, and the neurobiological substrate, which we term the *nanosystem,* concerned with brain processes, temperamental

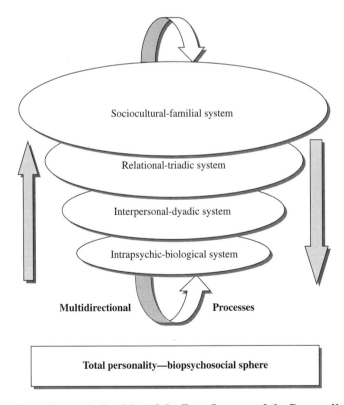

Figure 8.2   The Interrelationships of the Four Systems of the Personality Sphere

bias, and so on. The findings of neuroscience are beginning to provide crucial insight into this system and its interrelationship with attachment—interpersonal systems responsible for the regulation of affect and development of the self (A. N. Shore, 2003a, 2003b).

Interpersonal-Dyadic Triangle/System

The *interpersonal-dyadic system* concerns itself with interpersonal, attachment, or dyadic processes such as those that occur in marriage and other two-person relationship configurations. Attachment theory provides a crucial model for understanding dyadic processes and schema (Cassidy & Shaver, 1999). In the interpersonal-dyadic subsystem, it is useful to imagine that all relationships are subject to interpersonal or relational schema that influence shape and exert pressure on the other to respond in a familiar if not unhelpful way. For example, an anxious defiant-oppositional male often pulls for control and authoritarian type responses in others. This may be characterized as having a dominant-submit theme. The potency of psychotherapy is often in the individual personality system's pull to establish a familiar, albeit dysfunctional, dyadic balance. In this subsystem, we observe representations of the relational schema in how the patient reacts to the therapist or what he or she expects. This is the familiar transference-countertransference phenomenon. The interpersonal dyadic system is also manifest in current relationships in the way interpersonal conflicts are described and reported or observed if using a couple's modality.

Triadic-Relational System

The *triadic-relational system* is concerned with processes that occur in $2 + n$ relationships. This system operates when dyadic systems seek a third party for stabilization. Dyadic processes in and of themselves do not account for what was discovered by the family system's theorists in their groundbreaking work. Intensive affect can be aroused when individuals are excluded from or included in dyads (Emde, 1991). Triadic functions are ubiquitous and complex. Byng-Hall (1999) summarized Emde's work: "For instance, a triad has only three dyadic relationships influencing one another, whereas in a family of four there are 15, and in a family of eight 368!" (p. 626). When anxiety is activated at a certain threshold in a dyadic relationship, there is leakage and this anxiety can be absorbed, often by a vulnerable third person. For this process to occur, there has to be a level of differentiation that is generally low in the dyad, which means that each individual in the dyad has a low level of emotional differentiation and, referring back to the intrapsychic-biological subsystem, defenses that are poorly functioning.

Sociocultural-Family Triangle/System

The *sociocultural-family system* is essential to a unified model of personality. Psychologists have generally eschewed the cultural domain, leaving it to sociologists and anthropologists, thus limiting the perspective. Culture, physical, psychological, and familial development and the evolution of hominoids are inextricably interrelated. As others, such as Margaret Mead have espoused, anthropologist Bradd Shore (1996) believes that psychology and its sister discipline anthropology are enhanced when combined. He described the feedback system between the nervous system and cultural models:

> The eco-logical brain does not develop simply in a natural environment. Our nervous system unfolds in relation to two quite different kinds of environment, the one more "natural" and the other more cultural. Basic cognitive skills like perception, classification, and inference have evolved in the species and develop in individuals as ways in which a particular kind of body (human body) interacts with the contours of a particular physical world. (p. 4)

As is the primary assumption of a unified model, there exists a circular feedback loop between brain development and cultural systems, shaped by evolutionary processes and at times characterized by "punctuated equilibrium" (Gould, 2002). As Gould suggested, the gradual process of evolution can exist with states of punctuated equilibrium where major shifts characterized by chaos reshape cultural and political systems.

Angyal (1982) stated:

> The conception of organism and environment as entities separable in space is inadequate for the description of biological phenomena. They become fundamental biological concepts only if we define them as dynamic factors, as opposing direction in the biological process. The two presuppose each other, and external world becomes "environment" only when and insofar as it is in interaction with the organism. Every process, which results from this interaction, is part of the life process, irrespective of whether it occurs within the body or outside. (p. 8)

Lewin (1935) wrote: "An analysis of environmental factors must start from a consideration of the total situation. Such an analysis hence presupposes an adequate comprehension and presentation in dynamic terms of the total psychological situation as its most important task" (p. 73). One aspect of this matrix and of vital importance is culture. "Included in the concept of culture are value orientations and the norms governing behavior; knowledge, technology, and belief systems; language; and the meanings attributed to objects, events, and processes, including the uses of and the responses to time and space" (Germain, 1991, p. 28).

Another aspect of this matrix is "social settings," which "comprise the world of other human beings" (Germain, 1991, p. 30). Germain described this aspect:

> Its components include pairs (two-party systems such as friends or couples); families; neighborhoods and communities; natural groups and social networks; formal organizations, including systems of health care, education, and recreation, and workplaces, religious organizations, and political and economic structures at local, state, regional, and national levels; and social space and social time. (pp. 30–31)

A third component is the family system and network of extended family relationships, which occur over successive generations, as Germain (1991) described:

> The functionality of a family's value system and normative structure is reckoned by how values and norms operate and achieve the family's objectives and to facilitate the members' growth, health, and development. However, Walsh (1983) noted that what may be functional values and norms at one system level (individual, family, community, or society) may not necessarily be functional as others. Examples are found in culturally based differences in how families relate to societal institutions such as social agencies, schools, and health care organizations; how families perceive, define, and cope with a life issue; what pathways they use for seeking and obtaining help; and what their expectations are of help. . . . (Germain, 1991, p. 29)

The interrelationships between family dysfunction and societal pathologies can often be expressed in patterns of dysfunctional personologic systems, which were presented in a previous volume (Magnavita, 2000). These systems may spawn pathologies over successive generations via the multigenerational transmission process and culturally by memes.

In sum, within each of these systems, patterns-process-structure is expressed or manifest, patterns recognized as fractals, and intervention strategies made evident.

PERSONALITY-BIOPSYCHOSOCIAL SPHERE PROCESSES

Personality, as many view consciousness, may be viewed as an emergent phenomenon. Schwartz and Begley (2002) described this term: "An *emergent phenomenon* is one whose characteristics or behaviors cannot be explained in terms of the sum of its parts; if mind is emergent, then it cannot be wholly explained by brain" (p. 350). A number of processes have been identified as occurring in complex dynamical systems. These processes when repeated create structural entities within the personality-biopsychosocial sphere. For example, it is well established that learning creates neuronal connections and strengthens existing ones and that there is a fair amount of plasticity in the brain (Schwartz & Begley, 2002). Process and structure are intertwined. Changing process can change the structure or organization.

Homeostasis, Disequilibria

The general tend in any system is toward homeostasis—the point in the fluctuations in the system where processes are in a state of equilibrium. Systems may enter into states of disequilibria when perturbations in the system at any point are internal to a subsystem, which then may be amplified as well as external larger systems. Mahoney (1991) wrote: "When the perturbations challenging an open system exceed that system's current assimilative capacities, whole-system fluctuations are amplified. It is here, within the context of our episodes of 'disorder,' that reorganization occurs" (p. 419). This may result, for example, in what clinicians refer to as "downward spiraling," which can be observed in individuals, couples, families, and societies. In systemic parlance, a negative feedback state has developed. In couples, this state entails triggering in each partner increasingly more regressive defensive responding (Magnavita, 2000).

Strange Attractors

Strange attractors are forces that draw elements in a system together, as Gleick (1987) summarized:

> Given any number of points, it is impossible to guess where the next will appear—except, of course, that it will be somewhere on the attractor.
>
> The points wander so randomly, the pattern appears so ethereally, that it is hard to remember that the shape is an attractor. It is not just any trajectory of a dynamical system. It is the trajectory toward which all other trajectories converge. That is why the choice of starting conditions does not matter. As long as the starting point lies somewhere near the attractor, the next few points will converge to the attractor with great rapidity. (p. 150)

We have all heard or heard ourselves saying, "You are on a bad trajectory," "in a self-destructive pattern," "on a self-sabotaging course," "hitting rock bottom," and so on, in recognition of these attractor states and processes. Might it be better if we viewed personality systems as complex, prone to chaos at times, and capable of self-organization and restructuring? Attractor states are patterns of neurobiological, behavioral, affective, cognitive, interpersonal influences that converge in patterns in complex systems (see Figure 8.3). Complexity theory alerts us to the fact that strange attractor states make sense even though they may not appear so at first blush. Multiple subsystems and domains of the patient's personality-biopsychosocial sphere converge toward attractor states. For example, a patient reported feeling rejected and calling a friend who she "knows" is angry toward her only to discover she is not. The state of rejection is an attractor state for her that drives sequence and interpersonal patterns. She asks the therapist if he is thinking of terminating long-term therapy because she thinks he is bored, after returning from a vacation. Affect and cognition are intertwined, one leading to intensification of the other in a cascade of a negative feedback loop. She also scans her body noticing physiological signs that might lead to illness or catastrophe. She recalls her father leaving the family when she was a child and his return being brought about by her becoming ill so the mother could communicate her plight and stimulate his attachment system. These strange attractors find expression in the intrapsychic, dyadic, triadic, family, and cultural systems. The patterns can occur as fractals appearing in many levels and domains of the system.

Attractor Processes

Almost every domain system has identified attractors. These attractors include mechanism-process such as early maladaptive schema, reenactment patterns, kindling, transference reenactments, repetitive maladaptive schema, and so on.

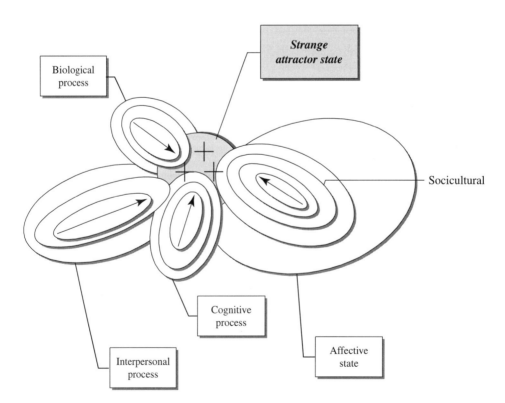

Figure 8.3   Strange Attractor States and the Biopsychosocial Personality Sphere

From Chaos to Reorganization—New Possibilities for Organization and Structure

Margaret Mead (1978) wrote: "Stated at its simplest, any whole system—a single organism, and island ecosystem, our planet, the solar system—is subject to imbalances within itself" (p. 150). Chaotic states may result in a reordering of a system or subsystem. Mahoney (1991) described this process:

> The new dynamic equilibrium that emerges is not a return to some prior (homeostatic) set point, however. Rather, it is an irreversible leap in the structural identity of the system. If and when such restructuring occurs, the more complex system that emerges is capable of assimilating perturbations like the ones that initiated its transformation (as well as others not yet encountered). The emergence of a more viable organization is not, however, an inevitable outcome of runaway fluctuations: some systems will settle into a less viable structure and suffer the consequences. In other words, the dynamics of disorder create opportunities for reorganization, but do not create or guide a system in its structural metamorphosis. Some systems will lack the capacities, resources, or good fortune to sustain a successful transformation, in which case they will struggle (chronically) and/or degenerate in the process. (p. 419)

Self-Organizing Features of Systems

An essential feature of a system is its tendency toward self-organization. "Every system, whether a rock or an animal, tends above all else to keep itself in an ordered state" (Csikszentmihalyi, 1993, p. 20). Chaos and self-organization go hand in glove and better depict how complex dynamical systems work than do linear models. For example, developmental processes are not linear but progress to points of disequilibria-chaos and reorganization such as occurs during developmental transitions seen in moving from childhood to adolescence and adolescence to early adulthood.

Differentiation and Integration

Systems generally tend to move in the direction of greater complexity requiring higher levels of differentiation among the various domains. Becoming increasingly differentiated means that there are increasing separations of various subsystems. Csikszentmihalyi (1993) described the terms differentiation and integration:

> *Differentiation* refers to the degree to which a system (i.e., an organ such as the brain, or an individual, a family, a corporation, a culture, or humanity as a whole) is composed of parts that differ in structure or function from one another. *Integration* refers to the extent to which the different parts communicate and enhance one another's goals. A system that is more differentiated and integrated than another is said to be *complex*. (p. 156)

Lewin (1935) wrote: "Great individual differences exist with reference to the way this delimitation of relatively closed subordinate wholes occurs: which parts are more strongly and which parts are more weakly developed, whether the degree of demarcation among parts of the personality are isolated" (p. 207). As Wilber (2000a) pointed out, "the differentiation-and-integration process can go wrong" (p. 93) and can result in dysfunction within the system. The process must be consistent with the aims of the organism and system. Thus, for example, in the early infant-maternal dyad, too rapid differentiation can result in abandonment and lack of future self-cohesion. Differentiation results in complex structures that then must become integrated within the total system.

Memes and Cultural Transmission

Dawkins (1982) coined the term *meme* to describe the cultural transmission process. "A meme has its own opportunities for replication, and its own phenotypic effects, and there is no reason why success in a meme should have any connection whatever to genetic success" (p. 110). Unlike genes, memes are units of information carried in consciousness and expressed in cultural systems. Memes are a critical part of the complex systems of personality and are expressions of human cultural systems, but they also shape the personality system. "The information we generate has a life of its own, and its existence is sometimes symbiotic, sometimes parasitic, relative to ours" (Csikszentmihalyi, 1993, p. 121). Memes also represent fractal patterns across systems and what Jung may have been describing as the "collective unconscious."

Multidirectionality

Complex systems both influence and are influenced by other subsystems in their total ecology in a multidirectional fashion. In the maternal-infant dyad, the mother shapes and influences the infant, and the infant conditions and shapes the maternal response system in a finely tuned communication pattern. A report published by the National Research Council/Institute of Medicine titled *From Neurons to Neighborhoods: The Science of Early Childhood Development* summarized a massive body of research and theory and concluded:

> At every level of analysis, from neurons to neighborhoods, genetic and environmental effects operate in both directions. On one hand, the gene-environment interactions of the earliest years set an important initial course for all of the adaptive variations that follow. On the other hand, this early trajectory is by no means chiseled in stone. (Shonkoff & Phillips, 2000, p. 24)

Entropy and Negentropy

Any system requires energy to keep functioning. A universal law is that systems break down over time. "*Entropy* is the amount of disorder in a system at a given point in time; negative entropy called *negentropy*, refers to the amount of order in a system" (Mahoney, 1991, p. 415). In biological systems, cells deteriorate and age. To prevent decline, systems need input. Plants need sun and water. Human beings need food, shelter, and nurturance. This requires energy to survive and fend off the forces of entropy. Human dynamical systems need an enormous amount of energy to sustain them. Every system must fight the forces of entropy, which is the process of disintegration. For systems to function, survive, and replicate, "an individual body, or a family, or social system—must always be at work repairing and protecting itself, becoming more efficient at transforming energy for its own purposes" (pp. 20–21). Higher functioning personality systems require less input of energy from other sources. For example, borderline personality requires more energy from other subsystems to maintain functioning.

The Interrelationship of Everything

Contemporary theorists from a number of perspectives and disciplines emphasize the interrelationship of all things. Csikszentmihalyi (1993) wrote:

It might have been already true in John Donne's time that "no man is an island," but the truth of this saying is certainly obvious now. And the interconnectedness of human activities and interests is going to increase even faster than we are accustomed to in this third millennium we are approaching. (p. 8)

The Recipe—"How It All Works, and So What?"

In this chapter on unification, I have assembled a number of components and summarized various processes that interconnect four domain systems of human personality functioning. You may wonder what all the effort is about and how it works. In other words, as the reviewer of this chapter reflected while watching a cooking show, how do all the ingredients come together and in what proportions? Although challenging this

Table 8.1   Personality System Components: Process, Structure, and Function

The Four Subsystems of the Personality Biosphere

- Intrapsychic—Biological Matrix
- Interpersonal—Dyadic Matrix
- Triadic—Relational Matrix
- Sociocultural-Familial Matrix

Function of the Human Personality System

Evolutionarily based: survive, adapt, replicate, and self-actualize

Structures

Physical or component regulatory systems that are associated with one another forming stable configurations or patterns, such as affective-cognitive, defensive-coping, neuro-cognitive, marital dyads, family, cultural, and others. The biopsychosocial model represents the basic structural components.

Processes of the Human Personality System

Just as the human body is composed mostly of water, the human personality system is composed mostly of complex and intricate processes among domain systems. Processes that occur include:

1. *Homeostasis—disequilibria:* The personality biosphere seeks to maintain a state of equilibrium of process and function, but experiences disequilibria as a result of developmental progression. Adaptation requires an alternation between these two states. States of dysfunction are characterized by irregularity of this process.
2. *Differentiation—integration:* Development requires a process of increasing differentiation among component systems and gradual integration. Systems that do not do so become maladaptive.
3. *Chaotic states and strange attractors:* Embedded as humans are in the total ecological system, part-whole relationships dominate. Complex systems are also prone to chaotic states of disequilibria often caused by small reverberating perturbations in components of the system.
4. *Fractals or elements of the whole evident in parts:* Complex systems converge at various domain levels and express common themes or patterns that therapists and social scientists discover and use in the process of pattern recognition. These are expressed as various convergences that have been variously termed transference, countertransference, reenactments, repetitive maladaptive patterns, neurotic complexes, family patterns, and others. These fractals are convergences of attractor states that require identification and narration or symbolization.
5. *Familial and cultural transmission:* Cultural (memes) and familial information (rituals, roles, etc.) are carried forth by complex transmission processes that both shape and are shaped by the system in a bidirectional manner.

effort at parsimony is extremely useful, a system that is so complex that it can't be reduced to a recipe will probably not be used by most clinicians and social scientists.

I address the "So what?" question first before tackling the more challenging one of "What is the recipe?" Continuing with our cooking metaphor, for the clinical psychological sciences to progress beyond a smorgasbord of seemingly disparate paradigms, methods, techniques, and systems, a unified model offers a scaffold that can localize structures, process, and functions within commonly acknowledged subsystems. The structure and function of these subsystems then can be explored, elaborated, and further delineated. More importantly, while doing so, clinicians, researchers, and theorists can engage in the joint task of understanding the way the human personality system functions and dysfunctions as we adapt to environmental challenges and are shaped by evolutionary forces. Pragmatically, as a theorist who is primarily a clinician, the more refined the map of the territory, the better able I am to navigate the complexity of the systems I am confronted with daily and develop strategies of intervention. I also believe, like Angyal, as described earlier in this chapter, that all clinicians use a model or bible, often a very personal or idiosyncratic one. A shared model can be open to scientific development.

It is far beyond the scope of this chapter to present the full edition of the cookbook comparable to Julia Child's tome *The Art of French Cooking.* A more detailed presentation describing the clinical application of this model is forthcoming (Magnavita, in press). The essential ingredients of the three domains of the unified model of clinical science (personality, psychopathology, and psychotherapy) presented in this chapter are depicted in Tables 8.1, 8.2, and 8.3.

Current Research Applications of Nonlinear Models

One of the most ambitious research applications of a nonlinear dynamical systemic model has been developed by Gottman et al. (2002). John Gottman, one of the cutting-edge researchers in the field of marital relationships, has, along with his associates, applied a nonlinear systemic paradigm to marriage research. In their landmark volume, *The Mathematics of Marriage: Dynamic Nonlinear Models,* Gottman and his associates built a mathematical

---

Table 8.2   Dysfunction and Psychopathological Expression and States

The human personality system malfunctions when there is a negative feedback loop that develops at any level of the four matrixes of the personality system. Negative feedback can be due to deviations, which may be amplified in any domain of the personality biosphere. Each of the four domains has varying degrees of vulnerability. The vulnerability may exist at the biological (faulty genes), intrapsychic (structural-process), interpersonal (attachment system), familial (dysfunctional personologic systems), or societal (poverty, suppression, etc.) level. The vulnerability and disruption of any aspect of the system can be best tracked and conceptualized by:

1. *Diathesis-stress:* The vulnerability of any of the four domains can be expressed in dysfunction of aspects of a system or reverberate throughout the system.
2. *Trauma:* Various types of traumata including physical, psychological, and sexual abuse as well as neglect can disrupt the homeostasis of a system and lead to negative feedback loops, which become consolidated over time. This may lead to personality dysfunction and symptomatic expression, which are reinforced and shaped by various components in the system.

This concept is consistent with Millon's (1990) notion of the personality as an "immune system" but carries it further to include the social and familial self—not just the intrapsychic functioning.

Table 8.3   Psychotherapeutic Implications

Clinical Treatment

The clinical treatment of a unified model organizes interventions based on an analysis of the process, structure, and function of the major subsystems. Various forms and methods of therapy attempt to reorganize and restructure these processes so that a higher level of adaptation can be achieved. Restructuring is a process of enhancing *differentiation* among the various components of the triangular systems and *reintegrating* them so they function more effectively. Methods of restructuring these component systems include:

1. Intrapsychic restructuring (IR).
2. Dyadic restructuring (DR).
3. Triadic restructuring (TR).
4. Mesosystem restructuring (MR; Magnavita, 2000, in press).

Within each of these categories of restructuring are submethods, which have been identified and used from various schools and modalities of psychotherapy.

Change Mechanisms and Processes

Change is conceptualized by balancing a *disruption* (creating disequilibria) of negative feedback systems, while *restructuring systems* creating positive feedback systems that are more adaptive. Especially in the case of personality disorders and complex clinical conditions, old patterns must be disrupted and new ones encouraged. Highly adaptive systems represent higher levels of differentiation and integration (communication) such as between affective response and cognition or self-other intimacy regulation functions.

model of marriage based on von Bertalanffy's (1968) system theory. Using a variety of mathematical equations, they were able to predict with a high degree of certainty which marriages in their sample would end in divorce.

CONCLUSION

In this chapter, the challenge of unification of clinical sciences is explored and a preliminary way of organizing the domains of the personality system is offered. Advances in a number of scientific disciplines can be annexed toward the goal of furthering the science of personology. We have at our disposal increasingly useful theoretical constructs that can be used in a stronger amalgam than if these models are used separately. The unification of personality-psychopathology-psychotherapy can be furthered by understanding the complexity of human functioning, adaptation, and dysfunction, as well as change processes by the incorporation of a dynamical systemic model as the foundation. Much of this work has been foreshadowed by the groundbreaking work of Theodore Millon, which has almost single-handedly led to a resurgence of one of the most exciting fields in the social sciences—personology.

REFERENCES

Adler, A. (1968). *Understanding human nature.* London: George Allen & Unwin Ltd.
Anchin, J. C. (2003). Cybernetic systems, existential-phenomenology, and solution-focused narrative: Therapeutic transformation of negative affective states through integratively-oriented brief psychotherapy. *Journal of Psychotherapy Integration, 13*(3/4), 334–442.

Angyal, A. (1941). *Foundations for a science of personality.* New York: Commonwealth Fund.

Angyal, A. (1982). *Neurosis and treatment: A holistic theory* (E. Hanfmann & R. M. Jones, Eds.). New York: Da Capo Press.

Bateson, G. (1972). *Steps to an ecology of mind.* New York: Chandler.

Bowen, M. (1978). *Family therapy in clinical practice.* New York: Aronson.

Bronfenbrenner, U. (1969). *The ecology of developmental process: Experiments by nature and design.* Cambridge, MA: Harvard Press.

Byng-Hall, J. (1999). Family and couple therapy: Toward greater security. In J. Cassidy & P. R. Shaver (Eds.), *Handbook of attachment: Theory, research and clinical application* (pp. 625–645). New York: Guilford Press.

Cassidy, J., & Shaver, P. R. (Eds.). (1999). *Handbook of attachment: Theory, research and clinical applications.* New York: Guilford Press.

Chamberlain, L. L., & Butz, M. R. (1998). *Clinical chaos: A therapist's guide to non-linear dynamics and therapeutic change.* New York: Brunner/Mazel.

Csikszentmihalyi, M. (1993). *The evolving self: A psychology for the third millennium.* New York: HarperCollins.

Dawkins, R. (1982). *The extended phenotype.* Oxford, England: Oxford University Press.

Emde, R. N. (1991). The wonder of our complex enterprise: Steps enabled by attachment and the effect of relationships on relationships. *Infant Mental Health Journal, 12,* 164–173.

Engel, G. (1980). The clinical application of the biopsychosocial model. *American Journal of Psychiatry, 137*(5), 535–544.

Erikson, E. H. (1950). *Childhood and society.* New York: Norton.

Freud, S. (1966). *The complete introductory lectures on psychoanalysis* (J. Strachey, Ed. & Trans.). New York: Norton.

Germain, C. B. (1991). *Human behavior in the social environment.* New York: Columbia University Press.

Gleick, J. (1987). *Chaos: Making a new science.* New York: Viking/Penguin Books.

Gottman, J. M., Murray, J. D., Swanson, C. C., Tyson, R., & Swanson, K. R. (2002). *The mathematics of marriage: Dynamic nonlinear models.* Cambridge, MA: MIT Press.

Gould, R. J. (2002). *The structure of evolutionary theory.* Cambridge, MA: Harvard University Press.

Herman, J. L. (1992). *Trauma and recovery.* New York: Basic Books.

James, W. (1890). *Principles of psychology* (Vols. 1–2). New York: Henry Holt.

Lewin, K. (1935). *A dynamic theory of personality: Selected papers.* New York: McGraw-Hill.

Lombardo, G. P., & Foschi, R. (2003). The concept of personality in the 19th-century American psychology. *History of Psychology, 6*(2), 123–142.

Magnavita, J. J. (1997). *Restructuring personality disorders: A short-term dynamic approach.* New York: Guilford Press.

Magnavita, J. J. (2000). *Relational therapy for personality disorders.* New York: Wiley.

Magnavita, J. J. (2002). *Theories of personality: Contemporary approaches to the science of personality.* Hoboken, NJ: Wiley.

Magnavita, J. J. (2003). Psychodynamic approaches to psychotherapy: A century of innovations. In F. W. Kaslow (Editor-in-Chief) & J. J. Magnavita (Vol. Ed.), *Comprehensive handbook of psychotherapy: Psychodynamic/object relations* (Vol. 1, pp. 1–12). Hoboken, NJ: Wiley.

Magnavita, J. J. (2004a). Classification, prevalence and etiology of personality disorders: Related issues and controversy In J. J. Magnavita (Ed.), *Handbook of personality disorders: Theory and practice* (pp. 3–23). Hoboken, NJ: Wiley.

Magnavita, J. J. (2004b). The relevance of theory in treating personality dysfunction. In J. J. Magnavita (Ed.), *Handbook of personality disorders: Theory and practice* (pp. 56–77). Hoboken, NJ: Wiley.

Magnavita, J. J. (2004c). Toward a unified model of treatment for personality dysfunction. In J. J. Magnavita (Ed.), *Handbook of personality disorders: Theory and practice* (pp. 528–553). Hoboken, NJ: Wiley.

Magnavita, J. J. (in press). *Personality-guided relational therapy: A component system model.* Washington, DC: American Psychological Association.

Mahoney, M. J. (1991). *Human change processes: The scientific foundations of psychotherapy.* New York: Basic Books.

Mandelbaum, D. G. (Ed.). (1963). *Selected writings of Edward Sapir in language, culture, and personality.* Los Angeles, CA: University of California Press.

Mandlebrot, B. (1977). *The fractal geometry of nature.* New York: Freeman.

Mead, M. (1978). *Culture and commitment: New relationships between the generations in the 1970's.* New York: Columbia University Press.

Millon, T. (1990). *Toward a new personology: An evolutionary model.* New York: Wiley.

Millon, T. (with Grossman, S., Meagher, S., Millon, C., & Everly, G.). (1999). *Personality-guided therapy.* Hoboken, NJ: Wiley.

Millon, T. (2003, August). *It's time to rework the blueprints: Building a science for clinical psychology* (Award for Distinguished Professional Contributions for Applied Research). American Psychological Association convention, Toronto, Ontario, Canada.

Monroe, S. M., & Simons, A. D. (1991). Diathesis-stress theories in the context of life stress research. *Psychological Bulletin, 110,* 406–425.

Murphy, G. (1947). *Personality: A biosocial approach to origins and structures.* New York: Harper & Brothers.

Murray, H. A. (1938). *Explorations in personality.* New York: Oxford University Press.

Ribot, T. (1885). *Les maladies de la personnalite* [Diseases of personality]. Paris: Alcan.

Schwartz, J. M., & Begley, S. (2002). *The mind and the brain: Neuroplasticity and the power of mental force.* New York: HarperCollins.

Shonkoff, J. P., & Phillips, D. A. (Eds.). (2000). *From neurons to neighborhoods: The science of early childhood development.* Washington, DC: National Academies Press.

Shore, A. N. (2003a). *Affect dysregulation and disorders of the self.* New York: Norton.

Shore, A. N. (2003b). *Affect regulation and the repair of the self.* New York: Norton.

Shore, B. (1996). *Culture in mind: Cognition, culture, and the problem of meaning.* New York: Oxford University Press.

Staats, A. W. (1983). *Psychology's crisis of disunity: Philosophy and method for a unified science.* New York: Praeger.

Sternberg, R. J., & Grigorenko, E. L. (2001). Unified psychology. *American Psychologist, 56*(12), 1069–1079.

Sullivan, H. S. (1953). *The interpersonal theory of psychiatry.* New York: Norton.

Taine, H. (1870). *De l'intelligence* [On intelligence] (Vols. 1–2). Paris: Hachette.

Vaillant, G. E. (2003). Mental health. *American Journal of Psychiatry, 160*(8), 1373–1384.

von Bertalanffy, L. (1968). *General system theory.* New York: Braziller.

Walsh, F. (1983). Normal family ideologies: Myths and realities. In J. D. Hansen (Ed.), *Cultural perspectives in family therapy* (pp. 2–14). Rockville, MD: Aspen Systems Corporation.

Wilber, K. (2000a). *Integral psychology: Consciousness, spirit, psychology, therapy.* Boston: Shambhala.

Wilber, K. (2000b). *A theory of everything: An integral vision for business, politics, science, and spirituality.* Boston: Shambhala.

Wilson, E. O. (1998). *Consilience: The unity of knowledge.* New York: Alfred A. Knopf.

Chapter 9

PSYCHODYNAMIC THEORY AND PERSONALITY DISORDERS

ROBERT F. BORNSTEIN

In one form or another, personality disorders (PDs) have been described and documented for thousands of years. It is reasonable to infer that once humans developed interpersonal strategies for maximizing adaptation and reproductive success, it did not take long for some of these strategies to go awry and evolve into the precursors of contemporary PDs. As Millon (1990, p. 21) noted, if personality represents "the more-or-less adaptive functioning that an organism of a particular species exhibits as it relates to its typical range of environments, [then disorders] of personality, so formulated, would represent particular styles of maladaptive functioning that can be traced to deficiencies, imbalances, or conflicts in a species' capacity to relate to the environments it faces."

Although PDs have existed for many centuries, interest in PD dynamics increased tremendously during the past several decades, due in part to the inclusion of Axis II in the third edition of the *Diagnostic and Statistical Manual of Mental Disorders* (*DSM-III;* American Psychiatric Association, 1980). Axis II of the *DSM-III* formalized a unique category of psychological syndromes characterized by longstanding difficulties in thought, behavior, impulse control, and emotional responding and provided a framework for understanding and exploring relationships among different PD categories (Millon, 1981, 1996; Pincus & Wiggins, 1990).

Clinicians' interest in personality pathology did not simply result from changes in the *DSM,* however: In recent years, psychologists have recognized that the intra- and interpersonal dynamics of PDs have important implications for theories of personality and psychopathology. Beyond basic theory testing, PD research can help refine existing diagnostic categories and point the way toward new ones (Widiger & Clark, 2000), aid in the formulation of novel therapeutic interventions (Turkat, 1990), and enable clinicians to develop strategies for minimizing the risk of a negative outcome in high-risk patients (Linehan, 1993). Externally imposed health care cost containment guidelines have caused clinicians to devote even greater effort to understanding and ameliorating PD pathology. Numerous theoretical frameworks have attempted to explain PD etiology and dynamics. Among the more influential of these are the psychoanalytic, behavioral, cognitive, trait, humanistic, biological, cultural, and systems perspectives. Although each of these frameworks has

Preparation of this chapter was supported by National Institute of Mental Health grant MH63723-01A1. Correspondence should be sent to Robert F. Bornstein, PhD, Department of Psychology, Box 407, Gettysburg College, Gettysburg, PA 17325 (phone 717-337-6175; Fax 717-337-6172; e-mail bbornste@gettysburg.edu).

something important to say about PDs, none provide a complete picture of the ontogenesis of PD symptoms and the intra- and interpersonal functioning of personality-disordered individuals. Each framework emphasizes one or more aspects of PD pathology but neglects certain aspects as well. Thus, cognitive models focus on dysfunctional thought patterns but underemphasize unconscious motives and defenses. Biological models capture the neurological underpinnings of PDs but ignore the impact of culture.

Given the limitations of individual PD models, there is a great need for an integrated perspective that combines the strongest elements of each approach and conceptualizes PDs from multiple vantage points (Millon, 1990). An integrated perspective on personality pathology has myriad advantages over narrower theoretical models, among the most important of which are:

- Exploration of PD processes from an array of complementary and contrasting perspectives.
- Delineation of pathways linking different PD features.
- Creation of a framework for connecting PD research to research in other domains within and outside psychology.

All but the most hard-nosed biologist and hard-core behaviorist would acknowledge the key role that psychodynamics must play in any integrated perspective on PDs. As Millon (1996, p. 44) pointed out, the "most fully conceptualized [models] of personality disorders are those formulated by psychoanalytic theorists. Their work was crucial to the development of an understanding of the causal agents and progressions that typify the background of these disorders." It is not surprising that psychoanalysis plays a key role in Millon's (1990, 1996) biopsychosocial model, providing a conceptual foundation for two major levels of analysis within the model: regulatory (defense) mechanisms and object relations. Psychoanalysis also provides more subtle context for other levels of analysis within the model, elucidating aspects of interpersonal conduct, cognitive style, self-image, and morphological organization.

This chapter discusses the psychoanalytic perspective on PDs. I begin by reviewing the psychoanalytic model of psychopathology, then apply this model to three key dimensions of PD functioning: reality testing, defense style, and object relations. I illustrate how these variables interact to shape underlying processes and surface behaviors by briefly describing the psychodynamics of three PDs: borderline, dependent, and narcissistic. Finally, I offer suggestions for further development of a psychoanalytic understanding of PD pathology and integration of the psychodynamic framework with other PD models.[1]

PSYCHOANALYTIC PERSPECTIVES ON PSYCHOPATHOLOGY

A complete understanding of PD pathology requires that the psychoanalytic perspective be placed in a broad context. In the following sections, I discuss the psychoanalytic model of psychopathology and the place of PDs within this model.

---

[1] A review of the psychodynamics of individual PDs is beyond the scope of this chapter. Indeed, numerous volumes have been written on this topic, with narcissistic, borderline, antisocial, and histrionic PDs receiving the greatest attention from theorists. Rather than evaluating the psychoanalytic model of each *DSM-IV-TR* PD, I evaluate the heuristic value of the psychoanalytic perspective *in toto,* with brief discussion of the psychodynamics of select PD syndromes.

The Etiology of Psychopathology

The psychoanalytic perspective on psychopathology has evolved considerably since Freud (1896) offered his first speculations in this area more than 100 years ago. Initially, psychological symptoms were presumed to result from early trauma, often involving sexual abuse by a parent or other caregiver. Clinical evidence—most prominently the cases of Dora, Anna O., and others (e.g., Freud, 1905a, 1920)—led Freud to revise his initial model, however, and conclude that it was the child's fantasies of sexual contact—not actual, experienced sexual contact—that led to the development of psychological symptoms. Freud's renunciation of his controversial "seduction theory" was sharply criticized, in part because it appeared to minimize the pathogenic role of actual sexual abuse and in part because it provided an alternative interpretation of sexual abuse accusations that could be exploited by perpetrators to escape responsibility for their actions (Torrey, 1992).

As with many clinical hypotheses, psychoanalytic and otherwise, Freud's early and later perspectives both proved to be partially correct. Studies demonstrated that sexual abuse of young children: (1) is far more common than many people believed and (2) has long-lasting negative effects on psychological functioning (Briere & Elliott, 1994; Finkelhor & Dziuba-Leatherman, 1994). However, studies also indicated that children's misperceptions, misattributions, and false memories can lead to erroneous reports of sexual abuse (Loftus, 1996; Williams, 1995). Contemporary psychoanalytic models acknowledge the impact of early trauma, neglect, and abuse in the etiology of psychopathology but recognize that less extreme variations in development can also play a role in the genesis of psychological symptoms. Factors such as inadequate parental empathy during the first years of life can lead to significant psychopathology later in life because lack of parental empathy interferes with the development of a stable self-concept, the internalization of cohesive mental images of other people, and the development of psychological resources (e.g., defenses, self-control strategies) that enable the person to modulate internal conflict and anxiety (Kernberg, 1976, 1984; Kohut, 1971, 1977). Along with this expanded psychodynamic view of trauma came a broadened perspective regarding the role of childhood fantasy: The work of Piaget (1954) and others on early cognitive development helped psychoanalysts and other mental health professionals realize that the child's egocentric perspective can exacerbate the psychological impact of events (e.g., divorce) that the child misconstrues as being the result of his or her thoughts or actions.

The Psychodynamics of Psychopathology

Psychoanalysis provides a useful framework for conceptualizing the pathogenic impact of major and minor variations in early experience, but the question remains: How do childhood events affect psychological functioning years—even decades—later? Three mechanisms underlie this persistence over time.

Ego Strength

A key tenet of classical psychoanalytic theory is that three mental structures—id, ego, and superego—play a central role in personality development and psychopathology. In the classical psychoanalytic model the id is conceptualized as the source of drives and impulses, whereas the superego represents the conscience (or moral code) and the ego is responsible for rational, reality-oriented thought. Early experiences help determine the developing child's *ego strength,* that is, the degree to which the ego carries out reality testing functions and deals effectively with impulses (Eagle, 1984). Adequate parenting and minimal trauma/disruption enable the child to devote considerable psychic energy to developing good reality testing skills and acquiring effective self-control strategies. Inadequate parenting and/or significant disruption in the child-caregiver relationship divert psychic energy from these adaptation-enhancing ego functions because at least some of the child's psychological resources must be used to cope with various stressful and hurtful experiences. Studies indicate that ego strength in adolescents and adults varies to some degree as a function of situational factors (e.g., mood, anxiety level), but also suggest that two key elements of ego strength—reality testing and impulse control—are relatively consistent over time, with enduring, trait-like qualities (Hoffman, Granhag, See, & Loftus, 2001; Nestor, 2002).

Defense Style

As children move through adolescence and into adulthood, they develop a stable *defense style*—a characteristic way of managing anxiety and coping with external threat (Cramer, 2000). Positive early experiences are associated with a flexible, adaptive defense style wherein mature defenses (e.g., sublimation, intellectualization) predominate (Vaillant, 1994). Negative early experiences lead to a less effective—and less mature—defense style characterized by coping strategies that entail greater distortion of internal and external events (e.g., repression, projection). Psychodynamic researchers have conceptualized defense style in myriad ways, but evidence from different research programs confirms that well-validated measures of defense style predict adjustment and functioning in a broad array of psychological domains (Cramer, 2000; Ihilevich & Gleser, 1986; Perry, 1991).

Object Relations/Object Representations

Early in life, the child internalizes mental representations of the self and significant others (e.g., parents, siblings). These object representations (sometimes called *introjects*) evolve over time, but they also have enduring qualities that are relatively resistant to change (Westen, 1991). Studies by Blatt (1991) and others (e.g., Bornstein & O'Neill, 1992) confirm that qualitative and structural aspects of an individual's object representations help determine interpersonal functioning and psychological adjustment throughout life: The person who has internalized introjects that are conceptually sophisticated and affectively positive is unlikely to develop significant psychopathology, whereas the person who has internalized introjects that are conceptually primitive and affectively negative is at increased pathology risk (see Bornstein, 2003, for a discussion of research in this area).

A Tripartite Severity Model

Psychoanalytic theory classifies psychological disorders into three levels of severity, with each level characterized by differences in ego strength, ego defenses, and introjects. Table 9.1 summarizes this tripartite model. The least severe level of psychopathology in the psychoanalytic model—neurosis—is characterized by high levels of ego strength, mature defenses, and relatively benign introjects. The middle level—personality pathology (sometimes called *character pathology* by psychoanalytic theorists)—is characterized by less adequate ego strength, immature defenses, and introjects that are structurally flawed and/or malevolent. The most severe form of psychopathology in the psychoanalytic

Table 9.1   Levels of Psychopathology in Psychodynamic Theory

Level	Ego Strength	Ego Defenses	Introjects
Neurosis	High	Adaptive/mature (displacement, sublimation)	Articulated/differentiated and benign
Personality disorder	Variable	Maladaptive/immature (denial, projection)	Quasi-articulated and/or malevolent
Psychosis	Low	Maladaptive/immature or nonexistent	Unarticulated/undifferentiated and malevolent

Source: Originally published as Table 5.5 in Psychodynamic Models of Personality, pp. 117–134, by R. F. Bornstein, in *Personality and Social Psychology,* T. Millon and M. J. Lerner, Eds., 2003, Vol. 5 in I. B. Weiner (Editor-in-Chief), *Handbook of Psychology,* Hoboken, NJ: Wiley. Reprinted with permission.

model—psychosis—is characterized by low levels of ego strength, immature (or even non-existent) defenses, and primitive, malevolent introjects.[2]

PSYCHOANALYTIC PERSPECTIVES ON CONTEMPORARY PERSONALITY DISORDERS: FROM FIXATION TO OBJECT RELATIONS

Freud's initial (1905b, 1908) speculations regarding the dynamics of PDs focused primarily on psychosexual fixation: He argued that problems during a particular developmental stage (i.e., oral, anal, Oedipal) would cause the child to remain preoccupied with the events of that stage and develop personality traits (including dysfunctional PD-related traits) associated with that period. Thus, Freud (1908, p. 167) argued that "one very often meets with a type of character in which certain traits are very strongly marked while at the same time one's attention is arrested by the behavior of these persons in regard to certain bodily functions." Other psychoanalytic theorists (e.g., Abraham, 1927; Reich, 1933) extended Freud's fixation model of personality pathology.

Freud's (1905b, 1908) fixation approach turned out to have limited heuristic value: Although certain PD-related symptoms are associated with oral, anal, and Oedipal traits (i.e., concerns about dependency, control, and status/competition), studies indicate that fixation as Freud conceived it does not provide a complete explanation for the development of these symptoms (Bornstein, 1996; Fisher & Greenberg, 1996). The evolution of the psychoanalytic model of PDs during the past 100 years has been characterized by a shift from psychosexual fixation to ego strength, defense style, and object relations. Just as these three variables determine the overall severity of pathology (see Table 9.1), they determine the form that pathology will take within a given level of severity/dysfunction.

[2] Characteristic forms of neurotic psychopathology include phobias and mild depression; representative psychoses include schizophrenia and dissociative disorders. Personality disorders in the psychoanalytic model (e.g., borderline, narcissistic) are discussed in the following sections.

In the following sections I discuss the role of ego strength, defense style, and object relations in the etiology and dynamics of PDs. Although these variables are discussed in separate sections for the sake of clarity, PD dynamics typically reflect the combined influence of all three variables. I briefly describe the psychodynamics of three PDs—borderline, narcissistic, and dependent—to illustrate how these variables interact to produce a more complete picture of the functioning of personality-disordered individuals.

Ego Strength: Differences in Reality Testing

Brenner (1974, p. 58) defined reality testing as "the ability of the ego to distinguish between the stimuli or perceptions which arise from the outer world, on the one hand, and those which arise from the wishes and the impulses of the id, on the other. If the ego is able to perform this task successfully, we say that the individual in question has a good or adequate sense of reality. If the ego cannot perform the task, we say that his sense of reality is poor or defective." Reality testing has proved an elusive concept to operationalize and quantify: Efforts to derive psychometrically sound assessment instruments have been only modestly successful, and in many instances projective measures have proved more useful than self-report tests in this regard (Hartmann, Sunde, Kristensen, & Martinussen, 2003; Weiner, 2000). This latter result is not surprising given that a person's ability to carry out reality testing functions effectively is not readily amenable to assessment via introspection and self-report.

From a psychodynamic perspective, two issues are central to the PD-ego strength relationship: overall impairment in reality testing and variability in reality testing over time and across situation. Certain PDs are characterized by a greater degree of ego impairment (and poorer reality testing) than other PDs, and certain PDs are associated with greater temporal and situational variations in ego functioning. A physiological analogue helps illustrate this process. Just as individuals differ in overall level of reality testing and variability in reality testing over time, they differ with respect to baseline (resting) heart rate, as well as variation in heart rate in response to internal and external stimuli (what physiologists refer to as *cardiovascular reactivity*).

Table 9.2 summarizes the links between reality testing and PD pathology, contrasting the 10 *DSM-IV-TR* (American Psychiatric Association, 2000) PDs with respect to overall impairment, variability, and common "triggers" (i.e., events that cause a temporary decline in reality testing, usually by increasing state anxiety). As Table 9.2 shows, most PDs are associated with at least moderate overall impairment in reality testing; dependent and obsessive-compulsive PDs are associated with somewhat lower degrees of impairment. Borderline, paranoid, and schizotypal PDs are associated with the greatest variability in functioning; antisocial, dependent, and obsessive-compulsive are associated with less temporal and situational variability than other PDs. The fourth column in Table 9.2 lists common triggers for different PDs. From a psychodynamic perspective, these triggers are particularly informative: Each PD-specific trigger reveals something important about the underlying vulnerabilities of the personality-disordered individual. Thus, borderlines' intense reaction to variations in interpersonal closeness-distance suggests an underlying preoccupation with boundary issues (Kernberg, 1975). Histrionics' exaggerated response to sexuality reveals an underlying fear of intimacy and confirms that their surface flirtatiousness is merely a self-presentation style designed to draw others in but still keep them at a safe distance (Horowitz, 1991). By scrutinizing the stressors that lead to diminished reality testing in personality-disordered individuals, the psychodynamic processes that underlie PD symptoms become readily apparent.

Table 9.2   Impairment and Variability in Reality Testing across Different PDs

PD Syndrome	Overall Impairment in Reality Testing	Variability in Reality Testing	Common Triggers
Antisocial	Moderate	Low	Challenges to status/autonomy; delay of gratification
Avoidant	Moderate	Moderate	Social interaction with unfamiliar people
Borderline	High	High	Variations in interpersonal closeness-distance
Dependent	Low	Low	Anticipated relationship disruption
Histrionic	Moderate	Moderate	Sexuality/emotional intimacy
Narcissistic	Moderate	Moderate	Loss of adulation, admiration, attention
Paranoid	High	High	Real or imagined external threats
Obsessive-Compulsive	Low	Low	Loss of control; disruption of routine
Schizoid	High	Moderate	Social contact
Schizotypal	High	High	Discordant/belief-contradicting information

Defense Style: Differences in Coping

Psychoanalytic theory contends that many PD symptoms reflect the characteristic defenses used by the individual. Thus, the emotional lability and impulsivity of borderlines reflect their overreliance on splitting and the associated tendency to perceive other people as either "all good" or "all bad" (Linehan, 1993). Histrionics' pseudosexuality is in part a product of their overreliance on denial (Apt & Hurlbert, 1994), whereas paranoids' tendency to attribute malevolent intent to others reflects their overreliance on projection (Bornstein, Scanlon, & Beardslee, 1989).

Defense style correlates of different PDs have been documented more extensively than other PD-related variables, in part because numerous self-report and projective indices of defense style have been developed over the years (see Cramer, 2000, for a review). Empirical research on defense styles offers mixed support for the psychodynamic model, however. Table 9.3 summarizes the results from two well-designed investigations of the PD-defense style link (Berman & McCann, 1995; Lingiardi et al., 1999). As this table shows, the defenses associated with specific PD syndromes are sometimes—but not always—as psychoanalytic theory contends. Thus, antisocial PD is associated with projection and acting out/turning-against-object in both investigations, but it is also associated with high levels of intellectualization in one study. Dependent PD is associated with a turning-against-self defense style, as psychoanalytic theory predicts, but it is also associated with high levels of self-assertion.

To be sure, these inconsistencies likely reflect several factors, including limitations in extant measures of defense mechanisms and flaws in the *DSM* PD criteria (Bornstein,

1998). At the very least, the results summarized in Table 9.3 suggest that traditional psychodynamic conceptualizations of the PD-defense style link require further refinement and additional empirical scrutiny.

Introjects: Differences in Perceptions of Self and Others

Contemporary psychoanalytic theorists agree that internalized mental representations of the self, other people, and self-other interactions play a key role in personality development and dynamics (see Gabbard, 1994; Kissen, 1995). Those who ascribe to a drive-oriented framework (e.g., Brenner, 1974) view these mental representations as ego and superego derivatives, whereas object relations theorists and self psychologists conceptualize introjects as free-standing entities that are independent of other psychic structures (Greenberg & Mitchell, 1983). Metatheoretical differences aside, psychoanalysts regard introjects as akin to relationship templates (or "blueprints"), that guide perception, thought, behavior, and emotional responding and create particular expectations for interpersonal interactions.

Table 9.3   Defense Styles Associated with Specific PDs

PD Syndrome	Psychodynamic Hypothesis	Empirical Findings	
		Berman & McCann (1995)	Lingiardi et al. (1999)
Antisocial	Acting out	High TAO, PRO; Low PRN	Intellectualization, projection, acting out
Avoidant	Fantasy	High PRO, TAS; Low PRN, REV	Self-absorption, reaction formation
Borderline	Regression, splitting	High TAS; Low PRN, REV	Acting out
Dependent	Introjection, reaction formation	High TAS, REV; Low TAO	Self-assertion
Histrionic	Denial	High TAO; Low TAS	Affiliation, splitting, omnipotence, acting out, idealization
Narcissistic	Reaction formation, denial	High TAO; Low TAS	Acting out
Paranoid	Projection	High PRO; Low PRN	—
Obsessive-Compulsive	Reaction formation, isolation	High PRN, REV; Low TAO	Humor, devaluation
Schizoid	Denial, isolation	High TAS	—
Schizotypal	Undoing, fantasy	High PRO, TAS; Low PRN, REV	—

Notes: R. F. Berman and J. T. McCann (1995) used the MCMI-II (Millon, 1987) to assess PD pathology, and the Defense Mechanisms Inventory (Ihilevich & Gleser, 1986) to assess defense style in a mixed-sex sample of 130 psychiatric inpatients and outpatients. Lingiardi et al. (1999) used the SCID-II (First, Spitzer, Gibbon, Williams, & Benjamin, 1994) to assess PD pathology, and the Defense Mechanisms Rating Scale (Perry, 1991) to assess defense style in a sample of 50 female psychiatric outpatients.

PRN = Principalization; PRO = Projection; REV = Reversal; TAO = Turning against object; and TAS = Turning against self. Dashes indicate no statistical association between PD pathology and defense style.

A number of empirical studies have explored self- and object representations in different PDs (e.g., Blatt, 1991; Blatt & Auerbach, 2000; Hibbard & Porcerelli, 1998; Soldz & Vaillant, 1998; Westen, Ludolph, Lerner, Ruffins, & Wiss, 1990). Table 9.4 summarizes the general patterns that have emerged in these investigations. Two conclusions emerge from Table 9.4 that are useful in the present context. First, there are predictable relationships between personality-disordered individuals' self-representation and their core representation of other people. For the most part, these self- and other representations represent contrasting and mutually reinforcing cognitive structures. Thus, avoidant persons' view of the self as unworthy is reified by their perception of others as critical and judgmental. Schizoids' perception of other people as frightening and intimidating exacerbates their sense of themselves as an isolated loner.

Second, it is easy to see how the characteristic behavior patterns of different PDs may be traced to these key introjects. Paranoid persons' distancing behaviors clearly reflect their view of others as threatening and intrusive. Dependent individuals' reflexive tendency to seek help when challenged stems in part from their belief that other people are more confident and powerful than they are.

INTEGRATING PSYCHODYNAMIC PERSONALITY DISORDER PROCESSES

Although every PD can be described in terms of ego strength, defenses, and introjects, it is the complex interplay among these variables that determines the underlying dynamics and surface manifestations of each syndrome. Brief reviews of borderline, dependent, and narcissistic PDs illustrate the interactions among these variables.

Table 9.4   Self and Object Representations in Different PDs

PD Syndrome	Self-Representation	Object Representation
Antisocial	Autonomous/Unrestrained	Naive/Trusting
Avoidant	Scrutinized/Unworthy	Critical/Judgmental
Borderline	Tenuous/Unstable	Overwhelming/Unreliable
Dependent	Weak/Ineffectual	Confident/Protective
Histrionic	Sociable/Desirable	Bland/Boring
Narcissistic	Important/Worthy	Unimportant/Unworthy
Paranoid	Scrutinized/Envied	Threatening/Intrusive
Obsessive-Compulsive	Industrious/Controlled	Impulsive/Uncontrolled
Schizoid	Independent/Loner	Frightening/Intimidating
Schizotypal	Different/Unconventional	Unreliable/Unavailable

Note: Discussions of self and object representations in PD syndromes are found in *Psychodynamic Psychiatrey in Clinical Practice,* by G. O. Gabbard, 1994, Washington, DC: American Psychiatric Press; *Affect, Object, and Character Structure,* by M. Kissen, 1995, Madison, CT: International Universities Press; *Toward a New Personology: An Evolutionary Model,* by T. Millon, 1990, New York: Wiley; and *Disorders of Personality: DSM-IV and Beyond,* second edition, by. T. Millon, 1996, New York: Wiley.

Borderline

Evidence suggests that cold, unresponsive parenting is central to the etiology of borderline personality disorder (BPD; Johnson, Cohen, Brown, Smailes, & Bernstein, 1999; Zanarini et al., 2000). As numerous clinicians have noted, individuals with BPD lack a cohesive sense of self: They have not internalized a stable self-image that provides a focal point for internal experience and external reality. In addition, BPD individuals cannot maintain stable mental representations of significant figures, and, as a result, they experience a failure in "evocative constancy": They cannot easily bring to mind images of people who are not physically present (Blatt, 1991). Because of these two interrelated deficits, persons with BPD are conflicted regarding interpersonal closeness-distance. They are preoccupied with maintaining ties to others (because of their inability to evoke images of absent objects) but fear being overwhelmed and annihilated by intimacy (because of their tenuous sense of self). Managing this intense ambivalence—and the affect that accompanies it—requires so much psychic energy that few cognitive resources are available to devote to other tasks of daily living. So much effort is devoted to managing anxiety and inner turmoil that other ego functions—most notably reality testing and impulse control—are significantly impaired. Moreover, because key self- and object representations have been internalized at a conceptually primitive level, BPD persons rely on splitting to structure their internal and external object worlds. Self and other people are seen as either "all good" or "all bad," with rapid and unpredictable fluctuations between the two. The self-destructive behaviors of BPD individuals (including substance use, self-mutilating tendencies, and parasuicidal episodes) are in part a product of their poor impulse control and inability to manage negative affect through internal means. These self-destructive behaviors help the BPD person avoid real or imagined abandonment by drawing others into a caregiving role (Davis, Gunderson, & Myers, 1999; Linehan, 1993), though the borderline typically has little insight into the underlying motives that drive these actions.

Dependent

The key psychodynamic factor in dependent personality disorder (DPD) is a representation of the self as vulnerable, weak, and ineffectual (Bornstein, 1996). This "helpless" self-concept results in part from a sustained pattern of overprotective and/or authoritarian parenting early in life (Head, Baker, & Williamson, 1991), which teaches the child that the way to survive is to accede to others' expectations and demands. Accompanying this helpless self-concept is a mental representation of other people as powerful and potent (Bornstein, 1993). As a result, the DPD person remains preoccupied with maintaining ties to potential caregivers (e.g., friends, supervisors, romantic partners) who can provide protection, guidance, and nurturance.

Although DPD persons show minimal impairment in reality testing in most situations, their exaggerated response to relationship disruption reveals that their perceptions of self and others are distorted in fundamental ways. Much of the dysfunctional dependency-related behavior of the DPD person (e.g., excessive help-seeking, breakdown threats) is aimed at precluding abandonment by a valued other, though in contrast to the BPD person, the person with DPD typically has some insight into the motives that drive these behaviors (Bornstein, 1996). Research has shown that dependent individuals have difficulty tolerating even minimal separation from caregivers and display features of an insecure attachment style in friendships and romantic relationships (Sperling & Berman, 1991). Studies examining defense style in DPD persons have produced less consistent results (see Bornstein, in press), but dependent individuals tend to direct anger and other negative emotions inward rather than expressing them directly. To some extent, the nurturant, protective relationships cultivated by DPD persons are themselves defensive in nature: They not only help dependent persons manage anxiety through external means but also prevent them from testing their perception of themselves as weak and ineffectual (Bornstein, 1993, in press). In this context, Pincus and Wilson (2001) noted that despite their surface differences, the myriad self-presentation patterns exhibited by dependent persons (e.g., devoted lover, exploited victim, submissive helper) all reinforce the preexisting belief that without the protection of others, they will not survive.

Narcissistic

Two contrasting psychodynamic models of narcissistic personality disorder (NPD) have emerged in recent years. Kohut (1971, 1977) argued that NPD results from a fundamental flaw in the development of the self that stems from inadequate parental empathy and ineffective parental mirroring early in life. As a result, the individual never fully differentiates from the primary caregiver, and subsequent relationships are characterized by boundary confusion and merging of self and other (Auerbach, 1993). Other theorists argue that NPD reflects defenses used to manage an overwhelming sense of failure that stems from the parents' inability or unwillingness to provide the positive feedback that fosters a sense of self-worth and self-esteem. As Kernberg (1975) noted, when parents do not respond with approval to their child's early displays of competency and initiative, the child protects him- or herself from overwhelming feelings of rejection and worthlessness by constructing a facade of exaggerated self-importance.

Whether the grandiosity of the NPD person is primary (as Kohut suggested) or the indirect result of defensive operations (as Kernberg argued), research confirms that NPD is characterized by a conscious perception of self as special and unique, along with a view of other people as inferior (Gabbard, 1994; Morf & Rhodewalt, 2001). A continuous stream of praise is required to prevent the narcissistic person from lapsing into depression, which results from the emergence into consciousness of underlying feelings of inadequacy (Rhodewalt & Morf, 1998). Narcissistic persons respond to even minor criticism with intense rage, denigrating those who criticized them in an effort to bolster their fragile self-image. Reality testing is at least moderately impaired, especially in the domains of self-evaluation and social comparison, although studies indicate that narcissistic people are capable of reasonably accurate information processing in domains unrelated to self-evaluation and self-worth. A combination of defenses including reaction formation and denial helps maintain the NPD person's inflated self-image and discount evidence inconsistent with the narcissistic illusion of importance and uniqueness (Gabbard, 1994).

CURRENT STATUS AND FUTURE DIRECTIONS

To refine a theoretical model of personality pathology, researchers must not only scrutinize the logic of that model and test the model empirically but also examine the place of the model relative to other theoretical frameworks. Where consistencies emerge among disparate frameworks, all are strengthened. Where inconsistencies emerge, a fruitful avenue for inquiry arises.

One of the great advantages of Millon's (1990, 1996) biopsychosocial perspective is that it represents the sort of broad, integrative framework that provides context for evaluation of narrower theoretical models. In the following sections, I discuss the place of psychoanalysis within the personological perspective and offer suggestions for future work in this area.

Primary and Secondary Personality Disorder Psychodynamics

Psychodynamic processes affect all PDs, but they do not affect all PDs equally. For certain syndromes, psychodynamic processes play a central role; for others, psychodynamics are subsidiary to other variables. It is useful to divide PDs into two broad categories with respect to psychodynamic relevance. Six *DSM-IV-TR* PDs are strongly affected by psychodynamic processes. These PDs—which form what can be termed a *primary psychodynamic cluster*—include dependent, narcissistic, histrionic, obsessive-compulsive, paranoid, and borderline. Each of these PDs can be traced to problematic early relationships that lead to impairments in ego functioning, dysfunctional introjects, and an ineffective defense style. Although other factors (e.g., inherited neurological variations, conditioning and learning effects) also play a role in the etiology of these syndromes, psychodynamic processes are central to each.

Four *DSM-IV-TR* PDs are influenced by psychodynamic processes, although for these syndromes psychodynamics are secondary to other variables. Antisocial, avoidant, schizoid, and schizotypal PDs may be grouped into this *secondary psychodynamic cluster*. All four syndromes are characterized by maladaptive perceptions of self and other people, problems in reality testing, and defense styles that impair interpersonal functioning and/or impulse control. However, in all four syndromes, identifiable neurophysiological diatheses play a central role in PD etiology, and precursors of dysfunctional interpersonal behavior are observable early in life as temperament differences. These temperament differences precede the psychodynamic processes that help shape subsequent inter- and intrapersonal functioning (see, e.g., Alden, Laposa, Taylor, & Ryder, 2002; Lenzenweger, 2001).

Understanding Intergenerational Personality Disorder Linkages

Research confirms that PD pathology in parents is associated with increased risk for PD pathology in offspring (Johnson et al., 1999). The specificity of these linkages varies from syndrome to syndrome, however, and while the presence of PDs in one or both parents is associated with a general increase in risk for personality pathology, there is no one-to-one correspondence between the form of PD pathology in parent and child.

At least five factors help explain the intergenerational transmission of PD pathology:

1. Genetics (i.e., inherited differences in temperament, neurophysiology, and other variables).
2. Relationship dynamics within the family (e.g., variations in parenting style and skill).
3. Faulty learning (e.g., flawed ways of thinking acquired within the family).
4. Generalized familial pathology (i.e., global milieu effects that reflect broader dysfunctional processes among family members).

5. System propagation factors (e.g., familial roles and alliances, both hidden and overt, that maintain dysfunctional behavior patterns over time).

An integrated model is needed to explain the interplay of these five factors and the pathways that link changes in one domain with changes in other areas. Psychoanalytic theory is particularly helpful in understanding one PD propagation process that seems, at first glance, counterintuitive: Many personality-disordered people select environments that perpetuate their dysfunctional patterns (see Auerbach, 1993; Linehan, 1993). This process (which parallels Freud's concept of the *repetition compulsion*) can be understood by focusing on: (1) the internalized object world of the personality-disordered individual (people tend to seek the predictable and familiar over the unfamiliar and unknown) and (2) the personality-disordered person's defense style (which may exacerbate distortions in perceptions of self, others, and self-other interactions).

Exploring Convergences among Personality Disorder Models

Although different models conceptualize PD dynamics in different ways, there is a surprising degree of convergence among these perspectives. Certain constructs emerge in many—even most—PD frameworks, and exploration of these constructs can be informative. For example, several models invoke the concept of an enduring mental representation of self and other people to explain personality-disordered behavior. Thus, the psychoanalytic concept *object representation* is echoed in the cognitive concept of *schema* and the humanistic construct of *experienced self.* Similarly, distortions in information processing are seen as central to many PDs, although psychoanalysts describe these distortions in terms of *defenses,* cognitive theorists describe them in terms of *automatic thoughts,* and humanistic theorists describe them in terms of a *constricted worldview.*

Just as there are convergences among different theoretical perspectives on PDs, there are common elements in different treatment approaches. To be sure, each model of PD pathology emphasizes intervention at a particular level dictated by the logic and assumptions of that model: Whereas psychoanalysts seek to effect change through exploration and insight (Bornstein, 2003), behaviorists intervene at the level of dysfunctional responding (Turkat, 1990), and humanistic therapists challenge the patient to confront aspects of the self that have been distorted or denied (Schneider, 1990). These treatment strategies can be integrated effectively, however, and their interventions made synergistic rather than contradictory (see Bornstein, in press, for a discussion of this issue).

Revisiting and Revising the Cluster Model

Although the cluster model of grouping *DSM-IV-TR* PDs is useful in identifying syndromes with similar surface characteristics, there are some difficulties with this model. Clinicians have questioned whether the three cluster labels (i.e., eccentric, dramatic, and anxious) are adequate representations of the PDs they purport to describe (Widiger, 2000). As Costello (1995) noted, there is as much behavioral and symptomatic heterogeneity within PD clusters as between them. It is not surprising that studies indicate substantial comorbidity among different PDs, and in many instances comorbidity is as high across clusters as within them (Bornstein, 1998). Numerous proposals for revising Axis II in future versions of the *DSM* have been offered. Some proposals aimed to recategorize PDs based on alternative criteria (Westen & Shedler, 1999) or do away with discrete PD categories altogether (Bornstein, 1998). The psychodynamic perspective offers a potentially useful framework for revising the *DSM* cluster model by grouping PDs based on underlying dynamics rather than surface presentation. Defense style, introject quality, and impairment in ego strength/reality testing could be used to group PD syndromes in future versions of the *DSM*. Alternatively, some or all of these variables could be coded on separate axes to complement existing information on Axis II diagnoses (see American Psychiatric Association, 2000, for a discussion of this issue and strategies for implementing it). It may be that multiple organizing clusters are the most useful way of codifying interrelationships among different PDs.

CONCLUSION

When PD syndromes are simultaneously described in terms of surface behavior, underlying dynamics, cognitive style, and other dimensions, a more complete picture of the personality-disordered person emerges, increasing treatment efficacy and facilitating diagnosis and theory testing. Millon's (1990, 1996) personological perspective represents an ideal framework for capturing the depth and complexity of personality pathology in future versions of the diagnostic manual, enhancing empirical and clinical work while celebrating the rich conceptual pluralism that has come to characterize contemporary research on personality and its disorders.

REFERENCES

Abraham, K. (1927). The influence of oral erotism on character formation. In C. A. D. Bryan & J. Strachey (Eds.), *Selected papers on psychoanalysis* (pp. 393–406). London: Hogarth Press.

Alden, L. E., Laposa, J. M., Taylor, C. T., & Ryder, B. A. (2002). Avoidant personality disorder: Current status and future directions. *Journal of Personality Disorders, 16,* 1–29.

American Psychiatric Association. (1980). *Diagnostic and statistical manual of mental disorders* (3rd ed.). Washington, DC: Author.

American Psychiatric Association. (2000). *Diagnostic and statistical manual of mental disorders* (4th ed., text rev.). Washington, DC: Author.

Apt, C., & Hurlbert, D. F. (1994). The sexual attitudes, behavior, and relationships of women with histrionic personality disorder. *Journal of Sex and Marital Therapy, 20,* 125–133.

Auerbach, J. S. (1993). The origins of narcissism and narcissistic personality disorder: A theoretical and empirical reformulation. In J. M. Masling & R. F. Bornstein (Eds.), *Psychoanalytic perspectives on psychopathology* (pp. 43–110). Washington, DC: American Psychological Association.

Berman, S. M. W., & McCann, J. T. (1995). Defense mechanisms and personality disorders: An empirical test of Millon's theory. *Journal of Personality Assessment, 64,* 132–144.

Blatt, S. J. (1991). A cognitive morphology of psychopathology. *Journal of Nervous and Mental Disease, 179,* 449–458.

Blatt, S. J., & Auerbach, J. S. (2000). Psychoanalytic models of the mind and their contributions to personality research. *European Journal of Personality, 14,* 429–447.

Bornstein, R. F. (1993). *The dependent personality.* New York: Guilford Press.

Bornstein, R. F. (1996). Beyond orality: Toward an object relations/interactionist reconceptualization of the etiology and dynamics of dependency. *Psychoanalytic Psychology, 13,* 177–203.

Bornstein, R. F. (1998). Reconceptualizing personality disorder diagnosis in the *DSM-V:* The discriminant validity challenge. *Clinical Psychology: Science and Practice, 5,* 333–343.

Bornstein, R. F. (2003). Psychodynamic models of personality. In T. Millon & M. J. Lerner (Eds.), *Personality and social psychology* (pp. 117–134). Vol. 5 in I. B. Weiner (Editor-in-Chief), *Handbook of psychology.* Hoboken, NJ: Wiley.

Bornstein, R. F. (in press). *The dependent patient: A practitioner's guide.* Washington, DC: American Psychological Association.

Bornstein, R. F., & O'Neill, R. M. (1992). Parental perceptions and psychopathology. *Journal of Nervous and Mental Diseases, 180,* 475–483.

Bornstein, R. F., Scanlon, M. A., & Beardslee, L. A. (1989). The psychodynamics of paranoia: Anality, projection, and suspiciousness. *Journal of Social Behavior and Personality, 4,* 275–284.

Brenner, C. (1974). *An elementary textbook of psychoanalysis.* New York: Anchor Books.

Briere, J. N., & Elliott, D. M. (1994). Immediate and long-term effects of child sexual abuse. *Future of Children, 4,* 54–69.

Costello, C. G. (1995). The advantages of focusing on the personality characteristics of the personality-disordered. In C. G. Costello (Ed.), *Personality characteristics of the personality disordered* (pp. 1–23). New York: Wiley.

Cramer, P. (2000). Defense mechanisms in psychology today: Further processes for adaptation. *American Psychologist, 55,* 637–646.

Davis, T., Gunderson, J. G., & Myers, M. (1999). Borderline personality disorder. In D. G. Jacobs (Ed.), *Harvard Medical School guide to suicide assessment and intervention* (pp. 311–331). San Francisco: Jossey-Bass.

Eagle, M. N. (1984). *Recent developments in psychoanalysis.* New York: McGraw-Hill.

Finkelhor, D., & Dziuba-Leatherman, J. (1994). Victimization of children. *American Psychologist, 49,* 173–183.

First, M. B., Spitzer, R. L., Gibbon, M., Williams, J. B. W., & Benjamin, L. (1994). *Structured clinical interview for DSM-IV Axis II personality disorders.* New York: New York State Psychiatric Institute.

Fisher, S., & Greenberg, R. P. (1996). *Freud scientifically reappraised.* New York: Wiley.

Freud, S. (1896). The aetiology of hysteria. In J. Strachey (Ed. & Trans.), *The standard edition of the works of Sigmund Freud* (Vol. 3, pp. 187–221). London: Hogarth Press.

Freud, S. (1905a). Fragment of an analysis of a case of hysteria. In J. Strachey (Ed. & Trans.), *The standard edition of the works of Sigmund Freud* (Vol. 7, pp. 1–122). London: Hogarth Press.

Freud, S. (1905b). Three essays on the theory of sexuality. In J. Strachey (Ed. & Trans.), *The standard edition of the works of Sigmund Freud* (Vol. 7, pp. 125–245). London: Hogarth Press.

Freud, S. (1908). Character and anal erotism. In J. Strachey (Ed. & Trans.), *The standard edition of the works of Sigmund Freud* (Vol. 9, pp. 167–176). London: Hogarth Press.

Freud, S. (1920). The psychogenesis of a case of homosexuality in a woman. In J. Strachey (Ed. & Trans.), *The standard edition of the works of Sigmund Freud* (Vol. 18, pp. 145–172). London: Hogarth Press.

Gabbard, G. O. (1994). *Psychodynamic psychiatry in clinical practice.* Washington, DC: American Psychiatric Press.

Greenberg, J. R., & Mitchell, S. A. (1983). *Object relations in psychoanalytic theory.* Cambridge, MA: Harvard University Press.

Hartmann, E., Sunde, T., Kristensen, W., & Martinussen, M. (2003). Psychological measures as predictors of military training performance. *Journal of Personality Assessment, 80,* 87–98.

Head, S. B., Baker, J. D., & Williamson, D. A. (1991). Family environment characteristics and dependent personality disorder. *Journal of Personality Disorders, 5,* 256–263.

Hibbard, S., & Porcerelli, J. (1998). Further validation of the Cramer Defense Mechanism manual. *Journal of Personality Assessment, 70,* 460–483.

Hoffman, H. G., Granhag, P. A., See, S. T. K., & Loftus, E. F. (2001). Social influences on reality-monitoring decisions. *Memory and Cognition, 29,* 394–404.

Horowitz, M. J. (1991). *Hysterical personality style and the histrionic personality disorder.* Northvale, NJ: Aronson.

Ihilevich, D., & Gleser, G. C. (1986). *Defense mechanisms.* Owosso, MI: DMI Associates.

Johnson, J. G., Cohen, P., Brown, J., Smailes, E., & Bernstein, D. P. (1999). Childhood maltreatment increases risk for personality disorders during early adulthood. *Archives of General Psychiatry, 56,* 600–606.

Kernberg, O. F. (1975). *Borderline conditions and pathological narcissism.* New York: Aronson.

Kernberg, O. F. (1976). *Object relations theory and clinical psychoanalysis.* New York: Aronson.

Kernberg, O. F. (1984). *Severe personality disorders.* New Haven, CT: Yale University Press.

Kissen, M. (1995). *Affect, object, and character structure.* Madison, CT: International Universities Press.

Kohut, H. (1971). *The analysis of the self.* New York: International Universities Press.

Kohut, H. (1977). *The restoration of the self.* New York: International Universities Press.

Lenzenweger, M. F. (2001). Reaction time slowing during high-load, sustained-attention task performance in relation to psychometrically identified schizotypy. *Journal of Abnormal Psychology, 110,* 290–296.

Linehan, M. (1993). *Cognitive behavioral treatment of borderline personality disorder.* New York: Guilford Press.

Lingiardi, V., Lonati, C., Delucchi, F., Fossati, A., Vanzulli, L., & Maffei, C. (1999). Defense mechanisms and personality disorders. *Journal of Nervous and Mental Disease, 187,* 224–228.

Loftus, E. F. (1996). Memory distortion and false memory creation. *Bulletin of the American Academy of Psychiatry and the Law, 24,* 281–295.

Millon, T. (1981). *Disorders of personality: DSM-III: Axis II.* New York: Wiley.

Millon, T. (1987). Millon Clinical Multiaxial Inventory—II manual. Minneapolis, MN: National Computer Systems.

Millon, T. (1990). *Toward a new personology: An evolutionary model.* New York: Wiley.

Millon, T. (1996). *Disorders of personality: DSM-IV and beyond* (2nd ed.). New York: Wiley.

Morf, C. C., & Rhodewalt, F. (2001). Unraveling the paradoxes of narcissism: A dynamic self-regulatory processing model. *Psychological Inquiry, 12,* 177–196.

Nestor, P. G. (2002). Mental disorder and violence: Personality dimensions and clinical features. *American Journal of Psychiatry, 159,* 1973–1978.

Perry, J. C. (1991). *Defense mechanisms rating scale.* Boston: Cambridge Hospital.

Piaget, J. (1954). *The construction of reality in the child.* New York: Basic Books.

Pincus, A. L., & Wiggins, J. S. (1990). Interpersonal problems and conceptions of personality disorders. *Journal of Personality Disorders, 4,* 342–352.

Pincus, A. L., & Wilson, K. R. (2001). Interpersonal variability in dependent personality. *Journal of Personality, 69,* 223–251.

Reich, W. (1933). *Character Analysis.* Leipzig, Germany: Sexpol Verlag.

Rhodewalt, F., & Morf, C. C. (1998). On self-aggrandizement and anger: A temporal analysis of narcissism and affective reactions to success and failure. *Journal of Personality and Social Psychology, 74,* 672–685.

Schneider, K. J. (1990). *The paradoxical self: Toward an understanding of our contradictory nature.* New York: Plenum Press.

Soldz, S., & Vaillant, G. E. (1998). A 50-year longitudinal study of defense use among inner-city men: A validation of the *DSM-IV* defense axis. *Journal of Nervous and Mental Disease, 186,* 104–111.

Sperling, M. B., & Berman, W. H. (1991). An attachment classification of desperate love. *Journal of Personality Assessment, 56,* 45–55.

Torrey, E. F. (1992). *Freudian fraud.* New York: HarperCollins.

Turkat, I. D. (1990). *The personality disorders: A psychological approach to clinical management.* New York: Pergamon Press.

Vaillant, G. E. (1994). Ego mechanisms of defense and personality pathology. *Journal of Abnormal Psychology, 103,* 44–50.

Weiner, I. B. (2000). Making Rorschach interpretation as good as it can be. *Journal of Personality Assessment, 74,* 164–174.

Westen, D. (1991). Social cognition and object relations. *Psychological Bulletin, 109,* 429–455.

Westen, D., Ludolph, P., Lerner, H., Ruffins, S., & Wiss, C. (1990). Object relations in borderline adolescents. *Journal of the American Academy of Child and Adolescent Psychiatry, 29,* 338–348.

Westen, D., & Shedler, J. (1999). Revising and assessing Axis II: Toward an empirically based and clinically useful classification of personality disorders. *American Journal of Psychiatry, 156,* 273–285.

Widiger, T. A. (2000). Personality disorders in the 21st century. *Journal of Personality Disorders, 14,* 3–16.

Widiger, T. A., & Clark, L. A. (2000). Toward *DSM-V* and the classification of psychopathology. *Psychological Bulletin, 126,* 946–963.

Williams, L. M. (1995). Recovered memories of abuse in women with documented child sexual victimization histories. *Journal of Traumatic Stress, 8,* 649–673.

Zanarini, M. C., Frankenburg, F. R., Reich, D., Marino, M. F., Lewis, R. E., Williams, A. A., et al. (2000). Biparental failure in the childhood experiences of borderline patients. *Journal of Personality Disorders, 14,* 264–273.

Chapter 10

SELF PSYCHOLOGICAL FOUNDATIONS OF PERSONALITY DISORDERS

MARSHALL L. SILVERSTEIN

During the past 30 years, the fields of personality disorders and psychoanalytic self psychology have developed important reformulations of personality. The contemporary period of conceptualizing personality disorders began by operationalizing diagnostic criteria and assigning these disturbances to their own axis of classification in the multiaxial structure that originated with the *Diagnostic and Statistical Manual of Mental Disorders,* third edition (*DSM-III;* American Psychiatric Association, 1980). Thus, continually refining criteria and differentiating personality disorders from syndromal disorders securely established a basis for investigating the clinical psychopathology of the personality disorders. This approach continued the neo-Kraepelinian tradition that substantially influenced contemporary American concepts of schizophrenia and affective disorders. It set the pace for the empirical studies that were to follow, emphasizing matters of diagnostic overlap or comorbidity, differential prevalence, genetic/familial characteristics, biological factors, and social-interpersonal influences. Contemporaneously, psychoanalytic theorizing was appreciably influenced by the introduction of psychoanalytic self psychology, also referred to as the psychology of the self (Kohut, 1971), one of the first major reformulations of classical psychoanalysis in several decades. Self psychology emerged first as a theory of narcissistic personality and behavior disorders. Kohut (1977, 1984) eventually extended his view of the self and its disorders beyond these conditions as he reconsidered other forms of psychopathology. Thus, the scope of self psychology expanded well beyond its origin in narcissism and the signature conditions of Kohut's psychology of the self.

Despite the interest generated by the fields of personality disorders and self psychology, neither of these areas substantially impacted the other. Axis II concepts of personality disorders were prominently influenced by refining diagnostic criteria and by examining relationships with Axis I disorders and how concurrent personality disorders affected course and outcome of Axis I disorders. As to narcissistic personality disorder, Kernberg's (1976) clinical description of narcissistic characteristics had a greater impact on devising Axis II diagnostic criteria than did Kohut's (1971) description, in part because Kohut's description of self disorders was less specific than Kernberg's. Nevertheless, neither

Ted Millon's career brought a level of broad scholarship to the integration of personality theory. This chapter acknowledges with admiration and respect how he influenced my thinking about extending self psychology to the field of personality disorders.

Kernberg's, Kohut's, nor any other psychodynamic theoretical viewpoint prominently influenced diagnostic conceptualizations of narcissistic personality disorder in any of the versions of the *DSM* since 1980 or in the mental disorders section of the *International Classification of Diseases* (ICD; World Health Organization, 1992). Therefore, Kohut's and others' evolving views about narcissism and the self remained largely within the field of psychoanalysis proper, even as Kohut's thoughts about conditions such as addictions, perversions, and depletion depression or anxiety expanded the range of clinical disturbances associated with self-cohesion and self-esteem deficits.

The neo-Kraepelinian tradition and psychoanalysis grew farther apart than ever before. As greater attention was directed toward understanding personality disorders, particularly as new pharmacologic agents were synthesized and as new instrumentation for defining symptoms and signs increasingly gained psychometric sophistication, the viewpoints and the methods of investigation of American psychiatry and psychoanalysis could not easily be joined. From a conceptual point of view, there were major divergences about what constituted crucial variables influencing personality development and its disorders. Thus, course and outcome characteristics, family history, and pharmacologic response defined the field in American psychiatry, while varying emphases on drives, ego, self, and object were central explanatory foci in psychoanalysis. Psychoanalytic theories increasingly favored concepts of self and object, which developed in part out of a need to explain an apparent shift in prevalence in clinical practice from symptom or character neuroses to more disturbed, pre-Oedipal, or primitive conditions resembling personality disorders.

Kohut's insights about the self were welcomed for their innovations in conceptualizing and treating narcissism in a way that classical psychoanalysis could not. His ideas met with interest in many quarters, because Kohut recognized a need to modify standard analytic approaches to treat narcissistic and other severely disturbed but nonpsychotic patients more effectively. But some of Kohut's ideas were also seen as being too revolutionary, particularly his emerging view that an entity of mental life, the self, was superordinate to drives and the ego as an explanation for psychological disturbances and as a foundation for a theory of therapeutic action. Galatzer-Levy and Cohler (1990) pointed out, however, that an impetus for regarding the self as superordinate to the ego could be located in other psychoanalysts' writings, such as the British independent movement. Galatzer-Levy and Cohler included George Klein (1976) together with Kohut as forerunners of the importance of experience-near observation and clinical investigation.

Kohut was also criticized by object relations theorists for not giving sufficient credit to important analytic thinkers, principally Winnicott, whose work probably influenced Kohut's ideas. It is now known that Kohut was guarded about how seriously ill he was for much of the decade during which his most creative work occurred. Thus, under the pressure of the limited time available to him, he emphasized formulating his ideas and placing them in the context of Freud's theories more than he considered relationships between his own contributions and those of other analytic theorists besides Freud. He thus left for his followers much of the work of placing his ideas in a broad theoretical perspective (Strozier, 2001).

While he was criticized by mainstream psychoanalysis for what seemed like radical technical recommendations, Kohut was simultaneously chided by other psychoanalytic theoreticians for not moving far enough or quickly enough to boldly rebuild clinical technique. Neither criticism may have been true, because Kohut's preference was to incorporate the far-reaching implications of the ideas he was developing only when the new theoretical and clinical reformulations compelled a necessity to either augment clinical technique or, if necessary, disassemble or abandon classical interpretive practices no longer suitable for a growing number of patients.

Some of these latter critics, mostly from the intersubjective and relational schools of psychoanalysis, regarded Kohut as being too wedded to the so-called one-person psychology of classical psychoanalysis with its emphasis on psychological experience almost entirely based on patients' intrapsychic lives. Drive theory and ego psychology defined psychopathology primarily through the interplay between libidinal and aggressive drives and ego functions. It was indeed Kohut who opened the door for what has come to be called a two-person psychology, a viewpoint that accorded greater meaning to analysts' influences (or what Stolorow & Atwood, 1992, preferred to regard as an intersubjective context) as a more mutative factor than contents of intrapsychic processes. Thus, Kohut's work was an important part of a sustained period of innovative psychoanalytic thinking questioning observations that no longer fit well with the predominant ego psychological viewpoint that had, until the 1970s, solidified the body of mainstream psychoanalytic theory.

Viewpoints of personality disorders have also undergone important changes over the past three decades, dominated by the innovations in diagnostic classification but extending beyond that arena as well. Like the major cleavages in psychoanalytic theory, where motivational loci shifted from drives and ego to self, object relations, and interpersonal emphases, concepts of personality disorder have also spanned a wide range of etiologic explanations, encompassing developmental, genetic, psychoanalytic, psychometric, and social-interpersonal traditions. Although viewpoints such as these are not independent points of reference, their similarities and mutual influences remain incompletely understood. There also persist disagreements concerning the relative importance of factors such as idiographic versus nomothetic bases for understanding personality; differential influences of genetic and environmental determinants; nonindependence among normal temperament, character dispositions, and pathological variants of such patterns or traits; and the consistency of personality or degree of resistance to change.

The neo-Kraepelinian influence of descriptive psychopathology continues to represent the categorical basis for the major diagnostic nomenclatures and how they identify reliable clinical features to define and delimit discrete personality disorders. Nevertheless, many critics of the categorical model characterizing the neo-Kraepelinian tradition call attention to the persisting problem of substantial comorbidity among the Axis II personality disorders (Clark, 1999; Widiger, 1992). These critics question the distinctiveness and validity of personality disorders as they are presently represented. Moreover, comorbid personality disorders may also mitigate the presentation of Axis I disorders and their prognosis. For these reasons, one of the major debates in the field concerns the matter of redefining personality disorders, either by retaining the current classification of these chronic disturbances as categorical entities but with better delineation or, alternatively, by reformulating personality disorders as points on continua of an uncertain number of dimensions or traits. Other heuristic approaches have been suggested in which flexible, hybrid prototypes might be developed, combining elements of both categorical and dimensional approaches (Livesley, 1991; Millon, 1990, 2000; Westen & Shedler, 2000).

EXTENDING SELF PSYCHOLOGY TO EXPLANATIONS OF PERSONALITY DISORDERS

This chapter suggests how a self psychological viewpoint of the personality disorders of Axis II adds to the theoretical and clinical understanding of these conditions. I present a selective discussion of several important concepts of self psychology by tracing the evolution of some ideas pioneered by Kohut, ideas that were developed further by colleagues with whom he worked closely. It is beyond the scope of this chapter to provide a summary or outline of self psychology; however, several sources for this purpose are available, notably Goldberg (1978), Kohut (1996), Ornstein (1978), Siegel (1996), Silverstein (1999), and Wolf (1988). For more recent self psychological viewpoints, such as intersubjectivity, motivational systems, and influences of infant development and attachment theory on views of the self, recommended sources include those by Goldberg (1998); Lichtenberg, Lachmann, and Fosshage (1992); Shane and Shane (1993); Shane, Shane, and Gales (1997); Stolorow and Atwood (1992); and Teicholz (1999).

I trace three concepts, noting how these concepts have been further developed or refined since Kohut's death. The first two of these concepts (optimal frustration versus optimal responsiveness and the forward edge) are both extensions of what is considered Kohut's paramount contribution—the importance of empathy for ensuring selfobject responsiveness and how its failure interferes with the consolidation of the self. These concepts are important for understanding how empathic responsiveness influences normal development and how faulty parental or caregiver attunement to young children's needs for admiration or mirroring leads to devitalization or diminished self-esteem. Self states dominated by devitalization or mirroring deficits are described later in this chapter as important influences on schizoid, schizotypal, and avoidant personality disorders.

The third concept of Kohut's I describe is the vertical split, which Goldberg (1999) recently expanded to better understand how disavowed experiences of the self may become split off or walled off in certain types of narcissistic behavior disorders. Although a vertical split can produce clinical manifestations such as perversions, lying or duplicity, and addictions, I consider the vertical split here to illustrate how this kind of mechanism can operate as one means of forestalling fragmentation, a central concern of a second group of personality disorders I describe. The vulnerability to experience the disintegration products of an enfeebled self requires an effort to contain or forestall the breakup or fragmentation of the self, an effort I later suggest is a crucial task occurring regularly in the paranoid, borderline, and obsessive-compulsive personality disorders.

I also describe how dependent, histrionic, and antisocial personality disorders may be viewed from a self psychological perspective as attempts to acquire alternative pathways to repair the self. Finally, narcissistic personality disorder as the paradigmatic self disorder is regarded as an admixture of all of these important mechanisms that are the foundations of self psychology.

RECENT ADVANCES IN SELF PSYCHOLOGY

This section incorporates the expanded view of a psychology of the self, a broader perspective extending beyond Kohut's (1966, 1971) initial description of the narcissistic personality and behavior disorders. This is a development in self psychology that may not be familiar to those primarily acquainted with self psychology's attempt to understand a previously untreatable group of narcissistic disorders. Thus, the self psychological formulations I discuss emphasize the self rather than drive states or ego functions as the central agent of mental life. I begin with a discussion of three recent advances in self psychology, which is followed by outlining a self psychological framework for conceptualizing personality disorders.

Optimal Frustration and Optimal Responsiveness

Kohut's (1977) concept of optimal frustration extended to the self a way of explaining how wishes and reality become differentiated. It was an explanation he considered a better fit than those based on drive theory and ego psychology. Beyond strengthening the ego, Kohut considered that in normal development, tolerating frustration and delay is also how the self becomes cohesive. Thus, the inevitable momentary empathic failures by children's caregivers led to a structure-promoting process that strengthened the self. He believed that empathic responsiveness from caregivers lays the groundwork for self-cohesion. The synchrony between caregivers' empathic attunement and children's needs for affirming the self is a measure of the efficacy of others' capacity to provide needed selfobject functions for consolidating the self. He regarded the inevitable frustrations of empathic misattunements to be optimal if they were gradual or nontraumatic and if they were responded to by a child's caregivers in a way that permitted empathic failures to be remedied.

Kohut regarded optimal frustration as a disruption-repair process that strengthened the self. It assumes that if the disruption caused by empathic failures or misattunement was not too severe or prolonged, it could be repaired sufficiently to prevent the depletion or devitalization affects that may turn into self disorders. Frustration was, therefore, Kohut's explanation for how the self is shored up or fortified in normal development. More extreme frustration does not foster self-cohesion, but it establishes the chronic disturbances he regarded as disorders of the self, some of which may also be understood as personality disorders. In this formulation, personality disorders result from levels of frustration that cannot be sufficiently metabolized to sustain a degree of self-cohesion necessary to invigorate or vitalize the self.

In contrast to Kohut's view, Bacal (1985) and Terman (1988) took the position that the self is strengthened neither exclusively nor even primarily by the frustrations of empathic failures. They regarded self development as being optimal when a certain level of empathic responsiveness was present in development, for example, the feeling of being deeply understood by a child's caregivers. Terman argued that frustration such as empathic misattunement occurs regularly in life and often enough in treatment, thus reviving or reactivating empathic failures from earlier stages of development. In Terman's view, experiencing empathic failures repeatedly, including their appearance in treatment, is not essential to promote development, although occurrences like these do represent occasions for clinicians to understand what went wrong in development. Conveying this understanding is the basis for interpretation, because it promotes the affective experience for patients of being understood in depth. Both Bacal and Terman argued that it is this affective component of empathic understanding that is the core element necessary for strengthening the self. Therefore, they regarded frustration to be unessential as a basis for consolidation of the self.

Although Bacal preferred the term *optimal responsiveness* to contrast this view with Kohut's concept of optimal frustration, the difference may be subtle and sometimes unimportant, because self psychologists generally believe the difference is imperceptible to many patients. Other self psychologists also commented on this problem, emphasizing different aspects of the quality of empathic attunement, such as affective engagement (P. Tolpin, 1988) or restoring empathic attunement following selfobject disruption (Wolf, 1993). Regardless of the terminology used by various self psychologists, it seems evident that Kohut's emphasis on optimal frustration was a concept several of his followers found troublesome. Thus, the view took hold that the crucial mutative factor that self psychology contributed to psychoanalysis was its focus on empathic attunement to unresponded-to affect states of the self.

As I suggest later, the unresponsiveness of a disengaged caregiver environment influences self states of devitalization or diminished self-esteem. When defects of caregiver engagement are persistently present and of long standing, they characterize the predominant clinical manifestations of personality disorders. Predominant self states brought about by insufficient affective responsiveness would seem to be another influence on the formation of personality disorders.

Forward Edge

Although Kohut regarded psychopathology in the traditional ego psychological approach as a dynamic interplay among conflicts, defenses, and symptoms (which he referred to as the *trailing edge* of psychological development), he was also aware that interpreting the traditional view or trailing edge often was not therapeutic. He became increasingly convinced that interpreting the reparative strivings of injured or undermined self states was at least as therapeutically advantageous as interpreting the trailing edge of the psychopathology. Although Kohut (1977) alluded to this idea as he was completing *The Restoration of the Self,* he did not develop it further during his lifetime. He referred to this form of clinical understanding and interpretation of patients' strivings as the *leading edge* (Miller, 1985; M. Tolpin, 2002). As his work proceeded, Kohut (1984) became even more convinced of the therapeutic importance of the leading edge, although he did not advocate abandoning the importance of the trailing edge.

Recently, M. Tolpin (2002) revived Kohut's view about the importance of the leading edge. Tolpin also preserved the traditional idea of a trailing edge to represent how development becomes derailed, but she stressed the importance of simultaneously looking for what she preferred to call the *forward edge* of how people attempt to find what they need to solidify a weakened self. Tolpin called attention to nascent or early beginnings of a healthy or vigorous self that frequently appear alongside the more easily seen trailing edge psychopathology. Such tendrils of a self become important, because they contain the strivings to continue and repair interrupted development of the self, however damaged or diminished the self may otherwise appear. Conventional interpretations of psychopathology, emphasizing the trailing edge as they characteristically do, may fail at times to produce mutative changes, because neglecting to include submerged, difficult-to-detect signs of forward edge strivings in such interpretations may impede securing what is most needed to mobilize these insights to produce genuine recovery.

Thus, while interpretation of the forward edge does not preclude simultaneously considering defenses or pathological processes, detecting forward edge strivings is what deepens understanding of affective experience. In this way, conceptualizing the origins of depletion of the self invariably includes considering what the injured self requires to restore sufficient vitality to sustain its cohesion.

It is but a short step to seeing that attentiveness to understanding the developmental precursors that propel the nascent forward edge strivings guides optimal responsiveness. Therefore, these concepts are conceptually as well as therapeutically linked. These are also concepts reflecting natural outgrowths of Kohut's thinking, although he may not have fully anticipated this link in his earliest writings. The particular significance of the forward edge for understanding personality disorders lies in appreciating the importance of responding to strivings or yearnings that patients have not abandoned, despite the longstanding deficits they continually experience over the lifelong course of chronic conditions such as the personality disorders.

Vertical Split

The vertical split is another concept Kohut introduced but did not develop further after *The Analyis of the Self* (Kohut, 1971) appeared. This concept served to explain Kohut's understanding of disparate experiences of the self that were at odds with one another but that also seemed to coexist. He suggested that the vertical split explained disavowed sectors of experience that become transformed into actions representing tension states walled off from the rest of ongoing experience. Disparate or split-off experiences usually develop in the service of soothing the self when affect states such as agitation or depression cannot otherwise be quieted or calmed. Patients with a vertical split are not patients who react with depression, anxiety, or related affective dysregulation states when selfobjects are unavailable or unresponsive rather than calming. These reactions also do not represent dissociative states, nor are these disavowed experiences that escaped repression, which was how Kohut denoted the repression barrier (the horizontal split) within the experiencing self. Rather, patients with a vertical split are the Jekylls and Hydes of the consultation room or clinic—the upstanding citizen who secretly shoplifts, the honest teacher who sporadically steals books he or she does not need and will never read, or the faithful wife or husband who has an involved and ongoing affair of several years' duration.

Goldberg (1999) expanded Kohut's thinking about this phenomenon, observing that a vertical split operates as if the patient were inhabiting two minds. Thus, an entire arena of these patients' experience, behavior, and affect is felt to be alien to themselves. The walled-off behavior represents something such patients typically do not experience as part of who or what they feel themselves to be. Nevertheless, these are also experiences of the self that are simultaneously familiar, and consequently, unlike repression, patients are aware of their existence. Goldberg's other examples of the vertical split include cross-dressing and binge eating, representing an expanded range of the clinical phenomena in which patients may seem to live parallel and contradictory lives. Such patients seem able to live with themselves despite some distress that coexists with full awareness of both sides of their experience. They are, on the one hand, looking the other way while still knowing about their other side and, on the other hand, not knowing how the other side or the behavior fits in with their predominant sense of who they believe themselves to be.

Basch (1988) suggested that parents who minimize or dismiss their children's anxiety foster these children's developing disavowal as an adaptation. Split-off behaviors are, therefore, how such children escape the distress of affects they are not helped to understand or to experience safely. This adaptation may also resemble the type of affective disconnection Balint (1969) suggested in his explanation of trauma—the trusted or loved parent suddenly or repeatedly traumatizes the child in some way, followed by the parent's indifference to what has occurred, thus betraying the child's trust. Goldberg (1999) described it thus:

> The parent is unable to see the fear of the child both because of his or her own limitations and because of the fact that the unhappy child is no longer around. The child has disappeared, has found a solution. He or she has discovered a split-off way of relieving the anxiety, and this is somehow registered and appreciated by the parent who implicitly prefers a misbehavior that can be ignored to a depression that cannot be. (p. 36)

Although Kohut regarded grandiosity as the core disavowed experience, Goldberg reformulated the source of the vertical split as a walled-off affect state typically resembling muted or subclinical depression. Often associated with the emotional unavailability of the caregiver, such disavowed affects are short-circuited and thus blocked by a parent's interest in preventing such affects from being fully experienced. Despite disdain and even moral repugnance for their acts, patients with a vertical split continue their misbehavior. Because the goals of the vertical split are sustaining self-cohesion or soothing self states that cannot otherwise be recognized or tolerated, a vertical split can be clinically differentiated from lying, stealing, or more severe forms of antisocial or sociopathic behavior that do not conceal underlying affect states threatening self-cohesion.

Treatment of the vertical split requires attention to the walled-off affects of the split-off segment of the self. Although it may be advantageous to consider the vertical split as a type of personality disorder, its relationship with antisocial personality disorder, an Axis I syndrome such as dissociation, and narcissistic or borderline personality disorders has not been investigated. It is, therefore, uncertain how to classify clinical phenomena that present as disturbances of functioning where contradictory, irreconcilable affect states co-exist but remain unintegrated. While its specific relationship to personality disorders or other clinical entities is unknown, the vertical split seems to represent a clinical phenomenon that operates like a stable but nevertheless chronic condition much like the personality disorders. It may promote a degree of self-cohesion when threats of fragmentation or disintegration might otherwise predominate.

A SELF PSYCHOLOGICALLY INFLUENCED FRAMEWORK FOR PERSONALITY DISORDERS

To this point, I have traced the diverging paths that self psychology and descriptive psychopathology followed. These paths were marked by the shift in emphasis in psychoanalytic theory from drive and ego to self and by the declining influence of psychoanalytic constructs associated with the multiaxial reconfiguration of psychopathology. Further, I have outlined several concepts representing evolutions of Kohut's original ideas, expanding his theories while still remaining within the traditional framework of self psychology. These concepts of optimal responsiveness, the forward edge, and the vertical split also bear on a self psychological formulation of the personality disorders.

Against this background, the self psychological framework I now propose is an additional or alternative way of grouping the personality disorders according to self psychological concepts of deficits and strivings or life tasks necessary for the repair of deficits of the self. I take the position that the particular stylistic behavior and symptoms of the various personality disorders represent different ways of attempting to repair the self. Attempting to repair the injuries of early caregiving deficits gives rise to self disorders that are characterized by different types of self-cohesion disturbances. These disorders are approximately synonymous with what is meant by personality disorders. These self-reparative paths, therefore, represent patients' attempts to: (1) sustain self-esteem by turning away in the face of devitalization or depletion, (2) devote predominant effort to maintain self-cohesion when it is threatened by fragmentation, or (3) preserve a thriving self through developing partially successful compensatory structures built up from idealization or twinship. (Twinship is a selfobject function derived from Kohut's original concept of the bipolar self, in which the self was composed of mirroring and idealizing sectors. He later [Kohut, 1984] differentiated the twinship selfobject function from mirroring to emphasize how one's experiencing oneself as being just like another may secure a needed sense of vitality.)

These three mechanisms represent the self-cohesion deficits that potentiate the personality disorders and the life tasks patients struggle to resolve in an effort to repair or revitalize the self. Thus, for example, sustaining buoyancy when the self has been exposed to chronic mirroring deficits becomes the focal task of avoidant, schizoid, and schizotypal disorders; forestalling fragmentation when threatened by varying degrees of destabilized self-cohesion predominates in obsessive-compulsive, paranoid, and borderline disorders; and preserving a thriving self through idealization may be a particularly crucial imperative in the histrionic, dependent, and antisocial personality disorders if a compensatory structure can be acquired. The prototypic disorder of the self, narcissistic personality disorder, can represent any of these three mechanisms, and admixtures also are not uncommon.

My intention in delineating these self psychological mechanisms is to emphasize how each promotes striving to manage a particular psychological task for consolidating a vulnerable self. These functions are neither pure forms nor are they identical to selfobject functions, although they clearly make important use of selfobject functions in how they operate. For example, the first mechanism I delineate, sustaining self-esteem when the self has been left substantially diminished or unmirrored, does presume a central mirroring selfobject disturbance. Schizoid, schizotypal, or avoidant personality disorders represent adapting to prominent mirroring selfobject deficits by distancing or aversion to protect a vulnerable self. Two of the concepts I described earlier, optimal frustration versus optimal responsiveness and trailing edge versus forward edge strivings, help to explain how the devitalization and depletion of an unmirrored self may themselves result from diminished attunement to mirroring needs and legitimate strivings to see the self as valued or admirable to others.

In a similar way, attempting to maintain self-cohesion by forestalling fragmentation may explain how obsessive-compulsive, borderline, or paranoid patients contend with appreciable, persistent threats to holding themselves intact. These patients experience threats associated with a self that is weakened more than it is diminished. Thus, much of the effort of such patients' lives is devoted to preserving the integrity of a self that can easily fall apart. These personality disorder patients are no less vulnerable to the deficits that patients with predominantly mirroring disturbances show. However, what is distinctive about this group of personality disorders is their prominent concern with preventing the breakup or fragmentation of the self. Kohut's original description of the vertical split and Goldberg's further development of this concept in relation to disavowal indicate other ways to consider how fragmentation may be short-circuited, although the vertical split appears to be a particular mechanism of compartmentalizing split-off or walled-off sectors of self experience.

Finally, preserving a stable or anchored self through idealization or twinship may represent struggling with a destabilized self that is fragile but still holding steady because a compensatory structure has been formed. Compensatory structures are ways of repairing self-cohesion when mirroring deficits have become too pronounced or extensive to be overcome. Forming a compensatory structure is based on there being a strong enough alternative route to cement self-cohesion when the damage in the mirroring sector is beyond repair. Usually taking the form of idealization or twinship, compensatory structures are not fleeting or temporary adjustments. Rather, they represent stable psychologically sustaining functions that operate internally to compensate for the devitalizing deficits of a relatively permanent and chronic mirroring selfobject failure (Kohut, 1977; Silverstein, 2001; M. Tolpin, 1997). It represents the kind of adaptation that histrionic, dependent, and antisocial personality disorder patients either reveal in varying degrees or fail to develop at all. This kind of adaptation capitalizes on idealizations that only partially compensate for mirroring deficits.

Devitalization: The Unresponded-to Self

The personality disorders characterized as devitalized are here regarded as emerging from injuries in the mirroring sector of the self. The central problem of the unmirrored self is that of maintaining its vitality or buoyancy when responsiveness to needs for affirmation or admiration has been ignored or is insufficient. Thus, efforts to secure an engaged, enthusiastic response to mirroring selfobject needs become undermined. Although unresponded-to mirroring selfobject needs are inevitably involved in most disorders, distanced withdrawal or aversiveness are predominant characteristics of avoidant, schizoid, and schizotypal personality disorders. These are disorders in which detachment and aversion to others are ways to which patients with these disorders resort in an effort to protect against further injury to an already devitalized or depleted self.

Thus, avoidant distancing can represent the maladaptive self-protectiveness of fearing that mirroring longings will be misunderstood or rebuffed. As a result, these yearnings are driven underground. Schizoid distancing may be thought to represent a more isolating denial of mirroring needs, perhaps because the selfobject failures of earlier mirroring attempts had been so traumatically injurious that the safest course was shutting down needs for empathic responsiveness. This represents the apparent turning away from the world that is particularly characteristic of schizoid detachment.

A related form is the schizotypal personality disorder, representing generally a more compromised adaptation having much in common clinically with schizoid personality. Because it is also linked with the genetic/familial influences of the "soft" schizophrenia spectrum, schizotypal disorder is likely associated with an inborn deficit of responsivity to maternal care coupled with chronic exposure to the impaired empathic capacities of genetically vulnerable mothers. Such mothers are undoubtedly compromised in anticipating or ministering to the needs of young infants. Perhaps this inborn deficit in such vulnerable children and infants represents an aspect of temperament related to the compromised neurodevelopmental disturbance of schizophrenia and schizophrenia spectrum conditions (Murray, O'Callaghan, Castle, & Lewis, 1992).

Difficulties may become apparent when a child early on shows subtle manifestations of a genetic vulnerability to a schizophrenia spectrum condition. Thus, in one type of clinical presentation, mothers who have themselves been relatively spared appreciable deficit nevertheless may find themselves confronted with and unprepared to respond empathically to the abnormal responses they receive from their children to their normal-enough maternal ministrations. Other mothers may show impaired empathic responsiveness resulting from their own genetically predisposed maternal deficiencies. These mothers' genetically compromised offspring may be doubly handicapped, first, by their own abnormalities and, second, by vulnerable mothers who cannot manage to respond adequately to children who react with aversiveness to maternal signals. The primary deficit that results in either case adversely affects mirroring, because the disturbance affecting mother and/or child interrupts self-cohesion that is built up from a substrate of empathic responsiveness. Mothers of such children are unable to notice and respond accurately to their children's moment-to-moment fluctuations in self states.

The prolonged empathic failures all of these disorders produce create the kind of children who typically feel forgotten about, psychologically dropped or ignored, and in whom the need to feel admired or affirmed fails to develop normally. Such self states become the prominent characteristics of a mirroring disturbance. Infants or young children thus withdraw from chronically unresponsive mothers, and a pattern of distancing, isolation, and self-sufficiency is set in motion as the predominant response to empathically unattuned maternal responsiveness. The injuries to self-esteem in which children who are exposed to considerably impaired mirroring leave them unable to sustain vitality or buoyancy. Efforts to secure an engaged, enthusiastic response to mirroring selfobject needs, therefore, become undermined.

Detachment and emotional constriction thus operate like self-protective defenses, particularly if alternative pathways to solidify self-cohesion through idealization or twinship do not develop as robust compensatory structures. In this way, self-cohesion fails to become established, because neither optimal frustration nor optimal responsiveness take hold. All that occurs is the trailing edge of psychopathology, taking the forms of aversiveness (in avoidant personality disorder) or withdrawal and disconnection (in schizoid and schizotypal personality disorders) from needed selfobjects. The resulting devitalized self does not lead to any meaningful opportunity for securing normal forward edge developmental strivings.

Patients exposed to developmental failures characterized by markedly diminished optimal empathic responsiveness typically reveal histories of an absent or minimal sense of feeling that they were special or uniquely valued, admired, or treasured. When the exhibitionistic or grandiose precursors giving rise to a healthy sense of feeling proud and desired are thus submerged, forward edge developmental strivings are forsaken. These forward edge strivings contain the beginnings of healthy pride and a sense of specialness as well as the basis for enthusiasm about an individual's abilities and value in the eyes of others. When such forward edge strivings are abandoned or driven underground, they become nearly totally given over to defensive, self-protective withdrawal from or aversion to the very selfobject needs patients most require. This kind of pattern results in diminished self-esteem, depression, and chronic boredom or ambitionless life goals. It also represents the failure of a compensatory structure such as idealization, favoring instead defensive insulation when mirroring needs become sufficiently unresponded to and consequently undermined.

Self-Cohesion: Forestalling Fragmentation

Although paranoid, borderline, and obsessive-compulsive personality disorders also have empathic failures in the mirroring sector of the self, their vulnerability to compromised self-cohesion makes them concerned predominantly with holding together an intact psychological structure. These disorders represent different degrees of managing self-cohesion ruptures, thus much of such patients' lives centers around forestalling the breakup of the self, called *fragmentation.*

Fragmentation phenomena take the form of intense tension states that are not readily dispelled but are instead experienced as overwhelming. States of fragmentation such as these leave patients feeling adrift or unanchored, resembling phenomena that Kohut (1971) first called *disintegration products,* such as outbursts of helpless anger (narcissistic rage). Fragmentation results from experiences with caregivers who could not provide the selfobject experiences of mirroring or idealization to bolster the self when normal developmental yearnings had not yet solidified to form a reliable psychological structure. It predisposes children to feel an overriding sense of lacking something vital, which is the quality of fragmented self-cohesion Kohut (1977) and M. Tolpin (1978) described as disintegration or depletion anxiety. The vulnerability to fragmentation produces an enfeebled self when a child's sense of normal healthy assertion breaks apart into disintegration products such as narcissistic rage or internal states of depletion depression.

In paranoid personality disorder, unreliable and inconsistent early mirroring may set the stage for an existence in which dependable selfobject responsiveness cannot be counted on. Rather than their concerns in life centering around the devitalization resulting from chronic or pervasive unempathic mirroring, such as that characterizing schizoid or schizotypal disorders, paranoid patients experience the selfobject environment as unsafe and untrustworthy. Their compromised self-cohesion is destabilized in such way that paranoid hypervigilant alertness to malevolent threat and danger is a greater concern in these patients' lives than are self states characterized by the injuries associated with depletion and devitalization.

Hypervigilance and wary suspiciousness are ways paranoid patients develop to forestall the fragmentation of a self in constant threat of being undermined or attacked. The world has become untrustworthy and undependable; thus these patients have come to replace enthusiastic welcoming of maternal involvement and the mirroring it provides with fearfulness that a mother will not be able to provide a sense of protective safekeeping. Being exposed chronically to the threat of a mother's empathic unresponsiveness to a child's need for holding or sustaining, the vulnerability to potential fragmentation begins to develop. In some patients, the danger of fragmentation of the self becomes infused with projected aggression, thus leading to a sense of the self as being endangered further by a selfobject world that has now become malevolent and attacking.

Such patients' malevolent orientation to others and to the world in general represents a selfobject environment in which empathic failures provoke the threat of breaking apart of a self insufficiently fortified to sustain itself as cohesive or solidified. This in turn produces the disintegration products of a fragmentation-prone self, which may take the form of narcissistic rage. In Kohut's reformulation of this process, aggression is understood not as the source but as an end product of the coming apart of self-cohesion.

Kohut did not address borderline personality disorder with any particular interest, even during the 1970s when Kernberg's (1976) object relations approach to this disorder dominated psychodynamic explanations. Kohut generally considered borderline personality as a severe self disorder, and he remained skeptical about the suitability of such patients for psychoanalytic treatment. Other self psychologists (Brandchaft & Stolorow, 1988) were more optimistic concerning this matter. However, Kohut stressed that borderline patients' difficulty turning with confidence to others to provide calming or stabilizing selfobject functions would seriously compromise, if not preclude, analytic treatment. Kohut also noted how his explanation of paranoia applied to self disorders that Kernberg and others described as borderline personality organization. Disagreeing with Kernberg about the primacy of aggression in borderline disorders, Kohut regarded the narcissistic rage seen frequently in such patients as secondary to the failures of mirroring and idealizing selfobjects to help secure stable self-cohesion.

Thus, Kohut did not emphasize a distinction between paranoid and borderline personality disorders. It would not be unreasonable, however, to infer that borderline personality disorder represents a more pervasive self disorder than paranoid personality disorder, because struggling with brittle self-cohesion perturbs more areas of psychological functioning in borderline patients. Although the pervasive damage found in borderlines may include, at times, paranoid hypervigilance, it appears that a generally greater degree of circumscribed distrust remains the most clinically prominent presentation of paranoid personality disorder.

Concerning obsessive-compulsive personality disorder, Kohut deemphasized the drive theory formulation centered around struggling with hostile impulses and structural conflict. Without entirely discounting the significance of hostility, Kohut also thought hostility reexposed patients to the threat of disintegration of the self. Kohut, like Freud, regarded defensive operations as serving a protective function, but Kohut thought protecting self-cohesion overshadowed in importance Freud's emphasis on protection of the ego. Kohut thus distinguished between signal anxiety, when the self is relatively cohesive, and disintegration anxiety, when self-cohesion is more fragile or vulnerable. Accordingly, he emphasized the point that drive states resulted from rather than set in motion symptomatic conditions and character pathology. In Kohut's view, this meant that obsessive and compulsive personality features or symptoms (without regard apparently for distinguishing between Axis II and Axis I clinical manifestations) were best considered to be forms of precarious self-cohesion. In this respect, the potential fragmentation or disintegration anxiety would represent what Kohut (1977) considered the "anticipation of the breakup of the self" (p. 104) resulting from selfobject deficiency or failure.

Kohut's concept of the vertical split, and Goldberg's expansion of this idea, represents another mechanism based on disavowal to dissipate affect or tension states that cannot be readily internalized into the self. In this way, disavowed or unintegrated self state experiences also may become walled off from how the self is experienced. Thus, sectors of the experience of the self are in effect sequestered, and these split-off aspects of self experience may prevent greater fragmentation. The vertical split may be a state of partial integration of the self, in which the split forestalls fragmentation but also interferes with establishing stable or cohesive self-regulation.

Alternative Pathways to Preserving a Thriving Self

A third group of disorders of the self, comprising the dependent, histrionic, and antisocial personality disorders, represents varying degrees of success at repairing mirroring deficits. Some patients with these disorders managed to establish compensatory structures of idealization or twinship, which are selfobject functions that serve to strengthen a fragile self when mirroring has become too unreliable or unavailable. Dependent personality disorder patients succeed somewhat well in this regard. Antisocial personality disorder patients may sometimes appear to show aspects of idealization or twinship, but generally to a less well-developed extent after the surface manifestations of idealization give way to the personality structure that inevitably emerges. Histrionic personality disorder is understood in this context as showing a poorly developed capacity for establishing compensatory structures of idealization or twinship selfobject functions. As a group of personality disorders, however, rather than being fragmentation-prone, patients with these chronic disturbances of personality functioning and structure attempt to sustain self-cohesion by strengthening alternative pathways to revitalize the self when mirroring selfobject functions cannot. It is true enough that such patients become reexposed to earlier experiences of unempathic mirroring such as feeling unresponded to, disappointed, or psychologically dropped. However, dependent and antisocial personality disorder patients attempt to solidify self-cohesion not through securing mirroring selfobjects but instead by compensatory structures centered on idealization or twinship selfobject functions. Histrionic personality disorder, on the other hand, represents a substantial incapacity to acquire other pathways; such patients seem inflexibly unable to move in any other direction, continually seeking mirroring selfobject responsiveness. It is as if they know only one way to orient themselves to the interpersonal world. They persist in pushing against a brick wall, striving for mirroring well beyond a point where this seems even remotely within reach.

Patients with dependent personality disorder reveal histories of impoverished mirroring selfobject responsiveness; however, these patients have managed to turn to others, perhaps excessively, for idealizing or twinship selfobject functions to compensate for the inner depletion or diminished invigoration of the self. Dependent personality disorder patients seem to submerge or abandon searching for mirroring responsiveness. They turn away from unsatisfying mirroring selfobjects, channeling needs for admiration or affirmation of their special qualities into idealization or twinship. Looking to others in such ways may indicate a measure of having successfully developed compensatory structures to bolster diminished self-esteem through another sector of the self. In this route to repairing the self, it becomes possible to at least partially revive another avenue of self-object functions, typically idealization or twinship when the primary deficit is in the mirroring sector of the self. If the self can be revitalized in a more durable or permanent way, compensatory structures thus formed may continue to operate to provide needed self-object functions in a regularly sustaining or reliable manner.

Histrionic patients display an unmistakably overt need for mirroring responsiveness, although the intensity of this need may be no greater than that of other patients, despite their dramatic presentation or clamoring for attention. What is particularly notable, however, is their relatively limited capacity to acquire compensatory idealizing or twinship selfobject functions. Such patients may manage to secure mirroring responses from many sources, but whatever gratifications these afford are typically short-lived and shallow, rarely providing the deeper sense of affirming responsiveness these patients seem to crave. There is little evidence of a capacity for idealization or twinship, thus the distinctiveness of the histrionic disorder, from a self psychological point of view, may well lie in the underdevelopment of idealization or twinship as workable compensatory structures.

Histrionic patients can do little else but turn repeatedly to sources of insufficient responsiveness for what they never manage to acquire to bolster the self. Remaining diminished and vulnerable to subsequent injuries, selfobject experience stays at a level of depletion with little capacity to repair the central deficiency of the self. It is as if they continually press for what they are least likely to get, thus their unwavering insistence on seeking mirroring selfobjects leaves them unfulfilled and stuck in a position of struggling for something they never realize will not be durable enough to coalesce into a stable psychological structure.

I also include the antisocial personality disorder in this category of self disorders where the principal concern is that of preserving a thriving self through idealization or twinship, although I regard this form of psychopathology as different in some important respects from histrionic and dependent personality disorders. Its prominent links with familial alcoholism and/or affective disorder undoubtedly represent important etiological factors. Moreover, psychophysiologic hyporeactivity impairs emotional learning that may also be under genetic influence. These influences contribute to the disposition to criminality, failure to learn or profit from experience, impaired empathy, and the characteristic deficiency in interpersonal concern, in which antisocial behavior in its various forms is the final common pathway of a biologically based disturbance. Antisocial personality disorder represents, therefore, a complex disorder that probably cannot be accounted for by any psychoanalytic theory, including self psychology. Nevertheless, the delinquent, irresponsible, and impulsive behavior manifestations may still be understood as being influenced in part by the early parenting environment such patients experience.

Deficient mirroring leaves such patients prone to grandiosity, perhaps of an unbridled or unrestrained variety, and idealization or twinship have very likely failed to take hold as alternative pathways to stabilize self-cohesion. Kohut did note that hidden yearnings for idealization could be discerned, concealed behind grandiose bravado and its related manipulative or ruthless behavioral manifestations. He speculated that the identification with the grandiosity of others, if mobilized in treatment, potentially could become transformed into the idealization of values and ideals. However, antisocial personality disorder can be understood as a surface appearance concealing a still unstable capacity to sustain over time a vigorous self in any of its sectors, including mirroring and idealization. In contrast, impaired idealization capacity is more characteristic of histrionic personality disorder, and an overdeveloped propensity for idealization may typify dependent personality disorder.

Kohut commented on the problem of stabilizing idealization in adolescent delinquency and milder subclinical variants of antisocial acting-out behaviors. Because clinically antisocial patients rarely present themselves for analysis and are hardly ever treatable when they do come for analysis, self psychologists may have had insufficient exposure to this form of psychopathology, at least in its more severe or entrenched forms. Nevertheless, despite this limitation, antisocial personality disorder seems to be a condition in which mirroring and idealization selfobject needs are diminished in ways that interfere with developing genuine rather than superficial ambitions, ideals, and values.

CONCLUSIONS

Despite the differences between self psychology and the empirically driven diagnostic nosology of the personality disorders and the controversies within each of these fields, self psychological concepts may augment understanding personality development and personality disorders. A central assumption of self psychology is that self-cohesion and self-esteem are consolidated in normal development when legitimate needs for being admired or valued are responded to with enthusiasm and vitality. This is a proposition that highlights the continuity between normal development and psychopathology, representing Kohut's belief that a robust self requires that its normal, healthy strivings be strengthened by empathically attuned responsiveness. Whether conceptualized as emerging from optimal frustration or from optimal responsiveness or whether paying equal attention to forward edge strivings of normal development as to pathological features of self disorders, consolidating a cohesive or invigorated self is the primary goal of psychological development. The disorders of the self result from caregivers' chronic and prolonged empathic failures, repeatedly producing experiences that leave patients feeling rebuffed, ignored, or unrecognized. Feeling as though they were invisible, patients are thus injured in ways that can be understood as representing the manifestations of an unmirrored self.

Personality disorders can be regarded as the most typical clinical manifestations of disorders of the self, in part because they represent enduring maladaptive attempts to sustain self-cohesion throughout life. The devitalization of a depleted or injured self and the compensatory self-restorative efforts to repair such injuries consequently explain in a different way how the personality disorders of Axis II may be conceptualized. Personality disorders thus emerge when self-cohesion becomes destabilized by compromised mirroring, idealization, or twinship.

These are conditions, therefore, that represent different ways of attempting to repair the self once the injuries of early caregiving deficits led to or influenced their formation. These self-reparative paths appear to take three forms. In schizoid, schizotypal, and avoidant patients, varying degrees of distancing and isolation are seen as representing attempts to maintain or preserve self-esteem when devitalization or depletion are predominant self states. Among borderline, paranoid, and obsessive-compulsive personality disorder patients, sustaining self-cohesion when it is threatened by fragmentation leads to the kinds of adaptations these Axis II disorders represent. Kohut's and Goldberg's concepts of the vertical split seem to merit further investigation in an attempt to understand further how split-off aspects of self experience may be still another path to forestall fragmentation. In a third self-reparative pathway, seen most prominently in the histrionic, dependent, and antisocial personality disorders, preserving a vitalized self relies on making use of compensatory structures built up from idealization or twinship, the selfobject functions derived from Kohut's original concept of the bipolar self. The signature disorder of self psychology, narcissistic personality disorder, represents varying combinations or degrees of all of these mechanisms of consolidating the self. Thus, narcissistic personality disorder is here considered a condition precipitated by a broad range of disturbances.

Representing independent paths of inquiry about personality disturbances, self psychology and the neo-Kraepelinian tradition in descriptive psychopathology had little influence on each other. Self psychology has become a broadened approach encompassing several points of view (Goldberg, 1998), and even the shape and direction of the diagnostic nomenclature pertaining to the personality disorders have been challenged such that it is difficult to predict what Axis II will look like upon the introduction of *DSM-V.* It may also be useful to examine self states as potential dimensions for consideration in further revisions of Axis II.

REFERENCES

American Psychiatric Association. (1980). *Diagnostic and statistical manual of mental disorders* (3rd ed.). Washington, DC: Author.

Bacal, H. A. (1985). Optimal responsiveness and the therapeutic process. In A. Goldberg (Ed.), *Progress in self psychology* (Vol. 1, pp. 202–227). New York: Guilford Press.

Balint, M. (1969). Trauma and object relationship. *International Journal of Psycho-Analysis, 50,* 429–435.

Basch, M. F. (1988). *Understanding psychotherapy: The science behind the art.* New York: Basic Books.

Brandchaft, B., & Stolorow, R. D. (1988). The difficult patient: An intersubjective perspective. In N. Slavinska-Holy (Ed.), *Borderline and narcissistic patients in therapy* (pp. 243–266). Madison, CT: International Universities Press.

Clark, L. A. (1999). Dimensional approaches to personality disorder assessment and diagnosis. In C. R. Cloninger (Ed.), *Personality and psychopathology* (pp. 219–242). Washington, DC: American Psychiatric Press.

Galatzer-Levy, R. M., & Cohler, B. J. (1990). The developmental psychology of the self and the changing world view of psychoanalysis. In Chicago Institute for Psychoanalysis (Ed.), *The annual of psychoanalysis* (Vol. 18, pp. 1–43). Hillsdale, NJ: Analytic Press.

Goldberg, A. (1978). *The psychology of the self: A casebook.* New York: International Universities Press.

Goldberg, A. (1998). Self psychology since Kohut. *Psychoanalytic Quarterly, 67,* 240–255.

Goldberg, A. (1999). *Being of two minds: The vertical split in psychoanalysis and psychotherapy.* Hillsdale, NJ: Analytic Press.

Kernberg, O. F. (1976). *Borderline conditions and pathological narcissism.* New York: Aronson.

Klein, G. (1976). *Psychoanalytic theory.* New York: International Universities Press.

Kohut, H. (1966). Forms and transformations of narcissism. *Journal of the American Psychoanalytic Association, 14,* 243–272.

Kohut, H. (1971). *The analysis of the self.* New York: International Universities Press.

Kohut, H. (1977). *The restoration of the self.* New York: International Universities Press.

Kohut, H. (1984). *How does analysis cure?* (A. Goldberg & P. Stepansky, Eds.). Chicago: University of Chicago Press.

Kohut, H. (1996). *The Chicago Institute lectures* (P. Tolpin & M. Tolpin, Eds.). Hillsdale, NJ: Analytic Press.

Lichtenberg, J. D., Lachmann, F. M., & Fosshage, J. L. (1992). *Self and motivational systems: Toward a theory of psychoanalytic technique.* Hillsdale, NJ: Analytic Press.

Livesley, W. J. (1991). Classifying personality disorders: Ideal types, prototypes, or dimensions? *Journal of Personality Disorders, 5,* 52–59.

Miller, J. (1985). How Kohut actually worked. In A. Goldberg (Ed.), *Progress in self psychology* (Vol. 1, pp. 12–30). New York: Guilford Press.

Millon, T. (1990). Classification in psychopathology: Rationale, alternatives, and standards. *Journal of Abnormal Psychology, 100,* 245–261.

Millon, T. (2000). Reflections on the future of *DSM* Axis II. *Journal of Personality Disorders, 14,* 30–41.

Murray, R. M., O'Callaghan, E., Castle, D. J., & Lewis, S. W. (1992). A neurodevelopmental approach to the classification of schizophrenia. *Schizophrenia Bulletin, 18,* 319–332.

Ornstein, P. H. (1978). The evolution of Heinz Kohut's psychoanalytic psychology of the self. In P. H. Ornstein (Ed.), *The search for the self: Selected writings of Heinz Kohut: 1950–1978* (Vol. 1, pp. 1–106). New York: International Universities Press.

Shane, M., & Shane, E. (1993). Self psychology after Kohut: One theory or many? *Journal of the American Psychoanalytic Association, 41,* 777–797.

Shane, M., Shane, E., & Gales, M. (1997). *Intimate attachments: Toward a new self psychology.* New York: Guilford Press.

Siegel, A. M. (1996). *Heinz Kohut and the psychology of the self.* London: Routledge.

Silverstein, M. L. (1999). *Self psychology and diagnostic assessment: Identifying selfobject functions through psychological testing.* Mahwah, NJ: Erlbaum.

Silverstein, M. L. (2001). Clinical identification of compensatory structures on projective tests: A self psychological approach. *Journal of Personality Assessment, 76,* 516–535.

Stolorow, R. D., & Atwood, G. E. (1992). *Contexts of being: The intersubjective foundations of psychological life.* Hillsdale, NJ: Analytic Press.

Strozier, C. B. (2001). *Heinz Kohut: The making of a psychoanalyst.* New York: Farrar, Straus and Giroux.

Teicholz, J. G. (1999). *Kohut, Loewald, and the postmoderns.* Hillsdale, NJ: Analytic Press.

Terman, D. M. (1988). Optimum frustration: Structuralization and the therapeutic process. In A. Goldberg (Ed.), *Progress in self psychology* (Vol. 4, pp. 113–125). Hillsdale, NJ: Analytic Press.

Tolpin, M. (1978). Self-objects and oedipal objects: A crucial developmental distinction. *Psychoanalytic Study of the Child, 33,* 167–184.

Tolpin, M. (1997). Compensatory structures: Paths to the restoration of the self. In A. Goldberg (Ed.), *Progress in self psychology* (Vol. 13, pp. 3–19). Hillsdale, NJ: Analytic Press.

Tolpin, M. (2002). Doing psychoanalysis of normal development: Forward edge transferences. In A. Goldberg (Ed.), *Progress in self psychology* (Vol. 18, pp. 167–190). Hillsdale, NJ: Analytic Press.

Tolpin, P. (1988). Optimal affective engagement: The analyst's role in therapy. In A. Goldberg (Ed.), *Progress in self psychology* (Vol. 4, pp. 160–168). Hillsdale, NJ: Analytic Press.

Westen, D., & Shedler, J. (2000). A prototype matching approach to diagnosing personality disorders: Toward *DSM-V. Journal of Personality Disorders, 14,* 109–126.

Widiger, T. A. (1992). Categorical versus dimensional classification: Implications from and for research. *Journal of Personality Disorders, 6,* 287–300.

Wolf, E. S. (1988). *Treating the self: Elements of clinical self psychology.* New York: Guilford Press.

Wolf, E. S. (1993). Disruptions in the therapeutic relationship in psychoanalysis: A view from self psychology. *International Journal of Psychoanalysis, 74,* 675–687.

Chapter 11

POLITICAL PSYCHOLOGY
AND PERSONALITY

AUBREY IMMELMAN

The study of personality in politics has a long past, but a short history as a distinct specialty within an organized academic discipline. Niccolò Machiavelli's political treatise, *The Prince* (1505/1908), an early precursor of personality-in-politics inquiry, has modern-day echoes in Richard Christie and Florence Geis's *Studies in Machiavellianism* (1970). The formal establishment of political psychology as a scholarly discipline, marked by the founding of the International Society of Political Psychology in 1978, was anticipated by notable precursors in the twentieth century with a focus on personality—Graham Wallas's *Human Nature in Politics* (1908), Harold Lasswell's *Psychopathology and Politics* (1930) and *Power and Personality* (1948), Hans Eysenck's *The Psychology of Politics* (1954), and Fred Greenstein's *Personality and Politics* (1969).

I entered the fledgling field of political psychology in the late 1980s in search of methodologies for assessing personality in politics as a vehicle for predicting the behavior of political leaders. Having been professionally trained as a clinician, I was baffled to discover that extant approaches to the assessment of political personality bore little resemblance to the tools and techniques of my trade. Increasingly, I became convinced that, both conceptually and methodologically, much of the work ongoing in political personality was psychodiagnostically peripheral, if not irrelevant. That is not to say that these studies were entirely worthless; indeed, their political-psychological formulations were frequently insightful and compelling. However, it seemed to me that some of these assessment models, particularly those relying on content analysis, did not exactly measure what they purported to measure—personality—raising troubling questions of construct validity. What could possibly account for the perplexing schism between conventional clinical practice and political personality assessment? Why, for example, would anyone want to infer personality indirectly from content analysis of speeches and published interviews when a wealth of direct observations from multiple sources—commonly referred to as *collateral information* in the parlance of psychodiagnostics—already existed in the public record, ready to be mined, extracted, and processed? And why would anyone construct, de novo, political

---

Portions of this chapter draw from the paper "A Research Agenda for Political Personality and Leadership Studies: An Evolutionary Proposal" (submitted for publication), coauthored by the present author and Theodore Millon, which integrates aspects of their respective contributions (Immelman, 2003; Millon, 2003) to the *Handbook of Psychology*.

personality taxonomies—as though politicians comprised a subspecies of Homo sapiens—when classification systems already existed with reference to the general population?

First—on a conceptual level—it was evident that the study of political "personality" had traditionally been more *political* than psychological or personological. For example, Lasswell's (1930) early formulation essentially identified three *leadership* (as opposed to personality) types: the agitator, the administrator, and the theorist. Lasswell formulated this typology before the modern systematization of major personality typologies, whose clinical variants would later come to be catalogued in classification systems such as the American Psychiatric Association's *Diagnostic and Statistical Manual of Mental Disorders.* But the same orientation to political personality was reflected in James David Barber's (1965) categorization, 35 years later, of four legislative types: the lawmaker, the advertiser, the spectator, and the reluctant. Barber (1972/1992) later reformulated his earlier typology, constructing a 2 × 2 model of presidential character by crossing a positive-negative affective dimension with an active-passive temperamental dimension. Barber's typology was rather well received in the nascent political psychology community. James Davies, for example, in the first *Handbook of Political Psychology* (1973), observed that analysis and description of leadership style had become increasingly sophisticated, pointing to the work of Barber, which he described as "the boldest step yet in establishing a typology applicable to all American presidents" (p. 25). Barber's four presidential character patterns are essentially temperamental dispositions rather than fully developed personality types. Though clearly relevant to personality, temperament in isolation from other personological attributes provides an insufficient basis for constructing a comprehensive taxonomy of personality patterns.

Second—on a methodological level—a degree of consensus began to emerge in the 1970s, converging around the notion that the proper route to political personality assessment was content analysis of verbal material rather than psychodiagnostic analysis of biographical data. For example, Margaret Hermann's (1974, 1978, 1980, 1984) influential conceptual scheme employed content analysis to assess four kinds of personal characteristics hypothesized to affect the content and style of political decision making: motives, beliefs, decision style, and interpersonal style. Hermann successfully applied her framework in illuminating studies of numerous world leaders. Hermann's landmark work was informed by social psychology (especially leadership studies), cognitive psychology (e.g., belief systems), and personality psychology (e.g., motives); however, it was at best only peripherally related to parallel personological and psychodiagnostic formulations. The same can be said of David Winter's (e.g., 1980, 1987) insightful content-analytic studies of the achievement, power, and affiliation motives of political leaders, inspired by the work of Henry Murray and David McClelland. Contemporaneously, Stephen Walker (1977, 1983, 1990) developed content-analytic scoring systems for the operational code construct introduced by Alexander George (1969) and Ole Holsti (1970) to political psychology. The operational code refers to an individual's beliefs about the fundamental nature of politics, narrowly conceived as "embedded in personality" or more broadly as "originating from the cultural matrix of society" (Walker, Schafer, & Young, 2003, p. 216). The construct is founded on the assumption that these political beliefs are instrumental in shaping a person's worldview and, hence, his or her choice of political objectives.

As organized political psychology approached the quarter-century mark, George Marcus (2002), pointing to recent advances in neuroscience, issued a call for "entirely new theories, new concepts, and new data" capable of rehabilitating political psychology from the limited, though currently dominant, social-psychological and cognitive conceptual frameworks (pp. 100–102). "Conventional wisdom," he noted:

whether as to substantive conclusions, methodologies, or typologies, is, by definition, well entrenched. As such, the "state of the field" often becomes resistant to self-examination due to our comfort with prevailing accounts. . . . Still, however circumspect we must be in advancing our current understandings, we should not shy away from the obligation to do an even better job of self-examination, for how else can political psychology become that scientific enterprise? (p. 104)

For political personality inquiry to remain a thriving scholarly endeavor, it will need to account, at a minimum, for the patterning of personality variables "across the entire matrix of the person" (Millon & Davis, 2000, pp. 2, 65). Moreover, it will be incumbent on political personology to advance an integrative theory of personality and political leadership performance, eventually to abandon its well-worn "patchwork quilt of concepts and data domains" (Millon, 1990b, p. 11). In the course of his long and illustrious career, Theodore Millon has both built the foundations and pointed the way for political psychology to proceed.

From a Millonian perspective, conceptual systems for the study of political personality and leadership performance should constitute a comprehensive, generative, theoretically coherent framework consonant with established principles in the adjacent sciences (particularly the more mature natural sciences; see Millon, 2003, pp. 3–8), congenial with respect to accommodating a broad array of politically relevant personal characteristics, and capable of reliably predicting meaningful political outcomes. In this regard, political psychologist Stanley Renshon (1996b) has been critical of unitary trait theories (such as those relying primarily on isolated personality traits, motives, or cognitive variables) that have dominated the study of personality in politics, noting that "it is a long causal way from an individual trait of presidential personality to a specific performance outcome" and that unitary trait theories fail to contribute to the development of an integrated psychological theory of leadership performance. In Renshon's view, "more clinically based theories . . . might form the basis of a more comprehensive psychological model of presidential performance" (p. 11).

Greenstein (1987), while acknowledging substantial progress since the publication of his seminal *Personality and Politics* (1969) "in grounding complex psychological typologies empirically," pessimistically proclaimed that "complex typologies are not easily constructed and documented" (Greenstein, 1987, p. xiv). However, as Millon has shown, recent advances in evolutionary theory, buttressed by flourishing neuroscientific understanding of the biological substrates of affect, behavior, and cognition at the molecular level, afford a timely resolution of this dilemma. Fundamentally, it offers the promise of "carving nature at the joints" by suggesting a generative framework for a model of political personality and leadership founded on latent phylogenetic-evolutionary principles rather than on observable characteristics and surface features.

THE CURRENT STATUS OF PERSONALITY-IN-POLITICS INQUIRY

Ironically, despite major advances in behavioral neuroscience, evolutionary ecology, personality research, and clinical science in the past two decades (see Millon, 2003), personality-in-politics inquiry appears to have stagnated, with little cross-pollination from these adjacent disciplines. At this juncture, all of the dominant trends in political personality assessment date back to the establishment of organized political psychology in the 1970s, and earlier. In addition, most are also at variance with conventional psycho-diagnostic frameworks and procedures—a difficulty alluded to in the previous section.

Jerrold Post's authoritative edited volume *The Psychological Assessment of Political Leaders* (2003c) covers seven methodologies for assessing leader personalities: two "integrated" methods, namely, psychobiographic/psychodynamic political personality profiling (Post, 2003a) and the closely related psychoanalytically oriented assessment of character and performance (Renshon, 2003); three trait/motivational approaches, namely, verbal behavior analysis (Weintraub, 2003), motivational analysis (Winter, 2003a), and trait analysis of leadership style (Hermann, 2003); and two cognitive methodologies, namely, operational code analysis (Walker et al., 2003) and the assessment of integrative complexity (Suedfeld, Guttieri, & Tetlock, 2003).

Integrated Psychodynamic Approaches

Post's (2003a) psychobiographically rendered psychodynamic profiling approach draws from an eclectic array of psychodynamically oriented approaches, including the theoretical frameworks of Erik Erikson (1950/1963) and Otto Kernberg (1984); however, it also references Axis II of the *Diagnostic and Statistical Manual of Mental Disorders,* fourth edition (*DSM-IV;* American Psychiatric Association, 1994), focusing primarily on the narcissistic, obsessive-compulsive, and paranoid personality patterns. The origins of Post's approach can be traced back at least as far as psychoanalyst Walter Langer's (1943/1972) study of Adolf Hitler, commissioned by the Office of Strategic Services (OSS), forerunner of the Central Intelligence Agency (CIA). Post, a psychiatrist, founded and led the CIA's Center for the Analysis of Personality and Political Behavior for 21 years, during which he used his integrated psychodynamic approach to develop the "Personality Profiles in Support of the Camp David Summit" (Post, 1979), which President Jimmy Carter commended for its instrumental role in his successful mediation of the peace accord between Anwar Sadat of Egypt and Menachem Begin of Israel (see Post, 2003b).

Renshon's (2003) psychoanalytic assessment of character and performance is firmly anchored to Kohut's (1971, 1977) psychoanalytic self theory, though it is also indebted to Erik Erikson's (1980) ego psychology and the social and interpersonal formulations of Karen Horney (1937), Harry Stack Sullivan (1953), and others (see Renshon, 1996b).

Trait/Motivational Approaches

Weintraub's application of language-based personality analysis, which focuses on syntax and paralinguistic variables, dates back to the 1960s (e.g., Weintraub & Aronson, 1964). This approach to psychological assessment is more rooted in psycholinguistics than in personality theory and references Chomsky (1957), who noted that syntactic structures are independent of meaning, easily recognized, and amenable to scoring (Weintraub, 2003, pp. 137–138).

Winter's motivational analysis of political behavior, organized in terms of three dimensions of motivated behavior—achievement, power, and affiliation (Winter, 2003b, p. 121)—was inspired by the work of Murray (1938) and McClelland (e.g., 1961). Winter (2003a, pp. 174–175) offers a cogent rebuttal of several validity issues that have been raised (e.g., Renshon, 2001, p. 235) about the logic of scoring speeches and other verbal material for motive imagery.

Hermann's (2003) trait analysis of leadership style, arguably the most prominent approach to political personality at the inception of political psychology as an organized discipline, remains influential. Hermann's (1980) elaborate scheme accommodates four kinds of personal characteristics: *beliefs* and *motives,* which shape a leader's view of the world; and *decision style* and *interpersonal style,* which shape the leader's personal political style. Conceptually, Hermann's notion of *beliefs* is anchored to the philosophical beliefs component of the operational code construct (George, 1969). The *motives* component is indebted to the work of Lasswell (1948) and Winter (1973). Hermann's construal of *decision style* overlaps with the instrumental beliefs component of George's (1969) operational code construct and aspects of Barber's (1972/1992) formulation of presidential character, focusing particularly on conceptual complexity (see Dille & Young, 2000). Finally, Hermann's *interpersonal style* domain encompasses a number of politically relevant personality traits such as suspiciousness, Machiavellianism, and task- versus relationship orientation in leadership (see Hermann, 1980, pp. 8–10), which—though informative— are much too restrictive for assessing personality in politics across the entire matrix of the person.

Cognitive Approaches

Walker et al.'s (2003) operational code analysis (now available in computer-enhanced automated form; Dille & Young, 2000) is the latest development in a World War II-era construct, revived by Holsti (1970) and George (1969), who asserted that perception and beliefs are more easily inferred than personality, given "the kinds of data, observational opportunities, and methods generally available to political scientists" (p. 195).

Suedfeld et al.'s (2003) integrative complexity approach to political personality assessment originated in the 1970s (e.g., Suedfeld & Rank, 1976; Suedfeld & Tetlock, 1977) and in some respects relates as closely to cognitive psychology and social cognition as to personality psychology.

As I show in the balance of this chapter, personality-in-politics inquiry is currently poised on the threshold of a new personology, due in no small part to the work of Theodore Millon.

MILLON'S DIMENSIONAL POLARITIES AS AN INTEGRATIVE FRAMEWORK FOR POLITICAL PERSONOLOGY

Over the past decade and more, Millon (1990b, 1996, 2003) has endeavored to build a clinical science of personology founded on universal evolutionary and ecological foundations and informed by parallel developments in the more mature adjacent sciences, most notably evolutionary ecology and neuroscience. Contemporaneously—and deeply indebted to Millon's uncommon insights and formulations—I (Immelman, 1993a, 1998, 2002, 2003), have endeavored to transpose these contemporary insights from the source disciplines of personology and clinical science to the target discipline of political personality and leadership, drawing liberally from the Millonian wellspring of knowledge.

To provide a conceptual background and furnish a rudimentary, though generative, model of personality and personality-based leadership styles, I must briefly recapitulate Millon's three interacting domains or spheres of evolutionary and ecological principles (detailed more extensively elsewhere in this volume). The three evolutionary domains are labeled *existence, adaptation,* and *replication.* The first domain, *existence* (the pain-pleasure polarity), relates to the serendipitous transformation of random or less organized states into those possessing distinct structures of greater organization. The second, *adaptation* (the passive-active polarity), refers to homeostatic processes employed to sustain survival in open ecosystems. The third sphere, *replication* (the other-self polarity), pertains to reproductive styles that maximize the diversification and selection of ecologically effective attributes. It is remarkable that these dimensions appear to reflect essentially the same evolutionary adaptations that Osgood, Suci, and Tannenbaum (1957) uncovered half a century ago with respect to person perception and object appraisal, namely, the three semantic differential dimensions of *evaluation* (good-bad; i.e., pleasure-pain), *potency* (strong-weak; i.e., self-other), and *activity* (active-passive)—dimensions that were later found to possess a high degree of cross-cultural universality (Osgood, 1977; Osgood, May, & Miron, 1975). Table 11.1 presents my taxonomy of politically relevant personality patterns derived from these principles, congruent with Millon's dimensional polarities and Axis II of *DSM-IV* (American Psychiatric Association, 1994).

Aims of Existence: The Pain-Pleasure Polarity

The two-dimensional (i.e., two linearly independent vectors) pain-pleasure polarity (Millon, 1990b, pp. 51–64, 2003, pp. 9–14) is conceptualized in terms of, respectively, life preservation (pain avoidance) and life enhancement (pleasure seeking): "behaviors oriented to repel events experientially characterized as painful (negative reinforcers)" versus "acts that are attracted to what we experientially record as pleasurable events (positive reinforcers)" (Millon, 2003, p. 10).

Personality Implications of the Pain-Pleasure Polarity

Although the tendency to minimize pain and maximize pleasure is undoubtedly an inherent part of human nature, individual differences in ontogenetic development of adaptive strategies—the shaping of latent potentials into manifest styles of perceiving, thinking, feeling, acting, and relating to others, engendered by the interaction of biological endowment and sociocultural experience—are overtly reflected in distinctive personality styles. (See Table 11.1 for all personality patterns described in this section.) *Reticent* (e.g., avoidant; Millon, 1996, p. 260) personalities display an excessive, pain-avoidant preoccupation with threats to their psychic security—a hyperalertness to signs of potential rejection—that leads these persons pessimistically to disengage from everyday relationships and pleasures. At the other extreme of the pain-pleasure polarity, we find pleasure seeking, *dauntless* (e.g., antisocial; Millon, 1996, p. 444) personalities with a risk-taking attitude and little countervailing caution and prudence to avoid danger and threat. Somewhat less sensation seeking—though still distinctly pleasure seeking—but more risk averse (i.e., pain avoidant) are *outgoing* (e.g., histrionic; Millon, 1996, p. 366) personalities. Less likely than either dauntless or outgoing personalities to throw caution to the wind are *ambitious* (e.g., narcissistic; Millon, 1996, pp. 403–404) personalities, who are intermediate on both pain avoidance and pleasure seeking; for them, risk taking is more commonly a function of self-enhancing hubris.

Both *conscientious* (e.g., obsessive-compulsive; Millon, 1996, pp. 513) and *contentious* (e.g., negativistic; Millon, 1996, pp. 548–549) personalities are low on the pleasure-seeking valence, experiencing relatively little joy in existence; they are more driven by self-preservation, though only average on the pain-avoidant polarity, which features less prominently in their adaptive strategy. Introverted, *retiring* (e.g., schizoid; Millon, 1996, pp. 228–229) personalities are notable for weakness on both the pain-avoidant and pleasure-seeking polarities, thus displaying a distinctively impassive, anhedonic quality.

Some personality patterns evince marked polarity reversals (see Millon, 1996, pp. 496–498, 597–600). *Aggrieved* (e.g., self-defeating; Millon, 1996, p. 584) personalities, rather than avoid circumstances that may prove painful and self-endangering,

Table 11.1   Taxonomy of Politically Relevant Personality Patterns: Millon Inventory of Diagnostic Criteria

Scale 1A: Dominant pattern
     a. Asserting
     b. Controlling
     c. Aggressive (Sadistic; *DSM–III–R*, Appendix A)

Scale 1B: Dauntless pattern
     a. Venturesome
     b. Dissenting
     c. Aggrandizing (Antisocial; *DSM–IV*, 301.7)

Scale 2: Ambitious pattern
     a. Confident
     b. Self-serving
     c. Exploitative (Narcissistic; *DSM–IV*, 301.81)

Scale 3: Outgoing pattern
     a. Congenial
     b. Gregarious
     c. Impulsive (Histrionic; *DSM–IV*, 301.50)

Scale 4: Accommodating pattern
     a. Cooperative
     b. Agreeable
     c. Submissive (Dependent; *DSM–IV*, 301.6)

Scale 5A: Aggrieved pattern
     a. Unpresuming
     b. Self-denying
     c. Self-defeating (*DSM–III–R*, Appendix A)

Scale 5B: Contentious pattern
     a. Resolute
     b. Oppositional
     c. Negativistic (Passive-aggressive; *DSM–III–R*, 301.84)

Scale 6: Conscientious pattern
     a. Respectful
     b. Dutiful
     c. Compulsive (Obsessive-compulsive; *DSM–IV*, 301.4)

Scale 7: Reticent pattern
     a. Circumspect
     b. Inhibited
     c. Withdrawn (Avoidant; *DSM–IV*, 301.82)

Scale 8: Retiring pattern
     a. Reserved
     b. Aloof
     c. Solitary (Schizoid; *DSM–IV*, 301.20)

Scale 9: Distrusting pattern
     d. Suspicious
     e. Paranoid (*DSM–IV*, 301.0)

Scale 0: Erratic pattern
     d. Unstable
     e. Borderline (*DSM–IV*, 301.83)

Note: Equivalent *DSM* terminology and codes are specified in parentheses. *Sources:* From *Diagnostic and Statistical Manual of Mental Disorders,* third edition revised, by the American Psychiatric Association, 1987, Washington, DC: Author. Copyright © 1987 by the American Psychiatric Association; *Diagnostic and Statistical Manual of Mental Disorders,* fourth edition, by the American Psychiatric Association, 1994, Washington, DC: Author. Copyright © 1994 by the American Psychiatric Association; and *Millon Inventory of Diagnostic Criteria,* second edition, by A. Immelman and B. S. Steinberg, compilers, 1999. Copyright © 1999 by Aubrey Immelman.

masochistically tend to set in motion situations in which they will come to suffer; in transmuting pain to pleasure, and thus self-inflicting rather than avoiding pain, they display a polarity reversal. *Dominant* (e.g., aggressive; Millon, 1996, pp. 482–483) personalities exhibit a different kind of polarity reversal; they avoid pain by preemptively imposing it on others—a tendency most clearly discernable in the extreme, sadistic variant of the dominant personality pattern. For some types, such as *accommodating* (e.g., dependent; Millon, 1996, pp. 330–331) personalities—intermediate on both the life preservation and life enhancement valences—the role of pain avoidance versus pleasure seeking is of minimal consequence in personality adaptation.

The hypothesized valences of the personality patterns catalogued in Table 11.1, with reference to Millon's three universal evolutionary polarities, are summarized in Table 11.2.

Political Implications of the Pain-Pleasure Polarity

The pain-pleasure polarity can be invoked to hypothesize a partial genetic basis for individual differences in ideological (e.g., liberal-conservative) resonance. In evolutionary terms, liberalism can be construed as a primary concern with "improvement in the quality of life" and "behaviors that improve survival chances," and conservatism as an avoidance of "actions or environments that threaten to jeopardize survival" (Millon & Davis, 2000, p. 58). Thus construed, liberals are motivated to maximize survival by seeking pleasure (life enhancement, or positive reinforcement), whereas conservatives seek to maximize survival by avoiding pain (life preservation, or negative reinforcement). In the context of personality correlates of the pain-pleasure polarity (summarized in the preceding section), evolutionary theory would predict that reticent and possibly dominant, conscientious, and contentious personalities are overrepresented among conservatives, that dauntless and possibly outgoing personalities are overrepresented among liberals, and that retiring personalities are the least ideological. Furthermore, it would be expected

Table 11.2 Millon's Three Domains of Evolution and Associated Personality Valences

Personality Pattern	Aims of Existence: Pain/Pleasure Polarity		Modes of Adaptation: Passive/Active Polarity		Strategies of Replication: Other/Self Polarity	
	Pain	Pleasure	Passive	Active	Other	Self
Dominant	High[a]	Medium	Low	High	Low	Medium
Dauntless	Low	High[b]	Low	High	Low	High
Ambitious	Medium	Medium	High	Low	Low	High
Outgoing	Medium	High[b]	Low	High	High	Low
Accommodating	Medium	Medium	High	Low	High	Low
Aggrieved	High[a]	Low	High	Medium	Medium	Low
Contentious	Medium	Low	Medium	High	Low[c]	Medium
Conscientious	Medium	Low	High	Low	High[c]	Low
Reticent	High	Low	Low	High	Medium	Medium
Retiring	Low	Low	High	Low	Low	Medium

[a] Polarity reversal.
[b] Millon regards this valence as medium.
[c] Conflict between polarities.
Source: From *Disorders of Personality: DSM–IV and Beyond,* second edition, by T. Millon with R. D. Davis, 1996, New York: Wiley. Copyright © 1996 by John Wiley & Sons, Inc.

that ideological resonance in accommodating and outgoing personalities is less determined by the pain-pleasure valence than by their strong other-nurturing orientation on
the other-self polarity (to be discussed), which predicts liberal resonance.

In Hermann's (1987) conceptual scheme, a core belief component shaping a leader's
worldview is *nationalism,* which emphasizes "the importance of maintaining national
honor and dignity" (p. 167). In evolutionary terms, the motivating aim of nationalism is,
in part, a life-preserving (pain-avoidant) orientation, emphasizing traditionalism (though
it likely also references the *self* valence of the other-self polarity).

The pain-pleasure dimension also provides evolutionary underpinnings for Barber's
(1972/1992) fourfold (active/passive × positive/negative) categorization of presidential
character, in which positivity-negativity is described in terms of enjoyment (i.e., positive
affect) derived from political office. Positive leaders have a generally optimistic outlook
and derive pleasure from the duties of public office, whereas negative leadership has a
more pessimistic tone, being oriented toward pain aversion.

Finally, the pain-pleasure polarity suggests a possible evolutionary basis for the three
management models proposed by Richard Johnson (1974) and employed by Alexander
George and Eric Stern (1998) to classify the policy-making structures and advisory systems favored by recent U.S. presidents:

- *Formalistic* chief executives prefer "an orderly policymaking structure, . . . well-
  defined procedures, hierarchical lines of communication, and a structured staff system" (George & Stern, 1998, p. 203). In evolutionary terms, their motivating aim is
  to *preserve* life by minimizing pain. In addition to the high-pain/low-pleasure reticent personality, a formalistic management style is likely for contentious and conscientious personalities, both of which are average on pain avoidance, in conjunction
  with low pleasure seeking (see Table 11.2).
- *Competitive* chief executives encourage "more open and uninhibited expression of
  diverse opinions, analysis, and advice" and tolerate or encourage "organizational
  ambiguity, overlapping jurisdictions, and multiple channels of communication to
  and from the president" (George & Stern, 1998, p. 203). In evolutionary terms, their
  motivating aim is to *enhance* life by maximizing pleasure. In addition to the high-
  pleasure/low-pain dauntless personality noted earlier, a competitive management
  style is likely for the outgoing personality, which is relatively high on pleasure seeking, in conjunction with a moderate level of pain avoidance (see Table 11.2).
- *Collegial* chief executives attempt to benefit from the advantages of both the competitive and formalistic approaches while avoiding their pitfalls. Thus, they strive
  for "diversity and competition in the policymaking system," balanced by "encouraging cabinet officers and advisors to identify at least partly with the presidential perspective" and "encouraging collegial participation" (George & Stern, 1998, p. 203).
  In evolutionary terms, collegial executives are intermediate on both the pleasure-
  seeking and pain-avoidant dimensions of the pain-pleasure polarity and strongly
  other-oriented on the other-self polarity (to be discussed). The accommodating pattern is noted for being average on both of these dimensions, in conjunction with
  strong other-directedness, which is also the case for outgoing personalities (see
  Table 11.2).

The systematic import of a generative theory is implicit in the suggestion that Johnson's (1974) management model fails to account for at least two additional (hypothesized)

executive styles: *complex* types high on both the pleasure-seeking and pain-avoidant polarities (e.g., mixed personality types; personalities with polarity reversals, such as aggrieved or dominant types; personality types whose adaptive strategies are defined more by the passive-active and other-self polarities than by the pain-pleasure polarity) and *undifferentiated* types low on both the pleasure-seeking and pain-avoidant polarities (i.e., introverted, retiring personalities).

Modes of Adaptation: The Passive-Active Polarity

The passive-active polarity (Millon, 1990b, pp. 64–77, 2003, pp. 14–18) is conceptualized in terms of ecological modification (active) and ecological accommodation (passive); that is, "whether initiative is taken in altering and shaping life's events or whether behaviors are reactive to and accommodate those events" (Millon, 2003, p. 14).

Personality Implications of the Passive-Active Polarity

At the ecologically accommodating end of the passive-active continuum are personality adaptations that exhibit an excess of passivity. Several personality patterns demonstrate this passive style, although their passivity derives from and is expressed in appreciably different ways. (See Table 11.1 for all personality patterns explicated in this section.) *Accommodating* (e.g., dependent; Millon, 1996, pp. 330–331) personalities, because of deficits in confidence, initiative, and autonomous skills, display a tendency to wait passively for others to provide nurturance, offer protection, and assume leadership. Passivity among *conscientious* (e.g., obsessive-compulsive; Millon, 1996, p. 513) personalities stems from their aversion to acting independently because of intrapsychic resolutions they have made to quell troubling thoughts and emotions generated by their self-other ambivalence. *Ambitious* (e.g., narcissistic; Millon, 1996, pp. 403–404) personalities presumptuously assume that they are unconditionally entitled to recognition and admiration and that good things will come their way with little or no effort on their part. *Retiring* (e.g., schizoid; Millon, 1996, pp. 228–229) personalities are passive because of their relative incapacity to experience pleasure and pain. *Aggrieved* (e.g., self-defeating; Millon, 1996, p. 584) personalities passively submit to others' wishes; however, unlike the acquiescence of accommodating types, for aggrieved types submission to suffering represents a measure of personal control in that anguish is perceived as the most desirable alternative among the range of seemingly inescapable options available to them.

At the ecologically modifying end of the passive-active continuum are personality adaptations that exhibit an excess of activity. *Outgoing* (e.g., histrionic; Millon, 1996, p. 366) personalities epitomize this tendency. These individuals achieve their goals of maximizing protection, nurturance, and reproductive success by energetically engaging in a series of manipulative, seductive, and attention-getting maneuvers. Approval and affection must constantly be replenished and are sought from every interpersonal source. Susceptible to boredom and intolerant of inactivity, they evince a restless, stimulus-seeking quality as they keep stirring up things, fleetingly enthusiastic about one activity after another. Ecological modification in *dominant* (e.g., aggressive; Millon, 1996, pp. 482–483) personalities is seen in the proactive manner in which they subjugate others (i.e., impose pain). A similarly active polarity focus is seen in *reticent* (e.g., avoidant; Millon, 1996, p. 260) personalities. The distinctive feature is the reticent personality's anticipatory escape from pain, which presents as a hypervigilant awareness and active avoidance of situations that portend failure, rejection, denigration, or humiliation. Activity in *contentious* (e.g., negativistic; Millon, 1996, pp. 548–549) personalities is seen in a perpetual shifting in thoughts, feelings, and behaviors because of conflict and ambivalence between the self-enhancing and other-nurturing polarities (to be discussed).

Major personality theorists (e.g., Kernberg, 1992) have noted strong similarities between the antisocial and narcissistic personality types. The evolutionary model, with its polarity schema, clarifies the central distinctions between the *dauntless* (e.g., antisocial; Millon, 1996, p. 444) and *ambitious* (e.g., narcissistic; Millon, 1996, pp. 403–404) personality patterns. Both patterns are below average in pain avoidance and above average in pleasure seeking, combined with high self-enhancement and low other-nurturance. The key distinction between these personality patterns appears on the passive-active dimension: Ecologically accommodating, ambitious, narcissistic personalities, with their characteristic sense of entitlement, assume that good things will come to them with minimal effort on their part; ecologically modifying, sensation-seeking, dauntless personalities assume the contrary—that they are undervalued and that little will be achieved without considerable effort on their part (including Machiavellian cunning and deception, should such means serve their aggrandizing ends).

Political Implications of the Passive-Active Polarity

The passive-active dimension provides evolutionary underpinnings for Barber's (1972/1992) fourfold (active/passive × positive/negative) categorization of presidential character, in which activity-passivity is described in terms of energy invested in political office. In evolutionary terms, a passive orientation can be construed as "a tendency to accommodate to a given ecological niche and accept what the environment offers," whereas an active orientation can be construed as "a tendency to modify or intervene in the environment, thereby adapting it to oneself" (Millon & Davis, 2000, p. 59).

The passive-active dimension also provides an evolutionary basis for Lloyd Etheredge's (1978) fourfold (high/low dominance × introversion/extraversion) classification of personality-based differences in foreign-policy operating style and role orientation. High-dominance introverts (*bloc* or *excluding* leaders such as Woodrow Wilson and Herbert Hoover) *actively* seek to reshape the world, typically by means of containment policies or by tenaciously advancing a personal vision. High-dominance extraverts (*world* or *integrating* leaders such as Theodore Roosevelt, Franklin D. Roosevelt, John F. Kennedy, and Lyndon B. Johnson) *actively* seek to reshape the world through advocacy and pragmatic leadership on a wide range of foreign policy fronts. Low-dominance introverts (*maintainers* such as Calvin Coolidge) tend to persevere with the existing order, *passively* pursuing a foreign policy that amounts to "a holding action for the status quo" (p. 449). Low-dominance extraverts (*conciliators* such as William McKinley, William Taft, Warren Harding, Harry Truman, and Dwight D. Eisenhower), though revealing a preference for *passively* accommodating to existing arrangements, are more flexible and open to change, tending "to respond to circumstances with the sympathetic hope that accommodations can be negotiated" (p. 450).

Finally, in Hermann's (1980, 1987) conceptual scheme, a core belief contributing to a leader's worldview, along with nationalism, is *belief in one's own ability to control events.* In evolutionary terms, a more efficacy-oriented, internal locus of control implies an active-modifying motivating aim, in contrast to a more external locus of control, which suggests a passive-accommodating mode of adaptation. Hermann's (1987) expansionist, active-independent, and influential orientations are more actively oriented, whereas her mediator/integrator, opportunist, and developmental orientations are more passively oriented. The likely personality correlates of these leadership and policy orientations are easily inferred from the exposition of passive and active modes of adaptation in the preceding section.

Strategies of Replication: The Other-Self Polarity

Somewhat less profound but no less fundamental than the first two polarities, the two-dimensional other-self polarity (Millon, 1990b, pp. 77–98, 2003, pp. 18–24) is conceptualized in terms of, respectively, reproductive nurturance (other) and reproductive propagation (self)—a nurturing tendency to value the needs of others, versus an individuating self-orientation that seeks to realize personal potentials before attending to the needs of others (Millon, 1994, p. 6, 2003, pp. 18–19). Evolutionary biologists (e.g., Cole, 1954; Wallen & Schneider, 2000) have recorded marked differences among species in both the cycle and pattern of their reproductive behaviors. Within most animal species, an important distinction may be drawn between male and female adaptive strategies (Daly & Wilson, 1983; Mealey, 2000; Trivers, 1972); it is this latter differentiation that undergirds what has been termed the self- versus other-oriented polarity.

Males lean toward being self-oriented, because their competitive advantages maximize the replication of their genes. Conversely, females lean toward being other-oriented, because their competence in nurturing and protecting their limited progeny maximizes the replication of their genes. It bears note, however, that these conceptually derived self-other extremes do not evince themselves in sharp and distinct gender differences (Hyde, 1996; Mealey, 2000). Such proclivities are matters of degree; consequently, most individuals exhibit intermediate characteristics on this, as well as on the other polarity sets.

Personality Implications of the Other-Self Polarity

In the other-nurturing quadrant of the two-dimensional other-self polarity are personality adaptations that exhibit a distinctively interdependent orientation and an external locus of control. Several personality patterns demonstrate this other-oriented style of self-denial, where self-actualizing autonomy is relinquished in favor of gaining the approbation of others. (See Table 11.1 for all personality patterns described in this section.) *Accommodating* (e.g., dependent; Millon, 1996, pp. 330–331) and *outgoing* (e.g., histrionic; Millon, 1996, p. 366) personalities have learned that feelings associated with pleasure or the avoidance of pain—that is, their personal sense of safety and security—are provided almost exclusively as a function of their relationships with others. Behaviorally, these persons display a strong need for external support (accommodating personalities) or attention (outgoing personalities); when deprived of affection, nurturance, or approval, they experience marked discomfort, if not sadness and anxiety. A centering on the wishes of others and denial of self is also seen in *conscientious* (e.g., obsessive-compulsive; Millon, 1996, p. 513) personalities. These persons display a picture of social compliance and interpersonal respect; however, beneath their veneer of conformity, they experience an intense desire to assert themselves. Managing this pervasive ambivalence requires rigid psychological controls, which leads to physical tensions that may find periodic relief in abrupt emotional outbursts directed at subordinates. *Aggrieved* (e.g., self-defeating; Millon, 1996, p. 584) personalities, like conscientious and accommodating types, are weak on the self-enhancement polarity; the key distinction is that aggrieved types are not nearly as strong on other-nurturing, ranking only average on this polarity.

In the self-enhancing quadrant of the two-dimensional other-self polarity are personality adaptations that exhibit a distinctively individualistic orientation and an internal locus of control. In *ambitious* (e.g., narcissistic; Millon, 1996, pp. 403–404) personalities, psychogenesis reflects the acquisition of a self-image of exceptional worth. Providing self-rewards is highly gratifying for individuals who value themselves or possess either a real or inflated sense of self-worth. Beneath their manifest confidence—and, in more extreme cases, arrogance and an exploitive egocentricity—these individuals believe they already possess what is most important—themselves; thus, they experience primary pleasure simply by passively being or attending to selfish needs, without much thought or even conscious intent, and benignly exploiting others to their own advantage. Although validation of others is both welcome and encouraged, their admirable self-concept requires little confirmation through social approval or—in more extreme cases—genuine accomplishment. *Dauntless* (e.g., antisocial; Millon, 1996, p. 444) personalities are skeptical about the motives of others, whom they judge to be unreliable, if not disloyal. To counter indifference or the expectation of pain from others, they strive for autonomy; in more extreme cases, they may actively engage in duplicitous behaviors and shamelessly exploit others for self-gain— which, from their strongly self-enhancing perspective, is simply just revenge for perceived past injustices. *Dominant* (e.g., aggressive; Millon, 1996, pp. 482–483) personalities are similar to ambitious and dauntless types in their weakness on the other-nurturing polarity; the key distinction in replication strategy is that dominant types are considerably less self-enhancing than ambitious and dauntless types, ranking only average on this polarity. Both *contentious* (e.g., negativistic; Millon, 1996, pp. 548–549) and *retiring* (e.g., schizoid; Millon, 1996, pp. 228–229) personalities are weak on the other-nurturing polarity; however, though self-involved, they are not self-enhancing, ranking only average on this polarity. Finally, for some types, such as *reticent* (e.g., avoidant; Millon, 1996, p. 260) personalities— intermediate on both the self-enhancing and other-nurturing polarities—the role of self versus other is of minimal consequence for personality adaptation.

Political Implications of the Other-Self Polarity

The other-self polarity provides one of the most clear-cut illustrations of the heuristic value of evolutionary theory in politics. Although humans can be both other-encouraging and self-enhancing, most persons will likely tend toward one side or the other. A balance that coordinates the two provides a satisfactory answer to the question of whether individuals are devoted to the support and welfare of others (in American politics, the underlying philosophy of the predominantly liberal Democratic Party) or fashion their lives in accord with their own needs and desires (in American politics, the underlying philosophy of the predominantly conservative Republican Party). More specifically, evolutionary theory predicts that in terms of party-political preference, women, in addition to accommodating and outgoing personalities generally, should disproportionately favor more liberal policy positions and the Democratic Party; in contrast, men, in addition to dauntless and ambitious personalities, should favor more conservative policies and the Republican Party.

With reference to political leadership, three social motives (which in Hermann's conceptual scheme are postulated to contribute to a leader's worldview) are considered to play a key role in leader performance: need for power, need for achievement, and need for affiliation (Winter, 1987, 1998). In evolutionary terms, the *need for power,* involving "the desire to control, influence, or have an impact on other persons or groups" (Hermann, 1987, p. 167), suggests a self-enhancing replication strategy, as does the *need for achievement,* which involves "a concern for excellence" and personal accomplishment (Winter, 1998, p. 369). Conversely, the *need for affiliation,* reflecting "concern for establishing, maintaining, or restoring warm and friendly relations with other persons or groups" (Hermann, 1987, p. 167), suggests an other-nurturing replication strategy. Hermann's expansionist, active-independent, and influential leadership orientations are more self-oriented, whereas her mediator/integrator, opportunist, and developmental orientations are more other-oriented.

Hermann (1980) also posits two key elements of interpersonal style that, in conjunction with decision style, shape a leader's personal political style: distrust of others and task orientation (see Hermann, 1987, pp. 163, 167). In evolutionary terms, the *trust-distrust* and *task-relationship* dimensions of leadership are easily reconceptualized as surface manifestations of the other-self polarity.

The two key elements of decision style in Hermann's (1980) framework are *conceptual complexity* and *self-confidence,* which she construes (following Ziller, Stone, Jackson, & Terbovic, 1977) as jointly determinative of "how ideological or pragmatic a political leader will be" (Hermann, 1987, p. 164). Stone and Baril (1979), elaborating on the findings of Ziller et al., used self-other orientation as a conceptual basis for postulating two distinctive political prototypes, each having a different motivational base. The *pragmatist*—akin to Barber's (1965) active-negative Advertiser—is motivated by power seeking to compensate for low self-esteem (as anticipated by Lasswell, 1948), being driven by self-enhancement and self-promotion. The second political personality type, the *ideologue*—akin to Barber's active-positive Lawmaker—is more other-oriented, apparently having a sincere interest in good legislation (defined as either pursuing ideological goals or as serving a constituency). Stone and Baril's construal of self- and other-oriented political personality types, in concert with Barber's (1965, 1972/1992) scheme, lends empirical and theoretical support for the utility of the other-self polarity in an overarching theory of political personality and performance.

The likely personality correlates of these leadership and policy orientations are readily inferred from the exposition of other-nurturing and self-enhancing strategies of replication in the preceding section.

OBSTACLES TO ADVANCING A MILLONIAN PERSPECTIVE IN POLITICAL PSYCHOLOGY

The advancement of a Millonian perspective in political psychology is beset by two general problems: broad objections to the relevance of studying personality in politics and specific objections to Millon's model of personality (including the empirical validity of Millon's evolutionary model and its suitability for personality inquiry in political psychology).

Scholarly Skepticism about the Relevance of Personality in Politics

Despite the conviction of personality-in-politics practitioners in the worth of their endeavor, the study of personality in politics is not without controversy (see Lyons, 1997, pp. 792–793, for a concise review of "controversies over the presidential personality approach"). Greenstein (1969, pp. 33–62) offered an incisive critique of two erroneous and three partially correct objections to the study of personality in politics, lamenting that the study of personality in politics was *not* a thriving scholarly endeavor, principally because "scholars who study politics do not feel equipped to analyze personality in ways that meet their intellectual standards . . . [thus rendering it primarily] the preserve of journalists" (p. 2). Four of the common objections noted by Greenstein (1969, p. 34) have been particularly prevalent among critics of personological analysis in politics:

1. Personality characteristics tend to be randomly distributed in institutional roles. Personality, therefore, "cancels out" and can be ignored in political analysis.
2. Personality characteristics are less important than social characteristics in influencing behavior.

3. Personality is irrelevant, because individual actors are severely limited in the impact they can have on events.

4. Personality is not an important determinant of behavior, because individuals with varying personal characteristics tend to behave similarly when placed in common situations.

Greenstein shows convincingly that the first two objections are erroneous on, respectively, empirical and conceptual grounds. The third objection is partially correct, but should be rephrased in terms of the circumstances under which the actions of individual actors are likely to exert a greater or lesser influence on the course of events (Greenstein, 1969, pp. 40–41). Greenstein offers three propositions in this regard:

- "The likelihood of personal impact increases to the degree that the environment admits of restructuring." In unstable systems, "modest interventions can produce disproportionately large results" (p. 42). Here, Greenstein (p. 44) cites the instrumental role Lenin played in bringing about the Russian Revolution. Furthermore, political systems vary in the degree of constraint they impose on the leader. In this regard, Greenstein (p. 45) points to Robert Tucker's (1965) observation that the political machinery of totalitarian systems serves as "a conduit of the dictatorial psychology." A fitting contemporary example is Iraq's former totalitarian Baathist regime and its malignantly narcissistic (Post, 1991) leader Saddam Hussein.

- "The likelihood of personal impact varies with the actor's location in the environment" (Greenstein, 1969, p. 44). In short, the higher the level of leadership, the greater the impact of personality. Thus, personality analysis is more relevant to the assessment of high-level leadership than it is with reference to regional or local politics.

- "The likelihood of personal impact varies with the personal strengths and weaknesses of the actor" (Greenstein, 1969, p. 45). For example, a highly skilled, talented leader can actively orchestrate a favorable position and a manipulable environment, thus altering the course of political events. Hitler is an exemplar of this type of leader-situation interaction.

The fourth objection, which concerns personal control versus situational power, is partially correct in that the power of the situation sometimes subdues individual differences. Nonetheless, as Greenstein (1992) has noted, "environments are always mediated by the individuals on whom they act; environments cannot shape behavior directly" (p. 109). In what may well be the most concise statement of the case for studying personality in politics, Greenstein concludes, "Political institutions and processes operate through human agency. It would be remarkable if they were *not* influenced by the properties that distinguish one individual from another" (p. 124).

In summary, skepticism concerning the pertinence of personality in politics no longer poses a significant obstacle to scholarly inquiry. More serious, however, are objections to Millon's model—both with reference to psychological assessment generally and specifically with regard to personality inquiry in political psychology.

Skepticism about the Logic and Empirical Validity of Millon's Dimensional Polarities

My purpose here is not to review critiques of Millon's theoretical model and applied measures. Rather, I address a few common oversimplifications, if not misconstruals, of Millon's model that complicate the evaluation of conceptual objections and empirical findings that have been presented to call into question the logic and empirical validity of Millon's evolutionary model and measures. Because of space constraints, I focus on two related critiques, by Widiger (1999) and Piersma, Ohnishi, Lee, and Metcalfe (2002), of Millon's dimensional polarities.

Widiger (1999), while acknowledging that the pain-pleasure, passive-active, and other-self polarities can indeed be employed to generate the basic personality patterns posited by Millon, asserts that it is not evident that these patterns are, in fact, logical derivations from the three polarities (p. 367); instead, they are "an imbalanced or uneven mixture of the three polarities" (p. 366). More important, he notes the "conceptual ambiguities" of representing the pain-pleasure and other-self polarities on single dimensions (p. 373). However, it is clear that this is not Millon's intent. Millon (1990b) is unambiguous in noting that "the pleasure-pain distinction . . . can ultimately be placed on *two* contrasting dimensions" [my emphasis] (p. 51). Moreover, as I have suggested elsewhere (Immelman, 2003, p. 617), the pain and pleasure dimensions should be conceptualized in multidimensional space as *two linearly independent vectors*. That is, they are bipolar but not orthogonal, which further implies that these dimensions cannot be simply represented in a 2 × 2 contingency table or located on a circumplex model. This accounts, in part, for the difficulty with simple tabular representation of Millon's patterns, as aptly pointed out in Widiger's critique. On a related note, Millon's two-dimensional pain-pleasure polarity is consistent with Jeffrey Gray's (e.g., 1991) biologically based reinforcement sensitivity theory, which posits two independent neuropsychological systems: a behavioral activation system (BAS) responsive to cues for reward and a behavioral inhibition system (BIS) sensitive to cues for punishment. The BAS mediates approach behavior and is equivalent to Eysenck's (e.g., 1990) and the five-factor model's (e.g., McCrae & Costa, 1999) introversion-extraversion dimension. The BIS mediates avoidance behavior and is equivalent to Eysenck's and the five-factor model's neuroticism-emotional stability dimension (see Pickering, Corr, & Gray, 1999).

Millon's other-self polarity also is two-dimensional and should be conceptualized as linearly independent vectors instead of a single bipolar dimension. This construal is implicit in Millon's own writing:

> The converse of other-nurturance is not self-propagation, but rather the lack of other-nurturance. . . . Although the dimension of self-other is arranged to highlight its polar extremes, it should be evident that many if not most behaviors are employed to achieve the goals of both self- and kin reproduction. Both ends are often simultaneously achieved; at other times one may predominate. (Millon, 2003, p. 22)

Piersma et al. (2002) conducted an investigation of Widiger's (1999) concerns about the logic of Millon's evolutionary model and the empirical validity of his dimensional polarities, as operationalized in the Millon Clinical Multiaxial Inventory (MCMI-III; Millon, Davis, & Millon, 1996). Like Widiger's original critique, the work of Piersma and his associates makes a worthy contribution to the advancement of clinical science, which cannot proceed solely on the strength of theoretical systematization and systematic import (see Immelman, 2003, pp. 604–605; Millon, 2003, pp. 4–5). In the simplest of terms, scientific progress requires hypothesis testing. Table 11.3 presents Millon's three polarities, the hypothesized polarity valences of the 10 basic personality patterns assessed by my inventory for assessing personality in politics (Immelman & Steinberg, 1999), and empirically established correlations among Millon Index of Personality Styles (MIPS; Millon, 1994) Motivating Aims and Interpersonal-Behaviors (reported in Millon, 1994, pp. 69–70) or MCMI-III (reported in Piersma et al., 2002, p. 155) scales. Piersma and his associates

Table 11.3   Three Domains of Evolution, Hypothesized Polarity Valences of MIDC Personality Patterns, and Correlations among MIPS Motivating Aims and MIPS Interpersonal-Behaviors or MCMI–III Scales

Personality Pattern	Aims of Existence: Pain/Pleasure Polarity		Modes of Adaptation: Passive/Active Polarity		Strategies of Replication: Other/Self Polarity	
	Pleasure	Pain	Active	Passive	Self	Other
Dominant	Medium	High[a]	High	Low	Medium	Low
Controlling (FIS)	.25	−.14	.63	−.46	.72	−.32
Controlling (NOI)	.12	.09	.39	−.14	.40	−.09
Sadistic	−.27	.39[d]	.08	.32	.36[d]	−.05
Dauntless	High[b]	Low	High	Low	High	Low
Dissenting (FIS)	−.48	.58	−.08	.35	.58	−.26
Dissenting (NOI)	−.07	.29	.11	.17	.37	−.13
Antisocial	−.12	.32	.04	.26	.32	.10
Ambitious	Medium	Medium	Low	High	High	Low
Asserting (FIS)	.63	−.51	.79	−.77	.38	−.04
Asserting (NOI)	.42	−.20	.56	−.36	.24	.08
Narcissistic	.60[d]	−.39	.40[d]	−.25	.30	.20
Outgoing	High[b]	Medium	High	Low	Low	High
Outgoing (FIS)	.57	−.43	.78	−.66	.26	.17
Outgoing (NOI)	.34	−.08	.38	−.21	.09	.25
Histrionic	.62[d]	−.45[d]	.32	−.39[d]	−.25	.64[d]
Accommodating	Medium	Medium	Low	High	Low	High
Agreeing (FIS)	−.14	.11	−.46	.43	−.72	.68
Agreeing (NOI)	−.09	.25	−.17	.44	−.10	.30
Dependent	−.53[d]	.59[d]	−.31	.56[d]	−.22	.24
Aggrieved	Low	High[a]	Medium	High	Low	Medium
Yielding (FIS)	−.70	.74	−.54	.68	−.15	.23
Yielding (NOI)	−.29	.62	−.10	.37	.18	.13
Masochistic	−.59[d]	.63[d]	−.19	.47[d]	.19	−.03
Contentious	Low	Medium	High	Medium	Medium	Low[c]
Complaining (FIS)	−.61	.72	−.10	.38	.45	−.19
Complaining (NOI)	−.29	.67	−.04	.44	.25	.12
Negativistic	−.53[d]	.73[d]	−.10	.49[d]	.22	.00
Conscientious	Low	Medium	Low	High	Low	High[c]
Conforming (FIS)	.31	−.23	.49	−.30	.01	.37
Conforming (NOI)	.14	−.02	.21	.07	−.01	.32
Compulsive	.52[d]	−.60[d]	.26	−.44[d]	−.15	.01
Reticent	Low	High	High	Low	Medium	Medium
Hesitating (FIS)	−.81	.80	−.50	.64	.01	−.00
Hesitating (NOI)	−.32	.54	−.19	.47	.13	.03
Avoidant	−.66[d]	.70[d]	−.31	.49[d]	−.00	−.23
Retiring	Low	Low	Low	High	Medium	Low
Retiring (FIS)	−.56	.56	−.36	.48	.28	−.26
Retiring (NOI)	−.18	.41	−.02	.33	.34	−.06
Schizoid	−.49[d]	.51[d]	−.12	.35	.33	−.46[d]

Table 11.3   *(Continued)*

Paranoid	−.37[d]	.50[d]	−.04	.32	.34	−.11
Borderline	−.60[d]	.73[d]	−.14	.49[d]	.14	.16

Notes: FIS = MIPS full-item set; NOI = MIPS nonoverlapping (prototypal) items. Millon (1994), $N = 1,000$; Piersma et al. (2002), $N = 50$. The first two rows of correlation data under each personality pattern are from the *Millon Index of Personality Styles Manual* (pp. 69–70), by T. Millon, 1994, San Antonio, TX: Psychological Corporation. Copyright © 1994 by Dicandrien, Inc. Adapted with permission of the author. The third row of correlation data under each personality pattern are from "An Empirical Evaluation of Millon's Dimensional Polarities," by H. L. Piersma, H. Ohnishi, D. J. Lee, and W. E. Metcalfe, 2002, *Journal of Psychopathology and Behavioral Assessment, 24,* p. 155. Copyright © 2002 by Plenum Publishing Corporation. Adapted with permission of the authors.

[a] Polarity reversal.
[b] Millon characterizes antisocial and histrionic personalities as average (medium) rather than high on the pleasure-seeking polarity.
[c] Conflict between polarities.
[d] $p < .01$ (Significance data not available for Millon, 1994).

suggest that if a particular personality pattern is hypothesized to be low on a particular polarity dimension, we would expect a significant negative correlation; if a pattern is hypothesized to be high on a polarity, we would expect a significant positive correlation; and if a pattern is hypothesized to be medium on a polarity, we would expect a nonsignificant correlation. Piersma et al. found the majority of correlations to be inconsistent with Millon's hypothesized polarity valences. In their study, they offer several caveats and conditional hedges, to which I might add that their conclusions rest on the assumption that Millon's evolutionary polarities are adequately operationalized in the MIPS Motivating Aims scale.

Millon (1999) offers a cogent and eloquent rebuttal of Widiger's (1999) concerns—and, by extension, the findings of Piersma et al. (2002)—focusing on the inherent absurdity of harnessing factorial techniques to authenticate "the predominant polythetic structure and overlapping relations that exist among clinical conditions" (p. 448). Simply stated, the personality patterns informed by Millon's evolutionary theory are not linear, orthogonal constructs. However, there is at least one anomaly in Millon's evolutionary derivations, namely, that *no* personality pattern is hypothesized to be high on life enhancement, the pleasure-seeking polarity (see Table 11.2). Based on an emerging consensus that Gray's (e.g., 1991) BAS is associated with extraversion and sensation seeking, I consider outgoing (e.g., histrionic) and dauntless (e.g., antisocial) personality patterns to be high on pleasure seeking—both objectively and relative to other personality patterns (see Table 11.3).

Skepticism about the Adequacy of the Millonian Approach for Assessing Personality in Politics

Scrutiny of peer and editorial reviews of Millon-based political psychology manuscripts submitted for publication offer interesting insights into common reservations concerning the adequacy of Millon's model for personality inquiry in political psychology and the validity and reliability of its measures.

Validity and Reliability Concerns

As a limitation or deficiency of political-psychological studies employing the conceptual framework and methodology that I adapted from Millon's work, reviewers have pointed to the difficulty of judging the reliability and validity of the Millon Inventory of Diagnostic Criteria (MIDC; Immelman & Steinberg, 1999), given that no reliability or validity coefficients are reported. The issue of reliability, in particular, occupies major status in the literature on indirect personality assessment in politics—to the extent, in my opinion, that it has overshadowed equally important validity concerns. The reason for this can probably be traced to the dominant status of content-analytic procedures in political psychology, which rely on the coding of verbal material by independent judges or by a single judge with demonstrable interjudge reliability. Winter, in his chapter on "Personality and Political Behavior" in the *Oxford Handbook of Political Psychology* (2003b), wrote:

> The most widely used at-a-distance technique is probably content analysis of written text or verbatim transcripts of spoken words (e.g., speeches or interviews) from individual leaders . . . taken as reflecting the psychological characteristics or personalities. . . . Typically, content analysis measures are carefully designed with examples and training procedures to enable previously inexperienced scorers to apply them with high reliability (percent agreement and correlation ≥ .85). (p. 114)

The critical issue of validity is relegated to a footnote:

> Of course most documents and speeches that bear the name of a major political leader are actually written by one or more speechwriters, and even "spontaneous" press conference responses to questions and "informal" comments may be highly scripted. Thus, one may ask whether a content analysis of such materials produces personality estimates of the leader or of the speechwriters. Suedfeld (1994) and Winter (1995) discuss this issue, and conclude that because leaders select speechwriters and review their drafts, and speechwriters "know" their clients, personality "scores" based on content analysis (at least of major speeches) can be taken as a valid indicator of the personality and psychological state of the leader—a claim that has generally been validated by research with such scores. (Winter, 2003b, footnote 1, pp. 114, 134)

I readily admit to immense admiration for the landmark work of Peter Suedfeld, David Winter, and other eminent scholars in political psychology who rely on content analysis, such as Stephen Walker and Margaret Hermann—all of whom count among the great pioneers of personality-in-politics inquiry. However, it should be recognized that the case for the validity of content analysis constitutes, in part, an article of faith. For a brief review of validity problems concerning content-analytic assessment methodologies in political psychology, along with references to recent overviews of the current state of content-analytic at-a-distance assessment, its major conceptual and methodological issues, and future research directions, see Immelman (2003, p. 613).

Preliminary reliability and validity data are now beginning to accrue for Millonian studies conducted in the first decade since the development, in 1993, of the original version of the MIDC. As reported in the MIDC manual:

> There is strong empirical evidence for the validity and reliability of commercial personality instruments derived from Millon's theory (see, for example, Millon, 1994; Millon, Davis, & Millon, 1996). As for the present adaptation of Millon's theory, the concordance between MIDC-based findings in the present author's work and the findings of other investigators (e.g., similar findings by Immelman, 1998, and Renshon, 1996a, with reference to U.S. President Bill Clinton) using alternative conceptual frameworks and methods, provides convincing evidence for the convergent validity of the MIDC. In addition, the reliability of the MIDC has been established empirically. For example, in comparing the results

of separate studies (Immelman, 1993b, 1994) of the personalities of South African presidents F. W. de Klerk and Nelson Mandela, the present author's psychodiagnostic meta-analysis correlated highly (De Klerk, r_s = .80, p < .01; Mandela, r_s = .64, p < .05) with the mean MIDC scale scores derived from expert ratings by two South African political scientists (Geldenhuys & Kotzé, 1991; Kotzé & Geldenhuys, 1990) who had interviewed and independently studied De Klerk and Mandela. In another study (Immelman & Hagel, 1998), provisional MIDC scale scores in a trained student rater's psychodiagnostic meta-analyses of Eleanor Roosevelt (r_s = .86, p < .01) and Hillary Rodham Clinton (r_s = .99, p < .01), correlated highly with the final scale scores yielded by the supervisor's re-coding of the data collected by the student. (Immelman, 1999, pp. 11–12)

In contrast, however, to content-analytic procedures—where reliability is established by coefficients of interrater reliability—the MIDC's psychodiagnostic approach relies on *replicability*. All diagnostic criteria endorsed on the 170-item MIDC must be documented by at least two independent sources (i.e., extractions from biographical source materials in support of item endorsements). Whereas the task of coding written text in content-analytic procedures can be measured in hours or days, the Millon-based process of extracting psychodiagnostically relevant content from biographical source materials requires weeks or months of bibliographic research. In practice, duplication of this task is not a viable option. However, the cost prohibitiveness of formally establishing conventional coefficients of reliability for individual MIDC-based studies is largely offset by the explicit nature of the documentation process, which renders MIDC-based research easily replicable—a basic requirement of the scientific method. Stated differently, studies employing the MIDC easily lend themselves to replication, enabling independent investigators to validate for themselves the consistency and accuracy of the measure.

From the perspective of measurement theory, a major distinction between traditional content-analytic approaches and the current psychodiagnostic approach is that the former emphasizes interrater reliability, whereas the Millonian approach to political personality assessment places a premium on predictive validity. For example, in a study (Immelman, 1998) conducted during the 1996 presidential campaign—two years before public knowledge of the Lewinsky affair—I made the following worst-case prediction for President Clinton's second term, based on his MIDC assessment:

> [Bill Clinton] may commit errors of judgment stemming from a combination of strong ambition, a sense of entitlement, and inflated self-confidence. . . . [Narcissistic] characteristics may also predispose him to dissemble or equivocate, not only ego-defensively to protect and bolster an admirable self-image, but instrumentally to have his way with others. Concurrent Outgoing features in President Clinton's MIDC profile suggest a strong need for public recognition, approval, and validation, along with a willingness to use his social skills to influence and charm others (though lacking some fidelity in consistently fulfilling his promises). . . . Finally, there is a danger that Outgoing presidents such as Bill Clinton may be oversensitive to public opinion and neglectful of role demands relating to oversight. (p. 355)

In the article's abstract, the implications of President Clinton's personality profile for high-level political leadership were summarized as follows: "The profile . . . is consistent with a presidency troubled by ethical questions and lapses of judgment, and provides an explanatory framework for Clinton's high achievement drive and his ability to retain a following and maintain his self-confidence in the face of adversity" (Immelman, 1998, p. 335). The ensuing Lewinsky scandal, President Clinton's subsequent (albeit partisan) impeachment, consistently high public approval ratings throughout the impeachment proceedings, and his success in averting efforts to remove him from office offer suggestive evidence for the predictive validity of the MIDC.

Another case in point is a similar study (Immelman, 2002) of then-governor George W. Bush, conducted in 1999—more than a year before his election as president of the United States. While the verdict of history is still out on the Bush presidency, in its third year at the time of this writing, this volume offers a fitting forum for recording that study's broad predictions for a prospective Bush presidency, based on his MIDC assessment:

> George W. Bush's major personality-based leadership strengths are the important political skills of charisma and interpersonality—a personable, confident, socially responsive, outgoing tendency that will enable him to connect with critical constituencies, mobilize popular support, and retain a following and his self-confidence in the face of adversity. Outgoing leaders characteristically are confident in their social abilities, skilled in the art of social influence, and have a charming, engaging personal style that tends to make people like them and overlook their gaffes and foibles.
>
> Bush's major personality-based limitations include the propensity for a superficial grasp of complex issues, a predisposition to be easily bored by routine (with the attendant risk of failing to keep himself adequately informed), an inclination to act impulsively without fully appreciating the implications of his decisions or the long-term consequences of his policy initiatives, and a predilection to favor personal connections, friendship, and loyalty over competence in his staffing decisions and appointments—all of which could render a Bush administration relatively vulnerable to errors of judgment. (pp. 101–102)

The essence of validity is the determination that a measurement procedure accurately assesses the theoretical constructs it purports to measure. As Millon (1994) has noted, "no single number can represent the validity of a test. There are many forms of validity. When researching the validity of an instrument, it is necessary to conduct the investigation with reference to the intended applications of the test" (p. 87). He notes that the central consideration is whether the test achieves its purpose. Clearly, the MIDC achieves the purpose of its design: at-a-distance personality assessment grounded in "a coherent psychodiagnostic framework capable of capturing the critical personological determinants of political performance, embedded in a broad range of attribute domains across the entire matrix of the person—not just the individual's motives, operational code, integrative complexity, or personality traits" (Immelman, 2003, p. 621).

Millon's Framework May Not Be Sufficiently Comprehensive or Relevant

This is essentially a straw man argument. The same can be said of *any* of the established approaches to studying personality in politics: Margaret Hermann's conceptual scheme, the Kernbergian notion of narcissistic personality organization in the work of Jerrold Post, Kohutian self psychology in the work of Stanley Renshon, integrative complexity in the work of Peter Suedfeld, operational code analysis in the work of Stephen Walker, and Murray's classes of motives in the work of David Winter. The Millonian framework (e.g., as represented in the MIPS and MCMI-III) has gained broad acceptance in applied psychology; for example, the *Journal of Personality Assessment* devoted an entire special issue (Strack, 1999a) to the work of Millon, and, in 2003, Theodore Millon was the recipient of the American Psychological Association's prestigious award for Distinguished Professional Contributions to Applied Research, given annually to a psychologist whose research has led to important discoveries or developments in the field of applied psychology. Beyond the narrower confines of clinical psychology and personality assessment, Millon (1990a) has contributed to the *Handbook of Personality* and coedited the *Personality and Social Psychology* volume of the first comprehensive (12-volume) *Handbook of Psychology* (2003). Furthermore, studies informed by my adaptation of Millon's model have been published in the journals *Political Psychology* (Immelman, 1993a) and *Leadership Quarterly* (Immelman, 1998).

Millon's Model Perpetuates a "Pathology" Orientation in Political Psychology

One anonymous reviewer has claimed that "the origins of Millon's model in abnormal psychology tend to perpetuate the 'pathology' orientation that gave much of early psychohistory a bad name." Indeed, Millon's model evolved from an original interest in personality disorders, as witnessed by his monumental texts, *Modern Psychopathology* (1969) and *Disorders of Personality* (1996). In its preface, Millon wrote that his 1969 work was an attempt on his part:

> to gather and to render the disparate facts and theories of psychopathology into a coherent and orderly framework . . . [founded on the conviction that the time had come] for the development of a new and coherent theoretical framework, . . . that interwove both psychological and biological factors, and from which the principal clinical syndromes could be derived and coordinated. (Millon, 2002, pp. 182–183)

However, the Millonian approach transcends both the traditional concerns and syndromes of abnormal psychology and psychiatry and descriptive *DSM* diagnostic categories. In Millon's words:

> Instead of rephrasing traditional psychiatric categories in the language of modern theories, as several able psychopathologists had done, I sought [in *Modern Psychopathology,* 1969] to devise a new classification schema, one constructed from its inception by coalescing what I considered to be the basic principles of personality development and functioning. (Millon, 2002, p. 183)

The related critique from within political psychology, that the application of Millon's model to political personality assessment tends to perpetuate the "pathology" orientation that gave much of the early psychohistory a bad name, simply is not a fair assessment. As Stephen Strack (1999b) has noted:

> Millon's . . . *normal* [italics added] personality styles and dimensions emanate from his broadly based evolutionary model of personality that differentiates and links healthy and pathological character on a continuum. . . . The continuous relations between the domains of normality and pathology in Millon's model allows personologists to study the ways that healthy and disordered personalities are similar and different [and] the developmental processes that lead to various outcomes. (p. 426)

In short, the Millonian approach is a far cry from the Lasswellian *Psychopathology and Politics* (1930) orientation implied in the present critique. It is even farther removed from the specious genetic reconstructions that have most tainted psychohistory. What gave some brands of psychohistory a bad name are unfalsifiable, impressionistic, psychoanalytically oriented genetic reconstructions such as the *Psychohistory Review* article, "François Mitterand: Personality and Politics" (Guiton, 1992), which attributed the former French leader's stiffness, obstinacy, shyness, anxiety, and power orientation to toilet training and separation during the pre-Oedipal period. To paint Millon with this selfsame brush is patently unfair and a disservice to political psychology; in transplanting Millon's model to political psychology more than a decade ago (Immelman, 1993a), I have been unambiguous in stating that the kind of developmental causal analysis caricatured in Guiton's study, cited earlier, is unsuitable for political personality assessment:

> For the majority of present-day personality-in-politics investigators, who generally favor a descriptive approach to personality assessment, developmental questions are of secondary relevance; however, an explicit set of developmental relational statements is invaluable for psychobiographically oriented analysis. Moreover, precisely because each personality pattern has characteristic developmental antecedents, in-depth knowledge of a subject's experiential history can be useful with respect to validating the results of descriptive personality assessment, or for suggesting alternative hypotheses. . . . This benefit notwithstanding, *genetic reconstruction does not constitute an optimal basis for personality assessment and description* [italics added]. (Immelman, 2003, p. 612)

In summary, common critiques of the Millonian approach to personality-in-politics inquiry, at best, are weak and misinformed; at worst, they reflect bias against the psychodiagnostically oriented approach to political personality assessment and ignorance of Millon's evolutionary model and clinical measures.

CONCLUSION

Despite major progress in personology and clinical science since the publication of Theodore Millon's landmark *Modern Psychopathology* in 1969, personality inquiry in the emerging field of political psychology remains largely divorced from these advances. In this chapter, I have attempted to expound the fruitful possibilities of Millon's evolutionary theory for advancing a generative model of personality and political leadership.

In a recent study, Camara, Nathan, and Puente (2000) reported that the MCMI-III counts among the 10 most frequently used assessment devices in forensic psychology. The demonstrated usefulness of the Millonian approach in forensic settings—arguably the area of application in clinical practice that most closely approximates the concerns of political personality assessment—strongly suggests that it should be similarly well suited to the psychological examination of political leaders.

Other psychological tests in the "forensic top 10" include the Rorschach Inkblot Test, mirroring the political-psychological concerns of psychodynamically oriented scholars such as Jerrold Post and Stanley Renshon; the Thematic Apperception Test (TAT), underscoring the relevance of David Winter's inquiry into the motive profiles of political leaders; the Wechsler Adult Intelligence Scale (WAIS-R), reflecting the interest of scholars such as Peter Suedfeld in the integrative complexity and related cognitive attributes of political leaders; and the Minnesota Multiphasic Personality Inventory (MMPI-2), consistent with the importance that investigators such as Post, Renshon, and I attach to the psychodiagnostic classification of political leaders as a tool for risk assessment and general understanding and prediction of political performance.

The publication of this volume coincides with an important milestone in the evolution of the Millonian era in professional psychology: the 25th anniversary of the Millon Inventories. Contemporaneously, in the adjacent field of political psychology, the seed Millon planted nearly two decades ago has taken root and begun to blossom. In addition to my published work in the United States (e.g., Immelman, 1998, 2002), the first phase (Steinberg, in press) of a major project in Canada to examine the relationship between Millon's personality patterns and the leadership styles of prominent twentieth-century female leaders has been concluded. And in Europe, a textbook in political communication (De Landtsheer, 2004) with a distinctively Millonian perspective and personality profiles of Dutch and Belgian leaders has been published.

The mark of Millon has transcended clinical science and crossed the threshold of adjacent disciplines in ways that even Theodore Millon could not have anticipated 35 years ago when *Modern Psychopathology* burst on the scene and forever changed the landscape of modern psychology.

REFERENCES

American Psychiatric Association. (1987). *Diagnostic and statistical manual of mental disorders* (3rd ed., rev.). Washington, DC: Author.

American Psychiatric Association. (1994). *Diagnostic and statistical manual of mental disorders* (4th ed.). Washington, DC: Author.

Barber, J. D. (1965). *The lawmakers: Recruitment and adaptation to legislative life.* New Haven, CT: Yale University Press.

Barber, J. D. (1992). *The presidential character: Predicting performance in the White House* (4th ed.). Englewood Cliffs, NJ: Prentice-Hall. (Original work published 1972)

Camara, W. J., Nathan, J. S., & Puente, A. E. (2000). Psychological test usage: Implications in professional psychology. *Professional Psychology: Research and Practice, 31,* 141–151.

Chomsky, N. (1957). *Syntactic structures.* The Hague, The Netherlands: Mouton.

Christie, R., & Geis, F. L. (1970). *Studies in Machiavellianism.* New York: Academic Press.

Cole, L. C. (1954). The population consequences of life history phenomena. *Quarterly Review of Biology, 29,* 103–137.

Daly, M., & Wilson, M. (1983). *Sex, evolution, and behavior* (2nd ed.). Boston: Willard Grant Press.

Davies, J. C. (1973). Where from and where to? In J. N. Knutson (Ed.), *Handbook of political psychology* (pp. 1–27). San Francisco: Jossey-Bass.

De Landtsheer, C. (2004). *Politiek impressiemanagement in Vlaanderen en Nederland* [Political impression management in Belgium and the Netherlands]. Louvain, Belgium: Acco.

Dille, B., & Young, M. D. (2000). The conceptual complexity of Presidents Carter and Clinton: An automated content analysis of temporal stability and source bias. *Political Psychology, 21,* 587–596.

Erikson, E. H. (1963). *Childhood and society* (2nd ed.). New York: Norton. (Original work published 1950)

Erikson, E. H. (1980). *Identity and the life cycle.* New York: Norton.

Etheredge, L. S. (1978). Personality effects on American foreign policy, 1898–1968: A test of interpersonal generalization theory. *American Political Science Review, 72,* 434–451.

Eysenck, H. J. (1954). *The psychology of politics.* London: Routledge.

Eysenck, H. J. (1990). Biological dimensions of personality. In L. A. Pervin (Ed.), *Handbook of personality: Theory and research* (pp. 244–276). New York: Guilford Press.

Geldenhuys, D., & Kotzé, H. (1991). F. W. de Klerk: A study in political leadership. *Politikon, 19,* 20–44.

George, A. L. (1969). The "operational code": A neglected approach to the study of political leaders and decision-making. *International Studies Quarterly, 13,* 190–222.

George, A. L., & Stern, E. (1998). Presidential management styles and models. In A. L. George & J. L. George, *Presidential personality and performance* (pp. 199–280). Boulder, CO: Westview Press.

Gray, J. A. (1991). The neuropsychology of temperament. In J. Strelau & A. Angleitner (Eds.), *Explorations in temperament: International perspectives on theory and measurement* (pp. 105–128). New York: Plenum Press.

Greenstein, F. I. (1969). *Personality and politics: Problems of evidence, inference, and conceptualization.* Chicago: Markham.

Greenstein, F. I. (1987). *Personality and politics: Problems of evidence, inference, and conceptualization* (New ed.). Princeton, NJ: Princeton University Press.

Greenstein, F. I. (1992). Can personality and politics be studied systematically? *Political Psychology, 13,* 105–128.

Guiton, M. V. (1992). François Mitterand: Personality and politics. *Psychohistory Review, 21,* 27–72.

Hermann, M. G. (1974). Leader personality and foreign policy behavior. In J. N. Rosenau (Ed.), *Comparing foreign policies: Theories, findings, and methods* (pp. 201–234). New York: Wiley.

Hermann, M. G. (1978). Effects of personal characteristics of political leaders on foreign policy. In M. A. East, S. A. Salmore, & C. F. Hermann (Eds.), *Why nations act: Theoretical perspectives for comparative foreign policy studies* (pp. 49–68). Beverly Hills, CA: Sage.

Hermann, M. G. (1980). Explaining foreign policy behavior using the personal characteristics of political leaders. *International Studies Quarterly, 24,* 7–46.

Hermann, M. G. (1984). Personality and foreign policy decision making: A study of 53 heads of government. In D. A. Sylvan & S. Chan (Eds.), *Foreign policy decision making: Perception, cognition, and artificial intelligence* (pp. 53–80). New York: Praeger.

Hermann, M. G. (1987). Assessing the foreign policy role orientations of sub-Saharan African leaders. In S. G. Walker (Ed.), *Role theory and foreign policy analysis* (pp. 161–198). Durham, NC: Duke University Press.

Hermann, M. G. (2003). Assessing leadership style: Trait analysis. In J. M. Post (Ed.), *The psychological assessment of political leaders: With profiles of Saddam Hussein and Bill Clinton* (pp. 178–212). Ann Arbor: University of Michigan Press.

Holsti, O. R. (1970). The "operational code" approach to the study of political leaders: John Foster Dulles' philosophical and instrumental beliefs. *Canadian Journal of Political Science, 3,* 123–157.

Horney, K. (1937). *The neurotic personality of our time.* New York: Norton.

Hyde, J. S. (1996). Where are the gender differences? Where are the gender similarities? In D. M. Buss & N. M. Malamuth (Eds.), *Sex, power, conflict: Evolutionary and feminist perspectives* (pp. 107–118). New York: Oxford University Press.

Immelman, A. (1993a). The assessment of political personality: A psychodiagnostically relevant conceptualization and methodology. *Political Psychology, 14,* 725–741.

Immelman, A. (1993b, July). *A Millon-based study of political personality: Nelson Mandela and F. W. de Klerk.* Paper presented at the sixteenth annual scientific meeting of the International Society of Political Psychology, Cambridge, MA.

Immelman, A. (1994, July). *South Africa in transition: The influence of the political personalities of Nelson Mandela and F. W. de Klerk.* Paper presented at the seventeenth annual scientific meeting of the International Society of Political Psychology, Santiago de Compostela, Spain.

Immelman, A. (1998). The political personalities of 1996 U.S. presidential candidates Bill Clinton and Bob Dole. *Leadership Quarterly, 9,* 335–366.

Immelman, A. (1999). *Millon inventory of diagnostic criteria manual* (2nd ed.). Available from Dr. Aubrey Immelman, Dept. of Psychology, St. John's University, Collegeville, MN 56321, USA.

Immelman, A. (2002). The political personality of U.S. president George W. Bush. In L. O. Valenty & O. Feldman (Eds.), *Political leadership for the new century: Personality and behavior among American leaders* (pp. 81–103). Westport, CT: Praeger.

Immelman, A. (2003). Personality in political psychology. In T. Millon & M. J. Lerner (Eds.), *Personality and social psychology* (pp. 599–625). Vol. 5 in I. B. Weiner (Editor-in-Chief), *Handbook of psychology*. Hoboken, NJ: Wiley.

Immelman, A., & Hagel, J. J. (1998, July). *A comparison of the personalities of Eleanor Roosevelt and Hillary Rodham Clinton*. Paper presented at the twenty-first annual scientific meeting of the International Society of Political Psychology, Montreal, Quebec, Canada.

Immelman, A., & Steinberg, B. S. (Compilers). (1999). *Millon Inventory of Diagnostic Criteria* (2nd ed.). Available from Dr. Aubrey Immelman, Dept. of Psychology, St. John's University, Collegeville, MN 56321, USA.

Johnson, R. T. (1974). *Managing the White House: An intimate study of the presidency*. New York: Harper & Row.

Kernberg, O. F. (1984). *Severe personality disorders: Psychotherapeutic strategies*. New Haven, CT: Yale University Press.

Kernberg, O. F. (1992). *Aggression in personality disorders and perversions*. New Haven, CT: Yale University Press.

Kohut, H. (1971). *The analysis of the self*. New York: International Universities Press.

Kohut, H. (1977). *The restoration of the self*. New York: International Universities Press.

Kotzé, H., & Geldenhuys, D. (1990, July). Damascus road. *Leadership South Africa, 9*(6), 12–28.

Langer, W. (1972). *The mind of Adolf Hitler: The secret wartime report*. New York: Basic Books. (Original report commissioned 1943)

Lasswell, H. D. (1930). *Psychopathology and politics*. Chicago: University of Chicago Press.

Lasswell, H. D. (1948). *Power and personality*. New York: Norton.

Lyons, M. (1997). Presidential character revisited. *Political Psychology, 18,* 791–811.

Machiavelli, N. (1908). *The prince* (W. K. Marriott, Trans.). London: J. M. Dent. (original work c. 1505)

Marcus, G. E. (2002). Political psychology: A personal view. In K. R. Monroe (Ed.), *Political psychology* (pp. 95–106). Mahwah, NJ: Erlbaum.

McClelland, D. C. (1961). *The achieving society*. Princeton, NJ: Van Nostrand.

McCrae, R. R., & Costa, P. T., Jr. (1999). A five-factor theory of personality. In L. A. Pervin & O. P. John (Eds.), *Handbook of personality: Theory and research* (2nd ed., pp. 139–153). New York: Guilford Press.

Mealey, L. (2000). *Sex differences: Development and evolutionary strategies*. New York: Academic Press.

Millon, T. (1969). *Modern psychopathology: A biosocial approach to maladaptive learning and functioning*. Philadelphia: Saunders. (Reprinted 1985 by Waveland Press, Prospect Heights, IL)

Millon, T. (1990a). The disorders of personality. In L. A. Pervin (Ed.), *Handbook of personality: Theory and research* (pp. 339–370). New York: Guilford Press.

Millon, T. (1990b). *Toward a new personology: An evolutionary model*. New York: Wiley.

Millon, T. (with Weiss, L. G., Millon, C. M., & Davis, R. D.). (1994). *Millon Index of Personality Styles manual*. San Antonio, TX: Psychological Corporation.

Millon, T. (with Davis, R. D.). (1996). *Disorders of personality: DSM-IV and beyond* (2nd ed.). New York: Wiley.

Millon, T. (1999). Reflections on psychosynergy: A model for integrating science, theory, classification, assessment, and therapy. *Journal of Personality Assessment, 72,* 437–456.

Millon, T. (2002). A blessed and charmed personal odyssey. *Journal of Personality Assessment, 79,* 171–194.

Millon, T. (2003). Evolution: A generative source for conceptualizing the attributes of personality. In T. Millon & M. J. Lerner (Eds.), *Personality and social psychology* (pp. 3–30). Vol. 5 in I. B. Weiner (Editor-in-Chief), *Handbook of psychology*. Hoboken, NJ: Wiley.

Millon, T., & Davis, R. D. (2000). *Personality disorders in modern life*. New York: Wiley.

Millon, T., Davis, R. D., & Millon, C. (1996). *Millon Clinical Multiaxial Inventory–III*. Minneapolis, MN: National Computer Systems.

Murray, H. A. (1938). *Explorations in personality*. New York: Oxford University Press.

Osgood, C. E. (1977). Objective cross-national indicators of subjective culture. In Y. H. Poortinga (Ed.), *Basic problems in cross-cultural psychology* (pp. 200–235). Amsterdam: Swets & Zeitlinger.

Osgood, C. E., May, W. H., & Miron, M. S. (1975). *Cross-cultural universals of affective meaning*. Urbana: University of Illinois Press.

Osgood, C. E., Suci, G. J., & Tannenbaum, P. H. (1957). *The measurement of meaning*. Urbana: University of Illinois Press.

Pickering, A. D., Corr, P. J., & Gray, J. A. (1999). Interactions and reinforcement sensitivity theory: A theoretical analysis of Rusting and Larsen. *Personality and Individual Differences, 26,* 357–365.

Piersma, H. L., Ohnishi, H., Lee, D. J., & Metcalfe, W. E. (2002). An empirical evaluation of Millon's dimensional polarities. *Journal of Psychopathology and Behavioral Assessment, 24,* 151–158.

Post, J. M. (1979, Spring). Personality profiles in support of the Camp David summit. *Studies in Intelligence,* 1–3.

Post, J. M. (1991). Saddam Hussein of Iraq: A political psychological profile. *Political Psychology, 12,* 279–289.

Post, J. M. (2003a). Assessing leaders at a distance: The political personality profile. In J. M. Post (Ed.), *The psychological assessment of political leaders: With profiles of Saddam Hussein and Bill Clinton* (pp. 69–104). Ann Arbor: University of Michigan Press.

Post, J. M. (2003b). Leader personality assessments in support of government policy. In J. M. Post (Ed.), *The psychological assessment of political leaders: With profiles of Saddam Hussein and Bill Clinton* (pp. 39–61). Ann Arbor: University of Michigan Press.

Post, J. M. (Ed.). (2003c). *The psychological assessment of political leaders: With profiles of Saddam Hussein and Bill Clinton*. Ann Arbor: University of Michigan Press.

Renshon, S. A. (1996a). *High hopes: The Clinton presidency and the politics of ambition*. New York: New York University Press.

Renshon, S. A. (1996b). *The psychological assessment of presidential candidates*. New York: New York University Press.

Renshon, S. A. (2001). The comparative psychoanalytic study of political leaders: John McCain and the limits of trait psychology. In O. Feldman & L. O. Valenty (Eds.), *Profiling political leaders: Cross-cultural studies of personality and behavior* (pp. 233–253). Westport, CT: Praeger.

Renshon, S. A. (2003). Psychoanalytic assessments of character and performance in presidents and candidates: Some observations on theory and method. In J. M. Post (Ed.), *The psychological assessment of political leaders: With profiles of Saddam Hussein and Bill Clinton* (pp. 105–133). Ann Arbor: University of Michigan Press.

Steinberg, B. S. (in press). Indira Gandhi: The relationship between personality profile and leadership style. *Political Psychology*.

Stone, W. F., & Baril, G. L. (1979). Self-other orientation and legislative behavior. *Journal of Personality, 47,* 162–176.

Strack, S. (Spec. Ed.). (1999a). Millon's evolving personality theories and measures [Special series]. *Journal of Personality Assessment, 72*(3).

Strack, S. (1999b). Millon's normal personality styles and dimensions. *Journal of Personality Assessment, 72,* 426–436.

Suedfeld, P. (1994). President Clinton's policy dilemmas: A cognitive analysis. *Political Psychology, 15,* 337–349.

Suedfeld, P., Guttieri, K., & Tetlock, P. E. (2003). Assessing integrative complexity at a distance: Archival analysis of thinking and decision making. In J. M. Post (Ed.), *The psychological assessment of political leaders: With profiles of Saddam Hussein and Bill Clinton* (pp. 246–270). Ann Arbor: University of Michigan Press.

Suedfeld, P., & Rank, A. D. (1976). Revolutionary leaders: Long-term success as a function of changes in conceptual complexity. *Journal of Personality and Social Psychology, 34,* 169–178.

Suedfeld, P., & Tetlock, P. E. (1977). Integrative complexity of communications in international crises. *Journal of Conflict Resolution, 21,* 169–184.

Sullivan, H. S. (1953). *The interpersonal theory of psychiatry.* New York: Norton.

Tucker, R. C. (1965). The dictator and totalitarianism. *World Politics, 17,* 555–583.

Walker, S. G. (1977). The interface between beliefs and behavior: Henry Kissinger's operational code and the Vietnam War. *Journal of Conflict Resolution, 21,* 129–168.

Walker, S. G. (1983). The motivational foundations of political belief systems: A re-analysis of the operational code construct. *International Studies Quarterly, 27,* 179–201.

Walker, S. G. (1990). The evolution of operational code analysis. *Political Psychology, 11,* 403–418.

Walker, S. G., Schafer, M., & Young, M. D. (2003). Profiling the operational codes of political leaders. In J. M. Post (Ed.), *The psychological assessment of political leaders: With profiles of Saddam Hussein and Bill Clinton* (pp. 215–245). Ann Arbor: University of Michigan Press.

Wallas, G. (1908). *Human nature in politics.* London: Archibald Constable. (Reprinted 1981 by Transaction Books, New Brunswick, NJ)

Wallen, K., & Schneider, J. E. (Eds.). (2000). *Reproduction in context: Social and environmental influences on reproductive physiology and behavior.* Cambridge, MA: MIT Press.

Weintraub, W. (2003). Verbal behavior and personality assessment. In J. M. Post (Ed.), *The psychological assessment of political leaders: With profiles of Saddam Hussein and Bill Clinton* (pp. 137–152). Ann Arbor: University of Michigan Press.

Weintraub, W., & Aronson, H. (1964). The application of verbal behavior analysis to the study of psychological defense mechanisms: II. Speech patterns associated with impulsive behavior. *Journal of Nervous and Mental Diseases, 139,* 75–82.

Widiger, T. A. (1999). Millon's dimensional polarities. *Journal of Personality Assessment, 72,* 365–389.

Winter, D. G. (1973). *The power motive.* New York: Free Press.

Winter, D. G. (1980). An exploratory study of the motives of southern African political leaders measured at a distance. *Political Psychology, 2,* 75–85.

Winter, D. G. (1987). Leader appeal, leader performance, and the motive profiles of leaders and followers: A study of American presidents and elections. *Journal of Personality and Social Psychology, 52,* 196–202.

Winter, D. G. (1995). Presidential psychology and governing styles: A comparative psychological analysis of the 1992 presidential candidates. In S. A. Renshon (Ed.), *The Clinton presidency: Campaigning, governing, and the psychology of leadership* (pp. 113–134). Boulder, CO: Westview Press.

Winter, D. G. (1998). A motivational analysis of the Clinton first term and the 1996 presidential campaign. *Leadership Quarterly, 9,* 367–376.

Winter, D. G. (2003a). Measuring the motives of political actors at a distance. In J. M. Post (Ed.), *The psychological assessment of political leaders: With profiles of Saddam Hussein and Bill Clinton* (pp. 153–177). Ann Arbor: University of Michigan Press.

Winter, D. G. (2003b). Personality and political behavior. In D. O. Sears, L. Huddy, & R. Jervis (Eds.), *Oxford handbook of political psychology* (pp. 110–145). New York: Oxford University Press.

Ziller, R. C., Stone, W. F., Jackson, R. M., & Terbovic, N. J. (1977). Self-other orientations and political behavior. In M. G. Hermann (Ed.), *A psychological examination of political leaders* (pp. 174–204). New York: Free Press.

PART III

Taxonomy, Classification, and Syndromes

Chapter 12

CONCEPTS OF NORMALITY AND THE CLASSIFICATION OF PSYCHOPATHOLOGY

MELVIN SABSHIN

My interest in concepts of normality as they relate to the classification of psychopathology has been a central part of my career since the early 1960s. While fascinated by intellectual questions about the nature and boundaries of normality and pathology, I have always been interested equally in the implications of normality's definition to the emergence of a scientifically grounded psychiatry.

I have had three close colleagues in different aspects of this work: a psychiatrist, a sociologist, and a psychologist. The psychiatrist is Dr. Daniel Offer, with whom I have written three books (Offer & Sabshin, 1966, 1984, 1991) and several articles on normality. Dr. Offer has continued his work on the subject and has made numerous contributions to specific formulations about normal behavior (Offer, Ostrov, & Howard, 1981). Professor Anselm Strauss, the sociologist, was deeply interested in the career models of psychiatrists, and we collaborated on a book on ideologies of psychiatrists (Strauss, Schatzman, Bucher, Ehrlich, & Sabshin, 1978), which included the ways in which varying ideological models of pathology and normality affected psychiatric concepts and practices. Professor Strauss continued to include work on health careers studied in a symbolic interactional model until his death in 1996 (Strauss, 1977; Strauss & Corbin, 1993).

Professor Theodore Millon, the honoree of this book, was a close colleague in psychology whose work is relevant to my contribution of this chapter. Dr. Millon and I worked together from 1969 to 1974 at the University of Illinois College of Medicine where I headed the Department of Psychiatry and he was in charge of the Psychology Division within Psychiatry. Our relationship transcended the formal academic system. To Dr. Millon, I was perceived as a good, if young, father figure. For me, the relationship was extraordinarily stimulating, and I learned a great deal from him. When I moved to the American Psychiatric Association as its medical director in 1974, I was pleased that Dr. Millon had already been placed on a task force involved in the formulation of the third edition of the *Diagnostic and Statistical Manual of Mental Disorders* (*DSM-III;* American Psychiatric Association, 1980). He was an active contributor to the final product, including to its multiaxial formulations. Our careers diverged in the late 1970s, but we continued to be colleagues over the next 25 years. Dr. Millon's subsequent work has been extraordinarily productive and creative. He has been one of the most influential figures in the nosological and general clinical advances of the late twentieth century, including contributions to normality from an evolutionary perspective (Millon, 1990, 1996; Millon & Davis, 1996). His Institute for Advanced Studies in Personology and Psychopathology has afforded him the opportunity in recent years to conduct research and to teach as well as to reflect.

My collaboration with Dr. Millon had given me many ideas on encouraging greater interest in studies in normal behavior. Gradually, however, my work on normality became a central part of my career; it influenced my pathway toward becoming the medical director of the American Psychiatric Association. The work on normality and the contributions to therapeutic ideologies coalesced in my mind as a basis for substantive concerns about the whole field of psychiatry (Sabshin, 1989, 1990). I had become determined to be one of those active in changing psychiatry from a field dominated by ideology to a more rationally oriented specialty. During the early part of my career, I had become convinced that psychiatry in several important areas lacked a clear enough commitment to scientific research: Rather, the field was divided among at least three ideological approaches to diagnosis and to treatment (Strauss et al., 1978). We labeled these ideologies as *psychotherapeutic, sociotherapeutic,* and *somatotherapeutic,* referring to profound differences in the concept of the independent variables involved in the cause of various mental illnesses and in the processes required for therapeutic effectiveness.

The psychotherapeutic ideology supported the position that psychological factors were the key elements in producing mental illness. They were also the most important part in effecting successful treatment (Brenner, 1976; Fenichel, 1945; Ogden, 1994). Sociotherapeutic ideologies postulated the power of social variables (societal, familial, cultural, or group) as the most important systems in stimulating the presence of mental illness (Hollingshead & Redlich, 1958; Kleinman, 1986; Montagu, 1961). Alterations of these systems were necessary for reduction of mental illness. Somatotherapeutic ideology emphasized the role of biological systems in the causation of mental illnesses and in their treatment (Ketty, 1959; Wortis, 1960). Varying groups of psychiatrists preferred each of these ideologies without acknowledging that they were, in fact, ideologies. As part of our studies, we designed scales for the measurement of these particular positions, and we were able to demonstrate significant differences among the three groups (Strauss et al., 1978).

Furthermore, the members of each group tended to work in different settings, to join separate professional organizations, to publish in specialized journals, and to employ markedly different therapeutic approaches. These differences were enhanced by the presence of charismatic leaders for each ideology, each of whom advocated a particular approach and depreciated the value of the others. Research was not visualized as the method to resolve these differences. Passionate advocacy ruled the day in publications as well as in educational curricula.

During the latter half of the 1940s, the 1950s, and most of the 1960s, the psychotherapeutic ideology was particularly strong, influenced intensively at that time by the power of psychoanalysis, especially in the United States. Psychoanalytic institutes had a very significant impact on basic psychiatric education; indeed, some institutes were located in medical school settings, in close proximity to, or even embedded within, the department of psychiatry. Many trainees in psychiatry had plans to become psychoanalysts, perhaps even to assume leadership positions in psychoanalytic organizations and institutions.

From my perspective, one of the most important influences that psychoanalysis had on psychiatry was its *implicit* concept of normality (Sabshin, 1990). This concept was not often stated or acknowledged in clear terminology; nevertheless, it was a vital part of the influence of psychoanalysis. This concept was grounded primarily in the assumption that each of us endured varying degrees of trauma in our psychological development, in our internal psychological structure, in our resolution of the turmoil of adolescence, and in achieving the maturity of adult life. With the exception of the most traumatized, each of us could be helped by analytic treatment although, of course, such a universal recommendation was not suggested except in the case of psychoanalytic candidates. To complete psychoanalytic training, an individual had to be analyzed. While this practice was intended to improve the therapeutic capacity of those who were becoming psychoanalysts, psychological problems were always discerned in those undergoing a training analysis. Also, during the course of their developmental progression, each of them demonstrated areas in which they failed to surmount the developmental hurdles optimally. The implication of the universality of at least some modicum of character neurosis, or symptomatic neurosis, related to developmental difficulties and current functioning was very important. In reaching these conclusions, psychoanalysts drew on their theory rather than advocating nosological studies. Nevertheless, the importance of psychoanalytic theory on the concept of normality was, and is still, very large. The emphasis was on the universality of the development of at least some form of minimal pathology. Normality, however, was not a major subject for specific studies (Freud, 1953–1964). Freud had defined *normality* as possessing "the capacity to work and to love." These words are full of implications but not specific enough to allow precise measurement.

The somatotherapeutic ideologues in psychiatry had very little interest in normality, per se, but for quite a different reason than the psychotherapists. They postulated that psychiatric illnesses were discrete problems, most often involving qualitatively altered behavior or extreme levels of distribution of variables on rating scales. From their perspective, psychiatric illness was not pervasive in the general population but involved varying degrees of incidence and prevalence. Normal behavior was a gross phenomenon and essentially included all those people not suffering from a mental illness. In classical medical tradition, the focus was on those with the mental illnesses. The normal population could serve as the controls in psychiatric research to contrast with the ill. Variations within the psychological behavior of the control group were not a significant interest for the somatotherapists. Normality was what existed in those members of the population without definitive mental illnesses.

The sociotherapists tended to focus on how social phenomena produced signs and symptoms of mental illness. They rarely asked why some people were not affected by these same social events, so in this sense they were like the somatotherapists. Their attention was on the way in which certain cultural processes produced personality disorders and illnesses. Some of the sociotherapists postulated that various cultures produced particular types of personality in their population (Kardiner, 1956).

The net effect of the various ideologies was a low interest in normality as such. The specific power of the psychoanalysts was to extend, at least implicitly, the number of individuals subsumed in the "illness" category. In the absence of a clear nosology, the analysts often struggled to find functional terminology to characterize illness; labels such as "pervasive regression" or "adolescent turmoil" were employed as diagnoses. Often they resisted providing a specific diagnosis, believing that a case formulation was more important than a label. They retained such an approach until external requirements for providing a diagnosis were significantly altered.

Ultimately, the environment for psychiatric practice began to change in the United States (Frank, Salkever, & Sharfstein, 1981). Reimbursement for psychiatric treatment by third-party providers became the mode, and the need to define eligibility for psychiatric treatment became increasingly important. By the 1980s, for the practice to receive reimbursement, a formal diagnosis had become mandatory (Fein, 1958). It also became a central question in the definition of eligibility for psychiatric treatment. As health insurance emerged as the chief source of payment, regulation of those patients who were eligible for reimbursement became central. The absence of clear, objective criteria for defining illness and the very large number of people undergoing psychiatric treatment were criticized. Arbitrary decisions concerning eligibility for treatment became widely employed, and many of those seeking reimbursement were turned down. The length of various forms of treatments was also questioned and arbitrary limits were set. Public criticism of psychiatric practice had been common, and often it was implied that "normal people" had been placed mistakenly in psychiatric treatment. Indeed, in some quarters this became a scathing criticism of psychiatry. The psychiatrists were accused by some of inventing nosological terms to receive payment.

Many psychiatrists were concerned by the widespread denial of reimbursement by peer reviewers and realized that psychiatry's failure to define illness more precisely was a distinct vulnerability. Equally important, the lack of a clear nosology hindered reliable studies of prevalence and incidence of mental illness. It became increasingly apparent that a rational nosological system was crucial for psychiatry, both theoretically and practically. Treatment procedures needed to vary for specific illnesses, and establishing boundaries between normality and illness became a very important goal (Sabshin, 1989). The psychoanalysts at first tended to resist the establishment of specific nosological categories of illnesses, preferring to use a more general language of case formulations.

The need of psychiatry for the establishment of a new nosological system was ultimately accepted by the American Psychiatric Association. Two choices were possible: the creation of a new American diagnostic system or joining the World Health Organization in the further development of the *International Classification of Diseases* (ICD; World Health Organization, 1993a, 1993b). American psychiatry was not ready for a complete change and wished to preserve relative independence as it sought a new nosological system. The decision was to extend and change the *DSM-II* (American Psychiatric Association, 1968) to create a much more elaborate and scientifically based *DSM-III* (American Psychiatric Association, 1980). This introduced a new system of classification requiring objective criteria for the diagnoses of specific mental illnesses. Attention was also paid to establishing boundaries for these mental illnesses.

It was realized, however, that subthreshold conditions existed that made some individuals more vulnerable than others to illness. *DSM-III* employed empirically determined descriptors for each illness. It did not use an etiological basis for its classification, since etiology was rarely understood. It was hoped that work on etiology would be part of future research and when it became widely understood, a superior nosological system would be developed. This system would also include a better understanding of normal behavior per se. The recognition of the importance of normality was primarily indicated by the inclusion of a multiaxial system that would include data on the status of prior adaptation in the patient. *DSM-III* was much more successful than anticipated, quickly became popular all over the world, and work continued with the publication of *DSM-III-R* (American Psychiatric Association, 1987) and *DSM-IV* (American Psychiatric Association, 1994).

The preparation of *DSM-V* has now begun, and this process of periodic revision should continue to evolve throughout the twenty-first century. The need to understand the meaning of normal behavior along with a new formulation of pathology has become evident to many researchers, but we are still in an early phase of this evolution. While some believe that mental illness should be defined in qualitatively precise categorical terms, many psychiatrists believe that the full panoply of mental illness will include dimensional characteristics of health and illness. Understanding these dimensions will require knowledge of the normal variance of these variables. It is also unlikely that most mental illnesses will be found to be fully categorical as, for example, in general medicine there are some infectious illnesses that possess a highly specific etiology and pathology: They are fundamentally discrete conditions. In all likelihood, an understanding of why some people with vulnerabilities to psychiatric illnesses remain normal may become a vital part of understanding the illness itself. Research on this question is currently limited, but it is highly likely to progress over the twenty-first century. Dr. Millon has been a major contributor to this subject. His hypotheses on evolutionary forces in determining variations in adaptive behavior are very important in defining general pathways to normal behavior. Indeed, Millon has initiated a taxonomy of normal behavior derived from evolutionary principles. While evolution has contributed significantly to an understanding of personology, Millon's contribution has opened the field of "normatology" to its evolutionary derivation (Millon, 1991).

In psychiatry, for most of its history, the concepts of normality have been distinctly secondary to concepts of pathology. The definition of normality has also varied considerably, often parallel with the concepts of pathology as understood by varying clinical groups within psychiatry. As psychiatry develops toward a more objectifiable etiological system in the twenty-first century, it must begin to find a more rational conceptual basis for normality. To achieve greater rationality, we need to start by understanding the current employment of normality as it is used by various groups.

The first view of normality is the classical equation of normality and health (Offer & Sabshin, 1966). This is a dominant concept in all medicine, including psychiatry. Whether illness is formulated in categorical or dimensional fashion, the absence of illness implies that the person is normal. The differences between illness and normality (or health) are clearer when the illness is defined in categorical terms; that is, illness is purported to be qualitatively distinct from normality. All persons who do not possess the categorical qualities of illness are, therefore, essentially normal. Next is the dimensional approach in which an arbitrary line based on prior medical experience is drawn. All who fall above the line, in this measurement, are defined as ill. High blood pressure is a good example of the arbitrary line being drawn, and all whose measurements of blood pressure fall above the line can be defined as hypertensive. Low blood pressure involves findings below another arbitrary line. It is relevant that the arbitrary lines can be changed periodically when reliable data emerges from long-term research.

In psychiatry, this classification of illness is common and useful, but it also has limitations. The present lack of strong interest in normality makes it unlikely that successful adaptation to the stresses inducing illness will be studied by psychiatrists with the same intensity as the study of illness. Even in the case of infectious diseases, many individuals may be relatively immune to illness even without receiving vaccination. The absence, for example, of the development of schizophrenia in an individual who is part of a family with a high incidence of the illness poses a major research question. Borderline schizophrenia also raises important questions about what brings on its symptoms as well as what prevents the patient from becoming overtly schizophrenic. As an example of defining the difference between normality and illness, the differentiation of normal mourning from depression is an area of intense interest. Freud's (1963) formulations on this subject remain relevant, although it is highly likely that biological and psychological factors other than those postulated by Freud are also involved.

Many psychiatric illnesses are currently conceived to be caused by hereditary factors; it is often stated, however, that environmental factors may interact with the genetic etiology. How this interaction takes place is one of the major areas of psychiatric interest. Many illnesses have a long-term course, perhaps in some cases a lifetime course. To assume that individuals between cycles of illness can be conceived as being normal is not necessarily valid. Whatever may be the ultimate formulations of some of these questions, the absence of sufficient interest in normality may weaken the exploration that is necessary to understand illness as fully as needed to unravel etiology and, importantly, to provide even more effective therapy. Furthermore, it is likely that greater interest in normality will open up many subthreshold states where there may be greater vulnerability to illness.

Currently, the formulation of normality as the absence of illness serves very practical functions, especially in day-to-day clinical medicine. It is interesting, however, that when physicians, while lecturing, describe a patient as "normal," they often add the phrase "whatever that means" as an aside. This is at least an implicit acknowledgment that more work needs to be done in defining normality, but it will continue to be difficult to achieve clarity.

Outside medicine, the most common definition of normality equates it with the concept of average (sometimes the mode or the median measure is employed; Offer & Sabshin, 1966). In medicine, this concept has significant use when a bimodal distribution of variables is observed. Illness is said to be present when measurements are both too high and too low. In psychiatry, bipolar illness includes manic behavior and depressive behavior, with normality being postulated as the in-between state as measured by a cluster of variables. Few psychiatric illnesses fall into this pattern, although many psychiatric and psychological symptoms such as motor behavior and affect follow a normal curve distribution. Psychiatrists sometimes employ the "normality as average" concept; often it is mixed in with other definitions of normality. The affect of schizophrenic patients may either be very limited or hyperactive, but the overall illness does not necessarily follow the bimodal pattern of some of the symptoms.

Important also for psychiatry has been the "normality as utopia" concept (Offer & Sabshin, 1966), which became very significant in the latter half of the twentieth century. Intrinsic to the psychotherapeutic ideology and correlated highly with psychoanalytic theory, this concept of normality has been employed primarily in the United States, reaching its zenith in the quarter of a century after World War II. In effect, it was postulated that all individuals proceed through developmental stages throughout their lives, but very few achieve full adaptation to the multiple tasks of child and adolescent development. Some individuals were noted to be psychologically arrested at earlier stages of development and subsequently demonstrated gross psychopathology, while others manifested less severe difficulties. For psychoanalysts, in the absence of an adequate nosology and with a focus on intrapsychic conflict, it was often postulated that some individuals experienced trauma severe enough to render them too sick for psychoanalytic treatment. But on the other hand, the net effect of psychoanalytic theory and practice was to overdiagnose and to concentrate on the presence of treatable psychiatric illness. Many people did not seem to manifest the full symptomatology of a neurosis as often as they demonstrated "character or personality" problems. These kinds of problems are common and have become a central part of psychoanalytic formulations and treatment. For example, the tendency of psychoanalysts to diagnose homosexuality as a mental illness, until very recently, was caused in part by their predisposition to view homosexuality as the result of significant deviations in basic developmental processes (Fenichel, 1945). The decision by the American Psychiatric Association to remove homosexuality from the psychiatric nosology (American Psychiatric Association, 1987; World Health Organization, 1993b) met powerful resistance from psychoanalysts who could not understand the normalizing of what they conceived as severe pathology in psychosexual development. The intensity of many psychoanalysts' resistance in accepting homosexuality as a "normal" type of development emerged as a major consequence of their rather fixed system of interpreting child development. Recently, this position has begun to change, and homosexuality in some psychoanalytic centers is now perceived as one of many possible types of normal sexual adaptation. Other psychoanalytic theories have also begun to change during the past decade (Gabbard, 2000; Kandel, 1999).

Some nonanalyst psychiatrists and psychologists have employed a concept of normality analogous to that of the psychoanalysts. They tended to focus on individuals who functioned very well on a wide variety of tasks: While most people have problems in at least a few of the variables under study (e.g., to be an astronaut, an individual had to function well in many areas; he or she was in effect in a class of "supernormals"), only a few individuals adapt extraordinarily well.

Normality was perceived by some investigators as "fully functioning behavior." Very few individuals achieved such a level of adaptation; hence normality was not present in most individuals.

Each of the concepts of normality discussed has some problems. This is especially obvious when individuals are studied at one stage of their life with a concentration on relatively few variables. In recent years, the tendency to study individuals from a biopsychosocial concept (Engel, 1977) of the processes of normality has begun to emerge and may become an approach that enables us to deal with some of the complexities and problems.

Under this newer concept, normality is looked on as a process that employs variables studied in transaction with one another over a significant period of time. Studies of people over a longer life span should be superior in many cases to cross-sectional description. Indeed, the study of behavior over the course of life, or long segments of life, may become a useful approach to the understanding of normality.

It is hoped that a transactional formulation of normal behavior may become a significant part of a clinical evaluation across all of psychiatry later in the twenty-first century. This will not be a simple task. In the development of *DSM-IV* (American Psychiatric Association, 1994), efforts were made to include additional attention to adaptation; these attempts have not yet proven to be widely accepted. First, there needs to be a more explicit awareness of which concepts of normality are being currently employed, then a determined effort to employ a biopsychosocial model of adaptation studied over time. This model will be facilitated by a greater understanding of the role of evolution in governing human adaptive behavior over a lifetime.

Cross-sectional assessments of normality in a biopsychosocial fashion may also become more practical as it becomes simpler to employ and to integrate many variables. To broaden such studies over various stages of life will also become more functional. The study of how individuals and groups of individuals adapt over these stages should also become more feasible. The biological variables will probably be easier to investigate over a life course than the psychological variables, but such biological measurements and their transactions with psychological functions studied over time will become a new system of understanding normality.

CONCLUSION

Dr. Offer and I have conceptualized the diverse systems of understanding normality as the field of *normatology*. Significant interest in such a field will take time to develop, but as theoretical concepts are clarified, new hypotheses concerning normal behavior will be formulated, studied over time, and become part of the taxonomy of nosology in the twenty-first century. Dr. Millon has opened new directions for the further understanding of normal be-havior, and this chapter honors his contributions.

REFERENCES

American Psychiatric Association. (1968). *Diagnostic and statistical manual of mental disorders* (2nd ed.). Washington, DC: Author.

American Psychiatric Association. (1980). *Diagnostic and statistical manual of mental disorders* (3rd ed.). Washington, DC: Author.

American Psychiatric Association. (1987). *Diagnostic and statistical manual of mental disorders* (3rd ed., rev.). Washington, DC: Author.

American Psychiatric Association. (1994). *Diagnostic and statistical manual of mental disorders* (4th ed.). Washington, DC: Author.

Brenner, C. (1976). *Psychoanalytic technique and psychic conflict.* New York: International Uni-versities Press.

Engel, G. (1977). The need for a new medical model: A challenge for biomedicine. *Science, 196,* 127.

Fein, R. (1958). *Economics of mental illness.* New York: Basic Books.

Fenichel, O. (1945). *The psychoanalytic theory of neurosis.* New York: Norton.

Frank, R. G., Salkever, D. S., & Sharfstein, S. S. (1981). A new look at rising mental health insur-ance costs. *Health Affairs, 10,* 116–123.

Freud, S. (1953–1964) *The standard edition of the complete psychological works of Sigmund Freud.* London: Hogarth Press.

Freud, S. (1963). Mourning and melancholia. *The standard edition of the complete psychological works of Sigmund Freud.* London: Hogarth Press.

Gabbard, G. (2000). A neurobiologically informed perspective on psychotherapy. *British Journal of Psychiatry, 177,* 117–122.

Hollingshead, A. B., & Redlich, F. C. (1958). *Social class and mental illness.* New York: Wiley.

Kandel, G. (1999). Biology and the future of psychoanalysis: A new intellectual framework for psychiatry revisited. *American Journal of Psychiatry, 156,* 505–524.

Kardiner, A. (1956). Adaptational theory: The cross-cultural point of view. In S. Rado & G. R. Daniels (Eds.), *Changing concepts of psychoanalytic medicine.* New York: Grune & Stratton.

Ketty, S. (1959). Biological theories of schizophrenia. *Science, 129,* 1528 –1532.

Kleinman, A. (1986). *Social origins of stress and illness.* New Haven, CT: Yale University Press.

Millon, T. (1990). *Toward a new personology: An evolutionary model.* New York: Wiley.

Millon, T. (1991). Normality: What may we learn from evolutionary theory? In D. Offer & M. Sabshin (Ed.), *The diversity of normal behavior* (pp. 356–404). New York: Basic Books.

Millon, T. (1996). *Personality and psychopathology: Building a clinical science–Selected papers of Theodore Millon.* New York: Wiley.

Millon, T., & Davis, R. D. (1996). *Disorders of personality: DSM IV and beyond* (2nd ed.). New York: Wiley.

Montagu, A. (1961). Culture and mental illness. *American Journal of Psychiatry, 118,* 15.

Offer, D., Ostrov, E., & Howard, K. I. (1981). *The adolescent: A psychological self portrait.* New York: Basic Books.

Offer, D., & Sabshin, M. (1966). *Normality: Theoretical and clinical concepts of mental health.* New York: Basic Books.

Offer, D., & Sabshin, M. (Eds.). (1984). *Normality and the life cycle: A critical integration.* New York: Basic Books.

Offer, D., & Sabshin, M. (Eds.). (1991). *The diversity of normal behavior: Further contributions to normatology.* New York: Basic Books.

Ogden, T. H. (1994). *Subjects of analysis.* Northvale, NJ: Aronson.

Sabshin, M. (1989). Normality and the boundaries of psychopathology. *Journal of Personality Disorders, 3,* 259–273.

Sabshin, M. (1990). Turning points in twentieth century American psychiatry. *Journal of American Psychiatry, 147,* 1267–1274.

Strauss, A. (1977). *Qualitative analysis for social scientists.* New York: Free Press.

Strauss, A., & Corbin, J. (1993). *Basics of qualitative research techniques and procedures for developing grounded theory.* New York: Free Press.

Strauss, A., Schatzman, L., Bucher, R., Ehrlich, D., & Sabshin, M. (1978). *Psychiatric ideologies and institutions.* New York: Free Press.

World Health Organization. (1993a). *The ICD-10 Classification of Mental and Behavioral Disorders: Diagnostic Criteria For Research.* Geneva, Switzerland: Author.

World Health Organization. (1993b). *International statistical classification of diseases and related health problems* (Rev. 10, Vol. 1). Geneva, Switzerland: Author.

Wortis, J. (Ed.). (1960). *Recent advances in biological psychiatry.* New York: Grune & Stratton.

Chapter 13

PROTOTYPE DIAGNOSIS OF PERSONALITY

DREW WESTEN AND REBEKAH BRADLEY

Despite the extraordinary progress made in the understanding of personality disorders (PDs) since the introduction of Axis II in the *Diagnostic and Statistical Manual of Mental Disorders,* 3rd ed. *(DSM-III),* a consensus has emerged that Axis II requires substantial revision (see Livesley & Jang, 2000). Although researchers largely agree on the diagnosis (e.g., categorical diagnosis is problematic, comorbidity is too high), little consensus exists on either prognosis (whether Axis II is going to survive another revision of the diagnostic manual) or the appropriate treatment. Some have called for changes that maximize the continuity with *DSM-III* through *DSM-IV* (e.g., Oldham & Skodol, 2000). Others have suggested more radical solutions, such as replacing PD diagnosis with trait diagnosis using the five-factor model (FFM; e.g., Widiger, Costa, & McCrae, 2002).

In this chapter, we describe an intermediate solution that represents an extension of the prototype approach to classification that guided the architects of the *DSM* since *DSM-II* (see Frances, 1982). We begin by reviewing the prototype concept, its use in psychiatric diagnosis, and research applying this construct to PDs over the past 20 years. Next, we examine some of the ways *DSM-IV* is limited in the way it has attempted to operationalize prototype diagnosis. We then describe an alternative prototype matching procedure that we believe better fulfills the goals of the framers of *DSM-IV*. Finally, we present a case study demonstrating the way this prototype matching approach might be applied in clinical practice.

PROTOTYPES, CLASSIFICATION, AND PERSONALITY DIAGNOSIS

The polythetic diagnostic decision rules characteristic of the recent editions of the *DSM* (i.e., diagnostic thresholds applied to criteria that are neither necessary nor sufficient for diagnosis of a given disorder) reflect the impact on the *DSM* of categorization research in cognitive science in the 1970s (Frances, 1982; Widiger & Frances, 1985). Research across a number of domains suggested that the classical "defining features" approach to classification, which

Preparation of this manuscript was supported in part by NIMH MH59685 and MH60892. Address correspondence to Drew Westen, Departments of Psychology and Psychiatry and Behavioral Sciences, Emory University, 532 Kilgo Cir., Atlanta, GA 30322, e-mail dwesten@emory.edu; or Rebekah Bradley, Psychological Center, Emory University, 1462 Clifton Road, Suite 235, Atlanta, GA 30322, e-mail rbradl2@emory.edu.

requires that all cases classified as members of a category share a list of features that are essential (necessarily present), is inadequate for describing many forms of categorization, including psychiatric diagnosis (Cantor & Genero, 1986; Cantor, Smith, French, & Mezzich, 1980; Smith, 1995). As numerous philosophers and psychologists observed (Rosch & Lloyd, 1978; Rosch & Mervis, 1975; Weber, 1949; Wittgenstein, 1953), most of the objects and concepts we encounter in daily life are not rapidly or easily categorized based on defining features. Rather, they belong to fuzzy categories, whose members share many features (likened to family resemblance) but do not share a set of necessary and sufficient features. Thus, people often categorize based on similarity to objects previously encountered; they are more likely to make explicit, rule-based judgments when they run into anomalous cases.

From this point of view, whether a given instance is a member of a category in many circumstances reflects a comparison between the instance and a *prototype,* or abstraction, across many instances. A related *exemplar* model suggests that people tend to compare a target object (or, in the present case, a set of symptoms or personality characteristics) to a salient example of the category considered to be particularly prototypical (e.g., a robin as an exemplar of the category "bird"). In this view, a clinician deciding whether to diagnose a patient with borderline PD is likely to compare the patient to a mental model of the disorder abstracted across dozens of cases and/or to highly salient, prototypic examples encountered over the course of clinical work and training.

The prototype concept was not without precedent in psychiatry. The philosopher and methodologist of social science Max Weber (1949) had described the related concept of *ideal types,* idealized constructs (e.g., a "Protestant work ethic" that spurred the development of capitalism) that do not correspond to any specific case but provide an idealized abstraction of a phenomenon across cases. The psychiatrist Karl Jaspers had drawn on this notion in developing his influential system for classifying psychopathology a half-century ago (Schwartz & Wiggins, 1987).

The late 1970s and 1980s saw a flurry of research applying the prototype concept to the classification of psychopathology and, particularly, PDs. Cantor and Mischel (1977) found evidence for prototype-based memory for personality features (introversion/extraversion) similar to the memory processes identified in cognitive psychology for simpler, nonsocial categorization tasks. Research by Horowitz and colleagues (Horowitz, Post, French, Wallis, & Siegelman, 1981; Horowitz, Wright, Lowenstein, & Parad, 1981) examined the extent to which prototypes could be identified and cases could be classified by expert and nonexpert raters based on the extent of prototypicality of the case. Several studies found that prototypes can be reliably generated and rated by clinicians (e.g., Blashfield, 1985; Livesley & Jackson, 1986; Sprock, 2003).

Some of the most cogent thinking about prototypes in the PD literature can be found in the work of Millon (1969, 1986, 1990), who drew extensively on prototype theory in the development of his biopsychosocial approach to PDs. Millon views the PD categories in *DSM-IV* (which he was instrumental in shaping) and the PD categories he deduced theoretically (and assessed empirically) as heuristic prototypes and argued that the underlying constructs should not be confused with the diagnostic algorithms used to operationalize them (Davis, 1999; Millon & Davis, 1996). When clinicians develop an understanding of a PD, they do not just remember a list of criteria. Rather, they form a complex mental representation of the disorder, which includes expectations about patterns of covariation. Thus, if a patient reports a history of self-mutilation, the clinician may suspect, until other evidence contradicts it, that the patient has difficulty regulating powerful emotions such as sadness or anger.

Further, Millon suggests that the criterion sets for PDs should not simply list criteria at varying levels of generality (from behaviors such as self-mutilation to broad constructs such as identity disturbance) but should reflect a prototype analysis of the underlying *functions* central to personality. The list of domains of functioning presumed to be impaired in patients with PDs delineated in the preamble to Axis II in *DSM-IV* (cognition, interpersonal functioning, affectivity, and impulse regulation) would suggest at least four domains for each disorder. Millon's point is both conceptual and psychometric: If we were to describe PDs using even this simple, relatively atheoretical list of personality functions, each PD prototype would be defined in terms of characteristic modes of cognition, impulse regulation, and the like, with examples or subcriteria used to anchor each of these domains in relatively concrete behavioral descriptions.

LIMITATIONS IN THE WAY PROTOTYPE CATEGORIZATION IS OPERATIONALIZED IN *DSM-IV*

The *DSM-IV* algorithms for diagnosing PDs, which involve counting the number of criteria met and applying diagnostic thresholds, represent one possible way of operationalizing prototype classification (which we hereafter refer to as the *count/cutoff method* of diagnosis). This was a substantial advance over prior approaches that implicitly or explicitly assumed a classical (defining features) model of categorization. The count/cutoff method of diagnosis, however, actually represents a mixed model of classification, in two senses. First, perhaps the most central feature of a prototype approach to classification is the recognition that for many categorization tasks, dichotomous classification (i.e., a case is either a member of a category or it is not) is inappropriate because the construct is a fuzzy set. (The same is true for dichotomous, present/absent diagnostic criteria.) Yet the *DSM* retains a categorical diagnostic system that requires clinicians and researchers to assume just the opposite (e.g., that a patient either has or does not have narcissistic PD). Second, although the *DSM* relies on polythetic decision rules, it delineates a list of features presumed in some combination to *define* the disorder rather than *exemplify* its most important features. This has led to a confusion between a set of constructs (prototypes) and their operationalization or measurement. Whereas the intent of providing a list of features was to provide a guide for reliable assessment of the underlying constructs, the constructs have become defined (reified) as the presence of a certain number of criteria selected out of the universe of criteria that might have been used to describe the disorder.

This method of operationalizing prototype diagnosis has several limitations. First, an accumulating body of research suggests that personality characteristics, including PD features, tend to be distributed continuously rather than categorically (Widiger, 1993; Widiger & Clark, 2000). Categorical diagnoses perform poorly relative to dimensional diagnoses most of the time in PD research, which has led many PD researchers to analyze their data primarily dimensionally (e.g., Lenzenweger, 1999). The dimensional distribution of many aspects of personality does not preclude the possibility that some personality characteristics can have categorically distinct variants (e.g., a heart attack is qualitatively different from a panic attack despite commonalities in subjective perception of symptoms). Taxometric analysis can be particularly useful in identifying such cases (Meehl, 1995; Waller & Meehl, 1998). There is little reason to believe, however, that the cutoffs currently used in *DSM-IV* optimally identify taxonic cases even in disorders such as schizotypal PD for which data support the likelihood of taxonicity (see Korfine & Lenzenweger, 1995).

Clinically, categorical diagnoses fail to capture the pathology of most patients with personality pathology, who fall short of diagnostic thresholds despite having enduring, maladaptive personality patterns such as repeatedly getting into unsatisfying relationships or having difficulty regulating self-esteem (Westen & Arkowitz-Westen, 1998). A significant challenge in moving to dimensional models, however, is to devise a way of describing the range of personality pathology that is clinically useful and parsimonious. Dimensional diagnosis using trait models, for example, tends to be cumbersome (e.g., "The patient is a 2 on conscientiousness, a 1 on agreeableness, and a 5 on the anger facet of neuroticism," versus "The patient has antisocial features").

Second, the use of lists of criteria assessed independently for their presence or absence places limits on the number of criteria that can be included for each disorder, which in turn renders the development of psychologically rich, internally consistent, and nonredundant diagnostic criterion sets psychometrically impossible (see Westen & Shedler, 1999a, 2000). Axis II includes 10 disorders with eight to nine criteria each. To the extent that several disorders share features or have latent traits in common, such as negative affectivity, lack of empathy, or externalizing pathology, criterion sets with eight to nine criteria each will inevitably produce problematic rates of comorbidity. The only way to reduce this artifactual comorbidity is to gerrymander diagnostic criteria to minimize diagnostic overlap at the expense of validity. Lack of empathy, for example, is empirically central to antisocial PD (see Shedler & Westen, 2004; Westen & Shedler, 1999a), yet it is not a diagnostic criterion, because including it would lead to undesirable comorbidity with narcissistic PD. Increasing the number of diagnostic criteria to 15 or 20 would minimize the problem, because two or three shared criteria among 20 would have little impact on comorbidity (as opposed to two or three of nine). However, this would require that clinicians and researchers make present/absent determinations about 200 criteria rather than the current 80, which would clearly be unwieldy. We do not see a way of resolving this problem using the current format of Axis II.

Third, the use of brief criterion lists selected atheoretically runs counter to naturally occurring cognitive processes that occur in most classification tasks. Research in cognitive science suggests that people do not typically identify objects as members of categories by simply counting the number of features in common. Rather, they develop rich concepts or mental models that reflect an understanding of causal relations and patterns of covariation among these features (Ahn & Kim, 2000). This renders the learning of noncausal lists of diagnostic criteria difficult and readily overridden by richer mental models that assume interrelations among diagnostic features. Thus, when a clinician identifies a tendency to become enraged in the face of slights in a patient who also shows signs of grandiosity, he or she begins to frame implicit and explicit hypotheses about the way the patient regulates self-esteem. The combination of sensitivity to slights and grandiosity lends what the philosopher and cognitive scientist Paul Thagard (1989) refers to as "explanatory coherence" to an emerging formulation of the patient as having narcissistic features or dynamics. Although such inferences, like all top-down or theory-driven cognitive processes, can render clinicians, like all human information processors, prone to confirmatory biases, inferences such as these are in fact central to human cognition and to our capacity to form mental models, make accurate probabilistic generalizations, and frame and test hypotheses.

Fourth, clinicians express considerable dissatisfaction with Axis II, do not use the cumbersome diagnostic algorithms specified in the manual to make diagnoses in clinical practice, and tend to make unreliable diagnoses even when compelled to do so (e.g., Lewczyk, Garland, Hurlburt, Gearity, & Hough, 2003; Morey & Ochoa, 1989; Rush et al., 2003; Westen, Shedler, Durrett, Glass, & Martens, 2003). Although we might explain the failure of clinicians to use the algorithms specified in the *DSM* in terms of failures in clinical judgment, part of the problem may lie in the fact that clinicians, like other information processors, tend to be guided in their cognitive processes by their *goals*. If clinicians of all theoretical orientations and disciplines gravitate toward diagnostic practices other than those prescribed in the diagnostic manual, which empirically they do (see, e.g., Westen & Arkowitz-Westen, 1998), it may be that the manual as currently configured is not optimally serving their purposes.

In fact, *DSM-III* emerged from the Research Diagnostic Criteria (RDC; Feighner et al., 1972) of the 1970s, whose goal was explicitly to allow researchers to generate consensual definitions of disorders that would allow comparability of samples across sites. The assumption in importing diagnostic decision rules like those in the RDC into the *DSM* was that the same diagnostic procedures useful for researchers would be useful for clinicians.

The goals of clinical and research diagnosis of personality clearly overlap, but they also diverge in some important respects. Researchers need to identify homogeneous diagnostic groups and hence require consensus as to what "counts" as obsessive-compulsive PD, even if based on relatively arbitrary decision rules. Although clinicians also presumably strive for accuracy in their diagnostic judgments (e.g., whether a patient appears schizoid), they tend to focus on whether and in what circumstances a patient is functionally impaired in a particular way. Whether the patient crosses or fails to cross a particular diagnostic threshold generally has little impact on treatment decisions; from a clinical point of view, it is generally enough to know that the patient is narcissistic or has borderline features, without knowing whether he or she meets four criteria (and hence is healthy) or five (and hence is ill). To our knowledge, no one has empirically demonstrated any treatment significance of any of the Axis II cutoffs. Thus, clinicians may not be behaving irrationally in ignoring *DSM* decision rules in personality diagnosis.

RETHINKING PROTOTYPE DIAGNOSIS: A PROTOTYPE MATCHING ALTERNATIVE

As applied to psychopathology, scientific classification involves two processes (see Sokal, 1974). The first is taxonomy, the development of diagnostic classes or groupings (categories, dimensions, or prototypes). The second is diagnosis, the application of those diagnostic groupings to individual cases. For several years, Westen, Shedler, and colleagues have been pursuing a prototype-matching approach to diagnosis that addresses both questions of taxonomy and of diagnosis (Westen, Heim, Morrison, Patterson, & Campbell, 2002; Westen & Shedler, 1999a, 1999b, 2000). We describe here, first, a proposal for personality diagnosis in clinical practice that represents an alternative to the count/cutoff approach, which we believe is more faithful to the prototype model of classification underlying the *DSM*. We then briefly describe ways of selecting the prototypes (taxonomy), ranging from methods that retain the diagnoses currently included on Axis II to others that are more strictly empirical. We then conclude this section by describing some preliminary data comparing prototype diagnosis with diagnosis using *DSM-IV* decision rules.

Implementing Personality Diagnosis: An Alternative to the Count/Cutoff Approach

The approach to diagnosis we have proposed presents clinicians with a set of personality prototype descriptions, each comprising 15 to 20 statements about the patient's patterns of thought, feeling, motivation, self-regulation, and interpersonal functioning (Westen & Shedler, 2000; Westen et al., 2002). The prototypes are psychologically rich, including statements about both manifest behaviors and readily inferable mental states. Instead of presenting the statements in list form in relatively random order, which minimizes the ability of clinicians to form *mental* prototypes of the disorders in the diagnostic manual, the prototypes are paragraph-long descriptions, with criteria grouped conceptually to maximize the formation of coherent mental models or representations. (The decision to move from list to paragraph form emerged in discussions with Michael First and Robert Spitzer, whose advice we gratefully acknowledge.)

The task of the diagnostician is to evaluate the extent to which the patient matches each personality prototype using a five-point rating system (Table 13.1). This system capitalizes on the advantages of dimensional diagnosis while simultaneously generating categorical diagnoses that can be useful clinically for summary communication. Patients receiving a score of 4 or 5 are considered to "have" the disorder ("caseness"); patients who receive a score of 3 are considered to have significant "features" of the disorder. The method parallels diagnosis in many other areas of medicine, where variables such as blood pressure are measured on a continuum, but physicians by convention refer to values in certain ranges as "borderline" or "high."

A guiding assumption of this approach is that the use of the diagnostic manual and the reliability of clinical diagnosis are likely to increase if clinicians are not forced to make dichotomous (present/absent) decisions about either diagnoses treated as a whole (one of the key flaws in *DSM-II*) or diagnostic criteria treated individually and then combined using thresholds that vary across diagnoses (*DSM-III* through *DSM-IV*). The task of the diagnostician using this prototype-matching method is, instead, to examine each diagnostic prototype

Table 13.1   Empirically Derived Narcissistic Prototype

Narcissistic Personality Disorder

Patients who match this prototype have fantasies of unlimited success, power, beauty, talent, brilliance, and so on. They appear to feel privileged and entitled, and expect preferential treatment. They have an exaggerated sense of self-importance, and believe they can only be appreciated by, or should only associate with, people who are high-status, superior, or otherwise "special." Individuals who match this prototype seek to be the center of attention, and seem to treat others primarily as an audience to witness their own importance, brilliance, beauty, and so on. They tend to be arrogant, haughty, or dismissive; to be competitive with others (whether consciously or unconsciously); to feel envious; and to think others are envious of them. They expect themselves to be "perfect" (e.g., in appearance, achievements, performance). They are likely to fantasize about finding ideal, perfect love. They tend to lack close friendships and relationships; to feel life has no meaning; and to feel like they are not their true selves with others, so that they may feel false or fraudulent.

1. Little or no match (description does not apply).

2. Some match (patient has *some features* of this disorder).

3. Moderate match (patient has *significant features* of this disorder).	Features
4. Good match (patient *has* this disorder; diagnosis applies).	Diagnosis
5. Very good match (patient *exemplifies* this disorder; prototypical case).	

taken as a whole, or as a gestalt, and to gauge the extent to which the patient's symptom picture matches the prototype. As should be clear, this approach to diagnosis differs from the method prescribed in *DSM-IV* in format but not in spirit; the task of the diagnostician is still to diagnose the patient using a set of personality diagnoses. What is different is simply how the clinician gauges whether (and to what extent) the diagnosis fits the patient.

This method has several advantages. First, it is simple, efficient, and parsimonious. Rather than making present/absent determinations on each of roughly 80 diagnostic criteria, counting them, and applying cutoffs, the clinician simply rates the extent to which the patient matches each prototype as a whole. The default is "1" (little or no match), so that clinicians do not need to read through or rate criteria that are clearly irrelevant to a given patient. Second, because this method is dimensional, it captures subthreshold pathology (i.e., ratings of 2 or 3, which indicate some resemblance to the prototype). (We have derived a psychological health prototype as well, which gauges degree of personality health/sickness and allows clinicians to assess strengths and measure progress over time.) Third, this method produces a diagnostic profile, similar to a Minnesota Multiphasic Personality Inventory (MMPI) profile, which describes the extent to which the patient matches each prototype. This provides substantially more information than simple present/absent determinations. The profile also translates directly into language that is meaningful to clinicians (e.g., a 4 on narcissistic and 3 on histrionic translates to "the patient has narcissistic PD with histrionic features"), hence solving many of the dilemmas entailed by moving to dimensional trait systems. Fourth, the procedure more closely reflects the cognitive processes that people naturally use in categorization tasks and, hence, is more likely to be implemented in clinical practice. Finally, as we suggest later, this method should reduce comorbidity—even using the categories in *DSM-IV,* which have built-in redundancies and conceptual overlap—because clinicians are rating gestalts rather than isolated symptoms.

Deriving Personality Prototypes

The obvious next question is how to derive the prototypes to be used in such a system. This could be done in three ways. The first is simply to weave the eight or nine criteria for each Axis II disorder into paragraph form. This has the advantage of being maximally continuous with *DSM-IV.* The corresponding disadvantage, as noted earlier, is that eight to nine items are unlikely to describe a relatively distinct personality style, particularly when PDs can be expected to share traits with one another. As Millon and others have observed, the current criterion sets do not systematically cover the domains of functioning outlined in the preamble to *DSM-IV,* let alone domains clinicians and researchers might hypothesize using more systematic models of personality (see Westen, 1998; Westen & Shedler, 1999a).

A second approach is to identify the central psychological features of the PDs as defined in Axis II by collecting personality data on a sample of patients with each *DSM-IV* PD and developing prototypes of personality characteristics modal in patients with each disorder. A third approach, more empirical still, does not assume the current Axis II diagnoses. Rather, it identifies prototypes of naturally occurring personality styles using statistical procedures designed to find commonalities among groups of patients with similar personality profiles. For several years, Westen, Shedler, and colleagues have pursued these latter two approaches (Shedler & Westen, 2004; Westen & Shedler, 1999a, 1999b). We briefly describe those efforts here.

Identifying Prototypes Using the SWAP-200 Q-Sort

To identify PD prototypes, Shedler and Westen developed the SWAP-200, a Q-sort instrument designed for taxonomic research and assessment of personality pathology. (We are currently norming the second edition of the instrument, the SWAP-II.) In designing the SWAP, we drew substantially on the work of Block (1971, 1978), who pioneered both the use of Q-sort techniques for personality assessment and the development of personality prototypes in normal populations. A Q-sort is a ranking procedure, in which the observer sorts items into piles, from least to most descriptive of the person. (On the advantages and limitations of Q-sorts for measuring clinical descriptions, see Block, 1978.) Following Block, our goal was to provide clinicians with a standard "language" with which to make their observations, so that we could use data from experienced clinical observers to generate reliable formulations of a case or disorder. The SWAP presumes a clinically experienced observer, who has either observed the patient clinically over an extended period or has administered a systematic, narrative-based interview, the Clinical Diagnostic Interview (Westen & Muderrisoglu, 2003).

The SWAP-200 includes 200 personality descriptors derived from multiple sources, including *DSM* diagnostic criteria, relevant clinical and empirical literatures, research on normal personality traits, clinical experience, videotaped interviews, and input from hundreds of clinicians who piloted initial versions. The items are written in jargon-free English close to the data (e.g., "Tends to be passive and unassertive"), so that they can be used by clinicians of any theoretical orientation. Items that require inferences about internal processes are written in simple and straightforward language (e.g., "Tends to blame others for own failures or shortcomings; tends to believe his or her problems are caused by external factors" or "Tends to see own unacceptable feelings or impulses in other people instead of in him/herself").

Although the item set includes statements that reflect all of the Axis II criteria from *DSM-IV* (and many from prior editions of the *DSM*), it differs from Axis II in three primary ways. First, it includes items that describe subtle, clinically important aspects of personality such as motives and affect regulation strategies (e.g., defenses) that were not included in Axis II because of concerns that they could not be measured reliably. Second, it addresses the range of personality pathology, from relatively healthy (including psychological strengths) to relatively severe. Third, to maximize content validity in item generation, we used a model of personality that specified domains of functioning (Westen, 1998) to ensure that we did not miss psychologically important processes not currently linked to any specific Axis II disorder. We refined the item set over several years using standard psychometric procedures, soliciting feedback from hundreds of clinicians using the instrument, and eliminating or combining items with redundancy or limited variance.

A growing body of evidence supports the reliability and validity of the SWAP. Research has shown high correlations between SWAP-200 descriptions made by treating clinicians and independent interviewers, between independent observers reviewing recorded interviews, and between clinician ratings and self-reported antisocial and borderline traits assessed by self-report (Bradley, Hilsenroth, & Westen, 2003; Shedler & Westen, 1998; Westen & Muderrisoglu, 2003). Scores derived from the SWAP-200 and its adolescent version (the SWAP-200-A) correlate with a range of criterion measures, such as history of suicide attempts, arrests, psychiatric hospitalizations, social support, Global Assessment of Functioning, and family and developmental history variables (Dutra, Campbell, & Westen, 2004; Nakash-Eisikovits, Dierberger, & Westen, 2002; Westen & Shedler, 1999a; Westen et al., 2003).

Deriving Prototypes of the DSM-IV *Axis II Disorders*

To derive prototypes of the disorders currently represented in *DSM-IV,* we collected data from a random national sample of experienced clinicians ($N = 530$), each of whom described a patient with one of the Axis II disorders (Shedler & Westen, in press; Westen & Shedler, 1999a). (To maximize comprehensiveness, a subgroup of these clinicians described instead a patient with a disorder included in the appendix to *DSM-IV* or in a prior edition of the manual.) This procedure yielded data on 26 to 43 patients with each Axis II disorder. We then averaged, or aggregated, the 200-item profiles of patients sharing a diagnosis to derive composite personality descriptions of each disorder. An important psychometric benefit of aggregation is that the idiosyncrasies of individual patients and clinicians (i.e., error variance) tend to cancel out in adequately sized samples (Horowitz, Inouye, & Siegelman, 1979; Rushton, Brainerd, & Preisley, 1983). This method of aggregating descriptions does not assume the reliability of any individual clinician's description of a patient. Rather, following Block (1978), we assess the reliability of composite descriptions using coefficient alpha. The logic is the same as computing the reliability of a psychometric scale, except that we are interested in the extent to which 200-item description of patients are consistent across observers, rather than the extent to which a set of items is internally consistent. Coefficient alpha for all composites was > .80, suggesting that we were, in fact, able to identify reliably shared features of all the *DSM-IV* PDs.

Thus, a composite description of patients with a given PD should identify the core psychological features shared by these patients. Because the item set of the SWAP-200 includes all the Axis II criteria from *DSM-IV,* we are able to determine, using this method, whether the criteria in the diagnostic manual provide the best criteria for each disorder or whether some other combination of criteria might provide a more empirically accurate description.

From these data, we can derive two kinds of composite descriptions of patients with each PD. The first most closely approximates the concept of a prototype (i.e., the "average" patient with the disorder) and is derived by taking the average item score for each item for patients who share a diagnosis and displaying the items in descending order of magnitude (i.e., of centrality to the construct). Table 13.2 presents the prototype for borderline PD aggregated in this way (Westen & Shedler, 1999a).

A second method more closely approximates the concept of an ideal type, that is, a portrait of the disorder that is somewhat idealized, which emphasizes its *distinct* features (i.e., those features that distinguish it from other PDs). Rather than aggregating the raw SWAP item scores, as before, we first standardize the SWAP items across patients, so that all 200 items have a mean of 0 and a standard deviation of 1. We then average item scores (Z-scores) across all patients who share a diagnosis to generate a *standardized prototype.* This second method reduces the centrality of items that are highly descriptive of the average patient with a given disorder but also highly descriptive of the average patient in the sample. Table 13.3 presents the composite standardized description of borderline PD aggregated this way.

As seen by comparing Tables 13.2 and 13.3, the two approaches yield similar but not identical diagnostic descriptions. The advantage of compositing the raw scores is that doing so identifies features of the disorder that might readily be overlooked, such as the desperate pain and despondency of borderline patients. This intense psychological pain is not reflected in the Axis II criteria for the disorder but likely plays a causal role in generating many features of the disorder, such as suicide attempts. The advantage of compositing Z-scores, in contrast, is that doing so provides a more pure description of the central features

Table 13.2   Borderline Prototype Based on Average Item Scores

SWAP Item	Mean Item Rank
Emotions tend to spiral out of control, leading to extremes of anxiety, sadness, rage, excitement, etc.	5.05
Tends to feel unhappy, depressed, or despondent.	4.88
Tends to feel s/he is inadequate, inferior, or a failure.	4.42
Tends to fear s/he will be rejected or abandoned by those who are emotionally significant.	4.40
Is unable to soothe or comfort self when distressed; requires involvement of another person to help regulate affect.	4.28
Tends to feel helpless, powerless, or at the mercy of forces outside his/her control.	4.19
Tends to be angry or hostile (whether consciously or unconsciously).	4.05
Tends to be anxious.	4.05
Tends to react to criticism with feelings of rage or humiliation.	3.95
Tends to be overly needy or dependent; requires excessive reassurance or approval.	3.93
Tends to feel misunderstood, mistreated, or victimized.	3.79
Tends to become irrational when strong emotions are stirred up; may show a noticeable decline from customary level of functioning.	3.74
Tends to get into power struggles.	3.56
Tends to "catastrophize"; is prone to see problems as disastrous, unsolvable, etc.	3.51
Emotions tend to change rapidly and unpredictably.	3.51
Lacks a stable image of who s/he is or would like to become (e.g., attitudes, values, goals, and feelings about self may be unstable and changing).	3.49
Tends to feel like an outcast or outsider; feels as if s/he does not truly belong.	3.47
Tends to express intense and inappropriate anger, out of proportion to the situation at hand.	3.40

that distinguish borderline patients from other PD patients and, hence, may, as a prototype (or ideal type), lead to reduced comorbidity, even though it is not quite as faithful to the empirical reality. Whether one or the other of these methods is superior or whether they should be combined in some way is an empirical question, which we are currently exploring.

Deriving Diagnostic Groupings Empirically

The approach described thus far assumes the diagnostic groupings (disorders) delineated in *DSM-IV*, but it attempts to generate psychologically richer, more clinically and empirically accurate personality descriptions for each disorder. A more thoroughgoing empirical approach to identification of prototypes does not assume either the categories or criteria currently outlined in *DSM-IV* but instead attempts to identify diagnostic groupings empirically. To generate more thoroughly empirical prototypes of this sort, we used SWAP data from the same large national sample to identify naturally occurring groups of patients with shared personality characteristics, using a clustering procedure called *Q-factor analysis* (also called inverse factor analysis). Q-factor analysis is a person-centered, rather than variable-centered, procedure that groups *people* rather than *items* based on their common variance. Using this approach, we derived 11 naturally occurring personality prototypes, most of which resemble current Axis II disorders but some of which do not (Westen

Table 13.3   Borderline Prototype Based on Standardized Item Scores

SWAP Item	Mean Z-Score
Tends to make repeated suicidal threats or gestures, either as a "cry for help" or as an effort to manipulate others.	1.14
Tends to engage in self-mutilating behavior (e.g., self-cutting, self-burning, etc.).	1.09
Emotions tend to change rapidly and unpredictably.	1.08
Emotions tend to spiral out of control, leading to extremes of anxiety, sadness, rage, excitement, etc.	.93
Struggles with genuine wishes to kill him/herself.	.83
Tends to enter altered, dissociated state of consciousness when distressed (e.g., the self or the world feels strange, unfamiliar, or unreal).	.82
Interpersonal relationships tend to be unstable, chaotic, and rapidly changing.	.70
Is unable to soothe or comfort self when distressed; requires involvement of another person to help regulate affect.	.65
Tends to become irrational when strong emotions are stirred up; may show a noticeable decline from customary level of functioning.	.65
Tends to elicit extreme reactions or stir up strong feelings in others.	.64
Manages to elicit in others feelings similar to those he or she is experiencing (e.g., when angry, acts in such a way as to provoke anger in others; when anxious, acts in such a way as to induce anxiety in others).	.64
Tends to act impulsively, without regard for consequences.	.64
Tends to become attached quickly or intensely; develops feelings, expectations, etc. that are not warranted by the history or context of the relationship.	.61
Appears to fear being alone; may go to great lengths to avoid being alone.	.55
Tends to express intense and inappropriate anger, out of proportion to the situation at hand.	.54
Repeatedly re-experiences or re-lives a past traumatic event (e.g., has intrusive memories or recurring dreams of the event; is startled or terrified by present events that resemble or symbolize the past event).	.53
Has uncontrolled eating binges followed by "purges" (e.g., makes self vomit, abuses laxatives, fasts, etc.); has bulimic episodes.	.52
Tends to oscillate between undercontrol and overcontrol of needs and impulses (i.e., needs and wishes are expressed impulsively and with little regard for consequences, or else disavowed and permitted virtually no expression).	.52
Expresses emotion in exaggerated and theatrical ways.	.52
Tends to get drawn into or remain in relationships in which s/he is emotionally or physically abused.	.50

& Shedler, 1999b). (We have also used conventional factor analysis to derive traits from the SWAP-200 but do not discuss these further here; see Shedler & Westen, in press.)

Table 13.4 describes the empirically derived prototype that best maps onto the borderline construct and has replicated across multiple samples, both adult and adolescent (Shedler & Westen, 1998; Westen & Shedler, 1999b; Westen et al., 2003; Zittel & Westen, 2004). As shown in the table, this prototype describes a disorder characterized by intense affective dysregulation and desperate efforts to escape from painful affective states. Unlike the borderline diagnosis in *DSM-IV,* this diagnosis is uncorrelated with

Table 13.4   Empirically Derived Borderline Prototype

Item	Factor Score (standard deviations)
Emotions tend to spiral out of control, leading to extremes of anxiety, sadness, rage, excitement, etc.	3.21
Struggles with genuine wishes to kill him/herself.	2.89
Is unable to soothe or comfort self when distressed; requires involvement of another person to help regulate affect.	2.76
Tends to feel life has no meaning.	2.58
Tends to make repeated suicidal threats or gestures, either as a "cry for help" or as an effort to manipulate others.	2.55
Tends to feel unhappy, depressed, or despondent.	2.47
Tends to "catastrophize"; is prone to see problems as disastrous, unsolvable, etc.	2.42
Tends to become irrational when strong emotions are stirred up; may show a noticeable decline from customary level of functioning.	2.16
Tends to be preoccupied with death and dying.	2.15
Tends to feel empty or bored.	2.05
Appears to find little or no pleasure, satisfaction, or enjoyment in life's activities.	2.00
Tends to be overly needy or dependent; requires excessive reassurance or approval.	1.94
Repeatedly re-experiences or re-lives a past traumatic event (e.g., has intrusive memories or recurring dreams of the event; is startled or terrified by present events that resemble or symbolize the past event).	1.85
Tends to engage in self-mutilating behavior (e.g., self-cutting, self-burning, etc.).	1.82
Tends to be angry or hostile (whether consciously or unconsciously).	1.70
Tends to feel like an outcast or outsider; feels as if s/he does not truly belong.	1.70
Tends to feel misunderstood, mistreated, or victimized.	1.70
Tends to feel s/he is inadequate, inferior, or a failure.	1.69
Emotions tend to change rapidly and unpredictably.	1.55
Tends to feel helpless, powerless, or at the mercy of forces outside his/her control.	1.44
Tends to enter altered, dissociated state of consciousness when distressed (e.g., the self or the world feels strange, unfamiliar, or unreal).	1.32
Tends to fear s/he will be rejected or abandoned by those who are emotionally significant.	1.32
Perception of reality can become grossly impaired under stress (e.g., may become delusional).	1.31

near-neighbor Axis II disorders such as antisocial and histrionic. The advantage of empirically derived prototypes of this sort is that they reflect the characteristics of patients seen in actual clinical practice as grouped empirically using a statistical procedure (factor analysis, with the matrix inverted so that patients, rather than items, are factored) designed to minimize diagnostic redundancy. Such empirically derived groupings need to be well replicated, however, before being considered a viable alternative to the current classification of PDs.

For research purposes, regardless of which method we use to generate personality prototypes using the SWAP, a patient's diagnosis (dimensional score) reflects the correlation between his or her 200-item profile (arrayed as a column of data) and a set of diagnostic prototypes (also arrayed as a column of data). This method nicely operationalizes prototype matching and is true to the construct of personality disorder, which refers to a *constellation* of personality characteristics that cut across many functional domains, rather than a set of eight or nine specific trait indicators. For most clinical purposes, the simple 1 to 5 rating system described earlier is likely to suffice, yielding data that are psychometrically somewhat less reliable, but using a process that is considerably more cognitively economical, taking only one or two minutes versus approximately 45 to make a proper Axis II diagnosis.

How Does This Prototype Matching Approach Fare Empirically?

In several studies, we have examined the reliability and validity of SWAP prototype diagnosis using both the *DSM* prototypes (composite descriptions of patients with a *DSM*-defined PD) and the empirically derived prototypes. Both approaches have demonstrated substantial validity and reliability. For example, interrater reliability for both sets of diagnoses averages > .80 (Pearson's correlation); SWAP PD scores obtained by interview correlate > .80 with PD scores obtained from the treating clinician's description of the patient using the SWAP (blind to interview results); and borderline and antisocial diagnosis made using the SWAP correlate in predicted ways with borderline and antisocial scales from well-validated self-report instruments (Bradley et al., 2003; Westen & Muderrisoglu, 2003).

We have recently completed our first test of the simple prototype rating system described earlier as an alternative in clinical practice to the *DSM* count/cutoff approach, focusing on the four Cluster B disorders (antisocial, borderline, histrionic, and narcissistic; Westen, Shedler, & Bradley, 2004). We chose the Cluster B disorders because they are the most studied, have the best-known correlates, and show high comorbidity. A random national sample of experienced psychiatrists and clinical psychologists ($N = 291$) described a randomly selected patient in their care. Clinicians completed an Axis II checklist, which provided present/absent data on each of the *DSM-IV* PDs, which we used to generate both categorical *DSM-IV* diagnoses (using *DSM-IV* decision rules) and dimensional diagnoses (number of symptoms met for each disorder). Half of the clinicians then diagnosed their patients using prototypes of the *DSM-IV* PDs (hereafter, *DSM* prototypes). The other half diagnosed their patients using prototypes derived empirically using Q-factor analysis (hereafter, empirical prototypes). Clinicians then completed a number of ratings comparing the *DSM* diagnostic method with the prototype approach they had used on several measures of clinical efficiency and utility.

We compared the two prototype systems (*DSM* and empirical) to the count/cutoff approach on three sets of criteria used to test the adequacy of a diagnostic system: diagnostic redundancy (comorbidity), validity (in this case, ability to predict ratings of adaptive functioning, treatment response, and variables relevant to etiology), and clinical utility (clinicians' ratings of ease of use, comprehensiveness, informational value, and utility in communicating with other clinicians). To control for the possibility that any observed differences between the prototype and count/cutoff approaches might simply reflect the differences between categorical and dimensional data, we compared the two prototype systems to both categorical (present/absent) and dimensional (number of symptoms met) *DSM-IV* diagnoses.

The two prototype systems performed as well or better than both categorical and dimensional *DSM-IV* diagnosis on each of the three sets of criterion variables, with the empirical prototypes generally faring the best. Prototype diagnosis yielded substantially reduced diagnostic overlap. The median intercorrelations among the *DSM-IV* PDs treated dimensionally (number of symptoms per disorder) was $r = .47$. The median intercorrelations for the two prototype approaches were substantially lower: $r = .28$ for the *DSM* prototypes and $r = .17$ for the empirical prototypes.

Did this reduced comorbidity not come at the expense of validity; that is, did each disorder carry less information when we eliminated regions of overlap? To assess the validity of the different diagnostic methods, we compared the correlations between each set of diagnoses and ratings of adaptive functioning, treatment response (to both psychotherapy and antidepressant medication), developmental and family history variables known to be associated with antisocial PD and borderline PD, and family history variables likely to show associations with antisocial and borderline PDs. (Correlates of histrionic and narcissistic PD are largely unknown, so we did not specify any a priori hypotheses with respect to these disorders.) The four diagnostic methods (*DSM-IV* categorical, *DSM-IV* dimensional, *DSM* prototypes, and empirical prototypes) correlated similarly with measures of adaptive functioning and etiology, such as global functioning, history of arrests, history of suicide attempts, and history of familial internalizing and externalizing pathology; however, *DSM-IV* categorical diagnosis consistently fared the worst and the empirical prototypes, the best in predicting relevant criterion variables. Of particular note, given the importance of prognosis and treatment response in validating a diagnostic method (Robins & Guze, 1970), neither categorical nor dimensional *DSM-IV* diagnosis predicted medication response, whereas both prototype systems did.

Clinicians also preferred both prototype rating approaches to the count/cutoff approach in *DSM-IV* on every measure of clinical utility. In general, 70% of clinicians rated the prototype systems more clinically useful than *DSM* diagnosis, 20% viewed the systems as about the same, and only 10% preferred the more familiar *DSM* algorithms.

We now illustrate the use of this prototype matching approach to diagnosis using data from a patient, whom we call Ms. Y, chosen from among the 1,200 patients in a study just completed.

CASE STUDY

Ms. Y is a 30-year-old, African American female with a college education who had been in psychotherapy for three months at the time the treating clinician described her. The clinician gave her an Axis I diagnoses of dysthymic disorder and eating disorder NOS and a GAF score of 50, indicating moderate impairment. As part of the assessment, the clinician completed a randomly ordered checklist of all of the symptoms comprising Axis II. When we applied *DSM-IV* diagnostic algorithms, the patient met criteria for borderline, histrionic, and dependent PDs. We also asked the clinician to rate this patient on each of the empirical prototypes of the Cluster B PDs using the rating system described earlier. The clinician rated the patient as meeting criteria for borderline PD (a rating of 5) and having significant features of histrionic PD (a rating of 3). She gave the patient ratings of 2 and 1, respectively, for narcissistic and antisocial PD. On a questionnaire that addresses developmental and family history variables, the clinician reported a history of sexual and physical abuse in childhood and rated the patient's childhood environment as low in family stability and warmth.

Narrative Description

The reporting clinician placed the following items from the SWAP-II in the top three (most descriptive) piles (5, 6, or 7). We reprint the items here verbatim with only minor grammatical changes to aid the flow of the text.

Ms. Y struggles with genuine wishes to kill herself and tends to make repeated suicidal threats or gestures, either as a "cry for help" or as an effort to manipulate others. She tends to feel unhappy, depressed, or despondent. She has a pervasive sense that someone or something necessary for happiness (e.g., a relationship, youth, beauty, or success) has been lost forever. Although she has a limited or constricted range of emotions, her emotions can also change rapidly and unpredictably. She tends to alternate between undercontrol and overcontrol of needs and impulses (e.g., she sometimes acts on desires impulsively while at other times denying them entirely). When upset, she has trouble perceiving both positive and negative qualities in the same person at the same time and tends to see others in black or white terms (e.g., swinging from seeing someone as caring to seeing him or her as malevolent and intentionally hurtful). She tends to deny, disavow, or squelch her own realistic hopes, dreams, or desires to protect against anticipated disappointment. She expresses anger in passive and indirect ways, such as making mistakes, procrastinating, forgetting, or becoming sulky. In addition, she tends to use her psychological or medical problems to avoid work or responsibility.

Ms. Y's relationships tend to be unstable, chaotic, and rapidly changing. She tends to feel misunderstood, mistreated, or victimized, and to feel like an outcast or outsider. She is critical of others and tends to hold grudges and to dwell on insults or slights for long periods. She is simultaneously needy of, and rejecting toward, others (e.g., craves intimacy and caring but tends to reject it when offered). She becomes attached quickly and intensely, developing feelings, expectations, and so on that are not warranted by the history or context of the relationship. She fantasizes about finding ideal, perfect love, but also becomes attached to, or romantically interested in, people who are emotionally unavailable. She tends to have numerous sexual involvements (i.e., is promiscuous) and to choose sexual or romantic partners who seem inappropriate in terms of age and status. She also tends to feel guilty or ashamed about her sexual interests or activities.

Ms. Y is articulate and can express herself well in words, but her verbal statements seem incongruous with accompanying affect or incongruous with accompanying nonverbal messages. She tends to describe experiences in generalities and is reluctant to provide details, examples, or supporting narrative. Her beliefs and expectations seem cliché or stereotypical, as if taken from storybooks or movies.

Ms. Y has a disturbed or distorted body image. She appears conflicted about her racial or ethnic identity (e.g., undervalues and rejects, or overvalues and is preoccupied with, her cultural heritage). She is also afraid or conflicted about becoming like a parental figure about whom she has strong negative feelings.

Discussion of Case

Two features of this case description are worthy of note. First, it is a rich depiction of the patient's character, which readily allows the reader to form a mental image of the patient and to "connect the dots" among multiple symptoms and personality characteristics. It is also suggestive of clinical hypotheses, such as potential links between her history of sexual abuse and her enduring sexual conflicts, concerns, and behaviors. This description seems to us much richer than a *DSM-IV* Axis II diagnosis.

Second, based on the SWAP-II description, it is readily apparent why the clinician saw Ms. Y as having primarily borderline PD, given the patient's suicidality, disturbed interpersonal relationships, and tendency to see people as all good or all bad or to shift her representations of them when upset. The patient also has a number of histrionic features, such as changeable emotions and promiscuous sexuality, although it is equally clear why the clinician did not see the patient as primarily histrionic in her personality style. As compared to her diagnosis using the *DSM-IV* diagnostic algorithms, the prototype ratings are not marked by high comorbidity; rather, they offer a consistent, more integrated picture of her overall functioning than a simultaneous diagnosis of borderline, histrionic, and dependent PD. Although we did not obtain Cluster C prototype ratings and, hence, do not have a rating for dependent PD, it is clear from her SWAP profile that she would not receive a prototype rating > 2 for dependent PD.

CONCLUSION

We have described a prototype approach to personality diagnosis that we believe yields clinically rich and sophisticated yet psychometrically sound descriptions of personality pathology. It can be applied to patients whether or not they have a severe enough personality disturbance to be diagnosable using Axis II of *DSM-IV* and, hence, captures a broader range of pathology. The prototype rating system we described could be readily implemented, either in combination with the current set of diagnoses (i.e., changing only the method of diagnosis, from symptom counting to prototype matching) or in combination with empirically refined diagnostic groupings (i.e., changing both the taxonomy and the method of diagnosis). It not only reduces diagnostic overlap but also yields diagnostic judgments that better predict criterion variables than the *DSM-IV* diagnostic algorithms and appears to be substantially more user-friendly and useful from a clinical standpoint.

REFERENCES

Ahn, W., & Kim, N. S. (2000). The causal status effect in categorization: An overview. In D. L. Medin (Ed.), *The psychology of learning and motivation, 40,* (pp. 23–65). San Diego, CA: Academic Press.

Blashfield, R. K. (1985). Exemplar prototypes of personality disorder diagnoses. *Comprehensive Psychiatry, 26,* 11–21.

Block, J. (1971). *Lives through time.* Berkeley, CA: Bancroft.

Block, J. (1978). *The Q-Sort method in personality assessment and psychiatric research.* Palo Alto, CA: Consulting Psychologists Press.

Bradley, R., Hilsenroth, M., & Westen, D. (2003). *Validity of SWAP-200 personality diagnosis in an outpatient sample.* Unpublished manuscript, Emory University, Atlanta, GA.

Cantor, N., & Genero, N. (1986). Psychiatric diagnosis and natural categorization: A close analogy. In T. Millon & G. L. Klerman (Eds.), *Contemporary directions in psychopathology: Toward the DSM-IV* (pp. 233–256).

Cantor, N., & Mischel, W. (1977). Traits as prototypes: Effects on recognition memory. *Journal of Personality and Social Psychology, 35*(1), 38–48.

Cantor, N., Smith, E. E., French, R. D., & Mezzich, J. (1980). Psychiatric diagnosis as prototype categorization. *Journal of Abnormal Psychology, 89*(2), 181–193.

Davis, R. (1999). Millon: Essentials of his science, theory, classification, assessment, and therapy. *Journal of Personality Assessment, 72*(3), 330–352.

Dutra, L., Campbell, L., & Westen, D. (2004). Quantifying clinical judgment in the assessment of adolescent psychopathology: Reliability, validity, and factor structure of the Child Behavior Checklist for Clinician-Report. *Journal of Clinical Psychology, 60*(1), 65–85.

Feighner, J. P., Robins, E., Guze, S. B., Woodruff, R. A., Winokur, G., & Munoz, R. (1972). Diagnostic criteria for use in psychiatric research. *Archives of General Psychiatry, 57–63.*

Frances, A. (1982). Categorical and dimensional systems of personality diagnosis: A comparison. *Comprehensive Psychiatry, 23,* 516–527.

Horowitz, L. M., Inouye, D., & Siegelman, E. (1979). On averaging judges' ratings to increase their correlation with an external criterion. *Journal of Consulting and Clinical Psychology, 47,* 453–458.

Horowitz, L. M., Post, D. L., French, R. S., Wallis, K. D., & Siegelman, E. Y. (1981). The prototype as a construct in abnormal psychology: 2. Clarifying disagreement in psychiatric judgments. *Journal of Abnormal Psychology, 90,* 575–585.

Horowitz, L. M., Wright, J. C., Lowenstein, E., & Parad, H. W. (1981). The prototype as a construct in abnormal psychology: I. A method for deriving prototypes. *Journal of Abnormal Psychology, 90*(6), 568–574.

Korfine, L., & Lenzenweger, M. F. (1995). The taxonicity of schizotypy: A replication. *Journal of Abnormal Psychology, 104,* 26–31.

Lenzenweger, M. F. (1999). Stability and change in personality disorder features: The Longitudinal Study of Personality Disorders. *Archives of General Psychiatry, 56*(11), 1009–1015.

Lewczyk, C. M., Garland, A. F., Hurlburt, M. S., Gearity, J., & Hough, R. L. (2003). Comparing DISC-IV and clinician diagnoses among youths receiving public mental health services. *Journal of the American Academy of Child and Adolescent Psychiatry, 42*(3), 349–356.

Livesley, W. J., & Jackson, D. N. (1986). The internal consistency and factorial structure of behaviors judged to be associated with *DSM-III* personality disorders. *American Journal of Psychiatry, 143*(11), 1473–1474.

Livesley, W. J., & Jang, K. L. (2000). Toward an empirically based classification of personality disorder. *Journal of Personality Disorders, 14*(2), 137–151.

Meehl, P. E. (1995). Bootstraps taxometrics: Solving the classification problem in psychopathology. *American Psychologist, 50*(4), 266–275.

Millon, T. (1969). *Modern psychopathology: A biosocial approach to maladaptive learning and functioning.* Philadelphia: Saunders.

Millon, T. (1986). A theoretical derivation of pathological personalities. In G. L. Klerman (Ed.), *Contemporary directions in psychopathology: Toward the DSM-IV.* New York: Guilford Press.

Millon, T. (1990). *Toward a new psychology.* New York: Wiley.

Millon, T., & Davis, R. D. (1996). An evolutionary theory of personality disorders. In J. F. Clarkin & M. F. Lenzenweger (Eds.), *Major theories of personality disorder* (pp. 221–346). New York: Guilford Press.

Morey, L. C., & Ochoa, E. S. (1989). An investigation of adherence to diagnostic criteria: Clinical diagnosis of the *DSM-III* personality disorders. *Journal of Personality Disorders, 3*(3), 180–192.

Nakash-Eisikovits, O., Dutra, L., & Westen, D. (2002). The relationship between attachment patterns and personality pathology in adolescents. *Journal of the American Academy of Child & Adolescent Psychiatry, 41*(9), 1111–1123.

Oldham, J., & Skodol, A. (2000). Charting the future of Axis II. *Journal of Personality Disorders, 14*(1), 17–29.

Robins, E., & Guze, S. (1970). The establishment of diagnostic validity in psychiatric illness: Its application to schizophrenia. *American Journal of Psychiatry, 126,* 983–987.

Rosch, E., & Lloyd, B. B. (Eds.). (1978). *Cognition and categorization.* Hillsdale, NJ: Erlbaum.

Rosch, E., & Mervis, C. B. (1975). Family resemblances: Studies in the internal structure of categories. *Cognitive Psychology, 7*(4), 573–605.

Rush, A., Crismon, L., Kashner, T., Toprac, M. G., Carmody, T. J., Trivedi, M. H., et al. (2003). Texas medication algorithm project, phase 3 (TMAP-3): Rationale and study design. *Journal of Clinical Psychiatry, 64*(4), 357–369.

Rushton, J. P., Brainerd, C. J., & Preisley, M. (1983). Behavioral development and construct validity: The principle of aggregation. *Psychological Bulletin, 94,* 18–38.

Schwartz, M., & Wiggins, O. (1987). Diagnosis and ideal types: A contribution to psychiatric classification. *Comprehensive Psychiatry, 28,* 277–291.

Shedler, J., & Westen, D. (1998). Refining the measurement of Axis II: A Q-sort procedure for assessing personality pathology. *Assessment, 5,* 333–353.

Shedler, J., & Westen, D. (2004). Refining *DSM-IV* personality disorder diagnosis: Integrating science and practice. *American Journal of Psychiatry, 161,* 1–16.

Smith, E. E. (1995). Concepts and categorization. In E. E. Smith & D. N. Osherson (Eds.), *Thinking: An invitation to cognitive science* (2 ed., Vol. 3, pp. 3–33). Cambridge, MA: MIT Press.

Sokal, R. R. (1974). Classification: Purposes, principles, progress, prospects. *Science, 185*(4157), 1115–1123.

Sprock, J. (2003). Dimensional versus categorical classification of prototypic and nonprototypic cases of personality disorder. *Journal of Clinical Psychology, 59*(9), 992–1014.

Thagard, P. (1989). Explanatory coherence. *Behavioral and Brain Sciences, 12,* 435–467.

Waller, N. G., & Meehl, P. E. (1998). *Multivariate taxometric procedures: Distinguishing types from continua* (Vol. 9). Thousand Oaks, CA: Sage.

Weber, M. (1949). *The methodology of the social sciences.* Glencoe, IL: Free Press.

Westen, D. (1998). Case formulation and personality diagnosis: Two processes or one. In J. Barron (Ed.), *Making diagnosis meaningful* (pp. 111–138). Washington, DC: American Psychological Association.

Westen, D., & Arkowitz-Westen, L. (1998). Limitations of Axis II in diagnosing personality pathology in clinical practice. *American Journal of Psychiatry, 155,* 1767–1771.

Westen, D., Heim, A. K., Morrison, K., Patterson, M., & Campbell, L. (2002). Simplifying diagnosis using a prototype-matching approach: Implications for the next edition of the *DSM.* In L. E. Beutler & M. L. Malik (Eds.), *Rethinking the DSM: A psychological perspective* (pp. 221–250). Washington, DC: American Psychological Association.

Westen, D., & Muderrisoglu, S. (2003). Reliability and validity of personality disorder assessment using a systematic clinical interview: Evaluating an alternative to structured interviews. *Journal of Personality Disorders, 17,* 350–368.

Westen, D., & Shedler, J. (1999a). Revising and assessing Axis II: Part 1. Developing a clinically and empirically valid assessment method. *American Journal of Psychiatry, 156,* 258–272.

Westen, D., & Shedler, J. (1999b). Revising and assessing Axis II: Part 2. Toward an empirically based and clinically useful classification of personality disorders. *American Journal of Psychiatry, 156,* 273–285.

Westen, D., & Shedler, J. (2000). A prototype matching approach to diagnosing personality disorders toward *DSM-V. Journal of Personality Disorders, 14*(2), 109–126.

Westen, D., Shedler, J., & Bradley, R. (2004). *A prototype matching alternative for diagnosing personality disorders in clinical practice.* Unpublished manuscript, Emory University, Atlanta, GA.

Westen, D., Shedler, J., Durrett, C., Glass, S., & Martens, A. (2003). Personality diagnosis in adolescence: *DSM-IV* Axis II diagnoses and an empirically derived alternative. *American Journal of Psychiatry, 160*(5), 952–966.

Widiger, T. A. (1993). The *DSM-III-R* categorical personality disorder diagnoses: A critique and an alternative. *Psychological Inquiry, 4*(2), 75–90.

Widiger, T. A., & Clark, L. A. (2000). Toward *DSM-V* and the classification of psychopathology. *Psychological Bulletin, 126*(6), 946–963.

Widiger, T. A., Costa, P. T., & McCrae, R. R. (2002). A proposal for Axis II: Diagnosing personality disorders using the five-factor model. In P. T. Costa Jr. & T. A. Widiger (Eds.), *Personality disorders and the Five-Factor Model of Personality* (2nd ed., pp. 431–456). Washington, DC: American Psychological Association.

Widiger, T. A., & Frances, A. (1985). The *DSM-III* personality disorders: Perspectives from psychology. *Archives of General Psychiatry, 42,* 615–623.

Wittgenstein, L. (1953). *Philosophical investigations* [Philosophische Untersuchungen]. Oxford, England: Blackwell.

Zittel, C., & Westen, D. (in press). Borderline personality disorder as seen in clinical practice: Implications for *DSM-V. American Journal of Psychiatry.*

Chapter 14

A FIVE-FACTOR MODEL PERSPECTIVE ON PERSONALITY DISORDERS

PAUL T. COSTA JR. AND ROBERT R. McCRAE

The idea that personality disorders (PDs) might be understood as variants of the general personality dimensions summarized in the five-factor model (FFM; McCrae & John, 1992) was inspired by a reading of Millon's (1981) classic volume on PDs. In a review of personality stability for a clinical journal (Costa & McCrae, 1986), we noted that "his conception of personality disorders as persistent styles of thought, feeling, and behavior, and his explicit recognition that personality disorders represent more-or-less extreme standing on continuous dimensions (rather than discrete categories) is entirely consistent with a trait model of personality" (p. 416). From our understanding of the PDs as he described them, we offered a series of hypotheses on how specific disorders might be related to the dimensions of Neuroticism (N), Extraversion (E), Openness to Experience (O), Agreeableness (A), and Conscientiousness (C). For example, Millon characterized antisocial PD as "the aggressive pattern," and we predicted it would be associated with low A. Most of those hypotheses were subsequently confirmed (Wiggins & Pincus, 1989), and by now a large literature has linked the PDs conceptually and empirically to these five broad factors and their specific facets (Costa & Widiger, 2002; Dyce & O'Connor, 1998).

The convergence of the diagnostic categories of the *Diagnostic and Statistical Manual of Mental Disorders,* fourth edition (*DSM-IV;* American Psychiatric Association, 1994) with the factors of the FFM brings face-to-face two of the most influential contemporary models of personality. We know that there is substantial overlap in the constructs they assess, but we do not yet know how best to use that information for psychiatric diagnosis and clinical assessment. In this chapter, we consider how the FFM can be used in conjunction with the existing *DSM-IV* system and then outline and illustrate a new four-step approach to the assessment of PDs that is scientifically grounded and, we hope, clinically useful (Widiger, Costa, & McCrae, 2002).

Some of the data in this chapter were drawn from Personality and Personality Disorders in the People's Republic of China project. We thank our collaborators on that project, Jian Yang, Xiaoyang Dai, Shuqiao Yao, Taisheng Cai, and Beiling Gao, as well as the psychiatrists and psychologists who assisted in data collection. We thank Tom Widiger and Jack Samuels for comments on this chapter, Jerry Wiggins and Krista Trobst for orchestrating the Madeline G assessments, and Ralph Piedmont for his contributions to understanding her personality.

THE FIVE-FACTOR MODEL IN THE SERVICE OF *DSM-IV* CATEGORIES

It is now well established that measures of the FFM correlate with *DSM-IV* PD symptom counts (e.g., Ball, 2002) and that individuals diagnosed with specific PDs have distinctive personality profiles (Clarkin, Hull, Cantor, & Sanderson, 1993). It should, therefore, be possible to use trait information in diagnosing PDs. An individual who scores low in A, especially the Trust facet, might be a candidate for the diagnosis of paranoid PD; one who is high in Neuroticism might qualify for a borderline diagnosis. Some system is needed, however, to apply these insights in practice.

DSM-IV diagnoses are based on the presence of a specified number of criteria from a defined set. For example, a paranoid PD diagnosis requires the presence of four or more of seven criteria, such as "persistently bears grudges." Self-report PD instruments such as the PDQ-4+ (Hyler, 1994) typically formulate these criteria into questionnaire items and generate categorical diagnoses by using *DSM-IV* rules about the number of endorsements necessary to cross the diagnostic threshold. There is no directly comparable way to score PDs from trait data, such as the facets in the Revised NEO Personality Inventory (NEO-PI-R), because for the most part there is no one-to-one correspondence between traits and criteria. A disagreeable person is likely to hold grudges, but some disagreeable people do not. To establish a *DSM-IV* diagnosis, the clinician must ascertain for this particular patient whether he or she holds grudges. There are 80 such criteria in the *DSM-IV* (plus 14 others if the provisional passive-aggressive and depressive PDs are included), and a thorough assessment may take 2 to 4 hours (Widiger, Costa, et al., 2002). The practical function of personality assessment is to narrow the diagnostic focus to likely PDs that can be rigorously assessed by direct interview.

The computer-administered version of the NEO-PI-R (Costa & McCrae, 1992b; Costa, McCrae, & PAR Staff, 1994) generates an Interpretive Report, which includes a section of Clinical Hypotheses that is intended to serve that function. For each PD, a characteristic profile was first identified, based on judgments of the relevance of NEO-PI-R facets to its criteria and associated features (see Widiger, Trull, Clarkin, Sanderson, & Costa, 1994). For example, low A1: Trust was judged to be relevant to the criteria of the paranoid PD and assigned a prototypic *T*-score of 30 (very low). N1: Anxiety was judged to be an associated feature and assigned a *T*-score of 60 (high). Traits not relevant to a PD are not included in the profile. The computer plots the patient's profile, and overlays of the prototypic PD profiles can be used to judge how similar the person is to the prototype.

The computer also generates a quantitative assessment of profile similarity, using the coefficient of profile agreement, r_{pa} (McCrae, 1993). That index is based on the elevation of the trait scores and the distance between the patient and prototype scores for each profile element. The distribution of r_{pa} values in the normative sample was used to select cutoff scores. For example, because paranoid PD was said (in *DSM-III-R;* American Psychiatric Association, 1987) to be uncommon, only r_{pa}s above the 99th percentile in the normative group were considered indicators of that disorder. The Interpretive Report evaluates r_{pa}s for all disorders and lists those PDs that the patient is likely to have. These statements are not diagnoses; they are research-based hypotheses that the clinician can address with more focused assessment. The report also lists those PDs that are so far from the prototypical profile they can safely be ruled out as diagnoses.

McCrae and colleagues (2001) provided empirical evidence for the validity of this system. They gathered self-report personality and PD data from nearly 2,000 psychiatric patients in the People's Republic of China; clinicians rated more than 300 of them using a structured interview, the PDI-IV (Widiger, Mangine, Corbitt, Ellis, & Thomas, 1995). As shown in Table 14.1 (columns 2 and 4), r_{pa} was significantly related to PD symptom counts for each disorder. Although the correlations are generally not large, they are almost as large as correlations between the two PD assessment instruments themselves (column 1). Kappa was used to quantify categorical agreement (present versus absent) between the psychiatric diagnosis and the cut-point rules of the Interpretive Report; in 7 of 10 cases, it was significant (see McCrae et al., 2001).

A Simplified Alternative to r_{pa}

The profile agreement system of the NEO-PI-R Interpretive Report was originally adopted because it seemed to be most consistent with the categorical approach of the *DSM:* Diagnoses were based on overall similarity to a complete pattern. However, the elaborate procedures of calculating r_{pa}s may be unnecessary. A much simpler approach can be adopted that can be used without the need for computer assistance: NEO-PI-R PD scales.

In its original application, r_{pa} was intended to compare the profiles of two raters of a single target, and it was, therefore, designed to allow elements from both profiles to vary. The prototypic PD profiles, however, are fixed, and it is much simpler to compare individuals to a fixed standard. In the simplified approach, we create a scale for each PD using the theoretically relevant NEO-PI-R facets (Widiger, Trull, Clarkin, Sanderson, & Costa, 2002). The scale adds the raw scores from facets positively related to the disorder and subtracts the scores from facets negatively related; adding a constant eliminates negative values. Consistent with recent practice, we use only facets related to criteria (not associated features). Thus, the NEO-PI-R paranoid PD scale is defined as:

96 + N2: Angry Hostility – A1: Trust – A2: Straightforwardness – A4: Compliance

Table 14.1   Correlations of Self-Report PD Symptoms and NEO-PI-R Scores with Continuous Scores from Two PD Instruments

| | Criterion | | | | |
| | PDI-IV Score | | | PDQ-4+ Score | |
Disorder	PDQ-4+	r_{pa}	Scale	r_{pa}	Scale
Paranoid	.34**	.29**	.25**	.41**	.49**
Schizoid	.19**	.16**	.25**	.20**	.40**
Schizotypal	.23**	.16**	.18**	.37**	.42**
Antisocial	.47**	.20**	.23**	.44**	.49**
Borderline	.39**	.34**	.32**	.59**	.61**
Histrionic	.29**	.14*	.08	.44**	.37**
Narcissistic	.31**	.24**	.23**	.37**	.40**
Avoidant	.43**	.50**	.54**	.50**	.55**
Dependent	.35**	.36**	.29**	.39**	.34**
Obsessive-compulsive	.32**	.16**	.01	.23**	.11**
Median	.33	.22	.24	.40	.41

Note: Columns 2 through 5 report correlations between continuous scores on the PD instruments and the corresponding scores calculated from the NEO-PI-R. Correlations with r_{pa} taken from *Revised NEO Personality Inventory (NEO-PI-R) and NEO Five-Factor Inventory (NEO-FFI) Professional Manual* by P. T. Costa Jr. and R. R. McCrae, 1992, Odessa, FL: Psychological Assessment Resources. Scale = NEO-PI-R PD Scale. For PDI-IV, N = 317-350. For PDQ-4+, N = 1,909. *p < .01. **p < .001.

Columns 3 and 5 of Table 14.1 present correlations of these scales with PD symptom scores in the Chinese sample. This simplified system appears to work about as well as the more elaborate profile matching system: With two exceptions, the correlations are all significant, and the median values are slightly higher than those based on profile agreement.

As with r_{pa}, it is possible to develop cutoff scores that can be used to suggest the presence of a PD. Distributions of the NEO-PI-R PD scale scores, calculated as shown in Table 14.2, were examined in the NEO-PI-R normative sample (Costa & McCrae, 1992b; $N = 1,000$). The cutoff points were determined by prevalence estimates in the general population listed for most PDs in *DSM-IV*. For example, the estimated prevalence of schizoid PD is 1%, so the cutoff score of 79 was selected because 1% of the normative sample scored at or above 79. As a test, these values were applied to the Chinese psychiatric data. Note that this procedure assumes that the Chinese NEO-PI-R has full-scale equivalence (van de Vijver & Leung, 1997) with the English NEO-PI-R, an assumption that has at least some support (McCrae, 2002; McCrae, Yik, Trapnell, Bond, & Paulhus, 1998).

Using these cutoffs, it appears that the most common PDs in Chinese psychiatric populations are schizotypal, antisocial (in males), and borderline. Psychiatrists' PDI-IV diagnoses concur that antisocial is relatively common, but schizotypal diagnoses are rare (0.9%; McCrae et al., 2001). In five cases, kappa is significant, and the magnitudes are comparable to those found using either r_{pa} or the PDQ-4+ (McCrae et al., 2001). However, neither the PDQ-4+ nor the NEO-PI-R is fully successful in identifying the majority of Axis II psychiatric diagnoses—presumably because single psychiatrists' diagnoses of PDs are relatively poor criteria (cf. Molinari, Kunik, Mulsant, & Rifai, 1998).

NEO-PI-R PD scale scores may be more useful in screening disorders out. Patients whose scores are less than the median in the normative sample are presumably unlikely to have the disorder, and the clinician might save time by dispensing with that portion of a PD interview. The last column of Table 14.2 shows the percentage of cases that would be missed if this screen were used; for most disorders, it is fairly small. Note, however, that the savings in time is not as great as it might first appear. When applied in a normal sample, the screen eliminates the need to assess PD criteria in half the sample, but when applied in a clinical sample, a smaller percentage meets the screen. For example, supplementary analyses showed that the borderline screen eliminated only one-quarter of the Chinese sample.

Why are general personality trait scores relatively inefficient in aiding the diagnosis of PDs? It is probably not because they are assessing different constructs. The PDQ-4+ was designed to assess exactly the same constructs as the PDI-IV, yet the median kappa predicting PDI-IV diagnoses from PDQ-4+ diagnoses was 0.11 (McCrae et al., 2001). Another possibility is that self-report instruments are imperfect, especially in psychiatric samples. The best available basis for evaluating the validity of self-reports is agreement with ratings by knowledgeable informants, and in this case we know that the NEO-PI-R data were reasonably valid: Correlations with spouse ratings ranged from .32 to .51 for the five domain scores (Yang, McCrae, et al., 1999), values that are comparable to those found in American volunteer samples (Costa & McCrae, 1992b).

Yet, correlations of such a magnitude leave considerable room for improvement. In a small subsample ($N = 24$), there was some suggestion that r_{pa}s based on spouse ratings instead of self-reports might show stronger convergence with clinician diagnoses. Even stronger results might come from combining self-reports with spouse ratings or other informant ratings. Clinicians themselves might provide personality ratings on their patients (Blais, 1997).

If data on general personality traits were useful to clinicians only as an aid to the diagnosis of PDs, they would probably be of limited appeal. But personality traits are also

Table 14.2 Composition and Diagnostic Accuracy of NEO-PI-R Personality Disorder Scales

Disorder	NEO-PI-R PD Scale Formula	M (SD)	US (%)	Cut	PCR (%)	κ	Screen	Missed (%)
Paranoid	96 + N2 − A1 − A2 − A4	47.0 (12.7)	2.5	75	4.5	.02	46	4
Schizoid	128 − E1 − E2 − E6 − O3	48.2 (12.6)	1.0	79	7.2	.25***	47	13
Schizotypal	128 + N1 + N4 − E1 − E2 − E6 + O1 + O4 + O5 − A1	127.8 (17.6)	3.0	164	11.8	−.02	127	0
Antisocial (Male)	224 + N2 + E5 − A2 − A3 − A4 − A6 − C3 − C5 − C6	109.5 (20.6)	3.0	148	12.4	.23***	110	13
Antisocial (Female)	224 + N2 + E5 − A2 − A3 − A4 − A6 − C3 − C5 − C6	102.9 (22.3)	1.0	161	2.3	−.04	103	40
Borderline	96 + N1 + N2 + N3 + N5 + N6 − A1 − A4 − C1	98.5 (23.7)	2.0	150	15.6	.12*	97	9
Histrionic	N3+ N4 + E1 + E2 + E5 + E6 + O1 + O3 + A1	160.7 (19.1)	3.0	197	2.9	−.05	161	38
Narcissistic	96 + N2 + N4 + O1 − A3 − A5 − A6 + C4	95.8 (13.7)	1.0	129	4.8	.02	95	12
Avoidant	96 + N1 + N3 + N4 + N6 − E2 − E3 − E5	98.2 (21.5)	1.0	154	9.0	.42***	97	5
Dependent	32 + N1 + N4 + N6 + E1 − E3 + A1 + A3 + A4 + A5	160.5 (17.8)	3.0	195	4.1	.15**	161	26
Obsessive-compulsive	64 + E3 − O6 − A4 + C1 + C2 + C3 + C4	124.2 (15.3)	1.0	161	1.5	−.04	125	56

Note: Formula elements are raw facet scores from the Revised NEO Personality Inventory. US% = Estimated prevalence in the U.S. population (American Psychiatric Association, 1994); Cut = Cutoff score; PCR% = Percentage of Chinese psychiatric patients (N = 1,980; Yang et al., 1999) at or above the cutoff; Screen = Score to rule out diagnosis; and Missed = Percentage of true cases missed by using screen. *p < .05. **p < .01. ***p < .001. *Source:* From *Revised NEO Personality Inventory (NEO-PI-R) and NEO Five-Factor Inventory (NEO-FFI) Professional Manual* by P. T. Costa Jr. and R. R. McCrae, 1992, Odessa, FL: Psychological Assessment Resources.

important indicators of Axis I diagnoses (Bagby et al., 1997; Trull & Sher, 1994), and personality profiles provide a wealth of information relevant to the development of rapport, the choice of therapies, and the prediction of treatment outcome (Costa & McCrae, 1992a; Mutén, 1991). T. Miller (1991) discussed the clinical presentation, treatment implications, and outcome expectations for each pole of each of the five factors. For example, he reported that patients low in A often report victimization because they are so easily offended (cf. McCullough, Emmons, Kilpatrick, & Mooney, 2003); that they are skeptical of the process of psychotherapy and of the skills of the clinician; and that, at extremely low levels, they might terminate treatment prematurely (if, indeed, they began it at all). Miller argued that information on early in the course of therapy was essential to build a satisfactory treatment alliance.

Given the close links between general personality traits and PDs, it follows that a complete PD diagnosis would yield some of the same information that assessment of the FFM does. For example, patients who have paranoid PD are very low in A and would probably show the same pattern of clinical presentation, treatment implications, and outcome expectations that T. Miller (1991) described for disagreeable patients. However, most patients do not meet criteria for any PD, whereas all patients have personality profiles. Further, measures of the FFM provide some information that PD diagnoses cannot. In particular, none of the PDs is a reliable indicator of standing on O (Ball, Tennen, Poling, Kranzler, & Rounsaville, 1997; Egan, Austin, Elliot, Patel, & Charlesworth, 2003), despite the fact that O is central to the way clients understand the therapeutic enterprise. As Miller (1991) said, "O influences the client's reaction to interventions. . . . Some treatment methods are more unconventional than others, and clients differ in the extent to which they feel comfortable with novelty" (pp. 425–426). The small literature on trait-by-treatment interactions in psychotherapy includes demonstrations that O does affect treatment efficacy. Weinstein and Smith (1992), for example, showed that anxious patients high in Absorption, a trait related to O, benefited more from meditation.

Five-factor model assessments, either from self-reports or from informant ratings, can rule out PD diagnoses, suggest (with modest accuracy) the presence of some PDs, and provide a broader portrait of the enduring characteristics of the individual, which can contribute unique information relevant to the choice of therapies.

A FOUR-STEP ALTERNATIVE

There are, however, a number of reasons to seek an alternative that improves on *DSM-IV* PD diagnosis. As noted in many critiques (e.g., Ball, 2001; Clark, Livesley, & Morey, 1997; D'Andrade, 1999), the *DSM* PD categories are arbitrary, not internally consistent, and prone to excessive comorbidity with one another and with Axis I diagnoses. Despite the fact that PDs are defined as enduring conditions, Shea and colleagues (2002) showed that PD diagnoses are not fixed for most patients even over as short an interval as one year. And although some attempts have been made to develop treatment guidelines (e.g., Gunderson, 2001; Quality Assurance Project, 1991), it is clearly not the case that correct PD diagnosis would effectively dictate the choice of therapies, the ultimate rationale for categorical diagnoses.

Widiger, Costa, and colleagues (2002) have proposed a four-step strategy that they suggest might provide a useful framework for Axis II diagnosis. In Step 1, personality is assessed; in Step 2, related problems in living are identified, some of which are targeted for intervention; in Step 3, the clinician determines whether the problems lead to significant impairment and thus constitute a psychiatric disorder; if so, in Step 4, the clinician may attempt to identify discrete PD patterns.

In disorders of personality, it makes sense to begin the process with an assessment of personality, and Widiger et al. recommend that both broad factors and specific facets be measured. This might involve use of self-reports or informant ratings on the NEO-PI-R or a structured interview covering the same traits (Trull & Widiger, 1997). The resulting personality profile should be of use to all clinicians who need to understand their clients, providing insight into their emotional, interpersonal, experiential, attitudinal, and motivational styles.

But personality traits, even at extreme levels, are not disorders, and knowledge of the personality profile does not automatically translate into knowledge about the problems in living, or psychiatric symptoms, that the client may have. The second step in PD assessment is thus a systematic evaluation of the problems in living that are associated with personality traits. The phrase "problems in living" may sound subclinical, but it is intended to apply to the whole range of maladaptations, from annoying habits to the most dangerous and debilitating symptoms that may warrant long-term residential care (Fenton & McGlashan, 1990). Step 2 is guided by the personality profile, because certain kinds of problems are associated with each of the five factors and 30 facets. The higher (or lower) a person's standing on a trait, the more likely such problems are to occur, so the clinician's attention should be turned first to the extreme scores. For example, someone with a very low score on A1: Trust might be asked first about interpersonal problems related to the patient's suspiciousness or about whether the patient perceives himself or herself to be cheated and victimized. All domain and facet scores that fall outside the average ($T = 45$ to 55) range should prompt inquiries into related problems.

A systematic survey of problems in living requires a taxonomy that, to date, has not been fully established. We could begin with the *DSM* criteria, arranged, however, not by PD but by their associations with personality factors. Yang, Dai, et al. (2002) provided empirical data on these associations using psychiatrist ratings of individual criteria in their Chinese sample. For example, low C is associated with "is irresponsible in work or finances" (antisocial PD), "shows chronic feelings of emptiness or lack of purpose" (borderline), "has difficulty making decisions" (dependent), and "has low self-esteem" (proposed depressive PD). A patient very low in C should be queried about each of these.

As Westen and Arkowitz-Westen (1998) pointed out, however, Axis II criteria are only a small subset of the personality-related problems that clinicians face in routine practice, which include problems with authority, perfectionism, and insecure attachment. A more comprehensive list of problems was offered by Widiger, Costa, et al. (2002). They noted problems with authority under low A4: Compliance, perfectionism under high C1: Competence, and insecure attachment under low E1: Warmth. Altogether, nearly 200 problems were enumerated. The clinician need not inquire about all of these because, on average, only about one-third will be relevant to a client's personality profile. Problems with authority, for example, would be a focus of attention only if the individual scored below the average range ($T < 45$) in A4: Compliance.

Widiger et al.'s list is a useful beginning in enumerating problems of living, which can be used now by clinicians who adopt the four-step approach. But future research could improve this taxonomy of problems. Conceptually, it should be compared with others, including the *DSM-IV* Axis II criteria and other lists of problems from various life domains (Farrell, 1999; Horowitz, Alden, Wiggins, & Pincus, 2000; Piedmont & Piedmont, 1996; Westen & Arkowitz-Westen, 1998) to ensure its comprehensiveness. Empirically, correlational studies are needed to confirm that these problems are in fact chiefly associated with the theoretically relevant personality factor or facet (for preliminary evidence, see Felker, 2000; Hammond, 2000). Base rates also need to be examined so that rare problems can be eliminated from routine consideration.

Step 2—the systematic assessment of personality-related problems in living—should be a part of all but the briefest and most focused psychotherapeutic encounters. The patient may not wish to deal with some of these problems, or the clinician may feel they do not merit attention, but a broad understanding of how the patient adapts to his or her world should facilitate almost any intervention, from pastoral counseling to psychiatric hospitalization. A focus on Step 2 problems constitutes what Westen and Arkowitz-Westen characterize as a *functional assessment of personality,* because it specifies concretely how the individual's personality traits create difficulties in his or her life.

The therapeutic focus on concrete problems is also justified by the relative imperviousness of traits to environmental intervention. There is some evidence that traits can be modified by effective therapy (Costa, Bagby, Herbst, Ryder, & McCrae, 2003; Piedmont, 2001), but change is typically limited in magnitude and of unknown duration. This fact has led some writers to assert that the focus of psychotherapy for personality disorders ought to be on the characteristic maladaptations that arise from traits, not on the traits themselves (Harkness & McNulty, 2002). It is useful to help patients understand themselves and what they can—and cannot—change.

For many purposes, particularly counseling, Steps 1 and 2 are sufficient. But for legal, medical, or insurance purposes, it is often necessary to make a formal determination of whether the patient has a psychiatric disorder, which is Step 3 in the alternative system. For that, it is necessary to show that the personality-related problems lead to significant personal distress or to significant impairment in social or occupational functioning. Widiger, Costa, et al. (2002) suggested that scores below 60 on the Global Assessment of Functioning (*DSM-IV* Axis V) might be used to define impairment, although clinical judgment is needed to assess Axis V. Once a clinician has decided that the patient has significant impairment due to personality-related problems in living, a diagnosis of personality disorder is warranted. The diagnosis might specify the relevant personality factor (e.g., Extraversion-related PD) or, consistent with the current *DSM-IV* system, might simply be designated as PD-NOS.

However, some clinicians or researchers may prefer a categorical judgment in the familiar terms of the *DSM-IV* PDs or in terms of other distinctive personality patterns, such as psychopathy or authoritarianism. Five-factor model PD patterns can be useful in communicating a great deal of information about personality traits. From the perspective adopted here, such a characterization is appropriate as long as it is understood that the pattern describes a cluster of personality traits, not a discrete psychiatric entity. Step 4, the optional identification of PD patterns among patients who qualify for a PD diagnosis in Step 3, is accomplished by noting the similarity of the patient's profile to a theoretical prototype. Either the r_{pa}-based decision rules used in the NEO-PI-R Interpretive Report or NEO-PI-R PD scale scores above the cutoffs in Table 14.2 could be taken as operationalizations of the presence of *DSM-IV*-based PDs. Other PD patterns might be based on prototypes generated by expert consensus (J. D. Miller, Lynam, Widiger, & Leukefeld, 2001) or the mean personality profiles of patient groups (Brooner, Schmidt, & Herbst, 2002). In the alternative recommended here, these Step 4 profile-matching procedures would supersede the criteria of *DSM-IV*. That is, an individual who was high in N2: Angry Hostility and low in A1: Trust, A2: Straightforwardness, and A4: Compliance would, by definition, have the paranoid PD pattern, whether or not he or she bore grudges or met others of the current criteria. The accuracy of the diagnosis would depend in such cases entirely on the accuracy of the personality assessments, so the use of multiple informants would be especially encouraged. The value of multiple perspectives on personality is illustrated in the following case study.

CASE STUDY

In *Paradigms of Personality Assessment,* Wiggins (2003) reports an extended case study of Madeline G, a young Native American woman. In a series of chapters, her personality is discussed by practitioners of several assessment paradigms, and a follow-up recounts some of the subsequent events in her life. Madeline had a troubled childhood that included a period of delinquency, but she overcame it to become a successful attorney, specializing in defending the rights of Native Americans. She is by all accounts a colorful and fascinating character, but one with a dark side that has had real-life consequences. She is in this sense an ideal case study for illustrating personality and its disorders.

Madeline G completed Form S of the NEO-PI-R, and her common-law husband rated her on Form R (Costa & Piedmont, 2003). Consistent with her dramatic self-presentation in daily life, she had an extreme style of response to the self-report questionnaire, using *strongly disagree* for a third of her answers and *strongly agree* for almost half. As a result, her personality profile is marked by extreme scores that probably exaggerate her characteristics. Yet, in general, her profile agrees with that provided by her husband's rating; r_{pa} between the two is .95. In particular, both agree that she is high in E and O and low in A. She sees herself as being low in N and high in C, whereas her husband sees her as high in N and low in C. Even in these domains, however, there is some agreement: Both see her as very high in N2: Angry Hostility and N5: Impulsiveness, high in C4: Achievement Striving, and low in C6: Deliberation.

Step 1 of the FFM four-step Axis II diagnostic process requires that the factors and facets of the FFM be assessed. The availability of data from two sources is desirable, but it complicates the assessment. How are discrepancies to be resolved? Ideally, the clinician would discuss their responses with both parties and form a clinical judgment of the "true" profile. That was not possible in the case of Madeline G, so Costa and Piedmont interpreted the adjusted mean scores that are provided by the NEO-PI-R Interpretive Report. According to this algorithm, Madeline G is very high in E and O and very low in A, and she scores outside the average range in 28 of 30 facets—consistent with the impression of all assessors that she is anything but average.

Step 2 requires a consideration of problems in living likely to be associated with extreme scores—in this case, high E and O and low A. Widiger, Costa, et al. (2002) suggested that people high in E may talk excessively and self-disclose inappropriately, seek attention, be overly dramatic in expressing emotions, and inappropriately seek to dominate others. Interviews with Madeline's friends and colleagues confirm that she is deeply concerned with being the focus of attention, even to the point of fabricating stories about her associations with famous people or claiming to have survived cancer. Her domineering nature—her inability to take orders—led quickly to failure when she joined a prestigious law firm (Trobst & Wiggins, 2003).

High O is likely to lead to a different set of problems. High scorers in O are prone to daydreaming, have eccentric thinking, and show "social rebelliousness and nonconformity that can interfere with social or vocational advancement" (Widiger, Costa, et al., 2002, p. 440). Although Madeline is highly imaginative, there is little in her life history to suggest excessive daydreaming or eccentric thinking (discounting those attention-getting fabrications). She does, however, exhibit social nonconformity: "Episodes of 'flashing' (flaunting her nudity) are not uncommon party behaviors for her, and on at least one occasion she reportedly bit the buttons off the shirt of a man she had just met. To some, these antics are amusing; to others, they are highly offensive" (Trobst & Wiggins, 2003, p. 313).

Finally, low A is associated with paranoid thinking and cynicism, exploitative and manipulative behaviors, and rude and inconsiderate actions that alienate others. Her peers agree that she is boastful and self-promoting and "a master of manipulation" (Trobst & Wiggins, 2003, p. 314) whose interpersonal shrewdness is a considerable asset to her as a trial lawyer. But her self-centeredness was apparently at the root of her failed relationship: Her husband left her a few months after her initial assessment, complaining that she never had time or concern for him. This was a devastating event for Madeline, who went into a yearlong depression and was still unattached three years later.

These examples make it clear that the problems listed by Widiger et al. are clinical hypotheses that must be individually evaluated. We cannot simply attribute a set of problems to a patient because the patient has the relevant personality characteristics. Some of the problems listed apply to Madeline, but others do not, and—as with her interpersonal cunning in the courtroom—some may not be problems at all or may be advantageous in some circumstances.

In addition to assessing the presence of the problems, the clinician needs to determine if they should be addressed in therapy. Outrageous behavior is apparently egosyntonic for Madeline and does not seem to have significantly affected her social adaptation. She might, however, be persuaded to deal with her egocentrism and inconsiderateness to others, especially those close to her, because these behaviors endanger her relationships.

Step 3 requires a judgment about the severity of the problems and whether they constitute a diagnosable personality disorder. Occupationally, Madeline is quite successful; she does not have problems with substance abuse; and she is a valuable member of her community, proudly upholding the rights of Native Americans. Her marriage, however, ended in failure and has not been replaced. With neither spouse nor children, one might argue that her low A has led to significant impairment in personal relationships.

The optional Step 4 consists of identifying applicable PD patterns. Costa and Piedmont (2003) used the r_{pa} algorithm applied to the mean personality profile and suggested that, if she were a treatment-seeking patient, Madeline might have antisocial, histrionic, or narcissistic PDs. Applying the cutoffs for NEO-PI-R PD scales given in Table 14.2 to mean raw facet scores, Madeline could be characterized by paranoid, antisocial, histrionic, or narcissistic PD patterns. Her own self-reports would add obsessive-compulsive, and her husband's ratings suggest borderline PD pattern. The histrionic and narcissistic elements of her character are clear, but whether these designations add to the understanding of Madeline's personality is for each clinician to decide. Perhaps it would be better to use Millon's (1981) terminology and say that Madeline exhibits gregarious and egotistic patterns.

CONCLUSION

The links between general personality traits and disorders of personality were noted by Millon decades ago, and recent research has confirmed substantial overlap. It is possible to use personality assessments on the dimensions of the FFM to suggest particular *DSM-IV* PD diagnoses, and personality profiles in some respects complement psychiatric diagnosis, providing information on personality strengths and on individual differences in openness to experience that can facilitate psychotherapy. But the *DSM-IV* PDs have been widely criticized, and we have described an alternative way to assess personality pathology. In this four-step process, comprehensive assessment of personality traits guides inquiries about problems in living. If they are severe enough, these problems may warrant a diagnosis of a PD; if not, they may still benefit from psychotherapy. Finally, clinicians or researchers may wish to determine whether the personality profile matches established patterns, based on *DSM-IV* PDs or other constructs such as authoritarianism. For patients who happen to match these patterns, the designations may be a convenient summary of traits and their functional significance; for those who do not, the four-step procedure offers an assessment of personality pathology that is as unique as the patients' personalities.

REFERENCES

American Psychiatric Association. (1987). *Diagnostic and statistical manual of mental disorders* (3rd ed., rev.). Washington, DC: Author.

American Psychiatric Association. (1994). *Diagnostic and statistical manual of mental disorders* (4th ed.). Washington, DC: Author.

Bagby, R. M., Bindseil, K., Schuller, D. R., Rector, N. A., Young, L. T., Cooke, R. G., et al. (1997). Relationship between the Five-Factor Model of personality and unipolar, bipolar and schizophrenic patients. *Psychiatry Research, 70,* 83–94.

Ball, S. A. (2001). Reconceptualizing personality disorder categories using personality trait dimensions: Introduction to special section. *Journal of Personality, 69,* 147–153.

Ball, S. A. (2002). Big Five, Alternative Five, and Seven personality dimensions: Validity in substance-dependent patients. In P. T. Costa Jr. & T. A. Widiger (Eds.), *Personality disorders and the Five-Factor Model of Personality* (2nd ed., pp. 177–201). Washington, DC: American Psychological Association.

Ball, S. A., Tennen, H., Poling, J. C., Kranzler, H. R., & Rounsaville, B. J. (1997). Personality, temperament, and character dimensions and the *DMS-IV* personality disorders in substance abusers. *Journal of Abnormal Psychology, 4,* 545–553.

Blais, M. A. (1997). Clinician ratings of the Five-Factor Model of personality and the *DSM-IV* personality disorders. *Journal of Nervous and Mental Diseases, 185,* 388–393.

Brooner, R. K., Schmidt, C. W., & Herbst, J. H. (2002). Personality trait characteristics of opioid abusers with and without comorbid personality disorders. In P. T. Costa Jr. & T. A. Widiger (Eds.), *Personality disorders and the Five-Factor Model of Personality* (2nd ed., pp. 249–268). Washington, DC: American Psychological Association.

Clark, L. A., Livesley, W. J., & Morey, L. (1997). Special feature: Personality disorder assessment: The challenge of construct validity. *Journal of Personality Disorders, 11,* 205–231.

Clarkin, J. F., Hull, J. W., Cantor, J., & Sanderson, C. (1993). Borderline personality disorder and personality traits: A comparison of SCID-II BPD and NEO-PI. *Psychological Assessment, 5,* 472–476.

Costa, P. T., Jr., Bagby, R. M., Herbst, J. H., Ryder, A. G., & McCrae, R. R. (2003). *Evidence for the validity of personality traits measured during Major Depressive Disorder: Reinterpretation of the state artifact issue.* Manuscript submitted for publication.

Costa, P. T., Jr., & McCrae, R. R. (1986). Personality stability and its implications for clinical psychology. *Clinical Psychology Review, 6,* 407–423.

Costa, P. T., Jr., & McCrae, R. R. (1992a). Normal personality assessment in clinical practice: The NEO Personality Inventory; Reply to Ben-Porath and Waller. *Psychological Assessment, 4,* 5–13; 20–22.

Costa, P. T., Jr., & McCrae, R. R. (1992b). *Revised NEO Personality Inventory (NEO-PI-R) and NEO Five-Factor Inventory (NEO-FFI) professional manual.* Odessa, FL: Psychological Assessment Resources.

Costa, P. T., Jr., McCrae, R. R., & PAR Staff. (1994). *NEO Software System* [Computer software]. Odessa, FL: Psychological Assessment Resources.

Costa, P. T., Jr., & Piedmont, R. L. (2003). Revised NEO Personality Inventory profiles of Madeline G. In J. S. Wiggins (Ed.), *Paradigms of personality assessment* (pp. 262–280). New York: Guilford Press.

Costa, P. T., Jr., & Widiger, T. A. (Eds.). (2002). *Personality disorders and the Five-Factor Model of Personality* (2nd ed.). Washington, DC: American Psychological Association.

D'Andrade, R. (1999, January). *Problems with DSM.* Paper presented at the Anthropology and Psychiatry Conference, University of California, San Diego, Department of Anthropology.

Dyce, J. A., & O'Connor, B. P. (1998). Personality disorders and the Five-Factor Model: A test of facet-level predictions. *Journal of Personality Disorders, 12,* 31–45.

Egan, V., Austin, E., Elliot, D., Patel, D., & Charlesworth, P. (2003). Personality traits, personality disorders and sensational interests in mentally disordered offenders. *Legal and Criminological Psychology, 8,* 51–62.

Farrell, A. D. (1999). Development and evaluation of problem frequency scales from Version 3 of the Computerized Assessment System for Psychotherapy Evaluation and Research (CASPER). *Journal of Clinical Psychology, 55,* 447–464.

Felker, C. S. (2000). CASPER as a typological classification system for college student problems: Verification and validation with the Five-Factor and Millon theoretical models. *Dissertation Abstracts International, 60*(7-B), 3561.

Fenton, W. S., & McGlashan, T. H. (1990). Long-term residential care: Treatment of choice for refractory character disorder? *Psychiatric Annals, 20,* 44–49.

Gunderson, J. G. (2001). *Borderline personality disorder: A clinical guide.* Washington, DC: American Psychiatric Publishing.

Hammond, M. S. (2000). Impact of client personality on presenting problems and symptoms. *Dissertation Abstracts International, 60*(12-B), 6408.

Harkness, A. R., & McNulty, J. L. (2002). Implications of personality individual differences science for clinical work on personality disorders. In P. T. Costa Jr. & T. A. Widiger (Eds.), *Personality disorders and the Five-Factor Model of Personality* (2nd ed., pp. 391–403). Washington, DC: American Psychological Association.

Horowitz, L. M., Alden, L. E., Wiggins, J. S., & Pincus, A. L. (2000). *Inventory of interpersonal problems.* San Antonio, TX: Psychological Corporation.

Hyler, S. E. (1994). *PDQ-4+ Personality Questionnaire.* New York: Author.

McCrae, R. R. (1993). Agreement of personality profiles across observers. *Multivariate Behavioral Research, 28,* 13–28.

McCrae, R. R. (2002). NEO-PI-R data from 36 cultures: Further intercultural comparisons. In R. R. McCrae & J. Allik (Eds.), *The Five-Factor Model of Personality across cultures* (pp. 105–125). New York: Kluwer Academic/Plenum Press.

McCrae, R. R., & John, O. P. (1992). An introduction to the Five-Factor Model and its applications. *Journal of Personality, 60,* 175–215.

McCrae, R. R., Yang, J., Costa, P. T., Jr., Dai, X., Yao, S., Cai, T., et al. (2001). Personality profiles and the prediction of categorical personality disorders. *Journal of Personality, 69,* 121–145.

McCrae, R. R., Yik, M. S. M., Trapnell, P. D., Bond, M. H., & Paulhus, D. L. (1998). Interpreting personality profiles across cultures: Bilingual, acculturation, and peer rating studies of Chinese undergraduates. *Journal of Personality and Social Psychology, 74,* 1041–1055.

McCullough, M. E., Emmons, R. A., Kilpatrick, S. D., & Mooney, C. N. (2003). Narcissists as "victims": The role of narcissism in the perception of transgressions. *Personality and Social Psychology Bulletin, 29,* 885–893.

Miller, J. D., Lynam, D. R., Widiger, T. A., & Leukefeld, C. (2001). Personality disorders as extreme variants of common personality dimensions: Can the Five-Factor Model adequately represent psychopathy? *Journal of Personality, 69*(2), 253–276.

Miller, T. (1991). The psychotherapeutic utility of the Five-Factor Model of Personality: A clinician's experience. *Journal of Personality Assessment, 57,* 415–433.

Millon, T. (1981). *Disorders of personality: DSM III: Axis II.* New York: Wiley.

Molinari, V., Kunik, M. E., Mulsant, B., & Rifai, A. H. (1998). The relationship between patient, informant, social worker, and consensus diagnoses of personality disorder in elderly depressed inpatients. *American Journal of Geriatric Psychiatry, 62,* 136–144.

Mutén, E. (1991). Self-reports, spouse ratings, and psychophysiological assessment in a behavioral medicine program: An application of the Five-Factor Model. *Journal of Personality Assessment, 57,* 449–464.

Piedmont, R. L. (2001). Cracking the plaster cast: Big Five personality change during intensive outpatient counseling. *Journal of Research in Personality, 35,* 500–520.

Piedmont, R. L., & Piedmont, R. I. (1996). *Couples critical incidents check list, manual.* Baltimore: Author.

Quality Assurance Project. (1991). Treatment outlines for Borderline, Narcissistic, and Histrionic personality disorders. *Australian and New Zealand Journal of Psychiatry, 25,* 392–403.

Shea, M. T., Stout, R., Gunderson, J., Morey, L. C., Grilo, C. M., McGlashan, T., et al. (2002). Short-term diagnostic stability of schizotypal, borderline, avoidant, and obsessive-compulsive personality disorders. *American Journal of Psychiatry, 159,* 2036–2041.

Trobst, K. K., & Wiggins, J. S. (2003). Constructive alternativism in personality assessment: Madeline G from multiple perspectives. In J. S. Wiggins (Ed.), *Paradigms of personality assessment* (pp. 296–324). New York: Guilford Press.

Trull, T. J., & Sher, K. J. (1994). Relationship between the Five-Factor Model of Personality and Axis I disorders in a nonclinical sample. *Journal of Abnormal Psychology, 103,* 350–360.

Trull, T. J., & Widiger, T. A. (1997). *Structured interview for the Five-Factor Model of Personality (SIFFM): Professional manual.* Odessa, FL: Psychological Assessment Resources.

van de Vijver, F. J. R., & Leung, K. (1997). Methods and data analysis of comparative research. In J. W. Berry, Y. H. Poortinga, & J. Pandey (Eds.), *Handbook of cross-cultural psychology: Vol 1. Theory and method* (pp. 257–300). Boston: Allyn & Bacon.

Weinstein, M., & Smith, J. C. (1992). Isometric squeeze relaxation (progressive relaxation) vs. meditation: Absorption and focusing as predictors of state affect. *Perceptual and Motor Skills, 75,* 1263–1271.

Westen, D., & Arkowitz-Westen, L. (1998). Limitations of Axis II in diagnosing personality pathology in clinical practice. *American Journal of Psychiatry, 155,* 1767–1771.

Widiger, T. A., Costa, P. T., Jr., & McCrae, R. R. (2002). A proposal for Axis II: Diagnosing personality disorders using the Five-Factor Model. In P. T. Costa Jr. & T. A. Widiger (Eds.), *Personality disorders and the Five-Factor Model of Personality* (2nd ed., pp. 431–456). Washington, DC: American Psychological Association.

Widiger, T. A., Mangine, S., Corbitt, E. M., Ellis, C. G., & Thomas, G. V. (1995). *Personality Disorder Interview-IV: A semi-structured interview for the assessment of personality disorders.* Odessa, FL: Psychological Assessment Resources.

Widiger, T. A., Trull, T. J., Clarkin, J. F., Sanderson, C., & Costa, P. T., Jr. (1994). A description of the *DSM-III-R* and *DSM-IV* personality disorders with the Five-Factor Model of personality. In P. T. Costa Jr. & T. A. Widiger (Eds.), *Personality disorders and the Five-Factor Model of Personality* (pp. 41–56). Washington, DC: American Psychological Association.

Widiger, T. A., Trull, T. J., Clarkin, J. F., Sanderson, C., & Costa, P. T., Jr. (2002). A description of the *DSM-IV* personality disorders with the Five-Factor Model of personality. In P. T. Costa Jr. & T. A. Widiger (Eds.), *Personality disorders and the Five-Factor Model of Personality* (pp. 89–99). Washington, DC: American Psychological Association.

Wiggins, J. S. (2003). *Paradigms of personality assessment.* New York: Guilford Press.

Wiggins, J. S., & Pincus, A. L. (1989). Conceptions of personality disorders and dimensions of personality. *Psychological Assessment, 1,* 305–316.

Yang, J., Dai, X., Yao, S., Cai, T., Gao, B., McCrae, R. R., et al. (2002). Personality disorders and the Five-Factor Model of personality in Chinese psychiatric patients. In P. T. Costa Jr. & T. A. Widiger (Eds.), *Personality disorders and the five-Factor Model of Personality* (2nd ed., pp. 215–221). Washington, DC: American Psychological Association.

Yang, J., McCrae, R. R., Costa, P. T., Jr., Dai, X., Yao, S., Cai, T., et al. (1999). Cross-cultural personality assessment in psychiatric populations: The NEO-PI-R in the People's Republic of China. *Psychological Assessment, 11,* 359–368.

Chapter 15

PSYCHOPATHY AS A PERSONALITY CONSTRUCT

RONALD BLACKBURN

Those who cannot remember the past are condemned to fulfil it.

—George Santayana

Incorrigible behavior in the absence of impaired reasoning has been attributed by psychiatrists to a disorder of the person for more than two centuries (Millon & Davis, 1996). In its twentieth-century guise, the concept of psychopathy came to denote a tendency or disposition to behave in socially unacceptable ways that impinge on the well-being of others, and there is some agreement on the surface regularities in behavior in which this disposition is manifested. Psychopaths are commonly held to be self-centered, deceitful, undependable, impulsive, to treat people as objects, and to be indifferent to the harm they inflict on others.

However, concepts are more than lists of attributes and depend on a theme that gives the attributes coherence (Medin, 1989). We might agree that the common theme is something about the impersonal and abusive treatment of people, or as Levenson (1992, p. 68) put it, "the trivialisation of the other," but the boundaries of the concept and the nature of the disposition of which this is an effect remain slippery. Boundary concerns, for example, are apparent in longstanding disputes about whether psychopathy should be construed as a disorder of personality, a type of criminal, or an unwelcome product of a competitive society. Psychological explanation and understanding have also been restricted by the dominance of an empiricist philosophy of science that reflects Hume's insistence on questions of "how" rather than "why" and a distaste for broader theorizing and mentalism (Leahey, 1980).

Nevertheless, empiricist demands for operational definition have produced measures of psychopathy in the form of the Psychopathy Checklist-Revised (PCL-R: Hare, 1991) and the antisocial personality disorder (APD) category of *Diagnostic and Statistical Manual of Mental Disorders,* fourth edition (*DSM-IV;* American Psychiatric Association, 1994) that have guided recent research. Measurement is crucial to advance knowledge, not because it provides a theoretically neutral or objective basis for research, but rather because it is shaped by, and in turn shapes, the construct that guides research (Faust & Miner, 1986;

Hogan & Nicholson, 1988). An examination of the construct of psychopathy, therefore, invites a consideration of this reciprocal relationship.

Messick (1981) emphasized this relationship in a nonempiricist (critical realist) analysis of how dispositions relate to constructs and their measurement. Dispositions or traits are real properties of the person manifest in behavioral consistencies but are understood only in terms of constructs. Constructs are integrative hypotheses that delineate the domain of the disposition and its boundaries and require a measurement model coordinated with the construct. A trait is analogous to a parameter, a construct to its fallible statistical estimate. Constructs can, therefore, be biased estimates of the trait because of incomplete theoretical networks or implicit value connotations, while measures of the trait may also be biased through loose coordination of the assessment model with the construct. Meehl (1978) similarly observed that *psychometric drift* through measurement operations can generate *conceptual drift* that changes the meaning of the construct away from what we started out to measure.

This analysis provides a framework for evaluating the conceptualization of psychopathy. The main considerations are the theory embodied by the construct, the domain it specifies, and the fidelity to the construct of its associated measurements. The first part of this chapter examines the currently dominant construct and measures of psychopathy in this light. I make no attempt to review the extensive literature on psychopathy, much of which is covered in several books and reviews (Cooke, Forth, & Hare, 1998; Hare, 1998; Harris, Skilling, & Rice, 2001; Millon, Simonsen, Birket-Smith, & Davis, 1998). The second part considers possible biases in the construct and some alternative conceptualizations that have been proposed.

THE CONSTRUCT OF PSYCHOPATHY

The concept of psychopathic personality has had a tortuous history and has varied in the extent to which it denotes a disorder of personality or socially repugnant behavior (Millon & Davis, 1996). In Britain, the nineteenth century notion of "moral insanity" inferred a disorder of the person from social deviance alone. This influenced mental health legislation and led to the characterization of psychopaths as individuals who exhibit antisocial conduct from an early age.

German psychiatrists, however, saw psychopathic personalities as a generic class of disorders of personality observable among psychiatric patients and offenders, but also detectable in law-abiding citizens. Schneider (1923/1950), for example, explicitly excluded antisocial behavior from the definition. Psychopathic personalities were defined, first, by their abnormal (i.e., statistically unusual) personality characteristics and, second, their tendency to cause suffering to themselves or others. Schneider's concept has not influenced recent concepts of psychopathy, but its legacy is the broad class of personality disorders in current psychiatric classifications. It remains relevant to psychopathy because of its influence on conceptions of the nature of personality disorder more generally (Livesley, 2001).

North American Concepts

Influenced by psychodynamic and sociological interest in crime, North American concepts of psychopathic, sociopathic, or antisocial personality focused on a narrower and specific kind of socially deviant person while emphasizing a constellation of deviant personality attributes as the defining characteristic. Millon and Davis (1996) noted the variety of concepts proposed in the clinical literature, such as instinct-ridden characters, manipulative personalities, or malignant narcissism, but the most influential concept has been that of Cleckley (1941/1982). Cleckley rejected detailed classifications of personality disorders, including Schneider's, seeing most categories as neurotic or psychotic disorders, but he proposed a "distinct clinical entity," which he considered to be a disorder of personality.

He described psychopaths as individuals incapable of leading normal lives who cause great distress in their community, despite an outer mask of robust mental health. By analogy with semantic aphasia, he hypothesized that their attributes resulted from a "deep" disorder in semantic processing, which impaired emotional awareness of what the most important experiences of life mean to others. He proposed 16 criteria, such as absence of psychosis or nervousness, superficial charm, unreliability, insincerity, lack of remorse, egocentricity, and interpersonal unresponsiveness, although some criteria seem peripheral to the construct (e.g., suicide rarely carried out, fantastic and uninviting behavior with or without drink).

Cleckley's concept has stimulated research for the past four decades, but it is instructive to compare it with two other near-contemporary conceptions. Drawing on the concept of the social self, Gough (1948) also specified a core theoretical construct that aimed to account for the behavioral manifestations. He distilled a pattern of traits from the literature that closely coincides with Cleckley's criteria, such as impulsive, emotionally shallow, and inability to form lasting interpersonal attachments, and proposed that a pathological deficiency in *role-taking ability,* the capacity to identify with another's point of view, synthesized the observed characteristics. Inability to experience the social emotions of contrition and group loyalty and lack of self-control were a consequence of this deficit. McCord and McCord (1964) provided an overlapping description, identifying the primary manifestations of a "psychopathic character structure" as persistent antisociality; a craving for primitive satisfaction or excitement; an inability to control aggressive impulsiveness; a lack of guilt, conscience, or sense of remorse; and a defective capacity for loving others. Persistent antisocial behavior was a necessary, but not sufficient, criterion and a function of a craving for excitement. The essential criteria were *guiltlessness* and *lovelessness.*

Although apparently similar, these concepts differ in significant ways. First, each identifies the core of the construct as a *deficit,* but where for Gough this is a cognitive dysfunction, for Cleckley and the McCords, it is affective. Second, they employ different embedding theoretical networks. Gough drew on the symbolic interactionism of social psychology, Cleckley on a disease model of traditional psychiatry, and the McCords on a psychodynamic developmental perspective. Concomitantly, Gough specifies the etiology of the deficit in social development, the McCords in family rejection, while Cleckley's quasi-neurological concept of *semantic dementia* implies a constitutional defect in the nervous system.

Third, the behavioral manifestations vary. Although Cleckley observed that psychopaths may become bored easily and seek out novelty, this does not appear among his criteria, whereas both Gough and the McCords include impulsiveness. Only the McCords specify aggressiveness as a manifestation. Moreover, only the McCords include criminal behavior as a core manifestation. They are clearly describing a type of criminal, although they do not clarify why guiltlessness and lovelessness are limited to persistent lawbreakers. Neither Cleckley nor Gough, on the other hand, see psychopathic traits as the prerogative of adjudicated offenders. Cleckley distinguished psychopathy from criminality, delinquency, consistent sexual deviation, hedonism, and clinical alcoholism, and noted that the typical psychopath ". . . is not likely to commit major crimes that result in long prison terms" (1982, p. 14). Similarly, Gough suggested that psychopaths would contribute more than their fair share to criminal behavior, but stressed that psychopathy was not explicitly dependent on illegal or asocial behavior.

Somewhat inconsistently, Cleckley regarded the *DSM-II* category of antisocial personality disorder as a fair summary of psychopathy. This category included the attributes of "chronically antisocial" and "hedonistic" excluded from his own concept. However, these three concepts may emphasize different, though related, personality constructs. Several of Cleckley's criteria, for example, appear in current descriptions of histrionic personality disorder (superficial charm, egocentric, emotionally shallow, suicide gestures, impersonal sex life). On the other hand, the McCords' focus on persistently antisocial behavior resulting from a craving for excitement reflects a hypothesis common in criminology that criminality results from impulsivity or *lack of self-control* (Blackburn, 1995). Gottfredson and Hirschi (1990), for example, contend that criminality is a disposition to seek short-term, immediate pleasure without regard for the consequences.

Although the explanatory power of Gough's construct is psychologically greater than that of Cleckley's, the latter is more reductionist and had greater appeal for hard-nosed empiricists. From the late 1950s onward, Cleckley's criteria provided operational criteria for research by psychologists, notably Lykken (1995) and Hare (1970, 1991). His specific hypothesis of semantic dementia has not itself been subjected to much empirical testing, but his proposal that an emotional deficit is the core of a psychopathic disposition has been central in research.

The Psychopathy Checklist-Revised

The PCL-R is now the most widely used measure of psychopathy. It was derived through factor analysis of Cleckley's criteria and other items and consists of 20 items each scored 0 to 2 from a semistructured interview and file information. A total score of 30 or more identifies psychopaths, but this has not been consistent in research, and a cutoff of 25 is commonly recommended in Europe. Early research focused on the PCL-R total score, but a 12-item screening version (PCL-SV) has been developed as a short form to facilitate assessment in civil populations. The PCL-R has good psychometric properties that generalize cross-culturally, and the psychopathy construct has been shown to apply to preadolescent children and adolescent boys, though less clearly to females (see Harris et al., 2001, for a review).

Hare (1991) argues that the "Cleckley psychopath" is the clinical basis for the PCL-R. However, there are several reasons for questioning the coordination of the measure with this construct. First, although the PCL-R contains several of Cleckley's defining traits, it goes well beyond them and includes several items not derived from Cleckley's construct, such as grandiosity, impulsivity, and juvenile delinquency. Factor analysis revealed two correlated factors (Harpur, Hare, & Hakstian, 1989), the first reflecting a selfish, callous, and remorseless use of others (e.g., superficial charm, egocentricity, lack of empathy); the second, social deviance or a chronically unstable and antisocial lifestyle (e.g., proneness to boredom, parasitic lifestyle, impulsivity, juvenile delinquency). For brevity, these factors are referred to as F1 and F2, respectively, in the following discussion. The former is considered to represent the core of psychopathy as described by Cleckley.

Harpur et al. (1989) found several differential correlates of the two factors. F2, but not F1, related inversely to intelligence and social class, suggesting its association with working-class criminality. F2 also related more strongly than F1 to *DSM-III* antisocial personality disorder, whereas F2, but not F1, correlated with narcissistic disorder. Self-report personality measures generally correlate only weakly with the PCL-R, but scales of narcissism, Machiavellianism, and lack of empathy correlate significantly with F1, while impulsivity and sensation seeking correlate with F2 (Hare, 1991).

Hare (1991) saw the total PCL-R score combining the two factors as a "unidimensional measure," and reported high correlations between this score and ratings of Cleckley's criteria. However, as Lilienfeld (1994) noted, the contribution of F2 implies that antisocial behavior is necessary to the concept of psychopathy, contrary to Cleckley's view. In fact, the description of F2 as "social deviance" is misleading, because it mixes traits (impulsivity, irresponsibility) with antisocial items (juvenile delinquency, revocation of conditional release). This factor can perhaps be construed as the disposition of self-control identified by Gottfredson and Hirschi (1990) to underlie criminality. Cleckley's construct may, then, be measured with some fidelity by F1, but the PCL-R total represents a drift away from this concept. The PCL-R may well be overall a comprehensive representation of psychopathy, but it is closer to the concept of the McCords than that of Cleckley.

A second example of conceptual drift is the current focus of research on the predictive utility of the PCL-R in assessing risk for violent recidivism. The PCL-R consistently identifies the more persistent offenders and is one of the best single predictors of both violent and nonviolent recidivism in released prisoners and mentally disordered offenders, as well as a predictor of institutional misconduct (Hare, Clark, Grann, & Thornton, 2000; Harris et al., 2001; Hemphill, Hare, & Wong, 1998; Salekin, Rogers, & Sewell, 1996). This is paradoxical given that neither aggression nor impulsivity appears as explicit traits among Cleckley's criteria. It is assumed that Cleckley's construct of an affective deficit accounts for an increased propensity for violence, but the validity of this requires first that the relationship is mediated primarily by F1 because it seems more obviously predictable from F2. The evidence is equivocal. In a meta-analysis, Hemphill et al. (1998) found that F2 correlated more highly with general recidivism than did F1, but both factors contributed equally to the prediction of violence. However, this was based on only a small number of studies, and Salekin et al. (1996) questioned the strength of the F1 relationship. Skeem and Mulvey (2001) found that although the PCL-SV total score was a relatively strong predictor of violence in a civil psychiatric sample, its predictive power came from the equivalent of F2 rather than. As Hart (1998) notes, the proximal cause of a violent crime is not psychopathy, but rather a decision to act violently. A psychopathic disposition may mediate such decision making through several possible mechanisms, such as perceptions of hostile intent, a generalized affective deficit, or lack of forethought. In the absence of research permitting a choice among these, the primacy of an affective deficit remains a tenuous assumption. For example, Woodworth and Porter (2002) found that among homicides, the offenses of psychopaths were primarily "instrumental." This was mediated mainly by F1 and was held to reflect murder "in cold blood." However, the violence of psychopaths was commonly motivated by vengeance and retribution, which are "hot" emotions more characteristic of "angry" than "instrumental" aggression, and their victims were more likely to be female. A more plausible interpretation is that their crimes reflected the narcissistic grandiosity of F1 and were an excessive reaction to threatened egotism (Baumeister, Smart, & Boden, 1996).

A further source of conceptual drift is the absence from the PCL-R of several items considered critical by Cleckley, notably absence of psychosis and absence of nervousness. The omission of these exclusionary criteria questions whether the measurement model matches that required by the construct (Messick, 1981). Cleckley's construct of psychopathy as "a distinct clinical entity" is clearly categorical. Exclusionary criteria are appropriate to categorical diagnosis, which does not require a homogeneous scale. The latter is more appropriate to a continuous variable. The measurement model of the PCL-R is ambiguous and reflects ambivalence about whether psychopathy should be construed as a discrete entity or a continuous dimension, an issue on which Hare (1970, 1998) declares himself agnostic. The total score reflects a homogeneous dimension (Hare, 1991), but it is often interpreted as the extent to which an individual meets the prototype of a psychopath and is used to create a dichotomy. This is not unreasonable for much research, but cutoff scores distinguishing psychopaths from nonpsychopaths can create the illusion that a discrete category has been identified. In fact, the common cutoff for dichotomizing the PCL-R is relatively arbitrary (Salekin et al., 1996).

The PCL-R measurement model more clearly meets the requirement of a quantitative dimension specified earlier by Hare (1970, p. 12) than that of a discrete category. In this dimensional concept, a single score on the PCL-R represents a person's degree of psychopathy, and psychopaths "exist" only as a convenient fiction representing an extreme degree. Implicitly, a dimensional conception acknowledges the absurdity of assuming that traits such as egocentricity, unreliability, or deceitfulness are limited to only a small section of humanity. However, Harris, Rice, and Quinsey (1994) argue that psychopathy is a discrete entity and not merely the end of a continuum. Applying taxometric methods to measures of psychopathy and childhood variables reflecting antisocial conduct, they found evidence for a taxon. However, chronic antisocial behavior beginning in childhood was the central feature rather than the affective and personality characteristics associated with F1. This was replicated by Skilling, Harris, Rice, and Quinsey (2002), who also included APD items. PCL-R and APD items were found to be highly correlated, and the level of prediction of violence was similar for both sets of items. Again, however, PCL-R F1 items were peripheral to the taxon. It, therefore, appears that a natural class may underlie the persistent rule-breaking assessed by APD and F2. This rediscovery of "the born criminal" should give us pause for thought.

The two-factor model has been questioned by Cooke and Michie (2001). Using confirmatory factor analysis, they developed a model in which three correlated factors are necessary to specify a superordinate construct of psychopathy: deceitful interpersonal style, deficient affective experience, and impulsive and irresponsible behavioral style. They contend that all factors contribute to a similar extent. In this model, F1 divides into the interpersonal and affective components and seven PCL-R items are deleted, most of them implicitly or explicitly entailing criminal behavior. Criminal behavior then becomes a correlate or a consequence of psychopathy rather than a core feature, consistent with Cleckley's views (Cooke, Michie, Hart, & Clark, in press). However, the three-factor model does not clarify whether the emotional deficit hypothesized to be the core of the disposition is reflected in the superordinate dimension or only one of the component factors. The model calls for a radical revision of the theoretical construct to accommodate this structure.

Primary and Secondary Psychopathy

Cleckley's concept is often described as the primary or classical concept of psychopathy, as distinct from *secondary* psychopathy. The distinction originated in psychodynamic conceptions, which differentiated socially deviant behavior resulting from deficient conscience from similar behavior arising from neurotic conflict or other psychopathology (e.g., McCord & McCord, 1964). Influenced by the learning theories of the time, early research linked the hypothesized emotional deficit of primary psychopathy to low anxiety and secondary psychopathy to high anxiety. This was the basis for theories that nonconformity in psychopaths resulted from problems created by low anxiety or fearlessness for socializing children through child-rearing methods relying on punishment. This theory is maintained by Lykken (1995), who now replaces the notion of secondary psychopaths with that of "sociopaths" who are criminal but not characterized by high fear. Although studies using personality questionnaires support the idea of secondary or anxious psychopaths (Blackburn, 1996), this questionnaire typology relates only weakly to the PCL-R (Blackburn, 1998), consistent with findings that self-reports do not readily tap the traits of F1. There is, nevertheless, a growing literature that suggests that psychopaths are not a homogeneous group (Skeem, Poythress, Edens, Lilienfeld, & Cale, 2003).

The issue of secondary psychopathy is theoretically critical to Cleckley's construct. Although it is assumed that the PCL-R measures primary psychopathy and is, hence, inversely related to anxiety, the omission of Cleckley's exclusionary criteria questions this. If absence of nervousness is equivalent to low trait anxiety, Cleckley's use of this exclusionary item means that his psychopaths were nonanxious *by definition*. Newman (1998) found that predictions from his hypothesis of a response modulation deficit in psychopaths are supported only when PCL-R psychopaths with high anxiety are excluded, and Schmitt and Newman (1999) found that PCL-R and F1 and F2 scores were all independent of trait anxiety or fearlessness. They conclude that the PCL-R does not measure primary psychopathy.

Consistent with this conclusion, we also found an absence of any inverse relationship between the PCL-R and Axis I anxiety or mood disorders (Blackburn, Logan, Donnelly, & Renwick, 2003). In another study, cluster analysis of the *DSM-III* personality disorders among violent offenders indicated three groups who scored equally highly on the PCL-R and its two subfactors (Blackburn & Coid, 1999). One group was primarily narcissistic and reported the lowest levels of Axis I anxiety and mood disorders. Another displayed borderline, avoidant, and other personality disorders associated with trait anxiety and reported the highest levels of anxiety and mood disorders. These two groups justify the distinction between primary and secondary psychopaths. These findings seem to reflect a failure of the PCL-R to provide an unbiased measure of Cleckley's construct. It could be argued, however, that the empirically derived PCL-R is a better measure of psychopathy and that Cleckley's inference of an emotional deficit in psychopaths was an artifact of excluding nonanxious people from his psychopathic category.

Our distinction suggests that primary and secondary psychopaths are *phenotypically* distinct groups having a similar extreme position on the psychopathy dimension, but distinguished by opposite extremes on an orthogonal dimension of anxiety. Some writers, however, make a *genotypic* distinction (see Skeem et al., 2003). Mealey (1995), for example, proposed two types falling at extremes of a continuum of "sociopathy," a product of evolutionary pressures manifested in predatory social interactions associated with emotional unresponsiveness. *Primary sociopaths* are a small but stable number of "cheaters" selected for in every culture through frequency dependent selection. *Secondary sociopathy* reflects a less extreme position on the genetic continuum and is the outcome of environmental conditions in which criminal behavior as a cheating strategy is more likely among individuals at a competitive disadvantage. In an addendum, Mealey suggested that primary sociopathy is reflected in F1 of the PCL-R, and secondary sociopathy in F2. However, as these are correlated variables, it is difficult to reconcile this suggestion with her proposal of two discrete types on a single continuum.

Porter (1996) proposed a similar etiological distinction between *fundamental psychopathy,* an inability to form interpersonal bonds together with a lack of empathy and conscience resulting from genetic predisposition, and *secondary psychopathy,* where the same outcome results from traumatic interpersonal experiences producing dissociation of affect. However, as Porter noted, etiological theories specifying different pathways to the same phenotypic outcome are untestable except by longitudinal research. Moreover, while such theories have implications for primary intervention, phenotypic discrimination of psychopaths based on variation along theoretically relevant personality dimensions has more immediate implications for construct validity, prediction, and secondary intervention.

Antisocial Personality Disorder

DSM-II described antisocial personalities as chronically antisocial, lacking in personal or group loyalties, callous, hedonistic, emotionally immature, and lacking responsibility or judgment. The *DSM-III* criteria, however, marked a return to the moral insanity tradition. They were a list of socially undesirable activities virtually devoid of reference to personality, prompting Millon (1981) to describe the category as "an accusatory judgment rather than a dispassionate clinical formulation" (p. 181).

These criteria were influenced by Robins (1978), who defined psychopathy as failure to comply with social norms, regardless of the psychological substrate, a definition that would equate all forms of social dissent with psychopathy (Levenson, 1992). More than other personality disorder categories, APD illustrates the folly of operational definitions (Leahey, 1980). Operational definitions are neither "operational" as originally conceived, nor are they "definitions" in a meaningful sense because the definition comes from the concept that binds the criteria. Although Robins (1978) appeared to accept Cleckley's concept, she defended her definition of psychopathy by arguing that "we rely on behavior to infer the psychological substrate" (p. 256). However, our prior assumptions about the substrate determine the behaviors we attend to in the first place. The substrate determining Robin's criteria does not clearly reflect Cleckley's construct. The related notion of *antisociality* similarly lacks any clear theoretical construct from which the manifestations are derived.

The *DSM-IV* criteria moved slightly in the direction of Cleckley, or more precisely, the PCL-R. Antisocial personality disorder is considered synonymous with psychopathy and is "a pattern of disregard for, and violation of the rights of others" (American Psychiatric Association, 1994, p. 629). The operational criteria defining APD are a mixture of socially deviant behavior (illegal behaviors, lying, physical fights, inconsistent work behavior, early conduct disorder) and concrete indicators of the traits of impulsivity, deceitfulness, recklessness, and lack of remorse. *DSM-IV* notes that individuals with APD frequently show traditional psychopathic criteria of callousness, arrogance, lack of empathy, or glib, superficial charm. However, because only three of the formal criteria are required for diagnosis, many individuals who meet the criteria for APD frequently do not in practice show these characteristics. Antisocial personality disorder is clearly a measure that is poorly coordinated with Cleckley's underlying construct and an illustration of conceptual drift.

The continued emphasis in APD on antisocial acts as primary manifestations of psychopathy fails to capture the traditional defining personality traits for two reasons. First, it confounds the two conceptual domains of personality and social deviance or antisociality. These are not competing conceptualizations of the same phenomenon as some maintain (e.g., Skilling et al., 2002) because they reflect different frames of reference and different areas of inquiry. The domain of personality is stylistic variations between people, while social deviance refers to departures from cultural and moral standards (Blackburn, 1988). It is of more than passing interest to inquire how personality contributes to persistent social rule-breaking. However, to define the former in terms of the latter confounds the dependent with the independent variable and precludes any understanding of the relationship.

Second, specific *acts* have multiple determinants and are poor criteria of a stable underlying *disposition* (Blackburn, 1995; Block, 1989; Gottfredson & Hirschi, 1990). Criminality or antisociality may be construed as a disposition of the person, but antisocial acts are only one of several possible manifestations of this disposition. Gottfredson and Hirschi (1990) conceptualized this disposition as a tendency to seek short-term, immediate pleasure, a disposition manifest in stable traits such as impulsivity or recklessness, which APD specifies. This same tendency is held to underlie using drugs, being in accidents, and smoking, but these are *events* arising from opportunities and external conditions as much as the attributes of the person. If antisocial behavior is simply a possible but not inevitable outcome of psychopathy, then social deviance is neither necessary nor sufficient to the definition.

It is not surprising that there is a close correspondence between APD and F2 of the PCL-R. However, the PCL-R criteria overall are more clearly weighted with Cleckley's traits, and, at best, APD provides no more than a crude approximation to Cleckley's concept. In terms of psychometric utility, the balance of evidence also suggests that the PCL-R is more valid for practical purposes than APD (Cunningham & Reidy, 1998). Nevertheless, both APD and the PCL-R are biased representations of the construct they purport to represent.

PSYCHOPATHY AS PERSONALITY DISORDER

Cleckley's acceptance of *DSM-II* antisocial personality and his concept of "a distinct clinical entity" encouraged the assumption that psychopathy is currently represented in *DSM-IV*, albeit inadequately, by the APD category. PCL-R criteria were, in fact, considered as a replacement for APD in *DSM-IV* (Hare, Hart, & Harpur, 1991). However, psychopathic traits appear in other personality disorders, notably narcissistic (grandiosity, lack of empathy) and histrionic (superficial charm, insincerity, shallow affect, egocentricity). *DSM-IV* adds that narcissistic disorder shares with APD the traits of tough-mindedness and exploitativeness, while impulsivity, excitement seeking, recklessness, and manipulativeness are common to both histrionic disorder and APD. Apart from criteria of seeking admiration or attention, histrionic and narcissistic disorders are distinguished from APD by usually lacking a history of conduct disorder or criminality. Given that criminal behavior was not intrinsic to Cleckley's concept, these categories could justifiably be regarded as variations of the same construct as much as representations of distinct disorders, and we wonder how many of Cleckley's psychopaths might have been labeled histrionic or narcissistic by clinicians with a different orientation.

Remarkably few studies have examined the relationship of the PCL-R to personality disorders other than APD, but these confirm significant associations of narcissistic and histrionic disorders with F1 and a stronger relationship of APD to F2 than to F1 (Harpur et al., 1989; Hart & Hare, 1989). Among violent offenders, Blackburn and Coid (1998) found positive correlations with the PCL-R of six of the *DSM-III* disorders (antisocial, paranoid, passive-aggressive, narcissistic, borderline, and histrionic) and negative correlations with compulsive and dependent disorders. In this study, the pattern of correlations with F1 and F2 was similar, except that F1 correlated slightly higher with narcissistic disorder, and F2 higher with APD and borderline disorder.

Factor analyses of the *DSM* disorders in nonoffender samples find with some consistency that four factors pervade the disorders. Mulder and Joyce (1997) described these as "the four As" (antisocial, asocial, asthenic, anankastic). The antisocial factor is defined mainly by the Cluster B scales, suggesting a broad factor equivalent to psychopathy underlying these disorders. We found the same four-factor structure in an analysis of the *DSM-III* disorders among violent offenders (Blackburn & Coid, 1998). Correlations of total PCL-R, F1, and F2 scores with the antisocial factor (or impulsivity as we identified it) were .75, .63, and .73, respectively. It is likely that the four personality disorder factors are not independent and may support two higher order factors. In a hierarchical analysis of the *DSM-III* personality disorder criteria, Morey (1988) found two superordinate clusters of "anxious rumination" and "acting out." The latter included items from APD, narcissistic and histrionic categories, and Morey noted the similarity to Cleckley's psychopathy.

These findings converge in challenging the conceptualization of psychopathy as "a distinct clinical entity." Rather do they suggest that psychopathy can be conceptualized hierarchically as a superordinate dimension in which narcissistic, histrionic, and antisocial disorders are correlated subcomponents (Blackburn, 1995). The superordinate factor of psychopathy identified by Cooke and Michie (2001) seems to be the factor underlying the acting out personality disorders, and their interpersonal, affective, and behavioral subfactors may broadly correspond, respectively, to narcissistic disorder, histrionic disorder, and the impulsivity of adult APD. This implies a further shift away from Cleckley's original concept.

PSYCHOPATHY AS HUMAN VARIATION

Cleckley's construct was scientifically restricted and displays several of the theoretical limitations and value connotations that can bias psychological constructs (Messick, 1981). First, it assumed the primacy of affect over cognition and lacked any broader theoretical context of personality or personality disorder. His "specific clinical entity" now appears to be neither specific nor an entity, although paradoxically, he seems to have identified a significant dimension relevant to personality disorders more generally. Second, his quasi-neurological hypothesis has encouraged a focus on research that bypasses the psychological level of explanation. Although some findings suggest an information processing deficits in psychopaths (Newman, 1998), a physiological deficit underlying psychopathy has yet to be clearly established (Harris et al., 2001) and may turn out to be a reductionist red herring. Even if forthcoming, it would not supply the proximal causal generative mechanisms that might explain socially offensive behavior.

Third, the construct of psychopathy as an underlying emotional deficit has restricted explanatory power, and it is unclear how this differs from the similar deficit held to underlie schizoid personality. At best, it may tell us why a psychopathic individual fails to *inhibit* harmful behavior, but it does not tell us *why* he or she engages in that behavior in the first place. Conspicuously absent from Cleckley's concept is a theory of motivation or goals or of the psychological functions that the behavior of psychopaths might serve. Evolutionary conceptions that identify psychopathy in terms of universal strivings may help to redress the balance (e.g., Beck & Freeman, 1990; Harris et al., 2001; Mealey, 1995; Millon & Davis, 1996), but these need to be set in the context of personality variation more generally.

The construct is also clearly biased by explicit and implicit value connotations. The shift from the earlier concept of psychopathic personality as a *psychologically damaged* person (i.e., suffering from psychopathology) to one of a *socially damaging* individual represented a morally biased conception of psychopathic personality as a type of criminal rather than a form of abnormal personality (Blackburn, 1988). This became most explicit in the pejorative antisocial personality, an enemy of society.

The focus on diagnosing this entity also creates a dichotomous way of thinking that exaggerates the differences between psychopaths and other offenders while minimizing similarities (Toch, 1998; Wulach, 1983). This is also seen in speculations about "successful psychopaths" in the community. If this means that some successful people have traits associated with Cleckley's psychopathy, it would hardly be surprising and is entirely consistent with a dimensional view of psychopathy. For example, narcissistic traits of grandiosity, lack of empathy, and exploitativeness are not uncommon among corporate leaders, and such traits may be valued by organizations, even though not by their employees (Hogan, Raskin, & Fazzini, 1990; see also Levenson, 1992). Often, however, "successful psychopaths" implies "subclinical psychopaths" getting away with undetected crimes, reflecting a dichotomous view of psychopathy as a dangerous diagnostic entity.

Operational definitions of psychopathy may also overpathologize common behavior because of moral biases. For example, Toch (1998) noted that the PCL-R items "sexually promiscuous behavior" and "frequent short-term marital relationships" reflect middle-class moral concerns. Another indicator is "deceitfulness" or "pathological lying." All psychopaths then become liars, never to be trusted. This moral stance influences assessment when researchers argue that psychopaths cannot be trusted to complete self-report measures. Yet, lying is commonplace human behavior that serves functions of self-presentation (DePaulo, Kashy, Kirkendol, Wyer, & Epstein, 1996). When psychopaths misrepresent themselves, it may be as much through self-deception as intended deceit.

Implicit social values also enter into the current focus of psychopathy research on the prediction of violent recidivism, which meets the demands of a managerial culture for a scientifically respectable way of incapacitating the dangerous. While behavioral scientists have an obligation to serve the interests of their clients, their clients in the criminal justice system include both the public and the offender. However, the ideological tensions between serving the interests of society and the welfare of individuals are frequently unacknowledged (Blackburn, 2002). These value biases are not inherent in Cleckley's concept, but the adoption of his biased construct has foreclosed alternative constructs of psychopathy that more readily permit psychological explanation and understanding. Some of these are considered here.

Psychopathy as Personality Variation

Schneider's notion of personality disorders as statistical abnormalities has reemerged in proposals that because personality disorders reflect extremes of normal personality traits, they are more appropriately conceptualized as variations along personality dimensions identified in the general population (Blackburn, 1988; Costa & Widiger, 2002). The dimensional system with the strongest empirical support is the *five-factor model* of personality (FFM), which represents variation in personality dispositions in terms of the higher order dimensions of neuroticism, extraversion, agreeableness, conscientiousness, and openness to experience. These dimensions represent the correlations of more specific traits lower in the hierarchy. For example, the facets of agreeableness versus antagonism include modesty versus arrogance, altruism versus exploitation, compliance versus aggression, and straightforwardness versus deception. Categories of personality disorder reflect different patterns across these dimensions (Costa & Widiger, 2002).

Widiger and Lynam (1998) proposed that psychopathy can similarly be understood in terms of the FFM and suggested that although the traits of the PCL-R vary in specificity, they are each represented in the dimensions and facets of the FFM. For example, grandiose, pathological lying, and callousness have clear representations in antagonism, while impulsivity and irresponsibility are closely linked to conscientiousness. Overall, psychopathy is a collection of personality traits rather than a qualitatively distinct condition. In their analysis, F1 is primarily measuring antagonism, F2 a mixture of antagonism and conscientiousness, and the correlation between them is carried by the common antagonism elements. Theories aiming to identify deficits in psychopaths may simply be focusing on different features of personality that are not unique to psychopaths.

Direct evidence favoring this hypothesis is currently sparse, and only one study to date has used the PCL-R. Among prison inmates, Harpur, Hart, and Hare (2002) found that agreeableness was negatively related to PCL-R total score and F1, but in a student sample, significant relationships were limited to negative correlations with conscientiousness. Harpur et al. suggested that the relationship between psychopathy and personality is complex and that psychopathic traits may not be fully captured by the FFM.

Although the factors of the FFM are generally considered independent dimensions, Digman (1997) found that they are correlated and that two higher order factors underlie them. The first factor was defined by high loadings of agreeableness, emotional stability (i.e., low neuroticism), and conscientiousness; the second, by high loadings of extraversion and intellect (openness). These higher order factors seem likely to be pervasive in personality measures (Blackburn, Renwick, Donnelly, & Logan, 2004). It is tempting to speculate that the higher order factor involving agreeableness is the acting out factor found by Morey (1988) to underlie personality disorders and that, in turn, these correspond to the higher order dimension of psychopathy found by Cooke and Michie (2001). Although the association of the first factor with neuroticism might not seem to fit the prototypical primary psychopath, Harpur et al. (2002) found that psychopaths score highly on some facets of neuroticism, notably hostility and impulsiveness. The possibility of a common higher order factor must await further research.

Psychopathy in Millon's Theory of Personality Disorder

Widiger and Lynam (1998) suggest that although psychopathy represents a "virulent" pattern of traits, it need not be considered a discrete entity. However, the FFM was derived atheoretically, and traits are only the doorway to personality, not explanations. Millon, in contrast, has long advocated the primacy of theory in identifying personality variation. In his theoretical model (Millon & Davis, 1996), he draws on evolutionary theory to derive three bipolarities of adaptation, linked to basic processes of life enhancement and individual survival (pleasure-pain polarity), ecological accommodation and modification (active-passive polarity), and reproductive individuation and nurturance (self-other polarity). Personality reflects psychological expressions of latent and fundamental evolutionary processes, and disorders of personality are maladaptive functioning arising from deficiencies, imbalances, or conflicts in capacities to relate to the environment.

Patterns of both normal and dysfunctional adaptation are derived from combinations of the three bipolarities. Millon links traditional concepts of psychopathy to both antisocial and narcissistic disorders. Both represent self-oriented extremes of the self-other bipolarity and a concern for independence but are differentiated by the active-passive bipolarity. The antisocial reflects an *aggrandizing pattern,* the core of the construct being active manipulation and exploitation of the environment in the service of self, marked by lack of concern for others. The narcissistic or *egotistical pattern* is also concerned with self-enhancement, status, and power but passively expects these to be delivered by the social environment. Where the relationships of the antisocial are dominated by mistrust and animosity, the narcissist is benignly arrogant.

Several manifestations follow from these core themes. The antisocial pattern is distinguished as impulsive, interpersonally irresponsible, cognitively deviant, has an autonomous self-image, is mistrusting and debasing, uncontrolled, aggrandizing, hedonistic, callous, irritable, and aggressive. Although prominent among offenders, this pattern can be seen in less extreme forms in law-abiding people. Millon also distinguishes several variants or subtypes, such as the covetous, the risk-taking, and the nomadic and considers the sadistic or *abusive pattern* a related form involving abnormalities of the pleasure-pain bipolarity. In the case of the narcissist, the primary manifestations are haughtiness, interpersonal exploitation, cognitive expansiveness, an admirable self-image, illusory object relations, self-deceptive rationalization, and flimsy internal coping strategies.

These characteristics of the antisocial and narcissistic personalities clearly overlap with the traits of psychopathy proposed by Cleckley, but go beyond them. The active striving, antagonism, and mistrust of the antisocial, for example, are absent from Cleckley's portrayal, and while affective deficits are accompaniments of these patterns in Millon's construct, they are part of a dynamic process centering on self-other orientation, much as in Gough's earlier account. Millon, nonetheless, identifies the narcissistic pattern with F1 of the PCL-R and the antisocial with F2. However, using questionnaire measures of Millon's patterns, Hart, Forth, and Hare (1991) failed to confirm this among prison inmates. While total PCL-R and F2 correlated significantly with several patterns, including antisocial and narcissistic, only the sadistic pattern correlated with F1, again reflecting the methodological problems of relating F1 to self-reports. Nevertheless, Millon's ideal types coalesce to form a distinct antisocial-narcissistic-histrionic personality pattern observable in questionnaire data among mentally disordered offenders (Blackburn, 1996).

Psychopathy as Malevolent Agency

Cleckley's construct focuses on an internal affective deficit, but the feature that he and most other writers emphasize is the destructive quality of the psychopath's relationships. This is not readily accounted for by deficient emotional responsiveness and requires an explanation in terms of the interpersonal goals and functions of the psychopath's behavior. This is directly addressed by Millon's theory, and a similar conceptualization is found in the interpersonal theory originating with Leary (1957) and subsequently developed by others (e.g., Kiesler, 1996; Wiggins & Trapnell, 1996).

The theory comprises an empirically established structural model of interpersonal behavior embedded in a rich theoretical network. The structural model portrays interpersonal variables as blends of two orthogonal dimensions of power or control (dominance versus submission) and affiliation (hostility versus love or nurturance) forming the coordinates of a circular structure or circumplex known as *the interpersonal circle.* These dimensions represent the themes most commonly negotiated in social exchanges, and the circle provides a map from which the characteristics of dyadic interactions can be identified. *Interpersonal style* refers to regularities in the way in which a person manages interactions across many social encounters and relationships, different styles reflecting an emphasis on different areas of the circle. Interpersonal theory conceptualizes such styles as relatively consistent modes of self-presentation that are maintained by the reactions they elicit from others. Different interpersonal styles are hence underpinned by beliefs about the self and others, which are organized around the fundamental social motives of power (dominance) and affiliation (nurturance).

Leary (1957) construed personality disorders as modal styles falling at different points around the circle. Psychopathy represented a hostile or *aggressive-sadistic style* in which fear is inspired in others through subtle forms of critical, humiliating, and punitive interactions, and not simply physical violence. It was not defined by delinquency, and people with this style often identify with law and moral codes they employ to humiliate others. Adjacent to this style in the circle was the hostile-dominant or *competitive style* represented by the narcissistic personality and reflected in self-love, arrogance, self-enhancement, and exhibitionism. Where the aggressive-sadistic style was motivated by desire to humiliate, the narcissistic style was driven to compete with and exploit others by a need for status. Again, this pattern was not defined by antisocial behavior, although Leary found that the aggressive and narcissistic styles were identifiable in 15% and 13%, respectively, of a sample of stockade prisoners.

Research supports the association of psychopathy with hostile-dominance. Harpur et al. (2002) found that PCL total and F1 and F2 scores projected significantly onto the hostile-dominant quadrant of the circle as measured by both self-ratings and observer ratings on an adjective checklist. Using interview-based ratings of the same measure in a small sample of prisoners, they also found that the PCL-SV was aligned closely with the hostile-dominant axis. Kosson, Steuerwald, Forth, and Kirkhart (1997) similarly found that among students, self and observer ratings of dominance and hostility were significantly related to their scores on both F1 and F2 of the PCL-SV. Ratings of hostile-dominant verbal and nonverbal interactions during the assessment interview also correlated with PCL-R scores, particularly F1, in prisoners.

In our own research (Blackburn, 1998), we assess the interpersonal circle by simple observer ratings of everyday institutional behavior (Chart of Interpersonal Reactions in Closed Living Environments [CIRCLE]). Following Leary, we construe the core features of psychopathy to be exemplified by extreme interpersonal styles falling in the hostile-dominant quadrant of the circle. However, in CIRCLE, the *coercive* axis between hostility and dominance represents both the aggressive-sadistic and competitive styles described by Leary.

Recent studies with CIRCLE provide further support for the association of psychopathy and interpersonal style (Logan & Blackburn, 2003). A coercive style correlates moderately strongly with PCL-R total score in mentally disordered offenders ($r = .45$: $N = 162$) and between .35 and .42 with the PCL-R F1 and F2 and with *DSM-IV* narcissistic, histrionic, and adult antisocial disorders, suggesting that it taps a common underlying factor. A coercive style was highly predictive of future institutional misconduct over two years and exceeded the predictive power of the PCL-R in this respect. Among non-mentally ill offenders, a coercive style also correlated strongly with a history of chronic offending (Blackburn, 1998).

Interpersonal styles express fundamental motivational concerns, and in interpersonal theory, interpersonal behavior sends signals to others that function to elicit anticipated reactions. For example, a coercive individual has learned to expect hostile-dominant reactions from others and behaves in ways that get them. This has affinities with Millon's suggestion that the aggression of antisocial personalities is a preemptive counterattack in the face of anticipations that others will exploit them. Explanations for the behavior of psychopaths may, therefore, be found in cognitive schemas and scripts (Beck & Freeman, 1990; Hart, 1998). Some of our data support the hypothesis of an association of coercive style with hostile expectations of others (Blackburn, 1998), but there is as yet no evidence that this also applies to the PCL-R. However, consistent with the theory, Kosson et al. (1997) found that the emotional reactions of interviewers, such as avoidance of confrontation or trepidation, were significantly related to interviewees' PCL-R scores and to ratings of their hostile-dominant style. Because antagonism of the FFM coincides with the coercive axis of the interpersonal circle, these results converge with the proposal that psychopathy is linked to the agreeableness-antagonism dimension.

Wiggins and Trapnell (1996) proposed that the dimensions of the interpersonal circle are concrete representations of the metaconcepts of *agency* (dominance) and *communion* (nurturance). Agency (versus passivity) refers to being a differentiated individual manifest in strivings for mastery and power that enhance that differentiation. Communion (versus dissociation) describes being part of a larger social or spiritual entity manifest in strivings for intimacy and solidarity with that entity. In these terms, the hostile-dominant styles of psychopaths can be construed as dispositions to engage in interpersonal transactions that communicate a high degree of concerns about power and status in social hierarchies (agency) but also the rejection or avoidance of intimacy (communion). Their behavior, including criminal activities, can be understood in this light as an attempt to maintain status or mastery of a social environment from which they feel alienated. This is in agreement with Millon's theory that the primary motive of antisocial and narcissistic personalities is self-enhancement.

This conception of psychopathy is also consistent with evolutionary perspectives that see strivings for status in the face of competition for resources as a universal adaptation. Competition for resources, including mates, involves impeding others' chances of acquiring resources that may take the form of stealing, cheating, attacking, humiliating, or ensuring compliance of the other, and several writers associate psychopathy with a "cheating" strategy (Beck & Freeman, 1990; Harris et al., 2001; Mealey, 1995; Millon & Davis, 1996). Although not addressing psychopathy, Gilbert (1989) suggested that competitiveness is a major source of individual differences reflected in the hostile-dominance described by the interpersonal circle.

PSYCHOPATHY AS A MENTAL DISORDER

Psychopaths have long posed problems for the courts because of uncertainty about whether their disorder exempts them from legal responsibility, and clinicians often assert that psychopaths are not "ill." Hart and Hare (1989) found that psychopaths were less likely to receive an Axis I diagnosis except for substance abuse, but while confirming a greater likelihood of substance abuse in psychopaths, we found that psychopathy is orthogonal to Axis I disorders (Blackburn et al., 2003). This indicates that some psychopaths suffer from mental disorders but that psychopathy itself is not directly related to Axis I disorders.

If psychopathy represents an extreme of normal personality variation (Widiger & Lynam, 1998), it would seem not to be discrete disorder. Harris et al. (2001) also argued that pychopathy is not a mental disorder but rather an evolutionary adaptation of a "cheater" lifestyle and that psychopaths are biomedically healthy. They suggest that a neurocognitive defect could not enhance attributes such as lying, conning, or manipulation. This argument assumes that physical abnormality is an appropriate criterion of mental disorder, but the "disease as lesion" view has generally not been considered a sufficient criterion.

Wakefield (1992) argued from an evolutionary standpoint that what defines mental disorder is *harmful dysfunction,* that is, conditions depriving a person of some socially valued benefit, which result from the inability of some mental mechanism to perform its natural function. This is challenged by Lilienfeld and Marino (1999), who pointed to a large number of exceptions and contended that mental disorder is an open (prototypical) concept that lacks clear boundaries in nature. Their objection to Wakefield's "essentialism" appears to be the empiricist argument that entities do not have a specific nature that we can detect. Wakefield's argument is, however, compatible with an alternative critical realist perspective that mental disorder is a real capacity (or liability) that we know from its effects, and, exceptions notwithstanding, many clinicians find the harmful dysfunction criterion useful. On this criterion, the information processing deficits found in psychopaths by Newman (1998) would meet the criterion of mental disorder, even though they may lie on a continuum of normal variation.

Livesley (2001) follows Schneider's argument that statistical abnormality of personality is not enough to define dysfunction and draws on the harmful dysfunction criterion in arguing that personality disorder should be defined by reference to the *functions* of personality. From an evolutionary perspective, these functions include attaining the universal life tasks of a stable identity of self and others; satisfying interpersonal functioning in the areas of attachment, intimacy, and affiliation; and prosocial, cooperative group relationships. Dysfunction or disorder arises from impairment in the organization, integration, or regulation of underlying personality processes involved in these tasks. The attributes of psychopathy clearly imply impairment in all three areas.

CONCLUSION

Cleckley's thoughtful clinical observations identified a pattern of deviant personality traits that stimulated research and theorizing, and there is little doubt that he recognized a real disposition of the person. He also attempted to move away from the moral insanity tradition by describing a type of disordered person that can be found outside penal institutions. However, Cleckley was a reluctant personality theorist, and the significant drift away from his concept in the PCL-R and APD has made it difficult to get beyond the narrow moralistic view of the psychopath as a criminal type. Yet the construct is not simply an attempt to understand the contribution of the person to social rule-breaking. The core features about which there seems little disagreement are the destructive ways in which some people conduct their relationships.

Progress in conceptualizing psychopathy, therefore, calls for the adoption of broader perspectives grounded in theories of personality, some of which have been highlighted in this chapter. This is a necessary prerequisite to further exploration and refinement of measurement. As Hogan and Nicholson (1988) observed, all personality research entails construct validation, and there is a need to work back and forth between the indicators making up a measure and its defining construct. The PCL-R represents only an early stage in this process, and recent work on its factor structure indicates how eliminating some of the items, particularly those related to criminality, may bring it closer to Cleckley's original concept (Cooke & Michie, 2001; Cooke et al., 2004). Alternative measures of psychopathy have also been developed in the form of self-report scales that may facilitate research in noncriminal populations (Levenson, Kiehl, & Fitzpatrick, 1995; Lilienfeld & Andrews, 1996). However, these developments remain tied to Cleckley's concept and have not so far led to a refinement of the construct itself. Although this concept has proved a useful starting point, it may have outlived its usefulness. Alternative conceptualizations would point to further trait indicators that could be incorporated into measures of psychopathy.

Construct validation also requires further evidence that psychopathy is clearly discriminated from other constructs. For example, it needs to be determined whether psychopathy is anything more than an extreme of identified personality dimensions such as agreeableness-antagonism or whether the traditional core features of psychopathy go beyond those identified in personality disorder constructs such as narcissism. This poses challenges to measurement because current assessment of psychopathy using the PCL-R is heavily dependent on the interview method and produces only weak correlations with traditional self-report measures. It is possible that the interview or other observational methods are necessary for the evaluation of attributes that impact negatively on others, such as callousness or grandiosity. It is equally possible, however, that method variance in the PCL-R produces measurement artifacts. For example, for purposes of predicting recidivism, self-reports have been found to be as adequate as the PCL-R (Kroner & Loza, 2001). This is a critical measurement issue that urgently requires further research.

Further research is also needed on the likelihood that psychopathy covers more than one distinctive pattern of deviant personality (Skeem et al., 2003). This will perhaps lead us back to the broader notion of psychopathic personalities as conceptualized by Schneider and hence require us to confront the question of where the North American concept of psychopathy fits into recent classifications of personality disorder. It may also clarify how far psychopathy and its variations can be construed in terms of a hierarchical dimensional structure of personality rather than as the discrete clinical entity that Cleckley proposed.

A personality-based conceptualization of psychopathy also focuses attention on the psychological level of explanation and the need for more attention in theorizing and research to interpersonal goals or motives and beliefs. Despite the established practical utility of the PCL-R for the criminal justice system, our theoretical understanding of the disposition that leads to crime in some individuals has progressed very little. We have also yet to come to grips with understanding how the same disposition may motivate ambition, competitiveness, or risk-taking in the general population, or "The ruthless and cleverly conniving businessman, the intimidating and brutalizing sergeant, the self-righteous and punitive headmistress, the demanding and dominating surgical chief . . ." (Millon, 1981, p. 202). Arendt (1963) remarked on *the banality of evil,* but the notion that people can do bad things out of ordinary human motives remains widely resisted. Only by setting psychopathy in the wider theoretical context of human adaptation will the concept contribute to a science of personology.

REFERENCES

Arendt, H. (1963). *Eichmann in Jerusalem: A report on the banality of evil.* New York: Viking.

American Psychiatric Association. (1994). *Diagnostic and statistical manual of mental disorders* (4th ed.). Washington, DC: Author.

Baumeister, R. F., Smart, L., & Boden, J. M. (1996). Relation of threatened egotism to violence and aggression. *Psychological Review, 103,* 5–33.

Beck, A. T., & Freeman, A. (1990). *Cognitive therapy of personality disorders.* New York: Guilford Press.

Blackburn, R. (1988). On moral judgements and personality disorders: The myth of the psychopathic personality revisited. *British Journal of Psychiatry, 153,* 505–512.

Blackburn, R. (1995). *The psychology of criminal conduct: Theory, research and practice.* Chichester, England: Wiley.

Blackburn, R. (1996). Replicated personality disorder clusters among mentally disordered offenders and their relation to dimensions of personality. *Journal of Personality Disorders, 10,* 68–81.

Blackburn, R. (1998). Psychopathy and personality disorder: Implications of interpersonal theory. In D. J. Cooke, A. E. Forth, & R. D. Hare (Eds.), *Psychopathy: Theory, research and implications for society* (pp. 269–301). Amsterdam: Kluwer Press.

Blackburn, R. (2002). Ethical issue in motivating offenders to change. In M. McMurran (Ed.), *Motivating offenders to change: A guide to enhancing engagement in therapy* (pp. 139–155). Chichester, England: Wiley.

Blackburn, R., & Coid, J. W. (1998). Psychopathy and the dimensions of personality disorder in violent offenders. *Personality and Individual Differences, 25,* 129–145.

Blackburn, R., & Coid, J. W. (1999). Empirical clusters of *DSM-III* personality disorders in violent offenders. *Journal of Personality Disorders, 13,* 18–34.

Blackburn, R., Logan, C., Donnelly, J., & Renwick, S. (2003). Personality disorder, psychopathy, and other mental disorders: Comorbidity among patients at English and Scottish high security hospitals. *Journal of Forensic Psychiatry, 14,* 111–137.

Blackburn, R., Renwick, S., Donnelly, J., & Logan, C. (2004). Big Five or Big Two? Superordinate factors in the NEO Five Factor Inventory and the Antisocial Personality Questionnaire. *Personality and Individual Differences, 37,* 957–970.

Block, J. (1989). Critique of the act frequency approach to personality. *Journal of Personality and Social Psychology, 56,* 234–245.

Cleckley, H. (1982). *The mask of sanity* (6th ed.). St. Louis, MO: Mosby. (Original work published 1941)

Cooke, D. J., Forth, A. E., & Hare, R. D. (Eds.). (1998). *Psychopathy: Theory, research and implications for society.* Amsterdam: Kluwer Press.

Cooke, D. J., & Michie, C. (2001). Refining the construct of psychopathy: Toward a hierarchical model. *Psychological Assessment, 13,* 171–188.

Cooke, D. J., Michie, C., Hart, S. D., & Clark, D. (2004). Reconstructing psychopathy: Clarifying the significance of antisocial and socially deviant behaviour in the diagnosis of psychopathic personality disorder. *Journal of Personality Disorders, 18,* 337–357.

Costa, P. T., & Widiger, T. A. (Eds.). (2002). *Personality disorders and the Five-Factor Model of Personality* (2nd ed.). Washington, DC: American Psychological Association.

Cunningham, M. D., & Reidy, T. J. (1998). Antisocial personality disorder and psychopathy: Diagnostic dilemmas in classifying patterns of antisocial behavior in sentencing evaluations. *Behavioral Sciences and the Law, 16,* 333–351.

DePaulo, B. M., Kashy, D. A., Kirkendol, S. E., Wyer, M. M., & Epstein, J. A. (1996). Lying in everyday life. *Journal of Personality and Social Psychology, 70,* 979–975.

Digman, J. M. (1997). Higher-order factors of the big five. *Journal of Personality and Social Psychology, 73,* 1246–1256.

Faust, D., & Miner, R. A. (1986). The empiricist and his new clothes: *DSM-III* in perspective. *American Journal of Psychiatry, 143,* 962–967.

Gilbert, P. (1989). *Human nature and suffering.* Hillsdale, NJ: Erlbaum.

Gottfredson, M. R., & Hirschi, T. (1990). *A general theory of crime.* Stanford, CA: Stanford University Press.

Gough, H. G. (1948). A sociological theory of psychopathy. *American Journal of Sociology, 53,* 359–366.

Hare, R. D. (1970). *Psychopathy: Theory and research.* New York: Wiley.

Hare, R. D. (1991). *The Hare Psychopathy Checklist–Revised.* Toronto, Ontario, Canada: Multi-Health Systems.

Hare, R. D. (1998). Psychopaths and their nature: Implications for the mental health and criminal justice systems. In T. Millon, E. Simonsen, M. Birket-Smith, & R. D. Davis (Eds.), *Psychopathy: Antisocial, criminal, and violent behaviour* (pp. 188–212). New York: Guilford Press.

Hare, R. D., Clark, D., Grann, M., & Thornton, D. (2000). Psychopathy and the predictive validity of the PCL-R: An international perspective. *Behavioral Sciences and the Law, 18,* 623–645.

Hare, R. D., Hart, S. J., & Harpur, T. J. (1991). Psychopathy and the *DSM-IV* criteria for antisocial personality disorder. *Journal of Abnormal Psychology, 100,* 391–398.

Harpur, T. J., Hare, R. D., & Hakstian, A. R. (1989). Two-factor conceptualisation of psychopathy: Construct validity and assessment implications. *Psychological Assessment, 1,* 6–17.

Harpur, T. J., Hart, S. D., & Hare, R. D. (2002). In P. T. Costa & T. A. Widiger (Eds.), *Personality disorders and the Five-Factor Model of Personality* (2nd ed., pp. 299–324). Washington, DC: American Psychological Association.

Harris, G. T., Rice, M. E., & Quinsey, V. L. (1994). Psychopathy as a taxon: Evidence that psychopaths are a discrete class. *Journal of Consulting and Clinical Psychology, 62,* 387–397.

Harris, G. T., Skilling, T. A., & Rice, M. E. (2001). The construct of psychopathy. In M. Tonry (Ed.), *Crime and justice: An review of research* (Vol. 28, pp. 197–263). Chicago: University of Chicago Press.

Hart, S. (1998). Psychopathy and risk for violence. In D. J. Cooke, A. E. Forth, & R. D. Hare (Eds.), *Psychopathy: Theory, research and implications for society* (pp. 355–373). Amsterdam: Kluwer Press.

Hart, S., & Hare, R. D. (1989). Discriminant validity of the Psychopathy Checklist in a forensic psychiatric population. *Psychological Assessment, 1,* 211–218.

Hart, S. D., Forth, A. E., & Hare, R. D. (1991). The MCMI-II and psychopathy. *Journal of Personality Disorders, 5,* 318–327.

Hemphill, J. F., Hare, R. D., & Wong, S. (1998). Psychopathy and recidivism: A review. *Legal and Criminological Psychology, 3,* 139–170.

Hogan, R., & Nicholson, R. A. (1988). The meaning of personality test scores. *American Psychologist, 43,* 621–626.

Hogan, R., Raskin, R., & Fazzini, D. (1990). The dark side of charisma. In K. Clark & B. Clark (Eds.), *Measures of leadership* (pp. 343–354). West Orange, NJ: Leadership Library of America.

Kiesler, D. J. (1996). *Contemporary interpersonal theory and research: Personality, psychopathology, and psychotherapy.* New York: Wiley.

Kosson, D. S., Steuerwald, B. L., Forth, A. E., & Kirkhart, K. J. (1997). A new method for assessing the interpersonal behavior of psychopathic individuals: Preliminary validation studies. *Psychological Assessment, 9,* 89–101.

Kroner, D. G., & Loza, W. L. (2001). Evidence for the efficacy of self-report in predicting nonviolent and violent criminal recidivism. *Journal of Interpersonal Violence, 16,* 168–177.

Leary, T. (1957). *Interpersonal diagnosis of personality.* New York: Ronald Press.

Leahey, T. H. (1980). The myth of operationism. *Journal of Mind and Behavior, 1,* 127–143.

Levenson, M. R. (1992). Rethinking psychopathy. *Theory and Psychology, 2,* 51–71.

Levenson, M. R., Kiehl, K. A., & Fitzpatrick, C. M. (1995). Assessing psychopathic attributes in a noninstitutionalised population. *Journal of Personality and Social Psychology, 68,* 151–158.

Lilienfeld, S. (1994). Conceptual problems in the assessment of psychopathy. *Clinical Psychology Review, 14,* 17–38.

Lilienfeld, S. O., & Andrews, B. P. (1996). Development and preliminary validation of a self-report measure of psychopathic personality traits in noncriminal populations. *Journal of Personality Assessment, 66,* 488–522.

Lilienfeld, S. O., & Marino, L. (1999). Essentialism revisited: Evolutionary theory and the concept of mental disorder. *Journal of Abnormal Psychology, 108,* 400–411.

Livesley, W. J. (2001). Conceptual and taxonomic issues. In W. J. Livesley (Ed.), *Handbook of personality disorders: Theory, research, and treatment* (pp. 3–39). New York: Guilford Press.

Logan, C., & Blackburn, R. (2003). *Clinicians' judgements, psychopathy, interpersonal style, and risk, and their relationship to the institutional behaviour of detained mentally disordered offenders.* Paper presented at the International, Interdisciplinary Conference on Psychology and Law, Edinburgh, UK.

Lykken, D. T. (1995). *The antisocial personalities.* Hillsdale, NJ: Erlbaum.

McCord, W. M., & McCord, J. (1964). *The psychopath: An essay on the criminal mind.* New York: Van Nostrand.

Mealey, L. (1995). The sociobiology of sociopathy: An integrated evolutionary model. *Behavioral and Brain Sciences, 18,* 523–599.

Medin, D. L. (1989). Concepts and conceptual structure. *American Psychologist, 44,* 1469–1481.

Meehl, P. E. (1978). Theoretical risks and tabular asterisks: Sir Karl, Sir Ronald, and the slow progress of soft psychology. *Journal of Consulting and Clinical Psychology, 46,* 806–834.

Messick, S. (1981). Constructs and their vicissitudes in educational and psychological measurement. *Psychological Bulletin, 89,* 575–588.

Millon, T. (1981). *Disorders of personality: DSM-III: Axis II.* New York: Wiley.

Millon, T., & Davis, R. D. (1996). *Disorders of personality:* DSM-IV *and beyond* (2nd ed.). New York: Wiley.

Millon, T., Simonsen, E., Birket-Smith, M., & Davis, R. D. (Eds.). (1998). *Psychopathy: Antisocial, violent and criminal behaviors.* New York: Guilford Press.

Morey, L. C. (1988). The categorical representation of personality disorder: A cluster analysis of *DSM-III-R* personality features. *Journal of Abnormal Psychology, 97,* 314–321.

Mulder, R. T., & Joyce, P. R. (1997). Temperament and the structure of personality disorder symptoms. *Psychological Medicine, 27,* 99–106.

Newman, J. P. (1998). Psychopathic behavior: An information processing perspective. In D. J. Cooke, A. E. Forth, & R. D. Hare (Eds.), *Psychopathy: Theory, research and implications for society* (pp. 81–104). Amsterdam: Kluwer Press.

Porter, S. (1996). Without conscience or without active conscience? The etiology of psychopathy revisited. *Aggression and Violent Behavior, 1,* 179–189.

Robins, L. N. (1978). Aetiological implications in studies of childhood histories relating to antisocial personality. In R. D. Hare & D. Schalling (Eds.), *Psychopathic behaviour: Approaches to research* (pp. 255–271). Chichester, England: Wiley.

Salekin, R. T., Rogers, R., & Sewell, K. W. (1996). A review and meta-analysis of the Psychopathy Checklist–Revised: Predictive validity of dangerousness. *Clinical Psychology: Science and Practice, 3,* 203–213.

Schmitt, W. A., & Newman, J. P. (1999). Are all psychopathic individuals low anxious? *Journal of Abnormal Psychology, 108,* 353–358.

Schneider, K. (1950). *Psychopathic personalities* (9th ed.). London: Cassell. (Original work published 1923)

Skeem, J. L., & Mulvey, E. P. (2001). Psychopathy and community violence among civil psychiatric patients: Results from the MacArthur Violence Risk Assessment Study. *Journal of Consulting and Clinical Psychology, 69,* 358–374.

Skeem, J. L., Poythress, N., Edens, J. F., Lilienfeld, S. O., & Cale, E. M. (2003). Psychopathic personality or personalities? Exploring potential variants of psychopathy and their implications for risk assessment. *Aggression and Violent Behavior, 8,* 513–546.

Skilling, T. A., Harris, G. T., Rice, M. E., & Quinsey, V. L. (2002). Identifying persistently antisocial offenders using the Hare Psychopathy Checklist and *DSM* antisocial personality disorder criteria. *Psychological Assessment, 14,* 27–38.

Toch, H. (1998). Psychopathy or antisocial personality in forensic settings. In T. Millon, E. Simonsen, M. Birket-Smith, & R. D. Davis (Eds.), *Psychopathy: Antisocial, violent and criminal behaviors* (pp. 144–158). New York: Guilford Press.

Wakefield, J. C. (1992). The concept of mental disorder: On the boundary between biological facts and social values. *American Psychologist, 47,* 373–388.

Widiger, T. A., & Lynam, D. R. (1998). Psychopathy and the five-factor model of personality. In T. Millon, E. Simonsen, M. Birket-Smith, & R. D. Davis (Eds.), *Psychopathy: Antisocial, criminal, and violent behavior* (pp. 171–187). New York: Guilford Press.

Wiggins, J. S., & Trapnell, P. D. (1996). A dyadic-interactional perspective on the five-factor model. In J. S. Wiggins (Ed.), *The five-factor model of personality; Theoretical perspectives* (pp. 88–162). New York: Guilford Press.

Woodworth, M., & Porter, S. (2002). In cold blood: Characteristics of criminal homicide as a function of psychopathy. *Journal of Abnormal Psychology, 111,* 436–445.

Wulach, J. (1983). Diagnosing the *DSM-III* antisocial personality disorder. *Professional Psychology: Research and Practice, 14,* 330–440.

Chapter 16

BORDERLINE PERSONALITY DISORDER

NEIL BOCKIAN

At first glance, the symptoms of borderline personality disorder (BPD) are incoherent and internally inconsistent. A student of mind once diagnosed an individual as having both antisocial and dependent personality disorders. The student failed the assignment for having such a contradictory, thus inaccurate, diagnosis. How could someone be both dependent and antisocial? It made no sense. The correct diagnosis, of course, was borderline.

However, that raises the question: *How can someone appear to be both dependent and antisocial?* Within the criteria of BPD is an image of a person filled with chronic feelings of emptiness, yet, simultaneously, feelings of rage. It is an image of a person with impulsive behaviors, such as impulsive sexual behavior, drug taking, and stimulation seeking, while simultaneously presenting with clinging dependency. There is frequent acting out behavior, yet depression often accompanies BPD, with comorbidity estimates ranging from 24% to 87% (Shea, Widiger, & Klein, 1992). Similarly, we expect that the expression of anger will help to reduce depression, yet it appears to have no such effect for the person with BPD. Filled with desperation, many people with BPD make suicidal gestures and attempts, and their mood is wildly unstable; yet they report chronic feelings of emptiness. Few disorders are so perplexing and paradoxical—not only to clinicians and theorists, but even to the persons with the disorder.

The purpose of this chapter is to elucidate theories of BPD, providing an explanation for why the disorder occurs and an understanding of the developmental history of the person who has the disorder. The chapter is organized in alignment with a biopsychosocial approach; biological, psychological, then social theories are presented. In addition, I incorporate the perspective of the individual with the disorder, using artwork and poetry to illustrate key borderline features. I then finish with an integration of existing theories and an illustration of the disorder using poetry by people with BPD.

BIOLOGICAL FACTORS

It is my impression that clinicians, students, and clients generally underestimate the role of biology in personality disorders, including BPD. Perhaps our American individualism leads us to believe that we shape our own character, with a guiding influence from our parents and other significant figures (especially early on). Anyone who has ever tried to help a child (or the parent of a child) who has BPD tendencies, however, can see the powerful role that biology plays. The biological mechanisms that underlie fundamental features such as impulse control, synthesis, and integration of conceptual material, memory, and affect regulation shape individuals' perception of their environment, their response to it, and their capacity to cope with stressors.

Neurological and Neuropsychological Findings

The past 20 years have brought many developments in our understanding of the neurobiology of personality disorders. Brain scans and other neurological and neuropsychological evaluations support the existence of significant differences between people with BPD as opposed to healthy, nonpsychiatric comparison groups. PET scans on several samples have demonstrated reduced activity in the brains of adults with BPD, particularly in the orbital-frontal region (Goyer, Andreason, et al., 1994; Goyer, Konicki, & Schulz, 1994). Studies by Soloff et al. (2000) with a sample of people with BPD demonstrate reduced response to the serotonin agonist fenfluramine relative to a placebo control. Using PET scans and MRIs, Leyton et al. (2001) also found lower levels of brain activity were seen near the frontal lobes area and differences in the serotonin-rich areas of the brain, concluding that low serotonin synthesis capacity in the relevant pathways of the brain may promote impulsive behavior in individuals with BPD. In conclusion, brain-scan studies show that individuals who have difficulty with impulse control and aggression have reduced levels of activity in their brains in a number of key locations. This effect held up whether lifetime history of impulsive/aggressive acts or current impulsivity on an assigned task was used to define impulsivity. Increases in aggression are associated with low level of activity in the frontal cortex, as well as reduced activity in several areas within the limbic system. While further research is necessary, these preliminary results imply that memory and integration of sensory and emotional material are implicated in the difficulties experienced by people with BPD. There are also interesting neuroanatomical differences between individuals with and without BPD. For example, one study showed that when compared to controls (while controlling for overall brain volume), people with BPD had a 16% smaller hippocampus and a 7.5% smaller amygdala (Driessen et al., 2000).

Neuropsychological studies of individuals with BPD also provide highly useful and suggestive findings. Cowdry and O'Leary (in Silk, 1994) reviewed four neuropsychological studies done on people with BPD. They concluded that people with BPD demonstrate difficulties with visual discrimination and filtering and difficulties with recall of complex material. There also appear to be problems in visuomotor integration and figural memory. Neurological examinations and EEG studies show a high rate of subtle neurological dysfunction in individuals with BPD (Zanarini, Kimble, & Williams, 1994). These problems are generally in the mild to moderate range and are diffuse; thus, these problems are subtle and could easily be missed without testing.

Individuals with BPD have been found to have difficulty with both verbal and visual memory, especially complex material. Difficulty with recall of complex material may make it hard for people with BPD to learn from their experiences. We do not yet know whether individuals with BPD have difficulty with retrieval, recall, or both. Processing problems can also impact an individual's self-image. O'Leary and Cowdry (1994) noted that "such a memory deficit may contribute to difficulties borderline patients experience in maintaining a continuous sense of self and using the past to respond to present events and predict future consequences" (p. 147).

Thus, brain functioning and learning style may contribute to many of the difficulties that we see in BPD. A number of the findings are consistent with borderline psychopathology. Poor filtering often leads to confusion, which may contribute to excessive dependence on others and poor boundaries. Diffuse neuropsychological dysfunction may be related to dissociation and other neurocognitive functions. Sluggish functioning of the serotonergic systems, imbalances in the cholinergic and noradronergic systems, anatomical deficiencies in the amygdala, and dysfunction in the limbic system may lead the person to be extremely vulnerable to impulsivity and affective dysregulation. Deficiencies in the hippocampus may contribute to memory problems. Many of the distortions people with BPD evince may be seen as a function of neurological dysfunction. Splitting, for example, can be seen as a problem of recall especially in evidence under conditions of high emotional arousal.

In light of these various biological findings, it is not surprising that genetics play a major role in the development of BPD. A factor labeled *emotional dysregulation,* which corresponds to BPD, had a heritability estimate of 52% (Jang, Vernon, & Livesley, 2000). Coolidge, Thede, and Jang (2001), in their sample of children and adolescents, found that the heritability of BPD (h^2) is 76%. Silk (2000), in his extensive review of the relevant literature, estimated that the contributions of genetics and environment are approximately equal in the development of personality disorders.

Medications

Medications are more germane to treatment than to conceptualization, so their treatment in this chapter is very brief. However, unlike many medical illnesses and Axis I conditions, there is no specific medication to treat a personality disorder per se. Instead, when treating individuals with BPD, Soloff et al. (2000) recommends conceptualizing the individual as having difficulties that lie along four dimensions: cognitive-perceptual, affective dysregulation, impulsive-behavioral dyscontrol, and interpersonal psychopathology. Based on a comprehensive review of the literature, Soloff constructed an algorithm of treatment recommendations. Cognitive-perceptual disturbances such as suspiciousness, paranoia, and thought disorder are treated primarily with low-dose neuroleptics, switching to an atypical neuroleptic if that has inadequate efficacy, and adding an SSRI or MAOI for affective symptoms. For affective dysregulation, including depression, anger, anxiety, and lability, an SSRI is the first line of treatment; a low-dose neuroleptic can be added for anger and clonazepam for anxiety. If these are insufficiently effective, other medications to try include valproate, lithium, or carbamazepine. Impulsive aggression, including bingeing and self-injurious behavior, are also primarily treated with SSRIs, followed by lithium, MAOIs, valproate, and carbemazepine, depending on the exact symptoms and response. The use of SSRIs for affective dysregulation and impulsivity was based on the theoretical work (presented earlier) on serotonergic insufficiency in people with BPD and other affective/behavioral dysregulation problems. Interpersonal psychopathology (problems in interpersonal relationships) is not directly treated with medications (except as they are impacted by the other three dimensions) and falls within the domain of psychotherapy (Soloff, 1998).

PSYCHOLOGICAL THEORIES

How does BPD develop? How is it maintained? Given that the symptoms are painful, why don't they simply undergo behavioral extinction? How can we intervene to reduce psychopathology and increase healthy behaviors? How can the inner conflicts associated with the disorder be resolved? There are no prospective longitudinal studies that begin evaluating people at birth and follow them throughout the life span. However, there are several key theories with a great deal of explanatory power, supported by empirical evidence such as positive treatment outcomes.

Millon's Theory

According to Millon (1996), three dimensions underlie personality. Each serves an adaptive function and is rooted in the organism's evolutionary history. The first dimension reflects the aims of existence: life enhancement (seeking reward/pleasure) versus life preservation (avoiding danger and threat/pain). The second dimension reflects modes of adaptation: ecological accommodation (passive adaptation) versus ecological modification (active adaptation). The third dimension refers to strategies of replication: reproductive individuation (actualizing self) versus reproductive nurturance (constructively loving others).

What is notable about BPD is the conflict between the two polarities of each dimension, which emerges as a near-constant state of ambivalence and tension. This is not true of all people with personality disorders. The person with dependent personality disorder can feel comfortable in an environment in which he or she is consistently nurtured and supported; similarly, the individual with narcissistic personality disorder can feel comfortable if interacting with one or more admirers, but not so for the borderline. A persistently nurturing other person tends to elicit fears of engulfment; however, anything less than complete devotion at every moment elicits abandonment terror. Similarly, the person with BPD tends to alternate between passively hoping for attention and affection from others and actively seeking to have his or her emotional needs met. Millon describes this polarity conflict as signifying ". . . the intense ambivalence and inconsistency that characterizes the borderline, their emotional vacillation, their behavioral unpredictability, as well as the inconsistency they manifest in their feelings and thoughts about others" (1996, p. 660).

According to Millon (1981, 1996), the development of any personality disorder, including BPD, is a function of biological, psychological, and social factors. Borderline personality disorder, in Millon's conceptualization, is a dysfunctional, or extreme, variant of dependent, histrionic, and passive-aggressive personality disorders. As such, the etiology, including biological underpinnings and psychosocial experiences, is related to the subtype. The more dependent types generally have more sluggish temperaments and a history of being overnurtured (with the inevitable metamessage that the child is incompetent and requires care). The more histrionic types have highly active temperaments and were reinforced for performing for their parents and others. The passive-aggressive (negativistic) types tend to have moody, irascible temperaments and were raised with extreme inconsistency. In all cases, repeated failures of their attempts to cope with the world have led to increasing desperation. Rather than flexibly adapting to the environment, however, the incipient borderline tends to recycle the same coping efforts, but at a higher or more extreme level of intensity. Eventually, the individual engages in extreme behaviors much of the time. Overall, Millon views mundane, oft-repeated patterns in the environment (such as ongoing parental inconsistency), rather than dramatic but time-limited traumatic events (such as a single episode of sexual abuse), as more central to the development of personality disorders.

Consistent with the theory, then, the overarching principle of Millon's therapy (personality guided therapy; Millon, 1999) is to reestablish polarity balance. Individuals with healthy personalities are able to adapt as the situation requires. Thus, they can be other-oriented (appropriately deferential) with authority figures, while asserting authority (self-oriented) with subordinates. If the person is too consistently dependent (i.e., too "other oriented," in the language of the polarities), the primary goal is to help the person to become more independent and thus more flexible on the self-other dimension.

For the person with BPD, the problem is not so much a rigid adherence to one polarity or another, but rather the wild vacillation from one polarity to another. Thus, the person with BPD who is generally passive and clingy suddenly snaps and explodes in a rage. Others become puzzled or frightened or respond in kind. Relationships are typically damaged, despite sincere contrition. There can be excessive leaning toward one polarity or another, as seen in admixtures of the histrionic-borderline type (more active and other oriented), the dependent-borderline (passive-other), and the antisocial-borderline (active-self). In all cases, however, the person with BPD must find the middle path, a way of being that is less focused on the extremes.

Another key element of Millon's theory with profound implications for therapy is the concept of self-perpetuating patterns and vicious circles. Given the extreme polarity imbalances implicit in a personality disorder, the person elicits problematic interpersonal and environmental situations that perpetuate or worsen the existing pattern. For example, the person with BPD who engages in substance abuse to cope with emotional dysregulation elicits a host of psychosocial stressors (e.g., job loss, financial problems, relationship difficulties, and legal problems) that elicit further emotional dysregulation. The manner in which the person copes with that dysregulation (e.g., further substance abuse or other acting out behavior) maintains or worsens the borderline pattern. Countering perpetuations, then, is a key component of therapeutic intervention (Millon, 1996, 1999).

Psychodynamic

Psychodynamic formulations of BPD focus on a variety of developmental and constitutional factors that interact to form the disorder. The term *borderline* is derived from the conceptualization of Stern (1938/1986) that there is a group of clients who seem to dwell at the boundary—the borderline—between psychosis and neurosis. Stern's initial interest in this area was in a group that seemed as though they should be amenable to analysis, but they did very poorly. Comparing psychoanalytic treatment to a necessary surgery, Stern stated:

> A negative therapeutic reaction is nevertheless inevitable; in some, the reaction is extremely unfavorable, and, cumulatively, may become dangerous; patients may develop depression, suicidal ideas, or make suicide attempts. (1938/1986, p. 59)

The word *inevitable* is chilling in this context; classical psychoanalysis is not recommended for this population. However, with some modest modifications from psychoanalysis, psychodynamic methods are effective. The theories described later draw primarily on object relations theory. Thus, the key issue is not really the relationships with real people, such as the mother, but, rather, the individual's internal representation of the mother and, perhaps even more germanely, the relationship of various parts of the self (part self) to various parts of the other (part objects). Thus, for example, the person with BPD may see himself or herself as a denigrated, abused self, in relation to a sadistic, abusive other; each of these are really part self and part object relations.

Kernberg (1967; Clarkin, Yeomans, & Kernberg, 1999; Kernberg, Selzer, Koenigsberg, Carr, & Appeibaum, 1989) employs the concept of "borderline personality organization" rather than BPD. Borderline personality organization is conceptualized as a level of functioning, rather than a categorical conception. Theoretically derived from the interplay of psychodynamic processes related to how the developing child handles an excess of aggressive libidinal energy, borderline personality organization includes features of not only borderline, but also narcissistic, schizoid, schizotypal, paranoid, histrionic, antisocial, and dependent personality disorders (Clarkin et al., 1999; Kernberg, 1967). Excess aggression can be caused by constitutional factors or by childhood frustration. The individual then defends against the aggressive impulses using splitting and related defenses.

Splitting occurs in normal development as a way of experiencing the positive and negative aspects of significant others in the environment. The newborn coos in the presence of the warm, loving mother and wails when the mother is unable to immediately provide for his or her needs. In normal development, the child at some point integrates whole views of others, so that he or she recognizes that the father who is nurturing at one time is still the same person as the one who is withholding at another. However, when the child has a massive excess of aggressive libidinal energy, good internalized objects are at risk for being completely overwhelmed by negative object representations. In other words, if the child were to see the other person, for example, the mother, as a whole, she would be invested with a massive amount of hostile, aggressive energy and a relatively small amount of loving, nurturing energy and, hence, would be seen as essentially all bad. Splitting, then, protects the fragile internalized good objects from being overwhelmed by the aggressive, malevolent bad object representations.

Splitting, the primary defensive operation to cope with excess aggression, elicits several other defensive operations. In primitive idealization, one side of splitting, external objects are seen as all good. Omnipotent control is overvaluation of the self and is related to devaluation, which is deflation of others. Projective identification is a three-part process:

1. Projection of an unacceptable impulse onto another, while continuing to experience the impulse.
2. Viewing the individual onto whom the impulse is projected as under the sway of the projected impulse and thus frightening.
3. Attempts to control the person, often in a way that provokes the feared behavior.

An example of projective identification is the client who repeatedly and with thinly veiled hostility accuses the therapist of being angry with her; eventually, the therapist does in fact become irritated and angry, "confirming" the client's suspicions. Denial, according to Kernberg (1986), is not so much denial of the existence of a perception, thought, or feeling, but rather the splitting off of the emotion, so that the phenomenon is seen as emotionally irrelevant.

Kernberg recommends the traditional analytic techniques of clarification, confrontation, interpretation, and technical neutrality (placing oneself equidistant from the id, ego, and superego in helping the client to resolve conflicts). The sine qua non of his treatment, however, is analysis of the transference in the here-and-now; in fact, he now labels his therapy *transference focused psychotherapy* (TFP). Transference focused psychotherapy has been manualized to promote consistent use in different settings (Yeomans, Clarkin, & Kernberg, 2002). Kernberg often combines his confrontations with accurate and empathically attuned statements. For example, he described the following case:

Therapist: I notice that you're making some marks on your pad whenever I speak.
Patient: Yes, I'm counting how many times you talk.
Therapist: Why do you do that?

Patient: It helps me know if you care about me. I count up the number of times you speak, and when I go home I compare that number to the last session. That's how I tell how much you're giving me.

Therapist: Does it matter what I say?

Client: Not so much. What really counts is how many times you tell me why you think I'm doing what I'm doing. Then I know you're really listening to me and concerned about me.

Therapist: *So it's very important that I care about you,* and you've devised a scheme to answer that question for yourself. Can you see you're also treating what I'm saying as if it were worthless? (Kernberg et al., 1989, p. 115, emphasis added)

This fragment is an illustration of several key aspects of Kernberg's approach. One is the splitting that occurs: The client simultaneously idealizes and devalues the therapist, without any integration of the two. The therapist is simultaneously the longed-for caring nurturer, while he or she is seen, projectively, as devalued and empty. Kernberg uses both clarification and confrontation concerning the relationship between the therapist and the client (i.e., the transference) to push the client to integrate the split self and object relations implied in the interaction.

Masterson (1981) has a different perspective. Rather than emphasizing the child's internalized aggression, he sees the primary problem as the mother's "libidinal withdrawal" from the child, frustrating the child's separation-individuation process. In the most common pattern, the mother discourages separation, instead encouraging dependency and clinging. The mother, according to Masterson, is generally a person with BPD herself, who has her own problems with separation anxiety. Attempts for the child to individuate provoke extreme anxiety in the mother, which in turn elicits caretaking behavior from the child. Another pattern is for the child to regress and cling to the mother, failing to individuate, thus gratifying the mother's emotional needs. Alternatively, the mother may withdraw, unable to handle the child's dependency needs.

For Masterson, like Kernberg, the key to understanding the individual with BPD is understanding the part self and part object relations that compose the psyche. The mother is divided into two part objects as a function of splitting. There is the rewarding object relations unit (RORU), which is the all-good object, and the withdrawing object relations unit (WORU), which is all bad (hostile, withdrawing, and rejecting). The child can defend against feelings of abandonment in one of two ways. The first way is to project the rewarding unit onto others (including the therapist), while internalizing the withdrawing unit. This leads to clinging subordination. The second path is to project the withdrawing unit onto others, while the rewarding unit is internalized. Others are thus seen as hostile, critical, and distancing. The client avoids thoughts and feelings that interfere with this defense, primarily through denial, and psychotherapeutic progress once again grinds to a halt.

Abandonment depression, and the defenses built around it, for Masterson, constitutes the heart of borderline psychopathology. Masterson calls this constellation the "borderline triad: separation-individuation leads to depression which leads to defense" (Masterson, 1981, p. 133). Similar to Kernberg, Masterson recommends confrontation as the path through which to break this stalemate. The purpose of the confrontation is to "render the functioning of the split object relations unit/pathologic ego alliance ego alien" (p. 136). That is, clients must experience their perceptions of others as part objects (e.g., as entirely hostile, withdrawing, bad, or good) as something foreign and in need of repair, rather than as a necessary and adaptive response to reality. According to Masterson:

The clinging transference calls for the confrontation of the denial of destructive behavior . . . while the distancing transference calls for the confrontation of the negative, hostile projections, usually on the therapist. (1981, p. 137)

Confrontation, when effective, thus *increases* anxiety because clients become aware of conflicts that were formerly suppressed, denied, or defended against via acting out. When clients recognize that these defenses are self-destructive, they control their behavior, thus experiencing the abandonment depression. This promotes a healing cycle:

There results a circular process, sequentially including resistance, confrontation, working through the feelings of abandonment (withdrawing part unit), further resistance (rewarding part unit) and further confrontation, which leads in turn, to further working through. (Masterson, 1981, p. 137)

According to Masterson, borderline clients do not have transference in the classical sense because transference requires whole object relations. Instead, they engage in "transference acting out." The concept is similar to Freud's repetition compulsion, in which events are repeated not in memory, but in behavior. Just as the resolution to the repetition compulsion is interpretation, which releases repressed memories, the resolution to transference acting out is confrontation in the transference, which brings awareness of the meaning of the behavior. This allows the client to increasingly perceive the therapist as a whole object, which permits working through. As Masterson stated: "The more he invests in the therapist as a real object, the more he turns to therapy to work through his feelings of abandonment rather than to the rewarding unit/pathologic ego alliance to relieve them" (1981, p. 151).

Masterson and Kernberg are similar in a number of ways, especially in the area of technique. Both emphasize confrontation, especially confrontation of the transference, as the path to resolution of borderline psychopathology. Both employ rather traditional psychoanalytic techniques (e.g., technical neutrality). The main differences are their etiological assumptions, with Kernberg emphasizing excess aggression, while Masterson emphasizes maternal unavailability.

Cognitive-Behavioral Therapy Theories

Cognitive-behavioral therapy (CBT) for BPD is built primarily on the notion that people who have the disorder are prone to a variety of beliefs that are then logically related to their emotions. The acquisition of these beliefs and behaviors is generally thought to follow the principles of social learning (e.g., Bandura), reinforcement (e.g., Skinner), and associational learning (e.g., Pavlov). The relationship that is encouraged between client and therapist is that of teacher and student, who engage in "collaborative empiricism" to shine the light of reason on the client's potentially irrational beliefs.

Young's work with schemas, originally labeled *schema-focused cognitive therapy* (Young, 1983, 1987; cited in Beck & Freeman, 1990) and now known as *schema therapy* (Young, Klosko, & Weishaar, 2003), examines typical beliefs held by people with personality disorders, including BPD. Young explicates typical beliefs that persist in people with BPD. By educating clients about schemas, the therapist can align with the client against the maladaptive schema. Examples of schemas that typify BPD are listed in Table 16.1.

Beck and Freeman (1990) argued that dichotomous thinking plays a central role in BPD pathology. Dichotomous thinking is the tendency to think in black-and-white terms

Table 16.1   Maladaptive Ways of Thinking Learned in Early Childhood by People with BPD

Early Maladaptive Schemas	Possible Expression
Abandonment/ Instability	I worry that people I feel close to will leave or abandon me.
Mistrust/Abuse	I have been physically, emotionally, or sexually abused by important people in my life.
Emotional Deprivation	Most of the time, I haven't had someone to nurture me, share him/herself with me, or care deeply about everything that happens to me.
Defectiveness/ Shame	I am unworthy of the love, attention, and respect of others.
Dependence/ Incompetence	I do not feel capable of getting by on my own in everyday life.
Undeveloped self	I feel that I do not really know who I am or what I want
Insufficient self-control/ Self-discipline	I often do things impulsively that I later regret
Subjugation	I feel that I have no choice but to give in to other people's wishes, or else they will retaliate or reject me in some way.
Punitiveness	I'm a bad person, who deserves to be punished.

Sources: The Young Schema Therapy Questionnaire, Short Form and Long Form, adapted from *Cognitive Therapy for Personality Disorders: A Schema Focused Approach, third edition,* Sarasota Professional Resource Press, 1999, pp. 12–16, and personal communication, May 3, 2002. Reprinted by permission of Jeffrey E. Young, PhD. Reproduction without written consent of the author is prohibited.

and is the phenomenological parallel of the psychodynamic construct, splitting. All-or-none thinking is seen as having broad-reaching implications:

> Since dichotomous thinking can produce extreme emotional responses and actions and can produce abrupt shifts from one extreme mood to another, it could be responsible to a considerable extent for the abrupt mood swings and dramatic shifts in behavior that are a hallmark of BPD. (p. 187)

Beck and Freeman (1990) further noted that relationship issues with the therapist will be much more prominent with people with BPD than with people with other disorders. Although coming from a perspective that is very different from Kernberg's and other dynamic therapists, they came to similar conclusions about some key aspects of the therapeutic relationship:

> Since the borderline has discovered through painful experience that it can be very dangerous to trust other people and realizes that the therapist-client relationship is a relationship in which he or she will be quite vulnerable at times, it rarely is productive to try to establish trust through persuasion, arguments, or pointing to one's credentials. The borderline is not foolish enough to trust others simply because they say they can be trusted or because they have diplomas. Trust is most effectively established by explicitly acknowledging and accepting the client's difficulties in trusting the therapist (once this becomes evident), and

then be careful to behave in consistently trustworthy manner. It is important to exercise more than the usual amount of care in communicating clearly, assertively, and honestly with the client; in avoiding misunderstandings; in maintaining congruence between verbal statements and nonverbal cues; and in following through on agreements. Over time, this approach will provide the evidence on which trust can be based. (p. 191)

People with BPD are also likely to have intense emotional reactions that appear to be highly inappropriate to the situation. The structured, task-focused nature of CBT tends to minimize what analysts would call "transference" with most clients; nonetheless, individuals with BPD are likely to have strong emotional reactions that are not a direct function of the therapist's behavior. From a cognitive-behavioral perspective, transference can be viewed as stimulus generalization from a previous relationship to the current one or, as Beck and Freeman noted, applying previously held general beliefs rather than responding to the therapist as an individual. The therapist must be prepared to help the client to unpack the meaning of these intense reactions, based on prior experiences and strongly held beliefs. The client's intense emotional reactions can then provoke a powerful emotional response, akin to countertransference, in the therapist. Although Beck and Freeman recommend professional consultation when the therapist is confused by his or her strong emotional reactions, they also note the positive aspects of attending to one's emotional responses:

> Far from being an impediment, strong feelings can be quite useful if the therapist is able to understand them. Emotional responses do not occur randomly. If a therapist experiences an unusually strong response to a client, this is likely to be a response to some aspect of the client's behavior, and it may provide valuable information if it can be understood. It is not unusual for a therapist to respond emotionally to a pattern in the client's behavior long before that pattern has been recognized intellectually. Accurate interpretation of emotional responses can speed recognition of these patterns. (1990, pp. 195–196)

Other aspects of borderline pathology also interfere with the development of a productive cognitive-behavioral therapeutic relationship. Identity confusion interferes with setting goals because individuals often experience rapidly shifting agendas. Their fear of intimacy can provoke discomfort, premature termination, or acting out even with the modest intimacy typically seen in CBT. Their fear of, and anticipation of, rejection, can lead to premature termination.

The establishment and continued maintenance of a positive therapeutic relationship provides the context in which the client can be provided with skills training in particular areas of deficit (such as assertiveness and other relationship skills) and encouraged to engage in behavioral experiments. The goal is to persistently identify the client's beliefs, particularly those that may be distorted or irrational, and challenge these beliefs against reality.

Dialectical Behavior Therapy Theory

Perhaps it is fitting, given the paradoxical nature of BPD, that a treatment developed specifically to address BPD, in its essence, is designed to address paradox. According to Linehan (1993), dialectical behavior therapy (DBT) is so named because Linehan sees the principal issues with BPD as the resolution of diametrically conflicting tendencies (thesis and diathesis) that must be brought to resolution (synthesis). Drawing on Zen Buddhism, Linehan views the synthesis as transcending the rational, similar to a Zen koan (paradox). The resolution to the polarities, rather than a rational solution, is an experience.

A crucial environmental precursor to BPD, according to Linehan (1993), is the "invalidating environment." Invalidation indicates that significant others are sending messages that an individual's feelings, thoughts, and perceptions are not real or do not matter. Such invalidation, according to Linehan, can contribute to the development of BPD. Examples include the girl whose interests in mechanical pursuits do not fit society's gender stereotyping and who is punished or told her interests are bad or wrong; conversely, the boy who's told he should be able to control his emotions and that his yearning for nurturance is a show of weakness is also being invalidated. Consistent invalidation leads to confusion and poor self-esteem. As is emphasized later, BPD results when the biologically vulnerable individual is raised in a persistently invalidating environment.

The concept of invalidation explains the finding that sexual abuse is common among people with BPD. Sexual abuse is the ultimate invalidation. The victim's well-being is irrelevant to the abuser, who is gratifying his or her needs. As described by Linehan (1993):

> Sexual abuse, as it occurs in our culture, is perhaps one of the clearest examples of extreme invalidation during childhood. In the typical case scenario of sexual abuse, the person being abused is told that the molestation or intercourse is "OK," but that she [or he] must not tell anyone else. The abuse is seldom acknowledged by other family members, and if the child reports the abuse she [or he] risks being disbelieved or blamed. (pp. 53–54)

The prototypical dilemmas are emotional vulnerability versus self-invalidation, active passivity versus apparent competence, and unrelenting crisis versus inhibited grieving, which are explained briefly later. Linehan defines emotional vulnerability as ongoing and extreme emotional sensitivity, intense emotional reactions, and the experience of persistent negative emotional reactions. She compared this to the physical hypersensitivity of the burn patient:

> The net effect of these emotional difficulties is that borderline individuals are the psychological equivalent of third-degree burn patient. They simply have, so to speak, no emotional skin. Even the slightest touch or movements can create immense suffering. Yet, on the other hand, life is movement. Therapy, at its best, requires both movement and touch. Thus, both the therapist and the process of therapy itself cannot fail to cause intensely painful emotional experiences for the borderline patient . . . it is the experience of their own vulnerability that sometimes leads borderline individuals to extreme behaviors (including suicidal behaviors), both to try to take care of themselves and to alert the environment to take better care of them. (Linehan, 1993, p. 69)

This phenomenon is strikingly conveyed by an artist who was attempting to convey his experience of BPD (see Figure 16.1). Clearly, the artist experiences the extreme vulnerability associated with having "no skin," or no emotional skin, as Linehan would put it. (I contacted the artist, who did not recall whether he had heard Linehan's theory before or after he had made his digital painting; personal communication, 6/24/03.)

Linehan believes that emotional vulnerability is the core feature of BPD, with many of the other symptoms making sense as an attempt to cope with it. Excessive emotional arousal interferes with cognitive functioning and behavioral responses that would facilitate coping. Attempts to regulate painful emotions are the precursors of impulsive behaviors, such as drug/alcohol use or unprotected sex, which then lead to further problems. Attempts to modulate emotions through social interactions can lead to excessive dependency and concomitant fears of abandonment. Thus, emotional vulnerability becomes a focal point around which many borderline symptoms make sense. As indicated in Figure 16.1, this tendency

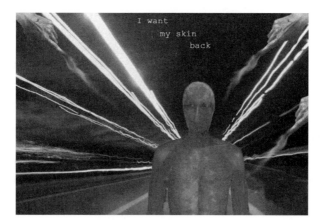

Figure 16.1   Borderline Personality Disorder. Reprinted by permission of the artist, who prefers to remain anonymous.

toward affective dysregulation is largely biological, while its counterpart, self invalidation, is predominately learned. Self-invalidation indicates a tendency on the part of the individual to respond with shame, guilt, and intropunitiveness to environmental stimuli and represents the internalization of the invalidating environment. "Active passivity" is Linehan's eye-catching phrase that captures the phenomenon of demanding clinginess and neediness seen in people with BPD. It is something of a hybrid between the passivity of the dependent, who waits and hopes for support, and the activity of the histrionic, who provides entertainment in "exchange" for nurturance. The likely experiential history of people experiencing active passivity is a history of failure when they attempt to cope actively with situations (i.e., learned helplessness), presumably accompanied by at least some instances of soothing by others.

Apparent competence is present when a person is competent in some areas, while behaving completely inappropriately at times. Others are surprised, perhaps even shocked, when a person who appears to be a typical colleague suddenly has a meltdown or behaves inappropriately for no apparent reason. Linehan explains this phenomenon as occurring due to (1) a lack of stimulus generalization; (2) a failure on the part of the person with BPD to communicate his or her vulnerability clearly, since he or she has learned to inhibit emotional expression as a form of coping; and (3) variations in competence based on perceived support—when a person with BPD is with a supportive individual or believes he or she is in a secure, supportive relationship, he or she does relatively well, which means that the person will function deceptively well during therapy sessions.

Unrelenting crisis is the phenomenon in which people with BPD tend to go from one crisis to the next. Linehan explains this as being due to a combination of low stress tolerance and poor coping skills. *Inhibited grieving* "refers to a pattern of repetitive, significant trauma and loss, together with an inability to fully experience and personally integrate or resolve these events" (Linehan, 1993, p. 89). Studies show that approximately two-thirds to three-quarters of people with BPD have a history of being abused sexually; thus, a majority of people with BPD are coping with trauma-related symptoms (Linehan, 1993, pp. 52–53). The problem, as Linehan sees it, is that the individual is unable to regulate his or her emotions well enough to handle normal grieving; if the individual were to process the loss, he or she would "fall apart." Therefore, like many people with posttraumatic stress disorder, the individual avoids contact with any reminders of the stressors, both external and internal. This strategy is only partially successful because reminders are common in the environment (especially in interpersonal relationships), and mental representations based on the traumatic events influence many aspects of the person's life. What unfolds, then, is a chronic, partial grieving, with frequent emotional dysregulation. Thus, in working through the traumatic past, the person with BPD may require substantial support to avoid an intolerable worsening of symptoms.

Client-Centered and Humanistic Conceptualizations

An important theoretical perspective within the client-centered/humanistic therapy domain is Margaret Warner's *fragile process* (Warner, 1998, 2000). Given the antilabeling orientation of most humanistically oriented therapists, it is relatively difficult to find theoretical work on personality disorders from that perspective. However, assuming that Linehan's theory about the invalidating environment is correct, it is likely that a therapeutic approach based on validation and unconditional positive regard would be effective; the one outcome study I could find (Eckert & Wuchner, 1996) indicated results comparable to those of DBT (Linehan, 1993) and TFP (Clarkin et al., 1999). Warner defined *fragile process* as follows:

> "Fragile" process is a style of process in which clients have difficulty modulating the intensity of core experiences, beginning or ending emotional reactions when socially expected, or taking the points of view of other people without breaking contact with their own experience. Clients in the middle of a fragile process often feel particularly high levels of shame and self-criticism about their experience. (Warner, 2000, p. 145)

Integrating fragile process with developmental theory, especially attachment theory, Warner hypothesized that individuals who are prone to fragile process are insecurely attached. Individuals with insecure attachment to adult figures find that high arousal leads to emotional overload and disorganization, which neither they nor their caregivers are able to soothe. The child would thus often feel either fearful (because he or she cannot be soothed) or angry (if the child expects the caregiver to help and is disappointed or frustrated). The infant, then, would either constantly seek out attachments to find sustaining nurturance or self-protectively withdraw from others.

The dilemma throughout life, then, is that if persons with fragile process (BPD) express their feelings, they are often misunderstood; if they withdraw, they feel empty. As Warner put it:

> Clients who have a fragile style of processing often experience their lives as chaotic or empty. If clients with high-intensity fragile process choose to stay connected with their experience in personal relationships, they are likely to feel violated and misunderstood a great deal of the time. When they express their feelings, others in their lives are likely to see them as unreasonably angry, touchy, and stubborn. These others are likely to become angry and rejecting in return, reinforcing clients' sense that there is something fundamentally poisonous about their existence. Clients who continue to express their feelings are likely to have ongoing volatile relationships or a succession of relationships that start out well and then go sour. If, on the other hand, they give up on connecting or expressing their personal reactions they are likely to feel frozen or dead inside. Many alternate, holding in their reactions while feeling increasingly uncomfortable and then exploding with rage at those around them. (Warner, 2000, p. 152)

Warner noted that there are pitfalls for the therapist treating people with fragile process: "The client may be able to talk about feelings of rage at the therapist and very much want them understood and affirmed. Yet, therapist comments to explain the situation or disagree with the client will be felt as attempts by the therapist to annihilate his experience" (Warner, 2000, p. 150).

So what is the proper intervention with someone with fragile process? Warner stressed that it is essential to try to understand the person from his or her own perspective:

> Empathic understanding responses are often the only sorts of responses people can receive while in the middle of fragile process without feeling traumatised or disconnected from their experience . . . clients in the middle of fragile process are asking if their way of experiencing themselves at that moment has a right to exist in the world. Any misnaming of the experience or suggestion that they look at the experience in a different way is experienced as an answer of "no" to the question. (Warner, 2000, p. 151)

One error that therapists frequently make with people in general, and especially those with fragile process, is to assume that they have words for their feelings. Often, they do not. People with fragile process often act out their feelings (such as taking drugs, self-mutilating, or attempting suicide). If the client is struggling for words, the therapist needs to support him or her through it and avoid the temptation to guess or hypothesize about the client's feelings. A comment such as, "Something about that feels uncomfortable, but you're not quite clear what it is," is often very effective and will allow the person with fragile process to continue to explore his or her experience (Warner, 2000, p. 153). If the therapist fills the space by putting words into the person's mouth, the client will often feel misunderstood—this being the core problem for people with BPD.

SOCIAL AND CULTURAL FACTORS

Borderline personality disorder appears to be increasing in frequency. This increase may be explained, in part, by clinicians' increasing awareness of Axis II disorders and the concomitant increase in diagnoses; however, there are also forces at work that are genuinely increasing the number of new cases. Since our genetics have not changed appreciably, social changes appear to be the most likely causal factors. If we were to design a society most likely to create BPD among its citizens, our current American society would be almost ideal.

Millon (1987) outlined a series of social factors that have contributed to this increasing prevalence. We live in a world of rapid technological and sociological change, the pace of which is constantly accelerating. In our highly mobile society, it is becoming less likely that children will grow up in one stable environment, in one home, in one city, or even in one family. Formerly stable institutions, such as religious institutions and marriage, are no longer so stable. Participation in religious institutions is down (Clark, 2000; Hadaway & Marler, 1993; Smith, Denton, & Faris, 2002). More than 50% of marriages end in divorce, and second marriages have an even higher failure rate. The breakup of parents makes it more difficult for the developing child to internalize stable role models. Further, it is not uncommon for a divorcing couple to line up on opposite sides of a courtroom, each painting himself or herself as all good and the other as all bad. The developing child can internalize this kind of real-life splitting.

Many women with children are now engaged in full-time careers, but few fathers have chosen to stay home with their children. Today, children are often raised by a patchwork of others, including day care workers, baby sitters, and aides working in early education programs. Extended kinship networks, although still a positive and stabilizing force in African American, Asian American, and Hispanic American subcultures (Sue & Sue, 2002), have had a declining role in White majority culture. Working parents often come home relatively late, exhausted from workday demands. They have difficulty spending the few precious moments they have with their children providing firm, consistent discipline. Instead, they often assuage their guilt by being lax or lavishing the child with gifts.

Television and other video media also have a profound impact on personality development. Role models and heroes have become increasingly violent, unstable, and outwardly sexual. Emotional shallowness and instability often dominate TV programs. Problems develop and are resolved in 30 to 60 minutes, often as a result of a dramatic, two-minute confrontation. The sincere expression of feelings and negotiations that comprise real conflict resolution does not happen on TV. It is reasonable to theorize that as our children watch television, they are learning how to be impulsive, cynical, sexually unrestrained, explosively angry, and melodramatic—that is, *more borderline.* According to Millon (1987):

> TV may be nothing but simple pablum for those with comfortably internalized models of real human relationships, but for those who possess a world of diffuse values and standards, or one in which parental precepts and norms have been discarded, the impact of these "substitute" prototypes is especially powerful, even idealized and romanticized. And what these characters and story plots present to vulnerable youngsters are the stuff of which successful half-hour "life stories" must be composed to capture the attention and hold the fascination of their audiences—violence, danger, agonizing dilemmas, and unpredictability, each expressed and resolved in an hour or less—precisely those features of social behavior and emotionality that come to characterize the affective and interpersonal instabilities of the [person with borderline personality disorder]. (p. 365)

Finally, the increasing prevalence of sexual abuse (Sedlak & Broadhurst, 1996) is likely a contributing factor in the increasing prevalence of BPD. The causal role of sexual abuse in BPD is complex. We do know that not all individuals with sexual abuse develop BPD, and not all people with BPD have been sexually abused. Zanarini et al. (1998) have shown that BPD cannot be reduced to complex posttraumatic stress disorder. Nonetheless, borderline symptoms logically relate to sexual abuse. In addition to Linehan's observations about the connection between invalidation and sexual abuse, those who have been sexually abused commonly employed defenses that are used by people with BPD. Dissociation (to mentally escape from the abuse) and splitting (to allow the person to have a relationship with the abuser) are associated with criteria 9 and 2 in the *DSM-IV,* respectively. Low self-esteem, a common concomitant of abuse, often leads to dependency and fear of abandonment (criterion 1), suicidal feelings (criterion 5), and depression (criterion 6). Thus, unless proven otherwise, it is wise to assume that sexual abuse plays a contributing role in BPD and that, as rates of abuse rise, so will rates of BPD.

While on the topic of sexual abuse, it is important to note that therapists may erroneously blame families or assume that family members were abusive when in fact the family members are often the greatest source of support to the person with BPD. John Gunderson, MD, put it this way:

> I (JG) was a contributor to the literature that led to the unfair vilification of the families and the largely unfortunate efforts at either excluding or inappropriately involving them in

treatment. So it is with some embarrassment that I now find myself presenting a treatment that begins with the expectation that families of borderline individuals are important allies of the treaters and that largely finesses the whole issue of whether they had anything to do with the origins of psychopathology. . . . The parents generally saw the families as much healthier than did the borderline offspring. Much of the preceding literature about the families of borderline patients derived solely from reports provided by the borderline patients, and rarely included the families' perspective. (Gunderson, Berkowitz, & Ruiz-Sanchez, 1997, p. 449)

We must exercise caution in our assumptions about families and be open to an inclusive approach when appropriate.

INTEGRATION

Millon (1996) has uncovered an ingenious way to integrate various and disparate theoretical interpretations. Rather than integrating at the level of theory, he integrates at the level of the *person*. Each theory best describes some aspect of a person's functioning. Millon described eight clinical domains that provide a comprehensive conceptualization of the person. The first two domains are observable and thus considered the behavioral level of analysis. Expressive Acts are connected to behaviorism, while Interpersonal Conduct is related to the interpersonal school. The next three domains are related to the person's experience of himself or herself and are thus labeled phenomenological by Millon. Cognitive Style is associated with the cognitive school (e.g., Beck, Ellis, Young), Self-image is the person's predominately conscious view of himself or herself and connects to nearly all schools of thought, while Object Representations refers to the individual's internalized image of significant others and is connected to object relations theory. The next two domains are intrapsychic in nature. Regulatory Mechanisms are essentially the ego defense mechanisms (Sigmund Freud, Anna Freud), and Morphologic Organization is related conceptually to fragmentation and cohesiveness of the self (e.g., Kohut). Finally, the Mood/Temperament dimension refers to the biological predispositions of the individual. Table 16.2 provides a list of the domains and the description of the prototypical person with BPD from the perspective of the domain. The domains provide a cohesive framework for organizing the disparate emphases of various theoretical orientations and allow for a comprehensive understanding of the person.

Bringing a person to wholeness generally involves progress in several, and in some cases, all, of the domains. However, the intervention should not be haphazard; a sequential and integrated plan is most likely to yield success. In general, it is best to start with interventions that will bring about relatively rapid relief to enhance motivation and compliance. Approaches that entail greater depth or more complex systemic intervention are generally reserved for somewhat later in treatment. When arranged optimally, interventions will interact synergistically, with each intervention supporting and enhancing the others. For example, a cognitive intervention (e.g., challenging the belief that a person is all bad) can be paired with a family intervention (meeting with the family to clarify boundaries); undermining the belief that a family member is all bad will facilitate creating more comfortable and realistic boundaries. In this example, the family intervention is properly timed once the irrational belief of the client has begun to falter.

Millon (1999) discussed typical catalytic sequences for the person with BPD. First and foremost, a strong therapeutic alliance must be formed. The therapeutic relationship is subject to the same strains as other relationships in the client's life; the erratic and

Table 16.2 Millon's Eight Clinical Domains

Behavioral Level

(F) *Expressively Spasmodic.* Displays a desultory energy level with sudden, unexpected, and impulsive outbursts; abrupt, endogenous shifts in drive state and inhibitory controls; not only places activation and emotional equilibrium in constant jeopardy, but engages in recurrent suicidal or self-mutilating behaviors.

(F) *Interpersonally Paradoxical.* Although needing attention and affection, is unpredictably contrary, manipulative, and volatile, frequently eliciting rejection rather than support; frantically reacts to fears of abandonment and isolation, but often in angry, mercurial, and self-damaging ways.

Phenomenological Level

(F) *Cognitively Capricious.* Experiences rapidly changing, fluctuating and antithetical perceptions or thoughts concerning passing events, as well as contrasting emotions and conflicting thoughts towards self and others, notably love, rage, and guilt; vacillating and contradictory reactions are evoked in others by virtue of one's behaviors, creating, in turn, conflicting and confusing social feedback.

(S) *Uncertain Self-Image.* Experiences with confusions of an immature, nebulous, or wavering sense of identity, often with underlying feelings of emptiness; seeks to redeem precipitate actions and changing self-presentations with expressions of contrition and self-punitive behaviors.

(S) *Incompatible Objects.* Internalized representations comprise rudimentary and extemporaneously devised, but repetitively aborted learnings, resulting in conflicting memories, discordant attitudes, contradictory needs, antithetical emotions, erratic impulses, and clashing strategies for conflict reduction.

Intrapsychic Level

(F) *Regression Mechanism.* Retreats under stress to developmentally earlier levels of anxiety tolerance, impulse control, and social adaptation; among adolescents, is unable to cope with adult demands and conflicts, as evident in immature, if not increasingly infantile behaviors.

(S) *Split Organization.* Inner structures that exist in a sharply segmented and conflictful configuration in which a marked lack of consistency and congruency is seen among elements; levels of consciousness often shift and result in rapid movements across boundaries that usually separate contrasting percepts, memories, and affects; this leads to periodic schisms in what limited psychic order and cohesion may otherwise be present, often resulting in transient, stress-related psychotic episodes.

Biophysical Level

(S) *Labile Mood.* Fails to accord unstable mood level with external reality; has either marked shifts from normality to depression to excitement, or has periods of dejection and apathy, interspersed with episodes of inappropriate and intense anger, as well as brief spells of anxiety or euphoria.

Notes: (F) = Functional Domain; (S) = Structural Domain

Source: Disorders of Personality: DSM-IV and Beyond, p. 662, by T. Millon, 1996, New York: Wiley. Reprinted with permission.

unpredictable moods and behaviors present a challenge in establishing a therapeutic bond. The therapist must establish a firm, realistic therapeutic contract and stick to it. He or she must also remain persistently empathic. Having established a sound working alliance, behavioral interventions, such as skills training, may provide noticeable gains that will establish feelings of hope. If the client is very anxious or depressed, psychopharmacological interventions can be considered. Group interventions, if structured to be supportive rather than confrontational, may be extremely useful adjuncts to individual treatment. Cognitive therapy can help change beliefs that may be destabilizing the client's moods. Once preliminary gains have been made, family therapy may be extremely useful for establishing appropriate boundaries and working through past hurts. A caveat here is that clinicians have noted that families in which sexual abuse has occurred are likely to be steeped in denial that will further invalidate the client, so caution must be used in establishing an appropriate agenda for such meetings. Although Millon does not specifically mention psychodynamic approaches in his section on making synergistic arrangements (Millon, 1999), it is likely that depth approaches would ideally be undertaken once the client has developed some distress tolerance skills and some capacity to challenge irrational beliefs. The strength of the psychodynamic approach is to encourage (or simply watch for) reenactment of important patterns in the therapeutic relationship and work through them in the here-and-now. Although anxiety provoking, such a method of learning is extremely powerful and has the potential to induce long-lasting change. In addition, psychodynamic theorists have given substantial attention to countertransference issues; therapist self-awareness of such issues is critical to the success of treatment, regardless of the specific interventions or theories employed. The aforementioned guidelines should be implemented flexibly rather than rigidly; in some cases, family therapy, psychodynamic therapy, or milieu therapy should be implemented immediately, based on the particulars of the case and/or the available resources.

Illustration

In teaching graduate students about BPD, I have found that poetry and other artwork often illustrate the disorder even better than case material because of the powerful emotional evocativeness of the material. The following poem is by Brooke Bergan, who was in high school when she wrote it. The poet identifies the lamb as symbolically representing her "mental illness" (personal communication, 12/20/02, reprinted with permission).

Mary's Lamb

Mary had a little lamb,
it's fleece as black as coal.
And everywhere that Mary went,
that lamb she'd have to scold.

It followed her to school one day,
it was against the rules.
It made the children laugh and say
that Mary was a fool.

So Mary took her lamb back home,
and went inside and thought:
"If I am such an awful girl,
maybe I should be shot."

Then Mary found her daddy's gun,
and wished that she were dead.
She heard the bang and then she fell . . .
she died on Daddy's bed.

Her daddy found her on his bed,
just minutes after death.
And in her hand, clutched oh so tight,
the gun that he had left.

She knew that she was different,
she knew that she was bad.
She knew she needed punished,
that she made others sad.

Her friends just could not understand,
they made her feel so little.
But they would not have hurt her
had they known she was so brittle.

Mary had a little lamb,
it's fleece as black as coal.
And everywhere that Mary went,
that lamb she'd have to scold.

From the perspective of psychodynamic theory, we can see the split-off, "bad self" being represented by the lamb. The poet's intropunativeness is a function of poorly integrated partial self-representation. Her view of herself as defective and destructive (making others sad) led to guilt and suicidal impulses. Others—especially her schoolmates—are seen as malevolent and punitive. She identifies with the aggressors, scolding the lamb, the bad self, just as others do. The frightening fantasy of shooting herself with her father's gun on his bed is vengeful, sadistic, and masochistic, and represents Masterson's talionic impulse. While the image of the gun and the father's bed may appear Oedipal, I believe that analytic thinkers such as Kernberg would argue that the primary pathology is pre-Oedipal in nature and represents primitive aggression.

Humanistic works, such as Linehan's and Warner's models, suggest that the poet is expressing feelings of intense alienation, which are primarily a function of an invalidating environment (Linehan), or experiencing conditions of worth, which thwarted the actualizing tendency (Warner). The poet recognizes her differentness from others, her hypersensitivity, and her emotional dysregulation (brittleness). Linehan, Millon, and perhaps the other theorists as well would note the self-defeating cycles entailed within the poem.

From any theoretical orientation, the poem illustrates the intense suffering that occurs with people with BPD. However, it is equally clear that the poems and artwork presented in this chapter are the products of exceptionally sensitive and intuitive individuals. As clinicians, we tend to focus on psychopathology—finding out what is wrong, so that we can help fix it. However, there is a growing movement to more fully integrate "positive psychology" (Seligman & Csikszentmihalyi, 2000) into our formulations. To ignore the power of the human spirit, the resiliency within all people, and, perhaps above all, the power of love, would be to paint only half the picture. The following poem is an illustration of the power of love between mother and child. According to the poet, Lori Fechhelm, the angel is her mother, who stayed with her and saw her through a terrifying psychotic episode (personal communication, 12/11/02, reprinted with permission).

The Face of an Angel

I was an infant. And you were an angel.
You held me and sang to me and rocked me to sleep.
Exhausted, you still comforted your screaming child.
Your endurance was great.
You sent me off to school, where you knew I only cried for you.
You told me you would return, and you always did.
You never let me down.

The patience you showed was amazing.
And when tough times set in, you were by my side.
I know my agony broke your heart.
And I would look at your face, and knew I was safe,
Because I saw the face of an angel.
I wanted to be happy to stop your pain.
You were never once too busy to listen to me.
And when you thought things were getting better,
I told you I did not want to live.
But you did not want to believe, You would not believe,
Because you could not bear to see me in pain again.
Despairing, you still comforted your sobbing child.
Because you were my angel.
Demons swirled about my head
and skeletons danced on my bed—but you stayed.
And I was ashamed.
To you I owe my life,
My sanity,
And my dignity.
And thanks to you I will do great things with my life.
A life that I once thought would never be.
How can I ever repay you?
I will find a way, because when I look at your face,
I see the face of an angel.

Is the angel/mother the "idealized part object?" Is there evidence of "poor differentiation" in the poet's difficulty being separated from her mother? Perhaps. But what is more important is the universal human quality of the experience—the experience of love, gratitude, and triumph over severe adversity. This song stands as a reminder of the strength and love that can exist in these families, love strengthened rather than weakened by shared adversity.

FUTURE DIRECTIONS

We have come a long way in our understanding of BPD. Outcome data for the approaches described in this chapter have shown that while there is no "cure" for BPD, most people can be helped substantially (Clarkin et al., 1999; Eckert & Wuchner, 1996; Koerner & Linehan, 2000). Currently, there is an ongoing study that randomly assigns patients to Linehan's DBT, Kernberg's TFP, or a control group (Kernberg, 2002); this study should help us to understand more about the disorder by seeing the differential effects of different treatments. More studies that employ neuropsychological testing could greatly improve our understanding of how people with BPD process information. In his review, Soloff et al. (2000) concludes that many medications are being used without an adequate research base; further research into the use of medications is not only warranted but, I would argue, an ethical necessity. To date, alternative medicine approaches, such as herbal remedies, acupuncture, and homeopathy, have demonstrated good success with depression and other mental health conditions; I am hopeful that the research will be extended to BPD symptoms (see Bockian, Porr, & Villagran, 2002, for a review). Humanistic and client-centered approaches would benefit from additional studies. In addition to Kernberg's studies, other psychodynamic approaches would benefit from validation using randomized group designs. All of the theories would benefit from longitudinal studies that look at the development of BPD from an early age, perhaps even prospective studies, to test the various theoretical assertions that are based on clients' recollections. Assessing the invalidating environment, excesses in aggression, or maternal withdrawal would greatly clarify existing theories.

CONCLUSIONS

Progress in our understanding of borderline personality disorder has been impressive over the past several decades. A nearly untreatable disorder littered with iatrogenic outcomes at the time of its discovery in 1938 (Stern, 1938), borderline personality disorder now bears a relatively sanguine prognosis. Millon's (1969) seminal theoretical work marked a turning point in the history of the disorder. Currently, psychodynamic, cognitive-behavioral, dialectical behavioral, and client-centered therapies have shown dramatic results. As a rough guideline, a meta-analytic review of 15 outcome studies for personality disorders suggests that personality disorders remit at seven times the rate when given focused, specific treatments, as opposed to running their natural course or receiving typical community care; the majority of studies reviewed were for BPD (Perry, Banon, & Ianni, 1999). The meta-analysis also showed that after 2 years of treatment, 75% of the participants no longer met the criteria for a personality disorder. Millon's newly developed therapy, personality guided therapy (Millon, 1999) promises further improvements in conceptualization and treatment.

Even with such tremendous accomplishments, we still have a long way to go. Even the person who is "remitted" (no longer meets the criteria for the disorder) still generally has several "residual" symptoms. A person could no longer meet the criteria for BPD but still suffer from chronic emptiness, frantically avoid abandonment, and engage in impulsive, self-damaging acts. Such an individual may still be suffering greatly. Until the average person with the disorder can obtain complete relief—or, better yet, the disorder can be prevented—then the research must continue.

REFERENCES

Beck, A. T., & Freeman, A. (1990). *Cognitive therapy of personality disorders.* New York: Guilford.

Bockian, N. R., Porr, V., & Villagran, N. E. (2002). *New hope for people with borderline personality disorder.* Roseville, CA: Prima.

Clark, W. (2000). Patterns of religious attendance. *Canadian Social Trends, 59,* 23–27.

Clarkin, J. F., Yeomans, F. E., & Kernberg, O. F. (1999). *Psychotherapy for borderline personality.* New York: Wiley.

Coolidge, F. L., Thede, L. L., & Jang, K. L. (2001). Heritability of personality disorders in childhood: A preliminary investigation. *Journal of Personality Disorders, 15,* 33–40.

Driessen, M., Herrmann, J., Stahl, K., de Zwaan, M., Meier, S., Hill, A., et al. (2000). Magnetic resonance imaging volumes of the hippocampus and the amygdala in women with borderline personality disorder and early traumatization. *Archives of General Psychiatry, 57,* 1115–1122.

Eckert, J., & Wuchner, M. (1996). Long term development of borderline personality disorder. In R. Hutterer, G. Pawlowsky, P. F. Schmid, & R. Stipsits (Eds.), *Client centered and experiential psychotherapy: A paradigm in motion* (pp. 213–233). New York: Peter Lang.

Goyer, P. F., Andreason, P. J., Semple, W. E., Clayton, A. H., King, A. C., Compton-Toth, B. A., et al. (1994). Positron-emission tomography and personality disorders. *Neuropsychopharmacology, 10*(1), 21–28.

Goyer, P. F., Konicki, P. E., & Schulz, S. C. (1994). Brain imaging in personality disorders. In K. R. Silk (Ed.), *Biological and neurobehavioral studies of borderline personality disorder* (pp. 109–125). Washington, DC: American Psychiatric Press.

Gunderson, J. G., Berkowitz, C., & Ruiz-Sanchez, J. (1997). Families of borderline patients: A psychoeducational approach. *Bulletin of the Menninger Clinic, 61,* 446–457.

Hadaway, C. K., & Marler, P. L. (1993, December). What the polls don't show: A closer look at U.S. church attendance. *American Sociological Review, 58,* 741–752.

Jang, K. L., Livesley, W. J., Vernon, P. A., & Jackson, D. N. (1996). Heritability of personality disorder traits: A twin study. *Acta Psychiatrica Scandinavica, 94:* 438–444.

Kernberg, O. F. (1986). Borderline personality organization. In M. H. Stone (Ed.), *Essential papers on borderline disorders.* New York: New York University Press. (Original work published 1967)

Kernberg, O. F. (2002). *Weill Medical College, Cornell University* [Research study]. Retrieved April 30, 2002, from, http://www.borderlineresearch.org/current_projects/index.html.

Kernberg, O. F., Selzer, M. A., Koenigsberg, H. W., Carr, A. C., & Appelbaum, A. H. (1989). *Psychodynamic psychotherapy of borderline patients.* New York: Basic Books.

Koerner, K., & Linehan, M. M. (2000). Research on dialectical behavior therapy for patients with borderline personality disorder. *Psychiatric Clinics of North America, 23*(1), 151–167.

Leyton, M., Okazawa, H., Diksic, M., Paris, J., Rosa, P., Mzengeza, S., et al. (2001). Brain regional alpha-[-sup-1-sup-1C]Methyl-l-tryptophan trapping in impulsive subjects with borderline personality disorder. *American Journal of Psychiatry, 158,* 775–782.

Linehan, M. M. (1993). *Cognitive behavioral treatment of borderline personality disorder.* New York: Guilford Press.

Masterson, J. (1981). *The narcissistic and borderline disorders.* New York: Brunner/Mazel.

Millon, T. (1969). *Modern psychopathology: A biosocial approach to maladaptive learning and functioning.* Philadelphia: Saunders.

Millon, T. (1981). *Disorders of personality: DSM-III: Axis II.* New York: Wiley.

Millon, T. (1987). On the genesis and prevalence of the BPD. *Journal of Personality Disorders, 1,* 354–372.

Millon, T. (1999). *Personality guided therapy.* New York: Wiley.

Millon, T., & Davis, R. D. (1996). *Disorders of personality: DSM-IV and beyond* (2nd ed.). New York: Wiley.

O'Leary, K., & Cowdry, R. (1994). Neuropsychological testing results in borderline personality disorder. In K. R. Silk (Ed.), *Biological and neurobehavioral studies of borderline personality disorder* (pp. 127–157). Washington, DC: American Psychiatric Press.

Perry, J. C., Banon, E., & Ianni, F. (1999). "Effectiveness of Psychotherapy for personality disorders." *American Journal of Psychiatry, 156,* 1312–1321.

Sedlak, A. J., & Broadhurst, D. D. (1996). *Executive summary of the third national incidence study of child abuse and neglect.* Washington, DC: U.S. Department of Health and Human Services. Available from http://www.calib.com/nccanch/pubs/statinfo/nis3.cfm#national.

Seligman, M. E. P., & Csikszentmihalyi, M. (2000). Positive psychology: An introduction. *American Psychologist, 55*(1), 5–14.

Shea, M. T., Widiger, T. A., & Klein, M. H. (1992). Comorbidity of personality disorders and depression: Implications for treatment. *Journal of Consulting and Clinical Psychology, 60,* 857–868.

Silk, K. R. (Ed.). (1994). *Biological and neurobehavioral studies of borderline personality disorder.* Washington, DC: American Psychiatric Press.

Silk, K. R. (2000). Overview of biologic factors. *Psychiatric Clinics of North America, 23*(1), 61–75.

Smith, C., Denton, M. L., & Faris, R. (2002). Mapping American adolescent religious participation. *Journal for the Scientific Study of Religion, 41,* 597–612.

Soloff, P. (1998). Algorithms for pharmacological treatment of personality dimensions: Symptom-specific treatments for cognitive-perceptual, affective, and impulsive-behavioral dysregulation. *Bulletin of the Menninger Clinic, 62*(2), 195–214.

Soloff, P. (2000). Psychopharmacology of borderline personality disorder. *Psychiatric Clinics of North America, 23*(1), 169–192.

Soloff, P. H., Meltzer, C. C., Greer, P. J., Constantine, D., & Kelly, T. M. (2000). A fenfluramine-activated FD8-PET study of borderline personality disorder. *Biological Psychiatry, 47,* 540–547.

Stern, A. (1986). Psychoanalytic investigation of and therapy in the border line group of neuroses. In M. H. Stone (Ed.), *Essential papers on borderline disorders* (pp. 54–73). New York: New York University Press. (Original work published 1938)

Sue, D. W., & Sue, D. (2002). *Counseling the culturally diverse: Theory and practice.* Hoboken, NJ: Wiley.

Warner, M. (1998). A client-centered approach to therapeutic work with dissociated and fragile process. In L. S. Greenberg & J. C. Watson (Eds.), *Handbook of experiential psychotherapy.* New York: Guilford.

Warner, M. (2000). Person-centered psychotherapy at the difficult edge: A developmentally based model of fragile and dissociated process. In D. Mearns & B. Thorne (Eds.), *Person-centered therapy today: New frontiers in theory and practice* (pp. 141–171). London: Sage.

Yeomans, F. E., Clarkin, J. F., & Kernberg, O. F. (2002). *A primer of transference-focused psychotherapy for the borderline patient.* Northvale, NJ: Aronson.

Young, J. E., Klosko, J. S., & Weishaar, M. E. (2003). *Schema therapy: A practioners guide.* New York: Guilford.

Zanarini, M. C., Frankenburg, F. R., Dubo, E. D., Sickel, A. E., Trikha, A., Levin, A., et al. (1998). Axis I comorbidity of borderline personality disorder. *American Journal of Psychiatry, 155*(12), 1733–1739.

Zanarini, M. C., Kimble, C. R., & Williams, A. A. (1994). Neurological dysfunction in borderline patients and axis-II control subjects. In K. R. Silk (Ed.), *Biological and neurobehavioral studies of borderline personality disorder* (pp. 159–176). Washington, DC: American Psychiatric Press.

PART IV

Assessment Themes

Chapter 17 ————————————————————————

INTEGRATIVE PERSONALITY ASSESSMENT WITH SELF-REPORT AND PERFORMANCE-BASED MEASURES

IRVING B. WEINER

Effective selection of measures for conducting personality assessments begins with an adequate conceptualization of the nature of personality functioning. To guide this selection process, personality can be conceived as a composite of what people are like and how they are likely to think, feel, and act. In more formal language, these defining characteristics of personality reside in each individual's states and traits. Personality states consist of the current content of a person's thoughts and feelings; as such, they comprise a broad range of relatively transitory affects and attitudes that arise in response to situational circumstances, for example, being happy or deeply in thought at the moment. Personality traits consist of a person's abiding dispositions to behave in certain ways in certain kinds of situations; as such, they comprise a broad range of fairly stable characteristics and orientations of the individual, for example, being a persistently enthusiastic or reclusive kind of person.

As an additional dimension of functioning relevant to instrument selection in personality assessment, people tend to be fully aware of some of their attitudes, affect, and action tendencies; only partially or vaguely aware of some of their other states and traits; and mostly or totally unaware of certain aspects of what they are like and how they are inclined to behave. The influence on human behavior of thoughts and feelings existing outside as well as within conscious awareness is recognized across a gamut of perspectives, from psychoanalytic formulations of the dynamic unconscious to cognitive and research-based conceptualizations of how underlying emotional meanings and automatic self-regulation shape behavior without awareness (see Bargh & Chartrand, 1999; Bornstein, 2003; Bornstein & Masling, 1998; Samoilov & Goldfried, 2000). McClelland, Koestner, and Weinberger (1989) formulated this dual determination of behavior by distinguishing between explicit or self-attributed motives, which people recognize and acknowledge as being characteristic of themselves, and implicit motives, which exert their influence automatically and largely without the person's awareness.

Although the relationships between state characteristics and explicit motives are not isomorphic, there is some overlap between them. The same can be said for the relationship between trait characteristics and explicit motives. Generally speaking, people are likely to be more fully aware of what they are thinking, feeling, and doing at the moment (their states) than they are of behavioral dispositions that are shaping their current experiences and actions (their traits). Correspondingly, those personality characteristics of which people are fully aware in themselves are more likely to be their states than their traits, whereas those characteristics of which people are largely or totally unaware are more likely to be their traits than their states.

This being the nature of personality, then, a personality assessment battery should be constituted to measure both the states and traits of respondents and to provide information about both their self-attributed personality characteristics, of which they are aware, and underlying features of their personality, of which they are partially or totally unaware. This chapter on integrative personality assessment first reviews the nature and origins of two types of instruments for assessing these aspects of personality functioning: self-report inventories and performance-based measures. The discussion then identifies some relative advantages and limitations of each type of instrument and concludes by describing how both congruence and complementarity between them can enrich psychological evaluations and facilitate clinical decision making. Integrative personality assessment involving selection of a multifaceted test better emerges as a conceptually sound and empirically supported procedure that merits a prominent place in educational and practice guidelines for clinical psychology.

This last assertion is consistent with the findings of the Psychological Assessment Work Group (PAWG), a task force appointed by the Board of Professional Affairs of the American Psychological Association and charged with assembling evidence on the efficacy of psychological assessment in clinical practice. Based on its review of the literature, this task force concluded that "logical and empirical considerations support the multimethod battery as a means to maximize assessment validity" and that "by relying on a multimethod assessment battery, practitioners have historically used the most efficient means at their disposal to maximize the validity of their judgments about individual clients"(Meyer et al., 2001, p. 150).

HISTORICAL BACKGROUND

Two types of personality assessment instruments have evolved for measuring personality states and traits and providing information about self-attributed and implicit personality characteristics (see Weiner, 2003a). Originating with Woodworth's Personal Data Sheet (1920), one of these types of instruments is the self-report inventory. As currently represented by well-known and widely used tests such as the Minnesota Multiphasic Personality Inventory (MMPI; Butcher, Dahlstrom, Graham, Tellegen, & Kaemmer, 1989), the Millon Clinical Multiaxial Inventory (MCMI; Millon, 1994), the Personality Assessment Inventory (PAI; Morey, 1991), and the NEO-PI (Costa & McRae, 1992), self-report inventories ask respondents to describe themselves by indicating whether or to what extent certain statements apply to or are true about them (e.g., "I have a good appetite"; "I show my feelings easily and quickly"; "It's easy for me to make new friends").

The second type of personality assessment instrument arose from Rorschach's (1921/1942) analyses of the percepts reported by people who were asked what a series of inkblots might be. The Rorschach Inkblot Method (RIM) remains in widespread use, as do subsequently developed and similarly open-ended personality measures involving telling stories about pictures (e.g., the Thematic Apperception Test [TAT]; Murray, 1943/1971), drawing figures (e.g., the Draw-A-Person [DAP]; Machover, 1948), and finishing incomplete sentences (e.g., the Rotter Incomplete Sentences Blank [RISB]; Rotter, Lah, & Rafferty, 1992; see also Camara, Nathan, & Puente, 2000).

Following an influential article by Frank (1939), in which he suggested that personality tests in which there is little structure induce a respondent to "project upon that plastic field . . . his private world of personal meanings and feelings" (pp. 395–402), this second type of personality measure became known as *projective* methods. Over time, these so-called projective methods were contrasted with and differentiated from the more *objective* methods represented by self-report inventories. The objective-projective distinction in referring to these types of tests is well entrenched in the language of psychology and, regrettably, may be destined to remain so, just as other habitual categorizations sometimes outlive their usefulness and become more misleading than informative.

The objective-projective distinction is misleading by virtue of implying that, inasmuch as one of these types of measures is objective, the other type must be subjective. In truth, however, self-report inventories are not entirely objective, nor are projective tests entirely subjective. In the case of self-report inventories, being asked to indicate true or false to a statement such as "I often get angry" does provide an unambiguous instruction to the respondent and an entirely objective coding choice for the examiner. However, the absence of specific benchmarks for self-report statements of this kind requires subjective interpretation on the part of the person taking the test. How often is "often," for example, and what constitutes "getting angry"? Some people who get angry on a daily basis but rarely more than once a day may regard their anger arousal as infrequent and respond "False" to the item. Other people who lose their temper only once weekly but regret doing so may consider themselves to be excessively anger-prone and answer the item "True." Similarly, people who shout and scream but do not hit anybody or break anything may not see themselves as being angry at the time (answer "False"), whereas people who prefer to avoid even raising their voice slightly to anyone may experience themselves as being angry whenever they do so (answer "True").

Subjectivity enters into the interpretation of so-called objective measures as well as into the response process that produces the test data. To be sure, self-report inventories feature an extensive array of quantified scale scores having empirically demonstrated behavioral correlates. In clinical practice, however, interpretation of these measures typically goes beyond identifying known corollaries of individual scale scores to include consideration of complex patterns of interaction among these scores. Some of these patterns of interactions have been examined empirically and others have not, in which case inferences and conclusions derive from the clinician's experience and reasoned judgment, not from objective data.

As for the so-called projective measures, in the RIM, for example, the inkblots do have relatively little objective reality and can be seen in many different ways. Added to the ambiguity of the inkblots, being asked what they might be is a relatively ambiguous instruction. Respondents are given little guidance concerning how many responses they should give or how long or detailed their responses should be. On the other hand, standard Rorschach administration also includes asking respondents where they saw their percepts and what made them look as they did, which are unambiguous instructions. Moreover, many features of Rorschach responses are coded in an objective manner. If the entire blot has been used for a response, for example, the response is coded *W* for Whole. If a response is one of 13 specific responses identified in the Rorschach Comprehensive System as occurring in one-third or more of the records produced by a database sample of 7,500 nonpsychotic adults, it is coded *P* for Popular. Both W and P are consistently coded with almost perfect agreement by trained examiners (Acklin, McDowell, Verschell, & Chan, 2000; Meyer et al., 2002).

The interpretation of Rorschach responses can be highly subjective, especially when inferences are drawn from the thematic imagery that respondents produce when they embellish their descriptions of the inkblots with various associations to them (e.g., "It looks like a bat, and it's black, and it's probably sad because of the way the wings are drooping"). At the same time, however, the interpretation of objectively coded Rorschach variables parallels the objectivity of interpreting self-report scale scores. For example, an unusual preponderance of W responses is taken to indicate a preference for forming global impressions of situations, sometimes at the expense of overlooking the details of these situations. An unusually high frequency of P responses suggests a strong commitment or at least lip service to conventionality, whereas infrequent P identifies difficulty or disinterest in recognizing and endorsing conventional modes of response (see Weiner, 2003b, chap. 5).

With respect to the storytelling, figure-drawing, and sentence-completion types of projective measures, each involves some fairly objective features in either the nature of the test stimuli, the instructions given to the respondent, or quantitative codes that can be correlated with externally observed or measured behavioral characteristics. The TAT shows real pictures of people and scenes, for example; the RISB gives precise instructions (e.g., "Complete these sentences to express your real feelings; try to do every one; be sure to make a complete sentence"); and the DAP can be interpreted with DAP-SPED, an actuarially derived and normatively based scoring system for identifying emotional disturbance (see Naglieri, 1988; Naglieri, McNeish, & Bardos, 1991).

Taken together, the subjective features of self-report inventories and the objective aspects of projective measures indicate the shortcomings of an objective-subjective distinction between these two types of instruments. Ambiguity is a dimensional and not a categorical characteristic of personality assessment measures, and none of these measures is completely objective or entirely subjective. Self-report and performance-based measures vary in their degree of ambiguity, and they differ among themselves as well as from each other in the extent to which the test stimuli and the respondent's task are ambiguous.

As one preferable alternative to the objective-subjective categorization, self-report inventories can appropriately be described as relatively structured measures and projective methods as relatively unstructured measures. Weiner and Kuehnle (1998) elaborated this distinction in terms of a "levels hypothesis" originally proposed by Stone and Dellis (1960). According to the levels hypothesis, there is a direct relationship between the degree to which a test is structured and the level of conscious awareness at which it taps personality processes. The more structured (hence, less ambiguous) a test is, the greater the likelihood that it will provide information about relatively conscious and apparent levels of personality. Conversely, the less structured (hence, more ambiguous) a test is, the more likely it is to access deeper levels of personality and provide information about underlying and unrecognized characteristics.

In a contemporary refinement of focusing on the degree of structure in different kinds of tests, the previously mentioned PAWG task force proposed differentiating between self-report inventories (SRIs) and performance-based measures (PBMs), which is the terminology that has been adopted in this chapter (see Meyer et al., 2001). The interpretive data of SRIs comprise what respondents say about themselves and are expected to provide relatively direct information about their personality characteristics. The primary inferences drawn from PBMs are based on how respondents deal with various tasks they are given to do and are expected to provide relatively indirect clues to their personality characteristics.

ADVANTAGES AND LIMITATIONS

The method differences between the primarily direct SRIs and the primarily indirect PBMs give rise to some relative advantages and limitations of each in conducting personality assessments. These advantages and limitations pertain mainly to differences between these two assessment approaches in (1) their sensitivity to state and trait aspects of personality functioning, (2) the dependability of the data they yield in certain circumstances, and (3) their susceptibility to impression management.

Differential Sensitivity to Personality States and Traits

As previously noted, SRIs ask respondents fairly directly to indicate what they think ("I think I am a very sociable and outgoing person"), how they feel ("I am happy most of the time"), how they spend their time ("I like to study and read about things that I am working at"), and whether they are experiencing various symptoms of psychological disorder ("I often hear voices without knowing where they are coming from"; "Lately, I have gone all to pieces"; "Sometimes I am afraid for no reason"). Hence, these measures are particularly likely to identify personality states, explicit motives, and other characteristics that people recognize in themselves. Moreover, to the extent that SRI statements parallel the content of interview questions used to establish *DSM* diagnoses, SRIs prove especially helpful in determining the presence and severity of specific psychological disorders.

With respect to drawing distinctions between SRIs and PBMs, however, it should not be overlooked that SRIs may include indirect as well as direct items. For example, items on the clinical scales of the original MMPI that were considered difficult for respondents to detect as indicating emotional disturbance were labeled *subtle* items, and several *subtle scales* have been created for comparison with *obvious scales*. According to available research, however, significant relationships between MMPI variables and external criteria are attributable mainly to the obvious items on the test, and the subtle items may even detract from, rather than contribute to, these relationships (Graham, 2000, pp. 186–187).

Because of the direct nature of most self-report items and the questionable validity of subtle items, SRIs are likely to be relatively limited in how much light they shed on behavioral dispositions and influences that respondents do not fully recognize in themselves. On the other hand, PBMs provide relatively limited information about what people are thinking or feeling at the moment and about what symptoms they are presently experiencing. However, these indirect measures gain advantage from their lack of obvious content or purpose and by capturing a representative sample of respondents' actual behavioral tendencies. By sampling how people deal with relatively unstructured tasks instead of asking them to describe themselves, PBMs are particularly likely to reveal underlying attitudes, coping styles, behavioral dispositions, and implicit motivations of which people are not fully aware. As Skinner (1953) observed, behavior related to ambiguous stimuli can "reveal variables which the individual himself cannot identify" (p. 289).

Neither the particular sensitivity of SRIs to personality states and explicit motives nor the particular sensitivity of PBMs to personality traits and implicit motives constitutes an absolute advantage of one type of approach over the other. There is good reason to believe that self-report data can speak to abiding dispositions of the individual and that performance-based test data help to identify personality states and psychological disorders. Nevertheless, as elaborated by Meyer (1997) in discussing differences between the MMPI and the RIM formats, there is clear conceptual basis for expecting these two types of measures to tap different levels of conscious awareness and, consequently, differ in their relative sensitivity to state and trait dimensions of personality functioning.

Empirical findings provide confirmation for this differential sensitivity of self-report and performance-based personality measures in the case of the MMPI and the RIM, which are the two most widely researched as well as the two most frequently used personality assessment instruments (see Butcher & Rouse, 1996; Camara et al., 2000). Hiller, Rosenthal, Bornstein, Berry, and Brunell-Neuleib (1999) examined the validity of these two instruments as measured against external (i.e., nontest) variables in a meta-analysis of 5,007 MMPI protocols and 2,276 Rorschach protocols used in a random sample of research studies published in the 20-year period 1977 to 1997 (see also Rosenthal, Hiller, Bornstein, Berry, & Brunell-Neuleib, 2001). These investigators found virtually identical overall effect sizes for the two instruments, with unweighted mean validity coefficients of .30 for the MMPI and .29 for the RIM. However, consistent with the preceding conceptual formulation of their differential sensitivity, MMPI variables were superior to RIM variables in correlating with psychiatric diagnoses (mean validity coefficients of .37 and .18, respectively), whereas RIM variables were more predictive than MMPI variables of behavioral outcomes, such as whether patients in psychotherapy remain in or drop out of treatment (.37 versus .20).

In a meta-analytic study involving a broader range of measures than the Hiller et al. (1999) work but a more specifically focused dependent variable, Bornstein (1999) examined the predictability of dependency-related behavior observed in laboratory, clinical, and field settings in 51 studies involving eight different self-report dependency scales (3,013 participants) and dependency indices on four different projective measures (1,808 participants). The effect sizes obtained in this study indicated superiority of projective dependency indices over self-report dependency scales in assessing underlying dependency needs, whereas the self-report scales were superior to the projective indices in assessing participants' perception of themselves and their public self-presentation with respect to being dependent persons.

As one further illustration of this difference between the likely criterion validities of SRIs and PBMs in personality assessment, Asendorpf, Banse, and Mucke (2002) observed shyness behavior in 139 participants who completed self-concept measures of both kinds. Implicitly measured self-concepts using an association test were more predictive of spontaneously emerging shy behavior in realistic social situations than were explicit self-ratings. Explicit self-ratings, on the other hand, were more predictive of controlled shyness behavior than was the implicit measure.

Differential Dependability of Obtained Data

The previously discussed differential sensitivity of self-report and performance-based measures derives primarily from the *ability* of persons to respond (i.e., how fully aware they are of their personality characteristics). The differential dependability of these types of measures reflects the *willingness* of persons to respond (i.e., how fully committed they are to being open and forthcoming in revealing aspects of themselves). Willing respondents provide ample test protocols that make it possible to generate the full range of interpretive hypotheses associated with a measure, and they respond in an honest and forthright manner, which enhances the dependability of inferences based on their test data. Unwilling respondents, by contrast, are motivated to limit as much as possible what the examiner is able to learn about them, and they approach personality tests in a guarded and defensive manner. They may hesitate to respond to certain test stimuli, decline to answer certain questions, object to taking particular tests, or refuse to be tested at all. Alternatively, if they have been adequately prepared for the examination and want to avoid appearing resistive, unwilling respondents may go through the motions of cooperating with the test procedures, and they may even be pleasant and deferential while doing so. While being overtly cooperative, however, these guarded and defensive respondents compromise the dependability of the test data they produce by efforts to avoid revealing themselves.

When unwilling examinees cooperate at least to the extent of not refusing to respond, SRIs have two advantages in dependability over PBMs. First, individual items are answered in full (e.g., true or false), and there is a complete or almost complete set of answers that allows reliable calculation of all of the scales and indices used in interpreting the test. Second, the validity scales usually generated on SRIs help to identify the extent to which the test data may be of questionable dependability as a consequence of the respondent having answered in a guarded manner.

By contrast, the open-ended format of PBMs allows respondents to be overtly cooperative while restricting the number and richness of their responses. On the RIM, for example, short records may satisfy the minimum validity criterion of at least 14 responses but lack enough responses to ensure the reliability of key summary scores and indices. Even while giving long Rorschach records with many responses, respondents are free to give only brief and bland answers that reveal very little about what they are like as people. With respect to the other types of performance-based personality tests, respondents can opt to tell brief and unelaborated stories to pictures, to draw stick or sketchy figures, and to write banal and uninformative sentence completions (e.g., "THE HAPPIEST TIME is when you're enjoying yourself"; "THE FUTURE lies ahead"). Although guardedness may be inferred in such instances, performance-based personality measures (aside from the minimum requirement of 14 responses on the RIM) do not provide objective indices of whether and to what extent the test findings can be considered dependable.

On the other hand, the indirect nature and lack of obvious item content in PBMs may at times help to circumvent guardedness. Respondents who are unwilling to admit their shortcomings or reluctant to report difficulties they are experiencing when asked about them directly may unwittingly reveal such shortcomings and difficulties in their manner of dealing with the relatively ambiguous test stimuli and unstructured task requirements of performance-based personality measures. Without obvious content to guide them, guarded respondents typically find it more difficult to choose their course of action on PBMs than on SRIs, and they may consequently provide more PBM information about their personality characteristics than was their intent.

A related method difference that can affect respondents' openness and the dependability of the test data they produce is that some people feel more comfortable in structured than unstructured situations and vice versa. For example, people who like to be told what to do, to know what is expected of them, and to conform to a clearly specified set of behavioral guidelines—which constitutes what has been called an authoritarian frame of reference—are more likely to be relaxed and cooperative when being asked specific questions about themselves than when they have to contend with an open-ended examination procedure. Respondents who are inclined to resent authority and shun conformity, on the other hand, may dislike or resist being pinned down by structured test items that must be answered in certain ways, and they may be more cooperative and forthcoming when they have more freedom to say as much or as little as they want in their own words and in their own preferred manner.

In summary, there are several implications of defensiveness for test dependability. SRIs are more likely than PBMs to elicit full protocols from guarded respondents, whereas

PBMs are more likely than SRIs to reveal personality characteristics that guarded respondents would like to conceal. However, in the examination of unwilling respondents, denials in the case of SRIs, limited productivity in the case of PBMs, and aversion either to highly structured or open-ended situations may result in either or both types of instruments being undependable as a source of information about the individual's personality characteristics.

Research studies examining correlations between MMPI-2 and Rorschach variables provide some indirect empirical evidence that respondent unwillingness can render either self-report or performance-based test results undependable. This line of research followed a review by Archer and Krishnamurthy (1993) in which the authors identified limited or minimal relationships between conceptually similar variables on these two measures. This seeming lack of convergent validity has been taken in some quarters to reflect poorly on the psychometric adequacy of the RIM (e.g., Hunsley & Bailey, 1999), even though Archer and Krishnamurthy (1993) concluded otherwise: ". . . it does not appear likely that these results are attributable to differential reliability or validity of these two instruments" (p. 286). However, as noted by Weiner (1993) and Ganellen (1996, chap. 2) and restated here in discussing the differential sensitivity of these measures, modest correlations between conceptually similar MMPI and RIM variables can for the most part be attributed to differences between these measures in their degree of structure and in the level of respondents' conscious awareness of what their answers might signify.

Meyer (1997, 1999) and Meyer, Riethmiller, Brooks, Benoit, and Handler (2000) have elaborated these implications of the method variance between the MMPI-2 and the RIM and noted in addition that correlations between these two tests are moderated by the manner in which respondents approach taking them. Meyer et al.'s (2000) data demonstrated substantial positive correlations between conceptually similar MMPI-2 and Rorschach indices among people who responded to both of these measures in an open, spontaneous, and engaged manner. Among respondents who approached one of the measures in a relatively open fashion and the other one in a relatively guarded manner, however, these same test indices tended to be negatively correlated. Hence, the Meyer et al. (2000) findings appear to confirm that the results of either self-report or performance-based measures may be undependable when respondents are reluctant to be open and forthcoming.

Differential Susceptibility to Impression Management

The utility of psychological test data can be attenuated not only by guarded respondents, who seek to restrict the amount of information they provide and thereby limit the examiner's ability to form impressions of them, but also by respondents who strive purposefully to create certain impressions of themselves. Impression management typically takes the form of attempts to malinger psychological disorder (faking bad) or of efforts to present a deceptively positive picture of psychological capability and well-being (faking good). Efforts to fake good sometimes result in test protocols that resemble the undependable records produced by guarded respondents who are seeking to conceal what they are like as people. There is nevertheless a subtle difference between the motivations of reluctant respondents, who aim to deny their imperfections and prevent the examiner from forming any clear impression of them, and deceptive (fake good) respondents, who extol their virtues and want the examiner to form a definite and distinctly positive impression of them.

The relatively direct and obvious item content of SRIs makes them generally more susceptible than PBMs to malingering and deception. Respondents who want to appear psychologically better or worse off than they are can usually decide with little difficulty whether to answer true or false on self-report items such as "Most of the time I feel blue."

Impression managers cannot so easily determine how to appear more depressed or better adjusted than is actually the case when dealing with relatively unstructured performance-based measures that provide few clues to the interpretive implications of how they respond. This difference between types of personality tests has been expressed as a general principle that the fakability of a measuring instrument is likely to be directly related to its face validity (see Bornstein, Rossner, Hill, & Stepanian, 1994).

With specific respect to the susceptibility of the MMPI-2 to impression management, the face validity of its obvious items is supplemented by readily available textbooks in libraries and bookstores that identify the scales to which items relate and elaborate the personality correlates of high and low scores on these scales (see Graham, 2000; Greene, 2000). Research findings indicate that enterprising respondents who inform themselves beforehand by reading the literature or who receive coaching in how to answer certain kinds of items can sometimes shape their MMPI-2 responses to give a misleading impression without elevating the validity scales (Baer & Miller, 2002; Ben-Porath, 2003; Storm & Graham, 2000; Walters & Clopton, 2000).

The interpretation of performance-based personality assessment instruments is also discussed in textbooks, and accessible coaching for the RIM even includes web sites that provide lists of supposedly good and bad percepts for each of the inkblots. However, no matter how much prior information or test familiarity impression managers acquire about PBMs, the relatively unstructured nature of these instruments still makes it difficult for them to anticipate and monitor the interpretive implications of what they say, write, or draw while responding to them. Would-be malingerers and deceivers can alter their responses on PBMs and perhaps confuse the issue, but only rarely can they avoid detection and succeed in creating a false impression.

On the RIM, for example, even clever and well-coached respondents attempting to malinger or deceive are likely to have trouble keeping track of the cumulative import of their response elaborations and judging how much is enough. The records they produce are consequently likely to contain exaggerations and inconsistencies that alert experienced examiners to their efforts to mislead. Especially common in the Rorschach protocols of persons who are attempting to fake bad is a markedly greater frequency of disturbed responses than even seriously disturbed people ordinarily give. As for inconsistencies, Rorschach malingerers often combine bizarre thematic elaborations seemingly indicative of gross cognitive or affective abnormality with response structure falling within the normal range. Such differences between dramatic Rorschach content and unremarkable or only moderately deviant Rorschach structure have been documented in research studies in which participants were given disorder-relevant information and instructed to malinger schizophrenia, depression, or posttraumatic stress disorder (Caine, Frueh, & Kinder, 1995; Frueh & Kinder, 1994; Netter & Viglione, 1994). Similarly, in a study reported by Ganellen, Wasyliw, Haywood, and Grossman (1996), the only Rorschach variable that was found to differentiate groups of identified malingerers and honest responders was an ad hoc measure of Dramatic Content.

Typical among Rorschach respondents who are attempting to fake good is a greater emphasis on common responses than usually characterizes the records of well-adjusted people. For example, respondents who have turned to the Internet for guidance on what constitutes a "good" response may end up giving all 13 Popular responses, compared to a normative range of 3 to 10 and a mean nonpatient expectancy of 6.58. Whether their goal is to malinger or deceive, clever and well-coached respondents may be able to prevent Rorschach examiners from learning very much about their actual personality characteristics. Only infrequently, however, will they achieve their goal of convincing examiners that they are more or less disturbed than is the case. The RIM is not impossible to fake, either bad or good, but faking on this measure is difficult to accomplish and fairly easy to detect.

Grossman, Wasyliw, Benn, and Gyoerkoe (2002) examined a forensic sample with strong motivation to minimize or deny psychological problems. Their participants were 74 men who were undergoing forensic psychological evaluations because of alleged sexual misconduct, in 80% of the cases with minor-age children, and who were cautioned that the results of the assessment could be used against them. This sample was expected to have a high base rate of psychopathology and to be experiencing situational distress in relation to the charges they were facing. MMPI validity scales were used to divide the sample into 53 minimizers and 21 nonminimizers. The minimizers showed significantly lower scores than the nonminimizers on virtually all of the clinical scales of the MMPI. Moreover, 74% of these minimizers, compared to just 38% of the nonminimizers, were able to produce limits profiles that were within normal limits.

By contrast, the minimizers were not able to appear more psychologically healthy than the nonminimizers on Rorschach indices of emotional distress, impaired judgment, interpersonal dysfunction, and psychopathology. The minimizers also fell short of appearing similar to the general population on the RIM. Instead, they showed abnormal elevations on several Rorschach indices of psychological dysfunction and were unsuccessful in concealing various psychological problems they had.

CONGRUENCE AND COMPLEMENTARITY

Integrative personality assessment is a complex and multifaceted process that extends beyond the standardized measuring instruments with which this chapter is concerned. In addition to formal psychological testing, potentially valuable sources of information in personality assessments include structured and unstructured interviews, observations of behavior in natural and contrived situations, collateral reports from persons familiar with an individual's previous life history and current behavior patterns, and historical documents, particularly school and medical records and the results of previous personality evaluations (see Beutler & Groth-Marnat, 2003; Weiner, 2003c). There is little way of anticipating in advance of collecting assessment data how revealing each of these information sources will be and which ones will provide reliable information about the problems and potentialities of the person being evaluated.

Similarly, with respect to the psychological testing component of personality assessments, the contribution of SRIs and PBMs to clinical decision making in the individual case can rarely be known before the test data are in hand. What can be known in advance of conducting an evaluation is that personality assessment proceeds most effectively when (1) the tests being used combine to measure both state and trait characteristics adequately, (2) the obtained data are sufficiently extensive to provide a dependable basis for drawing inferences from them, and (3) adequate procedures are in place to detect or minimize impression management. In light of these requisites for effective assessment, the previously presented comparisons between self-report and performance-based methods demonstrate the benefits of selecting measures of both kinds for inclusion in personality test batteries.

To reprise these comparisons, SRIs are likely to be particularly though not exclusively sensitive in measuring personality states, and PBMs are likely to be particularly though not exclusively sensitive in measuring personality traits; either type of instrument may at times yield data of questionable dependability, especially when respondents choose to be guarded and avoid giving information about themselves or when they are differentially comfortable in relatively structured and relatively unstructured situations. In addition, SRIs have the advantage of validity scales to help identify when respondents are attempting to give misleading information about themselves, whereas PBMs have the advantage of being less susceptible than SRIs to malingering or deception.

In addition, because of the method differences between SRIs and PBMs, conjoint use of both types of instruments can enrich personality evaluations and facilitate clinical decision making by virtue of either congruence or complementarity between the findings they yield. Congruent findings point in the same direction and identify similar personality characteristics. Except when the data are invalidated by impression management, congruence confirms that certain characteristics are both present in and recognized by the person being evaluated and, furthermore, that these characteristics are likely to be evident in both relatively structured and relatively unstructured situations. If both the SRI and the PBM protocols in a test battery appear valid and suggest substantial psychological disturbance, for example, respondents are very likely to be disturbed, to be aware of their disturbance, and to show this disturbance in a variety of contexts, both structured and unstructured. The same can be said for virtually any personality state or trait, such as being anxious or depressed, being compulsive or dependent, or being a socially gregarious or emotionally reserved person.

By identifying phenomena that are sufficiently marked and pervasive to appear in both self-report and performance-based test data, confirmatory findings clarify decision making in personality assessment. Clear indications from diverse sources of information that certain characteristics exist in a person, are recognized by that person, and are broadly manifest in that person's behavior increase the confidence and certainty with which examiners can draw diagnostic inferences, formulate treatment plans, and recommend dispositions of various kinds (e.g., child custody, fitness for duty, parole from prison).

Complementary findings in conjoint personality assessments, on the other hand, point in different directions, as when indications of substantial psychological disorder appear in either SRI or PBM protocols but not in both. Divergence between SRI and PBM data can be relative as well as absolute. Respondents may look definitely anxious, depressed, compulsive, dependent, socially gregarious, or emotionally reserved on one kind of test but not at all on the other kind, or they may show a mild extent of such states and traits on one kind of test and a marked extent of them on the other kind.

Whereas congruence between SRI and PBM findings clarifies clinical decision making, divergence in these data, whether absolute or relative, complicates the examiner's interpretive task. However, being divergent does not mean being contradictory, nor does complexity preclude clear clinical conclusions. To the contrary, valid SRI and PBM test protocols are each meaningful in their own right, and divergence between them provides information to be understood, not discarded. SRIs and PBMs pointing in different directions does not mean that one type of measure is correct and the other type in error or that one of these is to be believed and the other discredited.

Instead, divergence poses the question of why a respondent has shown different characteristics or a different extent of certain characteristics on SRIs as opposed to PBMs. The possible answers to this question enrich rather than detract from what examiners can learn about people from their responses to a multifaceted test battery. It is in this sense that divergent test findings can be complementary, with either an SRI or a PBM tapping aspects of personality functioning not identified by the other and, in the process, providing valuable information about respondents' attitudes toward ambiguity and their level of openness and self-awareness. Finn (1996) has illustrated the utility of both convergent and complementary test findings by showing how patterns of MMPI-2 and RIM results can be translated into guidelines for client feedback. Specifically, Finn provided samples of clinical formulations, statements to clients, and expected feedback reactions in four alternative situations: a high degree of disturbance indicated by both the MMPI-2 and the RIM, a low degree of disturbance indicated by both, and a high or low degree of disturbance on one of the instruments and the opposite finding on the other.

Finally, with respect to congruence and complementarity, it is fitting to include this chapter on integrative personality assessment in a tribute to Theodore Millon's contributions to clinical psychology. A pervasive theme running through Millon's work has been his advocacy for a "comprehensive structure" of clinical psychological science that coordinates universal laws of nature, a theoretical frame of reference, a systematic clinical and personality taxonomy, configurally integrated assessment tools, and person-appropriate remediation techniques (Millon, 1990, 2003). Millon's influence is clearly reflected in the discussion here of integrated application of self-report and performance-based personality assessment instruments.

CONCLUSIONS

This chapter reviewed the conceptual and empirical basis for a multimethod approach to personality assessment that integrates self-report and performance-based measures. Personality consists of both state and trait dimensions, and behavior is influenced by both self-attributed (conscious) and implicit (unconscious) motives. Test batteries should accordingly include instruments that will adequately measure these dimensions and motives and, in addition, sample behavior in both relatively structured and relatively unstructured settings, maximize the dependability of the findings, and minimize the likelihood of undetected malingering (faking bad) or deception (faking good). These requirements for effective personality assessment are best met by conjoint administration of self-report and performance-based measures. Assuming validity of the individual protocols, congruent findings between these types of measures provide confirmatory data that facilitate clinical decision making, and divergent findings provide complementary information that enriches clinical formulations of a respondent's attitudes, preferences, and self-awareness.

REFERENCES

Acklin, M. W., McDowell, C. J., Verschell, M. S., & Chan, D. (2000). Interobserver agreement, intraobserver agreement, and the Rorschach Comprehensive System. *Journal of Personality Assessment, 74,* 15–57.

Archer, R. P., & Krishnamurthy, R. (1993). A review of MMPI and Rorschach interrelationships in adult samples. *Journal of Personality Assessment, 61,* 277–293.

Asendorpf, J. B., Banse, R., & Mucke, D. (2002). Double dissociation between implicit and explicit personality self-concept: The case of shy behavior. *Journal of Personality and Social Psychology, 83,* 380–393.

Baer, R. A., & Miller, J. (2002). Underreporting of psychopathology on the MMPI-2: A meta-analytic review. *Psychological Assessment, 14,* 16–26.

Bargh, J. A., & Chartrand, T. L. (1999). The unbearable automaticity of being. *American Psychologist, 54,* 462–479.

Ben-Porath, Y. S. (2003). Assessing personality and psychopathology with self-report inventories. In J. R. Graham & J. A. Naglieri (Eds.), *Assessment psychology* (pp. 553–578). Vol. 10 in I. B. Weiner (Editor-in-Chief), *Handbook of psychology.* Hoboken, NJ: Wiley.

Beutler, L. E., & Groth-Marnat, G. (2003). *Integrative assessment of adult personality* (2nd ed.). New York: Guilford Press.

Bornstein, R. F. (1999). Criterion validity of objective and projective dependency tests: A meta-analytic assessment of behavioral prediction. *Psychological Assessment, 11,* 48–57.

Bornstein, R. F. (2003). Psychodynamic models of personality. In T. Millon & M. J. Lerner (Eds.), *Personality and social psychology* (pp. 117–134). Vol. 5 in I. B. Weiner (Editor-in-Chief), *Handbook of psychology.* Hoboken, NJ: Wiley.

Bornstein, R. F., & Masling, J. M. (Eds.). (1998). *Empirical perspectives on the psychoanalytic unconscious.* Washington, DC: American Psychological Association.

Bornstein, R. F., Rossner, S. C., Hill, E. L., & Stepanian, M. L. (1994). Face validity and fakability of objective and projective measures of dependency. *Journal of Personality Assessment, 63,* 363–386.

Butcher, J. N., Dahlstrom, W. G., Graham, J. R., Tellegen, A., & Kaemmer, B. (1989). *Minnesota Multiphasic Personality Inventory (MMPI-2): Manual for administration and scoring.* Minneapolis: University of Minnesota Press.

Butcher, J. N., & Rouse, S. V. (1996). Personality: Individual differences and clinical assessment. *Annual Review of Psychology, 47,* 87–111.

Caine, S. L., Frueh, B. C., & Kinder, B. N. (1995). Rorschach susceptibility to malingered depressive disorders in adult females. In J. N. Butcher & C. D. Spielberger (Eds.), *Advances in personality assessment* (Vol. 10, pp. 165–173). Hillsdale, NJ: Erlbaum.

Camara, W. J., Nathan, J. S., & Puente, A. E. (2000). Psychological test usage. *Professional Psychology, 31,* 141–154.

Costa, P. T., Jr., & McCrae, R. R. (1992). *Revised NEO Personality Inventory (NEO-PI) and NEO Five-Factor Inventory (NEO).* Odessa, FL: Psychological Assessment Resources.

Finn, S. E. (1996). Assessment feedback integrating MMPI-2 and Rorschach findings. *Journal of Personality Assessment, 67,* 543–557.

Frank, L. K. (1939). Projective methods for the study of personality. *Journal of Psychology, 8,* 389–413.

Frueh, B. C., & Kinder, B. N. (1994). The susceptibility of the Rorschach Inkblot Test to malingering of combat-related PTSD. *Journal of Personality Assessment, 62,* 280–298.

Ganellen, R. J. (1996). *Integrating the Rorschach and the MMPI-2 in personality assessment.* Mahwah, NJ: Erlbaum.

Ganellen, R. J., Wasyliw, O. E., Haywood, T. W., & Grossman, L. S. (1996). Can psychosis be malingered on the Rorschach? An empirical study. *Journal of Personality Assessment, 66,* 65–80.

Graham, J. R. (2000). *MMPI-2: Assessing personality and psychopathology* (3rd ed.). New York: Oxford University Press.

Greene, R. L. (2000). *The MMPI-2: An interpretive manual* (2nd ed.). Boston: Allyn & Bacon.

Grossman, L. S., Wasyliw, O. E., Benn, A. F., & Gyoerkoe, K. L. (2002). Can sex offenders who minimize on the MMPI conceal psychopathology on the Rorschach? *Journal of Personality Assessment, 78,* 484–501.

Hiller, J. B., Rosenthal, R., Bornstein, R. F., Berry, D. T. R., & Brunell-Neuleib, S. (1999). A comparative meta-analysis of Rorschach and MMPI validity. *Psychological Assessment, 11,* 278–296.

Hunsley, J., & Bailey, J. M. (1999). The clinical utility of the Rorschach: Unfulfilled promises and an uncertain future. *Psychological Assessment, 11,* 277–277.

Machover, K. (1948). *Personality projection in the drawing of the human figure.* Springfield, IL: Charles C Thomas.

McClelland, D. C., Koestner, R., & Weinberger, J. (1989). How do self-attributed and explicit motives differ? *Psychological Review, 96,* 690–702.

Meyer, J. G. (1997). On the integration of personality assessment methods: The Rorschach and the MMPI-2. *Journal of Personality Assessment, 68,* 297–330.

Meyer, J. G. (1999). The convergent validity of MMPI and Rorschach scales: An extension using profile scores to define response-character styles on both methods and a re-examination of simple Rorschach response frequency. *Journal of Personality Assessment, 72,* 1–35.

Meyer, J. G., Finn, S. E., Eyde, L. D., Kay, G. G., Moreland, K. L., Dies, R. R., et al. (2001). Psychological testing and psychological assessment: A review of evidence and issues. *American Psychologist, 56,* 128–165.

Meyer, J. G., Hilsenroth, M. J., Baxer, D., Exner, J. E., Jr., Fowler, J. C., Pers, C. C., et al. (2002). An examination of interrater reliability for scoring the Rorschach Comprehensive System in eight datasets. *Journal of Personality Assessment, 78,* 219–274.

Meyer, J. G., Riethmiller, R. J., Brooks, R. D., Benoit, W. A., & Handler, L. (2000). A replication of Rorschach and MMPI-2 convergent validity. *Journal of Personality Assessment, 74,* 175–215.

Millon, T. (1990). *Toward a new personology: An evolutionary model.* New York: Wiley.

Millon, T. (1994). *Manual for the MCMI-III.* Minneapolis, MN: National Computer Systems.

Millon, T. (2003). It's time to rework the blueprints: Building a science for clinical psychology. *American Psychologist, 58,* 949–961.

Morey, L. C. (1991). *The Personality Assessment Inventory professional manual.* Odessa, FL: Psychological Assessment Resources.

Murray, H. A. (1971). *Thematic Apperception Test manual.* Cambridge, MA: Harvard University Press. (Original work published 1943)

Naglieri, J. A. (1988). *Draw-a-Person: A quantitative scoring system.* New York: Psychological Corporation.

Naglieri, J. A., McNeish, T. J., & Bardos, A. N. (1991). *Draw-a-Person: Screening procedure for emotional disturbance.* Austin, TX: ProEd.

Netter, B. E. C., & Viglione, D. J. (1994). An empirical study of malingering schizopherenia on the Rorschach. *Journal of Personality Assessment, 62,* 45–57.

Rorschach, H. (1942). *Psychodiagnostics.* New York: Grune & Stratton. (Original work published 1921)

Rosenthal, R., Hiller, J. B., Bornstein, R. F., Berry, D. T. R., & Brunell-Neuleib, S. (2001). Meta-analytic methods, the Rorschach, and the MMPI. *Psychological Assessment, 13,* 449–451.

Rotter, J. B., Lah, M. I., & Raffety, J. E. (1992). *Manual: Rotter incomplete sentences blank* (2nd ed.). Orlando, FL: Psychological Corporation.

Samoilov, A., & Goldfried, M. R. (2000). Role of emotion in cognitive-behavioral therapy. *Clinical Psychology, 7,* 373–385.

Schretlen, D. J. (1997). Dissimulation on the Rorschach and other projective measures. In R. Rogers (Ed.), *Clinical assessment of malingering and deception* (2nd ed., pp. 208–222). New York: Guilford Press.

Skinner, B. F. (1953). *Science and human behavior.* New York: Macmillan.

Stone, H. K., & Dellis, N. P. (1960). An exploratory investigation into the levels hypothesis. *Journal of Projective Techniques, 24,* 333–340.

Storm, J., & Graham, J. R. (2000). Detection of coached malingering on the MMPI-2. *Psychological Assessment, 12,* 158–165.

Walters, G. L., & Clopton, J. R. (2000). Effect of symptom information and validity scale information on the malingering of depression on the MMPI-2. *Journal of Personality Assessment, 75,* 183–199.

Weiner, I. B. (1993). Clinical considerations in the conjoint use of the Rorschach and the MMPI. *Journal of Personality Assessment, 60,* 148–152.

Weiner, I. B. (2003a). History of assessment psychology. In D. K. Freedheim (Ed.), *History of psychology* (pp. 279–302). Volume 1 in I. B. Weiner (Editor-in-Chief), *Handbook of psychology.* Hoboken, NJ: Wiley.

Weiner, I. B. (2003b). *Principles of Rorschach interpretation* (2nd ed.). Mahwah, NJ: Erlbaum.

Weiner, I. B. (2003c). The assessment process. In J. R. Graham & J. A. Naglieri (Eds.), *Assessment psychology* (pp. 3–25). Vol. 10 in I. B. Weiner (Editor-in-Chief), *Handbook of psychology.* Hoboken, NJ: Wiley.

Weiner, I. B., & Kuehnle, K. (1998). Projective assessment of children and adolescents. In A. S. Bellack & M. Hersen (Eds.), *Comprehensive clinical psychology: Assessment* (Vol. 4, pp. 431–458). New York: Pergamon Press.

Woodworth, R. S. (1920). *Personal data sheet.* Chicago: Stoelting.

Chapter 18

THE STUDY OF PSYCHOSOCIAL FACTORS INFLUENCING MEDICAL DISEASES

MICHAEL H. ANTONI

> The good physician will treat the disease, but the great physician will treat the patient.
> —Sir William Osler, the eminent nineteenth-century clinician

In this chapter, I highlight the contributions of Dr. Theodore Millon and his research associates to the study of psychosocial factors influencing health and disease outcomes and the application of psychosocial assessment in the medical arena. I begin by reviewing clinical and empirical literature that provide a rationale for the use of psychosocial assessment to facilitate health maintenance and optimize adjustment and recovery from medical disease conditions. I then describe a line of research that has produced practical and empirically validated instruments developed to meet this need. In doing this, the seminal theoretical and empirical contributions of Millon and his associates to contemporary clinical health psychology practice and behavioral medicine research are illuminated.

To best understand the potential role of psychosocial factors in medical disease, you must first understand how psychosocial factors contribute to health maintenance. Maintaining our nation's health has been one of the most challenging agendas for policymakers during the past decade. It is clear that chronic medical diseases—the most expensive diseases to treat—represent the major health challenge in the United States (Taylor & Aspinwall, 1990). These diseases include arthritis (Lawrence et al., 1989), cancers (American Cancer Society, 1989), diabetes (American Diabetic Association, 1986; Centers for Disease Control, 1993), stroke (American Heart Association, 1988), and coronary heart disease (American Heart Association, 1988). Other less prevalent conditions have emerged as being equally devastating and costly, including asthma, acquired immune deficiency syndrome (AIDS), kidney disease, liver disease, spinal cord injury, and neurological disease. Conditions characterized by physiologic dysregulation are also very prevalent in contemporary medicine. These conditions include disorders of circulation (e.g., hypertension), digestion (e.g., gastrointestinal disorders), respiration (e.g., chronic obstructive pulmonary disease), arousal (e.g., chronic fatigue syndrome), sensation (e.g., chronic pain), reproduction (e.g., gynecologic disorders), metabolism (e.g., thyroid disorders), and immune function (e.g., allergies and autoimmune diseases).

Health care costs for managing these chronic conditions can be astronomical. By 1992, the total cost of health care in the United States was $838 billion, accounting for one-seventh of the money spent on all domestic goods and services (1992 HCFA Statistics, 1992). Since then, the annual increase has been running at more than three times the general inflation rate. Importantly, up to 20% of the health care costs are incurred on unnecessary procedures (e.g., doctor visits, lab tests, X-rays; 1992 HCFA Statistics). The accelerating increases in overall health care costs in the 1990s, as well as the significant evidence for abuse in the use of medical interventions, led in part to the creation of *managed care* (Regier, 1994). Managed care was part of a movement targeting the long-term reform of our nation's health care system designed to increase the accessibility, efficacy, and cost efficiency of procedures and services to preserve health and manage disease.

A main premise of this chapter is that psychosocial phenomena represent a major, if often ignored, set of factors that may contribute to optimal management of many health concerns. One fairly recent review (Sobel, 1995) noted that psychosocial, educational, and behavioral interventions may reduce the frequency of medical utilization by 17% to 56% for services such as total ambulatory care visits, pediatric acute illness visits, acute asthma services, cesarean section, epidural anesthesia during labor and delivery, and major surgery. These interventions have also been associated with an average reduction of 1.5 hospital days for surgical patients. Moreover, Sobel's (1995) review pointed out that (1) many health care costs are for treatment of conditions with psychosocial sources (e.g., cigarette smoking), (2) increasing a person's sense of control and optimism can improve health outcomes and decrease health care costs, and (3) groups that focus on building social support for medical patients are cost-effective.

A multitude of studies conducted in the past 20 years have documented that patients with similar medical diagnoses and treatments show wide variability in the physical course and psychological sequelae of the disease being treated and that much of this variance can be predicted on the basis of the psychosocial characteristics that the patients presented at the time of screening or intake. There now exists convincing data for the health and cost benefits of psychosocial interventions in conditions such as minor and acute illnesses, stress-related disorders, chronic pain, diabetes, asthma, arthritis, surgery and childbirth, coronary heart disease, different forms of cancer, and AIDS, among others (Schneiderman, Antoni, Saab, & Ironson, 2001).

How do psychosocial processes relate to an optimization of health maintenance and health care delivery? I next review the evidence for a set of psychosocial factors that have been empirically associated with indicators of both health maintenance and health care delivery. Aspects of *health maintenance* include (1) health preservation and the primary prevention of disease as well as (2) patient responses to disease and secondary prevention efforts. Aspects of *health care delivery* include (1) medical utilization and health care cost containment in addition to (2) treatment success and rehabilitation or recovery from disease. After summarizing evidence for the role of psychosocial factors in these various health contexts, I describe two of the instruments that have been developed by Theodore Millon and his associates to tap related patient characteristics in medical settings. I summarize the empirical support for the use of the Millon Behavioral Health Inventory (MBHI; Millon, Green, & Meagher, 1982) to address both primary and secondary prevention questions in different medical populations. I also review the limitations of these instruments for addressing emerging issues in behavioral medicine and the contemporary health care environment and present a rationale for the domains targeted by a new instrument, the Millon Behavioral Medicine Diagnostic (MBMD; Millon, Antoni, Millon, Meagher, & Grossman, 2001). I end by demonstrating empirical support for the use of the MBMD with different medical populations and the ongoing research that has been stimulated by this new instrument.

IMPORTANCE OF PSYCHOSOCIAL FACTORS IN HEALTH MAINTENANCE

Health maintenance can best be achieved by primary, secondary, and tertiary prevention. Primary prevention refers to preserving a state of health and avoiding disease. Secondary and tertiary preventions refer to optimizing psychosocial and physical changes *after* a diagnosis of disease. We first review health prevention.

Psychosocial Factors and Health Preservation

The first aspect of health maintenance that may be influenced by psychosocial factors is health preservation. Health preservation processes encompass risk behaviors, preventative health behaviors, susceptibility to stress-related symptoms, and resistance to the onset of disease. Together, these processes represent efforts to preserve a healthy nondiseased state including those that reduce the likelihood of developing disease among healthy individuals who are at risk for the development of a specific disease (i.e., primary prevention).

Psychosocial Factors and Health Risk Behaviors

There is a growing interest in this country in primary prevention as a means to prevent morbidity and mortality and lower health care costs (Woolf, 1999). Evidence-based primary prevention methods such as smoking cessation, exercise, and lowering cholesterol and blood pressure can prevent significantly more deaths than do mainstream tertiary prevention techniques such as the use of ACE inhibitors, b-blockers, aspirin, and warfarin in patients with cardiovascular disease (Woolf, 1999). Primary prevention (e.g., stopping smoking and becoming physically active) is also superior to secondary prevention (e.g., mammography) for decreasing mortality risk in breast cancer (Woolf, 1999). Thus, isolating psychosocial factors that predict the adoption and maintenance of health behavior changes at the earliest time is a major mission of behavioral scientists and organizations such as the National Institutes of Health (NIH).

It has become clear, however, that bringing about and, especially, sustaining such behavior changes can be difficult and complex for most people. Health psychologists have been able to make a significant contribution through behavioral research that identifies psychosocial variables associated with the adoption and maintenance of specific health activities. These variables include cancer risk behaviors such as smoking, excessive exposure to ultraviolet rays, unprotected sexual behaviors, and obesity and overeating (e.g., L. Glanz, Lew, Song, & Cook, 1999; Rock et al., 2000). Psychosocial factors associated with engaging in these types of risk behaviors include, but are not limited to, an individual's: *cognitive appraisals* of self-worth, current health status, perceived susceptibility to disease, general outlook toward the future, the health protective effects of ceasing the risk behaviors, and the personal efficacy for making behavior changes (Becker, Maiman, Kirscht, Haefner, & Drachman, 1977; McCann et al., 1995; Rosenstock, 1974; Turk & Meichenbaum, 1989); repertoire of *coping strategies* for dealing with internal and external forces that perpetuate the practice of the behaviors; available *external resources* for gaining the tangible informational, spiritual, and emotional support necessary to make substantial lifestyle changes (Wallston, Alagna, DeVellis, & DeVellis, 1983); and the *life context* (e.g., external stressors, illness burden, functional capacity) in which the person is attempting to make these changes.

Accordingly, individuals who have a low sense of self-worth are often unconcerned with their health. They typically exhibit a low sense of self-efficacy, maintain a pessimistic outlook, practice maladaptive coping strategies, have few resources for gaining tangible or emotional support, and live in very stressful environments. It is not surprising that these are the persons who are most likely to continue to engage in health-compromising risk behaviors. We also know that certain psychosocial factors (e.g., depression) may interact with a genetic predisposition to engage in these risk behaviors (Lerman, Caporaso, Main, et al., 1998; Lerman, Caporaso, Audrain, et al., 1999). This research stresses developing a culture within health care organizations that understands the importance of assessing several psychosocial aspects of persons seeking health and primary care to prevent the development of serious and costly diseases.

Psychosocial Factors and Preventative Health Behaviors

Some psychosocial factors may act as obstacles to practicing positive self-care behaviors (McCann et al., 1995; W. Wilson et al., 1986). They might deter healthy individuals from getting annual physical exams, Pap smears, mammography, and other medical tests that can dramatically reduce morbidity and mortality as well as costs of care. Within the specialty of oncology, behavioral researchers (e.g., Lerman et al., 1993) have identified psychosocial factors that may act as obstacles to the use of cancer risk screening tests such as regular Pap smears (for cervical cancer), mammography (for breast cancer), Prostate-Specific Antigen (PSA) testing (for prostate cancer), occult fecal blood testing (for colorectal cancer), and skin cancer screening (for melanoma). Most of this work focuses on psychosocial factors that are associated with the communication of, and decisions to undergo, these tests. Understanding these processes may help to identify disease at its earliest stages so that biomedical treatments can have maximum effectiveness. Behavioral research has also focused on factors associated with adjustment to positive cancer or cancer risk test results, since initial reactions to these results may predict whether people make critical follow-up visits after positive Pap smears, mammograms, PSA tests, or colon cancer tests, wherein early interventions may be initiated (A. Baum & Posluszny, 1999).

We now know that psychosocial factors also affect decisions to engage in genetic testing that can identify those at elevated risk for specific cancers long before the first signs of cellular (i.e., neoplastic) changes occur (Lerman, Rimer, & Glynn, 1997), including testing for risk of breast and ovarian cancer (e.g., BRCA1 and BRCA2 genes; Lerman, Hughes, Lemon, et al., 1998; Lerman et al., 1996) and colorectal cancer (Hereditary Nonpolyposis Colon Cancer [HNPCC] genes such as msh2, mlh1, pms1, and pms2; K. Glanz et al., 1999). This work has identified demographic (e.g., socioeconomic status; Lerman et al., 1996), cognitive (e.g., perceived risk; Glanz et al., 1999), and emotional (e.g., depressive symptoms; Lerman, Hughes, Trock, et al., 1999) factors that identify those who may be in greatest need of genetic counseling. Health psychology research also evaluates the costs and benefits of making such test information available to identified populations (Croyle, Smith, Botkin, Baty, & Nash, 1997; Lerman, 1997). Several of these psychosocial factors may also contribute to a symptomatic patient's delay in seeking prompt medical attention following the initial onset of physical symptoms such as suspicious skin changes, abnormal bleeding, angina, or unexplained weight loss (Cameron, Leventhal, & Leventhal, 1995; Neale, Tilley, & Vernon, 1986). At the other extreme, a person's appraisals, coping strategies, external resources, and life context may also cause them to overutilize the health care system when their condition does not warrant such use (Pallak, Cummings, Dorken, & Henke, 1994). Psychosocial assessment can make a huge contribution to health psychologists attempting to make predictions about these complex decision processes, and such predictions can, in turn, contribute to lower morbidity, mortality, and health care costs.

Psychosocial Factors and Vulnerability to Developing Stress-Related Health Changes

Psychosocial factors may also contribute to an individual's susceptibility to stress-related symptoms and health changes. Stressful life events ranging from daily hassles and marital discord to more traumatic events such as sexual and physical abuse, a devastating diagnosis, war, and natural disasters have all been related to the onset or exacerbation of physical symptoms in a variety of populations. In addition, underlying physiologic changes that might act to mediate these associations have been demonstrated in both healthy people (Cohen, Tyrrell, & Smith, 1991; Ironson, Antoni, & Lutgendorf, 1995; Ironson et al., 1997) and those with a preexisting medical condition (Grady et al., 1991; Lutgendorf et al., 1995; Pereira et al., 2003).

Research into individual difference factors that may act as buffers of stressful events has identified several psychosocial factors that *moderate* the influence of stressors on physical health changes and physiologic regulatory processes such as endocrine and immune system functioning. These stress moderators include appraisals of self-efficacy (Bandura, Taylor, Williams, Mefford, & Barchas, 1985; Wiedenfield et al., 1990), maintaining an optimistic outlook toward the future (Lutgendorf et al., 1995), using adaptive coping strategies (Antoni et al., 1995; Carver et al., 1993; Folkman & Lazarus, 1980; Taylor & Brown, 1988; Taylor, Lichtman, & Wood, 1984), emotional expression and disclosure (Esterling, Antoni, Fletcher, Marguilles, & Schneiderman, 1994; Esterling, Antoni, Kumar, & Schneiderman, 1990; Pennebaker, Kiecolt-Glaser, & Glaser, 1988), and having adequate social support (Cohen & Wills, 1985; Helgeson & Cohen, 1996; Zuckerman & Antoni, 1995). These stress moderators may relate to health outcomes in healthy persons and medical patients by way of their effects on the regulation of endocrine factors that are known to affect immunologic, metabolic, and cardiovascular functioning (McEwen, 1998). It is equally plausible, however, that these psychosocial factors may relate to health outcomes by way of their influence on health behaviors (e.g., smoking, medication adherence).

Psychosocial Factors and the Promotion of Subclinical Disease Processes

Finally, psychosocial factors may also contribute to an individual's resistance or vulnerability to the promotion of a subclinical pathogenic or pathophysiologic process or the onset of clinically manifest disease. Subclinical processes that have been associated with psychosocial factors include coronary artery stenosis and related disease processes (Schneiderman et al., 2001), glucose control and insulin resistance (Frenzel, McCaul, Glasgow, & Schafer, 1988; Schneiderman et al., 2001), neoplastic cell growth (Antoni, 2003a), and viral infections (Antoni, 2003b; Cohen et al., 1991).

Psychosocial factors implicated as contributing to these processes include affective disorders and distress states (Frasure-Smith, Lesperance, & Talajic, 1993; Herbert & Cohen, 1993a, 1993b; Schneiderman et al., 2001); anger and hostility (Dembroski & Costa, 1987); appraisals of self-efficacy or personal control (Cohen & Edwards, 1989; O'Leary, 1992); pessimism (Byrnes et al., 1998; Peterson, Seligman, & Valliant, 1988; Scheier & Carver, 1985); various coping strategies such as denial, avoidance, and emotional suppression (Holahan & Moos, 1986; Ironson et al., 1994; Pettingale, Greer, & Tee,

1977); social isolation or a lack of effective social support (Cohen, 1988; Cohen & Wills, 1985; House, Landis, & Umberson, 1988; Zuckerman & Antoni, 1995); a lack of religion and spiritual faith (Levin, 1994); as well as contextual factors such as elevated stressful events (Antoni & Goodkin, 1989; Schwartz, Springer, Flaherty, & Kiani, 1986).

A number of clinical disease phenomena have also been associated with these psychosocial factors, including myocardial infarction (MI; Booth-Kewley & Friedman, 1987; Kamarck & Jennings, 1991), different cancers (Goodkin, Antoni, Sevin, & Fox, 1993; McKenna, Zevon, Corn, & Rounds, 1999), Type II diabetes mellitus (Glasgow, Toobert, Hampson, & Wilson, 1995; Surwit & Feinglos, 1988), gastrointestinal symptoms (Friedman & Booth-Kewley, 1987), rheumatoid arthritis (K. Anderson et al., 1985), and acquired immune deficiency syndrome (AIDS; Leserman, 2003).

In summary, many psychosocial factors have been associated with health-compromising risk behaviors; decisions to seek diagnostic screening and help-seeking following the onset of symptoms; susceptibility to stress-induced emotional, physiologic, and physical health status changes; and the promotion of pathophysiologic processes and development of clinical disease. These psychosocial factors, while not associated with all of these aspects of health preservation, do appear to cluster around a finite number of domains including affective and other psychiatric disorders (depression and anxiety conditions), cognitive appraisals (self-efficacy, optimism/pessimism, perceived control), coping strategies (active behaviors, acceptance and cognitive reframing, avoidance and denial), external resources (social, economic, familial, spiritual), and the individual's life context (stressful events, perceived stress level, and functional capacity).

Psychosocial Factors and Responses to Diagnosis of Disease

A second major domain encompassing health maintenance concerns the patient's responses that determine the sequelae of the initial diagnosis of disease (i.e., secondary prevention). Secondary prevention can refer to the prevention of extreme or maladaptive behavioral, emotional, or physical responses to a new diagnosis; treatment regime; or any of the life-changing aspects of a chronic medical condition with which an individual must deal. Tertiary prevention reflects processes that contribute to recovery from, relapse of, or progression of physical disease. Psychosocial factors may predict a patient's acute reaction to a new diagnosis or a stressful, invasive curative medical procedure, as well as his or her longer term adjustment to the burdens of a chronic disease and those regimens concerned with its management. These psychological adjustments may, in turn, affect the actual physical course of the disease.

Some of the factors that may act to buffer an individual from extreme reactions to serious or life-threatening diagnoses are similar to those noted in the previous section on health preservation and primary prevention (Antoni, 1991; Taylor & Aspinwall, 1990). These include appraisals (interpretation of the meaning of the diagnosis and its ramifications, outlook toward the future, self-efficacy, treatment efficacy), repertoire of coping strategies (active coping, denial, giving up, cognitive reframing, acceptance), available resources (support of friends and family, spiritual sources of support, economic means), and contextual factors (ongoing life stressors, prior experience with serious disease, functional ability). For instance, maintaining an optimistic attitude (Carver et al., 1993), accepting the reality of the diagnosis (Lutgendorf et al., 1998; Taylor & Aspinwall, 1990), and having social (Zuckerman & Antoni, 1995) or spiritual resources (Woods, Antoni, Ironson, & Kling, 1999a, 1999b) available for dealing with a serious medical diagnosis can be predictive of less distress in the weeks or months following the identification of conditions such as HIV and cancer.

Psychosocial Factors and Adjusting to Chronic Disease

The most widely studied psychological problems that occur in the period after initial reactions to diagnosis, and which are common across the course of chronic diseases, are those involving anxiety and depression (Taylor & Aspinwall, 1990). Anxiety and depression can act as obstacles to the patient's ability to make, and adapt to, lifestyle changes; to recover from demanding medical procedures; to engage successfully in a rehabilitation program; and in some cases, return to the workforce or to premorbid levels of physical, mental, and interpersonal functioning (Taylor & Aspinwall, 1990). Anxiety reactions may vary considerably across patients as a function of their premorbid personality characteristics and psychiatric history, their specific medical disease, its stage at the time of diagnosis, and the nature of the medical regimen. For instance, uncertainties about the risk that behaviors (e.g., sexual relations) carry for future heart attacks represent one key source of anxiety among MI patients (Christman et al., 1988). It is plausible that other psychosocial characteristics (e.g., dependency, self-esteem, pessimism) may delineate which of these potential anxiety sources is most salient for different patient populations.

Another very prevalent set of emotional sequelae to major medical diagnosis is symptoms associated with depression. It has been estimated that up to 36% of medical patients suffer from a major depressive episode (Kimmerling, Ouimette, Cronkite, & Moos, 1999; Lustman, Clouse, Griffith, Camey, & Freedland, 1997; Taylor & Aspinwall, 1990). Dysphoric affect and related symptoms may interfere with adjustment to the lifestyle changes and treatment regimens that accompany a variety of medical diseases (Lustman, Griffith, & Clouse, 1988). Finally, depression (and anxiety) may be associated with greater pain perceptions in many medical populations including cancer patients (Ahles, Blanchard, & Ruckdeschel, 1983; Breitbart & Payne, 1998). It seems clear that being able to identify the presence of psychiatric disorders or mood disturbance early in the medical diagnosis process may be a critical part of comprehensive health care. Identifying these disturbances early in medical interventions (e.g., the diagnostic phase) is likely to be more effective than waiting until a later time.

Coping strategies characterized by avoidance are associated with increased distress in people dealing with a variety of stressors (Holahan & Moos, 1986; Taylor & Aspinwall, 1990), including those associated with having specific diseases (Taylor & Aspinwall, 1990; Young, 1992). Across patients diagnosed with cancer, hypertension, diabetes, and rheumatoid arthritis, coping through use of cognitive restructuring predicted better emotional adjustment, while use of techniques such as self-blame and fantasizing was associated with poorer adjustment (Felton & Revenson, 1984). There is some evidence that those psychosocial characteristics associated with patients' immediate emotional reactions to diagnosis are also predictive of their psychological responses (depressive and anxiety symptoms) to the medical treatment regimens that are administered in the initial postdiagnosis period (Burgess, Morris, & Pettingale, 1988; Carver et al., 1993; Smith & Wallston, 1992; Stein, Wallston, Nicassio, & Castner, 1988).

Another psychosocial factor that has been widely related to patients' ability to adjust to the stress of their disease is social support. Having rewarding personal relationships has been associated with better psychological adjustment to conditions such as cancer (Helgeson & Cohen, 1996; Siegal, Calsyn, & Cuddlihee, 1987; Taylor, Lichtman, & Wood, 1984), end-stage renal disease (Siegel et al., 1987), and arthritis (Fitzpatrick, Newman, Lamb, & Shipley, 1988). Social support may affect patients' adjustment to a chronic illness by way of multiple pathways, including its role as a stress buffer (Cohen & Wills, 1985; Zich & Temoshok, 1987), in facilitating the use of adaptive coping strategies (Dunkel-Schetter,

Feinstein, Taylor, & Lazarus, 1987; Leserman, Perkins, & Evans, 1992; Thoits, 1987) and enhancing adherence to medication regimens (Wallston et al., 1983).

Religiosity and spirituality have also been associated with lower depression and anxiety in medical patients (Koenig, Pargament, & Nielsen, 1998). One group found that greater use of religious coping was associated with less depressed mood and anxiety in HIV-infected men (Woods et al., 1999a) and women (Woods et al., 1999b). Another study showed that religious coping predicted better adjustment after mastectomy in early-stage breast cancer patients, though these effects varied as a function of religious orientation (Alferi, Culver, Carver, Arena, & Antoni, 1999).

The influence of a patient's coping strategies and resources on his or her psychological adjustment must operate in the context of factors such as ongoing major life events and minor hassles, the person's prior skills in dealing with illness, and his or her actual functional ability to carry out daily responsibilities, vocations, and social activities. Recent or ongoing life events may overwhelm the patient's coping strategies, thereby impairing his or her ability to deal with the challenges of the disease and the associated treatment regime (Antoni, 1991; Antoni & Emmelkamp, 1995). Stressful life events may also interact with health-compromising behaviors such as alcohol consumption (Morrissey & Schuckitt, 1978; Newcomb & Harlow, 1986), which can, in turn, further hamper patients' attempts to cope with new challenges. While depressive symptoms may be most evident at the time of the initial medical disease diagnosis (Cassileth et al., 1984), they may worsen after the patient recognizes the extent of the limitations that the disease places on his or her life (J. Baum, 1982; Hughes & Lee, 1987). Here, maladaptive coping strategies, social isolation, and other stressful life events may play a major role in a patient's emotional adjustment to a chronic disease (Taylor & Aspinwall, 1990).

Conversely, many studies demonstrate that psychosocial intervention can be used successfully to help patients deal with the emotional challenges of their disease, including persons with cancer (Andersen, 1992; Trijsburg, van Knippenberg, & Rijma, 1992) and HIV infection (Antoni, 2003b). Many of these interventions feature a social support component, as well as offering patients the opportunity to challenge and change maladaptive cognitive appraisals and coping strategies. Psychosocial interventions have also been shown to facilitate adjustment to other chronic diseases such as coronary heart disease (CHD; Oldenberg, Perkins, & Andrews, 1985; Williams & Chesney, 1993), chronic obstructive pulmonary disease (COPD; Emery, Schein, Hauck, & MacIntyre, 1998), arthritis (McCracken, 1991), diabetes mellitus (Glasgow et al., 1995), and melanoma (Fawzy et al., 1990), as well as syndromes such as chronic pain (Compas, Haaga, Keefe, Leitenberg, & Williams, 1998; Keefe, Dunsmore, & Burnett, 1992) including chronic cancer pain (Thomas & Weiss, 2000). It follows that knowledge of the presence of a psychiatric disturbance or significant emotional distress in medical patients, as well as their relative strengths and weaknesses in the domains of cognitive appraisals, coping strategies, support derived from social or spiritual sources, and their ongoing life context, can be very useful in determining the ways in which they will adjust to a new diagnosis and the demands that a chronic disease places on them. This information can, in turn, be used to choose appropriate psychosocial interventions that can facilitate the adjustment process.

Psychosocial Factors and Disease Course

The psychosocial factors associated with the physical course (morbidity and mortality) of many chronic diseases are similar to those that predict psychological adjustment. Severity of depressed mood has been shown to be an independent predictor of mortality in general medical patients (Herrmann et al., 1998), of acute MI and mortality in patients with CHD (Barefoot & Schroll, 1996), and of progression to AIDS in HIV-infected persons (Leserman et al., 1999). In fact, it is plausible that factors such as appraisals, coping styles, and different support resources may relate to a better disease course by way of their ability to moderate the influence of disease-related (and contextual) stressors on emotional adjustment (e.g., depression). Better emotional adjustment might in turn relate to a better disease course through its association with physiological mechanisms that have a protective effect against pathogens (e.g., immune system) or homeostatic dysregulation (e.g., endocrine system) causing the primary disease. Alternatively, better emotional adjustment may confer health effects by influencing positive health behaviors such as exercise (Blumenthal, Williams, Wallace, Williams, & Needles, 1982) and medication adherence (Carney, Freedland, Eisen, Rich, & Jaffe, 1995).

Patients who use certain coping strategies (e.g., active coping, less denial, more acceptance) for dealing with the demands of major life-threatening diseases such as cancer and HIV infection, as well as life stressors in general, may show the ability to outlive their physician's prognosis for the course of their disease (Ironson, Solomon, Cruess, Barroso, & Stivers, 1995b). These coping strategies may also relate to a better physical course of chronic but non-life-threatening diseases such as arthritis (Blalock, DeVellis, & Giordino, 1995; Grady et al., 1991) and chronic fatigue syndrome (Antoni et al., 1994; Antoni & Weiss, 2003; Lutgendorf et al., 1995), which are usually tracked in terms of flare-ups.

The cognitive appraisals that patients use to process life stressors, as well as those that are specific to the burdens of a chronic disease, may be associated with the course of their disease. For instance, having a fighting spirit was associated with a slower development of HIV-related symptoms and slower decline in the immune system among HIV-infected men (Solano et al., 1993) and with greater survival time in women with breast cancer (e.g., Greer, Morris, Pettingale, & Haybittle, 1990). Others have found that HIV-infected individuals who show the longest survival time after a diagnosis of AIDS are more likely to maintain an attitude of hope, greater life involvement, and a greater sense of meaningfulness than do those who have shorter survival times (Ironson et al., 1995b). Other work has focused on the construct of optimism-pessimism or general outlook on life. Greater levels of optimism have been related to a lower risk of developing cervical neoplasia (Goodkin, Antoni, Sevin, & Fox, 1993) and less likelihood of being rehospitalized after Coronary Artery Bypass Graft (CABG) surgery for postsurgical complications such as wound infections, angina, and MI (Scheier et al., 1999).

Having adequate levels of social support is associated with faster recovery or rehabilitation from a wide range of diseases including stroke (Robertson & Suinn, 1968), leukemia (Magni, Silvestro, Tamiello, Zanesco, & Carl, 1988), congestive heart failure (Chambers & Reiser, 1953), and kidney disease (Dimond, 1979). There is also evidence that social support may influence the course of other chronic diseases by improving diabetes control (Marteau, Bloch, & Baum, 1987; Schwartz et al., 1986), by reducing the risk of mortality from MI (Wiklund et al., 1988), by reducing the risk of recurrence in breast cancer patients (Helgeson, Cohen, & Fritz, 1998; Levy, Herberman, Lippman, D'Angelo & Lee, 1991), and by slowing down the progressive decline in the immune system (Theorell et al., 1995; Zuckerman & Antoni, 1995) and progression to the clinical manifestations of AIDS in those with HIV infection (Ironson et al., 1995b; Leserman et al., 1999).

The use of spiritual and religious resources has been related to physiologic functions such as blood pressure (Levin & Vanderpool, 1989) and immune function (Woods et al., 1999a). Greater religiosity has been consistently associated with better physical health across a wide range of studies (Levin, 1994). For instance, elderly coronary patients who lacked a sense of strength and comfort from religion were more likely to die in the 6 months following open heart surgery as compared to their more religiously comforted counterparts (Oxman, Freeman, & Manheimer, 1995). Religious involvement or spirituality may influence health in medical patients by multiple pathways including enhanced social support through the fellowship of organized religious activities (attending services and praying together), less fear of death, a greater acceptance of the efficacy of self-regulation techniques, greater practice of health-enhancing behaviors (e.g., adequate sleep and balanced diet), and a decreased likelihood of engaging in health-compromising lifestyle behaviors (e.g., substance use; Jarvis & Northcott, 1987).

Many behaviors associated with the patient's daily lifestyle may play a role in health preservation or adjustment to disease. These behaviors include alcohol use (Vaillant, Schnurr, Baron, & Gerber, 1991), illicit drug use (National Institute on Drug Abuse, 1990), overeating patterns (Brownell & Wadden, 1992), caffeine use (Lovallo et al., 1996), tobacco smoking (Epstein & Perkins, 1988), and physical exercise (Dubbert, 1992). Importantly, contextual factors such as life stressors may increase the likelihood of engaging in health-compromising behaviors such as smoking and drug use (Duberstein, Conwell, & Yeates, 1993; King, Beals, Manson, & Trimble, 1992) and may also decrease the frequency of health-promoting behaviors such as maintaining a balanced diet, engaging in adequate physical exercise, and adhering to medication regimes (A. Baum, 1994; Epstein & Perkins, 1988). Stress moderator variables such as coping strategies (Marlatt, 1985; Myers, Brown, & Mott, 1993) and social support (S. Richter, Brown, & Mott, 1991) can mitigate these stress triggers because increases in negative health behaviors may be more likely in stressed individuals who use poor coping strategies or who are socially isolated. Poor emotional adjustment to a chronic disease or to related treatment demands may also increase the risk of relapse of smoking and drug or alcohol use or may decrease a patient's ability to maintain a restricted nutritional regimen. Identifying chronic disease populations at greatest risk for such negative health behaviors through the use of a comprehensive psychosocial assessment may be key in providing them access to psychosocial intervention.

Psychosocial interventions capable of modifying several of these psychosocial and behavioral processes may be associated with a decreased rate of clinical progression in conditions such as coronary heart disease (Frasure-Smith & Prince, 1989; Oldenberg et al., 1985; Ornish et al., 1998; Williams & Chesney, 1993), HIV infection (Antoni, 2003b; Ironson et al., 1994), breast cancer (Andersen, Kiecolt-Glaser, & Glaser, 1994; Classen, Sephton, Diamond, & Spiegel, 1998; Spiegel, Kraemer, Bloom, & Gottheil, 1989; van der Pompe et al., 1994), and malignant melanoma (Fawzy, Fawzy, et al., 1993), to name a few. These studies underline the importance of identifying medical patients who would be most likely to benefit from interventions that modify psychosocial and behavioral factors associated with disease recurrence and survival. Comprehensive psychosocial assessment plays a clear role in this mission.

In sum, a set of psychosocial factors associated with health preservation (primary prevention) and adjustment to disease (secondary and tertiary prevention) appears to cluster around a finite number of domains including psychiatric disorders and negative mood states such as anxiety and depression, cognitive appraisals (self-efficacy, optimism/pessimism, perceived control), coping strategies (active coping, acceptance and cognitive reframing, avoidance and denial, emotional suppression), resources (social, economic, familial, spiritual), and the individual's life context (stressful events and perceived stress level, functional ability). The influence of these psychosocial factors on health preservation may be mediated by changes in patients' decisions to engage in risk behaviors, decisions to seek diagnostic screening services, help-seeking responses following the onset of overt symptoms, or biological processes associated with the initiation of infectious, neoplastic, metabolic, or cardiovascular diseases. The impact of these factors on adjustment to disease and disease course may be mediated by changes in patients' susceptibility to stress-induced emotional (e.g., depressive and anxiety symptoms), physiologic (e.g., endocrine, immunologic, cardiovascular dysregulation), and physical (e.g., muscle tension, sleep disorders, pain perception) sequelae.

IMPORTANCE OF PSYCHOSOCIAL FACTORS IN HEALTH CARE DELIVERY

There is a growing awareness that many psychosocial factors may contribute to optimal health care delivery and related medical treatment success rates and costs of care. Identifying these factors through clinical research and integrating new information into medical practice are greatly facilitated by comprehensive psychosocial screening and assessment. In this section, I present research demonstrating empirical support for links between specific psychosocial factors and patient medical utilization patterns and how these associations, in turn, can affect health care costs in the short term. I also review research relating psychosocial factors to the success rates of certain treatments and patient recovery and rehabilitation rates from specific illnesses, outcomes that are both instrumental in longer term cost containment.

The Influence of Managed Care on Health Care Delivery

Most managed care systems attempt to manage escalating costs of medical care by providing increases in services to underserved populations, determining the basic criteria for medical need, setting fair prices for services, emphasizing the role of primary care, and monitoring public health through nationally funded research programs (Regier, 1994). I have proposed that addressing these missions could be greatly enhanced with systematic and valid methods for assessing physical and psychological status of the patients making use of health care services. Improved screening and assessment is relevant for identifying underserved populations who could benefit from enhanced services, determining whether a patient meets criteria for one medical procedure or another, and surveying the usual and customary costs for services and their relative cost-effectiveness. Cost-effective primary care can be realized by understanding the factors that predict patients' decisions to utilize early screening and detection services, detecting physical and mental disorders in adults at the earliest possible stage, and predicting and monitoring the effects of medical decisions on recovery and rehabilitation rates, as well as the quality of life of the patients receiving care.

In most health care settings, the amount and level of psychosocial/mental health assessment may be grossly disproportionate to the amount of effort and resources spent on high-technology biomedical assessments. In fact, in many cases, psychosocial assessment may be totally absent from the screening, intake, and follow-up procedures, despite the remarkably low cost/high payoff potential of these tests. Where psychosocial assessments have been incorporated into health care protocols, psychologists are often unable to obtain reimbursement from third-party payers for such assessments (Eisen et al., 1998). This has placed at risk the use of psychological assessment for referral and decision making pertaining to level of care, the best mode of treatment delivery, and risk for early termination from treatment and inadequate adherence to prescriptions and recommendations during convalescence and aftercare (Eisen et al., 1998). Having access to information on personality traits is important in making decisions about appropriate psychosocial treatment formats (e.g., group versus individual-based interventions), which may optimize effectiveness while containing costs (Harkness & Lilienfeld, 1997). Finally, because many health care systems view themselves as acute care providers, they may not appreciate that value of having a complete patient profile capable of predicting adjustment to treatment and adherence to medication and lifestyle changes that are critical in the management of more costly *chronic* medical conditions.

Comprehensive psychological assessments are designed to provide far more than information about patient pathology and, instead, can provide insights about assets including personal and social resources, coping skills, and key targets for psychosocial interventions (Eisen et al., 1998). Ultimately, the psychosocial assessment report is a highly synthesized product integrating information about patient history, test scores, current medical diagnosis, and comorbidities to provide predictions about the patient's responses to medical diagnosis and treatment procedures. This sort of information gathering and processing can require far more time and effort than that which is reimbursed by current managed care organizations—a trend likely to continue until health insurance companies can see a clear benefit offered by comprehensive psychosocial assessment. What are some of these potential benefits?

The Influence of Psychosocial Factors on Medical Utilization, Treatment Outcomes, and Health Care Costs

Evidence justifying the potential cost savings and quality assurance that is made possible by integrating psychosocial assessment and intervention into health care delivery comes from many sources including epidemiological investigations, health services research, health costs analyses, and treatment efficacy studies. By integrating epidemiological and health services research, we can identify disease comorbidities that account for the highest utilization patterns. Health costs analyses consider the cost of illness and cost of treatment and are used to define the amounts that should be allocated to benefits packages. Cost-effectiveness can be tracked through actual cash outlay or through hospital admissions, lengths of stay, number of outpatient visits for follow-up, and the use of expensive (e.g., surgery) and less expensive (e.g., medications) procedures. Some of the psychosocial factors associated with health care costs involve those directly related to medical utilization (short-term cost effects) while others relate more directly to treatment success and recovery and rehabilitation rates (longer term cost effects).

These forms of research are complemented by treatment efficacy studies that test the effects of interventions on the net costs of medical illnesses. These studies are helpful in developing empirically validated guidelines for primary prevention strategies as well as recommendations for treatment choices (i.e., triaging) for people already diagnosed with a medical condition. Successful triaging may result in a recommendation for a synergistic combination of pharmacological (e.g., antidepressant) and psychosocial interventions (e.g., supportive group therapy or individual counseling) that can complement the treatment of the primary medical condition (e.g., cancer) by enhancing adherence to a self-care routine/lifestyle change or adjustment to the side effects of the medication. I have proposed that such a synthesis depends on knowledge of patients' psychosocial characteristics and health behavior patterns. Realizing this synthesis on a routine basis could aid in the reduction of the costs of health care delivery across a wide range of medical conditions in affected or at-risk populations.

Psychiatric Disturbances

There is good evidence that medical patients who display psychiatric disorders or who are in some way evidencing a poor emotional adjustment to their illness (e.g., depressed mood) may generate greater health care costs than their better adjusted counterparts (Holland, 1997; Jacobs, Kopans, & Reizes, 1995; Kimmerling, Ouimette, Cronkite, & Moos, 1999; Roth et al., 1998). The National Comprehensive Cancer Network (NCCN), made up of 17 Comprehensive Cancer Centers in the United States, has proposed that psychosocial screening should begin in the waiting room at the initial visit with conditions such as dementia, delirium, anxiety disorder, substance abuse, and personality problems being grounds for a mental health treatment referral. By providing vulnerable patients with mental health and pastoral counseling, the NCCN report suggests that the benefits of distress management may include better patient-physician communications, enhanced compliance with treatment regimens, and lower mood disturbance and stress.

These findings are not limited to cancer populations. Medical patients with depressive disorders may also generate greater costs in the process of obtaining their health care (Greenberg, Stiglin, Finkelstein, & Berndt, 1993; Klerman & Weissman, 1992). Some work has indicated that depressed patients tend to show greater medical utilization (Barsky, Wyshak, & Klerman, 1986; Katon, VonKorff, Lipscomb, Wagner, & Polk, 1990; Kimmerling et al., 1999; Simon & VonKorff, 1995), have longer hospital stays (Cushman, 1986; Jacobs et al., 1995; Narrow, Regier, & Rae, 1993), require more custodial care (e.g., nursing homes; Cushman, 1986), are less able to maintain improvements made during rehabilitation (Thompson, Sobolew-Shubin, Graham, & Janigian, 1989), and may be less able to recapture their premorbid quality of life (Niemi, Laaksonen, Kotila, & Waltimo, 1988). There is also growing evidence that depressed cardiac patients may be at heightened risk for rehospitalization (Stern, Pascale, & Ackerman, 1977) and reinfarct (Carney, Freedland, Rich, & Jaffe, 1995; Frasure-Smith et al., 1993) in the years following their initial MI. Another study showed that patients displaying significant levels of psychopathology showed 40% longer hospital stays, 35% greater hospital charges, and used more procedures, independent of gender, race, age, and medical diagnosis (Levenson, Hamer, & Rossiter, 1990). A large study of more than 50,000 medical/surgical patients discharged from two major hospitals during 1984 found that patients with psychiatric comorbidity (mostly affective disorders and substance abuse disorders) had nearly double the length of hospital stays of patients without comorbidity (Fulop, Strain, Vita, Lyons, & Hammer, 1987).

Coping Strategies

Psychosocial factors related to the ways individuals cope with stressors may also affect health care outcomes. Stone and Porter (1995) suggest that a patient's coping efforts, guided in part by their appraisals of their physical symptoms, can affect their emotional response, their health behaviors, communications with their health care provider, and their adherence to primary, secondary, and tertiary prevention efforts. These intermediary outcomes may in turn predict the patient's further help-seeking behavior, sense of well-being, and possibly disease course (Stone & Porter, 1995). To the degree that maladaptive coping strategies (e.g., denial and disengagement) lead to poor emotional adjustment, resumption of health risk behaviors, disturbed patient-physician communications, and reduced adherence, they may require additional medical care with associated escalation in costs.

Stress Moderators

Many of the stress-moderating factors previously associated with emotional adjustment to illness are also associated with medical utilization patterns. These include social support, life context, and personality characteristics. For instance, among medical patients attending 43 family practices, those with lower confidante support and lower emotional support showed a significantly greater number of office visits and a greater number of total charges over a one-year period (Broadhead, Hehlbach, DeGruy, & Kaplan, 1989). Contextual factors such as elevated life stress predicted a greater frequency of medical visits, and this association was strongest among patients with personality traits characterizing a tendency toward somaticizing (Miranda, Perez-Stable, Munoz, Hargreaves, & Henke, 1991). This work provides evidence that external life stressors may interact with tendencies to be overly focused on illness concerns in predicting medical utilization. Thus, stress reduction interventions might be particularly cost-effective in reducing overutilization of outpatient medical services, especially among patients who (1) possess this personality characteristic and (2) are undergoing significant life stressors. This line of work underlines the notion that identifying psychological characteristics of medical outpatients within their life context may facilitate triaging to time-limited, focused psychological intervention to substantially contain health care expenditures.

Negative Health Behaviors

Negative behaviors such as substance use may be one of the most important factors influencing the cost of health care in this country. When 2,238 medical records were randomly sampled from more than 42,000 discharges from six different hospital populations, *negative health behaviors* such as alcohol use and cigarette smoking were found to be consistently higher among the 13% of patients classified as high-cost utilizers as compared to the 87% low-cost utilizers (Zook & Moore, 1980). Repeat hospitalizations and unexpected complications during treatment were among the primary causes for the expenditures in the high-cost group. Importantly, these are behaviors that may be modifiable by psychosocial interventions. Being able to identify these health behaviors in the context of a patient's mood state, coping strategies, cognitive appraisal and health attitudes, social and external resources, and ongoing life context may enhance the effectiveness of these psychosocial interventions.

Psychosocial Interventions

Psychosocial interventions have been shown to be effective and efficient means of reducing costs for medical patients over the past 10 years (e.g., Brown & Schulberg, 1995; Levenson, 1992; Simon & Katzelnick, 1997; Simon & VonKorff, 1995; VonKorff et al., 1998). Educational, behavioral, and psychosocial interventions have been used by behavioral medicine researchers to experimentally demonstrate the importance of psychosocial factors in cost containment (Caudill, Schnable, Zuttermeister, Benson, & Friedman, 1991; Hellman, Budd, Borysenko, McClelland, & Benson, 1990; Jacobs, 1987; Pallak, Cummings, Dorken, & Henke, 1994; Schneider, 1987; Vickery, 1983). Educational programs have been shown to reduce utilization by 21% to 33%, often resulting in a return of more than 200% on the costs invested in the intervention. A large meta-analytic review of this literature revealed that medical utilization was reduced by 10% to 33% and hospital stays were cut by 1.5 days after brief psychotherapy (Mumford, Schlesinger, Glass, Patrick, & Cuerdon, 1984). Schlesinger and colleagues observed that patients diagnosed with one of four major medical conditions (chronic lung disease, diabetes, ischemic heart disease, and hypertension) showed significantly lower costs for medical services after receiving mental health treatment (Schlesinger et al., 1983).

It is difficult to separate out the contribution of psychosocial factors to health care utilization versus treatment success. However, some studies have provided some additional information that may support the role of psychosocial intervention in improving the efficacy of a medical intervention regime. At least three major studies involving more than 20,000 total patients showed that psychosocial interventions substantially reduced costs incurred by diabetics. One of these studies found a reduction in hospitalization rates of 73% and lengths of stay of 78%, resulting in an estimated savings of more than $2,000 per patient participating in the program (Miller & Goldstein, 1972). Another found that an outpatient education program reduced the incidence of severe ketoacidosis by 65% and the frequency of lower extremity amputations by nearly 50% for a cost savings of more than $400,000 per year (Davidson, 1983). Finally, a brief outpatient education program reduced the number of hospital days by more than 50% in a group of diabetics (Mulhauser et al., 1983).

Among patients with asthma, psychosocial interventions delivered in small groups resulted in more symptom-free days, greater physical activity improvements, and 49% fewer office visits for acute attacks compared to patients receiving usual care over a 2-year follow-up period (S. Wilson et al., 1993). One study found that asthma and arthritis patients who were offered a brief psychological intervention involving written disclosure of emotions showed significant improvement in symptoms and other indicators of clinical status (Smyth, Stone, Hurewitz, & Kaell, 1999). Among chronic rheumatoid arthritis sufferers, one health education program was found to reduce pain reports by 20% and physician visits by 43%. The program saved an estimated $12 over a four-year period (or $3 annually) for each dollar invested.

There is some evidence that surgery patients may recover faster with preoperative psychosocial intervention. Interventions ranging from muscle relaxation to intensive psychotherapy have been associated with improvements in several surgery-related outcome variables including fewer days in intensive care, fewer total days in the hospital, and fewer incidents of congestive heart failure (e.g., Aiken & Henricks, 1971). Among the nearly 200 studies addressing this topic between 1963 and 1989, 79% to 84% have reported beneficial effects for various forms of psychosocial intervention (Devine, 1992). Similar to other work with hospital inpatients, length of hospital stay was reduced on average by 1.5 days. Using a conservative estimate of projected cost savings of such changes in length of stay, these programs may save up to $10 for each dollar invested. Across 13 other studies, psychosocial intervention reduced hospital days post-heart attack or postsurgery by 2 full days (Mumford, Schlesinger, & Glass, 1982). One study also revealed that conducting an adequate psychological screen and triaging surgery patients to receive psychiatric intervention reduced the average hospital stay by 2.2 days for a savings of more than $8 for each dollar invested (Strain et al., 1991). Here it is apparent that greater attention to the role of psychosocial factors is warranted to contain health care costs and improve success rates of medical regimens over a wide range of disease conditions.

Psychosocial interventions that reduce stress levels may also affect postsurgical complications by reducing stress hormone output (e.g., urinary cortisol, Doering et al., 2000), improving wound healing (Kiecolt-Glaser, Marucha, Malarkey, Mercado, & Glaser, 1995), or accelerating immune system recovery after surgery, blood transfusions, and anesthesia (van der Pompe, Antoni, & Heijnen, 1998). Another intriguing target for future intervention research in cancer patients involves the proposed link between stress and susceptibility to infectious disease (Bovjberg & Valdimarsdottir, 1996). It has been suggested that because stress is associated with increased susceptibility to upper respiratory infections (Cohen et al., 1991) and bacterial infections (Bovjberg & Valdimarsdottir, 1996), cancer patients, especially those who are emotionally distressed and receiving chemotherapy or other immunosuppressive adjuvant therapies, may be vulnerable to stress-associated opportunistic infections (Bovjberg & Valdimarsdottir, 1996). Surprisingly very little work has examined the effects of stressors or stress management interventions on the incidence of infectious disease in cancer patients receiving adjuvant therapy. Emerging findings suggest that breast cancer patients assigned to a time-limited stress management intervention may show reduced cortisol (Cruess et al., 2000) and a faster recovery of immune system functioning after receiving adjuvant chemotherapy and radiation (McGregor et al., 2004).

Psychosocial interventions may play a significant role in reducing long-term health care costs by reducing the likelihood of phenomena such as diabetic complications, recurrence of heart attacks in MI patients, and extended rehabilitation costs for spinal injury or stroke due to reinjury. Other long-term effects of psychosocial interventions are currently being explored in terms of reducing the progression rate of conditions such as HIV infection, the recurrence rate of certain cancers (e.g., breast cancer), and life-threatening and costly complications such as kidney failure that result from other disease processes.

It is entirely likely that there are subsets of patients who possess certain psychosocial characteristics that make them more or less likely to benefit from psychosocial interventions. The ability to identify these characteristics at the point of screening and intake could further increase cost savings because all patients in need of such services would be caught while those not in need of such services would not incur the costs or burden of psychosocial services unnecessarily.

Summary

I reviewed studies supporting the role of specific psychosocial factors in two major aspects of health maintenance: health preservation/primary prevention and adjustment to disease/secondary prevention. Psychosocial characteristics such as psychiatric status, personality/coping style, psychosocial issues (appraisals, resources, contextual factors), lifestyle behaviors, and patient communication styles may all contribute additively or interactively to the probability of optimal health preservation as manifest in engagement in risk behaviors, decisions to pursue diagnostic testing or medical help following the onset of symptoms, vulnerability to stress-related symptoms, and the promotion of subclinical pathophysiologic changes that may in turn increase the risk of developing clinically manifest physical disease. This review also provided evidence that many of these same psychosocial characteristics can potentially affect the patient's adjustment to disease in the form of their initial emotional reaction to diagnosis and their adjustment to the stressful demands, limitations, and lifestyle changes brought about by a chronic illness. These factors may also have direct or indirect effects on the physical course of the disease, possibly facilitating or thwarting secondary prevention efforts. A review of the health services literature noted a vast array of studies showing that many of these psychosocial patient characteristics are associated with optimal health care delivery at the level of both medical utilization and treatment success and recovery, these improvements corresponding to potential reductions in short-term and longer term health care costs, respectively. These psychosocial factors include psychiatric conditions such as anxiety and depressive disorders, personality/coping styles, stress moderators related to intrapsychic (cognitive appraisals) and interpersonal/external resources (social and spiritual support), and treatment prognosticators related to adjustment to medical procedures and health maintenance behaviors after treatment. Ideally, all of this information can be synthesized to predict a wide range of medical outcomes that are relevant to the management of the patient's health care. These treatment outcomes might include: possible adverse emotional reactions to major medical procedures, potential difficulties with or misuses of medications, the patient's comfort in communicating detailed medical information, tendency to overutilize medical services, and compliance with required lifestyle changes.

Knowledge of the latter set of patient characteristics may be critical in determining adjustment to a medical condition, as well as health care costs and success of the medical treatments chosen. These characteristics include:

1. The likelihood that a patient will have a negative psychological reaction to major medical procedures such as surgery, cardiac catheterization, chemotherapy, and radiation treatment.
2. The tendency to become confused about or deliberately abuse medications that are prescribed.
3. Receptivity to specific details about diagnostic, prognostic, and treatment procedures and outcomes.
4. Inclinations to present many minor as well as major symptoms, sensations, and experiences and to overutilize medical services.
5. Difficulties in adhering to a posttreatment self-care regimen.

The ability of the health care provider to identify some of these treatment prognosticators at the earliest point in care may improve the precision of history-taking and symptom monitoring and facilitate the patient-provider rapport, potentially resulting in improved help-seeking upon emergence of new symptoms and better adherence to prescribed and self-care regimens. The ultimate synthesis of all of this information would result in a profile of the patient's potential adjustment difficulties listing both liabilities that could exacerbate their condition and assets that could be used by the health care provider to offset these elements. Finally, based on the identification of specific challenges and difficulties, the information could be used to determine whether referral for specific mental health intervention would likely provide benefits.

PSYCHOSOCIAL INSTRUMENTS FOR ASSESSING MEDICAL PATIENTS

I have presented the rationale for the development and use of psychosocial assessment in medical patients and those at risk for developing disease—a line of research that Theodore Millon and his colleagues have been conducting over the past 25 years. This work has led to the development and validation of a number of psychosocial instruments now in wide use in behavioral medicine research and in the practice of contemporary clinical health psychology. The final section of this chapter highlights two of these instruments, the MBHI (Millon et al., 1982), developed in the early 1980s, and a new instrument, the MBMD (Millon et al., 2001). These tools provide integrated information on the psychosocial characteristics of medical patients for the purpose of optimizing health maintenance and health service-related activities. This extensive body of literature in combination with Millon's personality theory formed the rationale for the choice of the major domains and corresponding scales assessed in these instruments.

Use of the Millon Behavioral Health Inventory with Medical Patients

One objective instrument that has attempted to provide comprehensive information for health psychologists and health care providers in a systematic and explicitly synthesized format is the MBHI (Millon et al., 1982). The MBHI is a 150-item self-report instrument designed to provide information on patient coping strategies, health-related attitudes (e.g., pessimism and hopelessness), and probable responses to major medical treatments. A good deal of published research has demonstrated the efficacy of the MBHI for evaluating a wide range of medical populations including patients with cancer (Goldstein & Antoni, 1989; Goodkin, Antoni, & Blaney, 1986; Jensen, 1987), chronic pain (Barnes, Smith, Gatchel, & Mayer, 1989; Dufton, 1990; Gatchel, Mayer, Capra, Barnett, & Diamond, 1986; Labbe, Goldberg, Fishbain, & Rosomoff, 1989; Wilcoxin, Zook, & Zarski, 1988), renal disease (Tracy, Green, & McCleary, 1987), headache (Gatchel, Deckel, Weinberg, & Smith, 1985), gastrointestinal disorders (Alberts, Lyons, & Anderson, 1988; J. Richter, Obrecht, Bradley, Young, & Anderson, 1986), and cardiac conditions (Brandwin, Clifford, & Coffman, 1989; Green, Millon, & Meagher, 1983; Katz, Martin, Landa, & Chadda, 1985; Kolitz, Antoni, & Green, 1988; Lantinga et al., 1988). These studies have established the utility of MBMH scales predicting help-seeking behaviors after the onset of MI symptoms, the promotion of early neoplastic changes in women at risk for cervical cancer, initial psychological reactions to news of a life-threatening medical diagnosis, psychological adjustment to the burdens of chronic disease, the ability to make lifestyle changes required by certain diseases, appointment keeping and other indices of medical adherence, responses to rehabilitation efforts, decision making concerning treatment choices, the progression of physical disease and related physiological changes (immune system declines), and recovery from and survival after major medical procedures such as heart transplant. Thus, the MBHI represented a major contribution of the Millon team as it provided a research and clinical tool capable of predicting behavioral responses to the onset of new symptoms, reactions to medical diagnosis, adjustment to chronic disease and chronic pain, and ability to forecast the efficacy of secondary prevention efforts and the physical course of disease.

Use of the Millon Behavioral Medicine Diagnostic with Medical Patients

Despite the impressive results generated by studies using the MBHI to assess psychosocial characteristics relevant to a variety of primary and secondary prevention domains in different patient populations, there remained several important psychosocial characteristics for which this instrument did not provide explicit information:

1. The presence of psychiatric indicators that may influence the patients' adjustment to their medical condition.

2. Coping styles reflecting recently derived disorders such as depressive personality disorder, sadistic personality disorder, and masochistic personality disorder (Millon & Davis, 1995).

3. Other psychological factors related to cognitive appraisals (e.g., self-esteem, general efficacy), resources (e.g., spiritual and religious), and contextual factors (e.g., functional abilities).

4. Specific lifestyle behaviors (e.g., alcohol and substance abuse, smoking, eating patterns, inactivity, and exercise).

5. The patient's communication stylistics (tendencies toward disclosure, social desirability, devaluation when communicating).

6. Characteristics useful for predicting patient adherence, medication abuses, utilization of medical services, preference for more or less detail when receiving medical information, and emotional responses to stressful medical procedures, which in turn can be useful in informing health care management decision making and mental health treatment triaging.

Awareness of the potential usefulness of this information for maximizing health maintenance and minimizing health care costs provided the impetus for the development of the new instrument, the MBMD (Millon et al., 2001), which is designed to address all of these issues in addition to those already tapped by its predecessor, the MBHI.

Millon and his associates developed the MBMD as an instrument that would expand on the scope of the MBHI by providing a comprehensive set of information on those psychosocial characteristics of medical patients that contemporary behavioral medicine research has identified as potentially influencing several domains of health maintenance and health care delivery: (1) psychiatric indicators, (2) coping style, (3) stress moderators, (4) treatment prognostics, and (5) negative health habits. Three additional MBMD scales characterize components of the patients' communication style that may affect their test responses as well as the ways in which they interact with health care providers: Disclosure, Desirability, and Debasement scales. The Disclosure scale captures the tendency of the patient to be open about sharing personal self-information. The Desirability scale characterizes the patient's inclination to present himself or herself in an overly positive light, even at the expense of concealing symptoms. The Debasement scale describes the patient's tendency to present many minor as well as major symptoms, sensations, and experiences in his or her communications with the health care provider. The ability of the health care provider to identify systematic distortions, biases, and preferences in the patient's self-reports can improve the precision of history-taking and symptom monitoring and facilitate patient-provider rapport. This could potentially result in improved help-seeking on emergence of new symptoms and better adherence to prescribe pharmacological and self-care regimens.

Empirical work supporting the use of the MBMD in different medical populations includes patients recruited from comprehensive cancer centers, organ transplant centers, behavioral medicine research centers, diabetes research institutes, and general medical hospitals and clinics. This work has included studies using the MBMD to predict post-treatment health-related behaviors and medical utilization; outcomes in inpatients undergoing organ transplant; health behaviors, immune function, and disease outcomes in persons with HIV infection; and glucose control in persons with diabetes mellitus. Future research should employ prospective designs to test the viability of the MBMD in predicting patient psychological responses to major medical intervention, the incidence of success and medical complications following medical procedure, the costs of different medical treatments in focused randomized trials, the likelihood of medication abuse in different populations, the self-care abilities in patients with newly diagnosed chronic disease, and utilization and expenditures in large health care systems. Ultimately, the MBMD may be useful in the primary care setting for screening of patients at risk of certain medical disease and triaging patients for both psychosocial services and the best-matched medical intervention for that individual. There is a huge need to study how sociocultural forces contribute to the ways that the psychiatric indicators and coping style are expressed and the nuances of the patient's *communication style*. These factors may also affect access to and personal value attached to different resources (e.g., social versus spiritual), which in turn may contribute to patients' ability to adjust successfully to their illness, adhere to medication regimens, and make the lifestyle changes that their condition necessitates. Establishing the algorithms for how such modifying information can be used to optimize the accuracy of predictions based on the MBMD and other psychosocial measures and constructs in medical patients will require a series of studies using samples varying systematically in age, gender, ethnicity, and disease type and stage, along with a clear set of psychosocial adjustment and medical outcome variables that are monitored over time. This represents the next series of steps that Millon and his associates will take in the coming years to further elucidate the influence of psychosocial factors on health and medical disease outcomes.

CONCLUSIONS

This chapter reviewed the empirical literature to establish a rationale for the use of psychosocial assessment in persons at risk for or diagnosed with medical diseases. This literature specified a set of psychosocial factors, which when identified at the earliest point of contact with the health care system, might facilitate health maintenance, optimize adjustment and recovery, and minimize costs associated with a wide variety of major medical disease conditions. This work paved the way for the development of psychosocial assessment tools that could be used to translate this knowledge into clinical settings ranging from the neighborhood clinic to the major medical centers across our country. Dr. Theodore Millon and his research team have for three decades been leaders in the development of a widely accepted theory of personality and psychosocial instruments that reliably assess personality disorders in adult and adolescent populations. For more than 20 years, Millon and his associates have directly contributed to health psychology research and practice through the development of two comprehensive instruments targeted to medical disease issues—the MBHI and the MBMD. These two measures have been widely researched in the context of several major medical conditions ranging from cancer to heart disease, being shown to reliably predict outcomes ranging from delay time before seeking care after initial MI symptoms to medical complications and associated costs after heart transplant. These tests have also been shown to be able to predict health behaviors ranging from OB-GYN appointment keeping to strict adherence to HIV antiretroviral medication regimens. These tests are presently mainstays in the screening batteries of major institutions such as VA hospitals, pain clinics, cancer centers, and diabetes research institutes, to name a few. Thus, Theodore Millon can be credited for being one of the few pioneers in the field of health psychology to have successfully translated the fruits of behavioral medicine research into practical and empirically validated instruments that are in wide use in medical settings today.

REFERENCES

Ahles, T., Blanchard, E., & Ruckdeschel, J. (1983). The multidimensional nature of cancer-related pain. *Pain, 17,* 277–288.

Aiken, L., & Henricks, T. (1971). Systematic relaxation as a nursing intervention technique with open heart surgery patients. *Nursing Research, 20,* 212–217.

Alberts, M., Lyons, J., & Anderson, R. (1988). Relations of coping style and illness variables in ulcerative colitis. *Psychological Reports, 62,* 71–79.

Alferi, S., Culver, J., Carver, C. S., Arena, P., & Antoni, M. H. (1999). Religiosity, religious coping and distress: A prospective study of catholic and evangelical Hispanic women in treatment for early stage breast cancer. *Journal of Health Psychology, 4,* 343–356.

American Cancer Society. (1989). *Cancer facts and figures—1989.* Atlanta, GA: Author.

American Diabetes Association. (1986). *Diabetes: Facts you need to know.* Alexandria, VA: Author.

American Heart Association. (1988). *1989 heart facts.* Dallas, TX: Author.

Andersen, B., Kiecolt-Glaser, J., & Glaser, R. (1994). A biobehavioral model of cancer stress and disease outcome. *American Psychologist, 49,* 389–404.

Andersen, B. L. (1992). Psychological interventions for cancer patients to enhance the quality of life. *Journal of Consulting and Clinical Psychology, 60,* 552–568.

Anderson, K. O., Bradley, L. A., Young, L. D., McDaniel, L. K., & Wise, C. M. (1985). Rheumatoid arthritis: Review of psychological factors related to etiology, effects and treatment. *Psychological Bulletin, 98,* 358–387.

Antoni, M. H. (1991). Psychosocial stressors and behavioral interventions in gay men with HIV infection. *International Reviews in Psychiatry, 3,* 383–389.

Antoni, M. H. (2003a). Psychoneuroendocrinology and psychoneuroimmunology of cancer: Plausible mechanisms worth pursuing? *Brain Behavior and Immunity, 17,* S84–S91.

Antoni, M. H. (2003b). Stress management and psychoneuroimmunology in HIV infection. *CNS Spectrums, 8,* 40–51.

Antoni, M. H., Brickman, A., Lutgendorf, S., Klimas, N., Imia-Finns, A., Ironson, G., et al. (1994). Psychosocial correlates of illness burden in chronic fatigue syndrome. *Clinical Infectious Disease, 18,* S73–S78.

Antoni, M. H., & Emmelkamp, P. (1995). Editorial on HIV/AIDS [Special issue]. *Clinical Psychology and Psychotherapy, 2*(4), 199–202.

Antoni, M. H., Goldstein, D., Ironson, G., LaPerriere, A., Fletcher, M. A., & Schneiderman, N. (1995). Coping responses to HIV-1 serostatus notification predict concurrent and prospective immunologic status. *Clinical Psychology and Psychotherapy, 2*(4), 234–248.

Antoni, M. H., & Goodkin, K. (1989). Life stress and moderator variables in the promotion of cervical neoplasia: II. Life event dimensions. *Journal of Psychosomatic Research, 33*(4), 457–467.

Antoni, M. H., & Weiss, D. (2003). Stress and immunity. In L. Jason, P. Fenell, & R. Taylor (Eds.), *Handbook of chronic fatigue syndrome and fatiguing illnesses* (pp. 527–545). New York: Wiley.

Bandura, A., Taylor, C. B., Williams, S., Mefford, I., & Barchas, J. (1985). Catecholamine secretion as a function of perceived coping self-efficacy. *Journal of Consulting and Clinical Psychology, 53,* 406–414.

Barefoot, J., & Schroll, M. (1996). Symptoms of depression, acute myocardial infarction, and total mortality in a community sample. *Circulation, 93,* 1976–1980.

Barnes, D., Smith, D., Gatchel, R., & Mayer, T. (1989). Psycosocioeconomic predictors of treatment/success/failure in chronic low-back pain patients. *Spine, 14,* 427–430.

Barsky, A., Wyshak, G., & Klerman, G. (1986). Medical and psychiatric determinants of outpatient medical utilization. *Medical Care, 24,* 548–560.

Baum, A. (1994). Behavioral, biological, and environmental interactions in disease processes. In S. Blumenthal, K. Matthews, & S. Weiss (Eds.), *New research frontiers in behavioral medicine* (Proceedings of the National Conference; NIH Publication No. 94-3772, pp. 61–69). Washington, DC: U.S. Government Printing Office.

Baum, A., & Posluszny, D. (1999). Health psychology: Mapping biobehavioral contributions to health and illness. *Annual Review Psychology, 50,* 137–163.

Baum, J. (1982). A review of the psychological aspects of neumatic diseases. *Seminars in Arthritis and Rheumatism, 11*, 352–361.

Becker, M. H., Maiman, L., Kirscht, J., Haefner, D., & Drachman, R. (1977). The health belief model and dietary compliance: A field experiment. *Journal of Health and Social Behavior, 18*, 348–366.

Blalock, S., DeVellis, B., & Giordino, K. (1995). The relationship between coping and psychological well-being among people with osteoarthritis: A problem-solving approach. *Annals of Behavioral Medicine, 17*, 107–115.

Blumenthal, J., Williams, R., Wallace, A., Williams, R., & Needles, T. (1982). Physiological and psychological variables predict compliance to prescribed exercise therapy in patients recovering from myocardial infarction. *Psychosomatic Medicine, 44*, 519–527.

Booth-Kewley, S., & Friedman, H. S. (1987). Psychological predictors of heart disease: A quantitative review. *Psychological Bulletin, 101*, 343–362.

Bovjberg, D., & Valdimarsdottir, H. (1996). Stress, immune modulation, and infectious disease during chemotherapy for breast cancer. *Annals of Behavioral Medicine, 18*, S63.

Brandwin, M., Clifford, M., & Coffman, K. (1989). The MBHI Life Threat Reactivity Scale as a predictor of mortality in patients awaiting heart transplantation. *Psychosomatic Medicine, 51*, 256.

Breitbart, W., & Payne, D. (1998). Pain. In J. Holland (Ed.), *Psycho-oncology* (pp. 450–467). New York: Oxford University Press.

Bremer, B. (1995). Absence of control over health and the psychological adjustment to end-stage renal disease. *Annals of Behavioral Medicine, 17*, 227–233.

Broadhead, W., Hehlbach, S., DeGruy, F., & Kaplan, B. (1989). Functional versus structural social support and health care utilization in a family medicine outpatient practice. *Medical Care, 27*, 221–233.

Brown, C., & Schulberg, H. (1995). The efficacy of psychosocial treatments in primary care: A review of randomized clinical trials. *General Hospital Psychiatry, 17*, 414–424.

Brownell, K. D., & Wadden, T. A. (1992). Etiology and treatment of obesity: Understanding a serious, prevalent, and refractory disorder. *Journal of Consulting and Clinical Psychology, 60*, 505–517.

Burgess, C., Morris, T., & Pettingale, K. W. (1988). Psychological response to cancer diagnosis-II. Evidence for coping styles (coping styles and cancer diagnosis). *Journal of Psychosomatic Research, 32*, 263–272.

Byrnes, D., Antoni, M. H., Goodkin, K., Efantis-Potter, J., Simon, T., Munajj, J., et al. (1998). Stressful events, pessimism, natural killer cell cytotoxicity, and cytotoxic/suppressor T-cells in HIV+ Black women at risk for cervical cancer. *Psychosomatic Medicine, 60*, 714–722.

Cameron, L., Leventhal, E., & Leventhal, H. (1995). Seeking medical care in response to symptoms and life stress. *Psychosomatic Medicine, 57*, 37–47.

Carney, R., Freedland, K., Eisen, S., Rich, M., & Jaffe, A. (1995). Major depression and medication adherence in elderly patients with coronary heart disease. *Health Psychology, 14*, 88–90.

Carney, R., Freedland, K., Rich, M., & Jaffe, A. (1995). Depression as a risk factor for cardiac events in established coronary heart disease: A review of possible mechanisms. *Annals of Behavioral Medicine, 17*, 142–149.

Carver, C. S., Pozo, C., Harris, S. D., Noriega, V., Scheier, M. F., Robinson, D. S., et al. (1993). How coping mediates the effect of optimism on distress: A study of women with early stage breast cancer. *Journal of Personality and Social Psychology, 65*, 375–390.

Cassileth, B. R., Lusk, E. J., Strouse, T. B., Miller, D. S., Brown, L. L., Cross, P. A., et al. (1984). Psychosocial status in chronic illness: A comparative analysis of six diagnostic groups. *New England Journal of Medicine, 331*, 506–511.

Caudill, M., Schnable, R., Zuttermeister, P., Benson, H., & Friedman, R. (1991). Decreased clinic use by chronic pain patients: Response to behavioral medicine interventions. *Journal of Clinical Pain, 7*(4), 305–310.

Centers for Disease Control. (1993). *Diabetes surveillance, 1993.* Atlanta, GA: Author.

Chambers, W. N., & Reiser, M. F. (1953). Emotional stress in the precipitation of congestive heart failure. *Medicine, 15,* 38–60.

Christman, N. J., McConnell, E. A., Pfeiffer, C., Webster, K. K., Schmitt, M., & Ries, J. (1988). Uncertainty, coping, and distress following myocardial infarction: Transition from hospital to home. *Research in Nursing and Health, 11,* 71–82.

Classen, C., Sephton, E., Diamond, S., & Spiegel, D. (1998). Studies of life-extending psychosocial interventions. In J. Holland (Ed.), *Textbook of psycho-oncology* (pp. 730–742). New York: Oxford University Press.

Cohen, S. (1988). Psychosocial models of the role of social support in the etiology of physical disease. *Health Psychology, 7,* 269–297.

Cohen, S., & Edwards, J. R. (1989). Personality characteristics as moderators of the relationship between stress and disorder. In R. W. J. Neufeld (Ed.), *Advances in the investigation of psychological stress* (pp. 235–283). Hillsdale, NJ: Erlbaum.

Cohen, S., Tyrrell, D. A., & Smith, A. P. (1991). Psychological stress in humans and susceptibility to the common cold. *New England Journal of Medicine, 325,* 606–612.

Cohen, S., & Wills, T. A. (1985). Stress social support, and the buffering hypothesis. *Psychological Bulletin, 98,* 310–357.

Compas, B., Haaga, D., Keefe, F., Leitenberg, H., & Williams, D. (1998). Sampling of empirically supported psychological treatment from health psychology: Smoking, chronic pain, cancer, and bulimia nervosa. *Journal of Consulting and Clinical Psychology, 66,* 89–112.

Croyle, R., Smith, K., Botkin, J., Baty, B., & Nash, J. (1997). Psychological responses to BRCA1 mutation testing: Preliminary findings. *Health Psychology, 16,* 63–72.

Cruess, D. G., Antoni, M. H., McGregor, B. A., Boyers, A., Kumar, M., Kilbourn, K., et al. (2000). Cognitive-behavioral stress management reduces serum cortisol by enhancing positive contributions among women being treated for early stage breast cancer. *Psychosomatic Medicine, 62,* 304–308.

Cushman, L. A. (1986). Secondary neuropsychiatric complications in stroke: Implications for acute care. *Archives of Physical Medicine Rehabilitation, 69,* 877–879.

Davidson, J. K. (1983). The Grady Memorial Hospital Diabetes Programme. In J. I. Mann, K. Pyorala, & A. Teuscher (Eds.), *Diabetes in epidemiological perspective.* London: Churchill Livingston.

Dembroski, T. M., & Costa, P. R., Jr. (1987). Coronary prone behavior: Components of the Type A pattern and hostility. *Journal of Personality, 55,* 211–235.

Devine, E. C. (1992). Effects of psychoeducational care for adult surgical patients: A meta-analysis of 191 studies. *Patients Education and Counseling, 19,* 129–142.

Dimond, M. (1979). Social support and adaptation to chronic illness: The case of maintenance hemodialysis. *Research in Nursing and Health, 2,* 101–108.

Doering, S., Katzlberger, F., Rumpold, G., Roessler, S., Hofstoetter, B., Schatz, D., et al. (2000). Videotape preparation of patients before hip replacement surgery reduces stress. *Psychosomatic Medicine, 62,* 365–373.

Dubbert, P. (1992). Exercise in behavioral medicine. *Journal of Consulting and Clinical Psychology, 60,* 613–618.

Duberstein, P. R., Conwell, Y., & Yeates, E. (1993). Interpersonal stressors, substance abuse, and suicide. *Journal of Nervous and Nervous and Mental Disease, 181*(2), 80–85.

Dufton, B. (1990). Depression and the mediation of chronic pain. *Journal of Clinical Psychiatry, 51,* 248–250.

Dunkel-Schetter, C., Feinstein, L., Taylor, S. E., & Lazarus, R. S. (1987). Correlates of social support receipt. *Journal of Personality and Social Psychology, 53,* 71–80.

Eisen, E., Dies, R., Finn, S., Eyde, L., Kay, G., Kubiszyn, T., et al. (1998). *Problems and limitations in the use of psychological assessment in contemporary healthcare delivery: Report of the board of professional affairs, Psychological Assessment Work Group, Part II.* Washington, DC: American Psychological Association.

Emery, C., Schein, R., Hauck, E., & MacIntyre, N. (1998). Psychological and cognitive outcomes of a randomized trial f exercise among patients with chronic obstructive pulmonary disease. *Health Psychology, 17,* 232–240.

Epstein, L. H., & Perkins, K. A. (1988). Smoking, stress and coronary heart disease. *Journal of Consulting and Clinical Psychology, 56,* 342–349.

Esterling, B., Antoni, M. H., Fletcher, M. A., Marguilles, S., & Schneiderman, N. (1994). Emotional disclosure through writing or speaking modulates latent Epstein-Barr virus reactivation. *Journal of Consulting and Clinical Psychology, 62*(1), 130–140.

Esterling, B. A., Antoni, M. H., Kumar, M., & Schneiderman, N. (1990). Emotional repression, stress disclosure responses, and Epstein-Barr viral capsid antigen titers. *Psychosomatic Medicine, 52,* 397–410.

Fawzy, F. I., Cousins, N., Fawzy, N. W., Kemeny, M., Elashoff, R., & Morton, D. (1990). A structured psychiatric intervention for cancer patients: I. Changes over time in methods of coping and affective disturbance. *Archives of General Psychiatry, 47,* 720–725.

Fawzy, F. I., Fawzy, N. W., Hyun, C., Elashoff, R., Guthrie, D., Fahey, J. L., et al. (1993). Malignant melanoma: Effects of an early structured psychiatric intervention, coping, and affective state on recurrence and survival 6 years later. *Archives of General Psychiatry, 50,* 681–689.

Felton, B. J., & Revenson, T. A. (1984). Coping and adjustment in chronically ill adults. *Social Science and Medicine, 18,* 889–898.

Fitzpatrick, R., Newman, S., Lamb, R., & Shipley, M. (1988). Social relationships and psychological well-being in rheumatoid arthritis. *Social Science and Medicine, 27,* 399–403.

Folkman, S., & Lazarus, R. S. (1980). An analysis of coping in a middle-aged community sample. *Journal of Health and Social Behavior, 21,* 219–239.

Frasure-Smith, N., Lesperance, F., & Talajic, M. (1993). Depression following myocardial infarction. *Journal of the American Medical Association, 270*(15), 1819–1825.

Frasure-Smith, N., & Prince, R. (1989). Long-term follow-up of the ischemic heart disease life stress monitoring program. *Psychosomatic Medicine, 51,* 485–513.

Frenzel, M. P., McCaul, K. D., Glasgow, R. E., & Schafer, L. C. (1988). The relationship of stress and coping to regimen adherence and glycemic control of diabetes. *Journal of Social and Clinical Psychology, 6,* 77–87.

Friedman, H. S., & Booth-Kewley, S. (1987). The "disease prone" personality: A meta-analytic view of the construct. *American Psychologist, 42,* 539–555.

Fulop, G., Strain, J., Vita, J., Lyons, J., & Hammer, J. (1987). Impact of psychiatric comorbidity on length of hospital stay for medical/surgical patients: A preliminary report. *American Journal of Psychiatry, 144,* 878–882.

Gatchel, R., Deckel, A., Weinberg, N., & Smith, J. (1985). The utility of the Millon Behavioral Health Inventory in the study of chronic headaches. *Headache, 25,* 49–54.

Gatchel, R., Mayer, T., Capra, P., Barnett, J., & Diamond, P. (1986). Millon Behavioral Health Inventory: Its utility in predicting physical function in patients with low back pain. *Arch Physical Medicine and Rehabilitation, 67,* 878–882.

Glanz, K., Grove, J., Lerman, C., Gotay, C., & Le Marchand, L. (1999). Correlates of intentions to obtain genetic counseling and colorectal cancer gene testing among at-risk relatives from three ethnic groups. *Cancer Epidemiology, Biomarkers and Prevention, 8,* 329–336.

Glanz, L., Lew, R., Song, V., & Cook, V. (1999). Factors associated with skin cancer prevention practices in a multiethnic population. *Health Education and Behavior, 26,* 344–359.

Glasgow, R., Toobert, D., Hampson, S., & Wilson, W. (1995). Behavioral research on diabetes at the Oregon Research Institute. *Annals of Behavioral Medicine, 17,* 32–40.

Goldstein, D., & Antoni, M. H. (1989). The distribution of repressive coping styles among nonmetastatic and metastatic breast cancer patients as compared to non-cancer patients. *Psychology and Health: An International Journal, 3,* 245–258.

Goodkin, K., Antoni, M., & Blaney, P. (1986). Stress and hopelessness in the promotion of cervical intraepithelial neoplasia to invasive squamous cell carcinoma of the cervix. *Journal of Psychosomatic Research, 30,* 67–76.

Goodkin, K., Antoni, M. H., Sevin, B., & Fox, B. H. (1993). A partially testable model of psychosocial factors in the etiology of cervical cancer: I. A review of biological, psychological, and social aspects. *Psycho-Oncology, 2*(2), 79–98.

Grady, K., Reisine, S., Fifield, J., Lee, N., McVay, J., & Kelsey, M. (1991). The impact of Hurricane Hugo and the San Francisco Earthquake on a sample of people with rheumatoid arthritis. *Arthritis Care and Research, 2,* 106–110.

Green, C., Millon, T., & Meagher, R. (1983). The MBHI: Its utilization in assessment and management of the coronary bypass surgery patient. *Psychotherapy and Psychosomatics, 39,* 112–121.

Greenberg, P. E., Stiglin, L. E., Finkelstein, S. N., & Berndt, E. R. (1993). The economic burden of depression in 1990. *Journal of Clinical Psychiatry, 54,* 405–417.

Greer, S., Morris, T., Pettingale, K., & Haybittle, J. (1990). Psychological response to breast cancer and 15-year outcome. *Lancet, 1,* 49–50.

Harkness, A., & Lilienfeld, S. (1997). Individual differences science for treatment planning: Personality traits. *Psychological Assessment, 9,* 349–360.

Helgeson, V., & Cohen, S. (1996). Social support and adjustment to cancer: Reconciling descriptive, correlational, and intervention research. *Health Psychology, 15,* 135–148.

Helgeson, V. S., Cohen, S., & Fritz, H. L. (1998). Social ties and cancer. In J. Holland (Ed.), *Textbook of psycho-oncology* (pp. 99–109). New York: Oxford University Press.

Hellman, C. J. C., Budd, M., Borysenko, J., McClelland, D., & Benson, H. (1990). A study of the effectiveness of two group behavioral medicine interventions for patients with psychosomatic complaints. *Behavioral Medicine, 16,* 165–173.

Herbert, T., & Cohen, S. (1993a). Depression and immunity: A meta-analytic review. *Psychological Bulletin, 113,* 472–486.

Herbert, T., & Cohen, S. (1993b). Stress and immunity in humans: A meta-analytic review. *Psychosomatic Medicine, 55,* 364–379.

Herrmann, C., Brand-Driehorst, S., Kaminsky, B., Leibing, E., Staats, H., & Ruger, H. (1998). Diagnostic groups and depressed mood as predictors of 22-month mortality in medical inpatients. *Psychosomatic Medicine, 60,* 570–577.

Holahan, C. J., & Moos, R. H. (1986). Personality, coping, and family resources in stress resistance: A longitudinal analysis. *Journal of Personality and Social Psychology, 51,* 389–395.

Holland, J. C. (1997). Preliminary guidelines for the treatment of distress. *Oncology, 11,* 109–117.

House, J. S., Landis, K. R., & Umberson, D. (1988). Social relationships and health. *Science, 241,* 540–545.

Hughes, J. E., & Lee, D. (1987). Depression symptoms in patients with terminal cancer. In M. Watson & S. Greer (Eds.), *Psychosocial issues in malignant disease.* Oxford, England: Pergamon Press.

Ironson, G., Antoni, M., & Lutgendorf, S. (1995). Can psychological interventions affect immunity and survival? Present findings and suggested targets with a focus on cancer and human immunodeficiency virus. *Mind/Body Medicine, 1*(2), 85–110.

Ironson, G., Friedman, A., Klimas, N., Antoni, M. H., Fletcher, M. A., LaPerriere, A., et al. (1994). Distress, denial and low adherence to behavioral intervention predict faster disease progression in gay men infected with human immunodeficiency virus. *International Journal of Behavioral Medicine, 1,* 90–105.

Ironson, G., Solomon, G., Cruess, D., Barroso, J., & Stivers, M. (1995). Psychosocial factors related to long-term survival with HIV/AIDS. *Clinical Psychology and Psychotherapy, 2,* 249–266.

Ironson, G., Wynings, C., Schneiderman, N., Baum, A., Rodriquez, M., Greenwood, D., et al. (1997). Post traumatic stress symptoms, intrusive thoughts, loss and immune function after Hurricane Andrew. *Psychosomatic Medicine, 59,* 128–141.

Jacobs, D. (1987). Cost-effectiveness of specialized psychological programs for reducing hospital stays and outpatient visits. *Journal of Clinical Psychology, 43,* 729–735.

Jacobs, D., Kopans, B., & Reizes, J. M. (1995). Reevaluation of depression: What the general practitioner needs to know. *Mind/Body Medicine, 1,* 17–22.

Jarvis, G., & Northcott, H. (1987). Religion and differences in morbidity and mortality. *Social Science and Medicine, 25,* 813–824.

Jensen, M. (1987). Psychobiological factors predicting the course of breast cancer. *Journal of Personality, 55,* 317–342.

Kamarck, T., & Jennings, J. (1991). Biobehavioral factors in sudden cardiac death. *Psychological Bulletin, 109,* 42–75.

Katon, W., VonKorff, M., Lipscomb, P., Wagner, E., & Polk, E. (1990). Distressed high utilizers of medical care: *DSM-III-R* diagnoses and treatment needs. *General Hospital Psychiatry, 12,* 355–362.

Katz, C., Martin, R., Landa, B., & Chadda, K. (1985). Relationship of psychologic factors to frequent symptomatic verntricular arrhythmia. *American Journal of Medicine, 78,* 589–594.

Keefe, F., Dunsmore, J., & Burnett, R. (1992). Behavioral and cognitive-behavioral approaches to chronic pain: Recent advances and future directions. *Journal of Consulting and Clinical Psychology, 60,* 528–536.

Kiecolt-Glaser, J., Marucha, P., Malarkey, W., Mercado, A., & Glaser, R. (1995). Slowing of wound healing by psychological stress. *Lancet, 346,* 1194–1196.

Kimmerling, R., Ouimette, P., Cronkite, R., & Moos, R. (1999). Depression and outpatient medical utilization: A naturalistic 10-year follow-up. *Annals of Behavioral Medicine, 21,* 317–321.

King, J., Beals, J., Manson, S., & Trimble, J. (1992). A structural equation model of factors related to substance use among American Indian adolescents. *Drugs and Society, 6*(3/4), 253–268.

Klerman, G., & Weissman, M. (1992). The course, morbidity, and costs of depression. *Archives of General Psychiatry, 49,* 831–834.

Koenig, H., Pargament, K., & Nielsen, J. (1998). Religious coping and health status in medically ill hospitalized older adults. *Journal of Nervous and Mental Diseases, 186,* 513–521.

Kolitz, S., Antoni, M. H., & Green, C. (1988). Personality style and immediate help-seeking responses following the onset of myocardial infarction. *Psychology and Health, 2,* 259–289.

Labbe, E., Goldberg, M., Fishbain, D., & Rosomoff, H. (1989). Millon Behavioral Health Inventory norms for chronic pain patients. *Journal of Clinical Psychology, 45,* 383–390.

Lantinga, L., Sprafkin, R., McCroske, J., Baker, M., Warner, R., & Hill, N. (1988). One-year psychosocial follow-up of patients with chest pain and angiographically normal coronary arteries. *American Journal of Cardiology, 62,* 209–213.

Lawrence, R. C., Hochberg, M. C., Kelsey, J. L., McDuffie, F. C., Medsger, T.-A., Felts, W. R., et al. (1989). Estimates of the prevalence of selected arthritis and musculo-skeleto diseases in the U.S. *Journal of Rheumatology, 16,* 427–441.

Lerman, C. (1997). Translational behavioral research in cancer genetics. *Preventive Medicine, 26,* S65–S69.

Lerman, C., Caporaso, N., Audrain, J., Main, D., Bowman, E., Lockshin, B., et al. (1999). Evidence suggesting the role of specific genetic factors in cigarette smoking. *Health Psychology, 18,* 14–20.

Lerman, C., Caporaso, N., Main, D., Audrain, J., Boyd, N. R., Bowman, E. D., et al. (1998). Depression and self-medication with nicotine: The modifying influence of the dopamine D4 receptor gene. *Health Psychology, 17,* 56–62.

Lerman, C., Daly, M., Sands, C., Balshem, A., Lustbader, E., Heggan, T., et al. (1993). Mammography adherence and psychological distress among women at risk for breast cancer. *Journal of the National Cancer Institute, 85,* 1074–1080.

Lerman, C., Hughes, C., Lemon, S., Main, D., Snyder, C., Durham, C., et al. (1998). What you don't know can hurt you: Adverse psychologic effects in members of BRCA1-linked and BRCA2-linked families who decline genetic testing. *Journal of Clinical Oncology, 16,* 1650–1654.

Lerman, C., Hughes, C., Trock, B., Myers, R., Main, D., Bonney, A., et al. (1999). Genetic testing in families with hereditary nonpolyposis colon cancer. *Journal of the American Medical Association, 281,* 1618–1622.

Lerman, C., Narod, S., Schulman, K., Hughes, C., Gomez-Caminero, A., & Bonney, G. E. A. (1996). BRCA1 testing in families with hereditary breast-ovarian cancer: A prospective study of patient decision-making and outcomes. *Journal of the American Medical Association, 275,* 1885–1892.

Lerman, C., Rimer, B., & Glynn, T. (1997). Priorities in behavioral research in cancer prevention and control. *Preventive Medicine, 26,* S3–S9.

Leserman, J. (2003). The effects of stressful life events, coping and cortisol on HIV infection. *CNS Spectrums, 8,* 25–30.

Leserman, J., Jackson, E. D., Petitto, J. M., Golden, R. N., Silva, S. G., Perkins, D. O., et al. (1999). Progression to AIDS: The effects of stress, depressive symptoms, and social support. *Psychosomatic Medicine, 61,* 397–406.

Leserman, J., Perkins, D., & Evans, D. (1992). Coping with the threat of AIDS: The role of social support. *American Journal of Psychiatry, 149,* 1514–1520.

Levenson, J. (1992). Psychosocial interventions in chronic medical illness: An overview of outcome research. *General Hospitals in Psychiatry, 14S,* 43S–49S.

Levenson, J., Hamer, R., & Rossiter, L. (1990). Relation of psychopathology in general medical inpatients to use and cost of services. *American Journal of Psychiatry, 147,* 1498–1503.

Levin, J. (1994). Religion and health: Is there an association, is it valid, and is it causal? *Social Science and Medicine, 38*(11), 9–36.

Levin, J., & Vanderpool, H. (1989). Is religion therapeutically significant for hypertension? *Social Science and Medicine, 29,* 69–78.

Levy, S., Herberman, R., Lippman, M., D'Angelo, T., & Lee, J. (1991). Immunological and psychosocial predictors of disease recurrence in patients with early-stage breast cancer. *Behavioral Medicine, 17,* 67–75.

Lovallo, W., d'Absi, M., Pincomb, G., Everson, S., Sung, B., Passey, R., & Wilson, M. (1996). Caffeine and behavioral stress effects on blood pressure in borderline hypertensive Caucasian men. *Health Psychology, 15,* 11–17.

Lustman, P., Clouse, R., Griffith, L., Camey, R., & Freedland, K. (1997). Screening for depression in diabetes using the Beck Depression Inventory. *Psychosomatic Medicine, 59,* 24–31.

Lustman, P. J., Griffith, L. S., & Clouse, R. E. (1988). Depression in adults with diabetes: Results of a 5-year follow-up study. *Diabetes Care, 11,* 605–612.

Lutgendorf, S., Antoni, M. H., Ironson, G., Fletcher, M., Penedo, F., Baum, A., et al. (1995). Physical symptoms of chronic fatigue syndrome are exacerbated by the stress of Hurricane Andrew. *Psychosomatic Medicine, 57,* 310–323.

Lutgendorf, S., Antoni, M. H., Ironson, G., Starr, K., Costello, N., Zuckerman, M., et al. (1998). Changes in cognitive coping skills and social support mediate distress outcomes in symptomatic HIV-seropositive gay men during a cognitive behavioral stress management intervention. *Psychosomatic Medicine, 60,* 204–214.

Magni, G., Silvestro, A., Tamiello, M., Zanesco, L., & Carl, M. (1988). An integrated approach to the assessment of family adjustment to acute lymphocytic leukemia in children. *Acta Psychiatric Scandinavia, 78,* 639–642.

Marlatt, G. (1985). Coping and substance abuse: Implications for research, prevention, and treatment. In T. Wills & S. Shiffman (Eds.), *Coping and substance abuse.* Orlando, FL: Academic Press.

Marteau, T. M., Bloch, S., & Baum, J. D. (1987). Family life and diabetic control. *Journal of Child Psychology and Psychiatry, 28,* 823–833.

McCann, B., Bovbjerg, V., Brief, D., Turner, C., Follete, W., Fitzpatrick, V., et al. (1995). Relationship of self-efficacy to cholesterol lowering and dietary change in hyperlipidemia. *Annals of Behavioral Medicine, 17,* 221–226.

McCracken, L. (1991). Cognitive-behavioral treatment of rheumatoid arthritis: A preliminary review of efficacy and methodology. *Annals of Behavioral Medicine, 13,* 57–65.

McEwen, B. (1998). Protective and damaging effects of stress mediators. *New England Journal of Medicine, 338,* 171–179.

McGregor, B., Antoni, M. H., Boyers, A., Alferi, S., Cruess, D., Blomberg, B., et al. (2004). Effects of cognitive behavioral stress management on immune function and positive contributions in women with early-stage breast cancer. *Journal of Psychosomatic Research, 54,* 1–8.

McKenna, M. C., Zevon, M. A., Corn, B., & Rounds, J. (1999). Psychosocial factors and the development of breast cancer: A meta-analysis. *Health Psychology, 18,* 520–531.

Miller, L. V., & Goldstein, J. (1972). More efficient care of diabetes in a county hospital setting. *New England Journal of Medicine, 286,* 1388–1391.

Millon, T., Antoni, M. H., Millon, C., Meagher, S., & Grossman, S. (2001). *Test manual for the Millon Behavioral Medicine Diagnostic (MBMD).* Minneapolis, MN: National Computer Services.

Millon, T., & Davis, R. D. (1995). *Disorders of personality: DSM-IV and beyond* (2nd ed.). New York: Guilford Press.

Millon, T., Green, C., & Meagher, R. (1982). *The Millon Behavioral Health Inventory manual.* Minneapolis, MN: National Computer Services.

Miranda, J., Perez-Stable, E., Munoz, R., Hargreaves, W., & Henke, C. (1991). Somatization, psychiatric disorder, and stress in utilization of ambulatory medical services. *Health Psychology, 10,* 46–51.

Morrissey, E., & Schuckitt, M. (1978). Stressful life events and alcohol problems among women seen at a detoxification center. *Journal of Studies on Alcohol, 39,* 1559.

Muhlhauser, I., Jorgens, V., Berger, M., Graninger, W., Gurtler, W., et al. (1983). Bicentric evaluation of a teaching and treatment program for Type I (insulin-dependent) diabetic patients; improvement of metabolic control and other measures of diabetes care for up to 22 months. *Diabetologia, 25,* 470–476.

Mumford, E., Schlesinger, H. J., & Glass, G. V. (1982). The effects of psychological intervention on recovery from surgery and heart attacks: An analysis of the literature. *American Journal of Public Health, 72*(2), 141–151.

Mumford, E., Schlesinger, H. J., Glass, G. V., Patrick, C., & Cuerdon, T. (1984). A new look at evidence about reduced cost of medical utilization following mental health treatment. *American Journal of Psychiatry, 141*(10), 1145–1158.

Myers, M. G., Brown, S. A., & Mott, M. (1993). Coping as a predictor of substance abuse treatment outcome. *Journal of Substance Abuse, 5*(1), 15–29.

Narrow, W. E., Regier, D. A., & Rae, D. S. (1993). Use of services by persons with mental and addictive disorders: Findings from the National Institute of Mental Health Epidemiologic
Catchment Area Program. *Archives of General Psychiatry, 50,* 95–107.

National Institute on Drug Abuse. (1990). *Alcohol and health* (DHHS Publication No. ADM 87-
1519). Rockville, MD: Department of Health and Human Services.

Neale, A. V., Tilley, B. C., & Vernon, S. W. (1986). Marital status, delay in seeking treatment and
survival from breast cancer. *Social Science and Medicine, 23,* 305–312.

Newcomb, M., & Harlow, L. (1986). Life events and substance use among adolescents: Mediating
effects of perceived loss of control and meaninglessness in life. *Journal of Personality and
Social Psychology, 51,* 564.

Niemi, M. L., Laaksonen, R., Kotila, M., & Waltimo, O. (1988). Quality of life four years after
stroke. *Stroke, 19,* 1101–1107.

1992 HCFA Statistics. (1992). *U.S. Department of Health and Human Services, Health Care Fi-
nancing Administration, Bureau of Data Management and Strategy.* HCFA Pub No 03333
(pp. 212–216).

Oldenberg, B., Perkins, R., & Andrews, G. (1985). Controlled trial of psychological intervention
in myocardial infarction. *Journal of Consulting and Clinical Psychology, 53,* 852–859.

O'Leary, A. (1992). Self-efficacy and health: Behavioral and stress-physiological mediation. *Cognitive Therapy and Research, 16,* 229–245.

Ornish, D., Scherwitz, L. W., Billings, J. H., Gould, L., Merritt, T. A., & Sparler, S. (1998). Intensive lifestyle changes for reversal of coronary heart disease. *Journal of the American Medical Association, 280,* 2001–2007.

Oxman, T., Freeman, D., & Manheimer, E. (1995). Lack of social participation or religious
strength and comfort as risk factors for death after cardiac surgery in the elderly. *Psychosomatic Medicine, 57,* 5–15.

Pallak, M. S., Cummings, N. A., Dorken, H., & Henke, C. J. (1994). Medical costs, Medicaid, and
managed mental health treatment: The Hawaii study. *Management Care Questionnaire, 2,* 64–70.

Pennebaker, J. W., Kiecolt-Glaser, J. K., & Glaser, R. (1988). Disclosure of traumas and immune
function: Health implications for psychotherapy. *Journal of Consulting and Clinical Psychology, 56,* 239–245.

Pereira, D., Antoni, M. H., Simon, T., Efantis-Potter, J., Carver, C. S., Duran, R., et al. (2003).
Stress and squamous intraepithelial lesions in women with human papillomavirus and human
immunodeficiency virus. *Psychosomatic Medicine, 65,* 427–434.

Peterson, C., Seligman, M. E. P., & Vaillant, G. E. (1988). Pessimistic explanatory style is a risk
factor for physical illness: A thirty-five year longitudinal study. *Journal of Personality and
Social Psychology, 55,* 23–27.

Pettingale, K., Greer, S., & Tee, D. (1977). Serum IgA and emotional expression in breast cancer
patients. *Journal of Psychosomatic Research, 21,* 395–399.

Regier, D. (1994). Health care reform: Opportunities and challenge. In S. Blumenthal, K. Matthews,
& S. Weiss (Eds.), *New research frontiers in behavioral medicine* (Proceedings of the National
Conference; NIH Publication No. 94-3772, pp. 19–24). Washington, DC: U.S. Government
Printing Office.

Richter, J., Obrecht, W., Bradley, L., Young, L., & Anderson, K. (1986). Psychological comparison of patients with nutcracker esophagus and irritable bowel syndrome. *Digestive Disorder
Science, 31,* 131–138.

Richter, S., Brown, S., & Mott, M. (1991). The impact of social support and self-esteem on adolescent substance abuse treatment outcome. *Journal of Substance Abuse, 3*(4), 371–385.

Robertson, E. K., & Suinn, R. M. (1968). The determination of rate of progress of stroke patients
through empathy measures of patient and family. *Journal of Psychosomatic Research, 12,*
189–191.

Rock, C., McEligot, A., Flatt, S., Sobo, E., Wilfley, D., Jones, V., et al. (2000). Eating pathology and obesity in women at risk for breast cancer recurrence. *International Journal of Eating Disorders, 27,* 172–179.

Rosenstock, I. M. (1974). The health belief model and preventive health behavior. *Health Education Monographs, 2,* 354–386.

Roth, A. J., Kornblith, A. B., Batel-Copel, L., Peabody, E., Peabody, E., Scher, H. I., et al. (1998). Rapid screening for psychologic distress in men with prostate carcinoma: A pilot study. *Cancer, 82,* 1904–1908.

Scheier, M., & Carver, C. S. (1985). Optimism, coping, and health: Assessment and implication of generalized outcome expectancies. *Health Psychology, 4,* 219–247.

Scheier, M., Matthews, K., Owens, J., Schultz, R., Bridges, M., Magovern, G., et al. (1999). Optimism and rehospitalization after coronary artery bypass graft surgery. *Archives of Internal Medicine, 159,* 829–835.

Schlesinger, H. J., Mumford, E., Glass, G. V., Patrick, C., & Sharfstein, S. (1983). Mental health treatment and medical care utilization in a fee-for-service system: Outpatient mental health treatment following the onset of a chronic disease. *American Journal of Public Health, 73*(4), 422–429.

Schneider, C. J. (1987). Cost-effectiveness of biofeedback and behavioral medicine treatments: A review of the literature. *Biofeedback and Self-Regulation, 12*(2), 71–92.

Schneiderman, N., Antoni, M. H., Saab, P., & Ironson, G. (2001). Health psychology: Behavioral management of chronic disease. *Annual Reviews in Psychology, 52,* 555–580.

Schwartz, L. S., Springer, J., Flaherty, J. A., & Kiani, R. (1986). The role of recent life events and social support in the control of diabetes mellitus. *General Hospital Psychiatry, 8,* 212–216.

Siegal, B. R., Calsyn, R. J., & Cuddihee, R. M. (1987). The relationship of social support to psychological adjustment in end-stage renal disease patients. *Journal of Chronic Disease, 40,* 337–344.

Simon, G., & Katzelnick, D. (1997). Depression, use of medical service and cost-offset effects. *Journal of Psychosomatic Research, 42,* 333–344.

Simon, G., & VonKorff, M. (1995). Recognition, management, and outcomes of depression in primary care. *Archives of Family Medicine, 4,* 99–105.

Smith, C., & Wallston, K. (1992). Adaptation in patients with chronic rheumatoid arthritis: Application of a general model. *Health Psychology, 11,* 151–162.

Smyth, J., Stone, A., Hurewitz, A., & Kaell, A. (1999). Effects of writing about stressful experiences on symptom reduction in patients with asthma or rheumatoid arthritis: A randomized trial. *Journal of the American Medical Association, 281,* 1304–1309.

Sobel, D. (1995). Mind matters, money matters: The cost-effectiveness of clinical behavioral medicine. In S. Blumenthal, K. Matthews, & S. Weiss (Eds.), *New research frontiers in behavioral medicine* (Proceedings of a National Conference). Washington, DC: U.S. Government Printing Office.

Solano, L., Costa, M., Salvati, S., Coda, R., Aiuta, F., Mezzaroma, I., et al. (1993). Psychosocial factors and clinical evolution in HIV-1 infection: A longitudinal study. *Journal of Psychosomatic Research, 37*(1), 39–51.

Spiegel, D., Kraemer, H. C., Bloom, J. R., & Gottheil, E. (1989). Effect of psychosocial treatment on survival of patients with metastatic breast cancer. *Lancet, 2,* 888–891.

Stein, M. J., Wallston, K. A., Nicassio, P. M., & Castner, N. M. (1988). Correlates of a clinical classification schema for the arthritis helplessness subscale. *Arthritis and Rheumatism, 31,* 876–881.

Stern, M. J., Pascale, L., & Ackerman, A. (1977). Life adjustment postmyocardial infarction: Determining predictive variables. *Archives of Internal Medicine, 137,* 1680–1685.

Stone, A., & Porter, L. (1995). Psychological coping: Its importance for treating medical problems. *Mind/Body Medicine, 1,* 46–54.

Strain, J., Lyons, J., Hammer, J., Fahs, M., Lebovitz, A., Paddison, P., et al. (1991). Cost offset from a psychiatric consultation-liaison intervention with elderly hip fracture patients. *American Journal of Psychiatry, 148*(8), 1044–1049.

Surwit, R. S., & Feinglos, M. N. (1988). Stress and autonomic nervous system in Type II diabetes: A hypothesis. *Diabetes Care, 11,* 83–85.

Taylor, S. E., & Aspinwall, L. G. (1990). Psychosocial aspects of chronic illness. In P. Costa & G. van den Bos (Eds.), *Psychological aspects of serious illness: Chronic conditions, fatal diseases, and clinical care* (pp. 3–60). Washington, DC: American Psychological Association.

Taylor, S. E., & Brown, J. (1988). Illusion and well-being: A social psychological perspective on mental health. *Psychological Bulletin, 103,* 193–210.

Taylor, S. E., Lichtman, R. R., & Wood, J. V. (1984). Attributions, beliefs about control, and adjustment to breast cancer. *Journal of Personality and Social Psychology, 46,* 489–502.

Theorell, T., Blomkvist, V., Jonsson, H., Schulman, S., Berntorp, E., & Stigendal, L. (1995). Social support and the development of immune function in human immunodeficiency virus infection. *Psychosomatic Medicine, 57,* 32–36.

Thoits, P. A. (1987). Gender and marital status differences in control and distress: Common stress versus unique stress explanations. *Journal of Health and Social Behavior, 28,* 7–22.

Thomas, E., & Weiss, S. (2000). Nonpharmacological interventions with chronic cancer pain in adults. *Cancer Control, 7,* 157–164.

Thompson, S. C., Sobolew-Shubin, A., Graham, M. A., & Janigian, A. S. (1989). Psychosocial adjustment following a stroke. *Social Science and Medicine, 28,* 239–247.

Tracy, H., Green, C., & McCleary, J. (1987). Noncompliance in hemodialysis patients as measured by the MBHI. *Psychology and Health, 2,* 411–412.

Trijsburg, R. W., van Knippenberg, F. C. E., & Rijma, S. E. (1992). Effects of psychological treatment on cancer patients: A critical review. *Psychosomatic Medicine, 54,* 489–517.

Turk, D., & Meichenbaum, D. (1989). Adherence to self-care regimens: The patient's perspective. In R. H. Rozensky, J. Sweet, & S. Tovian (Eds.), *Handbook of clinical psychology in medical settings.* New York: Plenum Press.

Vaillant, G. E., Schnurr, P. P., Baron, J. R., & Gerber, P. D. (1991). A prospective study of the effect of smoking and alcohol abuse on mortality. *Journal of General Internal Medicine, 6,* 299–304.

van der Pompe, G., Antoni, M. H., & Heijnen, C. (1998). The effects of surgical stress and psychological stress on the immune function of operative cancer patients. *Psychology and Health, 13,* 1015–1026.

van der Pompe, G., Antoni, M. H., Mulder, N., Heijnen, C., Goodkin, K., de Graeff, A., et al. (1994). Psychoneuroimmunology and the course of breast cancer, an overview: The impact of psychosocial factors on progression of breast cancer through immune and endocrine mechanisms. *Psycho-Oncology, 3,* 271–288.

Vickery, D. M. (1983). Effect of a self-care education program on medical visits. *Journal of the American Medical Association, 250*(21), 2952–2956.

VonKorff, M., Katon, W., Bush, T., Lin, E., Simon, G., Saunders, K., et al. (1998). Treatment costs, cost offset, and cost-effectiveness of collaborative management for depression. *Psychosomatic Medicine, 60,* 143–149.

Wallston, B. S., Alagna, S. W., DeVellis, B., & DeVellis, R. F. (1983). Social support and physical health. *Health Psychology, 2,* 367–391.

Wiedenfield, S., O'Leary, A., Bandura, A., Brown, S., Levine, S., & Raska, K. (1990). Impact of perceived self-efficacy in coping with stressors on components of the immune system. *Journal of Personality and Social Psychology, 59,* 1082–1094.

Wiklund, I., Oden, A., Sanne, H., Ulvenstam, G., Wilhelmsson, C., & Wilhemsen, L. (1988). Prognostic importance of somatic and psychosocial variables after a first myocardial infarction. *American Journal Epidemiology, 128,* 786–795.

Wilcoxin, M., Zook, A., & Zarski, J. (1988). Predicting behavioral outcomes with two psychological assessment methods in an outpatient pain management program. *Psychology and Health, 2,* 319–333.

Williams, R. B., & Chesney, M. (1993). Psychosocial factors and prognosis in established coronary artery disease: The need for research on interventions (Editorial). *Journal of the American Medical Association, 279,* 1860–1861.

Wilson, S., Scamagas, P., German, D., Hughes, G., Lulla, S., Coss, S., et al. (1993). A controlled trial of two forms of self-management education for adults with asthma. *American Journal of Medicine, 94,* 564–576.

Wilson, W., Ary, D. V., Biglan, A., Glasgow, R. E., Toobert, D. J., & Campbell, D. R. (1986). Psychosocial predictors of self-care behaviors (compliance) and glycemic control in non-insulin-dependent diabetes mellitus. *Diabetes Care, 9,* 614–622.

Woods, T., Antoni, M. H., Ironson, G., & Kling, D. (1999a). Religiosity is associated with affective and immune status in symptomatic HIV-infected gay men. *Journal of Psychosomatic Research, 46,* 165–176.

Woods, T., Antoni, M. H., Ironson, G., & Kling, D. (1999b). Religiosity is associated with affective status in symptomatic HIV-infected African American women. *Journal of Health Psychology, 4,* 317–326.

Woolf, S. (1999). The need for perspective in evidence-based medicine. *Journal of the American Medical Association, 282,* 2358–2365.

Young, L. (1992). Psychological factors in rheumatoid arthritis. *Journal of Consulting and Clinical Psychology, 60,* 619–627.

Zich, J., & Temoshok, L. (1987). Perceptions of social support in men with AIDS and ARC: Relationships with distress and hardiness. *Journal of Applied Social Psychology, 17,* 193–215.

Zook, C. J., & Moore, F. D. (1980). High cost users of medical care. *New England Journal of Medicine, 302,* 996–1002.

Zuckerman, M., & Antoni, M. H. (1995). Social support and its relationship to psychological physical and immune variables in HIV infection. *Clinical Psychology and Psychotherapy, 2*(4), 210–219.

Chapter 19 ——————————————————————————

PERSONALITY-BASED ASSESSMENT OF POSTTRAUMATIC STRESS DISORDER

GEORGE S. EVERLY JR.

Treatment, it may be argued, should be the natural corollary of assessment, and assessment should be the natural corollary of phenomenology. Thus, it would seem that the most valuable assessment formulations would focus not only on florid symptomatic presentations but also on more core undergirding phenomenological substrates. By focusing on core foundational substrates, the key to the most efficient and effective treatments may reside in targeting the cause of the condition, rather than targeting only its symptoms. In this chapter, the assessment of posttraumatic stress disorder (PTSD) is examined. This examination, however, is not a review of the plethora of symptom-based diagnostic tools that are keyed to the *Diagnostic and Statistical Manual of Mental Disorders,* fourth edition (*DSM-IV*). Such tools are highly correlated to the specific *DSM-IV* diagnostic criteria for PTSD residing within diagnostic Clusters B, C, and D, that is, reexperiencing, withdrawal/numbing, and arousal, respectively. Rather, this examination focuses on that which may be more clinically relevant, albeit speculative, to treatment formulation and, therefore, diagnostic formulation, that is, the effects of the traumatic stressor on the foundational personologic structure.

NATURE OF POSTTRAUMATIC STRESS DISORDER

Posttraumatic stress disorder was first recognized as an official psychiatric diagnosis in 1980 with the creation of the third edition of the *Diagnostic and Statistical Manual of Mental Disorders (DSM-III)*. As it was when first categorized, PTSD is defined by the current nosological compendium of psychiatric disorders, the *DSM-IV,* as an anxiety disorder:

> The essential feature of Posttraumatic Stress Disorder is the development of characteristic symptoms following exposure to an extreme traumatic stressor involving direct personal experience of an event that involves actual or threatened death or serious injury, or other threat to one's physical integrity; or witnessing an event that involves death, serious injury, or a threat to the physical integrity of another person; or learning about unexpected

or violent death, serious harm, or threat of death or injury experienced by a family member or other close associate. . . . (American Psychiatric Association, 1994, p. 424)

There exist three key clusters of diagnostic criteria: Cluster B consists of ways in which the traumatic event may be "persistently reexperienced." Cluster C consists of persistent avoidance of people, places, and/or things associated with the trauma and a numbing of general responsiveness. Cluster D consists of persistent symptoms of excessive arousal, for example, exaggerated startle response. These manifest symptoms must be present more than one month and must cause clinically significant distress or impairment.

Everly (1989, 1993a, 1994) has proposed that PTSD is best understood phenomenologically as a manifestation of two inextricably intertwined, interacting factors:

1. Potentially self-sustaining limbicogenic autonomic nervous system hypersensitivity; and
2. A catastrophic insult to core personologic substrates, that is, a contradiction to some deeply held cognitive schema, assumption about the world (more about this notion later).

PREVALENCE OF POSTTRAUMATIC STRESS DISORDER

Although it is to be expected that virtually all those exposed to a traumatic event will develop some form of acute posttraumatic distress or dysphoria, the prevalence with which such dysphoria reaches the amplitude of a psychiatric "disorder" wherein it interferes with social or occupational functioning is another issue. Consider the following:

1. The lifetime prevalence experienced by adults for exposure to one or more traumatic events (as defined by the *DSM-IV*) has been estimated to be more than 89% in an urban community area investigation (Breslau et al., 1998).
2. "Overall, among those exposed to extreme trauma, about 9 percent ultimately develop post-traumatic stress disorder" (U.S. DHHS, 1999, p. 237), but this statistic may be misleading.
3. Given the especially severe forms of traumatic stressors, the risk of developing PTSD was found to be about 34% (current prevalence) in response to mass disasters (North et al., 1999), about 49% in response to rape, and about 53% (lifetime prevalence) in response to captivity, kidnapping, or torture (Breslau et al., 1998).
4. When considering the risk of developing PTSD within "high risk" occupational groups, the prevalence of posttraumatic stress disorder ranged from 15% to 31% for samples of urban firefighters based on a traumatic exposure prevalence ranging from 85% to 91% (Beaton, Murphy, & Corneil, 1996). The current prevalence of PTSD was psychometrically estimated to be about 18% in a random sample of Kuwaiti firefighters (Al-Naser & Everly, 1999). Finally, the current point prevalence of PTSD was psychometrically estimated to be about 13% in a sample of suburban police officers (Robinson, Sigman, & Wilson, 1997).
5. The current point prevalence of PTSD among Vietnam veterans was estimated to be about 15%, while the lifetime prevalence was estimated to be about 30% (Kulka et al., 1988).

PSYCHOLOGICAL TRAUMA: THE DEFINING MOMENT

We return to a notion posited earlier: The process of traumatization is predicated on a violation or contradiction to a deeply held belief. If exposure to a traumatic stressor alone was the necessary and sufficient condition for the development of PTSD, the conditional risk would be 100%. Data summarized earlier, however, suggest that the risk of developing PTSD subsequent to exposure to some traumatic condition is far less than 100%, and on average may be around 9%. The implications for assessment are significant. Should we focus on the signs and symptoms of posttraumatic distress alone? How would such a focus assist the clinician in formulating a treatment plan? Or, should we also attempt to understand the mechanism by which exposure to a traumatic stressor causes a subsequent conversion to the development of posttraumatic stress disorder? Is it important in diagnostic and treatment formulations to understand not only underlying mechanisms of pathogenesis but also the signs and symptoms they engender?

The greatest endocrinologist of his time, as well as the father of the "stress" concept, Hans Selye, once noted, "It is not what happens to you that matters, but how you take it." Perhaps the most acclaimed pioneer in the field of psychosomatic medicine, Stuart Wolf, said, "It is evident from the idiosyncratic nature of interpreting experience that to understand the impact of an event, the focus of inquiry must be the individual." The philosopher Epictetus once wrote that man is disturbed, not by things, but by the views that he takes of them. Even Shakespeare once wrote, "For there are no things good nor bad, but thinking makes them so." Finally, it was once suggested that stressors, like beauty, lie in the eye of the beholder. While clearly avoiding a "blame the victim" scenario, one point does emerge that is worthy of consideration, that is, the role of interpretational mechanisms. Much of the difference between an event that results in acute distress and an event that results in chronic PTSD appears to lie in the subjective severity of the event, that is, how the two events are differentially interpreted by the individuals who experience them (there are notable exceptions to the principle, e.g., torture, death, or serious injury of a child, especially your own).

Consistent with the *DSM-IV*, a pivotal element of such a model of human stress is the subjective interpretation of real, imagined, or anticipated stressor events. Everly (1989) proposed that the amplitude and chronicity of the human stress response is largely dictated by the nature of the subjective interpretational process in the wake of exposure to a traumatic, or otherwise distressing, event. Later, Smith, Everly, and Johns (1993), using mathematical modeling procedures, tested the plausibility of such a model. In a large-scale investigation of the stressor-to-disease process in a sample of more than 1,500 subjects, it was discovered that the subjective interpretation of work-related stressors played a more significant role in the development of stress-related disease than did exposure to the actual work-related stressor itself.

Later, Everly (1993b, 1994) constructed a model of the posttraumatic stress process wherein subjective interpretation played a key deterministic role in posttraumatic phenomenology. Everly proposed that subjective interpretation of the traumatic event was the defining moment of psychotraumatogenesis. This model is portrayed in Figure 19.1.

Figure 19.1 shows that subsequent to actual exposure to the stressor event, interpretational mechanisms come into play. It is posited that this process of subjective interpretation explains a significant amount of pathogenic variance. Furthermore, withdrawal, numbing, and depressive-like symptoms may be viewed as second-order symptoms emerging more as a result of the intrusive traumatic ideation and autonomic hypersensitivity, rather than the stressor in and of itself.

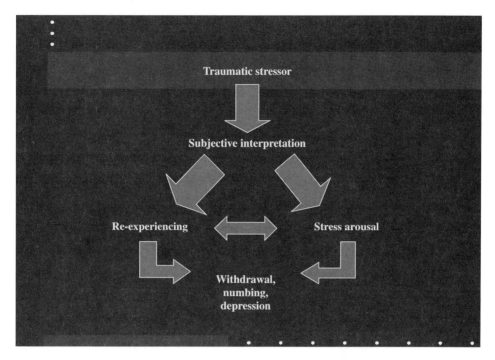

Figure 19.1   A Process Model of Posttraumatic Stress

Consistent with this formulation, in 1994, the *DSM-IV* dramatically altered its definition of a traumatic event and seemed to acknowledge the role of subjective interpretation in psychotraumatogenesis. The *DSM-IV* stated that to be considered a traumatic event, the event must engender "fear, helplessness, or horror" (American Psychiatric Association, 1994, p. 428). Clearly, fear, helplessness, and horror are all subjective states resulting from appraisal or interpretation.

It seems reasonable to assume that everything we consciously perceive undergoes a process of psychological filtering. Conceptually, an event that becomes a trauma is an event that breaches an individual's protective psychological filtering mechanisms. Many authors (Girdano, Everly, & Dusek, 2001; Rahe, 1974) concede that these psychological filters typically consist of factors such as personality traits, culture, prior related experiences, self-concept, and, certainly, an individual's coping mechanisms and resources. But some recent writers point to a far more specific factor when asking what makes a traumatic event traumatic. The factor is that of the person's extremely important and characterologically anchored schemas, or worldviews. From this perspective, a traumatic event is one that violates or destroys a very important and deeply held belief about yourself or your world (Everly, 1993b, 1994; Frank & Frank, 1991). In doing so, the traumatic event can be seen to threaten the structural integrity of the core foundations of personality. This notion has been recognized by the World Health Organization (WHO; 1992), which, in its *International Classification of Disease*-10, noted that traumatic experiences may lead to a fundamental alteration in personality. Under the category of "Enduring Personality Change after Catastrophic Experience" (F62.0), WHO recognizes the notion that personality can be lastingly altered by trauma.

In the final analysis, it may be argued that PTSD represents a phenomenological insult or injury to the structure and function of the essence of an individual's being, that is, the personality construction. PTSD represents a contradiction to some deeply held and imperative belief about self and/or the world in general. This contradiction causes chaotic upheaval within the core elements of personality, setting into motion a series of pathognomonic indicia and compensatory reactions.

THE ASSUMPTIVE BELIEFS AND EXPLANATORY WORLDVIEWS

In their critical work on psychotherapy, Frank and Frank (1991) further clarified the notion of characterologically anchored belief systems:

> Leading a successful life, even surviving, depends on the ability to predict future events from present ones, or at least the belief that one can do so. . . . Since prediction is based on understanding, the need to make sense of events is as fundamental as the need for food or water. (p. 24)

They went on to discuss what may be the most salient point within this context:

> To deal with the world and enjoy life, a person's assumptive world must correspond more or less closely to conditions as they actually are. . . . Thus, everyone is strongly motivated to monitor the validity of his or her assumptions. . . . If an act fails to produce predicted consequences, the person is in trouble. (p. 26)

Experiences that challenge, threaten, or invalidate core assumptions or general beliefs about the world serve as the potential foundations for dysphoria and/or maladaptive coping patterns. Traumatic events serve to challenge, threaten, or invalidate core characterologically based assumptions, hence their pathogenic nature.

Continuing this theme of pivotal assumptions, Everly (1993a, 1993b, 1994) noted that human beings require and, therefore, create, explanatory worldviews concerning themselves and their respective environments. Everly (1993, 1994, 1995), borrowing from the field of rhetoric, has referred to these deeply held belief systems as "Weltanschauung" (from the German *welt,* meaning "world" and *anschauung,* meaning "perspective"). These beliefs serve as important assumptive models, or explanatory worldviews, that bring order to what may be an otherwise chaotic environment. These worldviews, or Weltanschauung, as described by Everly (1995), serve not only as explanatory constructs with anxiolytic properties, but at the same time, potential diatheses, or psychological vulnerabilities, if threatened or destroyed.

Based on a review of relevant literature, there appear to be at least five core psychological themes that have relevance in understanding psychological trauma:

1. The need for attachment to, and trust in, others.
2. The need for a positive self-identity, view of self, that is, self-esteem, self-efficacy.
3. The belief in a fair and just world.
4. The need for physical safety.
5. The belief in some overarching order to life, for example, spirituality, or faith in a defining order, unifying paradigm, and so on.

Using these worldviews as our foundation, we see that events that threaten, violate, or destroy one or more of these worldviews serve as the psychological basis for the creation of a traumatic event. More specifically, using the basic beliefs just enumerated, psychological trauma emerges in the wake of their violation as described here:

1. The need for attachment and affiliation when violated yields the perception of abandonment, treachery, betrayal, especially if perpetrated by a trusted person, organization, or institution.
2. The need for a positive view of self when violated yields a self-deprecation and a sense of being unworthy of the good things in life. Guilt, for example, is a common psychotraumatogenic theme based on doing something you should not have done or not doing something you should have done, which ultimately resulted in a significant problem, injury, loss, catastrophe, and so on; there may even be guilt associated with survival, that is, "survivor guilt."
3. The need to believe in a fair and just world when violated gives rise to frustration, cynicism, and the belief that the end justifies the means (violence may be a common behavioral reaction). For example, a significant injustice (death or injury of a child), a criminal escaping justice, bad things happening to good people, and evil conquering over good all represent potential traumatic events.
4. The violation of the need for the physical safety of self or others (especially if involving children, loved ones, and/or people with whom there is a personal identification) gives rise to a chronic on-edge feeling, a sense of impending doom, and/or a pervasive pessimism; this condition is made worse if the threats are unpredictable.
5. The belief in some overarching order in life when violated gives rise to a disruption to the most deeply held assumptions about life and, perhaps, death. For example, some chaotic, unpredictable adversity without some explanation, rationale, meaning, or overarching explanatory schema may result in a crisis of faith or religion or an existential crisis.

Consistent with the notions of cognitive schemas and belief systems exerting important effects on behavior, Eidelson and Eidelson (2003) posited five core belief domains that may contribute to individual and group dysfunction:

1. *Superiority:* the enduring conviction that the individual is better than other people.
2. *Injustice:* the belief that the individual is the recipient of unjust and malevolent treatment.
3. *Vulnerability:* the belief that the individual is perpetually living "in harm's way" and lacking the ability to create a sense of safety.
4. *Distrust:* the belief that there exists individuals or groups that possess "malign intent."
5. *Helplessness:* the conviction that the individual is indeed helpless and, therefore, powerless to protect himself or herself.

Similar themes such as the violation of the need for safety, the violation of trust, a threat to self-esteem, the disruption of the need for intimacy, and the need for control have been postulated as themes that may undergird the process of vicarious traumatization, especially among helping professionals (McCann & Pearlman, 1990; Rosenbloom, Pratt, & Pearlman, 1995).

Why are these personal beliefs so critical to the maintenance of psychological well-being? And, why, if violated, do they create such havoc within an individual's psyche?

The answer appears to be twofold: First, as noted earlier, these personal beliefs serve to reduce anxiety and uncertainty in a world where much must be taken for granted. Second, these worldviews serve as substitutes for actual physical and psychological protection mechanisms, thus their extreme importance ontogenetically. This notion is consistent with the existence of a biological mandate to make sense of the world.

IMPLICATIONS FOR ASSESSMENT

Without understanding how the person views any given traumatic event (i.e., the meaning attached to the traumatic event), we cannot fully understand the nature of the trauma, the phenomenological course of the posttraumatic reaction, nor can we begin to formulate the best therapeutic intervention for that individual. In the final analysis, the defining moment of the traumatic event resides in the meaning. If the goal of assessment is not only to inventory signs and symptoms of distress and dysfunction but also to assist in the formulation of treatment options and facilitate the recovery or reconstruction process, we must seek to understand the nature of the traumatic experience far beyond that which is revealed by cataloging the person's reactions to trauma. This uncovering process can be achieved only by focusing on the "meaning" of the traumatic experience. Such a process necessarily involves delving into the core schemas of the pretrauma personality and a quest to understand how these core schemas, or assumptions, have been altered by the traumatic experience.

The use of objective personality tests such as the Millon Clinical Multiaxial Inventory can certainly be of assistance in such a quest. In using such tests, however, the psychologist must be careful not to misinterpret characterologic findings as premorbid traits without considering the possibility that any posttrauma psychometric assessment may be yielding data on the person's extant posttrauma character style. Interviews with friends and family members should always be conducted to ascertain some sense of the premorbid personality and determine how those findings compare with posttrauma psychometric data. For example, could it be that posttraumatic objective assessment findings of an aggressive personality (or even an antisocial personality) are more consistent with a "fighting back" posttraumatic compensatory style, rather than a pretraumatic personality disorder? Could it be that posttraumatic objective assessment findings of an avoidant personality are more consistent with a posttraumatic "flight" compensatory style, rather than a pretraumatic personality disorder? The implications are significant not only for diagnostic and treatment formulation purposes but also for litigation implications.

CONCLUSION

Dr. Henry Murray, one of the most noteworthy of personologists of the modern era, once admonished me to never lose sight of the fact that "there is nothing so powerful as the well-phrased question." The implication for the assessment of posttraumatic distress is clear . . . we must always inquire into the meaning of the traumatic event. Multimodal assessment strategies are certainly indicated. Projective tests, objective tests, and the well-structured interview are likely to yield more useful data than any one procedure alone.

In the final analysis, we must seek to discover what specific personality-based beliefs or assumptions were threatened or violated by the traumatic incident. Without understanding the meaning of the traumatic, we cannot understand how recovery can be best facilitated. This, then, is the challenge of the posttraumatic assessment process.

REFERENCES

Al-Naser, F., & Everly, G. S., Jr. (1999). Prevalence of posttraumatic stress disorder among Kuwaiti firefighters. *International Journal of Emergency Mental Health, 1,* 99–101.

American Psychiatric Association. (1994). *Diagnostic and statistical manual of mental disorders* (4th ed.). Washington, DC: Author.

Beaton, R., Murphy, S., & Corneil, W. (1996, September). *Prevalence of posttraumatic stress disorder symptomatology in professional urban fire fighters in two countries.* Paper presented to the International Congress of Occupational Health, Stockholm, Sweden.

Breslau, N., Kessler, R., Chilcoat, H., Schultz, L., Davis, G., & Andreski, P. (1998). Trauma and posttraumatic stress disorder in the community. *Archives of General Psychiatry, 55,* 626–633.

Eidelson, R. J., & Eidelson, J. (2003). Dangerous ideas: Five beliefs that propel groups toward conflict. *American Psychologist, 58,* 182–192.

Everly, G. S., Jr. (1989). *A clinical guide to the treatment of the human stress response.* New York: Plenum Press.

Everly, G. S., Jr. (1993a). Neurophysiological considerations in the treatment of PTSD: A neurocognitive perspective. In J. Wilson & B. Raphael (Eds.), *International handbook of traumatic stress syndromes* (pp. 795–801). New York: Plenum Press.

Everly, G. S., Jr. (1993b). Psychotraumatology: A two-factor formulation of posttraumatic stress. *Integrative Physiological and Behavioral Science, 28,* 270–278.

Everly, G. S., Jr. (1994). Brief psychotherapy for posttraumatic stress disorder: The role of Weltanschauung. *Stress Medicine, 10,* 191–196.

Everly, G. S., Jr. (1995). An integrative two-factor model of posttraumatic stress. In G. Everly, Jr. & J. Lating (Eds.), *Psychotraumatology: Key papers and core concepts in posttraumatic stress* (pp. 27–48). New York: Plenum Press.

Frank, J. D., & Frank, J. B. (1991). *Persuasion and healing* (3rd ed.). Baltimore: Johns Hopkins University Press.

Girdano, D., Everly, G. S., Jr., & Dusek, D. (2001). *Controlling stress and tension.* Boston: Allyn Bacon.

Kulka, R. A., Schlenger, W. E., Fairbank, J. A., Hough, R. L., Jordan, B. K., Marmar, C. R., et al. (1988). *The National Vietnam Veterans Readjustment Study (NVVRS): Description, current status, and initial PTSD prevalence estimates.* Washington, DC: Veteran's Administration.

McCann, L., & Pearlman, L. A. (1990). *Psychological trauma and the adult survivor: Theory, therapy and transformation.* New York: Brunner/Mazel.

North, C., Nixon, S., Shariat, S., Mallonee, S., McMillen, J., Spitznagel, E., et al. (1999). Psychiatric disorders among survivors of the Oklahoma City bombing. *Journal of the American Medical Association, 282,* 755–762.

Rahe, R. (1974). The pathway between subjects' recent life changes and their future illness reports. In B. S. Dohrenwend & B. P. Dohrenwend (Eds.), *Stressful life events: Their nature and effects* (pp. 341–365). New York: Wiley.

Robinson, H., Sigman, M., & Wison, J. (1997). Duty-related stressors and PTSD symptoms in suburban police officers. *Psychological Reports, 81,* 835–845.

Rosenbloom, D., Pratt, A., & Pearlman, L. A. (1995). Helpers' response to trauma work. In B. H. Stamm (Ed.), *Secondary traumatic stress* (pp. 65–79). Lutherville, MD: Sidran Press.

Smith, K., Everly, G. S., Jr., & Johns, T. (1993). The role of stress arousal in the dynamics of stressor-to-illness processes in accountants. *Contemporary Accounting Research, 9,* 432–449.

U.S. Department of Health and Human Services. (1999). *Mental health: A report of the Surgeon General.* Rockville, MD: Author.

World Health Organization. (1992). *International classification of disease, mental and behavioural disorders* (10th ed.). Geneva, Switzerland: Author.

Chapter 20 ————————————————————————

MEASURING NORMAL PERSONALITY THE MILLON WAY

STEPHEN STRACK

Until recently, students of clinical psychiatry, psychology, social work, and nursing were trained to see the pathology in their patients but not necessarily what is normal or healthy. Advances in theories of mental disorder and, especially, advances in treatment have given greater confidence to mental health professionals to think outside the box of psychopathology (Offer & Sabshin, 1984, 1991; Strack & Lorr, 1994). The multiaxial diagnostic format introduced in 1980 (i.e., the third edition of the *Diagnostic and Statistical Manual of Mental Disorders [DSM-III];* American Psychiatric Association, 1980) was both a consequence of this increased confidence and a catalyst for growth. Over the past 20-plus years, we have witnessed an explosion of ideas that have helped break down barriers between previously separate areas of scientific inquiry, such as normal-abnormal personality (Livesley, 2001; Markon, Krueger, Bouchard, & Gottesman, 2002; O'Connor, 2002; Strack & Lorr, 1994, 1997), and we are now witnessing a multidisciplinary integration of knowledge from many domains (Gold, 2005; T. Millon, 2000, 2003, 2005).

Among recent changes is a greater willingness to consider the normality and health of psychiatric patients in addition to their pathology—to understand the whole person, not just the presenting problems. In the twenty-first century, comprehending psychopathology is not just a matter of discerning symptoms, syndromes, and diagnoses; it is also grasping the biopsychosocial context of the individual, including his or her strengths and abilities (American Psychiatric Association, 2000; T. Millon, 1996; Sabshin, 2005; Sperry, 2003).

As conceived by Theodore Millon (e.g., 1990, 1996, 1999, 2003), personality may be an especially fruitful means by which to grasp and integrate a vast array of normal and abnormal psychological variables. In his way of thinking, personality represents an evolutionary, centrally organized (and organizing) system of perceiving, interpreting, and managing internal and external demands of all kinds—the executive system by which humans adapt to their environment:

> Persons are the only organically integrated system in the psychological domain, evolved through the millennia and inherently created from birth as natural entities rather than culture-bound and experience-derived gestalts. The intrinsic cohesion of persons is not merely a rhetorical construction but an authentic substantive unity. Personologic features may often be dissonant and may be partitioned conceptually for pragmatic or scientific

purposes, but they are segments of an inseparable biopsychosocial entity. (T. Millon, 2003, p. 951)

Within his model of personology and psychopathology, there is an appreciation that all mental health patients have a unique personality that must be considered to understand the nature of their Axis I disorders and to provide useful treatments. This is true whether the personality is "normal" or "disordered." From T. Millon's perspective, by knowing the personality of the individual, mental health professionals have the best opportunity to organize and synthesize their knowledge about the individual's symptoms and disorders within a rich developmental, biopsychosocial context, from which treatment planning naturally flows (T. Millon, 1996, 1999, 2003).

The focus of this chapter is on how T. Millon views and assesses healthy and adaptive personality. As implied by the foregoing, this is but one element of a larger model of personology and psychopathology. I present normal personality as a separate topic because most readers are already familiar with personality disorders (PDs), yet many lack training in how to understand and appreciate the normal personality features of their patients, including strengths.

NORMAL PERSONALITY IN MILLON'S MODEL

Theodore Millon's (1969/1983b, 1994; T. Millon, Antoni, C. Millon, Meagher, & Grossman, 2001; T. Millon, Green, & Meagher, 1982a, 1982b; Strack, 1987, 1991b) normal personality styles and dimensions emanate from his broadly based evolutionary model of personality that differentiates and links healthy and abnormal character on a continuum. The model is closely aligned with Axis II of the *DSM* (American Psychiatric Association, 1980, 1987, 1994, 2000). Thus, clinicians and researchers have at their disposal a framework for understanding a complete array of personality types and dimensions ranging from the healthy to the pathological. The continuous relationship between the domains of normality and pathology in Millon's model allows us to study the ways that personality contributes to Axis I disorders and their treatment, how healthy and disordered personalities are similar and different, the developmental processes that lead to various outcomes, and, perhaps most importantly, how disordered individuals may be restored to healthy functioning.

Early Formulations and Personality Prototypes

T. Millon (1969/1983b) presented his original biosocial-learning theory of personality in *Modern Psychopathology* (MP). There he proposed three axes—pleasure-pain, active-passive, and other-self—as the basic building blocks of normal and abnormal personality. Conceived in terms of instrumental coping patterns designed to maximize positive reinforcements and avoid punishment, the model crossed the active-passive axis with four reinforcement strategies—detached, dependent, independent, and ambivalent—to derive eight basic personality patterns (asocial, avoidant, submissive, gregarious, narcissistic, aggressive, conforming, negativistic) and three severe variants (schizoid, cycloid, paranoid). The basic patterns were thought to be present in both normal and disordered persons, while the severe styles were believed to be evident only in abnormal form. Millon described his personalities in prototype form, that is, by giving portraits of how particularly salient individuals might appear to a clinician or other observer.

T. Millon's (1969/1983b) assumptions about normal personality were outlined as follows: (1) Normal and abnormal personality are shaped according to the same basic processes and learning principles, (2) normal personality is on a continuum with pathological personality, (3) no sharp dividing line exists between normal and abnormal personality types, and (4) normal personality patterns may be distinguished from pathological patterns by their adaptive flexibility and balance on the active-passive, pleasure-pain, and self-other polarities:

> When an individual displays an ability to cope with his environment in a flexible and adaptive manner and when his characteristic perceptions and behaviors foster increments in personal gratification, then he may be said to possess a normal and healthy personality pattern. (p. 222)

By contrast, disordered persons tend to exhibit (1) tenuous stability, or a lack of resilience under conditions of stress; (2) an inability to respond flexibly and appropriately to internal and external demands; and (3) a tendency to foster vicious cycles of pathological behavior (T. Millon, 1969/1983b, 1996; T. Millon & Davis, 2000).

Although MP clearly addressed both normal and abnormal character types, the focus of that text on PDs overshadowed healthy personality development. Normal personality styles were not described there or in T. Millon's (1981) subsequent text, *Disorders of Personality.* In the early 1970s, T. Millon (1974) and his colleagues developed a research instrument, the Millon Personality Inventory, that assessed normal and abnormal personality traits. It was used primarily by students and was not widely distributed, but it did signal T. Millon's early interest in normal traits and served as a springboard for development of later measures.

Nondisordered personality styles were not disseminated to a large audience until the publication of the Millon Adolescent Personality Inventory (MAPI; T. Millon et al., 1982a) and the Millon Behavioral Health Inventory (MBHI; T. Millon et al., 1982b). These instruments were developed and normed for use in health care settings and presented personalities that were different from PDs. T. Millon did not alert test users to the essential differences between these styles and PDs. Nevertheless, careful readers could grasp the differences by comparing them with the personalities described in earlier texts and the Millon Clinical Multiaxial Inventory (MCMI) manual (T. Millon, 1977, 1983a). Significantly, T. Millon gave different names to the normal prototypes (see Table 20.1) and used terminology that was much less severe than that used for the PDs. For example, normal introversive personalities were described in the MBHI manual as "colorless," "quiet," and "unconcerned about their problems" (T. Millon et al., 1982b, p. 2), while T. Millon reported in the MCMI manual that disordered schizoid (asocial) persons demonstrated "an inability to display enthusiasm or experience pleasure," "obscure thought processes," and a "lack of vitality" (1983a, p. 4).

The first published work devoted exclusively to T. Millon's healthy personality styles was an article describing the development and validation of the Personality Adjective Check List (PACL; Strack, 1987). The instrument provided a self-report and rating measure of T. Millon's basic eight personality patterns, was normed solely on normal adults, and used *T* scores instead of *base rate* (BR) scores. In that initial report and several subsequent articles (Strack, 1991a, 1992, 1993, 1994; Strack & Guevara, 1999; Strack & Lorr, 1990a, 1990b; Strack, Lorr, & Campbell, 1990), my colleagues and I provided considerable empirical evidence in support of T. Millon's proposition that his normal prototypes are strongly related to their PD counterparts.

Table 20.1 Names for Millon's Normal Personality Styles by Source and Their Personality Disorder Counterparts

Modern Psychopathology 1969/1983b	MAPI 1982	MBHI 1982	PACL 1987	MIPS/MIPS-R 1994/2004	MIDC 1999	MBMD 2001	Personality Disorder Counterpart
Asocial	Introversive	Introversive	Introversive	Retiring/Asocial	Retiring	Introversive	Schizoid
Avoidant	Inhibited	Inhibited	Inhibited	Hesitating/Anxious	Reticent	Inhibited	Avoidant
						Dejected	Depressive
Submissive	Cooperative	Cooperative	Cooperative	Agreeing/Cooperative	Accommodating	Cooperative	Dependent
Gregarious	Sociable	Sociable	Sociable	Outgoing/Gregarious	Outgoing	Sociable	Histrionic
Narcissistic	Confident	Confident	Confident	Asserting/Confident	Ambitious	Confident	Narcissistic
Aggressive	Forceful	Forceful	Forceful	Dissenting/Unconventional	Dauntless	Nonconforming	Antisocial
				Controlling/Dominant	Dominant	Forceful	Sadistic
Conforming	Respectful	Respectful	Respectful	Conforming/Dutiful	Conscientious	Respectful	Compulsive
Negativistic	Sensitive	Sensitive	Sensitive	Complaining/Dissatisfied	Contentious	Oppositional	Negativistic
				Yielding/Submissive	Aggrieved	Denigrated	Masochistic

Notes: Numbers indicate the year the book or instrument was published or widely disseminated.
MAPI = Millon Adolescent Personality Inventory; MBHI = Millon Behavioral Health Inventory; MBMD = Millon Behavioral Medicine Diagnostic; MIDC = Millon Inventory of Diagnostic Criteria; MIPS = Millon Index of Personality Styles; MIPS-R = Millon Index of Personality Styles-Revised; PACL = Personality Adjective Check List. The table does not include the trait dimensions assessed by the MIPS and MIPS-R as these do not measure particular personality styles

The Evolutionary Model and Personality Dimensions

In the mid-1980s, T. Millon (1986, 1987, 1996, 1997; T. Millon & Davis, 1994) began altering his model and clinical measures to accommodate changes in *DSM* Axis II (American Psychiatric Association, 1987, 1994). He also widened his focus by placing his model in an evolutionary framework (T. Millon, 1990). From a structural perspective, these changes resulted in the addition of a discordant reinforcement strategy (where pleasure and pain have reversed value) and three personality styles—depressive, sadistic, and self-defeating—that were considered variants of his original avoidant, aggressive, and negativistic types, respectively.

The dimensional approach to normal personality presented by T. Millon in 1990 was his first effort to delineate healthy traits and styles of behavior independent of psychopathology. It was followed in 1994 with the publication of the Millon Index of Personality Styles (MIPS; T. Millon, 1994), a measure for use with normal adults that assesses trait dimensions as well as character styles.

The dimensional approach was anchored in his newly developed evolutionary view of personality and psychopathology (T. Millon, 1990), which expanded on his earlier framework (T. Millon, 1969/1983b). He retained his original axes and the concept of personality as a complex coping pattern that is shaped through reinforcement. What was new is that he linked personality development to the evolution of our species, added a fourth bipolar dimension (thinking-feeling) to the basic model, and added ways of distinguishing among personality subtypes (T. Millon, 1994, 1996):

> [A]n individual human organism must pass through four "stages" and must fulfill a parallel set of four "tasks" to perform adequately in life. . . . Each stage and task corresponds to one of four evolutionary phases: existence, adaptation, replication, and abstraction. Polarities . . . representing the first three of the phases (pleasure-pain, passive-active, other-self) have been used to construct a theoretically anchored classification of personality styles and disorders . . .
>
> Within each stage, every individual acquires personologic dispositions representing a balance or predilection toward one of the two polarity inclinations; which inclination emerges as dominant over time results from the inextricable and reciprocal interplay of intraorganismic and extraorganismic factors. (T. Millon, 1996, p. 97)

The four evolutionary phases or stages, and tasks, may be described as follows (and are summarized in Table 20.2):

1. *Existence:* A human being's first task is to survive. Evolutionary mechanisms associated with this stage relate to the processes of *life enhancement* and *life preservation.* The former are concerned with orienting individuals toward improving their quality of life; the latter, with orienting individuals away from actions and environments that decrease their quality of life or jeopardize existence. These superordinate categories may be called *existential aims* and are related to the polarity of *pleasure-pain.* A person's survival strategy is initially learned during the first year of life, what T. Millon (1996) calls the *sensory-attachment* phase. Developing a reliable survival strategy is partly a consequence of being able to trust those on whom a person depends and a willingness to share that trust with others.

2. *Adaptation:* Once survival is ensured, human beings learn to adapt to their environment through *ecological accommodation* and *ecological modification,* modes of being that are associated with *passive-active* behavior and coping strategies. These *modes of adaptation* refer to a person's tendency to move away from conflicts or problems (i.e.,

Table 20.2   A Developmental Framework for Normal Personality

Evolutionary Phase or Stage	Polarity	Survival Function	Neuropsychological Stage	Developmental Achievement
Existence	Pleasure-Pain	Life enhancement/ Life preservation	Sensory-attachment	Trust
Adaptation	Active-Passive	Ecological modification/ Ecological Accommodation	Sensorimotor-autonomy	Self-confidence
Replication	Other-Self	Progeny nurturance/ Individual propagation	Pubertal-genital identity	Gender identity and sex role
Abstraction	Thinking-Feeling	Intellective-reasoning/ Affective resonance	Intracortical integration	Balance of reason and emotion

Source: From *Disorders of Personality,* second edition, p. 110, by T. Millon, 1996, New York: Wiley. Reprinted with permission of the author.

be passive and compliant in response to challenges), versus moving toward them with the goal of confronting and/or changing them. Learning to adapt to one's environment is a complex process that begins roughly in the second year of life, what T. Millon (1996) calls the *sensorimotor-autonomy* stage, and may extend several years, although many individuals develop effective and often habitual adaptation patterns by the age of 5. Secure self-confidence is an important outcome of healthy adaptation.

3. *Replication:* Successful personal development includes the ability to leave offspring who, themselves, survive to reproduce. T. Millon believes that we develop a preference for either a *self-propagating* or *other-nurturing* strategy to achieve this aim. Linked to the *self-other* polarity and T. Millon's (1996) *pubertal-gender identity* stage of development (roughly 11 to 15 years of age), these modes of being are exemplified by tendencies toward self-advancement and agency in interpersonal pursuits, versus a preference for communality and nurturance. A secure gender identity and sex role orientation are major consequences of achieving a balance in this realm.

4. *Abstraction:* The first three evolutionary phases are common to other species, but human beings are unique in developing higher cortical functions that permit, among other things, complex language and reasoning. During the ages of 4 to 18, T. Millon's (1996) *intracortical integration* stage, people develop preferences for *intellective reasoning* or *affective resonance* in processing internal and external information. These preferences represent a *thinking-feeling* polarity exemplified by an inclination toward mental manipulation and abstraction in problem solving, versus a tendency to use emotions and intuition to tackle issues of personal import. Achieving a balance in the use of reasoning and emotion is a sign of success in this developmental arena.

T. Millon's (1994, 2004) dimensional perspective on personality was developed without reference to disorder, but it borrowed many concepts from his original model of psychopathology. In this approach, T. Millon considered the universe of traits and interpersonal styles that exist in the normal population and came up with three sets of personality variables to define and measure them. The first set, termed *motivating aims,* represents his three basic axes in evolutionary form. The original pleasure-pain polarity was called *enhancing-preserving,* active-passive was named *modifying-accommodating,* and other-self was labeled *individuating-nurturing.* The second set of variables, borrowed from Carl Jung (1936/1971), was termed *cognitive modes.* For T. Millon, cognition means an individual's primary source of obtaining information and the means by which that information is processed or transformed. Preferred sources of information can be the self (internal) or others (external) and either tangible or intangible. Favored methods of transforming information can be intellectual or affective and assimilative versus imaginative.

The last set of variables describes 10 common *interpersonal behaviors* or styles (T. Millon, 1994, 2004). Eight of the 10 styles (i.e., personalities) are essentially the same as those measured by the MAPI, MBHI, and PACL and are empirically related to PDs (see Table 20.1 under the column heading MIPS/MIPS-R). Two additional behavioral patterns, controlling/dominant and yielding/submissive, are conceptually related to sadistic and self-defeating PDs and are also found in two recently developed measures, the Millon Inventory of Diagnostic Criteria (MIDC; Immelman, 1999) and Millon Behavioral Medicine Diagnostic (MBMD; T. Millon et al., 2001).

INSTRUMENTS FOR ASSESSING NORMAL STYLES AND DIMENSIONS

There are currently six measures[1] available to clinicians and researchers for assessing T. Millon's normal personalities: the MAPI (T. Millon et al., 1982a) for adolescent counseling clients; the MBHI (Everly & Newman, 1997; T. Millon et al., 1982b) and the MBMD (C. Millon & Meagher, 2002; T. Millon et al., 2001) for medical patients; the PACL (Strack, 1987, 1991b, 2002) and revised MIPS, the MIPS-R[2] (T. Millon, 2004), for non-help-seeking normal adults, counseling clients, and employment candidates; and the MIDC (Immelman, 1999) for indirect ratings of political and historical persons. Among these, only the MIPS-R assesses T. Millon's personality dimensions.

Three of the measures (MAPI, MBHI, and PACL) were developed using T. Millon's (1969/1983b) original prototype model, while three (MIPS/MIPS-R, MIDC, MBMD) were developed using the evolutionary model (T. Millon, 1990, 1994, 1996). As shown in Table 20.1, the MAPI, MBHI, and PACL measure T. Millon's (1969/1983b) original eight normal personalities. The MIPS/MIPS-R and MIDC assess two styles added in 1986 (T. Millon, 1986), while the MBMD assesses a total of 11 styles, the number that is consistent with T. Millon's (1996, 2004) current taxonomy.[3]

---

[1] The *Millon Adolescent Clinical Inventory* (T. Millon, 1993), *Millon Clinical Multiaxial Inventory-III* (T. Millon, 1997), and the *Millon Personality Diagnostic Checklist* (Tringone, 1997) are not included because they measure disordered rather than normal personality traits.

[2] According to T. Millon (2004), the MIPS-R replaces the MIPS. Nevertheless, the MIPS-R uses the same scale items, scoring algorithms, and norms as the MIPS, so the two are equivalent for psychometric and research purposes.

[3] It is important to recognize that although T. Millon's model of personality and psychopathology has changed significantly over the past 25 years, what we have today is a more complex version of the original, not an entirely new set of formulations. This is exemplified by the way T. Millon added three personality styles (i.e., depressive, sadistic, and self-defeating) as *variants* of his original types (i.e., avoidant, aggressive, and negativistic) rather than introducing them as new elements of the model.

Following are descriptions of individuals who score highly on the various measures of normal personality styles and dimensions.

Personality Styles

1. *Asocial, introversive, retiring:* Aloof and solitary by nature, these individuals prefer limited social involvement. They are easygoing, slow-paced, and reserved. They rarely show strong emotion and may appear to others as dull and lacking in spontaneity. The PD counterpart is *schizoid.*

2. *Avoidant, inhibited, hesitating/anxious, reticent:* Shy and sensitive to criticism, these individuals keep others at an arm's distance and remain on the periphery of social gatherings. They are typically kind and considerate and do not like to draw attention to themselves. They are wary of novelty and seek stable rather than changeable environments. The PD counterpart is *avoidant.*

3. *Dejected:* A variant of T. Millon's (1969/1983b) avoidant style, these persons exhibit low self-esteem and pervasive pessimism. They frequently expect poor outcomes in their relationships and work efforts. They lack spontaneity, are retiring, and often don't follow through with complex tasks. They are self-focused and brooding. The PD counterpart is *depressive.*

4. *Submissive, cooperative, agreeing, accommodating:* These individuals value communality and seek others' approval. They are docile, obliging, and agreeable. They tend to think poorly of their own skills and seek stronger individuals to lean on. The PD counterpart is *dependent.*

5. *Gregarious, sociable, outgoing:* Active and extraverted, these individuals seek high levels of stimulation and attention. They are often spontaneous, colorful, and dramatic. Their interests and emotions change frequently, and others may experience them as shallow and fickle. The PD counterpart is *histrionic.*

6. *Narcissistic, confident, asserting, ambitious:* Typically bold and self-assured, these individuals think highly of themselves and expect others to cater to their wishes and demands. They can be charming and manipulative, and others may see them as lacking empathy. The PD counterpart is *narcissistic.*

7. *Aggressive, forceful, dissenting/unconventional, dauntless, nonconforming:* Assertive and socially dominant, these individuals are adventurous, competitive, and nonconforming. They persevere in difficult circumstances but can be inconsiderate of others' needs. They are often brusque and insensitive in their tactics and downplay the value of tender emotions. The PD counterpart is *antisocial.*

8. *Controlling/dominant, forceful:* A variation of T. Millon's (1969/1983b) aggressive style, these persons are interpersonally domineering and aggressive. They see themselves as being tough-minded and fearless in a world that is harsh and threatening. They are often exploitive and manipulative and don't mind stepping on others' toes if doing so will get them what they want. The PD counterpart is *sadistic.*

9. *Conforming, respectful, dutiful, conscientious:* Rule bound and scrupulous, these individuals are hard-working and respectful of those in authority. They tend to be perfectionistic and emotionally constricted. They are methodical and persistent but can be too rigid and moralistic in their efforts to live up to conventional standards. The PD counterpart is *compulsive.*

10. *Negativistic, sensitive, complaining/dissatisfied, contentious, oppositional:* Unconventional and moody, these individuals march to the beat of a different drummer and are not happy with the status quo. They are often loyal and forthright with their opinions but are also awkward, changeable, and fault-finding. The PD counterpart is *negativistic.*

11. *Yielding/submissive, aggrieved, denigrated:* A variant of T. Millon's (1969/1983b) negativistic type, high-scoring persons are typically submissive and self-demeaning. These individuals expect the worst and often contribute to their own unhappiness. They are frequently moody, irritable, and pessimistic. The PD counterpart is *self-defeating.*

Motivational Dimensions

1. *Enhancing versus preserving (pleasure-pain):* This dimension measures an individual's orientation toward life enhancement activities versus those aimed at life preservation. From a behavioral standpoint, this is translated into pleasure seeking versus avoidance of painful experiences. Those scoring high on the enhancing scale are outgoing and optimistic, while those scoring high on the preserving scale are worrisome and pessimistic.

2. *Modifying versus accommodating (active-passive):* This continuum assesses how individuals adapt themselves to their environment. For T. Millon, modifying persons are those who actively seek to manipulate and change their surroundings, while accommodating persons mold themselves to fit in with existing circumstances. Individuals who score high on the modifying scale take charge of their lives and play an active role in shaping the events that impact their lives. Those who score high on the accommodating scale tend to be dependent and acquiescent.

3. *Individuating versus nurturing (self-other):* This dimension assesses the behavioral manifestations of an individual's reproductive strategy. According to T. Millon, individuals tend toward propagation of the self or nurturance of others. There is an obvious parallel with masculinity-femininity, but this axis is more broadly based. Persons who score highly on the individuating scale are independent, egocentric, and seek to further their own aims. Those who obtain high scores on the nurturing scale value communality and tend to be gentle and protective of others.

Cognitive Dimensions

1. *Extraversing versus introversing:* Extraversing individuals look to others for information, attention, and stimulation. They are outgoing and feel most comfortable in social surroundings. Those with strong introversing traits tend to be private and closed off from external stimulation. They value their own thoughts and feelings as informational resources.

2. *Sensing versus intuiting:* High-sensing individuals seek information from tangible, literal, well-defined sources. For them, "seeing is believing." Those who are primarily intuiting place structure and fact in the background while focusing most intently on intangible sources of information such as personal insight.

3. *Thinking versus feeling:* Thinking individuals prefer to process information using cool logic and analytic reasoning. They downplay the value of emotions in evaluating problems and circumstances. By contrast, those who process information with feelings rely on subjective experience to assist them. They use empathy and affective responding in analyzing problem situations.

4. *Systematizing versus innovating:* Systematizing individuals tend to evaluate new experiences on the basis of past experiences. They seek reliability and consistency. They are conservative and tend to incorporate information into well-established modes of thought. Innovating persons are open to new experiences and seek novelty. They tend to be spontaneous, creative, and flexible.

EMPIRICAL FINDINGS

Basic studies of T. Millon's normal personality styles and dimensions have assessed their internal consistency, temporal stability, convergent and discriminant validity, factor structure, and comparability to PDs. Many subject populations have been sampled, including non-help-seeking adolescents, college students, noncollege adults, and the elderly; psychiatric patients; medical patients with a variety of diagnoses including cancer and chronic pain; employees in a variety of occupations including law enforcement; military personnel; military veterans; and prisoners. Included in the psychometric review are findings from the MAPI, MBHI, MBMD, MIPS/MIPS-R, and PACL. The recently developed MIDC (Immelman, 1999, in press) is unique in allowing indirect ratings of individuals (e.g., political figures) through work samples and written records. Because it is essentially a qualitative measure of personality, traditional research methods and criteria do not apply. See Immelman (1999, 2005) for psychometric information about this instrument.

Reliability and Validity

Internal consistency estimates (KR-20 or coefficient alpha) for the test scales are generally good, but there were a few exceptions in clinical samples: MAPI Range = .67 to .83, Median = .74 (T. Millon et al., 1982a, p. 51); MBHI Range = .66 to .86, Median = .73 (T. Millon et al., 1982b, p. 25); MBMD Range = .54 to .85, Median = .68 (T. Millon et al., 2001, p. 29); MIPS/MIPS-R Range = .74 to .87, Median = .78 (for the total sample, T. Millon, 1994, p. 61); and PACL Range = .76 to .89, Median = .83 (for the new sample; Strack, 1991b, p. 43).

Test-retest reliability has been generally impressive, even in clinical samples: MAPI Range = .69 to .82 over 5 months (Group A; T. Millon et al., 1982a, p. 51), MBHI Range = .77 to .88 over 4 to 5 months (T. Millon et al., 1982b, p. 25), MBMD Range = .71 to .90 over 1 to 4 weeks (T. Millon et al., 2001, p. 29), MIPS/MIPS-R Range = .74 to .90 over 2 months (uncorrected *r*s; T. Millon, 1994, p. 63), and PACL Range = .60 to .85 over 3 months (based on separate samples for men and women; Strack, 1991b, p. 44).

Scale scores have been linked in theoretically consistent patterns with measures from many self-report and rating instruments including the California Psychological Inventory (T. Millon, 1994; T. Millon et al., 1982a, 1982b; Strack, 1987), Life Orientation Test (T. Millon et al., 2001; Strack, 1987), Myers-Briggs Type Indicator (T. Millon, 1994),

Minnesota Multiphasic Personality Inventory (T. Millon, 1994; T. Millon et al., 1982b; Strack & Guevara, 1999), NEO Personality Inventory (T. Millon, 1994; Pincus & Wiggins, 1990; Wiggins & Pincus, 1989), Self-Directed Search (Strack, 1994), and Sixteen Personality Factors Questionnaire (T. Millon, 1994; T. Millon et al., 1982a; Strack, 1987). Findings are too numerous to present here, but summaries can be found in the appropriate test manuals as well as in C. Millon and Meagher (2002) for the MBMD, Strack (1993, 1997, 2002) for the PACL, and Weiss (1997, 2002) for the MIPS/MIPS-R. They convincingly demonstrate that the normal personalities exhibit trait patterns that are predicted by theory and are milder versions of their PD counterparts.

Factor Structure

Each of the assessment devices has yielded similar factor structures for the personality styles. In a large normal adult sample, PACL scales showed three bipolar dimensions labeled Neurotic versus Controlled, Assertive versus Compliant, and Introversion versus Extraversion (Strack, 1987, 1991b). Factor analyses of the MAPI (Hynan, Pantle, & Foster, 1998; T. Millon et al., 1982a), MBHI (T. Millon et al., 1982b), and MBMD (T. Millon et al., 2001) have been performed on clinical samples with symptom measures included. Nevertheless, their dimensional structure is comparable to that of the PACL. Recently, PACL and MIPS/MIPS-R scales were correlated and factor analyzed together in a sample of 148 college students (Guevara & Strack, 1998). Scales measuring the same personality styles were moderately associated (Range of rs = .35 to .71). Three of four varimax-rotated factors included basic personality styles. Factor 1, which was bipolar, linked three PACL introverted, neurotic personalities (Introversive, Inhibited, Sensitive) with pain-avoidance, passivity, a solitary thinking style, and MIPS/MIPS-R Hesitating/Anxious, Retiring/Asocial, Yielding/Submissive, and Dissenting/Unconventional interpersonal styles on one end of the continuum. Loaded in the opposite direction were three PACL extraverted, socially bold personalities (Sociable, Confident, Forceful), and the MIPS/MIPS-R Extraversing/Externally Focused, Outgoing/Gregarious, and Asserting/Anxious scales. Factor 2, which was also bipolar, linked PACL Confident and Forceful personalities with MIPS/MIPS-R Controlling/Dominant, Individuating/Self-Indulging, Dissenting/Unconventional, Asserting/Confident, Innovating/Innovation-Seeking, and Thinking/Thought-Guided scales on the positive pole and the PACL Cooperative style with MIPS/MIPS-R Nurturing/Other-Nurturing and Feeling/Feeling-Guided on the negative end. Factor 3 associated the PACL Respectful style and MIPS/MIPS-R Conforming/Dutiful, Systematizing/Conservation-Seeking, Thinking/Thought-Guided, Modifying/Actively Modifying, Sensing/Realistic, Asserting/Confident, Outgoing/Gregarious, and Enhancing/Pleasure-Enhancing scales on one end of the continuum and PACL Sensitive on the other. This dimension taps conscientiousness, emotional control versus lack of emotional control, and elements of extraversion.

Factor analyses of PACL, MCMI-I, and MCMI-II personality scales have revealed comparable results. PACL's three higher order dimensions (Strack, 1987, 1991b) correspond to the three factors found by Retzlaff and Gibertini (1987) for MCMI-I basic eight scales among psychiatric patients and normal adults and by Strack, Lorr, Campbell, and Lamnin (1992) for the 13 MCMI-II personality scales with patients. A joint factor analysis of PACL and MCMI-II basic personality scales among college students yielded three factors (using residual scores), with corresponding PACL and MCMI-II scales loading on the same dimensions (Strack, 1991a).

T. Millon et al. (2001) reported that many of the items for the MBMD personality style scales were drawn from the MBHI and MCMI-III. It is not surprising that correlations between comparable scales on the three measures were generally high: "[B]etween .55 and .75, with one or two exceptions . . ." (p. 31). They concluded that the personality scales for the three measures are "close cousins" (p. 31) and should yield common factors, although an empirical test is needed to verify this belief.

Experimental and Clinical Research

The experimental and clinical utility of these instruments has been demonstrated in numerous studies, a sample of which is presented here. The MAPI has been found useful in assessing the personality characteristics of aggressive (Kashani, 1990), depressed (Ehrenberg, Cox, & Koopman, 1990), and suicidal adolescents (Fritsch, Donaldson, Spirito, & Plummer, 2000); differentiating teens with and without conduct disorders (Holcomb & Kashani, 1991) and those who do and do not use steroids for athletic purposes (Burnett & Kleiman, 1994); identifying subgroups of substance abusers (Donat, Hume, & Hiner, 1992; Hart, 1995); and predicting treatment outcomes (Knapp, Templer, Cannon, & Dobson, 1991; Piersma, Pantle, Smith, Boes, & Kubiak, 1993) and overall adjustment (Nair, Nair, Kashani, Reid, & Rao, 2001).

The MBHI has been useful in predicting self-reported somatic complaints in military personnel (Watten, Vassend, Myhrer, & Syversen, 1997) as well as treatment outcomes in patients with chronic pain (Fishbain, Turner, Rosomoff, & Rosomoff, 2001), cardiac transplant candidates and recipients (Brandwin, Trask, Schwartz, & Clifford, 2000; Harper, Chacko, Kotik-Harper, Young, & Gotto, 1998), and those with visual impairments (Jackson, Taylor, Palmatier, Elliott, & Elliott, 1998). See Antoni, Millon, and Millon (1997) and T. Millon et al. (2001) for reviews.

Although the MBMD is new and has not yet developed an independent research base, T. Millon et al. (2001) report validation studies conducted while developing the test that demonstrate its ability to link personality with coping-style characteristics, such as medication use and compliance, and with positive or negative treatment outcomes among cancer, diabetes, HIV/AIDS, and heart disease patients (pp. 48–55).

The MIDC (Immelman, 1999, 2005) is also a new instrument, but it has already demonstrated its promise as an indirect rating measure of the personality characteristics of national presidents (Immelman, 2002) as well as presidential candidates (Immelman, 1998).

The MIPS has been found useful for employment screening and personnel selection (T. Millon, 1994; Weiss, 2002), assessing the personality characteristics of Navy divers (Beckman, Lall, & Johnson, 1996), and in identifying traits associated with different relaxation styles (Sohnle, 2001) as well as the theoretical preferences of counseling students (Scragg, Bor, & Watts, 1999). The MIPS Adjustment Index has been empirically demonstrated to identify individuals with poor work performance and those who may need psychological help (T. Millon, 1994; Weiss, 2002).

PACL scales have been used to study occupational preferences (Plante & Boccaccini, 1997; Strack, 1994), the characteristics of competitive athletes (Gat & McWhirter, 1998), family systems (Gontag & Erickson, 1996; Horton & Retzlaff, 1991), individual differences in social judgment (Moore, Smith, & Gonzalez, 1997), interpersonal problems (Pincus & Wiggins, 1990), and outcomes among elderly veterans with posttraumatic stress disorder (Hyer & Boyd, 1996). The PACL Problem Indicator scale successfully differentiates non-help-seeking normal adults from psychiatric patients (Strack, 1991b) and can be used as a screening measure to identify persons who may need referral for psychological help or additional assessment.

CONCLUSIONS

The MAPI, MBHI, MBMD, MIDC, MIPS, and PACL measures, from the perspective of T. Millon's (1969/1983b, 1996) evolving model of personality, have been successful in empirically validating his taxonomy of styles; in verifying the continuous relationship between normality and abnormality; in documenting the importance of personality for understanding a variety of behaviors, attitudes, and preferences; and in providing more effective treatments to counseling, psychiatric, and medical patients. The MACI, MBHI, MBMD, and MIDC were developed to assess personality within specific populations, while the MIPS and PACL were designed for use with more general populations, including college students, employees, military personnel, and the elderly.

As measures of normal personality, none of these instruments tap a sufficient range of problematic traits to diagnose PDs. Nevertheless, the MAPI, MBHI, MBMD, MIPS, and PACL have all been found useful in identifying persons who may have problems severe enough to warrant a clinical diagnosis, referral for clinically focused assessment, or psychiatric treatment. The MAPI, MBHI, and MBMD include multiple scales for measuring affective distress (e.g., depression), dysfunctional attitudes (e.g., chronic tension), and behaviors (e.g., impulsivity). The MIPS has an Adjustment Index, and the PACL contains a Problem Indicator scale, which are able to identify people with problems that may warrant further professional attention.

From an empirical standpoint, there is still much to be learned about the structure and behavior of T. Millon's normal personality styles and their relationship to PDs. Important housekeeping issues include further validation of the new Dejected (MBMD), Controlling/Dominant and Yielding/Submissive (MIPS/MIPS-R) personalities, the motivational and cognitive dimensions found on the MIPS/MIPS-R, and the relationship between T. Millon's evolutionary polarities and his taxonomy of personality styles and dimensions (T. Millon, 1996, 2003; Widiger, 1999). Studies that employ ratings and focus on real-life behavior are especially important for all of the T. Millon measures. As to differentiating normal and abnormal personalities, we need longitudinal investigations and side-by-side comparisons of matched groups of normals and patients to get at the essential similarities and differences between these populations (Lenzenweger, 1999; Livesley, 2001; Strack & Lorr, 1994, 1997). Evidence from correlational self-report studies suggests that T. Millon's normal personalities are healthier, more flexible, and more adaptive than their PD counterparts, but we need direct proof.

The continuous relationship between most forms of normal and abnormal personality has become increasingly accepted in the scientific community over the past decade (American Psychiatric Association, 2000; O'Connor, 2002; Sperry, 2003)—so much so that there is growing interest in adding a dimensional component to Axis II of the *DSM* (Endler & Kocovski, 2002; First, 2002). As noted throughout this chapter, T. Millon's model of personality is both dimensional in nature and strongly linked with current *DSM* taxonomy. Given these strengths and the fact that his model is the most comprehensive explication of personality and psychopathology ever developed, the American Psychiatric

Association should give serious consideration to adopting T. Millon's conceptualizations for a diagnostic manual that recognizes the importance of normality and dimensionality for understanding and treating all mental health patients.

REFERENCES

American Psychiatric Association. (1980). *Diagnostic and statistical manual of mental disorders* (3rd ed.). Washington, DC: Author.

American Psychiatric Association. (1987). *Diagnostic and statistical manual of mental disorders* (3rd ed., rev.). Washington, DC: Author.

American Psychiatric Association. (1994). *Diagnostic and statistical manual of mental disorders* (4th ed.). Washington, DC: Author.

American Psychiatric Association. (2000). *Diagnostic and statistical manual of mental disorders* (4th ed., text rev.). Washington, DC: Author.

Antoni, M. H., Millon, C., & Millon, T. (1997). The role of psychological assessment in health care: The MBHI, MBMC, and beyond. In T. Millon (Ed.), *The Millon inventories: Clinical and personality assessment* (pp. 409–448). New York: Guilford Press.

Beckman, T. J., Lall, R., & Johnson, W. B. (1996). Salient personality characteristics among Navy divers. *Military Medicine, 161,* 717–719.

Brandwin, M., Trask, P. C., Schwartz, S. M., & Clifford, M. (2000). Personality predictors of mortality in cardiac transplant candidates and recipients. *Journal of Psychosomatic Research, 2000,* 141–147.

Burnett, K. F., & Kleiman, M. E. (1994). Psychological characteristics of adolescent steroid users. *Adolescence, 29,* 81–89.

Donat, D. C., Hume, A., & Hiner, G. L. (1992). Personality subtypes of adolescent substance abusers: A cluster analysis of Millon Adolescent Personality Inventory (MAPI) personality scales. *Medical Psychotherapy: An International Journal, 5,* 95–102.

Ehrenberg, M. F., Cox, D. N., & Koopman, R. F. (1990). The Millon Adolescent Personality Inventory profiles of depressed adolescents. *Adolescence, 25,* 415–424.

Endler, N. S., & Kocovski, N. L. (2002). Personality disorders at the crossroad. *Journal of Personality Disorders, 16,* 487–502.

Everly, G. S., & Newman, E. C. (1997). The MBHI: Composition and clinical scales. In T. Millon (Ed.), *The Millon inventories: Clinical and personality assessment* (pp. 389–408). New York: Guilford Press.

First, M. (2002). A research agenda for *DSM-V:* Summary of the white papers. *Psychiatric Research Report, 18,* 10–13.

Fishbain, D. A., Turner, D., Rosomoff, H. L., & Rosomoff, R. S. (2001). Millon Behavioral Health Inventory scores of patients with chronic pain associated with myofascial pain syndrome. *Pain Medicine, 2,* 328–335.

Fritsch, S., Donaldson, D., Spirito, A., & Plummer, B. (2000). Personality characteristics of adolescent suicide attempters. *Child Psychiatry and Human Development, 30,* 219–235.

Gat, I., & McWhirter, B. T. (1998). Personality characteristics of competitive and recreational cyclists. *Journal of Sport Behavior, 21,* 408–420.

Gold, J. (2005). Personology, personality disorders, and psychotherapy integration. In S. Strack (Ed.), *Handbook of personology and psychopathology* (pp. 511–523). New York: Wiley.

Gontag, R., & Erickson, M. T. (1996). The relationship between Millon's personality types and family system functioning. *American Journal of Family Therapy, 24,* 215–226.

Guevara, L. F., & Strack, S. (1998). An examination of Millon's dimensional and stylistic descriptions of normal personality. *Journal of Personality Assessment, 71,* 337–348.

Harper, R. G., Chacko, R. C., Kotik-Harper, D., Young, J., & Gotto, J. (1998). Detection of a psychiatric diagnosis in heart transplant candidates with the MBHI. *Journal of Clinical Psychology in Medical Settings, 5,* 173–185.

Hart, L. R. (1995). MAPI personality correlates of comorbid substance abuse among adolescent inpatients. *Journal of Adolescence, 18,* 657–667.

Holcomb, W. R., & Kashani, J. H. (1991). Personality characteristics of a community sample of adolescents with conduct disorders. *Adolescence, 26,* 579–586.

Horton, A. D., & Retzlaff, P. D. (1991). Family assessment: Toward *DSM-III-R* relevancy. *Journal of Clinical Psychology, 47,* 94–100.

Hyer, L., & Boyd, S. (1996). Personality scales as predictors of older combat veterans with posttraumatic stress disorder. *Psychological Reports, 79,* 1040–1042.

Hynan, L. S., Pantle, M. L., & Foster, B. M. (1998). Factor structure of the Millon Adolescent Personality Inventory for psychiatric inpatients. *Psychological Reports, 82,* 267–274.

Immelman, A. (1998). The political personalities of 1996 U.S. presidential candidates Bill Clinton and Bob Dole. *Leadership Quarterly, 9,* 335–366.

Immelman, A. (1999). *Millon Inventory of Diagnostic Criteria manual-II-revised.* (Available from Dr. Aubrey Immelman, Department of Psychology, St. John's University, Collegeville, MN 56321-3000.)

Immelman, A. (2002). The political personality of U.S. president George W. Bush. In L. O. Valenty & O. Feldman (Eds.), *Political leadership for the new century: Personality and behavior among American leaders* (pp. 81–103). Westport, CT: Praeger.

Immelman, A. (2005). *Political psychology and personality.* In S. Strack (Ed.), *Handbook of personology and psychopathology* (pp. 198–225). New York: Wiley.

Jackson, W. T., Taylor, R. E., Palmatier, A. D., Elliott, T. R., & Elliott, J. L. (1998). Negotiating the reality of visual impairment: Hope, coping, and functional ability. *Journal of Clinical Psychology in Medical Settings, 5,* 173–185.

Jung, C. G. (1971). Psychology typology. In R. F. C. Hull (Trans.), *Psychological types.* Princeton, NJ: Princeton University Press. (Original work published 1936)

Kashani, J. H. (1990). Aggression in adolescents: The role of social support and personality. *Canadian Journal of Psychiatry, 35,* 311–315.

Knapp, J. E., Templer, D. I., Cannon, W. G., & Dobson, S. (1991). Variables associated with success in an adolescent drug treatment program. *Adolescence, 26,* 305–317.

Lenzenweger, M. F. (1999). Stability and change in personality disorder features: The Longitudinal Study of Personality Disorders. *Archives of General Psychiatry, 56,* 1009–1015.

Livesley, W. J. (Ed.). (2001). *Handbook of personality disorders.* New York: Guilford Press.

Markon, K. E., Krueger, R. F., Bouchard, T. J., & Gottesman, I. I. (2002). Normal and abnormal personality traits: Evidence for genetic and environmental relationships in the Minnesota Study of Twins Reared Apart. *Journal of Personality, 70,* 661–693.

Millon, C., & Meagher, S. E. (2002). Essentials of MBMD assessment. In S. Strack (Ed.), *Essentials of Millon inventories assessment* (pp. 52–105). Hoboken, NJ: Wiley.

Millon, T. (1974). *Millon Personality Inventory.* Philadelphia: Saunders.

Millon, T. (1977). *Millon multiaxial clinical inventory manual.* Minneapolis, MN: National Computer Systems.

Millon, T. (1981). *Disorders of personality: DSM-III: Axis II.* New York: Wiley.

Millon, T. (1983a). *Millon clinical multiaxial inventory manual* (3rd ed.). Minneapolis, MN: National Computer Systems.

Millon, T. (1983b). *Modern psychopathology.* Prospect Heights, IL: Waveland Press. (Original work published 1969)

Millon, T. (1986). A theoretical derivation of pathological personalities. In T. Millon & G. L. Klerman (Eds.), *Contemporary directions in psychopathology: Toward the DSM-IV* (pp. 639–670). New York: Guilford Press.

Millon, T. (1987). *Manual for the MCMI-II* (2nd ed.). Minneapolis, MN: National Computer Systems.

Millon, T. (1990). *Toward a new personology.* New York: Wiley.

Millon, T. (1991). Normality: What may we learn from evolutionary theory. In D. Offer & M. Sabshin (Eds.), *The diversity of normal behavior* (pp. 356–404). New York: Basic Books.

Millon, T. (1993). *MACI (Millon Adolescent Clinical Inventory) manual.* Minneapolis, MN: National Computer Systems.

Millon, T. (1994). *Millon index of personality styles manual.* San Antonio, TX: Psychological Corporation.

Millon, T. (1996). *Disorders of personality* (2nd ed.). New York: Wiley.

Millon, T. (1997). *Millon Clinical Multiaxial Inventory-III manual* (2nd ed.). Minneapolis, MN: National Computer Systems.

Millon, T. (1999). *Personality-guided therapy.* New York: Wiley.

Millon, T. (2000). Toward a new model of integrative psychotherapy: Psychosynergy. *Journal of Psychotherapy Integration, 10,* 37–53.

Millon, T. (2003). It's time to rework the blueprints: Building a science for clinical psychology. *American Psychologist, 58,* 949–961.

Millon, T. (2004). *MIPS-R (Millon Index of Personality Styles-Revised) manual.* Minneapolis, MN: Pearson Assessments.

Millon, T. (2005). Reflections on the future of personology and psychopathology. In S. Strack (Ed.), *Handbook of personology and psychopathology* (pp. 527–546). New York: Wiley.

Millon, T., Antoni, M., Millon, C., Meagher, S., & Grossman, S. (2001). *MBMD (Millon Behavioral Medicine Diagnostic) manual.* Minneapolis, MN: National Computer Systems.

Millon, T., & Davis, R. D. (1994). Millon's evolutionary model of normal and abnormal personality: Theory and measures. In S. Strack & M. Lorr (Eds.), *Differentiating normal and abnormal personality* (pp. 79–113). New York: Springer.

Millon, T., & Davis, R. D. (2000). *Personality disorders in modern life.* New York: Wiley.

Millon, T., Green, C., & Meagher, R. B. (1982a). *Millon adolescent personality inventory manual.* Minneapolis, MN: National Computer Systems.

Millon, T., Green, C., & Meagher, R. B. (1982b). *Millon behavioral health inventory manual.* Minneapolis, MN: National Computer Systems.

Moore, S. R., Smith, R. E., & Gonzalez, R. (1997). Personality and judgment heuristics: Contextual and individual difference interactions in social judgment. *Personality and Social Psychology Bulletin, 23,* 76–83.

Nair, J., Nair, S. S., Kashani, J. H., Reid, J. C., & Rao, V. G. (2001). A neural network approach to identifying adolescent adjustment. *Adolescence, 36,* 152–162.

O'Connor, B. P. (2002). The search for dimensional structure differences between normality and abnormality: A statistical review of published data on personality and psychopathology. *Journal of Personality and Social Psychology, 83,* 962–982.

Offer, D., & Sabshin, M. (Eds.). (1984). *Normality and the life cycle.* New York: Basic Books.

Offer, D., & Sabshin, M. (Eds.). (1991). *The diversity of normal behavior.* New York: Basic Books.

Piersma, H. L., Pantle, M. L., Smith, A., Boes, J., & Kubiak, J. (1993). The MAPI as a treatment outcome measure for adolescent inpatients. *Journal of Clinical Psychology, 49,* 709–714.

Pincus, A. L., & Wiggins, J. S. (1990). Interpersonal problems and conceptions of personality disorders. *Journal of Personality Disorders, 4,* 342–352.

Plante, T. G., & Boccaccini, M. T. (1997). Personality expectations and perceptions of Roman Catholic clergy members. *Pastoral Psychology, 45,* 301–315.

Retzlaff, P. D., & Gibertini, M. (1987). Factor structure of the MCMI basic personality scales and common-item artifact. *Journal of Personality Assessment, 51,* 588–594.

Sabshin, M. (2005). Concepts of normality and the classification of psychopathology. In S. Strack (Ed.), *Handbook of personology and psychopathology* (pp. 229–237. New York: Wiley.

Scragg, P., Bor, R., & Watts, M. (1999). The influence of personality and theoretical models on applicants to a psychology course: A preliminary study. *Counseling Psychology Quarterly, 12,* 263–270.

Sohnle, S. (2001). The Millon Index of Personality Styles and recalled relaxation states for one's preferred relaxation activity. In J. C. Smith (Ed.), *Advances in ABC relaxation: Applications and inventories* (pp. 132–137). New York: Springer.

Sperry, L. (2003). *Handbook of diagnosis and treatment of DSM-IV-TR personality disorders* (2nd ed.). New York: Brunner-Routledge.

Strack, S. (1987). Development and validation of an adjective check list to assess the Millon personality types in a normal population. *Journal of Personality Assessment, 51,* 572–587.

Strack, S. (1991a). Factor analysis of MCMI-II and PACL basic personality scales in a college sample. *Journal of Personality Assessment, 57,* 345–355.

Strack, S. (1991b). *Manual for the personality adjective check list (PACL)* (Rev. ed.). Pasadena, CA: 21st Century Assessment.

Strack, S. (1992). Profile clusters for men and women on the Personality Adjective Check List. *Journal of Personality Assessment, 59,* 204–217.

Strack, S. (1993). Measuring Millon's personality styles in normal adults. In R. J. Craig (Ed.), *The Millon Clinical Multiaxial Inventory: A clinical research information synthesis* (pp. 253–278). Hillsdale, NJ: Erlbaum.

Strack, S. (1994). Relating Millon's basic personality styles and Holland's occupational types. *Journal of Vocational Behavior, 45,* 41–54.

Strack, S. (1997). The PACL: Gauging normal personality styles. In T. Millon (Ed.), *The Millon inventories: Clinical and personality assessment* (pp. 477–497). New York: Guilford Press.

Strack, S. (2002). Essentials of PACL assessment. In S. Strack (Ed.), *Essentials of Millon inventories assessment* (pp. 175–223). Hoboken, NJ: Wiley.

Strack, S., & Guevara, L. F. (1999). Relating PACL measures of Millon's basic personality styles and MMPI-2 scales in patient and normal samples. *Journal of Clinical Psychology, 55,* 895–906.

Strack, S., & Lorr, M. (1990a). Item factor structure of the personality adjective check list (PACL). *Journal of Personality Assessment, 55,* 86–94.

Strack, S., & Lorr, M. (1990b). Three approaches to interpersonal behavior and their common factors. *Journal of Personality Assessment, 54,* 782–790.

Strack, S., & Lorr, M. (Eds.). (1994). *Differentiating normal and abnormal personality.* New York: Springer.

Strack, S., & Lorr, M. (1997). Invited essay: The challenge of differentiating normal and abnormal personality. *Journal of Personality Disorders, 11,* 105–122.

Strack, S., Lorr, M., & Campbell, L. (1990). An evaluation of Millon's circular model of personality disorders. *Journal of Personality Disorders, 4,* 353–361.

Strack, S., Lorr, M., Campbell, L., & Lamnin, A. (1992). Personality and clinical syndrome factors of MCMI-II scales. *Journal of Personality Disorders, 6,* 40–52.

Tringone, R. F. (1997). The MPDC (Millon Personality Diagnostic Checklist): Composition and clinical applications. In T. Millon (Ed.), *The Millon inventories: Clinical and personality assessment* (pp. 449–474). New York: Guilford Press.

Watten, R. G., Vassend, O., Myhrer, T., & Syversen, J. (1997). Personality factors and somatic complaints. *European Journal of Personality, 11,* 57–68.

Weiss, L. G. (1997). The MIPS (Millon Index of Personality Styles): Gauging the dimensions of normality. In T. Millon (Ed.), *The Millon inventories: Clinical and personality assessment* (pp. 498–522). New York: Guilford Press.

Weiss, L. G. (2002). Essentials of MIPS (Millon Index of Personality Styles) assessment. In S. Strack (Ed.), *Essentials of Millon inventories assessment* (pp. 224–268). Hoboken, NJ: Wiley.

Widiger, T. A. (1999). Millon's dimensional polarities. *Journal of Personality Assessment, 72,* 365–389.

Wiggins, J. S., & Pincus, A. L. (1989). Conceptions of personality disorders and dimensions of personality. *Journal of Clinical Child Psychology: Psychological Assessment, 1,* 305–316.

Chapter 21

EXPERIENCES IN TRANSLATING THE MILLON INVENTORIES IN A EUROPEAN COUNTRY

ERIK SIMONSEN

Theodore Millon introduced his assessment measures to Europe for the first time at the International Congress "Clinical Implications of the MMPI" held at the Department of Psychiatry, Nordvang Hospital, University of Copenhagen, in 1983. In adapting Jane Loevinger's three-stage validation model—*theoretical, internal,* and *external*—he launched a new paradigm for constructing clinical psychiatric and psychological inventories that differed from the Minnesota Multiphasic Personality Inventory (MMPI).

Millon presented pertinent historical literature and seminal papers on descriptive psychopathology (Millon, 1973), analyzed the differing approaches to research methodology in psychopathology (Millon & Diesenhaus, 1972), and elaborated on his fundamental perspectives on the interaction of personality and psychopathology (Millon, 1969). Impressed and inspired by his innovative, systematic, and timely insights into the varying schools of psychopathology, a group of Danish psychiatrists and psychologists formed a "Millon study group." The members of the group were a strong and creative mixture of experienced clinicians, psychoanalysts, behaviorists, neuropsychologists, and researchers, which gave all in the group the feeling of common genuine curiosity in psychopathology. Each one paid respect to others' ideas and experiences in understanding psychopathology, and all gained by this inspiration to broaden their own view.

By furthering their exploration of Millon's inventories and theories, the group sought to investigate the impact of understanding a patient's psychopathology and need for treatment. Instrumental sources for group discussions and clinical vignettes included Millon's newly released seminal book, *Disorders of Personality, DSM-III: Axis II* (Millon, 1981), select Millon Clinical Multiaxial Inventory (MCMI-I) patient profiles, and other available clinical evaluations and psychological tests, resulting in a pressing need to optimize the translation of the MCMI. The MCMI is one of the few self-report tests that focus on both symptoms and personality disorders and their relationship. It was developed in 1977 by Millon and colleagues and was subsequently revised in 1987 and 1994 (Millon, 1977, 1982, 1994).

Modeled after the success and productivity of the Millon study group, the members, in collaboration with Theodore Millon, organized the First International Congress on the Study of Personality Disorders, held in Copenhagen in 1988. Also implemented was an organization to enhance international collaboration, the exchange of ideas, and research promotion: the International Society on the Study of Personality Disorders (ISSPD). Subsequently, the Millon study group evolved into the Institute for Personality Theory and Psychopathology (IPTP). It is evident to all those involved that such landmark organizations came to fruition solely as a result of Millon's foresight, ingenuity, and organizational endeavors.

This chapter focuses on how the translation of the MCMI-I took place and the efforts to optimize and revise the subsequent translations under the guidance of empirical research.

INTERNATIONAL GUIDELINES FOR TRANSLATION OF PSYCHOLOGICAL TESTS

The translation of psychological tests should follow the guidelines adopted by a number of international associations, such as the International Association of Cross-Cultural Psychology (IACCP), International Union of Psychological Science (IUPsyS), and International Test Commission (ITC; Hambleton, 1994). In translating a test to another language, the test developers must consider the following 10 recommendations:

1. Present evidence that the wording of the items is appropriate for the target population after translation procedures have taken place.
2. Make sure that the test procedures (i.e., testing techniques, test conventions) are familiar to the target populations, the administrator, and the patient.
3. Present evidence that the purpose of the test and the content of the items are understood by the patient.
4. Provide empirical evidence to improve the accuracy of the translation and compile evidence of different language versions.
5. Use appropriate statistical techniques to establish item equivalence between language versions of the instrument.
6. Apply statistical techniques to identify problematic components or aspects of the instrument inadequate for the intended population.
7. Provide information about validity in the target population.
8. Provide statistical evidence of the equivalence of questions in the original and target population.
9. Ensure that nonequivalent questions intended for different populations are not used between versions in preparing a common scale.
10. Ensure that translations are done by translators fluent in both languages, providing both forward and back translations.

These recommendations and guidelines may seem rather strict and technical; yet, from a more practical and psychological point of view, we may formulate the ideal condition for a translation.

ISSUES IN TRANSLATION OF PERSONALITY SCALES

A psychological test consists of a set of items, a set of administration procedures, relevant scientific theory, and all empirical data that are relevant for the interpretation of the test.

Unfortunately, this complex set of procedures and knowledge often is simplified to the point of reification. An essential part of this simplification is to consider only the test items and ignore theoretical and empirical knowledge about a test; one of the consequences of this reification is a naïve attitude to the problem of translation: When words of the test items have been more or less literally changed from the source language to the target language, the same test is assumed to exist in both languages.

Before translating the MCMI, we made some general considerations of our intended aim. A personality test may be translated from two different perspectives: Either you want to observe how a good translation of a test empirically behaves differently in various cultures, or you want an empirically equivalent test in the target language. The first perspective may be called truly *cross-cultural* because its primary goal is to observe cultural differences. The second perspective may be called *psychometric* because the primary goal is to obtain a measurement instrument with certain characteristics in the target language.

An important difference between the two perspectives is that the success of the second approach, at least in principle, can be measured empirically: A translation is successful to the extent that the target version of a test has the same psychometric properties of the translated test; it must include both studies of the internal structure of the test and studies of correlations between the test, as well as other important psychological variables.

In this context, a good translation can be considered only one step in the successful transfer of a test from one culture to another, and it is important to realize that a translation may not be necessary in all areas of psychology: If a psychological theory within an area is developed so that it is possible to specify the characteristics of good test items to a sufficient degree, it may be a better procedure to simply construct new items in the target language.

The purpose of a translation of a personality inventory usually is to obtain an instrument that measures a specified number of personality constructs or personality traits. These constructs are the personality traits that the original inventory is supposed to measure in the source culture. One of the reasons that empirical validation of a translation may fail to relate to between-cultures variance in personality constructs is that the psychologically important personality constructs may not be the same in various cultures, and, even if they are, there may be both qualitative and quantitative differences in their development.

We have compared nonclinical samples from the source (U.S.) and the target (Danish) population. These comparisons give us an idea of the quality of the translation as well as whether there are any striking differences or similarities between the two populations.

Before discussing these comparisons, I first provide a short description of the most important methods used in the process of translating and validating the inventory in the target language. These methods are divided into the linguistic and the psychometric procedures.

Linguistic Procedures for Translation

Three different translation procedures should be taken into consideration. Each represents a step forward: (1) individual translation, (2) committee approach, and (3) back translation.

Individual Translation

Individual translation is limited by the translator's knowledge of the two languages and knowledge of the relevant scientific theories. Ideally, the translator should also possess good knowledge of the two cultures. If there is only one translator, he or she should have a basic linguistic education or have a basic training in psychological sciences. In most cases, knowledge of the relevant theory is more important than formal language training. The psychological meaning of the wording must be retained to ensure that the purpose of the test is fulfilled. In the case of multiconstruct questionnaires, such as the MCMI, knowledge of the included subscales for each item could be of great help in the translation process. On the one hand, translators with appropriate theoretical knowledge may be more able to use this kind of information, yet they may also be tempted to change individual items substantially. The purpose of these changes may be to make items easier to read and understand, for example, translators trying to avoid negations used in the source version of a questionnaire. This may be helpful, but in most cases, it can be argued that it is the original test constructor who should have avoided negations.

The Committee Approach

In the committee approach, two or more independent translators each produce a first translation. They then meet to discuss differences between their versions and work out an agreement on the most appropriate translation. This approach, in most cases, should reduce any bias that individual translators may have, and it is certainly an advantage that scientists and members with formal language training may supplement one another in a committee.

Back Translation

One way to investigate different translations is to have one or more translators make a first translation to the target language and then have one or more independent translators make a translation back to the original language (Brislin, 1970). Comparison of the original source version with the back-translated version is a valuable procedure for checking linguistic accuracy. In most cases, this method can detect items that have been poorly translated from a linguistic point of view, and, ideally, the complete process should be repeated for these items.

If the two versions are highly similar, the comparison suggests that the target version is equivalent to the source language form. However, it must be remembered that apparent equivalence may be created by factors that have nothing to do with the quality of the translation: Translators may have a shared set of rules for translating certain nonequivalent words and phrases, and some back translators may be able to make sense of a poor target language version.

Psychometric Procedures in Translation of the Danish Millon Clinical Multiaxial Inventory

In the analysis of empirical data of translations, a broad selection of psychometric procedures may be used. Most often used are: (1) comparing item endorsement frequencies and (2) correlations between each item and the total scale score (point biserial correlations).

The data might be collected in different ways. One way is to let bilingual responders answer both the source and the target versions. Another way is to have the same group answer a different version of the target questionnaire or to have two comparable groups answer different target versions.

The MCMI inventory of 20 clinical scales has a concise 175-item true-false self-report format sufficient to cover a span of nine clinical symptom syndromes (anxiety, somatoform, hypomania, dysthymia, alcohol abuse, drug abuse, psychotic thinking, psychotic depression, psychotic delusion), three pathological personality disorders (schizotypal, borderline, paranoid), eight basic personality patterns (schizoid, avoidant, dependent, histrionic, narcissistic, antisocial, compulsive, and passive-aggressive), and two correctional scales of denial versus complaint. The instrument identifies or calculates whether a patient is or is not a member of a diagnostic entity. Each scale is composed of a number of items. The raw score is transformed into base rate scores, and a conversion is determined by known prevalence data and by using cutting lines designed to maximize correct classification. The MCMI-I uses an item overlap keying for theoretical, practical, and empirical reasons. Because it is based on Millon's theory on psychopathology, you might expect that the avoidant and the dependent personalities share some common basic features, a finding gauged by empirical covariations. By using item overlap, the number of items in the 20-scale inventory could be kept to a minimum.

To check for translation problems, we carried out a study of two different versions in the field pretest phase (Simonsen & Mortensen, 1990). Two versions of the Danish translation of the MCMI were given randomly to subjects in a population survey study. Both versions were translated back to English. The item endorsement frequencies were compared by chi-square tests for all items. Those items with a significant group difference with *p* values of less than .01 were analyzed further for their impact on scales scores. Point biserial correlations between the item and the total scale score were calculated. Altogether, six items were used in significantly different ways. To illustrate the kind of problems that different, but still very close, translations have on scale homogeneity and scale scores, three examples are provided.

Table 21.1 shows the back translations of the two Danish versions of item 10. Neither translation agrees very well with the original English text, and it is noteworthy that considerably more Danes consider themselves satisfied with being a "rank-and-file member" than being "led by others."

According to the scoring instructions, the item should correlate positively with all four subscales, and these results indicate that neither of the two Danish versions performs ideally. None of the point biserial correlations are negative. Either items with substantial negative item-total correlations should be dropped from the scale, or the scoring should be reversed. Items with point correlations close to zero will introduce noise into the measurement and should also be dropped from the scale. In this particular example, neither of the two versions seems close to the original English version; therefore, we might try an improved translation. If a new translation does not work better, the best solution may be to construct a new Danish item from scratch.

Table 21.1 Text and Statistics for Item 10

Original version: I am content to be a follower of others.
Danish version 1: I am satisfied with being a rank-and-file member of a group.
Danish version 2: I am satisfied with being the type of person who is led by others.

Item endorsement frequencies: 72% (version 1) and 31% (version 2), respectively

Point biserial correlations between item and total scores

	Version 1	Version 2
Scale 1: schizoid	−.04	.15
Scale 3: dependent	.12	.04
Scale 7: compulsive	.10	−.20
Scale S: schizoptypal	−.03	.17

Table 21.2   Text and Statistics for Item 14

Original version: I think I am a very sociable and outgoing person.
Danish version 1: I believe that I am a very sociable and outgoing person.
Danish version 2: I think that I am a very sociable and outgoing person.

Item endorsement frequencies: 89% (version 1) and 50% (version 2), respectively

Point biserial correlations between item and total scale scores

	Version 1	Version 2
Scale 1: schizoid	.32	.19
Scale 2: avoidant	.24	.23
Scale 3: histrionic	.10	.33
Scale 5: narcissistic	.28	.37
Scale S: schizotypal	.29	.11
Scale N: hypomanic	.22	.44
Scale T: drug abuse	.23	.37

Table 21.2 shows the same data for item 14. Here there seems to be a very close agreement between the English original text and both translations (the only difference being between "believe" and "think"). The original text uses "think," and the tables show that version has the highest correlations for four scales, whereas version 1 has the highest correlations for three scales. This example illustrates a special problem with the MCMI. The fact that items load on several scales makes it even more difficult to obtain an ideal translation because one particular translation is not the best for all relevant scales.

Table 21.3 shows text and point biserial correlations for item 37. Danish version 1 has "always tried to avoid," and version 2, like the original, has "always avoided." The table also shows that the point biserial correlations unambiguously confirm that version 2 is most appropriate, and the item can be considered an example of agreement between linguistic and psychometric procedures. When the translation procedures are ended, the final translation should be reported for how its scale homogeneity is preserved (see later section on psychometric properties).

Table 21.3   Text and Statistics for Item 37

Original version: I have always avoided getting involved with people socially.
Danish version 1: I have always tried to avoid getting too involved in other people's affairs.
Danish version 2: I have always avoided associating much with other people.

Item endorsement frequencies: 53% (version1) and 25% (version 2), respectively

Point biserial correlations between item and total scale scores

	Version 1	Version 2
Scale 1: schizoid	.10	.57
Scale 2: avoidant	.05	.35
Scale S: schizotypal	.10	.53
Scale S: psychotic thinking	.01	.48

Comparison of Raw Scores in Nonclinical Samples across Cultures

Comparing nonclinical samples in the source and the target population gives a first-hand impression of how successful the translation is or how similar the people react cross-culturally (U.S.—Denmark) to the statements in the questionnaire (Simonsen, 1987). Raw scores are reported and compared in Table 21.4 (median raw score). The median scores are strikingly similar across all scales. Unfortunately, we had no available empirical data to test the apparent similarity. When we compared raw scores from a nonclinical population to a clinical population (both inpatients and outpatients), the nonclinical population had higher scores on the histrionic, narcissistic, antisocial, and compulsive subscales. Although the manual underlined the fact that the test was constructed to differentiate among patients, it was not validated as a screening instrument. Nevertheless, these findings encouraged the Millon study group to continue the work on the Danish version of the MCMI.

Psychometric Properties of the Millon Clinical Multiaxial Inventory

Another way of evaluating whether the translation has succeeded in adapting the MCMI-I to another language and culture is to compare the psychometric properties. In the MCMI manual, Millon reports the Kuder-Richardson formula 20 for each of the subscales and describes the structure of the subscales by reporting two MCMI varimax rotated factor matrixes. The same statistics for the Danish version and a Belgian translation are described here. The original MCMI sample consisted of 744 patients (Millon, 1977); the Danish sample, of 602 subjects (Mortensen & Simonsen, 1990); and the Belgian, of 427 patients

Table 21.4   MCMI Medians for Nonclinical Populations

Scale	United States	Denmark
Schizoid	7.9	9.8
Avoidant	4.8	5.7
Dependent	9.4	11.3
Histrionic	15.7	16.2
Narcissistic	21.9	21.4
Antisocial	14.7	15.2
Compulsive	27.6	27.7
Passive-aggressive	4.6	5.7
Schizotypal	3.5	6.4
Borderline	2.6	3.9
Paranoid	5.9	9.1
Anxiety	2.2	6.4
Somatoform	5.2	7.7
Hypomanic	14.7	15.2
Dysthymic	4.0	4.7
Alcohol abuse	5.8	6.5
Drug abuse	9.8	13.2
Psychotic thinking	0.8	3.7
Psychotic depression	1.1	2.1
Paranoid delusions	2.9	4.1

(Sloore, 1994). No details of sociodemographics on the subjects are reported here because, ideally, scale homogeneity and factor matrix are independent of external variables.

Coefficient Alpha

Coefficient alpha is a measure of the internal consistency of a scale, that is, whether there is a good correlation between each of the items. Between items and in relation to the total item score, maximum (ideal) score is 1.0. Coefficient scale scores should be between .7 and 1.0.

In Table 21.5, for the hypomanic, alcohol abuse, and the psychotic delusion scales, the differences are larger than .10, and for 15 of the 20 scales, the absolute difference between the U.S. and Danish coefficient is less than or equal to .05. All scales had a KR-20 at or above .70, the antisocial being the weakest at .70. The most remarkable result is the close agreement between the Danish and the U.S. results.

The Kuder-Richardson formula 20 for the Belgium translation showed similar, but not quite as satisfactory, results. The Belgian translation was adapted by the committee approach. Four psychologists each made a translation; then one version was agreed on and supported by a linguist. No empirical control was done for the Belgian translation. This

Table 21.5   Coefficient Alpha or KR-20 for MCMI Subscales

MCMI Scale	KR-20 U.S. $N = 978$	KR-20 DK $N = 602$	KR-20 B $N = 427$	Number Items	Difference p Level .05
Basic Personality Patterns					
Schizoid	.73	.78	.76	37	*
Avoidant	.91	.91	.90	41	
Dependent	.78	.78	.74	33	**
Histrionic	.85	.77	.64	30	*, **, ***
Narcissistic	.81	.77	.72	43	*, **, ***
Antisocial	.79	.70	.62	32	*, **, ***
Compulsive	.84	.81	.79	42	*, **
Passive-aggressive	.91	.87	.89	36	*, **, ***
Pathological Personality Disorders					
Schizotypal	.92	.92	.91	44	
Borderline	.95	.95	.94	44	**, ***
Paranoid	.82	.83	.81	36	
Clinical Symptom Syndromes					
Anxiety	.94	.94		37	
Somatoform	.91	.90		41	
Hypomanic	.70	.83		47	*
Dysthymic	.94	.93		36	*
Alcohol abuse	.81	.84		31	*
Drug abuse	.78	.79		46	
Psychotic thinking	.88	.85		33	*
Psychotic depression	.91	.89		24	*
Psychotic delusion	.58	.74		16	*

Notes: Significant difference at p value below .05. U.S. = United States; DK = Danish; B = Belgian.
* U.S. versus DK
** U.S. versus B
***DK versus B

explanation might be in favor of the Danish translation. Three scales had KR-20 in the .90s and two fell below .70.

An empirical evaluation showed that there are significant differences between several of the scales, when comparing coefficient alpha of the three different versions of the MCMI subscales. There seem to be mostly problems of keeping internal consistency of the histrionic, narcissistic, antisocial, compulsive, and passive-aggressive scales (significant differences between the original U.S. version and the Danish, as well as the Belgian) and, for the Belgian version, dependent and borderline as well. The Danish version has in addition significant higher coefficient alpha than the original U.S. version on the schizoid, hypomanic, alcohol abuse, and psychotic delusion subscales, but lower on dysthymic, psychotic thinking, and psychotic delusion subscales.

Factor Analysis

Factor analysis looks for underlying dimensions (factors) which might explain some common psychological features across the scales. Millon found three factors that accounted for 85% of the variance. Only these factors had eigenvalues greater than one, and Cattell's scree test also suggested interpreting only three factors (Cattell, 1966). The three factors in the U.S., Danish, and Belgian samples seem similar (see Table 21.6 factor loadings, varimax rotated matrix, MCMI U.S., Danish, and Belgian versions). Only positive loadings are included, and the loading factor reported highest is placed first.

We do not have enough empirical data to compare the factor loadings of the three versions. However, the findings seem to indicate that factor structure is best kept in the Danish

Table 21.6   Factor Loading of the MCMI by Country

U.S. Version		D.K. Version		B Version	
Scale	Factor	Scale	Factor	Scale	Factor
Factor 1					
C	0,95	C	0,95	8	0,94
D	0,91	D	0,95	D	0,93
A	0,91	A	0,94	C	0,92
CC	0,90	H	0,94	CC	0,91
H	0,89	CC	0,92	A	0,89
8	0,89	2	0,88	2	0,88
2	0,75	S	0,86	S	0,84
SS	0,71	8	0,85	H	0,78
Factor 2					
P	0,87	5	0,85	N	0,82
PP	0,83	T	0,83	4	0,81
5.	0,66	N	0,82	T	0,79
6	0,64	4	0,78	5	0,65
T	0,41	6	0,71	B	0,52
Factor 3					
1	0,78	PP	0,85	PP	0,93
S	0,64	P	0,78	P	0,79
2	0,61	SS	0,53	SS	0,55
SS	0,56	1	0,37	1	0,41

version, perhaps because of a better translation or because the U.S. and the Danish non-clinical populations are more similar.

Most of the scales have their highest loading on the first factor, which can be described as a general maladjustment factor. The second factor is the outgoing, novelty seeking, self-centered, interpersonal style; and the third factor is the withdrawn, insecure, alert, suspicious, near-psychotic style. Choca (Choca, Peterson, & Shanley, 1986) compared this pattern with results obtained in factor analytic studies of the MMPI and Eysenck's triad of neuroticism, extroversion, and psychoticism (Eysenck & Eysenck, 1975). These comparisons seem most relevant, and the first factor in MCMI is like that of the MMPI, in which many scales also have a strong relation to a general factor of "negative affectivity" (Watson & Clark, 1984).

CONSTRUCT VALIDATION OF THE MILLON CLINICAL MULTIAXIAL INVENTORY BY THE RASCH MODEL

To evaluate in more detail the issue of scale homogeneity and unidimensionality of the 20 MCMI subscales, a further step was taken using the item response theory. This theory and method have been adapted and further elaborated on by the Danish mathematician G. Rasch. His model, which is pure and statistically based, was used to look for scale validation (Kreiner, Simonsen, & Mogensen, 1990). No external validation is necessary if the scale proves to be homogeneous and unidimensional. The psychological phenomena then exist per se. Pure clinical syndromes, entities, or psychological traits (types) don't exist, but even if they do exist, it would still be interesting to see how the test reacts to this high demand for homogeneity. In the Danish study, the paranoia scale was used as an illustration of this statistical procedure and method. The response sets from a mixture of inpatients, outpatients, and a nonclinical sample were analyzed. The test question is meaningful in that some scores on the scales have a higher degree of responses for the nonclinical than for the group of patients. On the paranoia scale, significantly more from the nonclinical sample agreed to the following: "I enjoy intense competition," "I find it hard to sympathize with people who are always unsure about things," "I am ready to fight to the death before I'd let anybody take away my self-determination." The MCMI is not validated to differentiate between nonclinical and clinical samples, but identified patients.

The Rasch analyses showed that it was possible to achieve homogeneity, but only for the syndrome scales and for a psychopathological personality pattern (severe personality disorders). Item overlap could still be kept because it was only the higher scorings on each scale that mattered. The scales became homogeneous when a certain number of items on each scale were deleted and only as local homogeneity at the higher end of the scale. This finding correlates well with the clinical impression; that is, the more ill the patient, the more pure the syndrome is and the easier it is to recognize it as an entity—especially in the field of personality disorders where clinicians have great difficulties in delineating personality disorders. There is most often great overlap, and we seldom see any pure personality types. No personality test can find the pure types, which don't exist in real life.

EXTERNAL VALIDATION OF THE MILLON CLINICAL MULTIAXIAL INVENTORY

No documentation of the relation between the MCMI and appropriate external variables has been reported outside the United States. In Denmark, we have calculated only the internal structure of the test and procedures to optimize concurrence between the original and the translated test. We are fully aware that one of the weaknesses of the Millon inventories is that it has never been revalidated. Validation relies heavily on the sample. The MCMI is most useful if you work in a setting that is closest to the sample from which the test was originally validated. We were planning to do an external validation of the MCMI-I, but our controlling for errors and validating the translation procedures for the MCMI-I in the United States was changed to the MCMI-II in 1987 with new items, new scoring system, and so on. Subsequently, the MCMI-II was altered in 1994 to the MCMI-III; these relatively quick changes made validation difficult.

How do clinicians know in which populations the test is most valuable to differentiate? Most clinicians are pragmatic and experience the test's face validity as their measure for the utility of the test.

CROSS-CULTURAL ISSUES IN ASSESSMENT OF PERSONALITY AND PSYCHOPATHOLOGY

Issues of whether a personality trait is maladaptive or causes functional impairment or subjective distress are obviously related to the cultural context. Different cultures have tended to emphasize different traits as ideal. Buddhist monks in Asian countries are valued and highly respected for their behavior. Their essential traits include solitary activities, lack of emotional expression, lack of sexual desire, indifference to praise and criticism, and constricted affect—all traits that fall within the definition of a schizoid personality disorder in the *International Classification of Diseases* (ICD-10) and the *Diagnostic and Statistical Manual of Mental Disorders,* fourth edition (*DSM-IV*). They would not be regarded as personality-disordered people in their own society. The shamans in different cultures believe in magical thinking, enhance unusual perceptual experiences, show odd and eccentric behavior and inappropriate abstract speech, but are not regarded as schizotypal personality disordered. Each society has its own values and preferences. In a Western society, fashion models, showgirls, and actresses are valued for their histrionic traits; the grandiose political leaders and business men, for their narcissistic traits; academic scholars, scientists, and ministers, for their obsessive-compulsive traits; and dependent traits are valued in Inuit cultures. Thus, validation of a diagnostic system or a diagnostic instrument such as the MCMI has no golden standard. If the MCMI is to be valid and reliable in other cultures outside the United States, we must consider the issue of equivalence, which must be obtained in different ways:

1. *Linguistic equivalence:* Do the same content and grammar have similar denotative and connotative meanings across cultures? The wording of feelings, thoughts, and behavior often cannot be translated accurately. Each language has it own origin, and the vocabularies of words vary greatly in numbers and content. One way of checking how the psychological meaning is kept in the translation procedure is to ensure that a back translation is performed. An important example of the connotative problem is the different way in which *depression* is described in different cultures. Some refer to somatic sensations, others to a set of psychological terms, and still others refer to external things.

2. *Conceptual equivalence:* As discussed earlier, psychological terms are understood and valued in very different ways across cultures. To be dependent, undemanding, and submissive might be valued in one culture, but in another culture it might be regarded as immaturity.

3. *Scale equivalence:* Some cultures are not familiar with the principle of scaling their behavior. They may not be able to differentiate among "being sad sometimes, often, or all the time." They can react to a question with only a yes or no answer.

4. *Norm equivalence:* Patients should be evaluated against culturally applicable norms. Each culture has it own standards for normal and abnormal behavior. There isn't such a thing as a universal set of norms.

CONCLUSIONS

The MCMI was originally developed in 1977. It is now one of the most popular objective personality tests in the United States. It has stimulated hundreds of published papers and a steadily growing interest outside the United States. But we still know very little about the equivalence of the test across different cultures.

The next step in international research on the MCMI would, therefore, be to validate the test in other cultures. Our preliminary findings suggest that the distribution of raw scores of all MCMI subscales in nonclinical populations of an earlier version (MCMI-I) do not differ in a U.S. and a Danish population. Scale homogeneity is kept if a careful empirically guided translation has taken place. Our findings also suggest that the boundaries to normality were most difficult to draw for the histrionic, narcissistic, antisocial, and compulsive MCMI-I subscales. We must be careful to use the test in a clinical population similar to the original one. The MCMI personality scales are validated in U.S. culture, which educates and reinforces certain values in social behavior. Genetic factors are involved in the expression of these traits, and society values such traits mating patterns would select for them. Society not only idealizes certain traits, but also, in fact, because of cultural learning factors, realizes its own unique dimensions and patterns of personality, which would establish unique standards of normality. Consequently, we would expect that the prevalence of abnormal personality would differ from society to society. Differences in thresholds of abnormal behavior and prevalence of disorders might be a threat to validity of the MCMI subscales in different cultures because its validation is related to base rates. However, the MCMI-III is frequently used and has been well received among clinicians in Denmark. In the near future, we will be able to test the psychometric properties as we did with the earlier version, MCMI-I.

REFERENCES

Brislin, R. W. (1970). Back translation for cross-cultural research. *Journal of Cross-Cultural Research, 1,* 185–286.

Cattell, R. B. (1966). The screen test for the number of factors. *Multivariate Behavioral Research, 1,* 245–276.

Choca, J. P., Peterson, C. A., & Shanley, L. A. (1986). Factor analysis of the Millon Multiaxial Inventory. *Journal of Consulting and Clinical Psychology, 54,* 253–255.

Eysenck, H. J., & Eysenck, S. B. G. (1975). *Manual of the Eysenck Personality Questionnaire.* Sevenoaks, Kent, England: Hodder and Stoughton Educational.

Hambleton, R. (1994). Guidelines for adapting educational and psychological tests: A progress report. *European Journal of Psychological Assessment, 10,* 229–244.

Kreiner, S., Simonsen, E., & Mogensen, J. (1990). Validation of a personality inventory scale: The MCMI P-scale (paranoia). *Journal of Personality Disorders, 4*(3), 303–311.

Millon, T. (1969). *Modern psychopathology: A biosocial approach to maladaptive learning and functioning.* Philadelphia: Saunders.

Millon, T. (1973). *Theories of psychopathology and personality* (2nd ed.). Philadelphia: Saunders.

Millon, T. (1977). *Millon Clinical Multiaxial Inventory.* Minneapolis, MN: National Computer Systems.

Millon, T. (1981). *Disorders of personality: DSM-III: Axis II.* New York: Wiley.

Millon, T. (1982). *Millon Clinical Multiaxial Inventory manual* (2nd ed.). Minneapolis, MN: National Computers Systems.

Millon, T. (1994). *Millon Clinical Multiaxial Inventory-III manual.* Minneapolis, MN: National Computer Systems.

Millon, T., & Diesenhaus, H. (1972). *Research methods in psychopathology.* New York: Wiley.

Mortensen, E. L., & Simonsen, E. (1990). Psychometric properties of the Danish MCMI-translation. *Scandinavian Journal of Psychology, 31,* 149–153.

Simonsen, E. (1987). *Comparison of non-clinical profiles of the MCMI-I* (unpublished data). Paper presented at the Grand Rounds, the New York Hospital, Columbia University, Westchester Division, White Plains, NY.

Simonsen, E., & Mortensen, E. L. (1990). Difficulties in translation of personality scales. *Journal of Personality Disorders, 4*(3), 290–296.

Watson, D., & Clark, L. A. (1984). Negative affectivity: The disposition to experience aversive emotional states. *Psychological Bulletin, 96,* 465–490.

Chapter 22

ISSUES IN THE INTERNATIONAL USE OF PSYCHOLOGICAL TESTS

JAN DERKSEN AND HEDWIG SLOORE

The advantage of the use of internationally known tests such as the Wechsler Adult Intelligence Scale (WAIS), the questionnaire method on which the Minnesota Multiphasic Personality Inventory (MMPI-2) and Millon Clinical Multiaxial Inventory (MCMI-III) are based, and, for example, the Rorschach, is that small non-English-speaking countries such as Belgium and the Netherlands can greatly benefit from research conducted elsewhere—provided the relevant translation has led to an acceptable equivalent. In the case of Belgium and the Netherlands, the Dutch language domain is too small for the independent production of psychological tests with sufficient extratest correlations to increase the attractiveness of their use among clinicians. A marked disadvantage of frequently used tests, such as the WAIS, the MMPI, and the Rorschach, is the lack of a theoretical foundation. The only idea underlying the construction of the WAIS was general intelligence or the G factor. As the foundation and starting point for the construction of a general test of intelligence test, however, such a methodological-statistical construction is completely insufficient. A broadly constructed screening instrument such as the WAIS should be rooted in an explicit theory of intelligence, and the various facets or subscales are then adequately theoretically justified. In the revision of the WAIS, the addition of a subtest, such as matrix reasoning, appears to be more the result of pure pragmatism than thorough theoretical consideration and evaluation of the concept. The MCMI-III is a favorable exception in that Millon (1997) started from a theory of personality and personality disorders.

The majority of questionnaires in use today in the domain of personality and psychopathology have been developed in the United States. Many of these questionnaires have been translated into other languages and are used in different countries. Some of these translations are used only for research purposes, whereas other translations are used for research and in clinical practice.

This way of proceeding—making translations of existing questionnaires—has some very important advantages. Results of research and clinical experience with the questionnaire are accumulated in a much quicker way. Working the other way around means that clinicians or researchers in different countries develop their own instruments. This means disparity of techniques in use, and the different techniques are used on a much smaller scale. Another important advantage of the international use of questionnaires is the possible exchange of the clinical files of patients. In the context of a much more global world and a more mobile population (patients), the exchange of files can become of more importance. At the same time, clinical practice in all countries has become much more multicultural. This automatically raises the question of whether existing questionnaires can be used with clients or patients in different cultures or with patients with a different cultural background.

ADAPTATION PROTOCOL

Adaptation of tests such as the WAIS-III, the MMPI-2, or the MCMI-III for the Dutch language domain requires the completion of an adaptation protocol. Indeed, if an instrument, which may involve the questionnaire method, is to be referred to as a "psychological test," a number of prerequisites must be met. One of the prerequisites is that administration must occur under standard conditions. The standard conditions are those conditions that most resemble the conditions under which the norming of the test occurred. A second prerequisite is that norms representative of the people expected to complete the test be developed for the relevant language domain. Reliability and validity studies should also be conducted. Stated more precisely, the adaptation protocol for a psychological test appears to involve the following phases (also see Sloore & Derksen, 1997; Sloore, Derksen, de Mey, & Hellenbosch, 1996).

First, three psychologists must independently translate the different items, attempting to make the meanings of the items in the two languages identical to each other. Geisinger (1994) and Tanzer and Sim (1999) impose very high requirements and argue that the researchers responsible for the translation should be fluent in both languages, very familiar with both cultures, and expert on both the characteristics and the content of that which is being measured by the test. The researchers should also be aware of the manner in which the instrument is going to be used.

In the next phase, the translations are integrated. The integration proceeds in the form of a discussion aimed at the attainment of consensus on the translation of each item. Thereafter, a back translation should be made by a bilingual psychologist; that is, the Dutch items are translated back into English without inspection of the original English-language items. The two English versions of the test are then compared. In the case of problems, the translation process is again undertaken with a repeated back translation as well. Geisinger (1994) has pointed out one problem with the back-translation process, namely, that translators who know that their work is going to be translated back into the original language may opt for the use of words that they know will lead to the original language when translated back. This can obviously affect the meaning of the items in the second language. The translation of the original may be more literal, and the meaning of the original text slightly modified as a result. In addition, this method of translation excludes the introduction of any modifications to address certain cultural differences. Despite these differences, many experts use the single back-translation method (Geisinger, 1994). The solutions put forth by Geisinger to solve the aforementioned problems are the involvement of multiple translators for the back translation and the organization of a discussion for the integration of the different versions.

Depending on the publisher in the United States, it may be necessary to submit the translation for further checking of the quality. In the case of the MMPI-2 (567 items), the University of Minnesota Press indeed required this. They reported the results of their research to us three months later; the evaluation involved five categories, and 40 of the 42 suggestions for improvement proved useful. Should the publisher not require this step, research on the translation can be immediately undertaken. Following an ABBA design, about 40 bilingual subjects complete the test on two occasions; half complete the Dutch version first and the English version a few weeks later; the other half the opposite. On the basis of these results, whether the translation influenced the meaning of the items can be determined. When problems are indeed encountered with certain items, this cycle is repeated. In this phase of the evaluation, the test is also administered to a variety of subject groups (including the population for which the test is later intended). A test for the readability of the items is also administered. The index of reading difficulty and comprehension or the so-called Lexile value (Stenner, Horabin, Smith, & Smith, 1988) is then calculated on the basis of sentence length, word frequency among various types of popular literature, and sentence complexity. The index can range from 0 to 1,600. A Lexile value of 1,300 reflects a high school level of reading. In addition to this index, the test items can be presented, for example, to a group of sixth graders and a couple of high school classes. The feedback acquired in such a manner can then contribute to the revision of difficult items.

After completion of the preceding phase, norms can be developed by selecting a representative sample of the population for one of the key variables and administering the test to these people. Part of the norm group is then retested after a period of time. On the basis of the information gathered in such a manner, the reliability calculations can be performed. At the same time, factor analyses can be conducted and the psychometric properties of the new language version of the test compared to the properties of the original test. This is an important part of the evaluation research. Hereafter, validation research can be undertaken, and such research should never stop in principle. Publication of the test is recommended after psychometric analyses based on a norm group have been found to lead to acceptable results. Validation studies are promoted best by broad availability of the instrument.

CULTURAL DIFFERENCES

Timothy Church and Walter Lonner, in their article, "The Cross-Cultural Perspective in the Study of Personality," published in 1998, pointed to the fact that, from a historical point of view, anthropologists and sociologists were the first to pay attention and to research the relationships between culture and personality. Sociologists and anthropologists, however, are first interested in macrolevel phenomena and less in the microlevel of the individual person. Psychologists have been focusing most of the time on single aspects (e.g., neuroticism, locus of control, field dependence) and the cultural difference for these aspects and less on personality as a whole and the effect of culture on differences in personality.

Looking at some of the classical personality theories, we noticed that the original authors paid very little attention to the universality of their theories. In his developmental model of personality, Erikson (1950) presumed that the stadia in the life course are a kind of universals. One of the core aspects in Maslow's (1954) theory is the concept of self-actualization, and it is considered to be a fundamental aspect of all human beings in all countries. Markus and Kitayama (1991), however, have shown that the nature of the self and the self-actualization vary over different cultures. Are Murray's (1938) "needs" universal? Research done by Salili (1994) has shown that the meaning of these needs can vary in function of culture.

The trait psychologists in particular have always considered "their" traits to be universal. The literature on personality, for instance, has been dominated for the past 15 or 20 years by the Big Five, plus or minus two. Cross-cultural personality research has been dominated by research on the replicability of the Big Five over different cultures. Again and again, it has been shown that the Big Five can be identified in most languages and seem to be stable over cultures. The Big Five is perhaps too much in the eye of the beholder, and when the results are analyzed in detail, the results are not always that univocal (Block, 2002). Independently of this conclusion, we should ask ourselves to what degree the "universal" traits are a product of our European-American way of thinking and of our Western view on persons. Markus and Kitayama (1998) came to the following conclusion:

> Universal personality structure does not by itself imply that personality as understood in European-American framework is a universal aspect of human behaviour . . . nor does it imply that the variability that appears as an obvious feature of human life is a function of an internal package of attributes called a personality. (p. 67)

Triandis (1995) and others have pointed out that the concept of personality is less evident in collectivistic cultures and that the situation is considered to be more important as a causal factor for behavior. People in individualist countries, such as America and the European countries, attach much more importance to the personal self than people in collectivistic countries who stress the collective self. As a consequence, questionnaire items phrased in the "I" form, such as "Most of the time I am in an optimistic mood," are much closer to our way of thinking than to the collectivistic way of thinking or the "We" cultures.

Church (2000) makes a distinction between two different approaches when the relation between personality and culture is studied: (1) the cross-cultural trait psychology and (2) the cultural psychological approach. The first approach considers culture to be an independent variable external to the person. The basic idea is that universal personality dimensions can be identified, but that cultural differences are possible. The second approach is looking for "cultural universals" and studies how culture influences behavior and personality. The cross-cultural trait psychology has been dominating, probably because in Western psychology the individual differences have always been stressed. Initially, this way of thinking has been taken over by non-Western psychologists who just copied "our" way of thinking.

Personality dimensions identified on the basis of Western questionnaires could most of the time be replicated in other cultures. The question remains, however, to what degree "our" questionnaires impose the structures in other cultures. Cheung and Lueng (1998) developed a specific questionnaire, the Chinese Personality Assessment Inventory (CPAI) for use in Hong Kong and the mainland of China. The questionnaire revealed a number of dimensions that seemed to be specific for Eastern cultures. For example, a scale named "harmony" measures an individual's inner peace of mind, content, as well as interpersonal harmony; the scale "renqing" or relationship orientation is a more complicated social relationship concept in Chinese culture. The scale measures the individual's adherence to cultural norms of interaction. Forms of interaction involve courteous rituals, exchange of resources, reciprocity, maintaining and utilizing useful ties, and nepotism. These scales are part of a dimension that has been called "Chinese Tradition." The CPAI is a typical example of what we call an *etic-emic* measure, which measures universal concepts as well as indigenous constructs. The items were developed on the basis of the (clinical) experience of local clinicians and on the psychological literature and their own preliminary research. The questionnaire was developed following the empirical procedure. On the basis of the research results (combined factor analysis of the CPAI and the NEO-PI-R), a new set of openness scales was developed, and the questionnaire was restandardized. This resulted in the CPAI-2, a 541-item questionnaire in the true-false format (Cheung, Kwong, & Zhang, 2003).

We can eventually accept that there are (important) differences between Eastern and Western cultures. Most of the time, however, we consider the so-called Western cultures to be very similar or even identical so that American questionnaires can be used without any problems in all countries. However, when we have a close look at social life in different Western countries, many differences can be observed that could have an influence on the development of personality. In the same way, attitudes toward psychological problems and psychiatric disorders can differ greatly, and the question remains if these differences will influence, for instance, the responses given on items of psychopathology questionnaires.

In the cultural psychology approach, personality and culture are considered to be complementary and they influence each other (Markus, Kitayama, & Heiman, 1996; Miller, 1997; Shweder & Sullivan, 1993). The self is considered to be a social construction and, as such, variable over different cultures. Personality traits, seen as entities independent from culture, are questioned. Persons and culture are inseparably linked to each other and cannot be considered independent and dependent variables. Markus and Kitayama (1998) defended the standpoint that Western cultures consider personality to be individualistic and independent, while people from countries such as Asia, Africa, Latin America, and some countries from the southern part of Europe have a view of personality in which personality is considered to be dependent or interdependent. We must raise the question about the practical implications of these assumptions on the construction of questionnaires and the use of American questionnaires in other countries. However, Markus and Kitayama assume that the difference between the American and the European culture (at least with the exception of the southern part) are minimal.

In this conception, the words used to talk about personality are considered to be social constructs. When we are talking about *coherence,* for instance, in our Western culture, we are talking about the consistency of behavior. Coherence of personality in Eastern countries is seen much more in terms of a kind of equilibrium or harmony between different aspects of personality. The theories in which language is considered to be a social construction are not in favor of theories of personality in terms of universal traits, such as the Big Five. These theories are very skeptical about (1) the question of the universality of these concepts of personality, (2) the fact that these universal terms are capable of capturing the structure of personality in all cultures, and (3) the fact that the complexity of personality can be reduced to a limited number of concepts. The same restrictions can be formulated for the taxonomies in use today. Are the *Diagnostic and Statistical Manual of Mental Disorders,* fourth edition (*DSM-IV;* 1994) or *International Classification of Diseases* (ICD-10; 1992) universal classification systems, or are they products of the American and European way of looking at and defining psychopathology? The major differences between American-European and most of the other cultures have been summarized by Markus and Kitayama (1998; see Table 22.1).

Next, we analyze more concretely the cultural differences that may continue to be present even after adaptation of the test. Van de Vijver and Poortinga (1991) provided numerous examples of cross-cultural differences and emphasized that the psychological significance of numerically identical scores can be different depending on the relevant culture. In addition, these authors pointed out a number of other differences:

- *The test administrator:* The presence of the test administrator can have a different meaning depending on the culture; for example, a Black versus White test administrator in a Black versus White culture.
- *The group being tested:* Cultures can differ enormously, which greatly complicates the selection of comparable subject samples.

Table 22.1   Cultural Differences in Individualism and Interdependency

Individualism (Europe, America)	Interdependency (Asia, South America, Africa)
1. A person is an autonomous entity defined by a somewhat distinctive set of attributes, qualities, or processes.	1. A person is an interdependent entity who is part of an encompassing social relationship.
2. The configuration of internal attributes or processes determines or causes behavior (i.e., the origins of behavior are in the individual, and people are knowable through their actions).	2. Behavior is a consequence of being responsive to the others with whom one is interdependent. The origins of behavior are in relationships, and people are knowable through their actions within a social relationship.
3. Individual behavior will vary because people vary in their configurations of internal attributes and processes, and this distinctiveness is good.	3. The precise nature of a given social context often varies, so individual behavior will be variable from one situation to another and from one time to another. The sensitivity to social context and consequent variability is good.
4. People should express their attributes and processes in behavior so there should be consistency in behavior across situations and stability over time, and this consistency and stability is good.	4. The study of personality is significant because it will lead to an understanding of the relational and interpersonal nature of behavior.
5. The study of personality is significant because it will lead to an understanding of how to predict and control behavior.	

Source: "The Cultural Psychology of Personality," by H. R. Markus and S. Kitayama, 1998, *Journal of Cross-Cultural Psychology, 29,* pp. 63–87.

- *The interaction between test administrator and subject:* The official language at school is often a second or even a third language for the students in many cultures, and administration of the test in the official language as opposed to the mother language can, therefore, differ considerably.

- *Answer procedures:* In some cultures, the people being tested may never have used a pencil and paper. The use of multiple-choice questionnaires can, therefore, be problematic simply because this presupposes a particular type of problem-solving capacity.

- *Stimulus materials:* The familiarity of certain materials can greatly differ across cultures. The authors provided an example of Zambian children who have rarely or never had contact with photographs and can, therefore, "read" and recognize photographs less well than Western children can.

- *Emphasis:* In the cross-cultural use of questionnaires, the emphasis is on construct validity (Do we measure the same construct following translation of the test?), content validity (Are the test items representative of the original test items?), ecological validity (How often is the language used in the test used in daily life?), criterion-related validity, and/or predictive validity (Do the test scores provide information that can help predict future responding or behavior?).

The best way of using tests in multiple cultures is, according to Tanzer and Sim (1999), to develop the tests in both cultures at the same time. Thus, the possibility of certain cultural aspects of the test being overlooked can be avoided. In addition to application in other countries, the following question was correctly raised by Geisinger (1994): Is it also not possible for large differences to exist within the same country? Should research—in addition to the usual normative research among a group of subjects representative of the general population—also be undertaken within various subgroups? According to Geisinger, the validity and the utility of a particular test should again be evaluated for a new population even when the test itself remains unchanged.

A number of practical problems also arise in connection with the completion of questionnaires. Should the respondent have mistaken or untruthful intentions, it continues to be possible to mislead the researcher on most questionnaires. Some questionnaires, including the MMPI-2 and the MCMI-III, attempt to prevent this problem via the creation of a special scale to check the intentions of the person completing the test. A number of subjects are predisposed to provide socially desirable answers (Dawda & Hart, 2000; Paulhus & Reid, 1991). The extent to which a person provides socially desirable responses, nevertheless, constitutes a question that is not easy to answer.

The imposition of a response time limit appears to promote the provision of truthful answers (Holden, Wood, & Tomashewski, 2001). The provision of socially desirable answers or otherwise untruthful answers appears to take more time than the provision of the most accurate answer (for the person in question). The majority of questionnaires do not have a time limit, however. Subjects are given all the time that they need to complete the questionnaire and thus to provide answers that can possibly lead researchers astray. In addition, it is critical to recognize what has been reported by Weiner (2000) as to the validity of a test, namely, that a test can be very valid in certain situations and completely invalid in other situations. This makes it critical to always describe the situation in which a test is administered, the person who administered the test, and the type of background of the subjects.

THE MILLON CLINICAL MULTIAXIAL INVENTORY-III

When using questionnaires such as the MCMI-III, we are no longer in the field of personality, but we are talking about pathology in terms of normality versus pathology. Here, too, we should be really concerned about the possible influence of culture on the concepts in use. Although the taxonomies for psychopathology in use pay attention to cultural differences, they are typical products of the Western way of thinking. It has been shown repeatedly that the important categories of psychopathology are rather universal (the universalist perspective), but we should always remember that specific symptoms can be manifested in a (slightly) different way and can be understood differently (the relativist perspective). Shiraev and Levy (2004) described a list of 20 different culture-bound syndromes that are found in particular cultures and have received a proper name (pp. 244–246). Should such differences be reflected in the item pool when questionnaires are adapted to other cultures? Besides, in clinical practice, we should also take into account the possible influence of the societal context: To what degree are certain symptoms accepted in a specific society and by the patients themselves? Castillo (1997) pointed out that there are at least five areas in which culture can affect psychological disorders: the culture-based subjective experience of symptoms, the idioms of distress or the way in which the symptoms are expressed, the diagnoses, the treatment of disorders, and the culture-based outcome evaluation. Butcher (1996), however, demonstrated on the basis of MMPI-2 profiles that paranoid schizophrenics in the United States, Greece, and India produce very similar profiles on this questionnaire and that the differences between cultures are smaller than the individual differences in one culture. However, it seems important that local base rates are constructed or local norm groups are used when the technique is used in a country other than the country of origin.

If a questionnaire has to be adapted to another culture, we have to adopt the whole nomological network that is underlying the original questionnaire (Allen & Walsh, 2000). To get some insight into this nomological network, we can compare the internal structure of the questionnaire with the internal structure of the adapted form on the basis of the factor structure. A second way to obtain information on the equivalence of the two nomological networks is to research the correlation patterns with other instruments or constructs that are linked to the original instrument.

After translating the MCMI-III into Dutch/Flemish (Sloore, Derksen, & de Mey, 1994), following the previously mentioned procedures very strictly, the test was administered to a group of 656 inpatients, outpatients, and prisoners. Exploratory factor analyses were used to detect the internal structure. Exploratory factor analyses were used instead of confirmatory factor analyses (CFA) because the frequently used maximum likelihood estimation procedure assumes normality of the variables. It is one of the basic assumptions of the MCMI-III that the different scales are not normally distributed; this was confirmed by our research.

The results presented in Table 22.2 are the results of a principal components analyses (with varimax rotation) performed only on the personality disorder scales (Van den Brande, 2002).

Four factors with an eigenvalue larger than one are extracted and 76.37% of the variance is explained. The first factor seems to point in the direction of a *passive and dependent attitude;* the second factor could be indicative for *problematic impulse control;* the third factor is a component of *suspicion and skepticism,* while the fourth factor seems to be the classical *introversion-extraversion* dimension. Separate factor analyses

Table 22.2 Principal Components Analysis of MCMI-III Personality Disorder Scales

Scales	Factor 1	Factor 2	Factor 3	Factor 4
1 Schizoid	.00	.14	.37	.77**
2A Avoidant	.45	−.02	.32	.68**
2B Depressive	.74**	.14	.26	.30
3 Dependent	.83**	−.00	.15	.17
4 Histrionic	−.24	−.08	−.14	−.87**
5 Narcissistic	−.48	.10	.30	−.65**
6A Antisocial	−.08	.88**	.14	−.04
6B Sadistic	.10	.69**	.49	−.10
7 Compulsive	−.17	−.81**	.10	−.22
8A Negativistic	.45	.43	.60**	.18
8B Masochistic	.66*	.19	.29	.25
S Schizotypal	.36	.17	.62**	.44
C Borderline	.57	.61**	.26	.15
P Paranoid	.19	.08	.84**	.22

$*p \leq £.05$
$**p \geq £.01$

on the clinical and forensic populations resulted in very similar factors, although the range order of the factors is different.

A literature review on the results of factor analyses on the MCMI reveals rather inconsistent results, although on the basis of the item overlap, you could expect important similarities. This could be explained by the fact that the different studies are based on the MCMI, the MCMI-II, or the MCMI-III and that some of the studies are performed on patient populations while other factor analyses are done on "normal" subjects. Dyce, O'Connor, Parkins, and Janzen (1997) proposed a four-factor solution, too, although the factors are rather different. Factor analyses by Strack, Lorr, Campbell, and Lamnin (1992) done separately on the personality disorders scales for the MCMI-II revealed again four factors, but here, too, the factors are different although the names given are similar. A more recent study by Haddy, Strack, and Choca (2003) on the basis of the MCMI-III and on a very large sample of 2,366 patients (mostly VA patients) revealed only three factors: low versus high emotional constraint, introversion versus extraversion, and high versus low neuroticism. Again, the factors are different from the ones we found in our Belgian sample. Although the number of factor analyses done solely on the personality disorder scales is still limited, the results are not very univocal. However, there seems to be one factor identified in all the research: the dimension of introversion-extraversion. We also notice that the four factors obtained do not correspond to the four *DSM-IV* clusters, nor with Millon's classification of the personality disorders.

As mentioned earlier, another way to obtain information on the equivalence of the two nomological networks is to research the correlation patterns with other instruments or constructs that are linked to the original instrument. The correlations between the MCMI-III personality disorder scales and the MMPI-2 clinical scales were calculated (see Table 22.3).

Most of the correlations are in the expected direction, but are in general lower than the correlations represented in the manual (Millon, 1997). The scales measuring the

Table 22.3   Correlations between MCMI-III Personality Disorder and MMPI-2 Clinical Scales

MCMI-III / MMPI-2	1Hs	2D	3Hy	4Pd	5Mf	6Pa	7Pt	8Sc	9Ma	0Si
1 Schizoid	.21	.37	.13	.13	−.03	.24	.34	.38	.08	.48
2A Avoidant	.23	.50	.15	.13	.11	.31	.47	.45	−.01	.65
2B Depressive	.26	.49	.26	.22	.19	.43	.55	.51	.16	.39
3 Dependent	.22	.41	.16	−.02	.11	.33	.47	.36	.05.	.38
4 Histrionic	−.23	−.47	−.15	−.12	−.12	−.30	−.47	−.45	.03	−.66
5 Narcissistic	−.21	−.48	−.20	−.13	−.11	−.19	−.44	−.30	.21	−.56
6A Antisocial	−.07	−.05	−.05	.25	−.01	.01	.05	.16	.32	−.05
6B Sadistic	.07	.11	.06	.20	−.06	.24	.17	.30	.40	.07
7 Compulsive	−.08	−.17	−.09	−.26	−.13	−.10	−.28	−.34	−.25	−.12
8A Negativistic	.22	.36	.15	.21	.04	.40	.41	.47	.27	.36
8B Masochistic	.24	.44	.21	.21	.11	.37	.49	.45	.12	.42
S Schizotypal	.26	.37	.21	.22	.07	.42	.43	.48	.21	.43
C Borderline	.18	.36	.18	.26	.14	.35	.44	.47	.30	.27
P Paranoid	.17	.20	.08	.18	−.07	.40	.23	.36	.28	.28

Note: 1Hs = Hypochondriasis; 2D = Depression; 3Hy = Hysteria; 4Pd = Psychopathic deviate; 5Mf = Masculinity-feminity; 6Pa = Paranoia; 7Pt = Psychasthenia; 8Sc = Schizophrenia; 9Ma = Hypomania; 0Si = Social introversion.

histrionic, narcissistic, and compulsive personality disorders correlate mostly in a negative way with the different MMPI-2 scales. Although we know that the scale histrionic personality disorder in the MCMI-III and the scale 3Hy (hysteria) in the MMPI-2 are measuring different aspects, we could expect a positive correlation and not a negative one ($r = -15$). The same holds for the correlation between the compulsive personality disorder and scale 7Pt (psychasthenia). Scale 7Pt is presumed to measure aspects such as anxiety and compulsivity, so we should expect a positive correlation ($r = -.28$). However, these results are very similar to ones mentioned by Strack and Guevara (1999).

An important part of the correlational studies is the multimethod-monotrait correlations between the MCMI-III personality disorder scales and the personality disorder scales developed by Somwaru and Ben-Porath (1995). The correlations vary between .73 (borderline) and −.15 (compulsive). Most correlations, however, are in the low .60s or high .50s (Rossi, Hauben, Van den Brande, & Sloore, 2003). The negative correlation between the two compulsivity scales has been confirmed in other studies (Hicklin & Widiger, 2000).

In sum, researchers who adapt and use psychological tests developed in different countries and cultures are working in a complex field. They have to be aware of technical issues in the construction of tests as well as cultural aspects of the various language areas they are working in. Besides being highly qualified psychologists and bilingual in the languages used, they have to be at least amateurs in cultural anthropology.

CONCLUSION

The idea of using the same tests cross culturally will survive. The world in terms of communication is getting smaller and smaller, it not productive and not very wise to make tests separately in every language area. Translating and adapting high qualitative psychological tests is an example of good practice in science and has many advantages for the clinician. One of them is the process of including all the research done internationally. Theodore Millon made great contributions to this area.

REFERENCES

Allen, J., & Walsh, J. (2000). A construct-based approach to equivalence: Methodologies for cross-cultural/multicultural personality assessment research. In R. H. Dana (Ed.), *Handbook of cross-cultural and multicultural personality assessment* (pp. 63–85). London: Erlbaum.

American Psychiatric Association. (1994). *Diagnostic and statistical manual of mental disorders* (4th ed., text rev.). Washington, DC: Author.

Block, J. (2002). *Personality as an affect-processing system: Toward an integrative theory.* Mahwah, NJ. Erlbaum.

Butcher, J. (Ed.). (1996). *International adaptations of the MMPI-2.* Minneapolis: University of Minnesota Press.

Castillo, R. J. (1997). *Culture and mental illness.* Pacific Grove, CA: International Tests Publisher.

Cheung, F., Kwong, J., & Zhang, J. (2003). Clinical validation of the Chinese Personality Assessment Inventory. *Psychological Assessment, 15*(1), 89–100.

Cheung, F., & Leung, K. (1998). Indigenous personality measures: Chinese examples. *Journal of Cross-Cultural Psychology, 29,* 233–248.

Church, A. T. (2000). Culture and personality: Toward an integrated cultural trait psychology. *Journal of Personality, 68*(4), 651–703.

Church, A. T., & Lonner, W. (1998). The cross-cultural perspective in the study of personality: Rationale and current research. *Journal of Cross-Cultural Psychology, 29,* 32–62.

Dawda, D., & Hart, S. D. (2000). Assessing emotional intelligence: Reliability and validity of the Bar-On Emotional Quotient Inventory (EQ-i) in university students. *Personality and Individual Differences, 28,* 797–812.

Dyce, J. A., O'Connor, B. P., Parkins, S. Y., & Janzen, H. L. (1997). Correlational structure of the MCMI-III personality disorder scales and comparisons with other data sets. *Journal of Personality Disorders, 8*(1), 77–88.

Erikson, E. (1950). *Childhood and society.* New York: Norton.

Geisinger, K. F. (1994). Cross-cultural normative assessment: Translation and adaptation issues influencing the normative interpretation of assessment instruments. *Psychological Assessment, 6,* 304–312.

Haddy, C., Strack, S., & Choca, J. (2003). *Linking personality disorders and clinical syndromes on the MCMI-III.* Manuscript submitted for publication.

Hicklin, J., & Widiger, T. (2000). Convergent validity of alternative MMPI-2 personality disorder scales. *Journal of Personality Assessment, 54,* 502–518.

Holden, R., Wood, L., & Tomashewski, L. (2001). Do response time limitations counteract the effect of faking on personality inventory validity? *Journal of Personality and Social Psychology, 81,* 160–169.

Markus, H., & Kitayama, S. (1991). Culture and the self: Implications for cognition, emotion, and motivation. *Psychological Review, 98,* 224–253.

Markus, H., & Kitayama, S. (1998). The cultural psychology of personality. *Journal of Cross-Cultural Psychology, 29*(1), 63–87.

Markus, H., Kitayama, S., & Heiman, R. (1996). Culture and basic psychological principles. In E. Higgins & A. Kruglanski (Eds.), *The conceptual self in context* (pp. 13–60). New York: Guilford Press.

Maslow, A. (1954). *Motivation and personality.* New York: Harper & Row.

Miller, J. (1997). Cultural conceptions of duty. In D. Munro, J. Schumaker, & S. Carr (Eds.), *Motivation and culture* (pp. 115–145). New York: Routledge.

Millon, T. (1997). *MCMI-III, Millon Clinical Multiaxial Inventory-III: Manual* (2nd ed.). Minneapolis: National Computer Systems.

Murray, H. (1938). *Explorations in personality.* New York: Oxford University Press.

Paulhus, D., & Reid, D. (1991). Enhancement and denial in socially desirable responding. *Journal of Personality and Social Psychology, 60,* 307–317.

Rossi, G., Hauben, C., Van den Brande, I., & Sloore, H. (2003). Empirical evaluation of the MCMI-III personality disorder scales. *Psychological Reports, 92,* 627–642.

Salili, F. (1994). Age, sex, and cultural differences in the meaning and dimensions of achievement. *Personality and Social Psychology Bulletin, 20,* 635–648.

Shiraev, E., & Levy, D. (2004). *Cross-cultural psychology: Critical thinking and contemporary applications.* Boston, MA: Pearson Education.

Shweder, R., & Sullivan, M. (1993). Cultural psychology: Who needs it? *Annual Review of Psychology, 44,* 497–523.

Sloore, H., & Derksen, J. (1997). Issues and procedures in MCMI translations. In T. Millon (Ed.), *The Millon inventories: Clinical and personality assessment* (pp. 286–302). New York: Guilford Press.

Sloore, H., Derksen, J., & de Mey, H. (1994). *Vragenboekje voor de MCMI-III* [Item booklet for the MCMI-III]. Nijmegen (NL): PEN Tests Publisher.

Sloore, H., Derksen, J., de Mey, H., & Hellenbosch, G. (1996). The Flemish/Dutch version of the MMPI-2: Development and adaptation of the inventory for Belgium and The Netherlands. In J. Butcher (Ed.), *International adaptations of the MMPI-2: Research and clinical applications* (pp. 329–349). Minneapolis: University of Minnesota Press.

Somwaru, D., & Ben-Porath, Y. S. (1995). *Assessment of personality disorders with the MMPI-2.* Unpublished master's thesis, Kent State University, Kent, Ohio.

Stenner, A., Horabin, I., Smith, D., & Smith, M. (1988). *The Lexile framework.* Durham, NC: MetaMetrics.

Strack, S., & Guevara, L. (1999). Relating PACL measures of Millon's basic personality styles and MMPI-2 scales in patients and normal subjects. *Journal of Clinical Psychology, 55,* 895–906.

Strack, S., Lorr, M., Campbell, L., & Lamnin, A. (1992). Personality disorder and clinical syndrome factors of the MCMI-II scales. *Journal of Personality Disorders, 6*(1), 40–52.

Tanzer, N., & Sim, C. (1999). Adapting instruments for use in multiple languages and cultures: A review of the ITC guidelines for test adaptations. *European Journal of Psychological Assessment, 15,* 258–269.

Triandis, H. (1995). *Individualism and collectivism.* Boulder, CO: Westview Press.

van de Vijver, R., & Poortinga, Y. H. (1991). Testing across cultures. In R. K. Hambleton & J. N. Zaal (Eds.), *Advances in educational and psychological testing* (pp. 65–79). Boston: Kluwer Academic.

Van den Brande, I. (2002). *Empirische validering van de theorie van Th. Millon, m.b.t. de persoonlijkheidsstoornissen* [Empirical validation of Th. Millon's theory concerning personality disorders]. Unpublished doctoral dissertation, Free University of Brussels (VUB), Belgium.

Weiner, I. B. (2000). *Handbook of cross-cultural and multicultural personality assessment.* Mahwah, NJ: Erlbaum.

World Health Organization. (1992). *The ICD-10 classification of mental and diseases.* Geneva, Switzerland: Author.

PART V

Treatment Issues

Chapter 23

ADDRESSING INTERPERSONAL AND INTRAPSYCHIC COMPONENTS OF PERSONALITY DURING PSYCHOTHERAPY

LORNA SMITH BENJAMIN

Marianne, a 33-year-old, highly competent mother of six who held two jobs, was enrolled part time in college, and was caring effectively for her family. She suddenly drank household cleaner one afternoon for no known reason. Then she took to her bed and sobbed unrelentingly for 2 weeks. During that time, she repeatedly declared that her family would be better off without her. "They deserve someone who can do everything for everyone all the time." Eventually, her husband brought her to the hospital, saying he hoped staff could help her stop crying.

Despite her typically high level of functioning, Marianne had long been depressed. She had a history of several overdose attempts, one wrist slashing, and multiple hospitalizations. She had been given a variety of medications for anxiety and depression, which sometimes, but not always, gave some relief and respite. She explains: "I try to be on top of everything and that makes me anxious. When I am depressed, I go to a deep, dark, horrible place. I cannot stand the pain." She had one successful psychotherapy that lasted 2 years. It helped her deal with multiple rapes, but it terminated when the therapist moved to another city.

According to the hospital chart, her diagnoses were major depression, recurrent, severe; generalized anxiety disorder.

This chapter is about psychotherapy for people like Marianne—individuals who, despite receiving standard care by medications and psychotherapy, continue to suffer with more than one severe Axis I (clinical syndromes described in the *Diagnostic and Statistical Manual of Mental Disorders,* fourth edition [*DSM-IV*], American Psychiatric Association, 1994) mental disorder for a long time period. This population is sometimes called treatment-resistant depression, treatment-resistant anxiety disorder, or treatment-resistant X disorder. Alternatively, these people are called nonresponders. Virtually always, they also are eligible for a personality disorder diagnostic label (defined on Axis II in *DSM-IV,* American Psychiatric Association, 1994). In treating them, it is important to give a high priority to the personality component, utilizing understanding of the interface between the inner mental life and ongoing interpersonal as well as historical interpersonal contexts.

Thanks to my colleague, Ken Critchfield, who understands so well the clinical as well as research implications of IRT. He made helpful comments on an earlier draft of this chapter.

Having worked in two university psychiatric hospitals as a consultant for personality disorders for more than 25 years, I have seen many such individuals. These so-called nonresponder cases typically are referred for a consultation to "evaluate the Axis II component." As suggested earlier, they do, in fact, almost always qualify for the personality disorder labels.

DSM categories of personality disorder were described in terms of their prototypic interpersonal patterns and histories in Benjamin (1996). Treatment suggestions were sketched. In Benjamin (2003), the methods used in that earlier analysis of Axis II categories are explained so that clinicians and researchers can apply them to individuals instead of categories. Individual case formulations are used to link the person's presenting problems to interpersonal attempts to adapt that have evolved in relation to loved ones. In addition to explaining how to develop a case formulation for individuals, in Benjamin (2003), there are far more detailed discussions of treatment methods than in Benjamin (1996). The case formulation helps guide choices of therapy interventions that can be drawn from any school of therapy. The goal is to change problem personality patterns described by Axis II (e.g., Marianne's perfectionistic drivenness) and any directly associated Axis I symptom clusters (e.g., If Marianne's drivenness remits, she will not be so anxious, since she herself explains the anxiety is about trying to "be on top of everything").

A CLINIC IN INTERPERSONAL RECONSTRUCTIVE THERAPY

The treatment approach described in Benjamin (2003) is called interpersonal reconstructive therapy (IRT). The IRT individualized method of diagnosis identifies links among presenting behavioral problems (e.g., self-criticism and drivenness to take care of everyone), Axis I disorders (e.g., Marianne's anxiety and depression), current stresses (e.g., all her responsibilities), and developmental adaptations (described later in this chapter) that are specific and unique to each individual. The general idea is to account for the total symptom picture and understand the person in historical and current interpersonal contexts. If the case formulation can be used to change the intrapsychic beliefs that drive the problem personality patterns, the correlated Axis I problems also can remit.

The IRT approach has been successful enough at a clinical level for the University of Utah Neuropsychiatric Institute to be willing to sponsor an IRT clinic for nonresponders. The IRT clinic seeks to provide service, teaching, and research for this most difficult population. Supervisors include a postdoctoral fellow, the inpatient service chief, two other hospital staff members, and me. Therapist trainees enroll in a graduate student practicum in the Department of Psychology. Some come from related disciplines other than psychology, such as social work or counseling. Trainees usually do not see outpatients until their second year in the IRT sequence, which ideally lasts three years. These graduate students see nonresponder patients like Marianne as inpatients and, sometimes, as outpatients as well. A research protocol monitored by the University of Utah Institutional Review Board is in place to attempt to document changes during treatment as well as provide videotaped samples of the initial diagnostic interview (the consultation) and subsequent treatment sessions. A second IRT training program is directed by Kathleen Levenick, MD, in Madison, Wisconsin. About two dozen experienced clinicians have chosen to enroll for a fee in one of Dr. Levenick's three sequential levels of training to learn how to use IRT to help nonresponder patients change. In addition to receiving their clinical training, some of the Wisconsin group members view videotapes of the Utah patients and make independent case formulations to help assess reliability. Later, they will also test reliability of adherence assessments of Utah IRT therapists.

Some outcome measures include pre-post structured interviews and psychometrics (e.g., Structured Clinical Interview for *DSM-IV,* Axis I [SCID-I; First, Spitzer, Gibbon, & Williams, 1995]; Structured Clinical Interview for *DSM-IV,* Axis II [SCID-II; First, Spitzer, Gibbon, Williams, & Benjamin, 1997]; Beck Depression Inventory [BDI; Beck, 1996]; Beck Anxiety Inventory [BAI; Beck, 1990]) and provide simple clinical counts (e.g., number of rehospitalizations per year, number of suicide attempts, arrests, deaths, withdrawals from protocol). So far, results have been excellent, but the sample size includes subjects who were not in the current version of protocol, and it is small. Descriptions appear in Benjamin (2003, chap. 10) and Benjamin (in press).

Later in this chapter, the IRT case formulation and treatment methods are explained and applied to Marianne. But first, there will be an exploration of the general diagnostic and conceptual problems that arise when trying to understand, develop, and validate effective treatment methods for people like Marianne—whether from the perspective of IRT or any other approach.

DOCUMENTNG EFFECTIVE TREATMENT

IRT not only seeks to be effective in treating disordered patterns of personality, but it also explicitly addresses links among interpersonal and intrapsychic events and associated symptoms such as depression or anxiety. Although patients, Utah graduate student trainees, experienced clinician trainees in Wisconsin, and clinicians who attend IRT workshops and see videotapes of this work are convinced of its validity, IRT has not met, *and is unlikely to be able to meet,* current scientific standards that would permit it to be included on the list of "well-established" empirically supported therapies (ESTs; Chambless & Ollendick, 2001) within the usual time frameworks for research. This situation is not unique to IRT. It is a problem that has to be faced by any approach that seeks to treat severe personality disorder as it occurs in ordinary practice. Because of the relevance of this problem in documenting effectiveness to treatment of personality in general, the methodological issues are explored in some detail in the next few sections. The discussion leads to a suggestion for an alternative research paradigm that should supplement current rules for how to establish that a treatment is effective.

Problematic Attitudes about a Diagnosis of Personality Disorder

Although Marianne did not carry a label for personality disorder, she had one. As is explained later in this chapter, the personality disorder provided the key to understanding her particular constellation of Axis I symptoms and problem behaviors. There are reasons that her personality disorder had not been diagnosed until efforts at treating her depression and anxiety had clearly been established as not effective enough. First, training programs do not usually emphasize personality disorder diagnoses other than borderline, which in practice is likely inappropriately to be applied to those who are labile in anger, repeatedly cut on themselves, and often accuse health care providers of not caring or giving enough. Marianne had not been called borderline. She seemed appreciative of what she had received and blamed herself for any failures to cope. She did not rage at or demand much from health care providers. She mostly suffered "on her own."

A second reason for this diagnostic failure is that if a patient carries a diagnosis of personality disorder (*DSM-IV*, Axis II), the odds that insurers will cover the treatment are greatly reduced. There are several reasons for this default: (1) The belief that personality problems are "willful," while *DSM-IV* Axis I clinical syndromes are not; (2) serious definitional problems for personality disorders, including poor reliability and rampant comorbidity among them (Kupfer, First, & Regier, 2002; Widiger & Costa, 1995); and (3) relatively few recognized effective treatments for personality disorder (Chambless & Ollendick, 2001).

Clinician reluctance to file for reimbursement for treatment of personality disorder has absurd as well as negative consequences for personality-disordered patients. About 10 years ago, before dialectical behavior therapy (DBT; Linehan, 1993) had been articulated and so effectively brought to a higher level of clinician and administrator acceptance for treatment of borderline personality disorder, I heard from an administrator for the Public Employees Health Plan for the state of Utah that their database of cases treated shows, "There are essentially no personality disorders in our state." Despite the success of DBT, even today, insurers are likely simply to declare: "We do not cover treatment for personality disorders."

Although nearly invisible in the administrative world of practice, research studies have made it clear that if Axis I disorders are comorbid with personality disorder, the Axis I problems are likely to be more severe and longer lasting (Shea, 1993). Over and above the obvious need to help people mitigate their self- and other-defeating problem personality patterns, there is a clear need to better understand the impact of personality on Axis I problems and to use that understanding in developing more effective treatments for both Axis I and Axis II.

Personality Disorder and the Rules for Declaring That a Treatment Is Effective

Contemporary rules for research on the effectiveness of treatment of mental disorder first were put forth by a task force from Division 12 of the American Psychological Association. This group initiated a description of standards for establishing effectiveness that now is summarized by the term *Empirically Supported Therapy* (EST). According to a more recent summary, the optimum classification for an EST is Category I, "well established, efficacious." Category II is "probably efficacious," and Category III is "possibly efficacious" (Chambless & Ollendick, 2001).

These efficacy criteria for psychotherapy were adapted from standards of the U.S. Food and Drug Administration and describe what has been called the "horserace" model of research. In this model, a "well established" treatment competes against a contrast condition, scored in terms of reduction in symptoms or symptom clusters (*DSM* diagnoses). Briefly, there must be statistically significant differences between the treatment being tested and a contrast group, using "adequate" *N*. It is understood that subjects from the population under study will be randomly assigned to either group. This is the so-called randomized control trial design (RCT). Alternatively, there can be a large series of single case designs with *comparison of the intervention to another treatment*. In addition, there must be treatment manuals that detail what is done. The characteristics of the sample must be specified, and effects must be demonstrated by at least two different investigators or teams. The softer standards of "probably efficacious" or "promising" involve the same ideas in lesser quantities (e.g., fewer studies, smaller *n*, only one site conducting the research).

The list of psychotherapies that have been "well established" as effective according to these standards includes mostly behavioral approaches directed toward Axis I disorders.

There are "well established/efficacious" ESTs for anxiety, depression, bipolar disorder, schizophrenia, tobacco addiction, obesity, anorexia, cocaine abuse, and more. No treatment for personality disorder is listed as "well established/efficacious," but treatments for avoidant (social skills training) and borderline personality disorder (dialectical behavior therapy) have made it to the list of "probably or possibly efficacious" approaches (Chambless & Ollendick, 2001, Table 2).

Treatments for Personality Disorder and Performance of Contrast Conditions

The EST list notwithstanding, there are a number of studies suggesting there are effective treatments for personality disorder if the standard simply is that there be a significant difference between an experimental and a control condition. In fairness to EST reviewers of the literature, it should be noted that the surveys cited here did not systematically invoke each of the EST standards and, most importantly, rarely implemented the requirement that studies have randomly assigned subjects to experimental and contrast conditions.

Perry, Banon, and Ianni (1999) did a meta-analysis of literature from 1974 to 1998 considering studies that used systematic methods to diagnose personality disorder, validated outcome assessments, and provided data to permit estimates of within condition effect sizes or permitted determination of recovery from personality disorder. There were 15 studies that met these criteria. The authors concluded:

> Psychotherapy is an effective treatment for personality disorders and may be associated with up to a sevenfold faster rate of recovery in comparison with the natural history of disorders. The mean *pre-post effect sizes* [italics added] within treatments were large: 1.11 for self report measures and 1.29 for observational measures. (p. 1312)

They estimated that 25.8% of personality disorder patients recovered per year of therapy. Benjamin and Karpiak (2001) emphasized for American readers that there are a number of Canadian and European studies describing effective long-term treatments for personality disorder that combine individual with group and milieu approaches. These treatments yielded results that were stable on long-term follow-up.

These successful treatments of personality disorder were of longer duration (counted in years) than many of the (usually behavioral) treatments in the standard EST protocols (counted in weeks or months). Perry et al. (1999) concluded in their survey:

> Studies should include longer durations of treatment. Most patients with personality disorders do not recover rapidly. Some who do recover rapidly may in fact represent false positive cases. Treatments of less than 1 year's duration may better be characterized as treating crises, a series of crises, symptoms of distress, or a concurrent axis I disorder rather than core personality disorder psychopathology. (p. 1320)

Limits of Randomized Control Trials

It is not surprising that treatment approaches meeting the standards of EST are predominantly behavioral because their epistemology is strictly observational as is the case for the horserace model. Because they are so specifically defined in terms of technique (i.e., the therapy relationship is not expected to vary across techniques), behavioral treatments also can be implemented in the alternative acceptable design that switches techniques within single subjects. Under any design, the ultimate test is $p < .05$ when comparing two groups. By EST standards, there is no need to be concerned about mechanisms or to require a theory to account for the observed effects. "Why does it work" is not considered to be a necessary question. Nor is a statement about cause of the disorder or symptom cluster necessary to be ruled effective.

By contrast, concern about theory of causes and mechanisms of disorder and change had been emphasized by psychoanalysis during its heyday in the first part of the twentieth century. The concept of defenses, for example, was invoked to explain cognitive distortions. Instead of targeting the distortions themselves, as would be done in cognitive-behavioral therapy (CBT), the psychoanalytic idea was to get rid of the underlying need to defend (e.g., projection) by dealing directly with that which was defended against. Once the underlying (theoretical) cause was addressed, the derivative pathology (e.g., distorted cognition) was expected to remit. Focus on the symptom itself was said to be vulnerable to "symptom substitution." For example, changes in the distortion (projection) would be replaced by another distortion (e.g., denial), unless the underlying issue was successfully resolved.

In 1973, Walter Mischel gave psychodynamic theory a blow that was compounded by the *DSM-III* (American Psychiatric Association, 1980) in that it was guided by the rule that all diagnoses would be based on simple descriptions of symptoms. No theory was to be inferred on the basis of *DSM* labels. Mischel argued, apparently convincingly, that psychodynamic approaches have little or no effects or generality, while behaviorism focuses on objectively defined symptoms and is well substantiated by data. Since the 1970s, in tandem with the ascendance of use of medications that are increasingly effective in controlling behavior, affect, and cognition, behavioral therapies and their variants have ever more confidently come to dominate training, research, and practice of psychotherapy. There have even been initiatives from the American Psychology Association advocating that training programs that do not primarily teach ESTs should no longer be accredited. In sum, treatment approaches that invoke theory unsupported by data are to be avoided by true scientist practitioners.

If the raw empiricism reflected by the EST rules that presently control research validation studies[1] and threatening to control psychotherapy training programs continues to prevail, the potential for improving treatments for personality disorder will continue to be dim. Here are three of many reasons the EST rules can be expected to preclude development of effective treatments of personality-disordered individuals who have treatment-resistant comorbid Axis I conditions:

1. Personality disorders are highly comorbid with one another and with Axis I disorders. Hence, a pure, homogeneous diagnostic research sample (cf. EST rule, "Clearly describe sample characteristics") could not include many of these nonresponder individuals. Research samples are notably rarified and unlike those typically faced by clinicians. For example, Zimmerman, Mattia, and Posternak (2002) listed and applied published research standards for selecting research subjects to a sample of 803 successive depressed outpatients. If all selection criteria had been applied, as few as 14% of the depressed outpatients would have been eligible for a research study.

2. Severely personality-disordered individuals in the nonresponder population are very often suicidal, homicidal, and/or in legal trouble. Such logistic treatment challenges are

---

[1] Authoritative personal communications establish that NIMH reviewers presently do insist on the RCT design before funding treatment effectiveness studies. Moreover, published initiatives not withstanding, horseraces must have been won even before NIMH *developmental funds* can be granted for treatment development research, not to mention for full RCT protocols. NIMH practices tend to set the standards for other granting agencies as well.

often avoided in research studies. Subjects are commonly excluded from EST research studies because they are psychotic, at high risk for suicide, noncompliant with treatment, drug and alcohol abusers, have borderline (or other) personality disorders, have shown the targeted symptom for a very long time (e.g., dysthymic screened out of a depression study), or have a comorbid Axis I disorder (see Zimmerman et al., 2002, for an illustrative list of depression studies). The implication is that RCT studies do not generalize well to populations that clinicians face. There have been suggestions for how RCT studies could address this issue (e.g., they should report their rates and reasons for exclusion of subjects so that clinicians can determine whether their case would have been excluded; Stirman, DeRubeis, Crits-Christoph, & Brody, 2003), but the problem does not yet appear to be solved.

If high-risk subjects or patients with problematic personality problems are not eliminated at the outset, they are likely to be taken off protocol for safety or legal reasons after the study begins. They are then classified as "noncompleters." In some cases, such deterioration relates to effectiveness and should be included in outcome measures. Instead, this particular subgroup of *noncompleters* is most likely to be mentioned in a footnote in the section of the paper that describes the sample but rarely reported as a formal dependent variable measuring effectiveness. Adverse events are dealt with clinically, but they do not "count" in the research.

3. The requirement of large N is very difficult to achieve when working with the nonresponder population. Providing treatment for such severe personality disorders is time intensive for therapists and supervisors, and the patients take much longer to respond to treatment than do the well-screened subjects in the typical EST research studies. Given ordinary restrictions on investigators' and clinicians' time and resources, it is basically impossible to conduct a horserace between two approaches with adequate N in each nonresponder (highly comorbid, personality-disordered) group. Too much professional time is required to implement the treatment for each subject on a day-to-day basis. In addition, treatments need to last no less than 1 and, often, 2 or 3 or even more years. It would take at least a decade, probably more, to complete such a protocol with "adequate N." A different paradigm is needed to begin to approach the problem of how to establish effective treatments in this beleaguered group of personality-disordered nonresponders and their therapists.

A Practical and More Powerful Paradigm

One implication of this analysis is that the "rules" for thinking about and developing and validating treatments should be more flexible when it comes to nonresponders, who, in my experience, virtually always have comorbid severe personality disorders. *A reasonable alternative is to conduct replicated, small-scale, intensive studies that carefully define, continuously monitor, and directly relate adherence to outcome.* In the EST paradigm, adherence to the treatment approach is a moderator (nuisance) variable. After a criterion level of adherence is reached (typically assessed by supervisor opinion), the therapist is admitted to the study. Even within an approach that has many entries in the list of ESTs, "there was considerable variation among the 3 Controlled Trials, even when implemented in the current context of rigorous training, manualization, and adherence checks" (Malik, Beutler, Alimohamed, Gallagher-Thompson, & Thompson, 2003, p. 150). A recent survey of the literature also observed adherence variability and added that there is not strong evidence of associations between treatment fidelity and outcome (Miller & Binder, 2002). That failure appears to challenge claims that the treatments described in the manuals in outcome studies were what made the difference. This observation should underscore the proposal that adherence needs more emphasis—that adherence should become an independent variable. Under that alternative paradigm, patient-therapist dyads are assigned a position on the continuum of outcome measures based on their adherence to the treatment model. The dyads with highest adherence must have better outcomes if the null hypothesis is to be rejected; conversely, poor adherence must be associated with poor outcome. This design has at least three advantages compared to the group contrast model:

1.   Replicated, small N designs are both more efficient and more powerful than designs with a large N, whether correlational, randomized control, or other designs. Consider this simple example: The square of a correlation (e.g., between adherence and outcome) represents the percentage of variance shared by the two variables (i.e., the degree to which adherence and outcome vary together). With an N of 92, an r significant at the .05 level needs to be .205. With an N of 15, a significant r would have to be .514. The square of r significant at the .05 level for the larger sample is 4.2%, and for the smaller sample, it is 26.4%. Much more variance (i.e., in adherence) in the small sample has to be associated with outcome than in the larger sample before a .05 level is reported. In other words, to achieve significance in a smaller sample, there must be a larger effect size. The practicing clinician will notice the difference in effectiveness between a treatment that was identified as effective in a small sample and one that met the .05 test in a larger sample. A significant effect based on an N of 15 would have to improve symptoms in a much higher percentage of individuals than an effect identified at the .05 level in a sample of 92.

If such a small sample study is cross-validated and a second truly independent sample of 15 yields a comparable outcome, the combined results are significant at the (.05) (.05) = .0025 level. Thus, with one-third as many subjects ($15 \times 2 = 30$ rather than 92), the replicated small study adherence design establishes an effect at the .0025 level, while the large sample correlational study reports in at .05. This reasoning would apply in an identical fashion to p levels for group contrasts in the RCT design.

Some readers may be surprised to see this challenge to the longstanding belief that bigger N necessarily is better. Sampling theory provides substance to this tradition of having greater faith in studies with larger N. Continuing with the present example, it could be that the N of 15 happened not to be distributed around the population mean. Maybe it just happened to be skewed toward one extreme or the other. By contrast, the larger N is less likely to yield a result that is not an artifact of such unrepresentative sampling. But here is where the need for replication in the small sample design becomes relevant. If the small sample yields significant results in independent replications, the odds that the significant results were sampling artifacts are greatly reduced, as demonstrated in the present example (they shift from .05 to .0025).

Although this argument about the power of replications could be developed[2] for any design, the correlational design is preferable for psychotherapy treatment development research because adherence is likely to be more variable in early stages of a training and treatment development. Greater variance is a strength in correlational studies because a greater range of scores yields more power. By contrast, greater variance in adherence to the

---

[2] I have only argued by example here, and that does not constitute proof. A full exposition would require using formulae for the respective distributions involved in a particular test (r, F, t, z, for example) and compare their power under the two models (single sample large N; independent replications with smaller n). This issue probably has been addressed by the pollsters who are good at making predictions based on carefully defined small samples, but exploration (and development if necessary) of those mathematics is beyond the present scope. For now, simple rules of inference suffice. The percentage variance argument illustrated here for r can be repeated for any arbitrary number of df for r and for the other distributions if desired. Since I advocate only replicated small N correlational studies for developmental research and do agree that an eventual larger N RCT design is a good idea, there is no need to press this point further here.

treatment would be a liability in group comparison design—provided adherence to the treatment is in fact related to outcome as claimed.

In other words, in developmental stages of any but the simplest of treatment interventions (e.g., providing a particular drug or implementing a hierarchy of extinction procedures for a sharply defined phobia), adherence will vary quite a bit. This variability will reflect changes that accompany expected "noise," such as increases in therapist competence in adhering to the treatment model. If the design involves group comparisons, variations in adherence will cause a serious loss of power. If the design is based on adherence/outcome correlations, variability will instead increase the power of the design. The broader the range in therapist skills at adhering to the model, the wider the range in outcome and correlations will be—again, provided adherence relates directly to outcome as it should if the treatment performs as claimed.

Investigators may not like the recommendation in favor of the adherence/outcome correlational design for developmental research. It requires theorists and researchers to define and monitor adherence to the treatment model far more carefully than is typically the case. It is much easier simply to rely on generic supervisor opinion about adherence and assume thereafter that the manuals are being correctly implemented. By contrast, the recommended correlational design demands precision about and constant assessment of adherence to the model. Under this model, the presence of a manual is taken very seriously, and its proper use is integral to the study's design. For validation of effectiveness to obtain, outcome must be shown to be directly contingent on reliable assessments of adherence to the manual. This requirement is demanding on the theorists and researchers to be sure the manual says all that needs to be said and that the research measures relate specifically to that.

2. In addition to providing a more efficient and more powerful design, emphasis on developing and using reliable and valid measures of adherence would facilitate training. It would establish clear standards for certification in the given treatment approach. Competence would be more clearly defined than if it is simply the result of supervisor pass/fail judgments. Components of the model that perform poorly in the adherence outcome tests could be dropped from certification requirements. Critical ones could be weighed more heavily. Such well-operationalized standards for certification of competence in an approach would enhance exportability and generalizability of a treatment approach. Replication failures would be less likely and/or less vulnerable to claims that the failed replication did not "really" use the stated approach.

3. A set of reliable adherence measures that assess conformity to the model would also allow direct tests of any theory about mechanism and causality if included in the treatment approach. For example, if a theory of a therapy presumes to target underlying motivation, adherence measures should reflect the degree to which that was done, and if attention to causal mechanisms was as prescribed by the manual, outcome should be improved. This would comprise a databased test of the validity of the underling theory of the treatment approach. Despite psychology's present predilections to embrace raw empiricism as in the EST movement, validated theory has often turned out to have enhanced usefulness and generality in the history of science (Poincare, 1905).

NEW PARADIGMS FOR PSYCHOPATHOLOGY AND THEIR RELEVANCE TO TREATMENT

The earliest stage in the development of the American Psychiatric Association's *DSM-V* is complete. A collection of white papers that attempts to outline the issues that need to be addressed appeared in 2002 (Kupfer et al., 2002). Many of the shortcomings of the current diagnostic nomenclature are identified. Better definitions for personality disorders are called for, and the question of whether they should be separated from Axis I clinical disorders is raised. Shortcomings in Axis I definitions likewise are named and reflected on. Since the task was mainly to identify problem areas and mark avenues of exploration for possible solutions, no conclusions were reached. Here is an example of the broad questioning:

> Reification of *DSM-IV* entities, to the point they are considered to be equivalent to diseases, is more likely to obscure than to elucidate research findings. . . . *All these limitations in the current diagnostic paradigm suggest that research exclusively focused on refining the* DSM *defined syndromes may never be successful in uncovering their underlying etiologies.* For that to happen, an as yet unknown paradigm shift may need to occur. (p. xix)

It is unlikely that *DSM-V* will embrace any major paradigm shift, because whatever is proposed will need to have empirical support. But the invitation to leave behind the strict focus on *DSM*-based descriptions of symptom clusters and begin to think about psychopathology in ways that have more useable implications for the treatment of mental disorders in general, and personality disorders in particular, has been issued. The balance of this chapter shows how the IRT perspective[3] on personality and related forms of psychopathology can be used to enhance the effectiveness of psychotherapy. The approach is illustrated by application to Marianne.

THE INTERPERSONAL RECONSTRUCTIVE THERAPY CASE FORMULATION METHOD

Treatment-resistant patients, who typically are personality disordered, respond to internalized representations of important persons more than to persons in their present day real world. IRT, therefore, addresses their relationship with those internalizations. The assumption is that after old expectations and hopes in relation to the internalizations are given up, the usual and customary treatment procedures (e.g., medications, client-centered, cognitive behavioral, and psychodynamic therapy) have a better chance to work.

Copy Processes Link Problem Patterns to Key Internalizations

In an IRT case formulation, problem personality patterns and any associated Axis I symptoms are linked to patterns learned with important early loved ones via one or more of three copy processes:

1. Be like him or her (identification).
2. Act as if he or she is there and still in control (recapitulation).
3. Treat yourself as he or she treated you (introjection).

---

[3] This description of the IRT approach derives from and summarizes portions in *Interpersonal Reconstructive Therapy: Promoting Change in Nonresponders,* by L. S. Benjamin, 2003, New York: Guilford Press.

The person to whom the problems are linked mentally are called key figures, or Important Persons and their Internalized Representations (IPIRs). Consider how this applies to Marianne.

Marianne's Deep Dark Hole of Depression

Recall that for no known reason this extremely competent person, who usually took very good care of everyone at home and performed well in her two jobs and in school, suddenly drank poison and took to her bed sobbing and criticizing herself relentlessly for 2 weeks. The pattern was interrupted after 2 weeks by being taken to the hospital. This was one of many hospitalizations for depression and anxiety, some of which had been preceded by overdoses. She characterized her depression as a "deep, dark hole" and said the pain of feeling that way was simply unbearable. The IRT interviewer asked her to recall those days, imagining the sobbing again, and to talk about whatever came to mind. She associated to being sent to the "deep, dark hole" of a basement when she was a child. She explained that her extremely violent and unpredictable father often had banished her there "for being bad." His excessive violence is illustrated by her report that he once broke her hand by deliberately smashing it in a door. She vividly remembered all the times she was in that dark basement for many hours—frightened and filled with despair. She recalled that she was helpless to do anything but wait until her mother would come home. Then she could come out, but she could not tell her mother what had happened, lest her mother be beaten up, too.

Marianne's Copy Processes

The IRT interviewer then asked Marianne to go back in memory to the afternoon on which she drank the poison. It turned out that she had spent the morning with her father, whom she rarely saw. Having heard from him throughout childhood that she was responsible for whatever went wrong, Marianne had spent her lifetime taking responsibility to try to do "everything for everyone" so that no one (especially her father) would become stressed or upset. Yet on that morning, he had spent the whole time attacking her verbally, mostly for the very things she tried hardest to be. For example, she was always trying to meet others' needs, yet he called her selfish; she worked very hard and handled a lot of tasks very well, yet he called her a screw up; she agonized frequently about doing the right things, but he called her unrighteous.

The accusations her father made on the day she took the poison exactly matched the critical self-talk she used in her subsequent depressive condition. He called her a screw up, and she called herself a screw up. He said she was unrighteous, and she said she was unrighteous. After discussing these and other connections between what she did to herself while depressed and what her father had done to her just before the depressive episode, she realized that the compulsion to drink the poison was driven by the thought that she deserved harsh punishment for these alleged "crimes." Reflecting on the pattern of sobbing in her bed for 2 weeks, she realized *she had sent herself to "the basement" after her father told her she was bad.* She elaborated in amazement as she noted that the smells, sounds, feelings, darkness, helplessness, fear, and self-hatred of her 2-week depressive episode exactly matched those she had experienced when banished to the basement. In sum, after seeing him and being roundly condemned, she administered the "deserved" punishment to herself and then banished herself to the "basement" of depression.

The natural affective and cognitive correlations of this situation were extreme helplessness, merciless self-criticism, and a belief she was deserving of rejection and permanent aloneness. This represents three of the three likely interpersonal and intrapsychic correlates of depression that have been described (and substantiated by research of others such as Blatt, Quinlan, Chevron, McDonald, & Zuroff, 1982; Blatt, Zuroff, Bondi, Sanislow, & Pilkonis, 1998) in Benjamin (2003, chap. 2).

The sequence of events illustrated two of the IRT copy processes. By taking poison and by sending herself to the horribly painful basement, she treated herself as he had treated her (copy process 3). By staying in bed out of touch with everyone, she recapitulated the position of "deserved" isolation and despair.

Marianne and the observers of this case conference were astonished to hear her develop such explicit and simple links between the sequencing and phenomenology of her depression and the sequencing and phenomenology of her basement punishments.

When the IRT interviewer began to explore her remarkable habit of taking on an astonishing workload, another version of copy process 2 became clear to Marianne. In trying to do far too much for employers, spouse, and children, she was continuing her longstanding habit of accepting responsibility to make sure everything was in good order, thereby letting her father's rules and values for her prevail. The magnitude of her responsibilities was breathtaking, and it is easy to see why she might have been anxious about whether she could fulfill them all—particularly when her early learning had been that if she failed, catastrophe would follow.

Psychic Proximity Sustains the Copy Processes

The idea that Marianne was copying patterns from the past during her severe depressive episode is simple and did not require elaborate inference or special training on the part of the observers. Marianne's spontaneously offered words provided the raw data. The connections became clear to her and to observers of the consultation. Such simple connections have consistently become apparent in all referred personality-disordered nonresponder inpatients. Since this theory of copy process was first made explicit, there have been 166 recorded consultations, all supporting copy process theory as described in Benjamin (2003, chaps. 2 & 6).

Once clinicians become familiar with this idea of copy process (plus a few simple corollaries, such as how precisely to identify a copy process in negative image, as when an abused child grows up to be a kind parent), it is easy to see copying in their caseload. In fact, copy process can be seen in normal as well as in disordered individuals. The difference between normality and pathology lies primarily in what is copied. Normal individuals have had more adaptive models and more benign situations to copy. Their more benign, adaptive behaviors naturally are accompanied by pleasant affects and effective cognitions (definitions of normality and pathology in behavior, affect, and cognition are detailed in Benjamin, 2003, chap. 4, and appendix to chap. 4).

Attachment Provides the Assumed Support for Copy Processes

Neither patients nor clinicians find it difficult to accept the idea of copy processes. The more difficult question is why copying should be maintained when the person's situations change. For example, why do some personality-disordered people who grew up in dreadful situations self-sabotage when they find themselves in much better ones? Why can't people just stop doing maladaptive things, especially when they see they are only doing what they have learned to do in earlier situations? Psychoanalysis has chosen to deal with this problem of irrational self-destructiveness when much better choices would be possible by speaking of a death instinct and by considering anger and destructiveness to be primary driving forces. By contrast, IRT theory postulates that destructive (and other) behaviors simply reflect copy processes sustained by love for important persons with whom the patterns initially evolved.

By maintaining copy processes, individuals provide testimony to the rules and values of the important persons to whom they have been and still are attached. If the original patterns were normative, there is no disorder. If the original patterns were problematic, personality disorder is highly likely. Marianne had spent a lifetime trying to establish herself as righteous, hard working, competent, and very giving to others. Her need to meet these standards was so great that irrational self-denying depressive behaviors followed her father's annihilation of her on the morning that they were thrown together. Her acceptance of his criticism represented faithful implementation of his perceived rules and values for her. In that dreadful state, she treated herself as he had treated her and acted as if he were still in her life and in control of it. She resumed living as if she were in proximity to him and all that he represented. Being exposed to devastating criticism from this important person activated painful state-dependent memories that allowed her father's rules and values to take over and direct her internal mental processes.

When patients continue to treat themselves badly, or act entitled, or show any number of other problematic behaviors, IRT theory proposes they, like Marianne, are trying to receive affirmation and approval from the internalized representation of a key person. Internalized representations can be activated by a variety of reminders, but actual contact is one of the more potent possibilities. Behavior consistent with an old problematic relationship provides testimony to the importance of the internalized person and reflects wishes for loving acknowledgment from him or her. Like many nonresponder patients, Marianne insisted that she strongly disliked her father and wished to have as little to do with him as possible. However, toward the end of the consultation, she did say that she loved him. He was, after all, her father.

I have summarized this astonishing state of affairs with this phrase: *Every psychopathology is a gift of love.* The hypothesis is that destruction of self or others is done out of love and accompanied by the wish to receive love. According to IRT, even horribly destructive acts such as flying airplanes into the Twin Towers, killing thousands of people, are motivated by a wish to please important attachment figures.

Gifts of love stem from a wish to achieve *psychic proximity* to the person (or persons) who have become, as Bowlby suggested (1977), an "internal working model." By behaving in ways consistent with the rules and values of a beloved early figure (or figures), patients seek psychic proximity to the internalized representations of those figures, much as a toddler returns to his or her caregivers when frightened. Connections between this reasoning and ideas from important other theorists (especially Bowlby, 1977, and Fairbairn, 1952) are discussed in more detail in Benjamin (2003, chap. 2).

Guidelines for Developing an Interpersonal Reconstructive Therapy Case Formulation

Flow diagrams in Benjamin (2003) help the clinician address issues that need to be assessed before a case formulation can be assembled. An IRT assessment interview for inpatients is organized primarily by patients' stream of consciousness, but by the end of the assessment, the IRT clinician makes sure that the following tasks are completed:

1. *Identify presenting problems:* For Marianne, these included her depression, anxiety, inordinate self-criticism, self-punishment, and self-banishment. When not

immobilized by depression, her willingness to go to impossible lengths to provide for others was a problem.

2. *Link the presenting problems to key figures via copy processes:* Most of Marianne's lethal copy processes were connected to her father's specific ways of criticizing and punishing her, as discussed earlier.

3. *Connect the problem personality patterns to any associated Axis I symptoms or symptom clusters:* For Marianne, helplessness, hopelessness, and immobilizing depression followed her father's verbal abuse directed at all she held dear. The reactivation of memories of terrifying isolation exacerbated her senses of aloneness and loss. Her anxiety had been a natural correlate of her daily attempts to achieve the impossible, driven by expected catastrophe (e.g., Father would lose his temper) if she failed to keep everyone and everything in good order. Her personality patterns centered on perfectionism and attempts to be "on top of" everything. They were consistent with the description of obsessive-compulsive personality disorder (OCD-PD) in the *DSM-IV* and as described in interpersonal terms by Benjamin (1996, chap. 10). Obsessive-compulsive personality disorder often is comorbid with both depression and anxiety. Both are preceded by perceived overwhelming demand and differ depending on response disposition. If the patient is determined to cope, anxiety is likely; when the patient feels defeated and unable to cope, depression probably will be more salient (Zinbarg, Barlow, Brown, & Hertz, 1992).

In Benjamin (2003), additional Axis I symptoms are likewise connected to particular patterns of personality. A more complete exposition of these hypotheses about parallels between Axis I and Axis II is being drafted (Benjamin, in press). Arguments are based on clinical experience and selected aspects of the research literature. The idea of systematic parallels between particular patterns of behavior (personality) with specific types of cognitive and affective experiences may contradict popular belief that depression and anxiety are inherited "diseases." Nonetheless, the proposal is straightforward and already implicitly present in the literature, at least for some depressive and anxious presentations. For example, CBT has long been successful in treating depression by using the idea that depressive affect is a direct correlate of specific problem cognitions. Changing cognitions relieves depression. Similarly, if depressive affect is changed by medications, problem cognitions can diminish. Behavior therapists and the folk wisdom have long maintained that changing behaviors can change feelings and thoughts (e.g., take a pleasant walk and you will feel better). These examples suggest that parallelism among cognitions, behaviors, and affects have been *taken for granted* by many theorists, practitioners, researchers, and others.

In IRT, all three domains—affect, behavior, and cognition (ABCs)—are explicitly said to be directly connected and highly interactive. Comorbidity between Axis I and Axis II of the *DSM* and comorbidity within Axis I or Axis II is not a problem. If affect, behavior, and cognition move in concert, there *should be* comorbidity. Among other things, this perspective allows the clinician to approach a given defined problem (e.g., depression) from any direction: affect, behavior, or cognition. Formal arguments on behalf of parallelism appeared in Benjamin (2003, appendix 4), and further evidence and discussion is being developed (Benjamin, in press).

Connect the Copy Processes to the Underlying Gifts of Love

The treatment plan should attempt to target the sustaining underlying attachments as soon as possible. They are more difficult to identify and discuss with patients than are copy processes. Sometimes, gifts of love are not revealed until there have been many therapy sessions. For example, wishes for affirmation from a relevant IPIR may be buried beneath anger, resentment, and plans for revenge. The connection between the presenting problems and underlying love for an IPIR may take a while to emerge. Marianne, however, was able during the consultative interview to see that despite her terror of her father, she really did love him and want him to love her. She agreed that when depressed, she was treating herself as he had or would have treated her. She understood that represented providing testimony to his view of her. This realization offered treatment opportunities that are discussed later in this chapter.

The IRT clinician never argues about, confronts, or speaks of "resistance to the interpretation" concerning copy process, gifts of love, or attempts to achieve psychic proximity. The IRT therapy process should be collaborative, and the gift of love hypothesis is confirmed only if and when the patient thinks it makes sense. Nonetheless, my experience convinces me that structural personality change accelerates when patients understand at emotional, cognitive, and behavioral levels that their wishes for psychic proximity have not served them well and are very unlikely ever to be realized. They move out of their pain most easily after accepting the fact that their self-destructive gifts of love ensure only unending repetition of familiar disappointing and painful results. This claim is so concrete that it can and will be tested by research analyses of ongoing treatments in the IRT clinic.

Patients can be helped to give up their gifts of love in various ways discussed briefly in the treatment section later. One of the most important is to gain enough distance from their need that they begin to realize the IPIR was/is impaired. Wishes are then understood as "can't be realized" rather than "are deliberately being withheld." Once that reality has been embraced, the patient usually is more ready to grieve for and let go of *wishes for the past that never was.* (I am grateful to Dr. Sam Mikail, who told me that one of the Canadian Eskimo tribes uses this particular language to describe the need to stop yearning for what typically never was.)

Conflict Is Defined in Interpersonal Reconstructive Therapy in Concrete, Testable Ways

Although the IRT theoretical analyses of complex cases with multiple problems in behavior and symptomatology are parsimonious, they are not simplistic. For example, conflict, contradiction, and ambivalence are noted in every IRT case formulation and pervade every stage in IRT treatments. The part of the person that exhibits problem patterns while seeking approval of internalized representations is called "The Regressive Loyalist" or the "Red." The part of the person that comes to therapy for constructive change is called the "Growth Collaborator," or the "Green." Sometimes parts are fused. For example, Marianne's competence was fundamentally Green, but the fact that she pushed it to excess was Red. Her Red/Green conflict was literally played out on the morning her father shredded her psychically and resulted in her attempt to poison herself. She took his interpersonal process to heart and played it out internally for 2 weeks. After reaching the hospital, she began to reclaim her Green and do some things for herself. For example, she participated actively in the IRT consultation and in the brief inpatient therapy that followed.

In general, personality-disordered nonresponders begin treatment with their Red parts much larger than their Green. If a therapy progresses successfully, the Green grows and gradually predominates.

INTERPERSONAL RECONSTRUCTIVE THERAPY METHODS

IRT explicitly combines psychodynamic, cognitive-behavioral, client-centered (and other) treatment approaches. There are clear rules concerning how and when to draw on the various possibilities. The rules are so specific that it is possible objectively and reliably to assess each session for adherence. A brief summary of IRT methods follows.

The General Orientation of the Interpersonal Reconstructive Therapy Clinician

Every moment in IRT should be directed by the case formulation. The overarching priority is effectively to address the motivations that support the problem behaviors, namely, the wishes for psychic proximity to the IPIRs, the gifts of love. The more often the therapy process can be focused on the underlying fantasies that support the problem behaviors, the more efficient and effective the treatment. If unrealistic wishes can be left behind, the patient is then free to develop more adaptive ways of being via well-known interventions and technologies. In Marianne's case, for example, the core treatment challenge would be for her permanently to let go of her father's rules and values for her (e.g., that she was a screw up, immoral, responsible for whatever goes wrong). The part that is so difficult to face is that if she stops providing testimony for his views, she thereby gives up the hope that somewhere beneath the violence and cruelty, she will find the part of him that is a tender, caring, and loving father who will give her the affirmation she so desperately seeks. Giving up such a central, organizing wish and all the behaviors, feelings, and thoughts it supports usually is demoralizing (feeling the losses) and frightening ("If I am not this, then what; who am I?"). It is not easy to do and typically takes a long time.

Focus on underlying wishes has to be mutual and cannot be forced by the clinician. IRT interventions are delivered from a baseline of empathy and done in a collaborative manner. IRT therapists are not supposed to "tell" patients about their patterns and gifts. Rather, a shared understanding about patterns and links and wishes is lifted and highlighted as it emerges naturally from the therapy narrative. Attempts to discuss copy processes or gifts of love or wishes for psychic proximity when the patient is not ready and willing will destroy collaboration and will fail miserably.

If the patient and therapist are running a river in a canoe, the patient is in the back providing the power and choosing the direction. Except during the consultative interview, in times of crisis, or during blockade of therapy process, the IRT clinician is sitting in the front, softly stabilizing the course, but sometimes pulling hard to guide the canoe away from rocks or nudging it toward a more helpful current. These exceptions, when the IRT therapist can become extremely active, even challenging, are discussed in chapter 7 of Benjamin (2003).

The Interpersonal Reconstructive Therapy Goal

The IRT therapy goal is explained at the beginning of treatment, so the values of the approach can be known and accepted or refused at the outset. The Green goal is to work toward a baseline of friendliness, with moderate enmeshment (interdependent togetherness) and moderate degrees of differentiation (separation). Focus on others and on self is to be equally distributed. Extremes of enmeshment (interdependence) or differentiation (separation) are avoided. As mentioned in the prior discussion of parallel processes, these goal or normative behaviors are accompanied by pleasant affects and effective cognitive habits. As they prevail more of the time, hostile behaviors and their symptomatic correlates abate. These definitions of normality and pathology are defined by structural analysis of social behavior (SASB; Benjamin, 1979, 2003) and supported by many research studies involving highly ordered correlations between Axis I symptoms and interpersonal and intrapsychic behaviors measured by the SASB technology.

The Core Algorithm

Whether in inpatient or outpatient treatment, each moment in IRT therapy should be characterized by as many elements of the core algorithm as possible:

1. *Accurate empathy:* Empathy is fundamental to almost any version of psychotherapy, and IRT is no exception. Empathy supports collaboration and enhances the therapy relationship, which massive numbers of research studies have proved is one of the most potent enhancers of good therapy outcome (Norcross, 2002). In IRT, accuracy of the empathy is defined as a warm focus on other that is affirming or supportive (defined by SASB dimensional coding) and that corresponds well to the case formulation.

2. *Support the Green more than the Red:* Almost every therapy interaction involves the Red/Green conflict. Ideally, the therapist highlights Green implications of what the patient just said and minimizes the Red. Again, Red and Green are defined by the case formulation, which in turn is determined by the presenting problems and their copy process connections. For example, for someone who had identification copy process connections to a violent figure, the IRT therapist would be careful to say: (1) "You were able to control your temper, and the results were good," rather than, (2) "He made you so mad, you wanted to blow him away." The IRT reflection in alternative 1 shows understanding and contributes to Green interpersonal learning needed according to the case formulation. It slights the Red wish to deal with the situation with violence. The reflection in alternative 2 might come from a treatment model that highlights identification of anger. The IRT clinician could choose alternative 2 if the case formulation suggested that identification of anger was a needed corrective experience, but not otherwise. An example of an exception would be if there were strong prohibitions against anger in the patient's family, and he or she is just beginning to discover it.

Early in treatment, there is likely to be much more Red than Green. It is not possible or wise for the clinician to ignore Red behaviors, especially in severely disordered individuals. The Red will repeat its themes and escalate until it is heard, so it is best to acknowledge its presence explicitly as soon as it is noticed, no matter how subtle (e.g., "Please tell me more about what you mean when you say you may have to go away?"). It is better to talk about possible Red activity than to wait until it erupts in self-destructive behavior.

Sometimes, the clinician even has to "cozy up to the Red" (Benjamin, 2003, chaps. 3 & 5) to establish a working relationship and hold the patient in treatment. As time goes by, however, the clinician increasingly downplays Red wishes and promotes Green. In Benjamin (1996), I called this the Shaurette principle, meaning at first you must join the patient in hostile interpersonal space and at least implicitly accept, if not also agree with, his or her hostile processes, concerns, or thoughts. Gradually, the process moves into friendly space and ultimately ends with the patient able and willing to behave in ways that are Greener and more consistent with the therapy goal.

3. *Relate every intervention to the case formulation:* By now, the point may be clear that everything is directed by the case formulation. Examples appear throughout Benjamin (2003).

4. *Elicit detail about input, response, impact on self:* The IRT case formulation method shows how symptoms and problem behaviors are related to the impacts of earlier important interpersonal relationships, now translated into intrapsychic events involving IPIRs. Marianne's self-talk during her severe depressive episode made the connection between her interpersonal and intrapsychic experiences very clear. The boundary between interpersonal and intrapsychic typically is fluid. Although originally interpersonal, relationships with IPIRs have become internal events. It often does not matter much whether the person who originally provided the template for the IPIR is still living and in the person's life. Internal templates have weak time frames—then is now and now is then.

Since the case formulation is profoundly interpersonal, the treatment approach is, too. The interactive perspective pervades the therapy at the minute-to-minute level. Every conversation in IRT needs to begin with a clear and concrete sense of someone interacting with someone or something (any person, any idea, an animal, a broken fixture, just about anything at all that seems important to the interactant). If the patient is "sad," the clinician needs to know: Sad in relation to what or whom? The core algorithm requires that all such statements be explored in terms of their input (What was going on when you first felt sad this week?), response (What did you do, think, feel about it?), and impact on the self (How did you then feel about yourself?). When developed this way, almost every event can then easily be related to the case formulation. Such detail provides a constant check on and means to update and correct the case formulation (e.g., the patient did not curl up and withdraw, as was his childhood habit described in his case formulation up to now. Rather, he got into a street fight, like his older brother, suggesting a new template needs to be added to his case formulation.)

5. *Elicit ABCs associated with the story:* Every interactive event should, if possible, be explored in terms of Affect, Behavior and Cognition (ABCs). In IRT, no particular priority is assigned to any of these domains. All are interactive and all are relevant. Prototypic questions that explore the ABCs are: How did you feel? What did you do? What did you think?

6. *Relate the intervention to the five steps:* There are five steps or stages in IRT. They are so central to the approach that they are discussed separately in the next section.

The Five Steps in Interpersonal Reconstructive Therapy

The IRT therapist works from an empathic client-centered baseline and systematically requires therapy activities that facilitate self-discovery (psychodynamic) and self-management (cognitive-behavioral). The steps or stages, along with suggested interventions, are shown in Figure 23.1.

Interventions that facilitate self-discovery appear on the left-hand side of the figure, and they are mostly psychodynamic in nature. In IRT, the only reason to discuss the past is to motivate change. No inherent value is placed on remembering per se, as is the case in use of the cathartic model. The rationale for attending to the past in IRT is simple: By remembering relevant interactions that are related to the key figures and the organizing wishes, the patient is more aware of what is shaping his or her behaviors, feelings, and thoughts. He or she, therefore, has more choice. B. F. Skinner allegedly said: "The more you know about what determines your behavior, the freer you are to choose." Once the patient has a perspective on the past that permits him or her to let go of the old wishes it supported, he or she will be much more efficient in learning new ways of self-management.

Self-management activities are listed on the right-hand side of Figure 23.1, and most of these will be familiar to behavioral, cognitive-behavioral, and dialectical behavioral therapists.

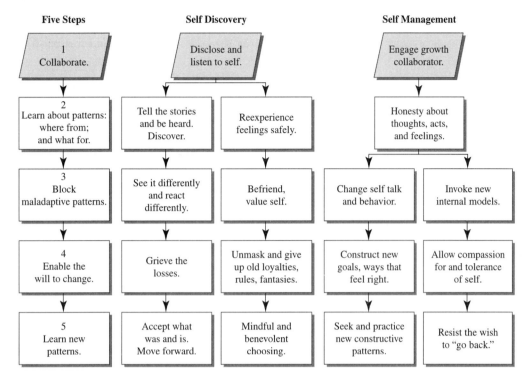

Figure 23.1 Therapy Steps and Tasks. From Benjamin (2003), p. 88. Copyright Guilford Press. Reprinted by permission.

Each of the five therapy steps invokes the Red/Green conflict. Red is everywhere at first with nonresponders, and trainees need to learn to be patient with it. When working with severe personality disorders characteristic of nonresponders, clinicians learn to expect dramatic ups and downs during the reconstruction of personality. Steps are listed in approximate sequential (and hierarchical) order, but there is much going back and forth, too. For example, there can sometimes be new learning at the beginning of therapy (Step 5), and toward the end of therapy, collaboration (Step 1) can reemerge as an issue.

*Step 1: Collaborate (Develop and Preserve a Good Working
Therapy Relationship)*

Empathy is key to IRT collaboration. But collaboration is far more than simple understanding or friendliness reflected in mutual liking between patient and therapists. Collaboration also includes a willingness to engage in the therapy work, as is the case if there is a good therapy alliance (Horvath, 1994). In IRT, that therapy task is to work to understand and appreciate the impact of copy processes and gifts of love—to try to give up addictions to the associated old habits and wishes and replace them with new, more adaptive ones. Good collaboration can lead sometimes to uncomfortable exchanges as the therapist receives and uses permission to press to confront perspectives that are uncomfortable, even frightening.

Collaboration begins in the first session, when the IRT therapist provides a clear description of the therapy approach via the "learning speech." In prototypic form, that speech is:

> Interpersonal Reconstructive Therapy starts with learning to recognize your patterns, where they came from and *what they are for.* Once you see that clearly, you can make a *decision* about whether to change. Finally, work can begin on learning new and better patterns. (Benjamin, 2003, p. 51)

Simple as it sounds, that speech has many implications. For example, it makes it clear that the patient, the learner, is responsible for therapy progress, and any progress is solely for his or her benefit. Second, it also makes it clear that the therapist is not a substitute parent ready to fulfill unrealized wishes. Nor is therapy about love and affirmation "for sale." Rather, the therapist is a teacher, a coach, who expects to provide expertise and hard work in exchange for a fee. Therapy is simply an intense relationship that is focused exclusively on the patient's learning about himself or herself. Its purpose is to facilitate awareness and choice so the patient may be more able to let go of old ways that are not working well and choose to learn new ones consistent with the therapy goals described earlier.

Step 2: Learn about Patterns, Where They Are From, and What They Are For

Once the therapy goals and methods are disclosed and agreed on, the process of discovering copy processes and copy links begins. Insight about copy processes, links to IPIRs, and discovery of gifts of love is not the cure. It just marks the beginning of the therapy work. For example, when Marianne discovered that her depression was a recapitulation of the horror with her father, she was not cured of depression. All that had happened was that she had learned that she must begin to separate herself from the internalized representation of her father. She will need to go on to other steps in the treatment. Approaching Step 3, block maladaptive behaviors, she must work on no longer reflexively trying to be all things to all people so that she can protect them from her (internalized) father's rage. Approaching Step 4, she must give up that hope that someday, somehow, he will become the loving and supportive father he never was. The process of letting go of old ways and wishes is sketched in a flow diagram in Benjamin (2003), called "Coming to terms," but a description of the suggested components is beyond the present scope. At Step 5, she will practice new patterns, such as taking time off to play or setting limits on her demanding children.

Step 3: Block Maladaptive Patterns

This step is crucial during crises (e.g., suicidal, homicidal, legal) and also when therapy seems to have come to a standstill. Suggested interventions appear in Figure 23.1 and in two flow diagrams. The first of these is about coming unstuck (Benjamin, 2003, chap. 3), and the other is about managing suicidal and homicidal threats (Benjamin, 2003, chap. 7).

Step 4: Enable the Will to Change

This step most directly addresses the wishes that support the copy processes. Insight at Step 2, the shared understanding of the case formulation, can contribute to enabling the will to change. For example, when Marianne realized she was providing testimony to her father's hostile views of her, she began to think perhaps she could respond differently to his verbal abuse. As she realized that sending herself to the depressive basement meant she was giving him control over her, she became very interested in learning how to resist that reaction. As she thought about the idea she was giving him so much control over her, she offered: "I don't think I will ever be that depressed again." As noted earlier, however, insight rarely is the end of the therapy story. Instead, it is a motivator that begins therapy and supports the discomfort of going through a slow and difficult process of learning to react in different ways in nearly every aspect of our lives.

This stage of enabling the will to change follows Prochaska's (Prochaska, DiClemente, & Norcross, 1992) transtheoretical model for stages of change: precontemplation, contemplation, preparation, action, and maintenance. Before the IRT consultation, Marianne was in the precontemplation stage. As she thought about the power she had been giving her father when she got so depressed, she entered the stage of contemplation. Therapy conversations before trying the new behaviors might constitute preparation. If she could begin to react and behave differently with her father and others, she would enter the stage of action.

As most severely disordered patients have trouble consistently giving up their old ways of responding, it becomes clear that Step 4 also can be described in terms of Kubler-Ross's (1969) stages of death and dying (denial, protest, despair, acceptance). Marianne might, for a little while, protest her lot in the family and become despairing about the fact she was treated so badly. She probably would grieve for her lost childhood as well as for the loss of the hope that she might be affirmed and warmly loved by her father. Ultimately, if she can accept that it was what it was, but never more need be, she can truly move on and not be troubled by such extreme episodes of depression or anxiety again.

Step 5: Learn New Patterns

After the past has been accepted and let go, it is much easier to respond to standard behavioral technology and interpersonal learning techniques offered in Step 5. Some personality-disordered nonresponders need instruction in adaptive techniques via parent training, assertiveness training, communication skills training, and the like. But many already have been in such programs without effect. Once they have engaged the will to change in adaptive directions, their "latent" learning becomes apparent as they go ahead and use those good skills. Personality-disordered nonresponders who have no idea of how to relate in relatively friendly, reciprocal, balanced ways will need to spend more time at Step 5. For them, supplementary group therapy focused on social, assertiveness, or other needed skills can be excellent adjunctive treatments.

New learning, like everything else in IRT, is directed by the case formulation. For example, Marianne realized during the consultative interview that she was responding to inappropriate demands from her teenage daughter. The daughter would yell at her mother for not having ironed a blouse for school. Marianne would then rush to iron the blouse even though she understood it would be better to help her daughter learn to take responsibility for herself and iron her own blouse. By complying with the daughter's name calling and commands to serve, Marianne observed that she was now "teaching" (her word) her child to repeat her father's controlling, degrading patterns with her. By the mechanisms of complementarity as defined in the SASB model[4] (Benjamin, 2003, chap. 4), abused, parentified children like Marianne end up "getting it" from all directions. First, they are abused by the family of origin and then again by the generation that follows.

Recognition of copy processes often is more effective in changing parenting behaviors than it is in changing behaviors toward the self. Many nonresponders can change for the benefit of others more easily than when it comes to changing for their own benefit.

---

[4] The SASB model codified interpersonal patterns and rigorously defines predictive principles that correspond directly to copy process. Patient phenomenology can be assessed by SASB questionnaires, and patient behaviors, by the SASB coding system. These data test IRT copy process predictions (e.g., Cushing, 2003; Smith, 2002) and can be related to measures of Axis I symptoms and provide test IRT hypotheses about connections between Axis II and Axis I. Questionnaires, manuals, and software are available to qualified users from the University of Utah via Intrex@psych.utah.edu.

RESEARCH ON THE EFFECTIVENESS OF INTERPERSONAL RECONSTRUCTIVE THERAPY

Earlier in this chapter, there was consideration of how to measure effectiveness of treatments of personality-disordered nonresponder patients. It was suggested that standard EST protocols are not well suited to this task, and an alternative paradigm of relating adherence to outcome was proposed. The first challenge when applying that paradigm to study effectiveness of IRT has been to assess reliability of the case formulations that direct every treatment intervention. Next, the IRT research team needs to be able to assess adherence to core algorithm and the five steps, with explicit attention given to the case formulation and the Red/Green conflict.

We decided not to let these problems be solved simply by constructing scales that range, in effect, from "not at all adherent" to "very much adherent." Numbers would be obtained, and they also might even correlate with outcome. But we could not be sure what the raters had in mind when they made those global judgments of adherence. We have chosen the more demanding course of trying to construct scales that explicitly invoke critical features of the treatment model. For example, Step 3, ratings of therapist activities related to blocking maladaptive patterns, may range from -10, anchored by "facilitates/enhances Red," all the way to $+10$, "optimally opposes/blocks Red." This scale may be used twice for the therapist: once when engaged in activities that relate to self-discovery and the second time when self-management activities are implemented. The same two sets of ratings will be repeated for the patient. In addition, similar ratings for aspects of the core algorithm will be made. We are hopeful that our breakdown of adherence is concrete enough to assert that our assessments of adherence do reflect critical components of the treatment model. There are many important decisions to be made when rating therapy sessions for adherence to the therapy model. First, the model's critical elements must be clearly identified. Then, there are the usual challenges of how to construct the scales that assess those critical elements, train raters, and assess their reliability. Units of sampling, as always, pose difficult questions. Dr. Kenneth Critchfield is the director of our team's efforts to develop and implement these adherence measures in IRT. His description of our decisions and early results will be forthcoming in the next year or so.

If an IRT trainee and his or her patient get high ratings on scales like these and if reliability is established by agreement from independent observers, it is reasonable to conclude that those trainees are adhering to the model. The numbers, if they relate to outcome, should be more informative than if a supervisor just rated trainees as, for example, 80% adherent. Nonresponders with highly adherent therapists should show significantly less depression after a year of IRT treatment than nonresponders with less adherent therapists. With the adherence outcome correlations, we also should be able to tell whether, for example, adherence to Step 4 (enabling the will to change) has a stronger relation with outcome than to some of the other steps. We could test whether the relation between Step 2 (learning about patterns) and Step 4 (enabling the will to change) is as expected—that is, that insight about copy process enables the will to change, and increased will to change is associated with better outcome. Or we can explore whether Step 1 (collaboration) must receive high ratings all of the time, as proposed. These and other uses of the adherence outcome correlations could help establish whether the treatment model is effective and, furthermore, might help identify which components of the model are more (or less) effective than others.

For any therapy treatment model, the adherence outcome paradigm demands careful articulation of its critical components as well as credible choices of how to assess those features. This exercise is daunting and demanding in terms of time and effort. Nonetheless, it is essential to carefully describe models in detail and develop closely corresponding measures of adherence if there are to be more truly effective treatments for individuals who are severely personality disordered and who have a record of nonresponsiveness to treatment.

CONCLUSIONS

The case formulation method in IRT proposes that patterns of personality are shaped by interactions with loved ones via one or more of three copy processes: (1) Be like him or her, (2) act as if he or she is still there and in control, or (3) treat yourself as he or she treated you. These interpersonal experiences with loved ones become encoded as internal working models (Bowlby, 1977) or internalized representations. Relationships with these internal models greatly affect a person's ways of relating to others and to himself or herself. They can become more important in determining behavior than whatever is happening at any given moment, as the individual seeks to remain loyal to the rules and values of the loved ones.

For example, Marianne, the illustrative patient, had a violent and condemnatory father. As a child, she scurried to keep everything in order, trying to protect herself and others from his rage. As an adult, she continued to try to manage things perfectly and sometimes became violent with and condemning of herself. Although usually highly functional, her relationship with her internalized father could take over her life and lead her to nonfunctional despair and dangerous suicidal actions. If he said she was nonfunctional ("a screw up") and unworthy, she lived out those expectations rather exactly. IRT proposes that such maladaptive loyalties are motivated by a desired to receive affirmation from the internalized figures. Although she said she hated him, Marianne acknowledged that she did love him, as he was her father.

IRT theory presumes that affect, behavior, and cognition evolved in support of one another and move in parallel. Hence, specific interpersonal and intrapsychic behaviors are directly and naturally linked to specific symptoms. Here is one of many possible examples: Helplessness can be associated with depression if the person has given up trying to cope successfully with a current situation that invokes the perceived rules and values of an internalized figure. These same conditions can be associated with anxiety if the person is still trying to cope but worries that he or she may not be able to do so.

The treatment implication of the IRT analysis is that the person who is behaving in maladaptive ways associated with presenting symptomatology needs help in letting go of any unrealistic wishes for affirmation that support the strategy of treating himself or herself according to the rules and values of an internalized figure. Once that intrapsychic goal is let go, more adaptive ways of relating to self and other can be learned. The idea that interpersonal (and intrapsychic) behaviors, cognitions, and affects move in parallel helps us understand why clinical syndromes such as anxiety or depression may be addressed by working with interpersonal and intrapsychic patterns driven by relevant internalized representations.

The IRT treatment manual (Benjamin, 2003) gives specific instructions for developing case formulations and using the case formulation in choosing therapy interventions to address the presenting symptoms. The overall orientation is detailed by a six-part core algorithm including: (1) Work from an empathic baseline; (2) support the Growth Collaborator (normative, healthy self) more than the Regressive Loyalist (problem patterns associated with a problem internalization); (3) relate every intervention to the case formulation; (4) elicit interpersonal detail in important therapy narratives so that input, response, and impact on the self is clear; (5) emphasize affect, behavior, and cognition equally; and (6) assure that every intervention relates to one or more of five therapy steps. These steps are: (1) collaborate; (2) learn about patterns, where they are from, and what they are for; (3) block maladaptive patterns; (4) enable the will to change; and (5) learn new patterns.

IRT was developed specifically to address treatment resistant or nonresponder cases. Research on its effectiveness with this population has not and could not conform to EST protocol rules because the population is too comorbid, too dangerous to be admitted to usual research protocol, too demanding of clinician time for large *N*s to cumulate, and more. There is a discussion of a feasible, more powerful and more efficient alternative model for testing efficacy. Replicated small *N* studies should show significant associations between carefully defined and measures adherence to the treatment model and outcome. IRT is specific enough in its linking of presenting problems to the presumably relevant internalizations, and about its rules of adherence when addressing those internalizations, that it is able to use this alternative model for testing effectiveness.

REFERENCES

American Psychiatric Association. (1980). *Diagnostic and statistical manual of mental disorders* (3rd ed.). Washington, DC: Author.

American Psychiatric Association. (1994). *Diagnostic and statistical manual of mental disorders* (4th ed.). Washington, DC: Author.

Beck, A. (1990). *Beck Anxiety Inventory.* San Antonio, TX: Psychological Corporation.

Beck, A. (1996). *Beck Depression Inventory-II.* San Antonio: Psychological Corporation.

Benjamin, L. S. (1978). Structural analysis of differentiation failure. *Psychiatry, Journal for the Study of Interpersonal Process, 42,* 1–23.

Benjamin, L. S. (1996). *Interpersonal diagnosis and treatment of personality disorders* (2nd ed.). New York: Guilford Press.

Benjamin, L. S. (2003). *Interpersonal reconstructive therapy: Promoting change in nonresponders.* New York: Guilford Press.

Benjamin, L. S. (in press). *Personality guided interpersonal reconstructive therapy for anger, anxiety and anhedonia.* Washington, DC: American Psychological Association.

Benjamin, L. S., & Karpiak, C. P. (2001). Personality disorders. *Psychotherapy: Theory, Research, Practice and Training, 38,* 487–494.

Blatt, S. J., Quinlan, D., Chevron, E., McDonald, C., & Zuroff, D. C. (1982). Dependency and self-criticism: Psychological dimensions of depression. *Journal of Consulting and Clinical Psychology, 50,* 113–124.

Blatt, S. J., Zuroff, D. C., Bondi, C. M., Sanislow, C. A., & Pilkonis, P. A. (1998). When and how perfectionism impedes the brief treatment of depression. *Journal of Consulting and Clinical Psychology, 66,* 423–428.

Bowlby, J. (1977). The making and breaking of affectional bonds. *British Journal of Psychiatry, 130,* 201–210.

Chambless, D. L., & Ollendick, T. H. (2001). Empirically supported psychological interventions: Controversies and evidence. *Annual Review of Psychology, 52,* 685–716.

Cushing, G. (2003). Interpersonal origins of parenting among addicted and nonaddicted mothers. Dissertation submitted for completion of the PhD., University of Utah, Salt Lake City.

Fairbairn, W. R. D. (1952). *An object-relations theory of the personality.* New York: Basic Books.

First, M. B., Spitzer, R. L., Gibbon, M., & Williams, J. B. W. (1995). *Structured clinical interview for DSM-IV Axis I clinical syndromes. (SCID-I).* Washington, DC: American Psychiatric Press.

First, M. B., Spitzer, R. L., Gibbon, M., Williams, J. B. W., & Benjamin, L. S. (1997). *Structured clinical interview for DSM-IV Axis II personality disorders. (SCID-II)*. Washington, DC: American Psychiatric Press.

Horvath, A. O. (1994). Research on the alliance. In A. O. Horvath & L. S. Greenberg (Eds.), *The working alliance: Theory, research, and practice* (pp. 259–286). New York: Wiley.

Kubler-Ross, E. (1969). *On death and dying*. New York: Macmillan.

Kupfer, D. J., First, M., & Regier, D. (2002). *A research agenda for DSM-V*. Washington, DC: American Psychiatric Press.

Linehan, M. (1993). *Cognitive-behavioral treatment of borderline personality disorder*. New York: Guilford Press.

Malik, M. L., Beutler, L. E., Alimohamed, S., Gallagher-Thompson, D., & Thompson, L. (2003). *Journal of Consulting and Clinical Psychology, 71*, 150–158.

Miller, S. J., & Binder, J. L. (2002). The effects of manual based training on treatment fidelity and outcome. A review of the literature on adult individual psychotherapy. *Psychotherapy: Theory, Research, Practice and Training, 39*, 184–198.

Mischel, W. (1973). On the empirical dilemmas of psychodynamic approaches: Issues and alternatives. *Journal of Abnormal Psychology, 82*, 335–344.

Norcross, J. C. (Ed.). (2002). *Psychotherapy relationships that work: Therapists' relational contributions to effective psychotherapy*. New York: Oxford University Press.

Perry, J. C., Banon, E., & Ianni, F. (1999). Effectiveness of psychotherapy for personality disorders. *American Journal of Psychiatry, 156*, 1312–1321.

Poincare, H. (1905). Science and hypothesis. In J. Bronstein, Y. H. Krekorian, & P. P. Wiener (Eds.), *Basic problems of philosophy* (pp. 279–291). New York: Prentice-Hall.

Prochaska, J. O., DiClemente, C. C., & Norcross, J. C. (1992). In search of how people change: Applications to addictive behaviors. *American Psychologist, 47,* 1102–1114.

Shea, M. T. (1993). Psychosocial treatment of personality disorders. *Journal of Personality Disorders, 7*(Suppl.), 167–180.

Smith, T. L. (2002). Psychosocial perceptions and symptoms of personality and other psychiatric disorders. Dissertation submitted for completion of the PhD. University of Utah, Salt Lake City.

Stirman, S. W., DeRubeis, R. J., Crits-Christoph, P., & Brody, P. E. (2003). Are samples in randomized controlled studies of psychotherapy representative of community outpatients? A new methodology and initial findings. *Journal of Consulting and Clinical Psychology, 71*, 963–972.

Widiger, T. A., & Costa, P. T. (1994). Personality and personality disorders. *Journal of Abnormal Psychology, 103*, 78–91.

Zimmerman, M., Mattia, J. I., & Posternak, M. A. (2002). Are subjects in pharmacological treatment trials of depression representative of patients in routine clinical practice? *American Journal of Psychiatry, 159*, 469–473.

Zinbarg, R. E., Barlow, D. H., Brown, T. A., & Hertz, R. M. (1992). Cognitive-behavioral approaches to the nature and treatment of anxiety disorders. *Annual Review of Psychology, 43*, 235–267.

Chapter 24

COGNITIVE THERAPY FOR THE PERSONALITY DISORDERS

ROBERT L. LEAHY, JUDITH BECK, AND AARON T. BECK

Cognitive therapy was first developed as a treatment for depression and the anxiety disorders (A. T. Beck, 1976; A. T. Beck, Emery, & Greenberg, 1985; A. T. Beck, Rush, Shaw, & Emery, 1979). According to this model, emotional disorders can be understood in terms of the biases in thinking that are activated with, for example, depressed individuals predisposed toward seeing events in terms of loss, failure, and depletion, and anxious individuals viewing events in terms of threat that is imminent. These biases are related to the latent *schemas* or models of reality through which information is filtered, in a manner that continually reinforces the biased model of thinking.

Schemas are expressed through the automatic thoughts that reflect these biases in thinking. For example, automatic thoughts—which arise spontaneously and seem plausible to the individual—might include common distortions such as mind reading ("He thinks I'm a loser"), fortune-telling ("I will fail the exam"), overgeneralizing ("I keep failing over and over again"), dichotomous thinking ("Everything I do is a failure"), and discounting the positive ("Passing those exams doesn't mean anything—they were easy"). These automatic thoughts serve the role of confirmation bias in supporting the negative schema—in the preceding example, the negative schema might contain the belief, "I am a loser." In addition to the schematic model, individuals activate strategies to cope with their vulnerable schemas—utilizing conditional rules—that are intended to prevent a negative outcome. For example, conditional rules might be: "If I try really hard to be perfect, then I won't fail," or "If I avoid difficult tasks, then I won't be exposed as a loser." Finally, schemas are further reinforced by the maladaptive assumptions that guide the evaluation of data. These more general and abstract beliefs include the imperatives—or "shoulds"— as well as the "If-then" rules, such as, "If you aren't perfect, then you are a failure," and "If someone doesn't like you, then it means there is something wrong with you."

Furthermore, the individual's schemas may contain not only beliefs about self and others but also beliefs about emotion, behavior, relationships, and the physical world. Schemas also have emotional, behavioral, physiological, and motivational components. Schemas may be coordinated into more general and encompassing *modes* (A. T. Beck, 1996). For example, the depressive mode coordinates schemas that are activated relevant to the self (incompetent), others (rejecting), affect (sad), behavior (inert), relationships (withdrawn), and the physical world (a barrier). Once the mode is activated, it functions like a self-preserving system—maintaining itself through feedback within the system and both selection of information consistent with the mode and discounting or ignoring information inconsistent with the mode.

Beck and his colleagues (A. T. Beck et al., 2003; Pretzer & Beck, in press) have extended the schematic processing model to an understanding of personality disorders. Influenced by the ego analysts—such as Alfred Adler (1924/1964), Karen Horney (1945, 1950), Harry Stack Sullivan (1956), and Victor Frankl (1992)—the cognitive model of personality stresses the importance of how thinking is organized to influence affect, behavior, and interpersonal relationships. Because personality is viewed in terms of its distinct cognitive characteristics, the cognitive model stresses the importance of developing a taxonomy for the specific schemas underlying each personality disorder. Furthermore, the cognitive model proposes that individuals with specific personality disorders use distinct strategies to adapt to these underlying vulnerabilities.

In this chapter, we review the schematic content for the major personality disorders, the cognitive model of how individuals use strategies to cope with their vulnerabilities, interventions that are used by cognitive therapists in the treatment of personality disorder patients, and empirical support for the model.

PERSONALITY DISORDERS AND SPECIFIC SCHEMAS

Each personality disorder reflects a distinct conceptualization of the self and other. For example, the avoidant personality has beliefs that others are rejecting and critical and that the self is incompetent or defective. Similarly, the dependent personality views others in terms of abandonment and views the self as helpless. The personality disorder schemas—like all personal schemas characteristics—are overgeneralized, inflexible, imperative, and resistant to change (A. T. Beck et al., 2003). Thus, the individual has difficulty differentiating when the schema is appropriate and when it is not—and experiences these schemas as demanding and difficult to modify. These schemas are similar to George Kelly's (1955) personal constructs, in that they vary in terms of breadth (narrow, discrete, broad), flexibility or rigidity (capability of being modified), and density (prominence in the cognitive hierarchy; A. T. Beck et al., 2003). Thus, a core schema that is difficult to modify and that confers greater impairment is broad, rigid, and highly prominent in the hierarchy of schemas and thoughts.

INFORMATION PROCESSING

These personality schemas will influence attention, recall, and the value attached to information. Thus, the dependent individual attends to information related to signs of abandonment and loss, and the avoidant attends to information about rejection and criticism. The information related to abandonment is experienced by the individual as highly representative of other information that is inferred by virtue of the schema. For example, an individual's idea that he or she has been rejected by a friend may become overgeneralized; the individual may believe that he or she will be generally rejected by other people. Automatic thoughts are also related to the schemas. For example, the dependent individual engages in mind reading ("He is getting less interested and is thinking of leaving"), fortune-telling ("He is going to leave"), and personalizing ("He's reading the paper because he is no longer interested in me"). The avoidant also engages in mind reading ("They think I'm boring and stupid"), fortune-telling ("If I open up more, they will really see how stupid I am"), and personalizing ("The reason they are not talking to me is that I look like a fool"). The selective focus on information—and the distortion or assimilation of information to the schema—further reinforces the strength of these negative beliefs.

Moreover, each personality disorder is marked by maladaptive assumptions that further maintain the schema. For example, the maladaptive assumption—"If I don't have a partner, I cannot survive"—magnifies the importance of signs of abandonment that the dependent individual sees. Information, filtered through the lens of the patient's beliefs, is evaluated according to these assumptions, which, in turn, are linked to the schemas. Thus, the avoidant personality, driven by the schema that contains a belief of incompetence and the view that others are rejecting and critical, puts a special meaning to not being liked: "If people don't like me, then I am a loser." When individuals confirm their belief that someone does not like them, this event confirms the belief that they are defective and incompetent.

The personality schemas are coordinated with other schemas in more general systems of modes (A. T. Beck, 1996). For example, the schemas with the belief that the individual is incompetent and boring may be coordinated with the schema with the belief that others are rejecting, which is coordinated with interpersonal behavior (withdrawal, caution), other behavior (isolated and deactivated), and affect (anxious and sad). As the mode is activated and these separate functions are engaged, the individual's belief that he or she is boring or incompetent is preserved through withdrawal from others, isolation, decreased behavioral activity, selective memory, and attention to signs of rejection. This core belief is not open to experiences that could potentially disconfirm the schema, and when the individual docs have positive experiences, he or she discounts or fails to attend to positive data contrary to the schema. Because of the automaticity of these coordinated functions within the personality disorder, the individual believes that the lack of disconfirming evidence is support for the underlying schema (boring, incompetent) and not a direct result of the self-protective and maintaining functions of the coordinated mode.

Further, these personal schemas are characterized by situational vulnerability. For example, the dependent individual is vulnerable to the end of relationships or threats to the relationship; the narcissist and the avoidant personality are vulnerable to criticism and meeting people or entering relationships. The specific vulnerability to situations is also reflected in the therapeutic—or transference—relationship in cognitive therapy—as in any therapy (Leahy, 1996, 2001). For example, in carrying out self-help homework in cognitive therapy, dependent individuals view themselves as helpless and prefer to seek reassurance from the therapist that they are okay. These dependent individuals may fear that the therapist will abandon them, favor other patients over them, or that the therapist's vacation is a precursor to a termination in the relationship. Narcissistic patients—who support a fragile ego by displaying a grandiose sense of entitlement—view self-help homework as beneath them and expect that the therapist's role is to join with them to condemn the people who do not appreciate their special talents.

CONTENT OF SCHEMAS

The specific schematic content and styles of adaptation of the various personality disorders are shown in Table 24.1, which indicates that each personality disorder consists of specific views (beliefs) of self and others, assumptions, and strategies for coping with the perceived vulnerability. (Although most patients who meet criteria for one Axis II disorder also have traits of other Axis II disorders, it is useful to appreciate the major beliefs and strategies of

Table 24.1   Personality Disorders

Personality Disorder	View of Self	View of Others	Main Beliefs	Main Strategy
Avoidant	Vulnerable to depreciation, rejection Socially inept Incompetent	Critical Demeaning Superior	It's terrible to be rejected, put down If people know the real me, they will reject me I can't tolerate unpleasant feelings	Avoid evaluative situations Avoid unpleasant feelings or thoughts
Dependent	Needy Weak Helpless Incompetent	(Idealized) Nurturant Supportive Competent	Need people to survive, be happy Need for steady flow of support and encouragement	Cultivate dependent relationships
Passive-aggressive	Self-sufficient Vulnerable to control, interference	Intrusive Demanding Interfering Controlling Dominating	Others interfere with my freedom of action Control by others is intolerable Have to do things my own way	Passive resistance Surface submissiveness Evade, circumvent rules
Obsessive-compulsive	Responsible Accountable Fastidious Competent	Irresponsible Casual Incompetent Self-indulgent	I know what's best Details are crucial People should be better, try harder	Apply rules Perfectionism Evaluate, control Shoulds, criticize, punish
Paranoid	Righteous Innocent, noble Vulnerable	Interfering Malicious Discriminatory Abusive motives	Motives are suspect Be on guard Don't trust	Wary Look for hidden motives Accuse Counterattack
Antisocial	Loner Autonomous Strong	Vulnerable Exploitative	Entitled to break rules Others are patsies, wimps Others are exploitative	Attack, rob Deceive Manipulate
Narcissistic	Special, unique Deserve special rules; superior Above the rules	Inferior Admirers	Since I'm special, I deserve special rules I'm above the rules I'm better than others	Use others Transcend rules Manipulative Competitive
Histrionic	Glamorous Impressive	Seducible Receptive Admirers	People are there to serve or admire me They have no right to deny me my just deserts	Use dramatics, charm; temper tantrums, crying; suicide gestures
Schizoid	Self-sufficient Loner	Intrusive	Others are unrewarding Relationships are messy, undesirable	Stay away

each personality disorder separately.) Thus, the dependent personality, characterized by beliefs of being vulnerable to depreciation, rejection, and of being socially inept or incompetent, views others as strong, nurturant, and competent. The strategy they develop is forming dependent relationships with strong and protective individuals who, in an idealized manner, will "take care" of the dependent individual. Because of their underlying schemas related to abandonment and incompetence, dependent individuals may cultivate specific interpersonal skills focused on pleasing the protective and stronger individual. However, because of the core belief that they are incompetent and helpless, these dependent individuals are sensitive to any signs of abandonment or rejection and may respond with clinging, reassurance seeking, or hypervigilance and jealousy.

The value of viewing personality disorders in these terms is that the cognitive therapist can assist the patient in modifying the central schemas related to the self and others by using cognitive, behavioral, and interpersonal interventions. Furthermore, the maladaptive strategies that serve to maintain the underlying schemas and beliefs can also be modified, allowing patients to learn that they can safely relinquish their safety strategies. Indeed, each point in the cognitive conceptualization provides an opportunity for intervention and change.

Overdeveloped and underdeveloped dimensions are shown in Table 24.2. Each personality disorder is characterized by specific styles of adaptation, with certain qualities or

Table 24.2   Typical Overdeveloped and Underdeveloped Strategies

Personality Disorder	Overdeveloped	Underdeveloped
Obsessive-compulsive	Control Responsibility Systematization	Spontaneity Playfulness
Dependent	Help seeking Clinging	Self-sufficiency Mobility
Passive-aggressive	Autonomy Resistance Passivity Sabotage	Intimacy Assertiveness Activity Cooperativeness
Paranoid	Vigilance Mistrust Suspiciousness	Serenity Trust Acceptance
Narcissistic	Self-aggrandizement Competitiveness	Sharing Group identification
Antisocial	Combativeness Exploitiveness Predation	Empathy Reciprocity Social sensitivity
Schizoid	Autonomy Isolation	Intimacy Reciprocity
Avoidant	Social vulnerability Avoidance Inhibition	Self-assertion Gregariousness
Histrionic	Exhibitionism Expressiveness Impressionism	Reflectiveness Control Systematization

behaviors overemphasized and other qualities or behaviors underdeveloped. For example, the dependent personality overemphasizes help-seeking and reassurance, while remaining underdeveloped in self-sufficiency and mobility. Thus, adaptation for the dependent individual who is characterized by the view of self as needy, weak, helpless, and incompetent, and the view of others as strong caretakers results in the beliefs, "I need other people to survive—I need someone to take care of me." The threat is one of rejection or abandonment; the strategy is to cultivate dependent relationships and to subordinate to others, and the behavior is to placate others. The expected affect will be anxiety about potential loss or abandonment and during loss, depression.

Histrionic individuals believe they must be glamorous and seductive to hold the attention of others. Others are viewed as seducible, admirers who are an audience for the dramatic displays of the histrionic. The main strategies are to put on dramatic displays, entice, and impress others. The overdeveloped areas are emotional impressions and exhibitionism, and the underdeveloped areas are reflectiveness, self-control, and systematic thinking. The central threat for the histrionic is to be ignored, to feel invisible, and to fail to make an impression.

STRATEGIES FOR INTERVENTION

A reasonable goal for Axis II patients is schematic reinterpretation, assisting patients in reducing the impact of the schema, and helping them understand and reinterpret events in more functional ways (A. T. Beck et al., 2003). This often leads to some degree of schematic modification; patients are able to view themselves, others, and the world in a more realistic and functional way. Since cognitive therapy with personality disorders usually requires many months, the clinician should be realistic about the goals that can be accomplished.

MODIFYING SCHEMAS

The cognitive approach to personality disorders incorporates many of the traditional cognitive therapy techniques used for the treatment of depression and anxiety (A. T. Beck et al., 1979, 1985; J. S. Beck, 1995; Leahy, 2003). However, the cognitive therapy of personality disorders also emphasizes case conceptualization of personality, developmental material, experiential techniques, impasses in the therapeutic relationship, and roadblocks in therapy. We next turn to specific interventions to accomplish these goals.

SOCIALIZATION TO SCHEMA-FOCUSED WORK

An essential component of cognitive therapy treatment is to educate patients as to the rationale for treatment and the expectation that they will engage in active self-help assignments. The clinician recognizes that treatment is likely to take longer than the treatment of patients with straightforward depression and anxiety disorders. Treatment will also be more demanding for both patients and therapists, and the very nature of the disorder will pose roadblocks to change. The initial focus of treatment is amelioration of Axis I symptoms, if present. When starting to work on Axis II issues, it is useful to provide patients with a description and rationale for schema-focused work, such as the one shown in Table 24.3 (which can be simplified or adapted as needed).

Table 24.3   Guide to Understanding Schemas

What are schemas?

People differ in what gets them depressed, anxious, or angry. We refer to these different issues as schemas. Schemas guide the habitual ways in which you see things. For example, depression is characterized by schemas related to loss, deprivation, and failure, anxiety is characterized by schemas related to threat or fear of failure, and anger is characterized by schemas related to insult, humiliation, or violation of rules. Research on personality indicates that people differ in the themes of their depression, anxiety, or anger.

Each of us looks at our experiences with certain habitual patterns of thinking. One person might focus a lot on achievement, another person focuses a lot on rejection, and someone else focuses on fears of being abandoned. Let's say that your schema—or your particular issue or vulnerability—is related to achievement. Things can be going well for you at work, but then you have a setback at work. This activates your schema about achievement—your issue about needing to be very successful so that you will not see yourself as a failure. So the setback at work might lead to the belief that you are a failure (or "average") and then you get anxious or depressed.

Or let's say that your schema is related to issues about abandonment. You might be very vulnerable to any signs of being rejected and left alone. As long as a relationship is going well, you are not worried. But because of this schema, you might worry about being left or being rejected. If the relationship breaks up, it leads you to feel depressed, because you can't stand being alone.

How do we compensate for our schemas?

If you have a schema about a specific issue, you might try to compensate for this vulnerability. For example, if you have a schema related to failure or "being average," you might work excessively—you are trying to compensate for your perception that you might turn out to be inferior or not live up to your standards of perfection. You might compensate by checking your work over and over again. As a consequence, people might see you as too absorbed in your work. And you might have a hard time relaxing, because you are worried that you are not working enough, something is left undone, or you are losing your motivation.

Or let's say that your schema is related to being abandoned. You might compensate for this by giving in to your partner. You might be afraid of asserting yourself, because you fear being abandoned. Or you might constantly seek reassurance from your partner—so that you can feel secure. But the reassurance doesn't work for very long. You keep seeing signs of your partner pulling away. Another way that you might compensate for your schema about abandonment is that you form relationships with people who do not meet your needs, but you are willing to commit to them because you don't want to be alone. Or you stay in relationships far beyond a point that seems reasonable to you—because you think you can't stand being on your own.

As you can see, trying to compensate for your underlying schemas can create problems of its own. The "compensation" may lead you to sacrifice your needs, work compulsively, pursue no-win relationships, worry, demand reassurance, and other behaviors that are problematic for you. And the most important thing about these compensations is that you never really address your underlying schema. For example, you might not ever question your belief that you have to be special, superior, avoid being average, avoid being alone, etc. Therefore, you never really change your schema. It's still there—ready to be activated by certain events. It is your continual vulnerability.

How do we avoid facing our schemas?

Another process that creates problems is *schema avoidance*. This means that you try to avoid facing any issues about your schema. Let's say that you have a schema related to being a failure—your view is that deep down inside you might really be incompetent. One way that you might avoid this is to never take on challenging tasks or to quit early on a task. Or let's say that you have a schema related to being "unlovable" or "unattractive." How do you avoid facing the schema? You might avoid socializing with people you think won't accept you. You might avoid

Table 24.3   *(Continued)*

dating. You might avoid calling friends because you already assume that people think you have nothing to offer. Or let's say that you are afraid of being abandoned. You could avoid this schema by not allowing yourself to get close to someone. Or you could break off with someone early in a relationship so that you don't get rejected later.

Another way that people avoid their schemas—whatever those schemas are—is by emotional escape and avoidance. This can involve behaviors such as drinking too much, using drugs to dull your feelings, binge eating, or even acting out sexually. You may feel that dealing with your thoughts and feelings is so painful that you have to avoid or escape from them by these "addictive" behaviors. These behaviors "hide" your underlying fears from you—at least while you are binge-ing or drinking or using drugs. Of course, the bad feelings come back again—since you are not really examining and challenging your beliefs. And, ironically, these addictive behaviors feed into your negative schemas—making you feel worse about yourself.

Where do schemas come from?

We learn these negative beliefs from our parents, our siblings, our peers, and from our partners. Parents might contribute to these negative beliefs by making you feel that you are not good enough unless you are superior to everyone, telling you that you are too fat or not attractive, comparing you to other people who are "doing better," telling you that you are selfish because you have needs, threatening to kill themselves, divorce, or abandon you, or intruding on you and ordering you around. There are many different ways that parents teach you these negative ideas about yourself and about others.

For example, think about the following actual experiences that some people recalled about how their parents "taught" them their negative beliefs:

1. "You could do better—why did you get that "B" ?" (I need to be perfect or I am inferior);
2. "Your thighs are too fat and your nose is ugly" (I am ugly and fat);
3. "Your cousin went to Harvard—why can't you be more like him?" (I am inferior and incompetent);
4. "Why are you always complaining? Can't you see that I have problems taking care of you kids?" (My needs don't count. I'm selfish);
5. "Maybe I should just leave and let you kids take care of yourself" (I am a burden and I'll be abandoned).

Another source of schemas—as we indicated—might be people other than your parents. Perhaps your brother or sister mistreated you—leading to beliefs of being abused, unlovable, rejected, or controlled. Or perhaps your partner has told you that you are not good enough—leading to beliefs of being unattractive, unworthy, and unlovable. We even get beliefs from popular culture. This includes images of being beautiful, having a perfect body, "what real men should be like," perfect sex, lots of money, and enormous success. These unrealistic images reinforce schemas related to perfection, superiority, inadequacy, and defectiveness.

How will therapy be helpful?

Cognitive therapy can help you in a number of important ways:

- Learn what your specific schemas and beliefs are.
- Learn how you are compensating for and avoiding your schemas.
- Learn how your schemas are maintained or reinforced by the choices that you have made or the experiences that you have had.
- Examine how your beliefs were learned.
- Challenge and modify these negative beliefs.
- Develop new, more adaptive, and more positive beliefs.

Source: Adapted from *Cognitive Therapy Techniques: A Practitioner's Guide,* by R. L. Leahy, 2003, New York: Guilford Press.

CASE CONCEPTUALIZATION

Another aspect of schema work is to develop a case conceptualization for each patient. This conceptualization is an ongoing and mutual effort on the part of both patient and therapist and draws on developmental and current information about relationships and work as sources of these schemas, automatic thoughts, and conditional assumptions that maintain the schema, and patterns of avoidance and compensation (J. S. Beck, 1995; Leahy, 1997, 2003). For example, a dependent woman had difficulty achieving her stated goal of leaving her husband. A case conceptualization, as presented next and summarized in Figure 24.1, helped guide treatment.

- *Current schemas:*
    1. *Self:* Helpless, incompetent, selfish
    2. *Other:* Strong, deserving, protective

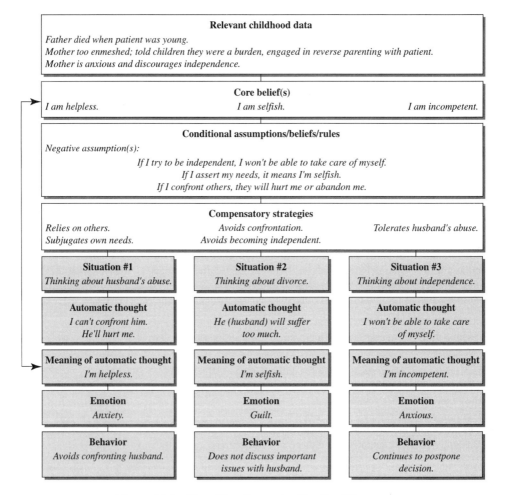

Figure 24.1   Cognitive Conceptualization Diagram

- *Developmental precursors:* Mother was enmeshed with daughter, told daughter that mother might have a heart attack if the daughter was not there, confided in daughter about her problems (reverse parenting). Mother worried that daughter would suffer harm if she became independent and discouraged her from working far from home. Mother told her she was selfish when she complained about her needs. Father had died when child was young.

- *Recent and current contributing factors:* Alcoholic and psychologically abusive husband who was overcontrolling and fearful that she would have any other relationships. Labeled her as stupid, dummy, fat, and selfish.

- *Conditional assumptions:*

    —If I try to be independent, I'll hurt others and won't be able to take care of myself. If I rely on others (husband, mother), I'll be okay.

    —If I subjugate my needs, I won't be abandoned or feel selfish. If I assert my needs (try to be independent, confront husband about abuse), others will get hurt or angry, criticize me, and refuse to take care of me.

- *Automatic thoughts and distortions:* Fortune-telling—My mother will get sick; catastrophic thinking—If I do anything independently, people will suffer and die; personalizing—If my husband loved me, he wouldn't drink; discounting positives—Even though I have earned a good living, I am still unable to take care of myself.

The case conceptualization assists the therapist in anticipating problems that might arise in treatment. For example, the patient's belief that she is helpless and needs someone to take care and protect her might lead her to believe that she cannot help herself through homework assignments. Moreover, her belief that she needs someone strong to protect her might result in her seeking reassurance from her therapist rather than actively engaging in examining her own thoughts and modifying her behavior. Her dependency might also lead her to avoid actions that could affect other people negatively and that would require some independence.

Another value of the case conceptualization is that it assists in identifying different levels of intervention. For example, therapy can focus on the automatic thoughts, assumptions, core beliefs, and/or behaviors. The cognitive case conceptualization diagram (Figure 24.1) allows the therapist to summarize a great deal of data and target the central beliefs and dysfunctional behavioral patterns (compensatory strategies; J. S. Beck, 1995). Developing the conceptualization with patients provides them with a level of understanding and targets for change that demystify the personality disorder.

Semantic Technique

To modify a schema, the clinician must discuss the criteria for the belief it contains. For example, the patient who views herself as helpless can identify what defines "helplessness." The patient may indicate that helplessness is characterized by the inability to accomplish anything on her own. As part of this definition, the therapist should inquire as to which behaviors would exemplify helplessness and which behaviors would exemplify the opposite of helplessness—effectiveness. Establishing what counts as evidence—given the definition—is an important part of being in a position to disconfirm a proposition. Thus, if the patient's definition is that helplessness is "at any time, not accomplishing your goal," it is unlikely that the proposition that she is helpless can ever be disconfirmed (Popper, 1959). Providing definitions that are open to disconfirmation allows the patient an opportunity to modify the schema. The clinician can ask, "How could we know that you are ever effective? What would count as evidence that you are effective at times?" Given the confirmation bias underlying schematic processing, it is often the case that personality schemas are not open to disconfirmation, since "contrary evidence" is not considered relevant and since the schema may lead the patient to believe, "If I am ever helpless, I am [characterologically] helpless."

Schema Monitoring

To further awareness of the pervasiveness of the schema, the patient can self-monitor any situations that elicit the core belief. Since many patients have more than one dysfunctional schema, this tracking will require identification of various beliefs and various situations. For example, the dependent personality patient described here monitored schemas related to being helpless, incompetent, and selfish. Components of the schema included anxiety, desire to withdraw, feelings of hopelessness and helplessness, and shame. Thus, her schemas related to being helpless and incompetent were activated when she thought of moving out. Other situational triggers for the helpless and incompetent schemas were driving in traffic, making purchases, or evaluating how to invest her savings. It is particularly informative to collect data about situations in which negative schemas *are not activated.* When she was at work, for example, a place where she experienced considerable support, her helpless and incompetent schemas were seldom activated. Recognizing that positive schemas can be activated helps the patient recognize the potential for modifying the rigidity and pervasiveness of these schemas.

Relating Schemas to Automatic Thoughts and Coping Styles

As part of the ongoing case conceptualization, the clinician can relate the beliefs to the patient's typical automatic thoughts and coping styles. For example, the belief, "I am helpless," is selectively confirmed through the cognitive distortions of mind reading, personalizing, discounting the positives, and overgeneralization. Indicating how these confirmatory biases consistently reinforce the belief can help the patient recognize that what "feels like reality"—"I am always messing up"—may be partly a function of the biased automatic thoughts. Recognizing that modifying these automatic thoughts—using traditional cognitive therapy techniques such as examining the evidence, considering the costs and benefits of the thought, and examining how a neutral person would view the situation—may decrease the credibility of both the automatic thoughts and the underlying beliefs.

Similarly, examining and modifying the coping styles that have been used to avoid or compensate for the schema can also modify the credibility of the belief. Thus, the dependent woman described earlier who believed that she needed to rely solely on her husband lest he threaten to abandon her for her disloyalty was urged to change her coping style of clinging and blind devotion. Rather, she was encouraged to share her views of the relationship with other friends and with her sister. They helped her view her husband as problematic—and that she was not entirely at fault. Moreover, rather than rely on the coping style of deference and suppression of her own feelings and opinions, they encouraged her to assert herself with her husband. This initially led to his verbal retaliation—but, encouraged to assert herself, she began to feel less helpless and was able to recognize that she could tolerate his verbal responses without blaming herself and fearing his abandonment.

Cost-Benefit Analysis

Developing motivation to change is a significant issue with personality-disordered patients because they may view their beliefs as realistic and their coping styles (or avoidance and compensation) as adaptive and self-protective. It is helpful to direct the patient to attend to short-term versus long-term consequences because schema maintenance, avoidance, and compensation often serve the role of reducing short-term anxiety (Young, Klosko, & Weishaar, 2003). For example, the benefit for the dependent patient in avoiding independent activity is that it immediately reduces her anxiety—but the costs of feeling trapped, subjugated, and helpless are longer term consequences. The clinician can help patients recognize that they are trading longer term costs for shorter term benefits. This also suggests that the process of change may require some investment of discomfort and tolerance of uncertainty.

Examining the Evidence

What counts as evidence for and against the core belief? As indicated, the semantic technique can draw attention to the confirmation bias in the patient's thinking—where nothing can be viewed as disconfirmation of the belief because it is discounted as irrelevant or offset by other factors. For the patient here, the evidence that she was helpless was, "I haven't left my husband; I am depressed, lonely, and I feel helpless." This evidence can be viewed as emotional reasoning and situational. Evidence that she is not helpless included "finishing college, doing well at work, learning new technical skills at work, learning how to drive, and having some friends at work." To bolster the legitimacy of the evidence, the clinician can ask, "What would your best friend say is the evidence for and against your idea that you are helpless?" In addition, the clinician can engage in active role plays, alternating with the patient the negative and positive voices, to evaluate these issues.

Viewing a Belief Along a Continuum

Beliefs are often expressed in dichotomous or polarized ways—either "helpless" or "completely competent." Modifying a belief may be difficult if the patient believes that the only changes that count are to the opposite extreme—"completely competent in everything." Thus, the belief can be differentiated into degrees—very much like the distinction between categorical and dimensional analysis in personality measurement. We find it useful to focus on degrees of a positive end of the continuum—that is, degrees of competence, rather than degrees of incompetence. A horizontal continuum can be drawn, with patients indicating the extent to which they view themselves as competent. Then the continuum scale can be applied to specific situations and behaviors—"How competent in this situation were you?" Further differentiation allows the patient to recognize that the belief has been overgeneralized and polarized. Encouraging the patient to use qualifiers—"sometimes, often, in this situation"—helps in this differentiation.

Setting Up Predictions

The belief can be tested by setting up behavioral experiments or opportunities to collect data relevant to the belief. For example, the dependent patient had the following predictions: "If I tell my husband I am upset with his drinking, he will leave me"; "If I do things with my other friends, I will be unhappy because he will be unhappy"; "If I leave him, I won't be able to take care of myself emotionally or financially." Some predictions are short term; others are longer term.

Competency tracking during the day can assist in testing predictions. Thus, the patient is asked to set up specific predictions—how he or she will perform in different situations. Beliefs can be tested by evaluating outcomes against these predictions—for each hour of the day. Although many of these situations may not be relevant to the schema, some of them will.

Acting against the Belief

The clinician can encourage patients to set up behavioral experiments that are contrary to their beliefs. For example, the dependent patient was hesitant to fly on her own on a business trip because this activated her fear that something terrible would happen—her husband would be angry, her mother might get sick, or she might end up depressed on the trip and have no support. These avoidant tendencies were addressed in therapy by evaluating the evidence and logic that a two-day trip would have such devastating effects. These dire predictions were then set up as a behavioral test of the belief. After she returned from the trip, she felt exhilarated by the fact that none of the dire outcomes ensued. In fact, this trip and several after served as a foundation for her consideration of separation from her husband. Moreover, she was encouraged to review her past dire predictions that her independent activity would result in terrible consequences for people she loved or for herself. She recognized that her actions had generally not led to negative outcomes and certainly not dire ones.

EXPERIENTIAL AND DEVELOPMENTAL TECHNIQUES

A number of techniques are used to activate the emotional salience of schemas and to link them with earlier developmental experiences that give the schema both personal significance and a personal historical context. These techniques are described below.

Role Play

Cognitive therapists often engage patients in active role plays in which various aspects of beliefs and automatic thoughts are played out and challenged. Role plays can consist of the patient playing the role of defending the belief, while the therapist plays the role of challenging the belief. These specific roles can then be reversed. The advantage of this kind of role play is that the patient can gain distance from his or her belief, examine its validity, and practice speaking a more adaptive perspective aloud. Another use of role play, described later, is to have the patient engage in challenging or questioning the original source of the belief—for example, the empty-chair technique to challenge critical parental messages. The role play will be more effective if the patient experiences moderate to intense affect because beliefs tend to change only when affect is aroused.

Imagery and Imagery Restructuring

Visual imagery is a powerful source of emotional meaning for patients—often more evocative than abstract, verbal sentences. Cognitive therapists use imagery induction in belief modification. Imagery can be used to activate the belief: "Close your eyes, try to experience the terrible feeling of loneliness that you fear. Once you have that feeling, imagine a blank screen. Project an image of a scene onto that screen. What do you see happening? What happens next? What feelings are you having in each of these scenes?" Another use of imagery induction involves identifying earlier experiences in which the belief was activated: "Try to get that terrible feeling of loneliness. Go back in your memory and try to recall the first time that you can remember feeling that way. What picture comes up in your mind? Who was there, what was happening, and what happened later? How did you feel about yourself? The other people there? What thoughts did you have? What parts of the image are particularly disturbing to you?" (see Brewin, 1996; Grey, Holmes, & Brewin, 2001; Smucker & Dancu, 1999; Young et al., 2003). "What is your younger self feeling and thinking? What messages are you getting?" (J. S. Beck, 1995).

Finally, disturbing visual images can be modified using imagery restructuring or rescripting. This involves collaboration between the therapist and patient in rewriting the feared image so that the outcome is more favorable. For example, a rescripting of an upsetting image of the patient as a young girl being told that her mother might get sick if the girl went off on her own was rescripted to, "I see myself telling my mother to stop being so demanding of me and stop being so selfish. I have to live my own life, and she has to take care of her problems herself."

Imagery rescripting can lead to schema defenses that maintain the schema. For example, in her rescripting she began to feel guilty and then afraid that something bad would happen to her mother because of her assertion. These thoughts were then evaluated using cost-benefit analysis, examination of the evidence, rational role play, and asking what a good friend might think of this. Replaying the rescripted image and writing out narratives to support it can be helpful in deepening the belief change.

Some patients do not respond well to rescripting the memory itself. It may be useful for these patients to imagine the period of time just after a very upsetting experience. They then imagine their current adult self entering the image and dialoguing with their younger self, helping the younger self understand what has happened in a different way that is less damaging to the child's sense of self.

Identifying the Source of the Belief

Belief modification can be enhanced by retrospective examination of the formative experiences that may have given rise to the belief. For example, the patient is asked to close his or her eyes, activate a negative mood, recall the issues related to the belief (e.g., fears of abandonment), and then recall an incident reminiscent of the belief and emotion (Hackmann, Clark, & McManus, 2000). In the case of the dependent patient, she recalled a memory when she was a girl of her mother threatening to abandon the family because she viewed the children as a burden. This activated continual fears for her as a child that her own demands or needs would lead to rejection and abandonment, thus leading her to feel ashamed, guilty, and fearful of having needs. The clinician can inquire during the memory exercise about any thoughts, feelings, sensations, or other images that may arise and ask if the patient had thoughts of how she would cope with these fears. These early memories are then related to similar patterns of triggers for the belief and the emotions and thoughts in current experiences that are conceptually related to early memories.

Writing Letters to the Source

Once the origin of the belief is identified, the patient can be assisted in challenging the individuals who contributed to these vulnerabilities. Writing assertive letters to the source of the belief can activate the patient's adaptive and self-esteem-building capability. For example, the patient described here wrote a letter to her mother (who was now dead) about how her mother had hurt her and made her afraid of having her own needs. The therapist can direct the patient to identify in the letter what was wrong about the messages conveyed and how the other person should have behaved. As in all assertive communication, the patient should identify the emotions that she experienced and "tell the source" what emotions she wished had been affected. Thus, this patient was able to say in her letter to her mother, "You made me suffer because of your own inability to handle your feelings. You made me afraid of having my own needs by threatening to leave us. I would like to forgive you— maybe someday I will. But you hurt me really badly. It affected my relationships with men and my ability to stand up to friends. I wish you had made me feel that I could always count on you—that you would be there no matter what. But you didn't."

It is helpful to have the patient read the letter aloud and to reflect on emotions that are experienced in reading the letter. Often the patient will report feeling afraid, guilty, or self-doubting. In this case, the patient said, "I feel my mother is dead—she suffered a lot. She had her own problems. Who am I to criticize her? I also feel afraid that I'm going to get punished. I always did." These fears of asserting against the source of the belief can then be examined as other examples of how the belief is maintained by beliefs that there is something dangerous or unethical in challenging a belief.

Developing More Adaptive Beliefs

Finally, the clinician can assist the patient in developing beliefs that can facilitate better relationships and self-confidence. Some patients are assisted in identifying their "Bill of Rights" if they are dependent or avoidant. Other patients can identify more adaptive schemas through a values-clarification exercise. They can be encouraged to describe ideally what they value in relationships, work, and life in general and to describe the kinds of experiences that constitute their ideal goals. These values can then be related to the kinds of beliefs that can assist in adaptation to these goals and values. For example, the dependent patient identified her rights to having her own feelings, not having to please everyone all the time, and her right to feel angry. She indicated that her values were to find a balance between intimacy and independence and to be able to do things on her own without feeling anxious. New beliefs—of being "good enough" and of "competence"—were identified. These new, adaptive beliefs were then examined for their costs and benefits to the patient, the evidence for and against them, and how others would see these as desirable new beliefs for the patient. Specific behavioral and interpersonal goals were identified—and these were incorporated into weekly self-help homework assignments. For example, independent behavior included going out to restaurants and theatres alone, and interpersonal goals included saying no to others, telling someone what you would prefer, initiating interactions with strangers, and calling people.

Schemas and the Therapeutic Relationship

The patient's core beliefs about the self and others are frequently also reflected in the therapeutic relationship and should be viewed as an opportunity to gain first-hand knowledge of the patient's interpersonal experience. Examples of how core beliefs are manifested in the therapeutic relationship are shown in Table 24.4.

These examples of resistance, noncompliance, or roadblocks provide the clinician with in vivo opportunities for testing the schemas. For example, a dependent patient views herself as incompetent, fails to state an agenda, and seeks continual reassurance. Her therapist can use the therapeutic relationship as an opportunity to test the idea that she cannot help herself and that the only means of gaining improvement is to get the therapist to reassure her. Self-directed homework can be employed, so that the patient can have a plan to examine and test these beliefs that she is unable to help herself. For

Table 24.4   Schemas in the Therapeutic Relationship

Schema	Example
Incompetent (Avoidant)	Avoids difficult topics and emotions. Appears vague. Looks for signs that the therapist will reject her. Believes that therapist will criticize her for not doing homework correctly. Reluctant to do behavioral exposure homework assignments.
Helpless (Dependent)	Seeks reassurance. Does not have an agenda of problems to solve. Frequently complains about "feelings." Calls frequently between sessions. Wants to prolong sessions. Does not think he can do the homework or believes that homework will not work. Upset when therapist takes vacations.
Vulnerable to control (Passive-aggressive)	Comes late to or misses sessions. Views cognitive "challenges" as controlling. Reluctant to express dissatisfaction directly. Vague about goals, feelings, and thoughts—especially as related to therapist and therapy. "Forgets" to do homework or pay bills.
Responsible (Obsessive-compulsive)	Feels emotions are "messy" and "irrational." Criticizes himself for being irrational and disorganized. Wants to see immediate results and expresses skepticism about therapy. Views homework as a test to be done perfectly or not at all.
Superior (Narcissistic)	Comes late or misses sessions. "Forgets" to pay for sessions. Devalues therapy and the therapist. Expects special arrangements. Feels humiliated to have to talk about problems. Believes that therapy will not work since the problem resides in other people.
Glamorous (Histrionic)	Focuses on expressing emotions, alternating rapidly from crying, laughing to anger. Tries to impress therapist with appearance, feelings, or problems. Rejects the rational approach and demands validation.

Source: Overcoming Resistance in Cognitive Therapy, by R. L. Leahy, 2001, New York: Guilford Press

example, the dependent patient described here was instructed to write out a thought-record and examine her negative beliefs about her competence and then to plan three independent behaviors that could test this belief.

Therapists may bring to the therapeutic relationship their own self-beliefs that may interfere with treatment—especially with patients with personality disorders. As illustrated in Table 24.5, therapists with various dysfunctional beliefs may experience considerable difficulty with patients who trigger these beliefs. For example, the therapist with schemas related to autonomy may feel constrained and pressured—even smothered—by the dependent patient. This may lead some to become overly focused on boundary-setting, which further exacerbates the dependent patient's vulnerability to rejection and abandonment. Examples of how to identify and modify these countertransference schemas are described elsewhere (Leahy, 2001).

EMPIRICAL EVALUATION OF COGNITIVE THERAPY FOR PERSONALITY DISORDERS

There is now support for the schema-content dimension of the cognitive model of personality disorders. O'Leary et al. (1991) found that borderline personality patients scored higher than others on dysfunctional beliefs, indicating that severity and type of disorder are related to maladaptive beliefs. More specifically related to the cognitive model as

Table 24.5   Therapist's Schema Questionnaire: Guide

Schema	Assumptions
Demanding standards	I have to cure all my patients. I must always meet the highest standards. My patients should do an excellent job. We should never waste time.
Special, superior person	I am entitled to be successful. My patients should appreciate all that I do for them. I shouldn't feel bored when doing therapy. Patients try to humiliate me.
Rejection sensitive	Conflicts are upsetting. I shouldn't raise issues that will bother the patient.
Abandonment	If my patients are bothered with therapy, they might leave. It's upsetting when patients terminate. I might end up with no patients.
Autonomy	I feel controlled by the patient. My movements, feelings, or what I say are limited. I should be able to do or say what I wish. Sometimes I wonder if I will lose myself in the relationship.
Control	I have to control my surroundings or the people around me.
Judgmental	Some people are basically bad people. People should be punished if they do wrong things.
Persecution	I often feel provoked. The patient is trying to get to me. I have to guard against being taken advantage of or hurt. You usually can't trust people.
Need approval	I want to be liked by the patient. If the patient isn't happy with me, then it means I'm doing something wrong.
Need to like others	It's important that I like the patient. It bothers me if I don't like a patient. We should get along—almost like friends.
Withholding	I want to withhold thoughts and feelings from the patient. I don't want to give them what they want.
	I feel I am withdrawing emotionally during the session.
Helplessness	I feel I don't know what to do. I fear I'll make mistakes. I wonder if I'm really competent. Sometimes I feel like giving up.
Goal inhibition	The patient is blocking me from achieving my goals. I feel like I'm wasting time. I should be able to achieve my goals in sessions without the patient's interference.
Self-sacrifice	I should meet the patient's needs. I should make them feel better. The patient's needs often take precedence over my needs. I sometimes believe that I would do almost anything to meet their needs
Emotional inhibition	I feel frustrated when I'm with this patient because I can't express the way I really feel. I find it hard to suppress my feelings. I can't be myself.

Source: Overcoming Resistance in Cognitive Therapy, by R. L. Leahy, 2001, New York: Guilford Press.

outlined here (A. T. Beck et al., 2001), 756 psychiatric outpatients completed the Personality Belief Questionnaire (PBQ) at intake and were also assessed for personality disorders using a standardized clinical interview. Patients with avoidant, dependent, obsessive-compulsive, narcissistic, and paranoid personality disorders preferentially endorsed PBQ beliefs theoretically linked to their specific disorders. Butler, Brown, Beck, and Grisham (2002) found that the PBQ's nine subscales, with 126 items, had good internal consistency for scales. Arntz, Dietzel, and Dreessen (1999) have found that the Personality Beliefs Questionnaire discriminates borderlines from Cluster C patients.

Kuyken, Kurzer, DeRubeis, Beck, and Brown (2001) have shown predictive validity of this scale with higher scores on the avoidant and paranoid scales predictive of poorer outcome in therapy.

There is growing evidence in support of a cognitive-behavioral approach to personality disorders. Nelson-Gray, Johnson, Foyle, Daniel, and Harmon (1996), in an uncontrolled study, found mixed results. Springer, Lohr, Buchtel, and Silk (1995) found significant improvement in hospitalized patients with personality disorders, and Luborsky, McLellan, Woody, O'Brien, and Auerbach (1985) found that patients receiving cognitive-behavioral treatment for antisocial personality maintained their improvement at seven-month follow-up. In studies of the treatment of avoidant personality patients, Greenberg and Stravynski (1985) and Feske, Perry, Chambless, Renneberg, and Goldstein (1996) found improvement with exposure-based cognitive-behavioral therapy. Brown, Newman, Charlesworth, and Crits-Christoph (in press) used a cognitive model for treatment of borderline personality based on a treatment manual (Layden, Newman, Freeman, & Morse, 1993), providing one year of treatment. Patients receiving cognitive therapy showed decreases in suicidal ideation, self-injury, hopelessness, depression, borderline symptoms, and dysfunctional beliefs, with only 48% on follow-up still meeting criteria for diagnosis of borderline personality disorder (Brown et al., in press).

CONCLUSIONS

The cognitive model of psychopathology has been extended effectively to the understanding and treatment of personality disorders. The value of this model is that it helps the clinician and patient collaborate effectively in developing a case conceptualization, rationale, and plan for effective treatment. Since the cognitive model articulates a model of core beliefs, assumptions, and strategies, it is open to empirical evaluation. Content areas, specified by this model, appear to coincide with the expected diagnostic groups, giving concurrent validity to the model. There is now promising evidence that treatment based on cognitive therapy principles can effectively help some of our most challenging patients.

REFERENCES

Adler, A. (1964). *Social interest: A challenge to mankind.* New York: Capricorn Books. (Original work published 1924)

Arntz, A., Dietzel, R., & Dreessen, L. (1999). Assumptions in borderline personality disorder: Specificity, stability and relationship with etiological factors. *Behaviour Research and Therapy, 37,* 545–557.

Beck, A. T. (1976). *Cognitive therapy and the emotional disorders.* New York: International Universities Press.

Beck, A. T. (1996). Beyond belief: A theory of modes, personality and psychopathology. In P. Salkovskis (Ed.), *Frontiers of cognitive therapy* (pp. 1–25). New York: Guilford Press.

Beck, A. T., Butler, A. C., Brown, G. K., Dahlsgaard, K. K., Newman, C. F., & Beck, J. S. (2001). Dysfunctional beliefs discriminate personality disorders. *Behaviour Research and Therapy, 39,* 1213–1225.

Beck, A. T., Emery, G., & Greenberg, R. L. (1985). *Anxiety disorders and phobias: A cognitive perspective.* New York: Basic Books.

Beck, A. T., Freeman, A., Davis, D. D., Pretzer, J., Fleming, B., Arntz, A., et al. (2003). *Cognitive therapy of personality disorders* (2nd ed.). New York: Guilford Press.

Beck, A. T., Rush, A. J., Shaw, B. F., & Emery, G. (1979). *Cognitive therapy of depression*. New York: Guilford Press.

Beck, J. S. (1995). *Cognitive therapy: Basics and beyond*. New York: Guilford Press.

Beck, J. S. (1996). Cognitive therapy of personality disorders. In P. M. Salkovskis (Ed.), *Frontiers of cognitive therapy* (pp. 165–181). New York: Guilford Press.

Brewin, C. R. (1996). Cognitive processing of adverse experiences. *International Review of Psychiatry, 8*(4), 333–339.

Brown, G. K., Newman, C. F., Charlesworth, S., & Crits-Christoph, P. (in press). An open clinical trial of cognitive therapy for borderline personality disorder. *Journal of Personality Disorders.*

Butler, A. C., Brown, G. K., Beck, A. T., & Grisham, J. R. (2002). Assessment of dysfunctional beliefs in borderline personality disorder. *Behavioral Research and Therapy, 40*(10), 1231–1240.

Feske, U., Perry, K. J., Chambless, D. L., Renneberg, B., & Goldstein, A. J. (1996). Avoidant personality disorder as a predictor for treatment outcome among generalized social phobics. *Journal of Personality Disorders, 10*(2), 174–184.

Frankl, V. E. (1992). *Man's search for meaning: An introduction to logotherapy* (4th ed.). Boston: Beacon Press.

Greenberg, D., & Stravynski, A. (1985). Patients who complain of social dysfunction as their main problem: I. Clinical and demographic features. *Canadian Journal of Psychiatry* [Revue Canadienne de Psychiatrie], *30*(3), 206–211.

Grey, N., Holmes, E., & Brewin, C. R. (2001). Peritraumatic emotional "hot spots" in memory. *Behavioural and Cognitive Psychotherapy, 29,* 367–372.

Hackmann, A., Clark, D. M., & McManus, F. (2000). Recurrent images and early memories in social phobia. *Behaviour Research and Therapy, 38,* 601–610.

Horney, K. (1945). *Our inner conflicts*. New York: Norton.

Horney, K. (1950). *Neurosis and human growth*. New York: Norton.

Kelly, G. A. (1955). *The psychology of personal constructs*. New York: Norton.

Kuyken, W., Kurzer, N., DeRubeis, R. J., Beck, A. T., & Brown, G. K. (2001). Response to cognitive therapy in depression: The role of maladaptive beliefs and personality disorders. *Journal of Consulting and Clinical Psychology, 69*(3), 560–566.

Layden, M. A., Newman, C. F., Freeman, A., & Morse, S. B. (1993). *Cognitive therapy of borderline personality disorder*. Boston: Allyn & Bacon.

Leahy, R. L. (1996). *Cognitive therapy: Basic principles and applications*. Northvale, NJ: Aronson.

Leahy, R. L. (1997). *Practicing cognitive therapy: A guide to interventions*. Northvale, NJ: Aronson.

Leahy, R. L. (2001). *Overcoming resistance in cognitive therapy*. New York: Guilford Press.

Leahy, R. L. (2003). *Cognitive therapy techniques: A practitioner's guide*. New York: Guilford Press.

Luborsky, L., McLellan, A. T., Woody, G. E., O'Brien, C. P., & Auerbach, A. (1985). Therapist success and its determinants. *Archives of General Psychiatry, 42*(6), 602–611.

Nelson-Gray, R. O., Johnson, D., Foyle, L. W., Daniel, S. S., & Harmon, R., Jr. (1996). The effectiveness of cognitive therapy tailored to depressives with personality disorders. *Journal of Personality Disorders, 10*(2), 132–152.

O'Leary, K. M., Cowdry, R. W., Gardner, D. L., Leibenluft, E., Lucas, P. B., & deJong-Meyer, R. (1991). Dysfunctional attitudes in borderline personality disorder. *Journal of Personality Disorders, 5*(3), 233–242.

Popper, K. R. (1959). *The logic of scientific discovery*. New York: Basic Books.

Pretzer, J., & Beck, A. T. (in press). Cognitive therapy of personality disorders. In J. J. Magnavita (Ed.), *Handbook of personality disorders: Theory and practice*. New York: Wiley.

Smucker, M. R., & Dancu, C. V. (1999). *Cognitive-behavioral treatment for adult survivors of childhood trauma: Imagery rescripting and reprocessing.* Northvale, NJ: Aronson.

Springer, T., Lohr, N. E., Buchtel, H. A., & Silk, K. R. (1995). A preliminary report of short-term cognitive-behavioral group therapy for inpatients with personality disorders. *Journal of Psychotherapy Practice and Research, 5*(1), 57–71.

Sullivan, H. S. (1956). *Clinical studies in psychiatry.* New York: Norton.

Young, J. E., Klosko, J. S., & Weishaar, M. (2003). *Schema therapy: A practitioner's guide.* New York: Guilford Press.

Chapter 25

SCHEMA THERAPY FOR PERSONALITY DISORDERS

DAVID P. BERNSTEIN

Schema-focused cognitive therapy, or *schema therapy,* is an integrative form of psychotherapy that was developed by Jeffrey Young (Young, 1990; Young, Klosko, & Weishaar, 2003) for difficult-to-treat cases, such as patients with personality disorders or chronic depression and anxiety disorders. These patients often respond poorly to more conventional forms of cognitive therapy because their interpersonal issues make it difficult for them to engage in the kind of collaborative partnership with the therapist that traditional cognitive therapy requires. Schema therapy combines treatment techniques that are taken from the cognitive, behavioral, psychodynamic, and existential/humanistic traditions. Its overarching theoretical framework is cognitive, but it was also highly influenced by psychodynamic object relations theory, attachment theory, and other theoretical perspectives.

In contrast to standard forms of cognitive therapy, which are focused primarily on the present, schema therapy is concerned with self-defeating patterns of thinking, feeling, and behavior that originate in childhood and play themselves out repeatedly over the course of a lifetime. In schema therapy terms, these patterns are referred to as *early maladaptive schemas.* Young has identified 18 early maladaptive schemas, such as Abandonment, Emotional Deprivation, and Mistrust, which are rooted in childhood experiences and color the way in which individuals perceive themselves, others, and the world. Early maladaptive schemas and the maladaptive coping mechanisms that operate in conjunction with them perpetuate themselves in an automatic and largely nonconscious way that interferes with the individual's ability to meet his or her basic emotional needs. In the schema therapy model, early maladaptive schemas and maladaptive coping mechanisms are considered to form the cognitive and affective core of personality disorders.

Schema therapy is a relatively recent therapeutic innovation. There are several randomized clinical trials of schema therapy currently in progress (Arntz, 2003; Ball, 1998; Hoffart & Sexton, 2002). In one of these studies, patients with borderline personality who were given schema therapy were much less likely to drop out of treatment after a period of two years, compared with patients who received a psychoanalytically informed treatment, transference focused psychotherapy (Arntz, 2003). Although these preliminary findings are encouraging, a more complete evaluation of the efficacy of schema therapy will have to await the completion of this and other studies.

In this chapter, I provide an introduction to the schema therapy conceptual model and treatment approach. I illustrate the schema therapy approach using an example of a patient with a severe personality disorder who was highly resistant to more conventional forms of cognitive therapy.

SCHEMA THERAPY CONCEPTUAL MODEL

Early Maladaptive Schemas: Definition

The fundamental unit of analysis in the schema therapy conceptual model is the *early maladaptive schema*. Early maladaptive schemas are pervasive themes or patterns that originate in unmet or frustrated developmental needs, are elaborated over the course of a lifetime, and are self-defeating to a significant degree (Young, 1990; Young et al., 2003). Early maladaptive schemas consist of memories, cognitive attributions, painful affects, and bodily sensations that typically arise in response to adverse childhood experiences. These experiences include ones that almost any child would find noxious, such as child abuse or neglect, abandonment or traumatic loss, or witnessing violence. However, early maladaptive schemas may also arise out of nontraumatic experiences, such as a mismatch between a child's innate temperament and his or her parents' childrearing style (e.g., a child with "difficult" temperament raised by a very anxious or very authoritarian parent). The impact of these experiences may be exacerbated or mitigated by other factors, such as the child's genetic makeup (e.g., a genetic vulnerability for anxiety or depression) or other features of the childrearing environment (e.g., a secure attachment to a nonabusive caregiver). In any case, when adverse or other childhood experiences are chronic or severe enough, the result may be a frustration of the child's basic developmental needs, such as the need for acceptance, support, guidance, belonging, autonomy, appropriate limits, respect, and protection. Early maladaptive schemas have their origins in the frustration of these basic emotional needs.

The 18 Specific Early Maladaptive Schemas and the Five Schema Domains

Young has identified 18 early maladaptive schemas, which are grouped into five schema domains (Table 25.1). Each schema domain represents "a grouping of schemas based on the frustration of related developmental needs" (Young, 1990; Young et al., 2003). The five domains are: Disconnection and Rejection, Impaired Autonomy and Performance, Impaired Limits, Other-Directedness, and Overvigilance and Inhibition.

The Disconnection and Rejection domain consists of five early maladaptive schemas—Abandonment/Instability, Defectiveness/Shame, Abuse/Mistrust, Emotional Deprivation, and Social Isolation/Alienation—that arise out of frustrated needs for acceptance, nurturance, safety, empathy, and respect. The Abandonment/Instability schema is the individual's expectation that he or she will invariably be abandoned. The Defectiveness/Shame schema is the individual's belief that he or she is fundamentally flawed, worthless, or unlovable. The Abuse/Mistrust schema is the expectation that he or she will be mistreated, manipulated, exploited, or abused. The Emotional Deprivation schema is the expectation that others won't meet the individual's need for a normal degree of emotional nurturance, empathy, and protection. The Social Isolation/Alienation schema is the expectation that the individual will always be alone and alienated from others.

The Impaired Autonomy and Performance domain consists of four early maladaptive schemas—Dependence/Incompetence, Vulnerability to Harm or Illness, Enmeshment/

Table 25.1   Early Maladaptive Schemas and Schema Domains

Disconnection and Rejection

1. Abandonment/instability
2. Mistrust/abuse
3. Emotional deprivation
4. Defectiveness/shame
5. Social isolation/alienation

Impaired Autonomy and Performance

6. Dependence/incompetence
7. Vulnerability to harm or illness
8. Enmeshment/undeveloped self
9. Failure

Impaired Limits

10. Entitlement/grandiosity
11. Insufficient self-control/self-discipline

Other-Directedness

12. Subjugation
13. Self-sacrifice
14. Approval-seeking/recognition-seeking

Overvigilence and Inhibition

15. Negativity/pessimism
16. Emotional inhibition
17. Unrelenting standards/hypercriticalness
18. Punitiveness

Source: Compiled from Young, 1990.

Undeveloped Self, and Failure—that arise out of frustrated needs for autonomy, separation, and independence. The Dependence/Incompetence schema is the expectation that the individual can't handle everyday responsibilities without considerable help from others. The Vulnerability to Harm or Illness schema is the exaggerated fear that catastrophe will strike at any time and that the individual cannot prevent it. The Enmeshment/Undeveloped Self schema is the excessive emotional involvement and closeness with others at the expense of full individuation or normal social development. The Failure schema is the expectation that the individual will inevitably fail or is fundamentally inadequate in areas of achievement.

The Impaired Limits domain consists of two schemas—Entitlement/Grandiosity and Insufficient Self-Control/Self-Discipline—that arise out of the frustrated need for appropriate limits, discipline, and ethical standards. The Entitlement/Grandiosity is the individual's belief that he or she is superior to others, entitled to special rights and privileges, or not bound by normal rules of social reciprocity. The Insufficient Self-Control/Self-Discipline schema is the pervasive difficulty or refusal to exercise self-control and frustration tolerance to achieve goals.

The Other-Directedness domain consists of three schemas—Subjugation, Self-Sacrifice, and Approval-Seeking/Recognition-Seeking—that arise out of frustrated needs for approval, recognition, and self-directedness. The Subjugation schema is the excessive surrendering of control to others because the individual feels coerced, or to avoid anger, retaliation, or abandonment. The Self-Sacrifice schema is the excessive focus on voluntarily meeting the needs of others at the expense of the individual's own gratification. The Approval-Seeking/Recognition-Seeking schema is the excessive emphasis on gaining approval, recognition, or attention from other people.

The Overvigilance and Inhibition domain consists of four schemas—Negativity/Pessimism, Emotional Inhibition, Unrelenting Standards/Hypercriticalness, and Punitiveness—that arise out of frustrated needs for spontaneity, joy/pleasure, emotional expression, flexibility, and compassion. The Negativity/Pessimism schema is a pervasive, lifelong focus on the negative aspects of life (e.g., pain, death, loss) while minimizing the positive or optimistic aspects. The Emotional Inhibition schema is the excessive inhibition of spontaneous action, feeling, or communication. The Unrelenting Standards/Hypercriticalness schema is the individual's belief that he or she must strive to meet very high internalized standards of behavior and performance. The Punitiveness schema is the belief that people should be harshly punished for making mistakes.

Perpetuation of Early Maladaptive Schemas

Early maladaptive schemas are like unshakeable truths. They are foundational beliefs that shape the way we view ourselves, other people, and the world in a manner that is largely nonconscious and automatic. They are self-perpetuating and self-reinforcing, in that they involve cognitive biases or distortions that filter incoming information in ways that confirm preexisting beliefs. For example, a person with a Defectiveness/Shame schema may ignore information about her successes and focus only on her failures, thus perpetuating the belief that she is fundamentally flawed. Early maladaptive schemas operate on the principle of *cognitive consistency* or *equilibration*—they operate in a manner that enables us to maintain stable, consistent beliefs about the self, others, and the world. As Young and colleagues (2003) have noted, in Piagetian terms, early maladaptive schemas reflect a predominance of *assimilation* over *accommodation*—we tend to rely on our existing schemas to make sense of the world, rather than modifying those schemas to take in new information (Piaget & Inhelder, 1969). Thus, to maintain cognitive homeostasis, we are more likely to filter out information that is discrepant with our schemas (i.e., assimilation) than to adjust our schemas to take new information into account (i.e., accommodation).

Early maladaptive schemas also perpetuate themselves by creating self-fulfilling prophecies—by producing the very outcomes that are feared. For example, a person with an Abandonment schema may set up tests of loyalty to see whether his intimate partners will leave him. When his partners tire of these tests and leave him, his basic belief that others will abandon him is confirmed and strengthened.

Early maladaptive schemas arise out of our early noxious life experiences, including those that occur in the preverbal period. As such, they occur during a period of development in which the brain has considerable plasticity, in which networks of neuronal connections are being formed and strengthened that will become more difficult to alter later in life (Kalat, 2001). Research suggests that traumatic experiences occurring in childhood can permanently affect brain structure and functioning (Driessen et al., 2002). Thus, from a neuropsychological perspective, early maladaptive schemas can be conceived of as neural networks that were formed as a result of early adverse life experiences and have been elaborated and strengthened by subsequent experience, becoming increasingly more difficult to modify. The origins of early maladaptive schemas in childhood experiences, during a period in which lasting patterns of neuronal connections are being formed, helps to explain the enduring nature of early maladaptive schemas and their resistance to change. They represent a neurobiological substrate or foundation on which our subsequent perceptions of self, others, and world are built.

Comparison of Schema Theory with Attachment Theory, Object Relations Theory, and Beck's Cognitive Model

Early maladaptive schemas share much in common with the working models described by attachment theorists, such as Bowlby (1969), and the internalized object representations described by psychoanalytic object relations theorists, such as Winnicott (1965) and Kernberg (1984). Like the attachment and object relations theorists, Young (1990; Young et al., 2003) has posited that our early experiences with significant figures, such as our primary caregivers, form a template or model on which our later experience of close relationships is based. Like the attachment theorists' concept of "secure attachment," Young proposes that our early experiences of safety, security, nurturance, and consistency form the basis for our ability to form healthy adult attachments. When our childhood attachments are disrupted, for example, by abuse, neglect, or other childhood traumas, our capacity to form trusting, mutually fulfilling relationships is impaired. The result is early maladaptive schemas, the expectation that close relationships will be abusive, depriving, demeaning, abandoning, and so on. Like the object relations theorists' concept of "internalized object representations," Young believes that memories of early painful relationships with caregivers are at the core of early maladaptive schemas. Unlike some object relations theorists, such as Kernberg (1984), however, Young is concerned with the effects of *actual* noxious experiences in childhood, rather than fantasies that may or may not correspond to real events. Moreover, Young does not posit the existence of instinctual drives, such as libidinal or aggressive drives, that object relations theorists such as Kernberg believe play an essential distorting role in interpersonal perceptions (e.g., splitting).

Early maladaptive schemas differ from traditional Beckian cognitive distortions (e.g., all or nothing thinking) in that the former are fundamentally *interpersonal* in nature—they concern our deepest convictions about our relationships with other people, particularly our core truths about intimate relationships. In contrast, traditional Beckian cognitive distortions are fundamentally *intellectual,* rather than interpersonal, constructs. They are distorted modes of reasoning or logical errors that are believed to be responsible for negative mood states, such as anxiety and depression (Beck, Rush, Shaw, & Emery, 1979). The goal of the cognitive therapist is to replace these illogical, irrational thoughts with more rational, balanced ways of thinking. The goal of the schema therapist, on the other hand, is to alter ways of relating to others—to modify longstanding, maladaptive ways of experiencing the self and others in relationships (i.e., early maladaptive schemas). This process includes modifying distorted, irrational cognitions about the self and others, but goes beyond the standard cognitive therapy approach because it fundamentally involves healing the early interpersonal wounds that are at the core of these distorted perceptions.

Schema therapy was developed to help those individuals who could not be helped by standard cognitive techniques—such as patients with personality disorders and histories of early trauma. Early maladaptive schemas resist correction by collaborative empiricism and other traditional cognitive methods, unless these techniques are accompanied by other approaches that more directly address interpersonal issues. For this reason, Young (1990; Young et al., 2003) created the schema therapy treatment model that combines multiple treatment methods, including cognitive, behavioral, psychodynamic, and experiential/

humanistic approaches, to access and modify early maladaptive schemas that are central to personality disorders and other dysfunctional modes of relating.

Egosyntonic Nature of Early Maladaptive Schemas

Early maladaptive schemas are nonconscious, in that they are triggered by stimuli that may be outside the awareness of the individual and have effects that often go unrecognized. As such, they are typically *egosyntonic*—they are so much a part of the individual's ongoing experience that they go unnoticed. For example, a person with an Abandonment schema may believe that it is his destiny in life to be "unlucky in love" or that his partners will end up leaving him because they will eventually see his flaws. If he has a little more self-awareness, he may recognize that he tends to choose the wrong kinds of partners—partners who reject him—but he probably doesn't know the reasons he does so. In either case, the themes or patterns are so much a part of the person's ongoing life experience that they are not recognized for what they are: largely automatic patterns of thinking, feeling, and relating that assert themselves repeatedly without conscious control.

For many patients, early maladaptive schemas are easily recognized, once they are pointed out. One of the primary goals of the initial assessment phase of schema therapy is to educate patients about their early maladaptive schemas by pointing out the evidence of repeating patterns that originated in early childhood and have played themselves out repeatedly. For many patients, it is both relieving and painful to understand the patterns that have shaped the course of their lives. For other patients, the recognition of early maladaptive schemas may proceed more slowly, because of the coping strategies that are used to keep the painful feelings associated with early maladaptive schemas outside awareness. A person with a Failure schema may avoid people and situations that trigger his schemas—for example, by avoiding taking on new challenges—and thus be unaware of the profound fear of failure that underlies his avoidance. Similarly, a person with a Defectiveness/Shame schema may use an overcompensating coping style—for example, acting superior to others and putting other people down—to avoid awareness of his painful feelings of inferiority.

Maladaptive Coping Mechanisms

Young's (1990; Young et al., 2003) model includes both schemas and coping mechanisms. When early maladaptive schemas are triggered, they produce intense, disruptive affects. Three coping mechanisms are used to manage the potentially disruptive effects of schematic activation: schema surrender, schema avoidance, and schema overcompensation. Young et al. (2003) have likened the three coping mechanisms to the evolutionary survival mechanisms of "freeze," "flight," and "fight," respectively.

Schema surrender is the tendency to give in to the schema. For example, people with a Defectiveness/Shame schema sometimes are attracted to people and situations that trigger their schema. Someone may continue to work for an emotionally abusive employer, despite the frequent humiliations that come with the position, because these episodes are unpleasant but familiar, confirming a core belief that the self is unworthy. This coping mechanism is largely automatic and nonconscious. It is a habitual way of coping with the schema, but one that is self-defeating, because it confirms and perpetuates the schema. Schema avoidance is the tendency to avoid people and situations that trigger our schema. For example, people with a Failure schema avoid taking on new challenges at which they might fail, because the risk of failure is one that is likely to trigger their schema. Schema overcompensation means doing the opposite of the schema. For example, people with a Defectiveness/Shame schema sometimes attempt to make other people feel ashamed, as a way of compensating for their own feelings of defectiveness. All of these coping mechanisms develop in childhood as a means of coping with early maladaptive schemas, but ultimately serve to perpetuate schemas, rather than resolving them. Most people have one or two predominant coping styles, although it is not unusual for some individuals to exhibit each of the three coping styles on different occasions.

Young et al. (2003) distinguish between the three basic coping mechanisms or styles of coping, and coping responses, which are more specific and individualized forms of each of the coping styles. For example, cognitive and behavioral avoidance are both coping responses that exemplify a more general avoidant coping style: avoiding thinking about stimuli that trigger schemas and avoiding situations that trigger schemas, respectively.

Schema Modes

The final concept in the schema therapy conceptual model, along with early maladaptive schemas and coping mechanisms, is *schema modes*. Schema modes are the statelike manifestation of schemas that appear when early maladaptive schemas are triggered or activated. Early maladaptive schemas are traitlike constructs representing long-term, enduring features of the personality. They are often latent, rather than active. In contrast, schema modes are states: They are the transient manifestations of schemas when they are activated. When schemas are triggered, they can manifest themselves in various ways along with their associated coping responses. Each one of these manifestations is referred to as a *schema mode*. Another related way of conceptualizing schema modes is that they are parts or aspects of the personality that may predominate in certain situations when schemas are triggered. Young et al. (2003) have identified 10 schema modes, which fall into four categories: Child Modes (Vulnerable Child, Angry Child, Impulsive/Undisciplined Child, and Happy Child), Maladaptive Coping Modes (Compliant Surrenderer, Detached Protector, and Overcompensator), Maladaptive Parent Modes (Punitive Parent and Demanding Parent), and Healthy Adult Mode (Table 25.2).

Table 25.2   Schema Modes

Child Modes

1. Vulnerable child
2. Angry child
3. Impulsive/undisciplined child
4. Happy child

Maladaptive Coping Modes

5. Compliant surrenderer
6. Detached protector
7. Overcompensator

Maladaptive Parent Modes

8. Punitive parent
9. Demanding parent

Healthy Adult Mode

10. Healthy adult

Source: Compiled from Young, Klosko, & Weishaar, 2003.

In patients with personality disorders whose personalities are poorly integrated, these modes are relatively dissociated from one another, and the person can flip back and forth rapidly between modes, appearing alternately vulnerable, angry, numb, and rational, all within a brief period of time. The most extreme version of this mode flipping is seen in dissociative identity disorder (i.e., multiple identity disorder), in which different modes are experienced as separate selves or "alters." In Young et al.'s (2003) conceptualization, dissociative identity disorder is at the extreme pathological end of a continuum of mode dissociation. Borderline personality disorder is viewed as a less extreme, but still pathological, variant, in which modes shift rapidly but are not so dissociated as to be experienced as separate selves. Young developed schema mode work as an intervention method for more disturbed patients, such as patients with borderline or narcissistic personality disorder or those with severe trauma histories, who frequently flip between modes. However, schema mode work can be fully integrated with standard schema therapy treatment techniques and is often highly useful in treating less disturbed patients as well.

To illustrate, I discuss four very common schema modes: Vulnerable Child, Angry Child, Detached Protector, and Health Adult. A discussion of all 10 schema modes can be found in Young et al. (2003).

Vulnerable Child mode is the state in which painful schema-related affects are being directly experienced. For example, a person with an Abandonment schema may be flooded with painful feelings of grief and longing when jilted by a sexual partner. This mode is referred to as Vulnerable Child mode because it feels as if the person experiencing it is in a state of childlike pain and vulnerability—he or she feels powerless, helpless, and overwhelmed by his or her feelings. In Vulnerable Child mode, the person is directly experiencing the affects that are associated with his or her schemas.

Angry Child mode is the state in which the predominant emotion is anger and in which other affects, such as those experienced in Vulnerable Child mode, are effectively blocked out. Thus, Angry Child mode protects the more vulnerable part of the self from painful feelings that accompany schemas when they are triggered. For example, some individuals, such as patients with borderline personality disorder, may be provoked to rage when their schemas are triggered. When in this state, the feelings underlying these reactions—schema-related affects such as grief, pain, terror, and loneliness—are blocked out of awareness.

Detached Protector mode is the state of numbing or detachment in which schema-related affects are blocked entirely out of awareness. This is not equivalent to feeling "nothing" when not in a state of schematic activation. Rather, it is an active, albeit unconscious, effort to avoid or block out feelings. For example, individuals may attempt to block out painful feelings by engaging in addictive behavior (e.g., drinking, drugging, pathological sex, or gambling), losing themselves in their work, isolating themselves from other people, or other means. In some individuals with severe personality disorders or histories of trauma, a Detached Protector mode is engaged in from a young age to ward off painful feelings associated with traumatic experiences. These individuals frequently report that for most of their childhood they felt "numb," "bored," or "nothing," despite undergoing severe predations. Thus, these individuals learn to avoid painful affects; detachment may then become an ongoing habitual mode of coping in which the person spends most of the time in a nonfeeling dissociated state.

Healthy Adult mode is a state of awareness in which a person is able to think through issues in an objective, rational way, without being too disrupted by painful feelings, although he or she may be aware. One of the primary aims of schema mode work is to identify schema modes in the therapy session so that patients can be moved out of modes that interfere with therapeutic progress (i.e., Angry Child and Detached Protector modes) and into modes that facilitate progress in treatment (i.e., Vulnerable Child and Healthy Adult modes). This type of therapeutic maneuver is often critical to the successful treatment of patients with personality disorders.

SCHEMA THERAPY TREATMENT APPROACH

Assessment Phase

Schema therapy is an integrative form of treatment that combines cognitive, psychodynamic, experiential/humanistic, and behavioral techniques (Young, 1990; Young et al., 2003). Treatment begins with an assessment and case conceptualization phase that can last for several sessions. During the assessment phase, the therapist gathers information about the patient's schemas, coping responses, and modes to formulate a case conceptualization. After the case conceptualization is made, it is shared with the patient, along with the basic concepts of schema therapy. Sometimes the therapist assigns the patient the popular self-help book, *Reinventing Your Life* (Young & Klosko, 1994), which illustrates schema therapy concepts.

Having a cognitive framework for understanding patients' problems is often very reassuring to them. It also helps to strengthen the therapeutic alliance, in that both the therapist and patient share an understanding of the problem and can begin to work together toward mutually agreed on goals.

Young and colleagues (2003) have developed several self-administered questionnaires that can assist in the assessment process, including the Young Schema Questionnaire (Young & Brown, 2001) and the Young Parenting Inventory (Young, 1994). The therapist gives the patient these questionnaires to fill out between sessions, explaining that they will provide useful information about the patient's core issues that the therapist will share with the patient. Thus, from the beginning, the therapist and patient work together collaboratively with the goal of better understanding the patient's problems. The therapist also takes a careful life history, because a primary goal of the assessment phase is to identify repeating maladaptive patterns that play themselves out over the course of the patient's lifetime. The therapist often gives a self-report life history questionnaire, such as Lazarus's Multi-Modal Life History (Lazarus, 2002), to gather detailed information that can be used for this purpose.

In many cases, the patient's core schemas, coping responses, and typical schema modes become evident to the therapist even after a few sessions. In other cases, they may seem more obscure. For example, patients who spend a good deal of time in Detached Protector mode—a state of emotional numbness—may have difficulty identifying life events that trigger their schemas because they are usually out of touch with their emotions. For this reason, the therapist also uses guided imagery exercises to identify core schemas, coping responses, and modes. Patients are asked to close their eyes and let an image float into their mind of an upsetting experience from childhood. They are asked to visualize the image as vividly as possible and to relate what is happening in detail, as if it is occurring in the present. The therapist asks questions about what the little child in the image is thinking, feeling, and doing, and what other people in the image (e.g., parents, siblings, peers, teachers) are doing, to identify core schemas and their origins and the origins of coping responses. For example, one patient, Sara, whose case is described later, visualized herself as a little girl alone in her house, sitting on the bedroom floor reading a book. Her room was stark and bare with no pictures on the walls. Her parents were working and had left her by herself.

When asked what the little girl in the image was feeling, Sara said that she wasn't feeling anything at all—that she had lost herself in her reading. She admitted, however, that the little girl might be feeling lonely. Sara was emotionally neglected as a child: Her parents left her alone for extended periods of time at an age when she was unequipped to cope with it. As a result, she experienced profound feelings of emotional deprivation and isolation, which she dealt with by emotionally detaching herself and withdrawing into a world of fantasy. Two of her core schemas, Emotional Deprivation and Abandonment, her predominant coping style, Avoidance, and her predominant mode, Detached Protector, were made palpable in the image she spontaneously produced.

Treatment Phase

The goal of the treatment phase is to help the patient change lifelong maladaptive patterns by ameliorating schemas, coping responses, and modes. Because schemas arise in childhood from the toxic frustration of basic emotional needs, the ultimate goal of schema therapy is to help the patient learn how to get those needs met—to heal the early emotional wounds that block the patient from fulfilling core needs such as self-acceptance, nurturance, security, and competence. Schema change methods include cognitive restructuring (collaborative empiricism) and schema dialogues to counter distorted beliefs and foster a healthy ability to take perspective on an individual's schemas; guided imagery exercises to release emotions and provide corrective emotional experiences in imagination (e.g., nurturing the deprived child, protecting the abused child, soothing the abandoned child); and role playing and homework assignments to counter maladaptive coping responses, such as avoidance and overcompensation, and to practice more effective means of getting needs met.

The therapy relationship is considered critically important in the schema therapy model (Young, 1990; Young et al., 2003). A key concept is limited reparenting, an active directive approach in which the therapist attempts to provide some of the warmth, guidance, and firm yet empathic limit setting that the patient may have lacked as a child. The aim of limited reparenting is to provide corrective emotional experiences within appropriate boundaries. In the case of many patients, empathy and compassion are crucial to counter feelings such as shame and deprivation. The therapist's ability to genuinely like, accept, and care about patients; to connect with them and help them feel understood; and to display compassion for their suffering is crucial to patients' ability to cultivate those attitudes toward themselves. Other important aspects of limited reparenting are the therapist's reliability and consistency and guidance to support healthy, responsible choices.

Another key ingredient of the therapy relationship is what Young has called "empathic confrontation" (Young, 1990; Young et al., 2003). Empathic confrontation is the therapist's ability to point out the patient's self-defeating or destructive behavior, while maintaining an attitude of acceptance toward the patient. By helping the patient to view self-defeating behavior in terms of schemas and coping mechanisms, the therapist is able to counter patients' beliefs that these behaviors are proof of their unworthiness. Instead, the patient can come to see these behaviors as unsuccessful and habitual ways of coping with painful experiences that they learned as a child and, over time, have become automatic and self-reinforcing.

Schema mode work is a relatively recent innovation in schema therapy theory and method. Its goal is to help patients integrate dissociated aspects of the self (i.e., schema modes) so that they can become accessible to, and therefore come under greater control of, the healthier part of the patient's personality (i.e., Healthy Adult mode). Schema mode work is particularly useful in working with more severely personality-disordered patients who may fluctuate rapidly between different emotional states or are rigidly stuck in one or more of the schema modes. For example, patients with borderline personality disorder may flip rapidly from Angry Child to Vulnerable Child to Detached Protector mode, all in the course of a single psychotherapy session. Alternatively, patients with narcissistic personality disorder may spend most of their time in a state of haughty superiority (i.e., Overcompensator mode), while schizoid personality disorder patients are usually stuck in a state of profound emotional detachment (i.e., Detached Protector mode).

In schema mode work, patients are helped to recognize and label their own schema modes. The therapist introduces the modes as parts of the self that developed when the patient was young to help him or her cope with painful events. Working collaboratively, the therapist and patient choose evocative labels for the schema modes to help the patient feel an emotional connection to them (e.g., "Little Sara," for the Vulnerable Child mode; "Angry Sara," for the Angry Child mode). Frequently, the therapist's aim is to move the patient from a therapeutically unproductive mode, such as Overcompensator, Detached Protector, or Angry Child, into a more productive mode, such as Vulnerable Child or Healthy Adult. For example, Sara often presented either in Detached Protector mode, a state in which she was out of touch with her emotions, or Overcompensator mode, a state in which she was haughtily devaluing of the therapist. Both of these modes had developed as a means of protecting her from considerable inner pain, resulting from the profound emotional deprivation she had experienced as a child. For the patient to make therapeutic progress, she needed to move into a more productive mode in which she could feel her inner pain more directly (i.e., Vulnerable Child mode) or take a more objective, balanced view of herself and her situation (i.e., Healthy Adult mode). It is in these more productive schema modes that some of the patient's original pain can be healed and therapeutic change can be accomplished.

Therapists have a variety of techniques at their disposal to help them move the patient from less productive into more productive schema modes. For example, they can have the patient engage in schema dialogues between maladaptive schema modes and the Healthy Adult mode. Sara could be asked to carry out a dialogue between the Detached Protector mode ("Detached Sara") and the Healthy Adult mode ("Rational Sara"), alternating between the two roles. This is a variation on the Gestalt therapy "two chairs" technique. "Detached Sara" might be asked to explain her function in Sara's life, to justify why it is so important that she protect Sara from the awareness of any feelings. For example, "Detached Sara" might explain that it is her job to protect Sara from feeling lonely and depressed. The therapist might ask "Rational Sara" to provide a healthy response by stating the disadvantages of remaining in a detached emotional state. "Rational Sara" might then reply that remaining in a detached state leaves her isolated and disconnected from other people. The therapist would then have the patient alternate back and forth, conducting a dialogue between the two modes, as each presents and elaborates on its own point of view and responds to the other's arguments. In doing this exercise, the therapist and patient gain greater insight into the functions served by maladaptive schema modes. In addition, by providing arguments to counter the maladaptive schema modes, the patient strengthens the healthy, rational side of himself or herself (i.e., the Healthy Adult mode).

Schema dialogues usually pave the way for imagery exercises that give the patient a vivid, emotional experience of the schema modes and their origins and afford the opportunity for corrective emotional experiences in imagination. For example, Sara could be asked to close her eyes and imagine an upsetting scene from her childhood. In one such exercise, Sara recalled a frequent scene from her childhood home in which her parents were fighting downstairs, while she was listening alone in her bedroom upstairs. When asked what "Little Sara" was feeling, Sara replied that the little girl in the image was reading a book and feeling nothing. As in the imagery exercise described earlier, the origins of Sara's Detached Protector mode are evident in the image of an isolated little girl trying to block out the pain of hearing her parents fighting. As a corrective emotional experience, the therapist could ask the patient for permission to enter the image himself or herself to comfort the lonely or abandoned child. In the imagery exercise, the therapist can speak directly to the Vulnerable Child, asking her how she is feeling and what might help to make her feel better. For example, "Little Sara" asked the therapist to sit with her while she read her book. This exercise enabled the patient to experience in imagery some of the comfort of a warm, empathic adult presence that she had been lacking in her childhood. Although such imaginal experiences cannot completely make up for damaging childhood events, they can help patients to experience directly some of their inner pain that is ordinarily inaccessible because of the self-protective function of maladaptive modes and coping responses. By grieving for the Little Child within herself and experiencing the therapist's comfort, empathy, and protection, the patient is able to heal some of the early emotional wounds that are at the heart of her longstanding difficulties.

Sara, a Case of Emotional Deprivation in a Patient with a Severe Personality Disorder

The following case illustrates some of the complexities presented by patients with severe personality disorders. The case serves as an introduction to the schema therapy conceptual model and illustrates why more conventional methods for treating common forms of psychopathology, such as depression and anxiety, often fail to work with these patients.

Sara was a woman in her 70s who had never married and had been suffering from major depression and dysthymia (double depression) for most of her life. She was severely personality disordered, with pronounced narcissistic, borderline, paranoid, and schizoid traits. She came to me for treatment, seeking cognitive therapy for her depressive symptoms. After much discussion, she agreed to a medication consultation. However, she refused to see the psychiatrist I recommended, later admitting that she hadn't wanted to give me "too much power" over her. She disliked the psychiatrist whom she saw and quickly discontinued the medication he gave her after developing some vocal irritation that she attributed to the medication. Trying another approach, I recommended a popular cognitive therapy self-help book for depression, which she agreed to read. However, after scanning the first chapter, she declared that there was "nothing in it" for her—the approach seemed superficial and irrelevant to her problems.

Sara had a history of severe childhood emotional deprivation—the failure to provide for a child's basic emotional needs, such as love, belonging, guidance, and support. Her father had been emotionally withdrawn throughout her childhood; in retrospect, Sara recognized that he had suffered from untreated depression. He worked long hours, and when he was home, he was barely communicative. Her mother was more emotionally available but worked outside the home and had left her daughter to fend for herself from a young age. Her parents had had a terrible marriage, fighting frequently and existing in a perpetual state of "cold war." To escape the marriage, her mother frequently stayed out late at night, attending meetings or socializing with friends. By the age of 7 or 8 years, Sara routinely returned from school to an empty house. Her mother had left her a prepared meal in the refrigerator, which Sara learned to heat up in the oven, eating dinner by herself. Often, she put herself to bed, staying awake until she heard her mother return. Not infrequently, the mother crawled into bed with her and they cuddled together. Cuddling in bed with her mother was among Sara's few happy memories of her childhood.

Sara remembered herself as having been a passive, withdrawn, and anxious child. Reading was the only refuge from her loneliness. She recalled herself as perpetually waiting for her mother to return home. In her mother's absence, she felt unable to cope with many decisions and tasks that had been thrust unwontedly on her at too early an age. As an adult, she felt empty inside, as if she were drifting aimlessly through life without any real goals or focus. She procrastinated terribly, ruminating over even minor decisions. She was an intelligent and educated woman but was unable to take any pleasure from her professional achievements; in fact, she considered herself a failure. She had had several romantic relationships but was emotionally detached and disengaged, a stance that her partners eventually found frustrating and disappointing. Although a few of her potential suitors had offered her the stability and security that she craved, she devalued them, focusing on their faults and depreciating their strengths. Inside, she felt that she was hopelessly flawed and that her partners would inevitably abandon her when they recognized her shortcomings. Moreover, she felt profoundly vulnerable in the world, believing that others could easily use, control, or manipulate her. To protect herself from rejection and mistreatment, she shared little personal information with anyone. When, inevitably, her partners lost patience and left her, she would plunge into despair, missing her partners terribly and regretting the opportunities she had wasted. On such occasions, she became seriously depressed. It was after the breakup of one such relationship that she sought treatment with me.

Conceptualizing Sara's issues in an integrated manner, her initial problems in therapy become more explicable. Her fundamental problem was an inability to form and maintain intimate connections with other people—a difficulty that was rooted in her history of emotional neglect. In schema terms, she had developed several early maladaptive schemas as a result of the profound experiences of disconnection and rejection she had suffered in childhood. These schemas were like absolute, unshakable truths that formed the basis for how she viewed herself, others, and the world. Thus, in intimate relationships, she anticipated that she would be deprived of love, safety, security, and support (Emotional Deprivation schema); that her partners would find that she was inherently flawed and, therefore, unlovable (Defectiveness schema); that her partners would take advantage of her vulnerability to control and manipulate her (Abuse/Mistrust schema); and that ultimately those whom she needed the most would abandon her (Abandonment schema). The lack of protection and supervision she had experienced as a child caused her to experience life as an adult as overwhelming and potentially dangerous. The world felt fundamentally unsafe (Vulnerability to Harm schema). Because, as a child, she had been overwhelmed by too much responsibility and given too little guidance, she felt that she was poorly equipped to handle even the mundane tasks of life, resulting in endless procrastination and indecision (Dependence/Incompetence schema).

The feelings associated with these schemas were so painful to her that she took drastic measures to avoid having her schemas triggered. From an early age, she had learned to wall off her feelings and distance herself from others, an avoidant coping style that she had probably modeled on her father's detachment and emotional withdrawal. As a child, she had sometimes felt sad, but most of the time felt "nothing." As an adult, most of the time she reported feeling "numb," "empty," or "depressed." Thus, she spent much of her time in Detached Protector mode—a state of emotional numbness that protected her from feelings such as loneliness, deprivation, and defectiveness. This coping style was formed in childhood and, by adulthood, was so automatic and reflexive that it asserted itself without her conscious awareness, particularly in situations that threatened to awaken these feelings. Thus, in intimate relationships, her emotional detachment, guardedness, and devaluation were understandable attempts to protect herself from the painful feelings that would be triggered if she allowed herself to get close to others. Ultimately, this coping style was self-defeating, because it caused the very abandonment that she feared and prevented her from getting the closeness that she craved. Thus, her maladaptive coping style served to confirm and strengthen the underlying beliefs about relationships—early maladaptive schemas—that had led her to take such drastic self-protective measures in the first place. The dissolution of her relationships left her feeling even more defective, deprived, mistreated, and abandoned.

In light of Sara's history of emotional neglect and her resulting early maladaptive schemas and coping styles, it is not surprising that my more conventional attempts at treatment had failed. Sara's guarded, mistrustful stance had thwarted my attempts to provide her with the medication I believed that she needed. She experienced the therapy relationship as one in which she was vulnerable and powerless—the way she felt in all close relationships—and in which she could be easily controlled, manipulated, or mistreated. Thus, my benign attempts to refer her for pharmacological treatment were experienced as an unwanted and threatening intrusion on her autonomy. As she probably experienced it, I was trying to collude with my psychiatrist colleague to give her a dangerous medication. It was no wonder she had rejected my recommendation of a psychiatrist in favor of someone she had chosen herself. And it was not surprising that at the first appearance of a possible side effect, she had discontinued the harmful—as she saw it—antidepressant. Thus, her fundamental belief that she was vulnerable and unprotected in the world (Vulnerability to Harm schema) and that close relationships gave others the power to manipulate and mistreat her (Mistrust schema) led her to experience my attempts to help her with medication in a profoundly distorted way.

Her coping response was to attempt to seize control in a situation in which she felt that she lacked it—first by rejecting the psychiatrist I recommended and then by ceasing to take the medication altogether. Thus, her coping style was to overcompensate for her feelings of vulnerability and fears of mistreatment by doing the opposite of her schemas: by attempting to assert her power when she felt powerless and taking matters into her own hands, rather than trusting me by putting her care into my hands. Thus, her early maladaptive schemas, combined with her maladaptive coping responses, led to a self-defeating result in which she was deprived of the medication that she needed. The upshot of all of this is that Sara was left bereft of the beneficial effects that the medication might have provided her. Every day, she suffered from painful feelings of depression, yet her schemas and coping responses had conspired to deprive her of relief from her suffering. In a sense, they had perpetuated the feelings of painful deprivation from which she had suffered as a child. As an adult, feeling powerless and trusting no one, she could not accept the help that others offered her, leaving her need for relief from suffering unmet.

When Sara rejected the self-help book that I recommended as being irrelevant to her problems, she was largely correct. The standard Beckian approach to cognitive therapy that the book propounded, namely the identification and correction of cognitive distortions that are common in depression (e.g., all or nothing thinking), missed the boat when it came to her issues. It was not the case that she failed to show the same cognitive distortions as other depressed patients. In fact, she exhibited them consistently. For example, she saw the glass as half-full, rather than half-empty (i.e., all or nothing thinking) when it came to her appraisal of her own accomplishments, the merits of her prospective suitors, and her assessment of her therapy's chances of succeeding. However, this form of cognitive bias was not her fundamental problem. Her basic problems were *interpersonal* rather than intellectual—that is, her inability to form and maintain intimate connections with others.

When I began to conceptualize Sara's issues in terms of her early maladaptive schemas, coping responses, and modes, and shifted the treatment emphasis from analyzing cognitive distortions to addressing the therapy relationship and her own shifting emotional states during and outside the therapy session, the treatment took a turn for the better. Sara became much more engaged and involved in her treatment, which no longer felt like an abstract intellectual exercise to her. Sara's fundamental problem was a lack of emotional connectedness, stemming from her history of severe emotional neglect. When I put that issue front and center, especially by addressing the barriers to closeness in her reactions to me, she felt that I was hitting the mark, and the treatment began to move forward. Treatment with Sara continued to be arduous because of the severity of her entrenched early maladaptive schemas, maladaptive schema modes, and coping responses. Nevertheless, we were managing to address the issues that had produced such desperation and despondency over the course of her lifetime.

CONCLUSIONS

Schema therapy is a conceptual model and treatment approach that was developed for patients with personality disorders and other severe, treatment-resistant problems. It offers therapists a method for working with patients who may not respond well to more traditional forms of psychotherapy. Although clinical trials of schema therapy have not yet been completed, schema therapy appears to hold considerable promise for treating otherwise intractable cases.

REFERENCES

Arntz, A. (2003). Cognitive therapy versus applied relaxation as treatment of generalized anxiety disorder. *Behaviour Research and Therapy, 41,* 633–646.

Ball, S. A. (1998). Manualized treatment for substance abusers with personality disorders: Dual focus schema therapy. *Addictive Behavior, 23,* 883–892.

Beck, A. T., Rush, A. J., Shaw, B. F., & Emery, G. (1979). *Cognitive therapy of depression.* New York: Guilford Press.

Bowlby, J. (1969). *Attachment and loss: Volume I. Attachment.* New York: Basic Books.

Driessen, M., Herrmann, J., Stahl, K., de Zwaan, M., Meier, S., Hill, A., et al. (2002). Magnetic resonance imaging volumes of the hippocampus and the amygdala in women with borderline personality disorder. *Archives of General Psychiatry, 57,* 1115–1122.

Hoffart, A., & Sexton, H. (2002). The role of optimism in the process of schema-focused cognitive therapy of personality disorders. *Behavior Research and Therapy, 40,* 611–623.

Kalat, J. W. (2001). *Biological psychology* (7th ed.). Stamford, CT: Thompson Learning.

Kernberg, O. F. (1984). *Severe personality disorders: Psychotherapeutic strategies.* New Haven, CT: Yale University Press.

Lazarus, A. (2002). The multimodal assessment therapy approach. In F. W. Kaslow (Editor-in-Chief) & J. Lebow (Vol. Ed.), *Comprehensive handbook of psychotherapy: Integrative/eclectic* (Vol. 4, pp. 241–254). Hoboken, NJ: Wiley.

Piaget, J., & Inhelder, B. (1969). *The psychology of the child.* New York: Basic Books.

Winnicott, D. W. (1965). *The maturational process and the facilitating environment: Studies in the theory of emotional development.* London: Hogarth Press.

Young, J. E. (1990). *Cognitive therapy for personality disorders.* Sarasota, FL: Professional Resources Exchange.

Young, J. E. (1994). *Young Parenting Inventory.* New York: Cognitive Therapy Center of New York.

Young, J. E., & Brown, G. (2001). *Young Schema Questionnaire.* New York: Cognitive Therapy Center of New York.

Young, J. E., & Klosko, J. S. (1994). *Re-inventing your life.* New York: Plume.

Young, J. E., Klosko, J. S., & Weishaar, M. E. (2003). *Schema therapy: A practitioner's guide.* New York: Guilford Press.

Chapter 26

THE ROLE OF COMMON FACTORS IN DOMAIN-FOCUSED PSYCHOTHERAPY FOR THE PERSONALITY DISORDERS

DARWIN DORR

This chapter discusses the interface between what have been called the *common factors* in psychotherapy and the domains of personality functioning as described by Theodore Millon (Millon & Davis, 1996) in working with the personality disorders. I begin with Millon's views of the state of our field.

In the Preface of *Personality-Guided Therapy,* Millon (1999) wrote:

> The great philosophers and clinicians of the past viewed their task as creating a rationale that took into account *all* of the complexities of human nature: the biological, the phenomenological, the developmental, and so on. Modern conceptual thinkers have actively avoided this complex and broad vision. They appear to favor one-dimensional schemata—conceptual frameworks that intentionally leave out much that may bear significantly on the reality of human life. (p. ix)

In this text, he also wrote:

> It is my hope that the book will lead us back to "reality" by exploring both the natural intricacy and the diversity of the patients we treat. Despite their frequent brilliance, most schools of therapy have become inbred; more importantly, they persist in narrowing clinicians' attention to just one or another facet of their patients' psychological makeup, thereby wandering even farther from human reality. They cease to represent the fullness of patients' lives when they consider as significant only one of several psychic spheres—the unconscious, biochemical processes, cognitive schemata, and so on. In effect, what has been taught to most fledgling therapists is an artificial reality. It may have been formulated in its early stages as an original perspective and one insightful methodology, but over time, it has drifted increasingly from its moorings and is no longer anchored to the clinical reality from which it was abstracted. (p. ix)

Thus, he begins a book that advocates reestablishing the person as the focus of treatment.

We recently witnessed the publication of *The Heart and Soul of Change: What Works in Therapy* (Hubble, Duncan, & Miller, 1999) and *Psychotherapy Relationships That Work: Therapist Contributions and Responsiveness to Patients* (Norcross, 2002). Both of these volumes were written to refocus us on common process, including person of the therapist and the patient. At this same time, Millon's *Personality-Guided Therapy* (1999) appeared in print, which began with the quotation cited at the beginning of this chapter. It would seem that the work of Millon is highly congruent with the renaissance of what we might call *process-oriented psychotherapy.* This chapter represents an effort to facilitate this interface. First, the elements of Millon's domain model are reviewed. Then, selected writings on the common factors are summarized. The third section is a discussion of special considerations in working with persons with personality disorder. The final section consists of a discussion of the role of the common factors in domain-focused psychotherapy with patients with personality disorders.

DOMAINS OF PERSONALITY

For more than 30 years, Theodore Millon has been developing an inclusive, integrative theory of personality and psychopathology, focusing especially on personality disorders. One of the major contributions of his theory has been to help us resolve the nature of how we approach our subject matter. That is, his theory helps us understand at what level we conduct our examination of the person.

Chapter 1 of the second edition of *Disorders of Personality: DSM-IV and Beyond* (Millon & Davis, 1996) offers nine principles for conceptualizing personality and its disorders. The fourth principle asserted that *personality consists of multiple units at multiple data levels.* In explaining this principle, Millon and Davis point out that much of the confusion in personality psychology (and psychology in general) stems from the fact that various investigators have traditionally examined different types of data. Further, proponents of one type of clinical data tend to be unaware of the work of others who focus elsewhere. Yet many levels of data are necessary for a complete perspective on psychotherapy with individuals. Although the dimensions of personality would seem to be almost endless, Millon suggests that there are four broad categories or levels of data that are prominent in the psychotherapy literature:

1. *Biophysical data* comprise one major area of knowledge. This area, favored mostly by advocates of biological psychiatry, focuses on a disease model of psychopathology and chooses chemical-biological elements for its unit of study, such as neurotransmitters, reuptake mechanisms, neuronal transmission, biological substrate of mood and temperament, and so on. As a result of intense focus at this level of analysis, marvelous advances have been made in the biological-chemical treatment of a broad range of psychological-psychiatric disorders.

2. The advocates of psychodynamic theories direct our gaze to *intrapsychic data.* Emphasizing the role of early experience and the demands of working through the various developmental stages, proponents of this point of view examine manifestations of the role of the unconscious, the control and direction of drives, the interplay among conflicting forces in the psyche, and the efficiency and adaptiveness of defenses.

3. Others prefer to examine *phenomenological data.* These individuals lean toward the humanistic and existential traditions and tend to prize the data of the conscious, apperceptive world. They ask: How does the human being perceive and experience his or her personal and unique world? No matter how distorted this worldview may be, it is the reality of that individual, and the therapist must enter this world with the

client as an essential part of the psychotherapeutic process. To do less would be to fall into an extraperspective and, thus, nontherapeutic position.

4. *Behavioral data* tend to be favored by those working in academic settings. Relevant data to these workers is objective, tangible, and directly measurable. Logical positivism reigns, and empiricism is valued over subjective inference.

In describing these various kinds or levels of data, Millon was introducing the concept of a "multireferential" perspective. This concept is essential because personality is multidetermined, and an integrative approach to treating personality must take into consideration multiple facets or dimensions of its complex nature. To do otherwise would be to eliminate the eclecticism of divergent points of view. But the process of integration is difficult. How do we select from among the broad range of domains of personal function the ones that are most important and relevant to the enterprise of psychological treatment?

Millon employed several criteria in selecting and developing the clinical domains in his model. First, they must be unique and varied in order to span the broad range of personal functioning. To select from a narrow band of domains would fail to honor the complexity of the human condition. Second, they must be reasonably isomorphic with prominent bodies of therapeutic knowledge. For example, phenomenological approaches have played a prominent role in psychological treatment for decades and should be represented as well as behavioral domains and so on. Third, the domains to be chosen must be reasonably coordinated with the dimensions of personality addressed by the prevailing *Diagnostic and Statistical Manual of Mental Disorders (DSM)* diagnostic system. The domains to be selected should allow discrimination of the distinctive features of disorders within each clinical domain.

Because the goal of his work was to offer a logical integration of psychotherapeutic traditions, Millon also considered both structuralism and functionalism in his conceptualization. Specifically, he included not only domains imbedded naturally in what might be called *American functionalism,* for example, behavioral domains, but also those that would fit more easily into structural schema such as object relations. Table 26.1 portrays the organization and nature of the domains Millon finally selected for his mode.

In selecting these eight domains, Millon presented a matrix that provides a means to consider the person in her or his complexity. The domains are not intended to be exhaustive, but they tend to cover a broad range of psychological functioning and describe avenues for intervention. Further, they are broad enough to allow additional points of view to be introduced. For example, C. R. Snyder's (1994) concept of hope can easily be incorporated under Cognitive Style, Self-Image, and even Object Representations.

Within the behavioral level of analysis are Expressive Acts, which are functional. Expressive Acts can be understood to be the realm of operant behavior. The observer can readily identify overt physical and verbal behavior. Patterns of behavior can be observed that reveal characteristic tendencies, which in turn make clear the individual's dispositions. Dispositions reveal what people actually do as opposed to what they say they will do. Behavioral therapeutic interventions naturally focus on this domain.

Also falling at the behavioral level is Interpersonal Conduct, which is also a functional domain. Interpersonal Conduct includes overt physical and verbal behavior in the social context. Sociocultural data reside within this domain. The person's style of interrelating with others resides here, and the dynamics between self and others are played out. Interpersonal Conduct also reflects attitudes and interpersonal schemas. Social,

**Table 26.1   Millon's Functional and Structural
Domains of Personality**

Functional Domains	Structural Domains
Behavioral Level	
Expressive acts	
Interpersonal conduct	
Phenomenological Level	
Cognitive style	Object representations
	Self-image
Intrapsychic Level	
Regulatory mechanisms	Morphologic organization
Biophysical Level	
	Mood/temperament

Adapted from *Disorders of Personality: DSM-IV and Beyond,* second edition, p. 138, by T. Millon with R. D. Davis, 1996, New York: Wiley. Reprinted with permission.

political, anthropological, and cultural attributes may be analyzed within this domain. Psychotherapeutic interventions informed by social-ecological considerations tend to access the individual by way of his or her interpersonal domain.

Falling at the phenomenological level is the Cognitive Style, which is considered functional. Cognitive Style reflects the person's manner of processing information, attentional focus, patterns of acquisition of information, cognitive filtering, styles of testing reality, and efficiency of thought processes. Naturally, all of the cognitive therapies target Cognitive Style as do phenomenological approaches.

The second phenomenological domain, Object Representations, is structural and grew out of classic and more contemporary psychodynamic thinking. In Freud's early work on libido theory, he found it necessary to distinguish between the aim of an instinctual drive versus its object. In later work by subsequent generations of psychodynamic workers, the term *object* came to be understood as "persons." Later writers recognized that person relations were heavily influenced by the richness and accuracy of internal representations of self and others, hence, the evolution of the term *object representations.* Object representations can occupy any of the sensory modalities and consist of cognitions, memories, images, and emotions that are associated with significant others. For example, it is believed that the borderline patient lacks object constancy, which means that soothing internal representations of nurturing persons do not live on internally when the actual caring person is physically absent. This helps explain the panicky telephone calls by borderline patients to their therapists in the middle of the night. They have difficulty retaining the internal image of the nurturing therapist when physically separated.

The third phenomenological domain is Self-Image. This structural domain considers the significant contributions of self psychology theorists. Linking conceptually to object relations, self-image consists of internalized images and emotions concerning identity, selfhood, and individuality. External experiences are perceived through the filter of self-perception. In the psychologically healthy person, selfhood is well established and consistent. The chaotic mélange of stimulation from the world is ordered and controlled by the sense of selfhood and a sense of predictability. In those with personality disorder, the sense of self is distorted, ambiguous, and variable.

At the intrapsychic level are Regulatory Mechanisms and Morphological Organization. Regulatory Mechanisms are functional and can be thought of as the defenses the individual employs in regulating stimulation from within and without. Need gratification, external pressures, motivation, and affect must be governed so that the individual can maintain a healthy degree of homeostasis and stability. Much of the psychotherapy with personality disorders involves helping these individuals develop healthy, natural, and reasonably automatic regulatory mechanisms. Morphological Organization refers to the form or structure of mind, and is, thus, structural. It refers to the degree of structural strength, orderliness, cohesion, or congruity.

Finally, Mood/Temperament falls at the biophysical level. The inclusion of this domain honors the contributions of Thomas and Chess (1977) on temperament and its pervasive impact on all aspects of an individual's personality functioning.

Most schools of psychotherapy tend to emphasize one or two of these domains. Millon's model helps us to remember that persons are complex and that attention to multiple domains will help us attend to this complexity in formulating and carrying out our psychotherapeutic endeavors.

Within Millon's conceptualization, all of the major personality disorders manifest significant pathology in each of the domains. For example, those with schizoid personality disorder are expressively impassive, interpersonally unengaged, cognitively impoverished, and have a complacent self-image. Their object representations are meager, they self-regulate through intellectualization, their morphological organization is undifferentiated, and their mood/temperament is apathetic. A summary of adjectival descriptions of expressions of all the personality disorders across the domains can be found on page 139 of Millon and Davis's *Disorders of Personality: DSM-IV and Beyond* (1996).

Most patients qualifying for *DSM-IV* Axis I diagnosis will likely present with difficulties in one or more of the domains described by Millon. However, unless the patient also has an Axis II disorder comorbid with the Axis I disorder, it is assumed that the difficulties within domains are secondary to the Axis I disorder and not a representation of chronic personality pathology. A brief case example illustrates this assertion. Recently, I had the opportunity to treat a young professional who was in considerable difficulty because of his behavior. Although his diagnosis was bipolar disorder I, mixed, his psychiatrist and I both sensed the presence of a personality disorder having antisocial and borderline features. He was not responding to medication, and he was acting out in professionally self-destructive ways. Eventually, however, his psychiatrist prescribed a new antibipolar medication, and his "personality disorder" went away! Obviously, his personality disorderlike condition was secondary to his bipolar disorder, not a lifelong condition of personality pathology.

In addition to his model of domains, Millon described a model of polarities, a theory emanating from basic science and evolutionary theory. Therapeutic interventions guided by the polarity theory are referred to as *strategic approaches*. Interventions focused on domain pathology are called *tactical psychotherapies*. Strategic approaches are broad and general whereas tactical approaches are more immediate and focused. For a presentation of this level of approach, consult *Tactical Psychotherapy of the Personality Disorders* (Retzlaff, 1995). Everly's (1995) chapter provides an excellent summary of domain-oriented tactics. Most reviews of domain (tactical) approaches to psychotherapy focus on schools or techniques of therapy. In the present chapter, however, an alternate approach is being introduced. It is the thesis of the chapter that the personality pathology within the domains of Millon's model may be impacted by a number of the common factors. Hence, we return to a review of the current literature on the common factors.

COMMON FACTORS

This chapter began with a quote by Millon to the effect that the great clinicians of the past took into account all of the complexities of human nature whereas modern thinkers seem to favor one-dimensional models that leave out much of the reality of human life. We can attain a much more fruitful and clinically real approach to the treatment of persons if we lessen our emphasis on procedures and again embrace the rich processes of therapy, which include the humanness of the patient, of the therapist, and of the relationship between them. It is believed that these factors are some of the major elements of what have been called the *common factors.* I next examine some of the major reviews of the common factors.

In 1936, Saul Rosenzweig asserted that common factors were shared among most effective therapies. He pointed out that similarities across treatments had more to do with common elements of practice than with their theoretical foundations. Rosenzweig articulated three factors common to all effective psychotherapies: (1) the personality of the therapist has more to do with treatment effectiveness than the preferred and habitual treatment modality (technique) of the therapist, (2) interpretation provides patients with alternative modes of thought and action and provides an explanation, making it easier for them to understand their problems, and (3) different theoretical orientations focus on or emphasize different domains, but all may be effective because of the synergistic effects one area of functioning may have on another.

In 1991, Frank and Frank, extending the work of the elder Frank, identified four features that are shared by all effective therapies: (1) "an emotionally charged, confiding relationship with a helping person"; (2) "a healing setting"; (3) "a rationale, conceptual scheme, or myth that provides a plausible explanation for the patient's symptoms and prescribes a ritual or procedure for resolving them"; and (4) "a ritual or procedure that requires the active participation of both patient and therapist and that is believed by both to be the means of restoring the patient's health" (pp. 40–43).

Michael Lambert (1992) outlined four essential variables in psychotherapy based on his extensive review of the extant literature. These are Client/Extratherapeutic factors; Relationship factors; Placebo, Hope, and Expectancy; and Model/Technique factors. Those therapists who place great emphasis on their techniques seem to forget that about 40% of the outcome variance is accounted for by client and social environmental variables outside the consulting room. Millon's domains provide us with a template for considering the patient's unique configuration of psychological variables. According to Lambert, relationship variables account for about 30% of the outcome variance. Included in these variables are empathy, warmth, acceptance, mutual affirmation, and encouragement of risk-taking. Hope and expectancy are all part of "placebo," which accounts for about 15% of the outcome variance. Last, technique accounts for about 15% of the outcome variance in psychotherapy.

Garfield's 1995 *Psychotherapy: An Eclectic-Integrative Approach,* second edition, drew on the earlier works of Rosenzweig (1936), Levine (1948), Heine (1953), and Rosenthal and Frank (1956) as well as his own considerable work in the area. He identified several common factors present in different forms of psychotherapy. His basic hypothesis is that despite the many apparent differences in theoretical orientations across various approaches, "many of the divergent schools of psychotherapy rely on essentially common factors for securing some to the changes believed occur in their respective psychothera-peutic endeavors" (p. 127). Garfield began his listing of common factors by describing a person in some sort of emotional/behavioral distress who is motivated to consult a thera-pist who is a socially sanctioned healer. The person is then given the opportunity to tell his or her story to an interested and compassionate listener, thus experiencing an unbur-dening of discomfort. A major factor in therapy is the relationship that develops between patient and therapist, which is strengthened by trust and predictability. Catharsis or un-burdening is a part of all therapies whether emphasized or not. Additionally, the therapist offers some sort of explanation for the patient's suffering, which offers a means of re-thinking or reframing the patient's view of the problem. Finally, the therapist presents with enthusiasm and conviction that the patient will be able to overcome problems; this fosters hope and self-efficacy, which seems to be essential to improvement.

In his 1995 book, Garfield, who is one of the main proponents of the importance of common factors in psychotherapy, omits the personality of the patient in his listing of com-mon factors. Elsewhere (1973), however, he has been critical of the emphasis of the impor-tance of the patient variables in therapy outcome because it allows us to place the blame for therapeutic failure too easily on the patient. He does admit, however, that patient variables are important to outcome.

There is considerable agreement that there are factors common to nearly all successful psychotherapies, but we do not have agreement on exactly what the common factors are. It is not the purpose of this chapter to decide this matter but rather to articulate the way in which common factors play a role in Millon's domain-focused psychotherapy with person-ality disorders. To achieve this goal, it will be necessary to select some of the most salient common factors from the extant literature for discussion. Most writers in the area of com-mon factors emphasize the role of patient variables. Millon's domains themselves are pa-tient variables; that is, most writers would consider them to be part of the common factors. However, unlike most approaches to common patient variables, Millon's domains are di-mensions of personality that are thoroughly developed and carefully articulated. Further, because of the manner in which the domains have been operationalized, they lend them-selves to measurement by clinical assessment and psychometric means. Thus, it is possible to be very precise in discussing the ways in which these person variables interrelate with the other common factors in psychotherapy.

Because Sol Garfield (1995) has been one of the major proponents of the role of com-mon factors in psychotherapy, this chapter employs his enumeration:

1. *Seeking help:* Psychotherapy begins when a person experiences some degree of emotional/behavioral discomfort and is motivated to consult a psychotherapist who is a socially sanctioned healer.

2. *Telling the story:* The patient is afforded an opportunity to tell the story of his or her difficulties to an interested and compassionate listener.

3. *Relationship:* Nearly all psychotherapies emphasize the central role of the therapeu-tic relationship, which is based on trust, predictability, empathy, and mutual respect.

4. *Catharsis:* A measure of catharsis and unburdening is an essential part of all thera-pies. Clients attain a degree of emotional release by relating their difficulties.

5. *Direct observation:* The patient exhibits habitual modes of feeling, thinking, and behaving in the sessions, giving the therapist an opportunity to observe and respond to the characteristic patterns of functioning.

6. *Reframing:* All therapies seem to encourage the patient to rethink or reframe customary ways of assessing life's problems, thus gaining a measure of hope and self–efficacy, which is central to recovery.

7. *Confidence in the therapy:* The therapist's conviction in what he or she is doing is communicated to the patient, which, in turn, strengthens the patient's belief that the therapy will be successful and that the work will result in permanent, positive change.

SPECIAL CONSIDERATIONS IN WORKING WITH PERSONALITY DISORDERS

Those writers who emphasize the role of common factors in psychotherapy have generally not articulated the role of these factors in the treatment of personality disorders. Yet, treatment of these persons generally requires sensitivity to certain elements of their psychopathology. For example, personality disorders are essentially disorders of selfhood. Self-image is very likely to be extremely distorted, either over- or undervalued, and split. The sense of selfhood is tenuous and fragile. Self-image may vary widely over time, and the various complex parts of the self are likely to be poorly integrated. In parallel, object representations are also poorly developed, vague, poorly formed, and inaccurate. It is not surprising that issues of selfhood and relationship are especially difficult for these persons. For example, one of my psychotherapy patients (borderline personality with narcissistic and antisocial tendencies) once wrote to me:

> Sometimes I could not swear by the validity of my experience when I am facing you; I feel somehow latent, invisible. But when I write, it seems that I can render myself onto a sheet of paper, and thence come to be in some real form. I wrote this—you didn't. You won't know what it says until I give it to you. This means to me that there is something of me that exists outside of you, independently of you. If I don't give this to you, you won't know what it says, but it will still be here on this sheet of paper. I am, I am, I am.

This passage demonstrates that the identity of the patient with personality disorder is likely to be in chaos, and it is essential that the therapist be acutely aware of this condition. Hence, the person of the patient, of the therapist, and the relationship between the two is of paramount importance. If this interface is managed poorly, the patient has experienced yet another crushing personal and interpersonal failure. If it is managed well, healing and integration will likely occur.

Because of their wildly vacillating representations of self and others, ego boundaries are often flimsy or virtually nonexistent. Many persons with personality disorder ooze (or, in some cases, barge) into the personal space of the therapist. The phenomenon of projective identification is one outgrowth of this aspect of the condition. That is, the patient projects his or her pathology (aggression, sexual urges, etc.) onto the therapist and then, acting as though this projection is real, battles with the projected forces in the therapist. For example, the patient noted earlier projected her sexual urges onto me and then fought with me as though I were pressing sexual urges on her.

These issues magnify the importance of transference and countertransference. The transference of the patient with personality disorder can be remarkably powerful and may exert enormous pressures on the countertransference vulnerabilities of the therapist. Indeed, according to Masterson (1983), the skillful management of the countertransference is the single most therapeutic act of the therapist. Thus, the therapist working with these remarkable patients faces special demands in establishing the holding environment so that neither the patient nor the therapist is harmed. This is at the core of the treatment of these persons.

Most clinicians working with these patients emphasize the importance of assessing the need for external structure. Patients with personality disorder tend to act out inner pathology. Some things to monitor are potential for acting out in the sessions, attempts to control the therapist's life, suicide attempts or persistent self-mutilation, use of drugs or alcohol, persistent antisocial behavior, and failure to manage physically dangerous conditions such as anorexia nervosa or diabetes. Therapists are advised to have clearly developed policies and procedures for dealing with these kinds of difficulties. Additionally, most writers suggest that, if possible, someone other than the therapist make arrangements for special care (e.g., medical care for suicide attempts) to discourage the patient from perceiving the therapist as a paternal caretaker.

A final principle focuses on the verbal exchange between therapist and patient. Patients with personality disorder act out their pathology in self-damaging ways, and it is the task of the therapist to bring this to the awareness of the patient. There are various ways to do this. Clarification, for example, is a fairly gentle intervention; it attempts to bring split object representations to awareness. An example of clarification might be: "I noticed that last week you felt your wife was the perfect woman for you, and this week you seem to believe she is completely wrong for you. Say more." Second, a number of authors have recommended using explanation (or educational) approaches. For example, Rinsley (1982) recommends using imagery training to help patients who have object inconstancy. He teaches them how to summon up images of significant others. One of his procedures is to ask patients to close their eyes and picture him in their inner world and then to open their eyes and actually see him again. This helps the patient gain greater control over object representations. A third common interaction technique in work with personality disorders is confrontation. Confrontation does not mean "attack." Rather, it is a verbal procedure used to target patients to externalize inner conflicts by acting out in destructive ways. The acting out generally feels good to the patient at the time but it results in regression and self-harm, and it halts the progress in the psychotherapy. Masterson (1976) wrote:

> Confrontation, the principal therapeutic technique of this (the early) phase, throws a monkey wrench in the patient's defense system by introducing conflict where there previously had been none . . . When the therapist points out the harm the patient can no longer act out without recognizing the harm. Therefore conflict and tension are created. . . . He [sic] has to recognize the cost of "feeling good." . . . It is important to keep in mind that confrontation is needed throughout the therapy. (pp. 100–101)

Confrontation must, however, be used judiciously and always in the service of the patient.

INTEGRATING A COMMON FACTORS APPROACH WITH MILLON'S DOMAIN-FOCUSED PSYCHOTHERAPY WITH PATIENTS WITH PERSONALITY DISORDER

I next attempt to interface the list of common factors with Millon's domains of psychological functioning. First is *seeking help* from a socially sanctioned healer. In the first place, the help-seeking is, by definition, an expressive behavior. The patient experiences discomfort of some kind and emits an operant behavior by seeking assistance from some new agent. Also, by definition, help-seeking reflects a change in interpersonal conduct. The patient seeks out an additional social contact in his or her efforts to overcome emotional difficulties. This represents a new form of social behavior, and it results in the patient's expanding the number of social agents with whom he or she interacts. Frequently, however, patients with personality disorder do not seek help themselves. They are often pressured into therapy by others. The therapist must be aware of all the reasons the person has presented for treatment. The fact that the patient may have been coerced into treatment does not preclude a positive outcome, but it changes the dynamics of the therapeutic strategy. For example, the therapist may need to do additional work on helping the patient to understand how the treatment might be personally beneficial in terms of success in life and happiness. The help-seeking behaviors also reflect activity in the phenomenological domains of object relations and self-image. The self may be experienced as insufficient to overcome personal difficulties and worthy of the soothing and therapeutic efforts of the healer. Further, object relations are altered by admitting a new representation into the phenomenological realm in the form of the socially sanctioned healer, who is likely to be experienced as trustworthy, benevolent, and helpful. The help-seeking of people with personality disorder is remarkably complex because of the marked deficiency of their object representations and self-image. Those patients who fall nearest the antisocial, sadistic, and narcissistic core are the least likely to have sought treatment voluntarily. The fact that they are in treatment poses a threat to their tough and independent self-image. Thus, they may exhibit considerable resentment of being in therapy in the first place. The patient's perception of the "socially sanctioned healer" must also be carefully considered because these persons are not likely to easily accept another's social sanctions, and they are not likely to experience the agent as healing. Often, healers are perceived as individuals to "get around."

Those patients with traits closer to the borderline, dependent, depressive, or self-defeating core may not only engage in help-seeking behavior but also surrender any personal strength to the healer and attempt to cling to the therapist in ways that impede personal growth. The internalized representation of the healer may be highly distorted, and the internalizations may vacillate considerably, placing great strain on the therapeutic relationship. Help-seeking for these individuals may be marked by primitive idealization or devaluation of the therapist. Further, as their self-images tend to be fragile, the socially sanctioned healer may be perceived as frightening, overpowering, and omnipotent.

Finally, the help-seeking behavior itself is a regulatory mechanism. Specifically, we can assume that the usual regulatory mechanisms or defenses are not sufficient to protect the individual from psychic pain, thus motivating the individual to seek outside help. The defenses of persons with personality disorder are primitive. They may be very powerful defenses in terms of protecting the individual from inner distress, but they are maladaptive and do not support personal adjustment. Thus, these defenses are likely to interfere greatly with the help-seeking behavior. The patients may even be overtly compliant with the treatment but because of the regressive valence of their defenses, they may not be able to adequately benefit from the help they seek in therapy. The healer must be extremely sensitive to the way in which the pathological defenses of the person with personality disorder complicate the help-seeking behavior.

Morphological organization is not immediately impacted by help-seeking behavior, but the act of turning to the therapist offers promise of reorganization. Because the personalities of these persons are so fragile, they could be easily overwhelmed and frightened. Yet, in most cases, acting out is what led to their being brought to treatment in the first place, and the acting out must be contained to protect them from themselves. It is essential that the containment be experienced as supportive to the integrity of their personalities and in their best interests.

Finally, the mood/temperament of persons with personality disorder interacts with seeking help from a healer. The affect of persons with personality disorder is often volatile, and anger may be ascendant. Indeed, the patient may be very angry about being in the position of seeking help in the first place. Clinicians working with these patients must be prepared to weather the affective storms calmly and compassionately, especially in the initial phases. It is essential, in the early contacts with the helper, that patients come to know their powerful affect will not destroy the therapist or cause the therapist to withdraw.

We turn next to *telling the story* to an interested and compassionate therapist. On the surface, this is an expressive act that promises to be a reinforcing event, for example, lessening of pain and personal growth. It also represents a new form of interpersonal conduct, expressing very personal information with a socially sanctioned healer. There is an implicit assumption that in emitting words, the patient is actually telling the story, linking affect with cognition in reasonably full communication with the listener. However, clinicians working with the personality disorders must pay special attention to this aspect of the therapy. Personality-disordered patients often communicate metaphorically. The words uttered on the surface may be unconnected with their inner meaning. It is probably safe to say that the use of language by persons with personality disorder often differs from that of other kinds of patients. Consider the semantic aphasia of the antisocial person. Words are a convenient means of keeping other people at bay, but they are devoid of deeper meaning. Consider also the discrepancy of the borderline person's utterances, which on one occasion describe a significant other in glowing, positive terms, yet on another find only hateful, negative words to describe the same person. Although all good therapists are taught to listen for material deeper than the words being shared in the session, because persons with personality disorder are poorly integrated, their language is poorly integrated. The split psychic structure sabotages their efforts to articulate what is really going on within themselves. The interested and compassionate listener must learn to move beyond the story of the patient and listen to the rest of the story, which may be communicated in very subtle and hidden ways.

The object relations of persons with personality disorder are either inchoate and/or inaccurate. Telling of the story to the listener offers an important way for the patient to develop stronger and more accurate object relations. If the therapist is experienced as understanding, compassionate, and accepting, the patient has an opportunity to revise internal representations of other people, finding a place for the development or reinforcing of a strong and benevolent internal symbol or figure. This is why it is especially important for the therapist to look beyond the surface story and to hear at a deeper level. Because of their difficulty in linking deeper aspects of themselves with their speech, they are isolated and alienated. If the therapist can hear what is really going on and reflect this awareness back to the patients, the latter has an opportunity to better experience the presence of the therapist, which strengthens the object representation. Likewise, there is an opportunity in the storytelling for a modification of the self-image. Specifically, the patient may learn that "I am worthy of being healed, and my story is important." This will likely serve to enhance the self-concept of worthiness and personal value.

Telling the story is a form of regulatory mechanism. Because acting out is one of the major defense mechanisms of the person with personality disorder, the telling of the story provides an essential vehicle for expression. Even if the patient's efforts toward verbal expression are initially compromised by pathology, the continued practice of this means of expression gives the patient and therapist a valuable means for developing higher levels of defense. Consider a patient who is a "cutter," who learned to express emotional pain verbally. The therapist may say something like, "It is extremely important that this time you told me how angry you were at me rather than cutting your wrists like you used to do. This represents how much better you are getting."

Telling the story may not directly impact morphological organization of the person with personality disorder, but as with help-seeking behavior, it has the potential for reorganization. Words provide a means of expressing disparate aspects of our personality. As the patient tells the story to the listener, expressing the inner chaos and confusion, clarity and order may emerge, helping to strengthen organization.

Finally, storytelling may have a major impact on the mood/temperament of the patient with personality disorder. Moods are more transient than temperament, which is more traitlike. Both are affective constructs, and persons with personality disorder have great difficulty with affect and the expression of affect. The telling of the story affords a means of expressing this affect in a more controlled and nonbehavioral way, thus lessening the likelihood of destructive acting out and its sequelae.

All therapies emphasize the importance of the therapeutic *relationship*. By definition, a therapeutic relationship is healthy and involves an alliance. Expressive acts do not necessarily require another person to be present. However, expressive acts carried out within an established relationship with a psychotherapist are amenable to redirection, modification, reassessment, and the like. Interpersonal conduct, however, within the relationship with the psychotherapist also is amenable to influence as much as expressive acts.

Object relations are formed and modified within relationships, and the psychotherapeutic relationship provides a wonderful opportunity to correct and enrich internalized representations of significant others. So it is with the self-image. Selfhood is defined and experienced within the context of relationships. If the patient experiences the self as acceptable, valued, appreciated, and prized in the therapeutic relationship, the chances of enhancement of the self-image are increased. The therapeutic relationship itself may function as a regulatory mechanism for the patient. Patients with personality disorder are notorious for having deficient regulatory mechanisms, both externally and internally. In the therapeutic relationship, the patient may introject the ego strength of the therapist and through the mechanism of identification, internalize ways of binding frustration, enhancing self-soothing, and managing conflicting urges. By this process, morphological organization is changed and strengthened. Finally, the enhancement of regulatory mechanisms provides the patient with new tools for dealing with disruption of mood.

The positive aspects of the therapeutic relationship will ideally impact deficiencies in all of the domains described by Millon. However, the therapeutic relationship presupposes an alliance (or therapeutic alliance), and it is here that we run into trouble with patients with personality disorder. In 1979, G. Adler described the "myth" of forming a therapeutic alliance with these patients. Because of deficiencies in the various domains of their personalities, these patients may be extremely vulnerable in any relationship, therapeutic or otherwise. For this reason, the therapeutic relationship may not serve the same function, or it might not function in the same way as it does with other kinds of patients. Indeed, the therapeutic alliance may be a myth, experienced only by the therapist. It is very difficult for an individual with a fragile, incomplete, split, or distorted self-image to enter into an emotional relationship. The risks of diminishment of selfhood are too great. Healthy relationships depend on a healthy sense of self and the capacity to form rich and accurate internalizations of others—two attributes that patients with personality disorder do not have. Patients with personality disorder are not integrated. Masterson (1976) used the term "part objects" to describe split internalized representations of significant others. Patients in the antisocial spectrum view others either as cockroaches (something to squash) or bon bons (having something they want). There is no basis for a relationship in this case. The more clingy borderlines, dependents, depressives, and so on expect the therapist to play the role of parent and satisfy every need, even if unexpressed. Again, in these cases there is no basis for the development of a healthy therapeutic relationship. In fact, with these kinds of patients, the therapeutic relationship tends to wax and wane. Masterson characterized this process as a "saw tooth" phenomenon. Specifically, the patient splits or engages in some sort of regressive maneuver, the therapist confronts this, the patient integrates momentarily and is, thus, able to relate to the therapist. Masterson warns us, however, that this "alliance" will be transitory. After a period of relatedness, the patient again regresses and the relationship evaporates. However, if the therapist again confronts in a therapeutic manner, the patient will likely recompensate; thus, integration is achieved and the alliance is reestablished. Thus, the role of the therapeutic relationship in domain-focused psychotherapy with these patients is an on again/off again matter. When the relationship is functioning, we are likely to see augmentation of structure and function in the relative domains as described earlier. When the relationship falters, progress stops temporarily and only resumes when it is reestablished.

When the patient shares emotionally laden material with the therapist, it is hoped that he or she will experience *catharsis* (bring conflictual material to awareness) and subsequent abreaction (discharge of the emotion), which plays an important role in mental healing. Articulation of a person's troubles to a psychotherapist is an expressive act that facilitates the experience of catharsis and, thus, relief, which is usually experienced as reinforcing. It is also a form of interpersonal conduct. The patient may find that this sort of expression with selected persons is a positive event, and this may, in turn, lead to enhanced anticipation that interpersonal relationships may be positive. Moreover, this experience may alter cognitive style by fostering more openness and fluidity. The positive experience associated with unburdening may help the patient to develop the beginnings of benevolent internal representations of human figures. The patient may come to see that some persons can be helpful (leading to more positive object representations), and "they can be helpful to me." This internalization may enhance self-image. While catharsis itself is a form of regulation, it can also produce a decided positive impact on mood and, for that matter, on temperament.

The phenomenon of catharsis in treating patients with personality disorder is complex, however. In the first place, the concepts of catharsis and abreaction emanate from psychodynamic thinking and presuppose a good measure of repression. Yet, many writers, at least of that orientation, believe that patients with personality disorder do not have well-developed repressive capacities and, instead, rely more on primitive defenses. Catharsis/abreaction requires a capacity to bind and control impulse while expressing emotion. Many persons with personality disorder do not have this capacity. For example, Samenow (1984), who specialized in treating the antisocial personality, strongly discourages allowing them to express anger. He reasons that it makes little sense to allow a person who is already angry to express it even more. Catharsis/abreaction is useful for individuals who tend to internalize their difficulties and who do not express them by acting out. Persons with personality disorder make a lifestyle of acting out. That is why Masterson recommends the technique of confrontation to help move the disturbance into the psyche of the patient where it can be managed psychologically rather than by externalization and acting out. Another potential difficulty of catharsis with these patients is the danger that they might be retraumatized in the cathartic moment. This is especially important when there has been abuse of some kind—not uncommon in these patients. At the very least, it is probably wise to help the person with personality disorder develop some positive self-soothing skills before attempting to facilitate cathartic expression (if possible).

Direct observation allows the therapist to view habitual and possibly maladaptive behaviors in the patient. This provides the therapist an opportunity to help the patient modify maladaptive self-perpetuating tendencies. Thus, the sessions can be viewed as a sort of laboratory in which the patient's behavior is played out for the therapist. This provides an opportunity to influence behavior. The behavior will nearly always be of an interpersonal nature; thus, the therapist has an opportunity to influence interpersonal conduct. So it is with all other domains. The therapist observes cognitive style, relatedness, self-image, regulatory mechanisms, and habitual mood and temperament tendencies, thus, having an opportunity to foster improvement in all of these areas.

The opportunity for direct observation is invaluable in working with persons with personality disorder because, initially, they tend to present as psychologically healthier than they really are. In outdated language, these patients tend to present as neurotics when, in fact, their psychological organization is below the neurotic level and above the psychotic level of psychic organization. As therapy progresses, the pathological personality organization reveals itself in the interaction with the therapist. This provides a valuable opportunity for corrective emotional learning experiences. It is common for the social history of these patients to be littered with the corpses of ruined relationships. These issues can be addressed within the immediate experience of the therapy relationship to the end that new ways of experiencing, thinking, relating, and being can be learned. For example, in the case mentioned earlier in the section on special considerations in working with personality disorders, the client entered treatment after she had taken an overdose of prescribed medication in a suicide attempt. Her diagnosis was borderline personality with narcissistic and antisocial tendencies. At 15, she had developed a predatory stance with middle-age men, seducing them sexually, then "destroying" them by exposing the affair to their wives. Her own father had nothing to do with her from the time she was conceived (her parents were in divorce proceedings at the time), and she longed for the support and nurturance of a male parent figure. She was very bright, highly manipulative, and suicidal. On one occasion, she called me to say that she had overdosed with acetaminophen 48 hours previously, but she had left her apartment (she was 17 at the time) and would not tell me where she was. She acted out both within and outside the sessions. She tried to compromise me sexually. She tried to provoke me into "firing" her from therapy. In short, she behaved exactly as her diagnosis would predict. This provided both of us with a magnificent opportunity for correction. I remained emotionally available and compassionate but fortified the boundaries of our relationship. She escalated, trying to seduce a colleague of mine (not a mental health professional). I continued to make it clear that to violate the nature of the therapeutic relationship would be ruinous for her and for me. Thus, I modeled self-protective behavior without rejecting her. This testing went on for months. Finally, one day she came in for her session and sat down, saying nothing for several minutes. I waited. Finally, she said quietly, "You win." I asked her what she meant. She told me that she could not compromise me, and she now knew she could trust me to care for her without exploiting her or being exploited by her own impulses. This is the first time she had ever experienced such a state. She was relieved but confused. She began internalizing, and the acting out diminished. She had a new kind of experience with an interpersonal relationship, which led to a new kind of object representation and self-representation. She could feel prized for being herself, not for sexual favors. This led to new ways of thinking about her world. Because she began to internalize, she acted out less and less, thereby changing her habitual defensive patterns. Her overall personality organization slowly changed. In the end, her temperament remained somewhat cold though she eventually discovered she had developed the capacity for jealousy. Before this, her narcissism led her to believe that people were interchangeable. She was not sure she liked jealousy, but she was reassured when told it was a sign that she was getting better. All this did not happen magically the day she told me she could trust me. It took months of therapy and a lifetime of her own personal work (she has kept in touch with me over the years). However, I strongly believe that what was said in the sessions was not as important as the fact that she brought her pathology to the relationship, which presented the opportunity for a corrective emotional experience.

The opportunity to reassess or *reframe* would appear to be especially salient to the cognitive style of the patient. Maladaptive cognitive habits and sets are addressed in therapy, and new ways of thinking about life's challenges are explored. These cognitive changes will then have an impact on functioning within other domains. Patients with personality disorder tend to function at a preverbal level, and they generally have little observing ego. Hence, cognitive interventions are not likely to be immediate or easy. As in the case described earlier, although cognitive interventions were employed, the actual work was at a more experiential level. My young patient had to experience me as compassionate and empathic, yet safe and stable. Only then could she develop a new way of thinking. It is in the way the therapy relationship plays out that the work gets done. I personally have little confidence that direct cognitive work alone (as in manualized cognitive-behavior therapy) with these kinds of patients is very effective.

Finally, Garfield (1995) notes that the therapist's *confidence in the therapy* is a powerful common factor. Bandura (1962) has taught us that much of operant behavior is learned through observation. The patient comes to introject the confidence of the therapist and, thus, gains new strength and self-efficacy. The therapist's conviction is a form of interpersonal conduct. It provides a model of such conduct that may also be emulated by the patient. Moreover, the therapist's confidence is a model of optimism, which itself is a cognitive style. That is, the therapist's confidence encourages enhancement of the patient's self-efficacy—"This is not something I cannot handle." The therapist's belief in the therapy provides a model of strength and conviction with which the patient can identify, thus encouraging the development of competent internal representation of others and the self. This conviction encourages confidence in the patient, which improves regulation, thus mood, which in turn strengthens the organization of the personality.

An important factor for all psychotherapy, confidence in the therapy, is especially important for people with personality disorder. Confidence in the therapy must include confidence in the patient. Patients with personality disorder are commonly disliked and shunned. (Some clinicians have come to my workshops on personality disorders so they can spot these persons better so as to avoid them as patients!) These patients are often desperate to be understood and desperate for a better life. They are typically disheartened. They identify with their pathology, not with their strength. Self-image is usually that of a damaged, weak, bad, incompetent person. It is essential that the therapist convey a rock-solid belief in their capacity to overcome serious difficulties. A two-pronged approach to this principle seems to lead to the best results. The therapist overtly conveys to the patient anticipation that he or she can and will do better. That is, the therapist more or less "colludes" with the healthy aspect of the personality, an aspect that may seem alien to the patient. However, the therapist privately expects regression and is not surprised, dismayed, or frustrated that the patient has again strayed into trouble. This permits the therapist to maintain a positive outlook about ultimate success while avoiding discouragement when the inevitable regression occurs. A brief case example illustrates.

CASE STUDY

A patient was referred to me by a psychiatrist colleague because of my interest in severe personality disorders. The diagnosis was borderline personality disorder with depressive and self-defeating tendencies. If it can be believed, the patient was ejected from two other psychiatric hospitals because of the lethality of her suicide attempts! Fortunately, the treatment philosophy at our institution differed on this point. Her pain was palpable. The first dozen or so therapy sessions consisted of her sobbing, saying nothing, and my simply being there with her. No conversation was possible. Finally, she asked me to leave her alone. She asked me why I cared. Slowly the relationship began to grow, and a sense of trust developed. She revealed parts of her life, including her hopes and fears, especially her fears of abandonment. Since I had been working for so many years with this kind of patient, I strongly believed in the power of the human spirit to overcome. But she had been seriously suicidal, and we needed to be aware of this. Then she had a bad moment and tried to hang herself with a belt in the closet of her room. Fortunately, her attempt failed, but she was absolutely devastated. She was convinced that she would once again be ejected from the hospital. I was not able to see her immediately. However, shortly after the event, one of the nurses sat with her and said, "Oh honey, it's all right. You just took *one* step backward, not 16." By the time I was able to meet with her, the patient was still very upset and still convinced I would reject her. But she was absolutely stunned by the remark the nurse had made. She could not believe what she heard. I confirmed that our philosophy was to stay with patients through whatever it took for them to overcome their difficulties. We had confidence that she would get better. She did get better. There was never another suicide attempt. She moved out of the hospital, found a job, joined a church, and established friendships in the community. She made peace with her parents and began to accept the fact that she had a future. Therapy acts holistically, but it is difficult not to believe that the nurse's reaction to the patient's last suicide attempt helped her gain the confidence that she could and would overcome her terrible emotional disorder.

CONCLUSION

This chapter attempted to interface what have been called the common factors in psychotherapy with Millon's domain-focused therapy with patients with personality disorder. Millon's brilliant integrative work is highly compatible with the efforts of the entire integrative (common factors) movement. It is my belief that we cannot help these fascinating, desperate individuals with personality disorder with technique alone. They need to be in the presence of the complex humanness of others who understand them well enough to contain their destructive acting out without blaming or rejecting them. They need compassion and empathy as well as strength and consistency. The heart and soul of the therapy is not in the technique but in the power of the human interaction. It is this that has the healing effect on the damaged and undeveloped domains of their personalities.

REFERENCES

Adler, G. (1979). The myth of the alliance with borderline patients. *American Journal of Psychiatry, 136,* 642–645.

Bandura, A. (1962). Social learning through imitation. In M. R. Jones (Ed.), *Nebraska Symposium on Motivation* (pp. 211–269). Lincoln: University of Nebraska Press.

Everly, G. S. (1995). Domain-oriented personality theory. In P. D. Retzlaff (Ed.), *Tactical psychotherapy of the personality disorders: An MCMI-III-based approach* (pp. 24–39). Needham Heights, MA: Allyn & Bacon.

Frank, J. D., & Frank, J. B. (1991). *Persuasion and healing: A comprehensive study of psychotherapy* (3rd ed.). Baltimore: Johns Hopkins University Press.

Garfield, S. L. (1973). Basic ingredients of common factors in psychotherapy? *Journal of Consulting and Clinical Psychology, 41,* 9–12.

Garfield, S. L. (1995). *Psychotherapy: An eclectic-integrative approach* (2nd ed.). New York: Wiley.

Heine, R. W. (1953). A comparison of patients' reports on psychotherapeutic experience with psychoanalytic, nondirective and Adlerian therapists. *American Journal of Psychotherapy, 7,* 16–23.

Hubble, M. A., Duncan, B. L., & Miller, S. D. (Eds.). (1999). *The heart & soul of change: What works in therapy.* Washington, DC: American Psychological Association.

Lambert, M. J. (1992). Implications of outcome research for psychotherapy integration. In J. C. Norcross & M. R. Goldfried (Eds.), *Handbook of psychotherapy integration* (pp. 94–129). New York: Basic Books.

Levine, M. (1948). *Psychotherapy in medical practice.* New York: Macmillan.

Masterson, J. F. (1976). *Psychotherapy of the borderline adult: A developmental approach.* New York: Brunner/Mazel.

Masterson, J. F. (1983). *Countertransference and psychotherapeutic technique: Teaching seminars on psychotherapy of the borderline adult.* New York: Brunner/Mazel.

Millon, T. (1990). *Toward a new personology: An evolutionary model.* New York: Wiley.

Millon, T. (1999). *Personality-guided therapy.* New York: Wiley.

Millon, T., & Davis, R. D. (1996). *Disorders of personality: DSM-IV and beyond* (2nd ed.). New York: Wiley.

Norcross, J. C. (Ed.). (2002). *Psychotherapy relationships that work: Therapist contributions and responsiveness to patients.* New York: Oxford University Press.

Retzlaff, P. D. (Ed.). (1995). *Tactical psychotherapy of the personality disorders: An MCMI-III-based approach.* Needham Heights, MA: Allyn & Bacon.

Rinsley, D. B. (1982). *Borderline and other self disorders: A developmental and object-relations perspective.* New York: Aronson.

Rosenthal, D., & Frank, J. D. (1956). Psychotherapy and the placebo effect. *Psychological Bulletin, 53,* 294–302.

Rosenzweig, S. (1936). Some implicit common factors in diverse methods in psychotherapy. *Journal of Orthopsychiatry, 6,* 412–415.

Samenow, S. E. (1984). *Inside the criminal mind.* New York: Times Books.

Snyder, C. R. (1994). *The psychology of hope: You can get there from here.* New York: Free Press.

Thomas, A., & Chess, S. (1977). *Temperament and development.* New York: Brunner/Mazel.

Chapter 27

INTERPERSONAL MOTIVES AND PERSONALITY DISORDERS

LEONARD M. HOROWITZ AND KELLY R. WILSON

When we say that a woman dresses dramatically *because* she wants to draw attention to herself, we are ascribing the cause of her behavior to a particular motive, namely, her desire to influence others to relate to her in a particular way. This chapter proposes a model that organizes the features of most personality disorders around an interpersonal motive that is unique to that disorder. We argue that the organizing motive became prominent for the person over many years as a way of protecting the self. Furthermore, according to our model, the defining features of most personality disorders in the *Diagnostic and Statistical Manual of Mental Disorders,* fourth edition, text revision (*DSM-IV-TR;* 2000), can be integrated around the frustrated motive and its sequelae (Horowitz, 2004). When the features are integrated in this way, the resulting formulation has specific implications that allow us to (1) describe the person's plight and behavior, (2) identify cognitive biases associated with the disorder, (3) explain why the disorder requires a fuzzy definition, (4) clarify the purpose of treatment, and (5) expose similarities and differences among the personality disorders. We begin by considering the concept of an interpersonal motive.

THE MOTIVE AS AN EXPLANATORY CONSTRUCT

Motivational approaches have a long tradition in the field of personality. Contemporary approaches date back to Murray (1938), F. Allport (1937), and G. W. Allport (1937). A number of writers, beginning with F. Allport (1937), have suggested that we need to understand an individual's motives (what the person is trying to do) if we are to understand the individual's personality. We use the term *motive* to refer to a very broad abstraction, a cluster of goals, desires, or needs that affect the person's well-being. A motive, according to our model, may be conscious or unconscious. When the motive is satisfied, the person experiences positive affect; when it is frustrated, the person experiences negative affect (Emmons, 1989; McAdams, 1988; McClelland, 1985).

Hierarchical Organization of Motives

Motivational constructs vary in their breadth or level of abstraction. A broad desire, such as a desire for intimacy or a desire to belong to a group, is more abstract than a narrow desire, such as a desire to spend time with a romantic partner. That desire, in turn, is more abstract than a still narrower desire, such as a desire to arrange a date with the woman who lives next door. These levels of abstraction may be conceptualized hierarchically (Emmons, 1989). That is, a desire for intimacy constitutes a superordinate (more abstract) category, which subsumes narrower categories; and, those categories each subsume still narrower categories.

When interpersonal motives are conceptualized this way, we commonly assume that two very broad, abstract categories are at the top of the hierarchy, namely, communion and agency (for a summary, see Horowitz, 2004). A communal motive is a motive for selfless connection with one or more others; it is a motive to participate in a larger union with other people. In contrast, an agentic motive emphasizes the self as a distinct unit, separate from other people; it focuses on the person's own performance as an individual. Bakan (1966) expressed the distinction this way:

> I have adopted the terms "agency" and "communion" to characterize two fundamental modalities in the existence of living forms, agency for the existence of an organism as an individual, and communion for the participation of the individual in some larger organism of which the individual is a part. Agency manifests itself in self-protection, self-assertion, and self-expansion; communion manifests itself in the sense of being at one with other organisms. Agency manifests itself in the formation of separations; communion in the lack of separations. . . . Agency manifests itself in the urge to master; communion in noncontractual cooperation. (pp. 14–15)

The earliest manifestation of a communal motive appears in the literature on infant attachment. The infant's motive to attach to an adult caretaker is the first expression of a communal motive (thereby increasing the child's chances of surviving infancy). Later, when the child feels sufficiently secure in this attachment, the child separates from the caretaker and explores the environment, a first step toward autonomy. The motive to separate and explore is thus the earliest manifestation of an agentic motive. Whenever the child's safety is threatened, however, the communal motive is again activated. Over time, each motive becomes differentiated into subordinate motives. Communion comes to include motives such as intimacy, sociability, and belonging to groups. Agency comes to include motives such as autonomy, individualism, achievement, control, and self-definition. Communion is always interpersonal, but agency may be interpersonal or intrapersonal. Agency includes a desire to influence other people, but a desire that is initially interpersonal (e.g., gaining approval, avoiding criticism) can become internalized and intrapersonal (e.g., striving for perfection).

Many behaviors stem from a *combination* of motives. A person who enjoys giving advice may find advice-giving gratifying for more than one reason—displaying competence and knowledge (agentic), influencing others (agentic), connecting with others (communal). Similarly, a person who loves a particular sport may enjoy that sport for various reasons— belonging to the team (communal), displaying a skill (agentic), winning competitions (agentic), being like his or her parent (communal), and so on.

Western culture emphasizes agency (initiative, individualism, accomplishment, productivity, uniqueness of the self), whereas other cultures emphasize communion (affiliation, group membership, cooperation). Nonetheless, we assume that communal and agentic motives are present, to some degree at least, in the behavior of every human being. Different cultures provide different outlets for satisfying these motives. If a culture discourages individualism, agentic motives may still be satisfied through the individual's own contribution to a group. Even in Western culture, a woman who chooses to enter a marriage primarily for closeness and intimacy may be willing to relinquish some autonomy, control, and decision making to her partner while still satisfying agentic motives through her domestic competence and a career outside the home.

The term *motive* is usually used to designate a very high level of abstraction (e.g., intimacy, autonomy). The term *personal striving* has been used to designate an intermediate level of abstraction, and the term *goal* (or *specific action unit*), to designate the narrowest, most specific category (Emmons, 1989). This way of conceptualizing motivation is very common in contemporary psychology (Austin & Vancouver, 1996; Cantor & Genero, 1986; Cantor & Kihlstrom, 1987; Cropanzano, James, & Citera, 1992; Klinger, 1987; Little, 1983).

A communal motive for sociability, then, would include personal strivings such as "getting to know new people" and "doing nice things for people." An agentic motive for achievement would include personal strivings such as "excelling academically" and "being competent at work." A personal striving, such as excelling academically, would, in turn, subsume still narrower goals, such as "preparing well for tomorrow's chemistry test." As shown in Figure 27.1, the hierarchy moves from the very abstract category to the very specific action units (goals). A simplified pathway through one person's hierarchy of motives might be: communion motive → intimacy motive → desire to feel close to an attractive woman → goal to call Maria for a date this weekend.

A Behavior, by Itself, Is Often Ambiguous

Suppose we know a man's goal, but nothing more—namely, that he intends to call Maria for a date this weekend. Can we infer the higher order motive from which this goal stems? If two men both plan to call Maria for a date this weekend, are they both necessarily trying to satisfy an intimacy motive? Clearly not. As shown in Figures 27.1 and 27.2, one may be seeking intimacy (a communal motive), whereas the other may be seeking the respect, admiration, or envy of his friends (an agentic motive). Thus, the meaning of a goal, by itself, is often ambiguous. Only when we can locate the behavior in the person's hierarchy of motives do we understand its meaning. If someone sitting next to us on an airplane started chatting amiably, we might assume a communal motive (to socialize). But if the person then asked in all seriousness, "Have you heard the Word of the Lord today?" we might quickly perceive an agentic goal (to proselytize, to influence) and revise our interpretation of the person's chattiness.

Symptoms of Axis I disorders are frequently ambiguous in this way. An individual with anorexia nervosa might aspire to lose weight, but the meaning of the person's behavior

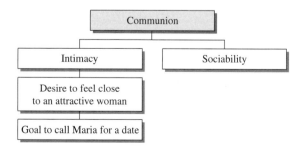

Figure 27.1   Hierarchy of Communal Motives

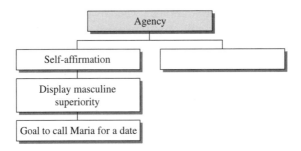

Figure 27.2   Hierarchy of Agentic Motives

(self-starvation) would not be clear until we could locate it in the hierarchy of motives. For one individual (Figure 27.3), self-starvation might have an agentic meaning: agentic motive → motive to exercise autonomy → desire to display self-control → desire to lose weight → goal to eat nothing but lettuce this weekend. For another individual (Figure 27.4), however, self-starvation might have a communal meaning: communal motive → motive to be nurtured by the family → desire to seem small, thin, and frail → desire to lose weight → goal to eat nothing but lettuce this weekend. (A blend of the two is also possible.) Minuchin's theory of anorexia emphasizes a communal motive to maintain family harmony (Minuchin, Rosman, & Baker, 1978), whereas Bruch's (1973) theory emphasizes an agentic motive to exhibit self-control and strength. Thus, the behavior (self-starvation) is ambiguous until we can describe the broader motive from which it emerged (Horowitz, 2004).

In the same way, a major depression or agoraphobia may result from a frustrated motive, and that motive may be communal or agentic (or both). Sometimes, the disorder is precipitated by a frustrated communal motive, sometimes by a frustrated agentic motive, and sometimes by a combination of motives. Similar views about the importance of motives in psychopathology have been expressed by Caspar (1995, 1997), Grawe (2003), and Grosse Holtforth and Grawe (2000, 2002).

The motive associated with a personality disorder, however, is usually unambiguous. First, personality disorders are defined in terms of enduring personality traits, and a personality trait, itself a high-order abstraction, often implies an abiding interpersonal motive. Generally speaking, for example, a sociable person wants company, an assertive person wants to have influence, a narcissistic person wants to be admired or respected, a dependent person wants to be cared for, and a theatrical person wants to be noticed.

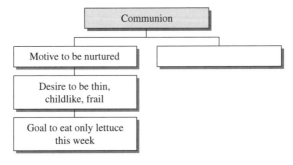

Figure 27.3   Communally Motivated Anorexia Nervosa

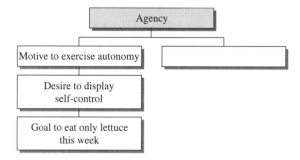

Figure 27.4   Agentically Motivated Anorexia Nervosa

Second, the features that define a personality disorder often include internal states (fears, preoccupations) that help clarify the interpersonal motive.

Consider the dependent personality disorder, for example. *DSM-IV-TR* (2000) emphasizes a pervasive and excessive need to be taken care of. Feature 8 states that the person "is unrealistically preoccupied with fears of being left to take care of himself or herself," and feature 2 states that the person "needs others to assume responsibility for most major areas of his or her life." Additional features describe strategies that the person uses to satisfy the motive. For example, feature 3 indicates that the person does not disagree with others, lest other people withdraw their support. Feature 5 indicates that the person goes to excessive lengths to obtain support from others, even volunteering to do unpleasant tasks.

The Frustrated Motive

When these strategies work and the motive is satisfied, we do not speak of a personality disorder. A personality disorder implies that the salient interpersonal motive is commonly frustrated. That is, behavioral strategies to get the motive satisfied have failed, thereby inducing subjective distress and causing an interpersonal problem. For example, feature 6 of the dependent personality disorder describes the person's emotional reaction to the frustrated motive as follows: "feels uncomfortable or helpless when alone because of exaggerated fears of being unable to care for himself or herself." Other features describe ways that the person then goes about reducing negative affect. For example, feature 7 indicates that the person "urgently seeks another relationship as a source of care and support when a close relationship ends."

THE ORGANIZATION OF FEATURES IN A PERSONALITY DISORDER

Every personality disorder in *DSM-IV-TR* is defined as a fuzzy set: The features (or criteria) of each disorder appear as a non-integrated list of n characteristics; a person must exhibit any m of those n characteristics to receive the diagnosis. No single feature (or subset of features) constitutes a necessary and sufficient requirement for the diagnosis. The features themselves are heterogeous, variously describing behaviors, motives, affects, cognitions, and preoccupations. Since every feature is weighted equally, no one feature serves to integrate or organize the other features. In brief, there is no overarching conceptualization that has implications for treatment, justifies the use of a fuzzy definition, or explains why some personality disorders co-occur more often than others. In this section we suggest that most (but not all) personality disorders may be organized around a single salient interpersonal motive. That interpersonal motive can then be used to integrate the other features.

In brief, we propose that the features of most personality disorders may be organized around a frustrated interpersonal motive. The resulting formulation has several advantages:

1. It enables us to conceptualize the corresponding personality disorder in interpersonal terms.
2. It provides a rationale for specific treatment procedures.
3. It explains why most personality disorders require a fuzzy definition.
4. It clarifies the relationship of the personality disorders to one another; for example, it shows which personality disorders are similar and commonly co-occur and which contrast and rarely co-occur.

Four types of features may be identified that appear among *DSM-IV*'s defining criteria for most personality disorders. Some features explicitly mention a specific self-protective motive. The clearest examples appear in the dependent, avoidant, borderline, narcissistic, histrionic, and paranoid personality disorders. Other features describe consequences of that motive. Altogether, the four types of features may be classified as follows:

1. The salient interpersonal motive.
2. Strategies that the person uses to satisfy the motive.
3. The type of negative affect that occurs when the motive is frustrated.
4. Ways in which the person characteristically reduces the resulting negative affect.

We now consider examples of each type of feature.

Personality Disorders for Which a Motive Is Explicitly Stated

The six personality disorders described in this section each possess a feature that explicitly names a salient interpersonal motive. In later sections, we examine two personality disorders for which the interpersonal motive is implied (but not explicitly named) and two personality disorders that cannot be organized around an interpersonal motive.

The Salient Interpersonal Motive

The organizing motive reflects a wish to attain a desired state or avoid an aversive one. For example, one feature of the borderline personality disorder (feature 1) describes an intense desire to avoid being abandoned. A prominent feature of the histrionic personality disorder (feature 1) describes an intense desire to be the center of attention. A feature of the narcissistic personality disorder (feature 4) describes an excessive need for admiration. A feature of the paranoid personality disorder (feature 3) mentions a motive to protect the self from malice, humiliation, and exploitation by others.

Features of the avoidant personality disorder emphasize a sense of inadequacy and the person's resulting desire to avoid rejection, disapproval, criticism, and ridicule (features 1, 2, 3, 4). Features of the dependent personality disorder emphasize an intense sense of helplessness and inadequacy and a resulting desire to have others take charge (features 2, 4, 5, 8). These motives all stem from a sense of vulnerability in relating to other people.

Thus, although *DSM-IV* generally tries to minimize clinical inference, the features discussed earlier all describe an intense motive to attain a desired state (another person's attention, admiration) or an intense motive to avoid an aversive state (abandonment, rejection, helplessness, or the malice of others).

Strategies for Satisfying the Motive

Other diagnostic features describe behaviors designed to satisfy the motive. For example, a person with a histrionic personality disorder typically uses physical appearance (feature 4) and exaggerated emotion (feature 6) to draw attention to the self. A person with a narcissistic personality disorder exploits other people (feature 6), adopts a sense of self-importance (feature 1), fantasizes unlimited success, power, brilliance, or beauty (feature 2), and holds beliefs about being special and entitled (features 3, 5). In these two disorders, the person is apparently trying to attain a desired state (other people's attention in one, admiration in the other). In treatment, histrionic and narcissistic people seem to want something from the clinician, and clinicians, at least initially, seem to feel more connected to those patients than to patients with any other personality disorder (Wagner, Riley, Schmidt, McCormick, & Butler, 1999).

People with other personality disorders exhibit defensive strategies for avoiding an aversive state. A person with an avoidant personality disorder strives to avoid rejection by minimizing social contact (feature 1); the person limits intimacy, new relationships, and risks (features 3, 5, 7). A person with a dependent personality disorder strives to avoid helplessness by getting others to take charge (feature 2) and finding ways to keep others happy (features 3, 5). A person with a paranoid personality disorder strives to avoid humiliation—guarding against possible malice (feature 1), disloyalty (features 2, 7), and abusive acts (features 3, 4, 5, 6).

Reactions When the Motive Is Frustrated

A third set of features describes the person's reaction when the strategy fails and the motive is frustrated. A dependent person becomes uncomfortable, anxious, or helpless when alone (feature 6). A borderline person shifts abruptly into a contrasting state of affect, identity, or interpersonal relationship (features 2, 3, 6, 8). A narcissistic person becomes envious (feature 8). A paranoid person gets angry at signs of malice (feature 6). These various reactions—anxiety, depression, anger, and envy—are common types of negative affect that occur when a motive is frustrated.

Ways of Coping with Negative Affect

Finally, the remaining features describe how the person copes with the negative affect produced by the frustrated motive. The dependent person urgently seeks another relationship when a close relationship has ended (feature 7). The borderline person acts out on the self or others through impulsive or suicidal behavior (features 4, 5). The narcissistic person becomes arrogant and haughty (feature 9), perhaps also exploitative (feature 6). The paranoid person counterattacks (feature 6). Kemperman, Russ, and Shearin (1997), for example, showed that people often mutilate themselves (e.g., by cutting their wrists) explicitly in an effort to feel better.

Personality Disorders for Which a Motive Is Implied, but Not Explicitly Stated

Features of the schizoid and obsessive-compulsive personality disorders also suggest a motive, but the features of *DSM-IV* do not explicitly name that motive. A person with a schizoid personality disorder seems to be very uncomfortable with closeness and strives to keep separate from other people. In some cases, a motive is clear—namely, to minimize contact with others to preserve the intactness of the self (Horowitz, 2004). This higher order motive to preserve the self would help clarify why the schizoid person chooses solitary activities (feature 2), shows little interest in sexual experiences (feature 3), appears indifferent to praise or criticism (feature 6), and is emotionally cold or detached (feature 7).

A person with an obsessive-compulsive personality disorder seems to be striving to protect the self from criticism and obtain approval (from others and from the self). Most features of this disorder describe strategies for demonstrating that the self is beyond reproach—perfectionism (feature 2), conscientiousness (feature 4), a rigid and detailed focus on rules and order (features 1, 8), and devotion to work (feature 3).

Personality Disorders without an Integrating Motive

Two personality disorders do not conform to our model, namely, the antisocial personality disorder and the schizotypal personality disorder. People with an antisocial personality disorder seem to feel little guilt or remorse (feature 7), and other features of the category primarily describe antisocial acts that reflect a lack of conscience—commits unlawful acts (feature 1), deceives other people (feature 2), and behaves impulsively, aggressively, and irresponsibly (features 3, 4, 6). These features do not seem to suggest an easily threatened motive.

Features of the schizotypal personality disorder also seem to lack an integrating motive. Instead, those features resemble mild symptoms of the schizophrenic disorders—ideas of reference (feature 1), odd beliefs and magical thinking (feature 2), unusual perceptual experiences (feature 3), odd thinking and speech (feature 4), inappropriate affect (feature 6), and eccentric behavior (feature 7). For the antisocial and schizotypal personality disorders, then, we cannot argue that the features describe a self-protective interpersonal motive that leads to strategies for satisfying the motive, or reactions when the motive is frustrated. Therefore, these two categories seem to be qualitatively different from the other eight personality disorders. This kind of heterogeneity has been discussed by McWilliams (1998).

In summary, most personality disorders highlight an important interpersonal motive: to connect with other people by getting attention (histrionic), to connect as a way of avoiding helplessness (dependent), to get admiration from other people (narcissistic), to keep other people at a distance (schizoid), to avoid feeling abandoned (borderline), to avoid contact with people who might reject or disapprove (avoidant), to defend oneself against the malice of others (paranoid), and to avoid criticism so as to maintain approval from others and from the self (obsessive-compulsive).

Clinicians sometimes speak of a "maladaptive interpersonal pattern" in describing the personality disorders (e.g., Benjamin, 1996; Carson, 1969; Kiesler, 1983, 1996; Leary, 1957; McLemore & Brokaw, 1987; Pincus & Wiggins, 1990; Strupp & Binder, 1984; Sullivan, 1953). That term is generally used to highlight the person's self-defeating interpersonal behavior. Our model attempts to highlight specific ways in which the person's behavior is maladaptive. For one, when a person meets the criteria for a personality disorder, the behavioral strategies for satisfying the interpersonal motive are not working. For example, a *behavioral* strategy (ambiguous to start with) may backfire: The histrionic person, rather than attracting others, seems manipulative; the obsessive-compulsive person, rather than appearing perfect, seems pedantic; the dependent person, rather than inviting nurturance, seems needy; the avoidant person, rather than protecting the self from rejection, seems disinterested in other people. Furthermore, as the person's efforts backfire, they frustrate the very motive that they were meant to satisfy. As a result, the person experiences subjective distress, which the person tries to alleviate in non-constructive ways (e.g., self-injurious behavior, counterattacking other people). According to this analysis, a treatment needs to focus on each step of the formulation—the self-protective interpersonal motive, the ineffective strategies for satisfying the motive, the resulting (uncontrollable) negative affect, and the self-defeating ways of coping with negative affect.

How Does an Interpersonal Motive Become Salient?

What makes an interpersonal motive so pressing that its frequent frustration leads to a personality disorder? Apparently, the person has acquired significant self-doubts as a result of accumulated frustrations over many years—for example, doubts about his or her appeal to others, efficacy, and respect from others. To disconfirm these unwanted hypotheses and dispel self-doubts, the person has apparently become very sensitive to potentially relevant evidence: Am I unappealing to others? Will I be abandoned by others? Am I not respected by others? Can I protect myself from humiliation? In brief, the person seems to have acquired a need to keep testing and disconfirming negative hypotheses, thereby reassuring the self. The greater the person's self-doubt, the greater the need (or motive) for reassurance.

The resulting vulnerability (or diathesis) appears to be a traitlike "person" variable that is probably acquired gradually through an interplay of temperament (biological endowment) and experience. Some vulnerable people are fortunate in that they do not often encounter situations that frustrate the now salient motive. Though vulnerable, they are spared the emotional distress of a frequently frustrated motive. An ideally suited spouse or best friend, for example, might reliably satisfy the motive, thereby shielding the vulnerable person from a borderline, dependent, or histrionic personality disorder. Other vulnerable people, however, are less fortunate and repeatedly encounter situations that frustrate the motive, thereby inducing a personality disorder.

The Pressing Motive Induces Cognitive Biases, Which Sustain the Maladaptive Cycle

The salient interpersonal motive amounts to an intense need to avoid an aversive state—to avoid such states as feeling abandoned (borderline), being rejected by others (avoidant), being the object of other people's malice (paranoid), or being the target of other people's criticism and disapproval (obsessive-compulsive). It therefore serves a self-protective function.

One extreme example is the paranoid personality disorder. To protect the self from malice, the person is highly suspicious of others. Suspiciousness seems to lower a person's objectivity in testing hypotheses about the self. The paranoid person has a single-minded purpose—namely, to avoid humiliation by detecting evidence of cheating, deceiving, exploiting, betraying, and so on. Therefore, the person conducts a *biased* search; evidence to the contrary is simply ignored. When individuals with a paranoid personality disorder detect hints of malice, they quickly become convinced that their suspicion has been confirmed: He *wanted* to cheat me. This "discovery" then reinforces the original need for vigilance.

Millon and Davis (2000) describe the paranoid attentional style in terms of signal detection theory. The person evaluates interpersonal evidence as though it were a blip on a radar screen: Does it signify malice or not? Some indicators genuinely reflect malice; others do not. If the person correctly judges a valid indicator to be real evidence of malice, we call it a "hit" or a "true positive." But if the person mistakenly judges an *invalid* indicator to be genuine evidence of malice, we call it a "false alarm" or a "false positive." Once in a while, a paranoid person makes a brilliant hit, but far more often, the person produces false alarms. The relatively high rate of false alarms reveals the person's bias. According to Millon and Davis, this tactic might be useful in warfare—where false alarms are tolerated to maximize the number of hits in detecting the enemy. But in everyday interactions, people with a paranoid personality disorder seem to be distorting reality (Shapiro, 1965, p. 64) and acquire a reputation for distorting and overreacting.

To some extent, a cognitive bias is probably associated with every personality disorder that is organized around a desperate motive to protect the self. The borderline person is probably biased toward perceiving signs of abandonment; the avoidant person, toward signs of rejection; the obsessive-compulsive person, toward signs of criticism; the schizoid person, toward signs that other people wish to connect; and so on. And the resulting false alarms increase the sense of frustrated motives and negative affect, thereby increasing the probability of some maladaptive way of reducing distress.

Why Does a Personality Disorder Require a Fuzzy Definition?

Every personality disorder in *DSM-IV-TR* is defined as a "fuzzy construct." To qualify for a particular diagnosis, a person needs to exhibit m of the n defining features. If the category were precisely defined, all criteria would be individually necessary and jointly sufficient; that is, every person who qualified for membership in the category would exhibit each and every one of the n defining features. But the members of a *fuzzy* category are heterogeneous: Some qualify through one subset of m criteria; others through other subsets. Therefore, two members of the category typically have some but not all features in common.

Why should a personality disorder require a fuzzy definition? First, various strategies allow a person to satisfy an important motive. Two people with an obsessive-compulsive personality disorder may both strive to avoid criticism or attain approval, but one may do so by being neat, careful, and orderly, whereas another may do so through prodigious amounts of work. The abstract *motive* would be the same, but alternate strategies (goals, specific action units) exist for satisfying the higher order motive.

Second, different people react differently when the motive is frustrated. Two people with a borderline personality disorder may both feel abandoned, but one may become depressed, whereas the other may become enraged. Third, different people may cope with negative affect in different ways. One may exhibit eating binges; another, a vengeful rage; and a third, suicidal gestures. Thus, the disorder is organized around the same fundamental motive, but different strategies, emotional reactions to frustration, and ways of coping with negative affect characterize people with the same organizing motive. Because of these individual differences in strategies and reactions to frustration, the diagnostic category has to be defined as a fuzzy set.

ASSESSING THE FUNDAMENTAL INTERPERSONAL MOTIVE

An interpersonal motive is not directly observable; it is always inferred from the person's self-report and overt behavior. Good self-report measures exist for assessing a person's salient motives and goals (Grosse Holtforth & Grawe, 2000, 2002; Locke, 2000), but a person cannot provide a valid self-report unless the person is somewhat psychologically minded, possesses a capacity for self-reflection, and is willing to self-disclose. Some people are probably unable or unwilling to provide the kind of information that is needed to identify the relevant motive.

Suppose a person is prone to frequent displays of temper and depression and seems to meet every criterion of the borderline personality disorder, with one exception: The person denies any concern over (or desire to avoid) real or imagined abandonment. That is, suppose the person claims to be unconcerned about abandonment, rejection, or the loss of close relationships. This hypothetical person, then, would possess eight of the nine features of a borderline personality disorder but would be claiming that other people's intentions or actions have nothing to do with his or her mood shifts, identity shifts, displays of temper, impulsive behavior, feelings of emptiness, and unstable relationships. If we accepted the self-report as valid, would we still judge the person to have a borderline personality disorder? Perhaps not. Interpersonal theorists, at least, would probably search for some other explanation and diagnosis—perhaps a purely biological explanation that did not require concepts such as a fear of abandonment or frustrated interpersonal motives (Horowitz, 2004). In particular, an interpersonal theorist would probably not use the label "borderline personality disorder" to describe someone whose traits were best explained biologically. For an interpersonal theorist, the interpersonal motive would make a significant difference both in diagnosis and in treatment.

On the other hand, an interpersonal theorist might question the validity of the person's claim to be unconcerned about abandonment. It is possible that the person who displayed eight of the nine borderline characteristics was, for some reason, unable to recognize, acknowledge, or describe the fundamental motive. An inference about an organizing motive is always a tentative hypothesis, not a logical deduction or observable fact. It is simply a guide to further inquiry. Like any hypothesis, it needs to be tested and either confirmed over time or rejected. If it is confirmed, it clarifies the person's problem, focuses the goal of treatment, and helps us empathize with the person's phenomenology. If it is disconfirmed, however, it needs to be abandoned in favor of an alternate formulation of the case.

Sometimes a person qualifies (or nearly qualifies) for two or more personality disorders. In that case, the person's disorder would be formulated in terms of two or more organizing motives. For example, the same person might crave attention (a histrionic motive) and strive to avoid abandonment (a borderline motive); both involve communal motives. Indeed, the histrionic and borderline personality disorders do frequently co-occur (e.g., Davila, 2001; Davila, Cobb, & Lindberg, 2001; Watson & Sinha, 1998). Likewise, a person might crave attention (a histrionic motive) and crave admiration (a narcissistic motive); one is communal, the other is agentic. It is very common for a person who qualifies for one personality disorder to qualify for other personality disorders as well (Marinangeli et al., 2000). Certain pairs of motives are more similar than others, so those personality disorders, according to the model, should co-occur more often.

PERSONALITY DISORDERS IN AN INTERPERSONAL SPACE

As noted earlier, interpersonal motives may be described in terms of two broad dimensions or factors, communion and agency. If the features of a personality disorder can be organized around a particular interpersonal motive, every personality disorder should occupy a particular location in the two-dimensional interpersonal space (Horowitz, 2004).

For example, the histrionic motive—"to connect with other people by getting their attention"—implies a desire to influence other people to connect. This disorder should, therefore, occupy the upper right-hand quadrant of a two-dimensional space (where the motive to connect implies high communion and the motive to influence implies high agency). Similarly, the dependent motive—"to connect with other people and get them to take charge"—implies that the dependent personality disorder should occupy the lower right-hand quadrant.

Several studies have scaled and graphed the personality disorders. Pincus and Wiggins (1990) administered questionnaires to a large sample of undergraduate students to assess the interpersonal problems (frustrated motives) associated with different personality disorders. Figure 27.5 shows, for each of six personality disorders, the graphical location of typical interpersonal problems. Two primary dimensions (corresponding to communion and agency) emerged from a principal components analysis. People with a histrionic, antisocial, or narcissistic personality disorder, by their own report, tend to "take charge of other people" too readily (high agency). Those with a histrionic personality disorder also tend to connect with others too readily (high communion), whereas those with an antisocial personality disorder fail to connect with others (low communion). People with a dependent, schizoid, or avoidant personality disorder tend to yield too readily as a result of feeling inferior and inadequate (low agency). Those with a dependent personality disorder also connect too readily (high communion), whereas those with a schizoid personality disorder avoid connecting (low communion).

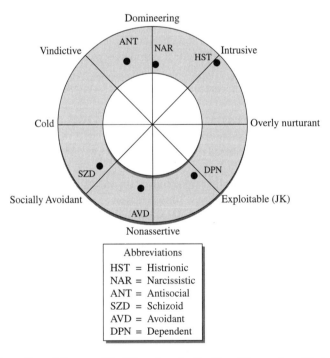

Figure 27.5   Location of Personality Disorders in the Two-Dimensional Interpersonal Space. Adapted with permission from "Interpersonal Problems and Conceptions of Personality Disorders," by A. L. Pincus and J. S. Wiggins, 1990, *Journal of Personality Disorders, 4,* pp. 342–352.

Other authors have obtained similar results for both patients and students (Blackburn, 1998; DeJong, Van den Brink, Jansen, & Schippers, 1989; Matano & Locke, 1995; Morey, 1985; Overholser, 1996; Sim & Romney, 1990; Soldz, Budman, Demby, & Merry, 1993; Trull, Useda, Conforti, & Doan, 1997). As summarized by Wagner et al. (1999), the following graphical locations are typical. People with a narcissistic personality disorder are high in agency and neutral in communion (they want respect and admiration). Those with a paranoid or antisocial personality disorder are high in agency and low in communion (they want to influence others without connecting). Those with an avoidant or schizoid personality disorder are low in both (they want to protect the self by remaining passive and disconnected). Those with a dependent personality disorder are low in agency and high in communion (they want others with whom they are connected to take charge). Those with a histrionic personality disorder are high in both (they want to influence others to become connected). The borderline personality disorder, with its many instabilities, does not seem to occupy a consistent graphical location.

Matano and Locke (1995) studied alcohol-dependent individuals who had a personality disorder. According to their results, subjective distress is greater for people with a sense of inadequacy. Therefore, people with a dependent, avoidant, or schizoid personality disorder generally report more overall distress than people with a narcissistic, antisocial, or histrionic personality disorder. The authors also noted that those patients who are motivated to influence others (narcissistic, antisocial, and paranoid people) seemed to "have a hard time relinquishing autonomy and control—whether to a treatment program or to a higher power in Alcoholics Anonymous." On the other hand, patients with a dependent personality disorder—who are too ready to relinquish control—seem to "have a hard time resisting social pressures to drink." The authors also suggested that patients who are highly communal (histrionic and dependent people) seem to "have a hard time respecting or maintaining boundaries in therapy," whereas those who are more disconnected (schizoid, avoidant, paranoid, and antisocial patients) seem to have problems allowing themselves to engage with others. Those people may, therefore, find it difficult to self-disclose as a way of promoting interpersonal relatedness in individual and group therapy.

The graphical arrangement of disorders also helps us predict which disorders are apt to co-occur. Disorders that are near one another would seem more likely to co-occur than disorders that are farther apart. Disorders that are diametrically apart are negatively related (e.g., antisocial versus dependent or histrionic versus schizoid); the motive associated with one contrasts with that of the other. Thus, an interpersonal formulation helps organize the features of most personality disorders, thereby highlighting similarities, differences, and patterns of co-occurrence among them.

We have discussed the 10 personality disorders as though each were a natural category that every person unambiguously matches or fails to match. We do not hold this view of personality disorders. In our view, a personality disorder is a construct that trained observers have created to help them describe and discuss observations of people in distress. Each personality disorder, as an abstract concept, may be regarded as a theoretical ideal that real people approximate to different degrees—along a continuum from "not at all" to "extremely." Although it is sometimes heuristically useful in discussions like the present one to speak of a personality disorder as a finite (discontinuous) category (Horowitz, 2004), empirical evidence favors a dimensional, rather than a categorical, view of psychopathology (e.g., Livesley, Schroeder, Jackson, & Jang, 1994; Widiger, 1989). If a personality disorder is viewed dimensionally, the salience of its organizing interpersonal motive must also be viewed dimensionally—along a continuum from "not at all salient" to "extremely salient" in the person's experience. Therefore, in our view, people who are not at all vulnerable to psychopathology would also recognize in their everyday experience some of the organizing motives described in this chapter. However, they are not vulnerable to a personality disorder because they are successful in satisfying the motive or because the motive is not pressing enough to cause great distress when it is frustrated.

CONCLUSIONS

Most personality disorders described in *DSM-IV-TR* (2000) may be organized around a particular interpersonal motive that has become salient for that person. Interpersonal motives, broadly speaking, may be classified as communal or agentic (or a combination of the two). Because these motives have a self-protective function, the person acquires a heightened sensitivity to interpersonal information that might satisfy or frustrate the interpersonal motive. When the strategies that are used fail to satisfy the motive, the person encounters significant frustration and experiences negative affect. The person may then adopt maladaptive ways of coping with the negative affect. In such cases, we speak of a personality disorder, and various outcomes of the process constitute the defining features of the disorder. In brief, however, we regard the interpersonal motive as the organizing feature of the personality disorder. Therefore, to understand the personality disorder, we must always ask, "What is the person trying to achieve interpersonally?" and "Why is the person unable to satisfy that motive?" We believe that the answer to such questions will better equip a clinician to empathize with the person's situation, conceptualize the person and the problem broadly, and devise appropriate treatment interventions to help resolve the problem.

REFERENCES

Allport, F. (1937). Teleonomic description in the study of personality. *Character and Personality, 5,* 202–214.

Allport, G. W. (1937). *Personality: A psychological interpretation.* New York: Holt, Rinehart and Winston.

American Psychiatric Association. (2000). *Diagnostic and statistical manual of mental disorders* (4th ed., text rev.). Washington, DC: Author.

Austin, J. T., & Vancouver, J. B. (1996). Goal constructs in psychology: Structure, process, and content. *Psychological Bulletin, 120,* 338–375.

Bakan, D. (1966). *The duality of human existence: Isolation and communion in western man.* Boston: Beacon Press.

Benjamin, L. S. (1996). *Interpersonal diagnosis and treatment of personality disorders* (2nd ed.). New York: Guilford Press.

Blackburn, R. (1998). Relationship of personality disorders to observer ratings of interpersonal style in forensic psychiatric patients. *Journal of Personality Disorders, 12,* 77–85.

Bruch, H. (1973). *Eating disorders: Obesity, anorexia nervosa, and the person within.* New York: Basic Books.

Cantor, N., & Genero, N. (1986). Psychiatric diagnosis and natural categorization: A close analogy. In T. Millon & G. L. Klerman (Eds.), *Contemporary directions in psychopathology: Toward the DSM-IV* (pp. 233–256). New York: Guilford Press.

Cantor, N., & Kihlstrom, J. F. (1987). *Personality and social intelligence.* Englewood Cliffs, NJ: Prentice-Hall.

Carson, R. C. (1969). *Interaction concepts of personality.* Chicago: Aldine.

Caspar, F. (1995). *Plan analysis: Toward optimizing psychotherapy.* Seattle, WA: Hogrefe & Huber.

Caspar, F. (1997). Plan analysis. In T. Eells (Ed.), *Handbook of psychotherapy case formulation* (pp. 260–288). New York: Guilford Press.

Cropanzano, R., James, K., & Citera, M. (1992). A goal hierarchy model of personality, motivation, and leadership. In L. L. Cummings & B. M. Staw (Eds.), *Research in organizational behavior* (Vol. 15, pp. 267–322). Greenwich, CT: JAI Press.

Davila, J. (2001). Paths to unhappiness: The overlapping courses of depression and romantic dysfunction. In S. R. H. Beach (Ed.), *Marital and family processes in depression: A scientific foundation for clinical practice* (pp. 71–87). Washington, DC: American Psychological Association.

Davila, J., Cobb, R., & Lindberg, N. (2001). *Depressive symptoms, personality pathology, and early romantic dysfunction among young individuals: A test of a romantic stress generation model.* Unpublished manuscript, State University of New York at Buffalo.

DeJong, C. A. T., Van den Brink, W., Jansen, J. A. M., & Schippers, G. M. (1989). Interpersonal aspects of *DSM-III* Axis II: Theoretical hypotheses and empirical findings. *Journal of Personality Disorders, 3,* 135–146.

Emmons, R. A. (1989). The personal striving approach to personality. In L. A. Pervin (Ed.), *Goal concepts in personality and social psychology* (pp. 87–126). Hillsdale, NJ: Erlbaum.

Grawe, K. (2003). *Psychological therapy.* Seattle, WA: Hogrefe & Huber.

Grosse Holtforth, M., & Grawe, K. (2000). Fragebogen zur Analyse Motivationaler Schemata (FAMOS) [Inventory for the Analysis of Motivational Themes]. *Zeitschrift für Klinische Psychologie, 29,* 170–179.

Grosse Holtforth, M., & Grawe, K. (2002). Bern Inventory of Treatment Goals: Part 1. Development and first application of a taxonomy of treatment goal themes. *Psychotherapy Research, 12,* 79–99.

Horowitz, L. M. (2004). *Interpersonal foundations of psychopathology.* Washington, DC: American Psychological Association.

Kemperman, I., Russ, M. J., & Shearin, E. (1997). Self-injurious behavior and mood regulation in borderline patients. *Journal of Personality Disorders, 11,* 146–157.

Kiesler, D. J. (1983). The 1982 interpersonal circle: A taxonomy for complementarity in human transactions. *Psychological Review, 90,* 185–214.

Kiesler, D. J. (1996). *Contemporary interpersonal theory and research: Personality, psychopathology and psychotherapy.* New York: Wiley.

Klinger, E. (1987). Current concerns and disengagement from incentives. In F. Halisch & J. Kuhl (Eds.), *Motivation, intention, and volition* (pp. 337–347). Heidelberg, Germany: Springer-Verlag.

Leary, T. F. (1957). *Interpersonal diagnosis of personality.* New York: Ronald Press.

Little, B. R. (1983). Personal projects: A rationale and method for investigation. *Environment and Behavior, 15,* 273–309.

Livesley, W. J., Schroeder, M. L., Jackson, D. N., & Jang, K. L. (1994). Categorical distinctions in the study of personality disorder: Implications for classification. *Journal of Abnormal Psychology, 103,* 6–17.

Locke, K. D. (2000). Circumplex scales of interpersonal values: Reliability, validity, and applicability to interpersonal problems and personality disorders. *Journal of Personality Assessment, 75,* 249–267.

Marinangeli, M. G., Butti, G., Scinto, A., DiCicco, L., Petruzzi, C., Daneluzzo, E., et al. (2000). Patterns of comorbidity among *DSM-III-R* personality disorders. *Psychopathology, 32,* 69–74.

Matano, R. A., & Locke, K. D. (1995). Personality disorder scales as predictors of interpersonal problems of alcoholics. *Journal of Personality Disorders, 9,* 62–67.

McAdams, D. P. (1988). Personal needs and personal relationships. In S. Duck (Ed.), *Handbook of research on personal relationships* (pp. 7–22). New York: Wiley.

McClelland, D. C. (1985). *Human motivation.* Glenview, IL: Scott, Foresman.

McLemore, C. W., & Brokaw, D. W. (1987). Personality disorders as dysfunctional interpersonal behavior. *Journal of Personality Disorders, 1,* 270–285.

McWilliams, N. (1998). Relationship, subjectivity, and inference in diagnosis. In J. W. Barron (Ed.), *Making diagnosis meaningful* (pp. 197–226). Washington, DC: American Psychological Association.

Millon, T., & Davis, R. D. (2000). *Personality disorders in modern life.* New York: Wiley.

Minuchin, S., Rosman, B. L., & Baker, L. (1978). *Psychosomatic families: Anorexia nervosa in context.* Cambridge, MA: Harvard University Press.

Morey, L. C. (1985). An empirical comparison of interpersonal and *DSM-III* approaches to classification of personality disorders. *Psychiatry, 48,* 358–364.

Murray, H. A. (1938). *Explorations in personality.* New York: Oxford University Press.

Overholser, J. C. (1996). The dependent personality and interpersonal problems. *Journal of Nervous and Mental Diseases, 184,* 8–16.

Pincus, A. L., & Wiggins, J. S. (1990). Interpersonal problems and conceptions of personality disorders. *Journal of Personality Disorders, 4,* 342–352.

Shapiro, D. (1965). *Neurotic styles.* New York: Basic Books.

Sim, J. P., & Romney, D. M. (1990). The relationship between a circumplex model of interpersonal behaviors and personality disorders. *Journal of Personality Disorders, 4,* 329–341.

Soldz, S., Budman, S., Demby, A., & Merry, J. (1993). Representation of personality disorders in circumplex and five-factor space: Explorations with a clinical sample. *Psychological Assessment, 5,* 41–52.

Strupp, H. H., & Binder, J. L. (1984). *Psychotherapy in a new key.* New York: Basic Books.

Sullivan, H. S. (1953). *The interpersonal theory of psychiatry.* New York: Norton.

Trull, T. J., Useda, D., Conforti, K., & Doan, B. T. (1997). Borderline personality disorder features in nonclinical young adults: II. Two-year outcome. *Journal of Abnormal Psychology, 106,* 307–314.

Wagner, C. C., Riley, W. T., Schmidt, J. A., McCormick, M. G. F., & Butler, S. F. (1999). Personality disorder styles and reciprocal interpersonal impacts during outpatient intake interviews. *Psychotherapy Research, 9,* 216–231.

Watson, D. C., & Sinha, B. K. (1998). Comorbidity of *DSM-IV* personality disorders in a nonclinical sample. *Journal of Clinical Psychology, 54,* 773–780.

Widiger, T. A. (1989). The categorical distinction between personality and affective disorders. *Journal of Personality Disorders, 3,* 77–91.

Chapter 28

PERSONOLOGY, PERSONALITY DISORDERS, AND PSYCHOTHERAPY INTEGRATION

JERRY GOLD

In this chapter I explore the ways in which the fields of personology, the psychopathology of personality disorders, and psychotherapy integration have existed, and do exist, in mutually helpful feedback relationships with one another, especially in connection to understanding and treating personality disorders. The chapter provides a brief history of psychotherapy integration, through which its increasing use of, and contributions to, personality theory and psychopathology are examined. This is followed by an examination of the theoretical utility of an alliance among these three disciplines. The bulk of the chapter is devoted to a review of some of the more important integrative models for the treatment of personality disorder.

DEVELOPMENTAL HISTORY OF PSYCHOTHERAPY INTEGRATION: FROM ATHEORETICAL INNOVATION TO FOUNDATIONS IN PERSONOLOGY

The term *psychotherapy integration* is of relatively recent usage, having become a commonly accepted descriptor following the organization of the Society for the Exploration of Psychotherapy Integration (SEPI) in 1983. Psychotherapy integration refers to the search for and study of the ways in which the various schools or models of psychotherapy can inform, enrich, and ultimately be combined, rather than a specific theory or method of psychotherapy. However, attempts to combine or integrate two or more versions of psychotherapy have been around for a relatively long time, given the relatively short history of the field of modern psychotherapy itself. Most of the early work in this area was clinically derived and was composed of an attempt to use concepts or techniques from one psychotherapeutic model (e.g., behavior therapy) within the context of another psychotherapeutic model (e.g., psychoanalysis). These integrative efforts, therefore, were relatively narrow in scope, and although they involved the synthesis or recombination of a limited number of theoretical constructs, they typically did not connect with a broader, personological view of patients, of psychopathology, or of psychotherapeutic change. Over time, however, as discussed later, psychotherapy integration in its most complex and sophisticated forms has displayed an implicit personological focus and has offered new insights into the field of personology as well. In addition, psychotherapy integration offers clinicians and theorists new and potentially more effective ways of treating and studying personality disorders.

Perhaps the earliest article that might be considered a forerunner of modern psychotherapy integration was concerned with the synthesis of the theory of Freudian psychoanalysis and the observable facts of Pavlovian classical conditioning (French, 1933). Another groundbreaking contribution was made by Rosenzweig (1936), who was the first to write about the shared change processes, or common factors, that contribute to progress and improvement in most, if not all, psychotherapies. Rosenzweig's article remains well known and is frequently cited even today in the psychotherapy integration literature. He usually is considered to be the founder of the *common factors* approach to psychotherapy integration (Hubble, Duncan, & Miller, 1999), in which interventions are selected from a variety of psychotherapy models on the basis of their utility in supplying the particular change factor that the therapist assumes would be helpful for a particular client. This work has eventuated in modern integrative systems such as the transtheoretical system proposed by Prochaska and DiClemente (2002) in which the patient is assessed to determine the most advantageous change factors that can be supplied.

As work in this area continued, integrative efforts were concerned largely with adding behavioral concepts and/or techniques to psychoanalytically based psychotherapies (Sears, 1944) or with the translation of psychoanalytic theory into behavioral, learning theory-based concepts that then could be tested with experimental methodology (Dollard & Miller, 1950). Work in this vein continued through the 1950s, 1960s, and 1970s with an increasing number of articles and books appearing, in which a methodological integration was described. For example, Marks and Gelder (1966) compared and found similarities between then-current versions of behavior therapy and psychoanalysis. Alexander (1963) and Beier (1966) argued that the therapist's influence on the patient could be understood within the perspective of conditioning theories, especially concerning the reinforcement value of the therapist's responsiveness and approval. In particular, Beier suggested that unconscious processes and conflicts were subject to shaping and to extinction within the interpersonal context of psychotherapy and described a therapy in which these operant processes could best be utilized. An early integration of client-centered therapy with behavior therapy can be found in Bergin's (1968) demonstration that the effectiveness of systematic desensitization could be improved by using that technique within the context of a psychotherapeutic relationship that supplied warmth, empathy, and unconditional positive regard. Feather and Rhodes (1973) developed a variant of psychotherapy, which they identified as "psychodynamic behavior therapy." This integrative approach involved using behavioral techniques, such as systematic desensitization, to reach and to resolve unconscious conflicts. These contributions, and others like them, were precursors to the psychotherapy integration literature that today is concerned with two modes of integration in which personology and theory are of secondary importance to clinical innovation (Gold, 1996). I refer here to the integrative modes known as *technical eclecticism* and *assimilative integration*.

Technical eclecticism refers to a commonly practiced version of psychotherapy integration in which the therapist selects interventions that are best suited to the immediate clinical need and to long-term goals, without reference to underlying theoretical principles. Technical eclecticism is guided, when possible, by empirical findings that have identified the most useful matches between the patient's problems and specific techniques. When this is not possible, techniques are selected on the basis of clinical experience. The most influential examples of this mode of integration are prescriptive psychotherapy (Beutler & Hodgson, 1993) and multimodal therapy (Lazarus, 2002). Assimilative integration refers to a form of integrative psychotherapy that is guided by a basic, or "home" theory, such as psychoanalysis, but into which selected constructs and techniques from other therapies are assimilated and to which the home theory must accommodate through expansion and revision.

A widely cited example of this mode of integration is *assimilative psychodynamic psychotherapy* (Stricker & Gold, 2002).

These seminal papers remain interesting and useful contributions to the theoretical and clinical literature even today. However, they reflect the distance that existed between the clinically oriented emerging field that would become known as psychotherapy integration and the more academic field of personology. Authors such as those just cited and their like-minded colleagues had little that was new to say about existing theories of personality and seemed to accept the status quo in such matters. A new era in the dialogue between personology and psychotherapy integration and a new mode of psychotherapy integration was ushered in by the publication of Wachtel's (1977) landmark volume, *Psychoanalysis and Behavior Therapy: Toward an Integration.* This book remains the single most influential and widely cited work in modern psychotherapy integration. It is the prototype of the most complex and sophisticated form of psychotherapy integration, namely *theoretical integration.* This label refers to an integration of two or more systems of psychotherapy in which the underlying theories of personality, on which those discrete forms of psychotherapy are based, are combined into a novel, integrative, overarching personality theory. Wachtel's integrative, psychodynamic psychotherapy is derived from his unique personality theory, which he calls "cyclical psychodynamics." Placed in an intermediate position between personality theory and intervention strategies is the conceptual framework for assessing psychopathology that derives from cyclical psychodynamic theory, which posits that all forms of psychological disorder are pathologies of character or personality.

It was this remarkable development and the introduction of other systems of theoretical integration like it that soon followed (see Gold, 1996, for a complete review of the various models of theoretical integration) that demonstrated the important ways in which personology and psychotherapy integration could be, and are, complementary to each other.

PERSONOLOGY, PERSONALITY DISORDERS, AND PSYCHOTHERAPY INTEGRATION: THEORETICAL CONNECTIONS AND TRENDS TOWARD SYNERGY

Personality disorders allow us a view of the strata of personality, much as the shifting of the Earth's tectonic plates reveals to us the layers of sediment and of geological development that lie beneath the obvious surface. In the "disordered" or dysfunctional behaviors; cognitive processes, patterns, and contents; emotional dysregulation; and ineffectual, inhibited, or exaggerated ways of engaging others, we find the fossilized remains of past experience and of the ways in which personality development has gone wrong. This conceptualization can be found in Millon's (1990) suggestion that we study personality disorders, and psychopathology in general, from an evolutionary perspective. In doing so, we must look beneath the surface to unearth the patient's successive attempts at adaptation to an ever more complex and more demanding series of internal and external environments. In this model, healthy or normal personality functioning is composed of the specific ways that the person has successfully adapted to the series of expectable environments with which he or she has been faced. The "disordered" aspects of personality disorder then can be understood to refer to failures of adaptation or to maladaptive styles of adapting, but which represented the patient's only psychological choices, given her or his psychological and environmental constraints. Literally, in the experience of such patients, a poor adaptation is better than no adaptation. It is probably incorrect to consider these adaptations to be complete failures. Rather, these attempts to adjust to and manage self in the face of new environmental and intrapsychic demands are limited successes in the short run but do not promote stable change and adaptive success over time. Thus, each successive adaptation is compromised as well.

Another integrative personality theory that has been suggested as a vehicle for assessing and treating personality disorders is the multilevel narrative theory developed by Gold (1996). This theory likens each person's developmental history and contemporary pattern of living to the various threads of a fictional, cinematic, or theatrical narrative. Personality disorders represent "broken" narratives in which the patient's ability to live effectively is hindered by narrative components that are discordant or in conflict with other narrative trends, for example, the patient whose conscious "story" of self results in self-deprecation, while at an unconscious level the narrative is filled with disavowed grandiose fantasies.

It is not possible, or perhaps even necessary, at this point in the evolution of the fields of personology, psychopathology, or psychotherapy integration to specify a personality theory of choice. Rather, the preceding discussion was meant to illustrate the advantages of establishing such theoretical linkages. When we turn to psychotherapy, we find that theoretically oriented, personality theory-based forms of psychotherapy integration seem to be particularly well suited to the examination and treatment of personality disorder, as such "broad-spectrum" methods (Lazarus, 2002) allow for intervening at and within as many of the strata of personality development as are necessary. Sectarian psychotherapies and the theories of personality development on which they are based force us into narrow perspectives on the evolution of psychopathology and of disorders of adaptation. To return to a geological metaphor: Each separate theory of personality development can account best for a limited group of strata and must avoid the fossil record of experiences that are outside, or which do not fit into, the range of application of that theory. An integrative model of personality broadens and deepens our perspective and understanding of these phenomena. Millon's (1988, 2000) evolutionary approach to personology and psychotherapy integration is highly applicable in this context, as are the other systems of theoretical integration that were mentioned earlier. Millon (1988) noted:

> I will seek . . . to outline some reasons why personality disorders may be that segment of psychopathology for which integrative psychotherapy is ideally and distinctively suited . . .
>
> The cohesion (or lack thereof) of complexly interwoven psychic structures and functions is what distinguishes the disorders of personality from other clinical syndromes; likewise, the orchestration of diverse, yet synthesized techniques of intervention is what differentiates integrative from other variants of psychotherapy. These two, parallel constructs, emerging from different traditions and conceived in different venues, reflect shared philosophical perspectives, one oriented toward the understanding of psychopathology, the other toward effecting its remediation.
>
> It is not that integrative psychotherapies are inapplicable to more focal pathologies but rather that these therapies are *required* for the personality disorders . . . it is the very interwoven nature of the components that comprise personality disorders that make a multifaceted approach a necessity. (p. 210, italics in original)

Millon's (1988) remarks on the nature of a truly integrative psychotherapy for personality disorders are highly instructive. He notes first that for a therapy to be integrative, rather than merely an eclectic collection of techniques, it must be based on an overarching theoretical gestalt, namely a personality theory that identifies the linkages among the various part-components (cognitive, interpersonal, psychodynamic, etc.) of the various personality disorders and that can specify how these components coalesce to form these psychopathological unities. In this article, he illustrates this position by applying his evolutionary model of personality to personality disorders. Millon is able to differentiate how the various personality pathologies differ in their patterns of adaptation (most notably in their various survival aims, modes of survival, and foci of survival) and how this evolutionary perspective can be used to guide preplanned sequences of integrative therapeutic interventions. True to his definition of personality disorder (cited earlier) as the failure of integration of personality components, he suggests that effective, and truly integrative psychotherapy, is aimed at and leads to a rebalancing of the components of personality, much as the conductor of an orchestra brings harmony to an initially discordant set of instruments. Some personality components must be tamed or muted, others must be brought up in volume, some must be added to the "orchestral profile," and others must be gently asked to leave the stage. The conductor cannot accomplish these tasks without a musical score, while the integrative therapist must be guided by a fully detailed theoretical model of the healthy personality and of the personality disorders. In this article and in a later contribution, Millon (1988; Millon, Everly, & Davis, 1993) made it clear that an atheoretical psychotherapy, one that attempts to "fix" symptoms without reference to a theory of personality and of psychopathology, is akin to medicine as it was practiced in the nineteenth century and certainly is not deserving of the label *integrative.*

In a subsequent article that was derived from a keynote address delivered to an annual conference of the Society for the Exploration of Psychotherapy Integration, Millon (2000) expanded and updated his earlier description of a posteclectic, integrative psychotherapy that was based on a foundation of his evolutionary theory of personality. Herein, Millon applied the critical argument that has marked all of his work in personality theory and the study of psychopathology, namely, that effective psychotherapy must treat the person as a whole, by evaluating all of the deficits, excesses, inhibitions, and deviations in functioning, rather than focusing on surface, target symptoms. In this article and in the book on which it was based, Millon (1999, 2000) introduced his model of *psychosynergy* as an overarching framework that could lead theorists and therapists from the understanding of the normal personality, through the process of conceptualizing and assessing psychopathology in general and personality disorders in specific, to the end goal of developing and implementing an integrative treatment plan. Such a personality-guided psychotherapy (Millon, 1999) flows through a series of stages, each of which is derived from the preceding stage, and each of which is bonded to, and supports, the stage that follows. Millon (2000) argued convincingly that only such a synergistic version of psychotherapy could treat the person in his or her entirety, and only such a person-centered approach can be a stable and enduring basis for true psychotherapy integration:

> Current debates regarding whether "technical eclecticism" or "integrative therapy" is the more suitable designation for our approach are mistaken. These discussants have things backward, so to speak, because they start the task of intervention by focusing first on technique or methodology. Integration does not adhere in treatment methods or in their theories, be they eclectic or otherwise. *Integration inheres in the person, not in our theories or in the modalities we prefer.* It stems from the dynamics and interwoven character of the patient's traits and symptoms. Our task as therapists is *not* to see how we can blend intrinsically discordant models of therapeutic technique, but to match the pattern of features that characterize each patient, and *then* to select treatment goals and tactics that mirror this pattern optimally. It is for this reason, among others, that we have chosen to employ the label "personality-guided synergistic therapy" to represent our brand of integrative treatment. (p. 49, italics in original)

By placing the locus of integration within the person who is the patient and in that person's interactions with the environment at any level, therapists are then free to work with any clinically significant "part-functions" such as unconscious processes, cognitive distortions, the family, or the social, economic, and political conditions that impact on the patient. Synergistic therapy offers a uniquely tailored, custom-fitted idiographic integrative psychotherapy that is based on empirically derived and tested theoretical principles and assessment instruments. This integration of the idiographic and the nomothetic avoids the pitfalls of each stance: the purely clinical basis of much of the former and the strictures and surface orientation of many empirically supported psychotherapies.

Millon's (2000) vision of this most optimal form of psychotherapy integration overlaps with the "local clinical scientist model" suggested by Trierweiler and Stricker (1998), which also attempts to base a person-focused approach on a nomothetic assessment foundation. It also dovetails well with another trend in psychotherapy integration, namely, that described by Bohart and Tallman (1999) as the "active client" model. In that model, promulgated by those authors and by others (Gold, 2000; Hubble et al., 1999), the patient is considered to be the source of, and the leader in, promoting integrative work. The therapist's task lies in understanding the patient's unique clinical needs, which can be derived only from understanding his or her personality and adaptive goals.

Millon is not the only student of the personality disorders who has called for an integrative, personological guided treatment for such patients. Livesley (2001) concluded a review of the extant literature on personality disorders by suggesting that the most effective treatment for these complex forms of psychopathology would be a model in which diverse interventions, based on an evidence-based personality theory, are implemented in a flexible way that recognizes the individuality and unique needs of each patient. Clarkson, McMain, Weston, and Young (2003), all recognized as authorities on research and treatment in this area, concluded a recent public symposium on progress in work with personality disorders by noting that the consensus in the field is that integration is necessary and the most advantageous way to think and work with this population.

PSYCHOTHERAPY INTEGRATION AND THE TREATMENT OF PERSONALITY: A REVIEW OF CONTEMPORARY TREATMENT MODELS

When we review the current status of psychotherapy integration against the standards set by Millon's (2000) proposal, we find a field that has made some significant progress toward synergistic, personality-guided psychotherapies for the personality disorders. A number of integrative psychotherapists have offered theoretically guided models of psychotherapy that approach, and that may to some degree satisfy, Millon's (1988, 2000) description and criteria. Several of these integrative models are reviewed here.

An early contribution to the psychotherapy integration literature that exemplifies a theory-driven, person-oriented approach was Guidano's (1987) cognitive-developmental model. Guidano was a careful student of Bowlby's (1980) innovations in attachment theory and perhaps the first psychotherapist to adapt this theory to uses within the perspective of psychotherapy integration. Cognitive-developmental theory is based largely on, and extends significantly, the concept of *internal working models* that was introduced by Bowlby. This term refers to conscious and unconscious patterns of organizing experience and of representing the self and significant persons in the patient's life. Internal working models are relatively realistic, though highly personalized, abstractions of repetitive experiences of attachment and exploration on the part of the child and of the attachment figure's typical responses to those behaviors.

By expanding Bowlby's (1980) research on patterns of secure and insecure attachment, Guidano (1987) was able to develop a taxonomy of early childhood attachment experiences that lead to psychological health or to psychopathology, resulting patterns of information processing that typify various psychopathological entities, and a cluster of critical psychological structures that organize information processing and the person's working models. In particular, Guidano was interested in what he termed "core structures," which were self-images and representations of significant others in the patient's life that were formed early in life in the context of highly charged attachments situations. These core representations remain operative outside of awareness and are not subject to revision during later periods of development. From this theoretical perspective and classificatory framework, Guidano was able to offer a technical framework that integrated a variety of intervention strategies. The goals of these interventions moved beyond surface concerns with overt problems and symptoms to reaching and modifying the central, core structures that were the key underlying issues.

A related, contemporary approach to personality disorders is Young's (Young, Klosko, & Weishaar, 2003) schema-focused therapy. This approach is based on an integrative theory of personality that, very much like Guidano's theory, is inspired by and apparently derived from a synthesis of cognitive, developmental, and attachment theories. Young et al. (2003) posit that maladaptive schemas lie beneath all behavioral, cognitive, emotional, and motivation components of psychopathology. Schemas are cognitive-emotional structures that govern the processing, patterning, and retention of all experience, past and present, and are identified clinically through the exploration of pervasive, emotionally tinged themes about the self and about important persons in the patient's past and current life. Maladaptive schemas are formed in the context of important interpersonal relationships in which the child's needs consistently are not met. Once established as the person's predominant structure for processing experience, maladaptive schemas give rise to redundant, repetitive patterns of relating and of constructing experience. These patterns usually express and confirm the patient's darkest, most pessimistic, and fearsome expectations about the world, themselves, other people, and the future.

Young and his colleagues (2003) have identified particular groups or clusters of schemas that may be linked to particular forms of psychopathology, most notably to the range of personality disorders. Schema therapists note, in agreement with the sentiments expressed by Millon (1988, 2000) and others cited in this chapter, that symptom-focused, single-modality psychotherapy is ineffective with, and clinically inappropriate for, the complex structural, information-processing issues that promote and maintain pathologies of personality. The assessment of schemas leads sequentially into the choice of interventions, which are selected once the patient's underlying constellation of pathogenic schemas has been identified.

Gold and Stricker (1993, 2001) described an integrative psychotherapy for personality disorders that is based on an expanded version of psychodynamic personality theory that they called the "three-tier model" (Stricker & Gold, 1988). This three-tier theory (behavior, cognition, psychodynamics) allowed the therapist to integrate a variety of nonanalytic ideas and methods in a flexible but systematic way into psychoanalytically oriented work.

This conceptual foundation resembles and was influenced by Wachtel's (1977) theory of cyclical psychodynamics, which posits that unconscious processes and structures (motivations, conflicts, and self- and object representations) both initiate thinking and behavior and are maintained by these experiences and ways of functioning. Central to this model is the traditional psychoanalytic notion that those memories and experiences that are painful and that contradict our cherished notions of who we are and of who our parents and other loved ones were are excluded from consciousness, yet continue to influence our thinking, behavior, and emotional experience. Yet, the three-tier model states that consciousness and its components (emotion, cognition, and perception) and behavior play significant roles in personality and psychopathology and often require direct intervention as well. Furthermore, a critical assumption in this theory is that there are dynamic linkages between the tiers that play significant roles in reinforcing and maintaining phenomena at all levels. In other words, dysfunctional cognitive processes and disturbed interpersonal patterns of relating often express and stabilize unconscious conflicts and representations and prevent interpretive work from being completely effective. Problems in thinking, feeling, and acting may reflect the disharmony among personality components that has been provoked through developmental failures and by ongoing psychodynamic issues, requiring a psychotherapy that can go beyond the limits of traditional psychodynamic psychotherapy. In this model, personality disorders are understood to be resultant of complex patterns of living with and relating to other people, which are unsuccessful and pained because of early failures of learning and development (Gold & Stricker, 1993; Stricker & Gold, 1988, 2002). Such an individual cannot adapt comfortably and successfully to the demands of inner and outer reality: to regulate emotion, to delay gratification and tolerate frustration, to have true concern and empathy for others, to perceive himself or herself realistically in the face of failure or success, and so on.

These extreme affective, cognitive, and behavioral difficulties manifested in and outside therapy by personality-disordered patients are the consequences of early, frequent exposure to interpersonal situations in which their limited adaptive capacities are overtaxed. While this approach shares the view of traditional psychodynamic therapies that many of these deficits can be "filled in" through insight and through corrective experience in the therapeutic relationship, this is not always the case. Patients with personality disorders often require a structured, didactic approach and the chance to learn and to practice those skills with which their early interpersonal environment did not equip them. In particular, Gold and Stricker (1993, 2001) employed active interventions, drawn from cognitive-behavioral and experiential therapies, to address components of personality disorders that may not be effectively remediated via traditional psychodynamic work. These components include:

- Using active interventions as a source of corrective emotional experiences and new object representations.
- Enhancing the therapeutic alliance by giving patients more immediate tools for managing painful emotions, symptoms, and relationship patterns.
- The active management and resolution of negative transferences.
- The resolution of defensive and resistive (noncompliant) interactions by shifting interventions sets.
- Exposure to and extinction of anxiety.
- Correction of developmental deficits through skill building and the provision of success experiences.
- Resolution of treatment destructive behaviors.

When the therapist sets out to help the patient in this way, a number of therapeutic processes are set in motion. The patient attains new cognitive, interpersonal, emotional, and behavioral skills. In addition, the therapist's active interventions can be the source of a powerful corrective experience in which representations of self and others are reworked in benign and positive ways.

Cognitive-analytic therapy (CAT; Ryle, 2001; Ryle & Low, 1993) is one of the more fully investigated and clinically elaborated integrative therapies that have been applied specifically to personality disorders and to borderline personality disorder in particular. Ryle was explicit in his assertion that an effective integrative therapy must be based on a comprehensive theory of personality that "must encompass the full complexity of being human" (p. 401). The integrative model of personality that informs and guides the cognitive-analytic therapist is a synthesis of psychoanalytic object relations theory and personal construct psychology. This personology elucidates the complex interrelationships between the way that the individual consciously processes information about the self and others and the unconscious developmental antecedents of the person's cognitive structures, beliefs, assumptions, and role definitions. The central theoretical concept used in this theory is the procedural sequence object relations model (PSORM), which refers to the unconscious representations of self and of others through which the person sequentially processes present-day experiences to construct and elaborate the meaning of ongoing interpersonal interactions (Ryle, 2001). The person's unconscious representations derive from childhood interactions with parents, other caretakers, and peers. These sequences of meaning construction manifest themselves in *reciprocal role procedures,* which are behaviors that are designed to express certain interpersonal needs and to evoke predictable and desirable responses from the other person. Reciprocal role procedures thus serve the functions of establishing and maintaining ongoing relationships and of organizing and controlling an individual's self-image and self-states. As we have seen previously, this integrative model leans heavily on concepts that are seemingly identical to attachment theory and that dovetail well with Millon's (2000) emphasis on the survival value of personality disorders.

Cognitive-analytic therapists are alert to certain behavioral patterns that denote maladaptive experiential processing and/or interpersonal engagement. These patterns include *traps, dilemmas,* and *snags.* Traps are acts that are prompted by negative interpersonal assumptions, with such acts leading to social consequences that seem to confirm those assumptions. Dilemmas are situations in which the person's choices of action are restricted to opposite or polarized opportunities. The discarding of healthy goals due to the person's perception that these goals are unacceptable to the self or others is labeled snags (Ryle, 2001; Ryle & Low, 1993). Patients with borderline personality disorder are assumed to experience many difficult traps, dilemmas, and snags due to their inability to maintain an integrated self-state. This failure of self-integration reflects the internalization of contradictory procedural sequences due to repeated, traumatic early experiences. The unintegrated self of the personality-disordered patient also is a product of the partially dissociated connections among reciprocal role procedures, which in themselves are frequently extreme and maladaptive (Ryle, 1996). Such a description again echoes the arguments made earlier in this chapter, wherein the lack of harmony and integration among the varied components of personality were offered as the critical structural components of the personality disorders.

Cognitive-analytic interventions are derived from this extensive, theoretically guided assessment model and are aimed at helping the patient to identify and work his or her way out of snags, traps, and dilemmas and to modify positively and integrate less extreme reciprocal role procedures. As the patient achieves greater interpersonal comfort and success, the work moves toward revision and reconstruction of the underlying representational structures and procedural sequences (Ryle, 2001).

Dialectical behavior therapy (DBT) is a system of integrative psychotherapy that originally was specified for chronically suicidal and "parasuicidal" or self-mutilating patients (Linehan, 1987) and has been widely studied and applied to borderline personality disorder (Linehan, 1993). Dialectical behavior therapy is not built on an explicit theory of personality, but in reading Linehan's (1993) descriptions of the etiology of borderline personality disorder, it is clear that she relies on a cognitive social learning model that is similar in its content, if not in its terminology, to the cognitive-developmental models proposed by Guidano (1987) and Young et al. (2003). Linehan and her colleagues (Robins, Ivanoff, & Linehan, 2001) have elaborated a highly specific theory of the development of this form of psychopathology. Borderline personality disorder is understood within a biosocial framework, that is, this pathology is understood to derive from the repeated interactions of a person who has difficulty regulating his or her emotions with an environment that is invalidating, dismissive, or punitive of the person's emotions and thoughts. The patient's emotional dysregulation may result from temperamental factors (low thresholds of emotion, rapid affective response rates, and intense levels of emotional reactivity) or from the failure to learn to modulate these emotions (Robins et al., 2001). Therapy in this model aims at correcting the patient factors that feed this pathology: validating the patient's unique perspective and experiences, while teaching tactics and strategies that better enable the patient to control, tolerate, and regulate his or her emotions. Dialectical behavior therapists rely on the establishment of the validating relationship to assist the patient in forming a viable therapeutic contract and to serve as the interpersonal foundation of the patient's active involvement in self-monitoring and in learning and applying new skills. Therapists use their assessment of the specifics of the patient's difficulties in self-regulation to suggest any viable technique drawn from the broad repertoire of cognitive-behavior therapy, as well as teaching Zen philosophy and meditation as aids in helping the patient to accept and tolerate painful aspects of reality (Robins et al., 2001).

Magnavita (2002) introduced a new therapy for complex clinical syndromes such as personality disorders, known as *integrative relational psychotherapy*. This theoretical and therapeutic synthesis is described by its author as a biopsychosocial approach in which basic psychodynamic concepts drawn from ego psychology, self psychology, drive theory, and object relations theory are integrated with systems concepts drawn from the work of family systems theorists such as Ackerman, Bowen, Bateson, and Kaslow. This theoretical integration leads to a personality theory and diagnostic system in which personality-disordered patients are assessed within a systemic conceptual framework that allows the categorization of the variables that lead to and maintain personality disorders. Magnavita introduced the term *dysfunctional personologic system* to describe the theoretically derived system of intrapsychic, interpersonal, and environmental processes that make up the various personality disorders. This therapy relies on what Magnavita has described as restructuring methods: interventions that are aimed at the systematic reorganization and modification of patterns of organizing experience and of integrating important relationships. The ultimate targets of all therapeutic efforts at restructuring are the schemas that organize and process new experience and that sort that experience into maladaptive or new and productive units of meaning. Magnavita suggests that the 10 dysfunctional personologic systems that he has identified can be conceptualized as having unique profiles of maladaptive cognitive, affective, and relational schema.

This therapy allows the therapist to target specific intrapersonal, interpersonal, familial, and larger units of person-environmental dysfunction for intervention once the specific dysfunctional personologic systems have been studied and carefully assessed. Therapists who employ this model may choose to intervene through techniques that are aimed at defense restructuring, affective restructuring, cognitive restructuring, dyadic restructuring, triangular relational restructuring, and self-other restructuring. As Millon (2000) suggested, the emphasis on particular symptoms and intervention selection follows from the patient's unique configuration of dysfunctional schema and the problem areas that derive from these information-processing structures.

Allen (2003) described a theoretically integrated psychotherapy for borderline personality disorder that is based on his model of unified psychotherapy (Allen, 1993).

This model attempts to bridge the gaps between individual and family-systems approaches to the treatment of severe, chronic psychopathology. Allen (1993) suggested that the three main clinical phenomena that bring these patients to treatment—namely, chronic emotional dysregulation, repetitive self-destructive behaviors, and chronic, visible familial conflict—could and should be seen as distinct but related manifestations of a common underlying set of psychological and interactional processes. In his later work, he specifically applied this conceptual formulation to the treatment of borderline personality disorder. Allen's (2003) clinical focus and strategies are concerned with identifying and resolving the "services" that members of a family or other social group provide for one another. The concept of services refers to the ways in which each member of the system behaves and interacts with people within and outside that system in the face of new adaptive pressures and changing environmental demands.

He argued that the dramatic symptoms of the patient with borderline personality disorder thus need to be understood within this context: How do these problems help this family system to maintain its expectable level of homeostasis, and how and where and with which set of interventions must the therapist enter and try to change that system?

Only when such interpersonal services are addressed can the patient free himself or herself of these influences and move on developmentally to explore other experiential, behavioral, and adaptive options.

CONCLUSIONS

Have we arrived at a truly integrative, synergistic psychotherapy for the personality disorders? It seems very clear that Millon (1988, 2000) and others who have called for an integrative treatment for the personality disorders have not been unheeded prophets, preaching in the wilderness. This very fruitful area has yielded a number of promising psychotherapies, which address at least several of the orchestral sections of personality that are discordant, even if, as yet, no single integrative treatment has managed to include and to conduct the entire orchestra.

There are still a number of limitations to these existing models other than the scope of their theoretical and clinical applications. Only two of the models reviewed in this chapter have been subjected to rigorous empirical testing: dialectical behavior therapy and cognitive-analytic therapy. The other approaches have been tested clinically by their authors and colleagues and are in need of such grounding in research.

In addition, it is unclear whether any of these therapies are applicable to the entire range of personality disorders—a question muddied by the lack of empirical support for the current *DSM*'s nosology of personality disorders.

Finally, this group of integrative psychotherapies runs the risk of developing into a new generation of segregated, sectarian schools, each with its own theory of personality and clinical methodology, much as did their psychoanalytic, humanistic, behavioral, cognitive, and systems predecessors. If this trend continues, in the future we will have a new, discordant orchestra of psychotherapies, which may be integrative, but which continues the tradition of remaining separate from other progress in the field. In this chapter, an attempt has been made to point out briefly where these therapies overlap and resemble one another. Several of these models rely explicitly on Bowlby's (1980) classic work on attachment theory, while others seem implicitly to have incorporated this perspective. Several of these models also share Millon's (1990) evolutionary, survival-value-based approach to personality and psychopathology. Yet, there is little cross-referencing among approaches. Such lack of meta-integration among these explorers of new treatment may keep us all from reaching the goal of a truly integrative, synergistic treatment.

REFERENCES

Alexander, F. (1963). The dynamics of psychotherapy in the light of learning theory. *American Journal of Psychiatry, 120,* 440–448.

Allen, D. M. (1993). Unified psychotherapy. In G. Stricker & J. Gold (Eds.), *Comprehensive handbook of psychotherapy integration* (pp. 125–137). New York: Plenum Press.

Allen, D. M. (2003). *Psychotherapy with borderline patients.* Washington, DC: American Psychological Association.

Beier, E. G. (1966). *The silent language of psychotherapy.* Chicago: Aldine.

Bergin, A. E. (1968). Techniques for improving desensitization via warmth, empathy, and emotional re-experiencing of hierarchy events. In R. Rubin & C. M Franks (Eds.), *Advances in behavior therapy* (pp. 20–33). New York: Academic Press.

Beutler, L. E., & Hodgson, A. B. (1993). Prescriptive psychotherapy. In G. Stricker & J. Gold (Eds.), *Comprehensive handbook of psychotherapy integration* (pp. 151–163). New York: Plenum Press.

Bohart, A. C., & Tallman, K. (1999). *How clients make therapy work.* Washington, DC: American Psychological Association.

Bowlby, J. (1980). *Attachment and loss: Volume III. Loss: Sadness and depression.* New York: Basic Books.

Clarkson, J., McMain, S., Weston, D., & Young, J. (2003, May). *Progress in research and treatment with personality disorders.* Panel discussion, 20th annual conference of the Society for the Exploration of Personality Disorders, New York.

Dollard, J., & Miller, N. E. (1950). *Personality and psychotherapy.* New York: McGraw-Hill.

Feather, B. W., & Rhodes, J. W. (1973). Psychodynamic behavior therapy: I. Theory and rationale. *Archives of General Psychiatry, 26,* 496–502.

French, T. M. (1933). Interrelations between psychoanalysis and the experimental work of Pavlov. *American Journal of Psychiatry, 89,* 1165–1203.

Gold, J. (1996). *Key concepts in psychotherapy integration.* New York: Plenum Press.

Gold, J. (2000). The psychodynamics of the patient's activity. *Journal of Psychotherapy Integration, 10,* 207–220.

Gold, J., & Stricker, G. (1993). Psychotherapy integration with personality disorders. In G. Stricker & J. Gold (Eds.), *Comprehensive handbook of psychotherapy integration* (pp. 323–336). New York: Plenum Press.

Gold, J., & Stricker, G. (2001). Relational psychoanalysis as a foundation for assimilative integration. *Journal of Psychotherapy Integration, 11,* 47–63.

Guidano, V. (1987). *Complexity of the self.* New York: Guilford Press.

Hubble, M., Duncan, B., & Miller, S. (1999). *The heart and soul of change.* Washington, DC: American Psychological Association.

Lazarus, A. A. (2002). The multimodal assessment therapy approach. In F. W. Kaslow (Editor-in-Chief) & J. Lebow (Vol. Ed.), *Comprehensive handbook of psychotherapy: Integrative/eclectic* (Vol. 4, pp. 241–254). Hoboken, NJ: Wiley.

Linehan, M. M. (1987). Dialectical behavior therapy: A cognitive-behavioral approach to parasuicide. *Journal of Personality Disorders, 1,* 328–333.

Linehan, M. M. (1993). *Cognitive-behavioral treatment of borderline personality disorder.* New York: Guilford Press.

Livesley, W. J. (2001). A framework for an integrated approach to treatment. In W. J. Livesley (Ed.), *Handbook of personality disorders* (pp. 570–600). New York: Guilford Press.

Magnavita, J. J. (2002). Relational psychodynamics for complex clinical syndromes. In F. W. Kaslow (Editor-in-Chief) & J. J. Magnavita (Vol. Ed.), *Handbook of psychotherapy: Vol. 1. Psychodynamic/object relations* (pp. 435–453). Hoboken, NJ: Wiley.

Marks, I. M., & Gelder, M. G. (1966). Common ground between behavior therapy and psychodynamic methods. *British Journal of Medical Psychology, 39,* 11–23.

Millon, T. (1988). Personologic psychotherapy: Ten commandments for a posteclectic approach to integrative treatment. *Psychotherapy, 25,* 209–219.

Millon, T. (1990). *Toward a new personology: An evolutionary model.* New York: Wiley.

Millon, T. (1999). *Personality-guided psychotherapy.* New York: Wiley.

Millon, T. (2000). Toward a new model of integrative psychotherapy: Psychosynergy. *Journal of Psychotherapy Integration, 10,* 37–54.

Millon, T., Everly, G., & Davis, R. (1993). How can knowledge of psychopathology facilitate psychotherapy integration: A view from the personality disorders. *Journal of Psychotherapy Integration, 3,* 331–352.

Prochaska, J. O., & DiClemente, C. C. (2002). Transtheoretical therapy. In F. W. Kaslow (Editor-in-Chief) & J. Lebow (Vol. Ed.), *Comprehensive handbook of psychotherapy: Integrative/Eclectic* (Vol. 4, pp. 165–184). Hoboken, NJ: Wiley.

Robins, C. J., Ivanoff, A. M., & Linehan, M. M. (2001). Dialectical behavior therapy. In W. J. Livesley (Ed.), *Handbook of personality disorders* (pp. 437–459). New York: Guilford Press.

Rosenzweig, S. (1936). Some implicit common factors in diverse methods of psychotherapy. *American Journal of Orthopsychiatry, 6,* 412–415.

Ryle, A. (1996). Cognitive-analytic therapy: Theory and practice and its application to the treatment of a personality disorder patient. *Journal of Psychotherapy Integration, 6,* 139–172.

Ryle, A. (2001). Cognitive-analytic therapy. In W. J. Livesley (Ed.), *Handbook of personality disorders* (pp. 400–413). New York: Guilford Press.

Ryle, A., & Low, J. (1993). Cognitive-analytic therapy. In G. Stricker & J. Gold (Eds.), *Comprehensive handbook of psychotherapy integration* (pp. 87–100). New York: Plenum Press.

Sears, R. R. (1944). Experimental analysis of psychoanalytic phenomena. In J. Hunt (Ed.), *Personality and the behavior disorders* (pp. 191–206). New York: Ronald Press.

Stricker, G., & Gold, J. (1988). A psychodynamic approach to the personality disorders. *Journal of Personality Disorders, 2,* 350–359.

Stricker, G., & Gold, J. (2002). An assimilative approach to integrative psychodynamic psychotherapy. In F. W. Kaslow (Editor-in-Chief) & J. Lebow (Vol. Ed.), *Comprehensive handbook of psychotherapy: Integrative/eclectic* (Vol. 4, pp. 295–316). Hoboken, NJ: Wiley.

Trierweiler, S. J., & Stricker, G. (1998). *The scientific practice of professional psychology.* New York: Plenum Press.

Wachtel, P. L. (1977). *Psychoanalysis and behavior therapy: Toward an integration.* New York: Basic Books.

Young, J. E., Klosko, J. S., & Weishaar, M. (2003). *Schema therapy: A practitioner's guide.* New York: Guilford Press.

PART VI

Future Perspective

REFLECTIONS ON THE FUTURE OF PERSONOLOGY AND PSYCHOPATHOLOGY

THEODORE MILLON

Significant in my life has been the opportunity to participate in the renaissance of personology as a field of study, a subject given its name by Henry Murray some 65 years ago (1938). Trends that led to a decline in personologic studies have reversed in the past two decades. Themes that were given short shrift in the 1960s and 1970s have not only reemerged but also moved into the limelight, especially in the clinical area. Some 40 to 50 years ago, the enthusiasm that once characterized personologic theories and instruments was buffeted by trivial, as well as just, criticisms. Once preeminent ideas and techniques were sundered by the value schisms that inevitably separate generations. Hence, the marvelous theories (e.g., Freud, Jung, Adler, Horney, Sullivan) and incisive methods (e.g., Rorschach, TAT, Bender-Gestalt, Figure Drawing) of yesteryear faded inexorably to a status befitting quaint historic notions and intriguing, albeit ancient, tools.

Were the powers that once proposed comprehensive personologic ideas a fantasy, impertinent, if not grandiose, thoughts by an immature and arrogant young science? Were these theories and instruments ill-considered and presumptuous aspirations of ill-informed and naive, if not cavalier, speculators who asserted knowledge to themselves far greater than "the facts" would warrant?

The splendidly astute and discriminating clinical portrayals of early and mid-twentieth century thinkers, each of whom stirred our curiosities and inspired us to further our desire to know, had become outdated curiosities, grandiose speculations that were to be replaced by tightly focused and empirically anchored constructs. The conceptual models and cogent insights of these early theorists resonated with our own personally more prosaic efforts to penetrate and give order to the mysteries of our patients' psychic worlds. But personality and psychopathology were no longer to be seen as an integrated gestalt, a dynamic and complex system comprising more than the sum of its mere parts. The pendulum swung toward empiricism and positivism; only what was "observable" came into ascendancy. Personality was segmented into its ostensive constituents and best disassembled into its component parts. Given that most quasi-empirical critics were nomothetically rather than idiographically inclined, they made a shambles of the "personality-as-a-coherent-whole" theories that nurtured those of us who began our clinical studies in the immediate post-World War II era.

HOW DO WE MOVE THE STUDY OF PERSONOLOGY AND PSYCHOPATHOLOGY INTO THE TWENTY-FIRST CENTURY?

Change in the fortunes of these subjects began to brew in the 1970s. Slow though this awakening may have been, there were signs of emerging new ideas and challenges that promised a revivification of the luster of the 1940s and 1950s. By virtue of time, reflection, and, not the least, a growing disenchantment with available alternatives, the place of these subjects began to regain its formerly solid footing. Especially promising was the observation that the essential element that gave substance to personology—the fact that people exhibit distinctive and abiding characteristics—has held fast, despite the attacks of its most fervent critics. This durability attests, at the very least, to its intuitive consonance with authentic observation. Its renaissance is particularly impressive when we consider the vast number of popular psychological and psychiatric ideas that have faded to a status consonant with their trivial character or have succumbed, under the weight of their scientific inefficacy, to scholarly boredom.

Personology and psychopathology weathered its mettlesome assaults and underwent a wide-ranging resurgence in the 1970s and 1980s. Notable here were the formulations of contemporary analytic theorists, particularly Kernberg (1975) and Kohut (1971). No less significant were theoretical ideas posited by a reactivated interpersonal school, led by post-Sullivan and post-Leary theorists such as Benjamin (1984), Wiggins (1982), and Kiesler (1986). Also notable were the formulations of social learning theorists such as Rotter (1954) and Bandura (1977), who "reconnected" behaviorism to cognitivism. Similarly significant was the bridging of neurophysiologic thinking to personologic processes, as in the work of Cloninger (1987), Siever and Davis (1991), and Zuckerman (1991). No less relevant to advances in the field was the special role assigned personality disorders in the multiaxial classification system of the *Diagnostic and Statistical Manual of Mental Disorders,* third and fourth editions (*DSM-III, DSM-IV*), and the *International Classification of Diseases* (ICD-10), each pointing to the growing diagnostic importance of these syndromes. The organization of the International Society for the Study of Personality Disorders in 1988, the initial publication of the *Journal of Personality Disorders* in 1987, and the cosponsorship of an International Congress on the Personality Disorders by the World Psychiatric Association in 1988 added further to the status and cross-cultural importance of personology as a science.

As the inherent significance of personality regained its former standing and became broadly established, perhaps its erstwhile adversaries soon will discover the merits of a psychoanalytic-cognitive-behavioral-neurochemical synthesis of personologic and psychopathologic functions, as well as promulgate the efficacy of parallel multidimensional approaches to treatment.

INTEGRATING THE SCIENCES OF NATURE

The twenty-first century will be a time of rapid scientific and clinical advances, a time for ventures designed to bridge new ideas and syntheses. The intersection between the study of psychopathology and the study of personology will continue to be a sphere of significant intellectual and clinical activity. Theoretical formulations that bridge this intersection represent a major and valued conceptual step, but to limit our scientific efforts to this junction alone will lead us to overlook other crucial elements in promoting fundamental progress, especially those realms that are provided by our connection to more mature sciences (e.g., physics and evolutionary biology). By failing to coordinate personologic and psychopathologic propositions to principles established in these advanced disciplines, our science may continue to float horizontally, that is, at its current level.

A major goal for the twenty-first century will be to connect the conceptual structure of our field to its foundations in the natural sciences, a goal akin to Freud's abandoned "Project for a Scientific Psychology" (1895) and a parallel effort seen in Wilson's highly controversial work on sociobiology (1975). Both were worthy endeavors to advance our understanding by exploring interconnections among human disciplines that evolved ostensibly unrelated bodies of research and manifestly dissimilar languages.

It seems necessary that we should go beyond our current disciplinary boundaries, more specifically to explore carefully reasoned, as well as intuitive, hypotheses that draw their principles, if not their substance, from more established, adjacent sciences. Such steps may not only bear new conceptual fruits but also provide a foundation that can undergird and guide our own discipline's explorations. Much of personology and psychopathology remains adrift, divorced from broader spheres of scientific knowledge, isolated from firmly grounded, if not universal, principles, leading us to continue building the patchwork quilt of concepts and data domains that characterizes our field. Preoccupied with but a small part of nature's larger puzzle or fearing accusations of reductionism, we fail to draw on the rich possibilities to be found in other realms of scholarly pursuit. With few exceptions, cohering concepts that would connect our subject to those of its sister sciences have not been adequately developed.

And what better sphere is there within the psychological sciences to undertake such syntheses than with the subject matter of personology? Persons are the only organically integrated system in the psychological domain, evolved through the millennia and inherently created from birth as natural entities, rather than culture-bound or experience-derived attributions. The intrinsic cohesion of persons is not a mere rhetorical construction, but an authentic substantive unity. Personologic features may often prove dissonant and may be partitioned conceptually for pragmatic or scientific purposes, but they are segments of an inseparable biopsychosocial entity.

To take this view is not to argue that different spheres of scientific inquiry should be equated, nor is it to seek a single, overarching conceptual system encompassing fields such as biology, psychology, and sociology. Arguing in favor of establishing explicit links among these subject domains calls neither for a reductionistic philosophy, a belief in substantive identicality, nor efforts to so fashion them by formal logic. Rather, we should aspire to their substantive concordance, empirical consistency, conceptual interfacing, convergent dialogues, and mutual enlightenment.

CONSTRUCTING A BLUEPRINT FOR A CLINICAL SCIENCE

As I have argued recently (Millon, 2000, 2003), if personology and psychopathology are ever to become a full-fledged science and profession, rather than a piecemeal potpourri of miscellaneous observations and ideas, the overall and ultimate architecture of the science must be refashioned, that is, given a scaffold or framework within which its elements can be properly located and ultimately coordinated. For example, our official diagnostic system should not stand alone, unconnected to other relevant realms of our clinical or scientific discourse; that is, it should be anchored to a foundation of an empirically supportable theory, on the one hand, and prove useful for formal assessment and therapeutic action, on the other. Comprehensively, the overall goal of our efforts should seek to coordinate the separate components and functions that comprise our field, namely, their relation to the universal laws of nature, their explanatory theories, their derived classification scheme, their diagnostic assessment instruments, and their therapeutic intervention techniques. As recorded in Millon (2000), rather than developing independently and being left to stand as autonomous and largely unconnected functions, a truly mature clinical science, one that is designed to create a synergistic bond among its components, will explicitly embody the following five elements:

1. *Universal scientific principles:* Science grounded in the ubiquitous laws of nature. Despite varied forms of expression (in physics, chemistry, psychology, for example), these principles should reflect fundamental evolutionary processes and thereby provide an undergirding framework for guiding and constructing subject-oriented theories.

2. *Subject-oriented theories:* Explanatory and heuristic conceptual schemas of nature's expression in what we call personology and psychopathology. These theories should be consistent with established knowledge in both its own and related sciences (e.g., biology, sociology) and from which reasonably accurate propositions concerning clinical conditions can be both deduced and understood, enabling thereby the development of a formal classification system.

3. *A taxonomy of personality patterns and clinical syndromes:* A classification and nosology derived logically from a coordinated personology/psychopathology theory. These should provide a cohesive organization within which its major categories can readily be grouped and differentiated, permitting thereby the development of relevant and coordinated assessment instruments.

4. *Integrated clinical and personality assessment instruments:* Tools that are empirically grounded and quantitatively sensitive. These should enable the theory's propositions and hypotheses to be adequately investigated and evaluated and the categories comprising its classification schema to be readily identified (diagnosed) and measured (dimensionalized), specifying therefrom target areas for interventions.

5. *Synergistic therapeutic interventions:* Coordinated strategies and modalities of treatment. These should be designed in accord with the theory, incorporate and synthesize diverse therapeutic techniques (interpersonal, cognitive, intrapsychic, biochemical), and be oriented to modify problematic clinical and personologic characteristics, consonant with professional standards and social responsibilities.

The coordination of all five elements (i.e., making them reciprocally enhancing and mutually reinforcing) constitutes the essence of a mature clinical science. Working together, these components and functions should produce integrated knowledge that is greater than the sum of its individual constituents. What should be aspired to is the synthesis of clinical elements that have been disconnected and pursued independently in the twentieth century. Just as each person is an intrinsic unity, each component of a clinical science should not remain a separate element of a potpourri of unconnected parts. Rather, each facet of our clinical work—its principles, theories, taxonomy, instrumentation, and therapy—should be integrated into a gestalt, a coupled and synergistic unity in which the whole will be coordinated and become more informative and useful than its individual parts.

ON THE IMPORTANCE OF A GUIDING THEORY

It was Kurt Lewin (1936) who wrote almost 70 years ago that "there is nothing so practical as a good theory." Theory, when properly fashioned, ultimately provides more simplicity and clarity than unintegrated and scattered information. Unrelated knowledge and techniques, especially those based on surface similarities, are a sign of a primitive science, as has been effectively argued by modern philosophers of science (Hempel, 1961; Quine, 1961).

All natural sciences have organizing principles that not only create order but also provide the basis for generating hypotheses and stimulating new knowledge. A good theory not only summarizes and incorporates extant knowledge but also is heuristic, that is, has "systematic import," as Hempel has phrased it, in that it originates and develops new observations and new methods.

It is unfortunate that the number of theories that have been advanced to explain personologic and psychopathologic functions is proportional to the internecine squabbling found in the clinical literature. Paroxysms of "scientific virtue" and pieties of "methodological purity" rarely are exclaimed by theorists themselves, but by their less creative disciples. Toward the ostensive end of pragmatic sobriety, those of an antitheory bias have sought to persuade the profession of the failings of premature formalization, warning that we cannot arrive at a desirable future by lifting science by its own bootstraps, so to speak. To them, there is no way to traverse the road other sciences have traveled without paying the dues of an arduous program of empirical research. Formalized axiomatics, they say, must await the accumulation of hard evidence that is simply not yet in. Shortcutting the route with ill-timed theories will lead us down primrose paths, preoccupying our efforts as we wend fruitlessly through endless detours, each of which could be averted by holding fast to an empiricist philosophy.

No one need argue against the view that theories that float on their own, unconcerned with the empirical domain, should be seen as the fatuous achievements they are. They make a travesty of the virtues of a truly generative conceptual system. Formal theory should not be pushed far beyond the data, and its derivations should be linked wherever feasible to established observations. Such a theoretical framework can prove a compelling tool for coordinating complex and diverse observations. By probing beneath surface impressions to inner structures and processes, previously isolated facts and difficult to fathom data may refine previous work, expose new relationships, and yield clearer meanings. Progress, however, does not advance far by brute empiricism, that is, by merely piling up more descriptive and more experimental data. What is elaborated and refined by theory is "making sense" of the data, seeing their relationships more plainly, conceptualizing their categories more accurately, and creating greater overall coherence to their subject, that is, integrating the elements of data in a logical, consistent, and intelligible fashion.

The formal structure of most personologic and psychopathologic theories of the past has been haphazard and unsystematic; concepts often were vague, and procedures by which empirical consequences were derived often were tenuous. Instead of presenting an orderly arrangement of concepts and propositions by which hypotheses could be clearly derived, many theories were composed of a loosely formulated pastiche of opinions, analogies, and speculations. Brilliant and insightful as many of these were, they often left the reader dazzled rather than illuminated. Ambiguous principles in structurally weak theories make it impossible to derive systematic and logical hypotheses; this results in conflicting derivations and circular reasoning. Many theories in both personology and psychopathology generated ingenious deductions, but few of these ideas could be attributed to their structure,

the clarity of their central principles, the precision of their concepts, or their formal procedures for hypothesis derivation. It is here where the concepts and laws of adjacent sciences
might come into play, providing models of structure and derivation, as well as substantive
ideas and data that could undergird and parallel the principles and observations of our
own field.

Despite these theoretical shortcomings, systematizing principles and abstract concepts
can "facilitate a deeper seeing, a more penetrating vision that goes beyond superficial appearances to the order underlying them" (Bowers, 1977). For example, pre-Darwinian
taxonomists, such as Linnaeus, limited themselves to apparent similarities and differences among animals as a means of constructing their categories. Darwin was not seduced
by appearances. Rather, he sought to understand the principles by which overt features
came about. His classifications were based not only on descriptive qualities but also on
explanatory ones.

EVOLUTIONARY PRINCIPLES AS A
THEORETICAL FOUNDATION

It has been my belief that the undergirding framework for personology and psychopathology should be guided by an evolutionary model. It is on the underpinnings of evolutionary
knowledge that the theory I have presented in recent years has been grounded and from
which a deeper future understanding will be developed concerning the nature of both
normal and pathological mental functioning. The principles I have employed and suggest
for the future are essentially the same as those that Darwin developed in seeking to explicate the origins of species. However, they are presented to derive not the origins of
species but the structure and style of each of the personality disorders and clinical syndromes that are formulated in the *DSM* on the basis of clinical observations alone. Aspects of these formulations have been published in earlier books of mine (Millon, 1969,
1981, 1990, 1999; Millon with Davis, 1996). Identified in earlier writings as a biosocial
learning model for personality and psychopathology, the theory has sought to generate the
recognized categories of mental disorder through formal processes of deduction. The goal
is not only to apply principles across diverse clinical realms but also to reduce the enormous range of trait concepts, clinical syndromes, and personality typologies that have
proliferated through history (Millon, 2004).

The power of evolutionary theory might aid us in simplifying and organizing previously disparate personologic and psychopathologic features. For example, all organisms
seek to avoid injury, find nourishment, and reproduce their kind if they are to survive and
maintain their populations. Each species displays commonalities in its adaptive or survival style. Within each species, however, there are differences in style and differences in
the success with which its various members adapt to the diverse and changing environments they face. In these simplest of terms, "normal personality" would be conceived as
representing the more-or-less distinctive style of adaptive functioning that an organism of
a particular species exhibits as it relates to its typical range of environments. Clinical syndromes and personality disorders, so formulated, would represent particular styles and
symptoms of maladaptive functioning that can be traced to deficiencies, imbalances, or
conflicts in a species' capacity to relate to the environment it faces.

A relevant and intriguing parallel may be drawn between the phylogenic evolution of a
species' genetic composition and the ontogenic development of an individual organism's
adaptive strategies (i.e., its personality style). At any point in time, a species will possess

a limited set of genes that serve as trait potentials. Over succeeding generations, the frequency distribution of these genes will likely change in their relative proportions depending on how well the traits they undergird contribute to the species' fitness within its varying ecological habitats. In a similar fashion, individual organisms begin life with a limited subset of their species' genes and the trait potentials they subserve. Over time, the *salience* of these trait potentials—not the proportion of the genes themselves—will become differentially prominent as the organism interacts with its environments. It learns from these experiences which of its traits fit best, that is, are most optimally suited to its ecosystem. In phylogenesis, then, actual *gene frequencies* change during the generation-to-generation adaptive process, whereas in ontogenesis it is the *salience* or prominence of gene-based traits that changes as adaptive learning takes place. Parallel evolutionary processes occur: one within the life of a species, the other within the life of an organism. What is seen in the individual organism is a shaping of latent potentials into adaptive and manifest styles of perceiving, feeling, thinking, and acting; these distinctive ways of adaptation, engendered by the interaction of biologic endowment and social experience, comprise the elements of what is termed personality styles and mental disorders. It is a formative process in a single lifetime that parallels gene redistributions among species during their evolutionary history.

EMPLOYING EVOLUTIONARY PRINCIPLES TO STRUCTURE A PERSONOLOGIC THEORY

Developments bridging psychological and evolutionary theories are well underway (D. M. Buss, 1994; Cosmides & Tooby, 1987; Symons, 1992; Wilson, 1978) and hence do offer some justification for extending their principles to human styles of adaptation. To provide a conceptual background from these sciences and to furnish a rough model concerning the styles of personologic and psychopathologic functioning, four psychological domains or processes in which evolutionary principles have been demonstrated are labeled as *Existence, Adaptation, Replication,* and *Abstraction.* The first relates to the serendipitous transformation of random or less organized states into those possessing distinct structures of greater organization, the second refers to homeostatic processes employed to sustain survival in open ecosystems, the third pertains to reproductive styles that maximize the diversification and selection of ecologically effective attributes, and the fourth concerns the emergence of competencies that foster anticipatory planning and reasoned decision making. I briefly elaborate in the following paragraphs (the interested reader may want to look into several of my earlier publications, most relevantly, Millon, 1990; Millon with Davis, 1996).

Existence relates to the formation and sustenance of discernible phenomena, to the processes of evolution that enhance and preserve life, and to the psychic polarity termed *pleasure* and *pain. Adaptation* relates to the manner in which extant phenomena adapt to their surrounding ecosystems, to the mechanisms employed in accommodating to or in modifying these environments, and to the psychic polarity labeled *passivity* and *activity. Replication* refers to the strategies utilized to replicate ephemeral organisms, to the methods of maximizing reproductive propagation and progeny nurturance, and to the psychic polarity termed *self* and *other. Abstraction* relates to a fourth polarity, the sources employed to gather knowledge about life and the manner in which this information is registered and transformed. In this final polarity, a distinctively human function, we are looking at *styles of cognizing*—differences (first) in what people attend to in order to learn about their experiences and (second) how they process this information internally. Comprising the most recent stage of evolution, abstraction and its polarities relate to the reflective capacity to transcend the immediate and concrete; interrelate and synthesize diverse experience; represent events and processes symbolically; and weigh alternatives, reason logically, and anticipate and appraise the unknown.

The first three polarity pairs articulated here—pain/pleasure, active/passive, self/other—have forerunners in psychological theory that can be traced as far back as the early 1900s. A number of pre-World War I theorists proposed a parallel set of three polarities that were generated time and again as the raw materials for articulating psychological processes. For example, Freud wrote in 1915 (1915/1925) what many consider to be among his most seminal papers, those on metapsychology and, in particular, the section titled "Instincts and Their Vicissitudes." Speculations that foreshadowed several concepts developed more fully later, both by Freud and others, were presented in preliminary form in these papers (see Millon, 1990). Although he failed to pursue their potentials, the ingredients he formulated for his tripartite polarity schema were drawn on by his disciples for many decades to come, seen prominently in the mid- and late-twentieth century growth of *ego psychology, self psychology,* and *object relations* theory.

PARALLELS WITHIN THE PSYCHOLOGICAL DISCIPLINES THAT CORRESPOND TO THE INITIAL THREE EVOLUTIONARY POLARITIES

A growing group of modern scholars has begun to illuminate these polar dimensions, albeit indirectly and partially. For example, a tripartite model has been formulated over the past 40-year period by the distinguished British psychologist Hans Eysenck (1957, 1967). A parallel, but more recent, conception anchored to biological foundations has likewise been developed by Eysenck's erstwhile student Jeffrey Gray (1964, 1973). A three-part model of temperament, grounded in behavioral and evolutionary theory and matching in most regards the three-part polarity model, has been formulated by the highly resourceful American psychologist Arnold Buss and his associates (Buss & Plomin, 1975, 1984). Circumplex formats based on factor analytic studies of mood and arousal that align well with my schema have been published by Russell (1980) and Tellegen (1985). Deriving inspiration from a sophisticated analysis of neuroanatomical substrates, Cloninger (1986, 1987) has deduced a threefold schema that is coextensive with my model's initial three polarities. Oriented less to biological foundations, recent advances in both interpersonal and psychoanalytic theory likewise exhibit strong parallels to one or more of the three polar dimensions. I elaborate these evolutionary-based polarities further.

Aims of Existence

Existence reflects a "to be" or "not to be" issue. In the inorganic world, "to be" is essentially a matter of possessing qualities that distinguish a phenomenon from its surrounding field, that is, not being in a state of entropy. Among organic beings, "to be" is a matter of possessing the properties of life, as well as being located in ecosystems that facilitate the preservation and enhancement of that life. In the phenomenological or experiential world of sentient organisms, events that extend life and preserve it correspond largely to metaphorical terms such as *pleasure* and *pain,* that is, eliciting positive sensations and emotions, on the one hand, and eschewing negative sensations and emotions, on the other.

Modes of Adaptation

The two primary modes by which living organisms adapt to their ecologic environments correspond closely, if somewhat imperfectly, to the evolution of the plant and animal kingdoms. Plants best characterize the mode of ecologic *accommodation,* an essentially *passive* style that disposes them to locate and remain securely anchored in a niche where the elements comprising their environment (e.g., soil, temperature, sunlight) furnish both the nourishment and protection requisite to sustaining individual homeostatic balance and promoting species survival. Animals, in contrast, typify what has been termed adaptation via ecologic *modification,* an essentially *active* style that intervenes and transforms the surrounds, a versatile mobility that enables the organism not only to seek out its needs and to escape threats to its survival but also to reconstruct or shift from one niche to another as unpredictable events arise.

Broadening the polarity to encompass human experience, the active-passive dimension means that the vast range of behaviors engaged in by humans may fundamentally be grouped in terms of whether initiative is taken in altering and shaping life's events or whether our behaviors are reactive and accommodate to those events. Often reflective and deliberate, those who are passively oriented manifest few overt strategies to gain their ends. They display a seeming inertness, a phlegmatic lack of ambition or persistence, a tendency toward acquiescence, a restrained attitude in which they initiate little to modify events, waiting for the circumstances of their environment to take their course before making accommodations. Descriptively, those who are at the active end of the polarity are best characterized by their alertness, vigilance, liveliness, vigor, forcefulness, stimulus-seeking energy, and drive. Some plan strategies and scan alternatives to circumvent obstacles or avoid the distress of punishment, rejection, and anxiety. Others are impulsive, precipitate, excitable, rash, and hasty.

Strategies of Replication

Recombinant replication achieved by sexual mating entails a balanced though asymmetric parental investment in both the genesis and nurturance of offspring. By virtue of her small number of eggs and extended pregnancy, the female strategy for replicative success that has evolved among most mammals is characterized by the close care of others and the protection of a limited number of offspring. Oriented to reproductive nurturance rather than reproductive propagation, most surviving adult females, at least until recent decades in Western society, bred close to the limit of their capacity, attaining a reproductive ceiling of approximately 20 viable births. By contrast, males not only are free of the unproductive pregnancy interlude following mating but also may substantially increase their reproductive output by engaging in repetitive matings with as many available females as possible. Although most human societies are organized to optimize a balance between genders in mating, nurturance, and protection, the male animal is biologically capable of following a *self-indulgent* strategy of maximizing propagation by profligate breeding, whereas the female of the species adheres more closely to the *other-nurturing* strategy of intensively caring for and thereby enhancing the survival of her few offspring. Crucial personological consequences flow from these contrasting replication strategies.

Predilections of Abstraction

The capacity to sort, to recompose, to coordinate, and to arrange the symbolic representations of experience into new configurations is in certain ways analogous to the random processes of recombinant replication, but processes enabling manipulation of abstractions are more focused and intentional. To extend this rhetorical liberty, replication is the recombinant mechanism underlying the adaptive progression of phylogeny, whereas abstraction is the recombinant mechanism underlying the adaptive progression of ontogeny. The powers of replication are limited, constrained by the finite potentials inherent in parental genes. In contrast, experiences, abstracted and recombined, are infinite.

Several polarities constitute this distinctly human abstraction function. The first two pairs refer to the *information sources* that provide cognitions. One set of contrasting polarities addresses the orientation either to look outward (external-to-self) in seeking information, inspiration, and guidance, versus the orientation to turn inward (internal-to-self). The second of this initial set of abstraction polarities contrasts predilections for either direct observational experiences of a tangible, material, and concrete nature with those geared more toward intangible, ambiguous, and inchoate phenomena. The second set of abstraction polarities relates to *cognitive processing*—that is, the ways in which people evaluate and mentally reconstruct information and experiences after they have been apprehended and incorporated. The first of this set differentiates processes based essentially on ideation, logic, reason, and objectivity from those that depend on emotional empathy, personal values, sentiment, and subjective judgments. The second component of this set of processing polarities reflects either a tendency to make new information conform to preconceived knowledge in the form of tradition-bound, standardized, and conventionally structured schemas versus the opposing inclination to bypass preconceptions by distancing from what is already known and instead to create innovative ideas in an informal, open-minded, spontaneous, individualistic, and often creative manner.

DEDUCING A TAXONOMY OF PERSONOLOGIC AND PSYCHOPATHOLOGIC SYNDROMES

Given the philosophic and multidimensional complexities of any category construct, we must resist the ever-present linguistic compulsion to simplify and separate constructs from their objective reality and then treat them as if these clinical constructions were fixed "disease entities." Constructs (e.g., clinical or personality prototypes) should be used heuristically, as guidelines to be reformulated or replaced as necessary; it is only the unique way in which the construct is seen in actual and specific patients that should be of primary clinical interest. The *DSM* disorders are nomothetic in that they comprise hypothetical or abstract taxons derived from historical, clinical, or statistical sources (biochemical, intrapsychic). Given the fixed nature in which each of these constructs is promulgated in the *DSM,* would it not be wise to generate a range of *subtypes* to represent trait-constellation variants that come close to corresponding to the distinctive or idiosyncratic character of our actual patients?

Not only is *DSM not* an exhaustive listing of clinical configurations that correspond to many of our patients, but it does not begin to scratch the surface of human individuality and variability. A *DSM-IV* diagnosis alone, unsupplemented by information from additional descriptive domains, constitutes an insufficient basis from which we can articulate the distinctive, complex, and often conflictual trait dynamics of a person. Nomothetic propositions and diagnostic labels are superficialities to be overcome as understanding is gained. They comprise a crude first step, but they are not sufficient for useful clinical work and, in fact, if left as they are, should be regarded as prescientific.

All experienced clinicians know that there is no such thing as a homogeneous schizophrenic group or bipolar category, nor is there a single schizoid (or avoidant, or depressive, or histrionic) personality pattern. Rather, there are innumerable variations, different forms in which the prototypal personality expresses itself. Life experience subsequently impacts and reshapes constitutional dispositions in a variety of ways, taking divergent turns and producing shadings composed of meaningfully discriminable psychological features. The course and character of each person's life experiences are, at the very least, marginally different from all others, producing influences that have sequential effects that may generate *recombinant mixtures* of clinical and personality syndromes, some of which result in contrasting inclinations within the same person, such as those that stem from parents who are strikingly different in their child-rearing behaviors, one rearing pattern conducive to the formation of an avoidant style in the child, the other to an obsessive-compulsive one. Internal schisms of character, so well understood by our analytic colleagues, are not at all uncommon, as are discrepancies we see between the overt and covert characteristics in many of our patients.

The inexact fit between a patient and his or her diagnostic label is a nagging and noisome reminder of the individuality of persons; it reflects the *idiographic* as contrasted with the *nomothetic* approach to psychological study. This incessant conceptual trouble has fueled the development of modern multiaxial taxonomies, but these taxonomies are at best only a beginning step in what might come to be the right direction for devising relevant and integrative diagnostic models.

Ideally, a diagnosis alone should be both necessary and sufficient to begin focused and integrative treatment—all you need to know. Were ideals realities, individuals would fit their diagnostic categories perfectly with pristinely prototypal presentations. Yet, such a thing seldom occurs. The monotypic categories of the *DSM* are but a crude and global beginning in a march toward specification and the accommodation of a taxonomy of individuality. Although the initial phases of a diagnostic taxonomy must consist of categories of broad bandwidth and little specificity, *DSM* diagnostic categories provide exceptionally gross distinctions, if not invalid ones. As clinical knowledge and empirical studies accrue, the manifestation of classification groupings must become more sharply delineated; that is, broad diagnostic taxons should be broken down into multiple, narrow taxons of greater specificity and individually descriptive value, as we begin to do when formulating category subtypes. All we ask is that we generate clinical syndromes and personality subtypes that reflect the individualities of human nature and pathology. Clinicians and students must learn not only *DSM* textbook categories but also subtype mixtures that are seen in clinical reality. In several of my recent books (Millon 1999, 2000; Millon with Davis, 1996), I have sought to describe a number of these early stage variants. They also can provide us with a foundation for developing a system of flexible and well-targeted therapies.

I limit my presentation here of the *DSM* personality disorders, describing and interpreting them briefly in terms of the polarity model. Noted also is reference to a number of the several personality *subtypes,* each more fully elaborated in Millon with Davis (1996). Each diagnostic prototype should be seen as merely an anchoring referent about which "real patients" vary. Because of the space limitations of this chapter, those interested in my theoretical explication of the *DSM* clinical syndromes may wish to review my recent therapy text (Millon, 1999).

Schizoid Personalities

On what basis can pathology represent the level or capacity of the pain and pleasure polarity? Several possibilities present themselves. For example, schizoid patients are those in which *both* polarity levels are deficient; that is, they lack the capacity, relatively speaking, to experience life's events either as painful or pleasurable. They are consequentially passive in orientation, appearing apathetic, listless, distant, and asocial. Affectionate needs and emotional feelings are minimal, and the person functions as an uninvolved observer detached from the rewards and affections, as well as from the demands and problems of human relationships. Among this prototype's subtypes we find *affectless* schizoids, noted by their partial compulsive traits, as well as their lackluster and passionless characteristics; the *languid* schizoids, with secondary depressive features, as evident in their phlegmatic behaviors; as well as two other subtype variants, the *remote* and *depersonalized*.

Avoidant Personalities

The second clinically meaningful combination based on problems in the pleasure-pain polarity comprises patients with an oversensitivity to pain and a diminished ability to experience pleasure. They evince an active stance, a foreboding anticipation, and responsiveness to psychic difficulties. To them, life is experienced as vexatious, one possessing few rewards and much anxiety. Among the major subtypes of the avoidant we find the *phobic* variant with dependent personality features evident in a general apprehensiveness and a seeking of institutional support; there are also *hypersensitive* subtypes that exhibit paranoid features such as suspiciousness and timorousness. Among other subtypes are the *self-deserting* and the *conflicted variants*.

Depressive Personalities

Akin to both the schizoid and avoidant personalities is the *DSM* depressive personality disorder, introduced recently in a *DSM-IV* appendix. All of these disorders share a deficiency in their ability to experience pleasure. Further, avoidants and depressives share an overreactivity to pain. The avoidant, however, actively eschews pain-generating experiences, anticipates them, and, as best as possible, attempts to distance from their occurrence, whereas depressives give up, passively accepting their psychically burdensome state. Depressive personalities fail to display efforts to elude and circumvent the pain they experience, resulting in a perennial state of hopeless anguish. Among the subtypes of the depressive prototype we find the *self-derogating* variant with dependent traits, evident in a tendency to be self-deriding and self-discrediting. Another variant is the *ill-humored* depressive, noted by negativistic features seen as irritability and general discontent. Other subtypes include the *voguish,* the *restive,* and the *morbid.*

Dependent Personalities

Those with a passively dependent pathology have learned that feeling good, secure, confident, and so on—that is, feelings associated with pleasure or the avoidance of pain—is provided by close relationships with others. Behaviorally, these persons display a strong need for external support and attention; they experience marked discomfort, if not sadness and anxiety, should they be deprived of affection and nurturance. Among the five subtypes recorded in Millon with Davis (1996), we find the *disquieted* variant with avoidant features, as seen in their fretful and foreboding attitude. Notable also is an *accommodating* subtype with histrionic traits and compliant and agreeable social behaviors. Among the others, we note the *ineffectual, immature,* and *selfless* subtypes.

Histrionic Personalities

Turning to others also as a lifestyle is a group of personalities that take an actively dependent stance. They seek the goal of maximizing protection, nurturance, and reproductive success by engaging in a series of manipulative, seductive, gregarious, and attention-getting maneuvers. Six subtype variants are noted, among them the *vivacious,* with narcissistic features, evident in their charming, impulsive, and ebullient behaviors. Also notable is the *disingenuous* type, with antisocial, calculating, and deceitful behaviors, and the *tempestuous* variant with negativistic features, as seen in moody complaints, sulking, and turbulent behaviors. Other variants include the *infantile, appeasing,* and *theatrical* types.

Narcissistic Personalities

This personality pattern is characterized by a passively independent orientation, noted by a self-image of superior worth, often learned in response to admiring and doting parents. Providing self-rewards is highly gratifying, if the individual possesses either a real or an inflated sense of self-worth. Displaying manifest confidence, arrogance, and an exploitive egocentricity in social contexts, this self-orientation has all that is important—himself or herself. The four subtypes of the narcissist include the *elitists,* who fancy themselves as demigods, flaunt their status, and engage in self-promotion. Other variants are the *compensatory* type with covert avoidant features, underlying feelings of inferiority, but public displays of superiority. Noteworthy also are the *amorous* and *unprincipled* subtypes.

Antisocial Personalities

Those whom we characterize as exhibiting the active-independent self-orientation resemble the outlook, temperament, and socially unacceptable behaviors of the *DSM* antisocial personality disorder. They act to counter the expectation of pain at the hand of others by actively engaging in duplicitous or illegal behaviors in which they seek to exploit others for self-gain. Skeptical about the motives of others, they desire autonomy and wish revenge for what are felt as past injustices. There are five subtypes of the antisocial; most common is the *covetous* variant, noted by enviousness, retribution seeking, and a greedy avariciousness. Also prevalent is the *risk-taking* type, seen in recklessness, impulsivity, and heedless behaviors; other variants include the *reputation-defending,* the *nomadic,* and *malevolent* subtypes.

Negativistic (Passive-Aggressive) Personalities

In both dependent (other) and independent (self) orientations, patients demonstrate personality pathologies in which the strategy of being oriented *either* toward others or toward themselves is grossly one-sided. This imbalance toward self or other is not the only pattern seen to reflect this polarity. "Normal" individuals, for example, exhibit a comfortable intermediary position with both bipolarities of self and others in balance. Certain pathological personalities, those whom we speak of as "ambivalent," also are oriented both toward self and others, but they are in *intense conflict* between the two. Those represented in the *DSM* negativistic personality vacillate between others and self, behaving obediently one time and reacting defiantly the next. Feeling intense, yet unable to resolve their ambivalence, they weave an erratic course from voicing self-deprecation and guilt, to expressing stubborn negativism and resistance. These patients' conflicts are overt, worn on their sleeves, so to speak; they are spoken of in the theory as actively ambivalent, a more varied lot than earlier *DSM* portrayals of the so-called passive-aggressive. There are four negativistic subtypes, the *circuitous,* with dependent traits prevalent, as seen in their inefficiency, forgetfulness, and procrastination. Also common is the *discontented* variant, seen frequently with depressive traits, and noted by their grumbling, petty, complaining, and embittered feelings. Other subtypes include the *abrasive* and *vacillating* variants.

Obsessive-Compulsive Personalities

Another major conflicted pattern, the *DSM* obsessive-compulsive personality, displays a picture of distinct other-directedness, a consistency in social compliance, and interpersonal respect: Their histories usually indicate their having been subjected to constraint and discipline, but only when they transgressed parental strictures and expectations. Beneath the conforming other-oriented veneer they exhibit are intense desires to rebel and assert their own self-oriented feelings and impulses. Five subtypes of the obsessive-compulsive are notable. The pure type, termed the *conscientious,* is noted by being earnest, meticulous, but also inflexible and indecisive. Also noteworthy is the *bureaucratic* subtype with modest narcissistic features, who acts in an officious, petty-minded, mettlesome, and close-minded manner. Three other variants are the *parsimonious,* the *bedeviled,* and the *puritanical.*

Borderline Personalities

The cardinal feature of the borderline pattern is the loss of hierarchical control of emotional reactivity. Affect regulation is poorly developed, inchoately modular rather than firm and integrated. In the relative absence of higher regulatory processes, there is an intense lability between competing cognitive-affective-behavioral structures, as one and then another co-opts control of the psychic system in reaction to fleeting and idiosyncratic events in the patient's environment. Several subtypes are notable among the borderline pattern. Common are *self-destructive* variants with depressive traits, a high-strung, inward turning of moody behaviors. Also prevalent is the *impulsive* type with histrionic and/or antisocial features, evident in capricious, agitated, irritable, and potentially suicidal behaviors. Two other variants are the *discouraged* and *petulant* subtypes.

Schizotypal Personalities

This personality disorder represents a cognitively dysfunctional and maladaptively detached orientation in the polarity theory. Schizotypal personalities may experience minimal pleasure, have difficulty consistently differentiating between other and self strategies, as well as active and passive modes of adaptation. Many prefer social isolation with minimal personal attachments and obligations. Inclined to be either autistic or confused cognitively, they think tangentially and often appear self-absorbed and ruminative. Two major subtypes are found among schizotypals. One, the *insipid* subtype, is an outgrowth of the schizoid pattern and is noted by its sluggish, inexpressive behavior and its vague and obscure thinking. The second, grounded in an avoidant base and labeled the *timorous* variant, is warily apprehensive, alienated from self, and tends to disqualify its own thoughts.

Paranoid Personalities

Here are seen a vigilant mistrust of others and an edgy defensiveness against anticipated criticism and deception. Driven by a high sensitivity to pain (rejection-humiliation) and oriented strongly to the self-polarity, these patients exhibit a touchy irritability, a need to assert themselves, not necessarily in action, but in an inner world of self-determined beliefs and assumptions. They are prepared to provoke social conflicts and fractious circumstances as a means of gratifying their confused mix of pain sensitivity and self-assertion. Among the five subtypes of the paranoid described in Millon with Davis (1996), we find the *fanatic,* exhibiting narcissistic features and evincing clinical signs such as grandiose delusions, arrogant expansiveness, and extravagant fantasies. Also typical is the *insular* variant with avoidant features, exhibiting a reclusive, hypervigilant, and defensive lifestyle. Other subtypes include the *querulous, obdurate,* and *malignant* variants.

DEVELOPING INTEGRATED ASSESSMENT TOOLS

A historic and still frequently voiced complaint about diagnosis, be it based or not on the official classification system, is its inutility for therapeutic purposes. Many clinicians, whatever their orientation, pay minimal attention to the possibility that diagnosis can inform the therapeutic philosophy and technique they employ. A schema of synergistic assessment instruments would be based on an overarching gestalt that gives coherence, provides an interactive framework, and creates an organic order that integrates the syndromes of Axis I with the disorders of Axis II. Each person being assessed is seen, therefore, as a synthesized and substantive whole that is greater than the sum of his or her multiaxial parts.

Our patients come to us as an inextricably interwoven pattern of behaviors, cognitions, intrapsychic processes, and so on, bound together by feedback loops and serially unfolding concatenations that emerge at different times and in dynamic and changing configurations, sometimes in the form of an Axis I syndrome, sometimes in the shape of an Axis II disorder, and sometimes in formations composed of both axes. As a consequence, the interpretation of the psychological inventories I have sought to construct, such as the Millon Clinical Multiaxial Inventory (MCMI), does not proceed through a serial interpretation of single scales. Rather, each scale contextualizes and transforms the meaning of the others in the configuration or profile of several interacting scales.

Formerly segmented instruments have begun to be analyzed as configural integrations that possess clinical significance and meaning as gestalt composites. Furthermore, the insistence that interpretation be anchored precisely to empirical correlates has given way to free-form clinical syntheses, as evident in the dynamics of the unfairly maligned projectives. Personality formulations are no longer conceived as arbitrary sets of syndromal and trait scales that must first be individually deduced and then pieced together, but as holistic or integrated configurations from the very start. The MCMI represents this trend toward holistic clinical and personality tools, bridging and coupling both the *DSM-IV* Axis I clinical syndromes and Axis II personality disorders in a single inventory (Millon, Millon, & Davis, 1997). The synergy of such assessment tools flows from their reciprocal clinical insights. To know that the patient is dysthymic is of value. Of greater value, however, is whether we know that the patient exhibits the core features of a histrionic personality with dysthymia, or the characteristics of an avoidant personality with dysthymia, and so on.

Paradoxically, the methodology through which most assessment instruments have been created in the past is in spirit opposed to the goal that directs their use. Proceeding initially to separate out one or another feature of a set of psychological traits, we have segmented and differentiated particular characteristics of the person from that of all others. Yet, our ultimate task is to reconstruct the very person we had just dismembered. We must build back and reintegrate what was decomposed. We have moved from idiographic individuality, to nomothetic commonalities, and, finally, to what might be called nomothetic individuality. Proper assessment is, at best, a self-regulatory process, the validity of which depends on our first giving up or segmenting the person in order to reassemble, restore, and, thereby, understand him or her fully.

An integrative assessment approach is concerned with the last two links of this process. The fractionated person, the person who has been dispersed across scales and instruments, must be put back together again as the organic whole he or she really is. We argue that this integrative assessment is eminently a theoretical process, indeed, a process that requires a weighing of this and a disqualifying of that across the idiosyncrasies and commonalities of methods and data sources through multiple iterations of hypothesis generation and testing. Such an integrative assessment theory of personology and psychopathology is *the theory of the patient*. Every loose end should be tied up in that person's theory, a theory so logical, comprehensive, and compelling that we feel that things could not be other than what the assessment concludes them to be.

Implicit in this idea is that not all patients with the same diagnosis can be considered as the same. Platitudinous though this assertion may be, we must take care not to force patients into the procrustean beds of our theoretical models or taxonomic entities. Whether they are derived from mathematical analyses, clinical observations, or systematic theories, all taxonomies are composed of prototypal classes, classes that may lead clinicians to exaggerate within-group homogeneity (Cantor & Genero, 1986). Instead, diagnostic categories must be conceived as flexible and dimensionally quantitative, permitting the full and distinctive configuration of characteristics of patients to be displayed (Millon, 1997). The multiaxial schema of the *DSM* is only a small step in the right direction. Its structural format does encourage multidimensional and contextual considerations (Axes I, II, and IV), as well as multidiagnoses that begin to approximate the natural heterogeneity of patients' lives, but it does not do so sufficiently to represent the subtleties and idiosyncratic character of even the subtypes we described earlier.

Turning to my own assessment tools, I note first that the well-regarded MCMI is *not* a general personality instrument to be used for purposes other than diagnostic screening or clinical assessment. It contrasts with other, more broadly applied, inventories whose presumed utility for diverse populations is highly questionable. Normative data and transformation scores for the MCMI are based on clinical samples and are applicable, therefore, only to persons who evince psychological symptoms or are engaged in a program of professional psychotherapy or psychodiagnostic evaluation. Other instruments associated with my theoretical work are designed also with special populations in mind, such as the Millon Adolescent Clinical Inventory (MACI) for troubled and troubling adolescents, the Millon Behavioral Medicine Diagnostic (MBMD) for appraising psychological influences that impact the experiences of medical patients, the forthcoming Millon Organizational Roles and Styles Indicator (MORSI) for evaluating industrial/organizational clients, and the Millon Index of Personality Styles-Revised Edition (MIPS-Revised) for run-of-the-mill normal personalities.

Further, there are distinct boundaries to the accuracy of the self-report method of clinical data collection; by no means is it a perfect data source (Allport, 1937; Ellis, 1946; Millon, 1997). The inherent psychometric limits of the tools, the tendency of similar patients to interpret questions differently, the effect of current affective states on trait measures, and the effort of patients to effect certain false appearances and impressions all narrow the upper boundaries of this method's potential accuracy. However, by constructing a self-report instrument in line with the several accepted techniques of validation

(Hase & Goldberg, 1967; Loevinger, 1957), an inventory should begin to approach these upper boundaries.

TOWARD SYNERGISTIC THERAPIES

If my wish for the twenty-first century takes root, this chapter should help promote a revolutionary call for a therapeutic renaissance that brings treatment back to the reality of patients' lives. Of course, a patient's reality presents a bewildering if not chaotic array of possibilities. Even the most motivated young therapist may wish to back away to a manageable and simple worldview, be it cognitive, pharmacologic, or otherwise. I contend, however, that this complexity need not be experienced as chaotic or overwhelming if a treatment plan has logic and order. This I have sought to do by illustrating, for example, that the systematic integration of Axis I syndromes and Axis II disorders is not only feasible but also conducive to briefer and more effective therapy.

Although my professional focus has been on the personality disorders, I believe that all the clinical syndromes that comprise Axis I can be understood more clearly and treated more effectively when conceived as an outgrowth of a patient's overall personality style. To say that depression is experienced and expressed differently from one patient to the next is a truism; so general a statement, however, will not suffice. Our task requires much more. My personality-guided therapy text (Millon, 1999) provides extensive information, often with accompanying illustrations, on how patients with different personality vulnerabilities perceive and cope with life's stressors.

Debates on whether the treatment approach recorded here should be designated as a variant of *technical eclecticism* or *integrative therapy* are mistaken. Both of these approaches have things backward, so to speak; they start intervention by focusing first on technique or methodology. Evolutionary thinking does not focus on either treatment methods or the subject-area theories that generated them. *Synergistic therapy, the term preferred here, states that the focus begins with the inherent characteristics of the person first, not in theories or technical modalities.* It starts with the interwoven character of the patient's extant traits and symptoms. The task is *not* to see how discordant therapeutic models or therapeutic techniques can be blended, but rather to select those methods that *match,* first and foremost, the integrated pattern of clinical features that are manifested by the patient. The synergistic therapeutic task is to select treatment goals and tactics that *mirror* each patient's intrinsic clinical pattern optimally.

Synergy is an important concept not only for the psychotherapy of an individual case but also for the role of psychotherapy in the broad sphere of clinical science. As noted earlier in this chapter, for the treatment of a patient to be fully integrative, the several elements comprising a broad clinical science should be integrated as well. One of the arguments advanced against technical eclecticism is that it explicitly insulates therapy from the context of a clinical science. In contrast to eclecticism, where techniques are justified methodologically or empirically, synergistic treatment reflects the logic of a comprehensive model of human nature.

Whether we work with part functions that focus on behaviors, cognitions, unconscious processes, or biological defects and the like, *or* whether we address contextual settings that focus on the larger environment—the family, the group, or the socioeconomic and political conditions of life—the crossover point, the unit that links parts to contexts, is the person. The individual is the *intersecting medium* that brings them together. Persons, however, are more than just crossover mediums. As noted previously, they are the only organically integrated system in the psychological domain. Persons are inherently created from birth as natural entities. Moreover, they are at the heart of the therapeutic experience. A person is a substantive being who gives meaning and coherence to expressive symptoms and traits—whether they are behaviors, affects, or mechanisms—as well as the singular being who experiences and gives meaning to family interactions and social processes. Therapists should be cognizant of the person from the start, therefore, because the expressive symptoms and the social contexts take on different meanings and call for different interventions in terms of the person to whom they are anchored. To focus on one psychic form of expression or one social structure, without understanding its undergirding or reference base, is to engage in potentially misguided, if not random, therapeutic techniques.

Synergistic therapy should be conceived as a configurational system of strategies and tactics in which each intervention technique is selected not only for its efficacy in resolving singular pathological features but also for its contribution to the overall constellation of treatment procedures, of which it is but one. The careful orchestration of diverse, yet synthesized, techniques is selected because those techniques mirror the characteristics of each patient's psychological makeup. The primacy given to the patient is what differentiates synergistic psychotherapy from its integrative counterparts. Therapies that conceptualize clinical disorders from any single theoretical perspective—be it psychodynamic, cognitive, behavioral, or physiological—may be useful at times, but is not sufficient in itself to undertake a therapy of *the whole person.*

The therapeutic "revolution" proposed asserts that clinical disorders are not exclusively behavioral or cognitive or unconscious, that is, confined to a particular expressive form. The overall pattern of a person's traits and psychic symptoms are primary; moreover, they are systemic and multioperational. No part of the system exists in complete isolation from the others. Every part is directly or indirectly tied to every other. The synergism of traits and symptoms of a patient accounts for a disorder's clinical tenacity. Persons are "real"; each of us is a composite of intertwined elements whose totality must be reckoned within all therapeutic enterprises. The key to treating our patients, therefore, lies in *therapy that focuses on the patient first and is designed afterward to be as organismically complex as is each patient himself or herself.*

Synergism in therapy may sound difficult, but its relative ease and utility has been demonstrated in several of my recent books (Millon, 1999; Millon with Davis, 1996). Two basic strategies are described. In the first, termed "potentiated pairings," treatment methods are *combined simultaneously* to overcome problematic characteristics that may be refractory to each technique if employed separately. These composites pull and push for change on several fronts. Treatment is oriented to *more than one* expressive domain of clinical dysfunction; a currently popular form of such treatment pairing is found in cognitive-behavioral therapy. The *second* synergistic procedure, labeled "catalytic sequences," considers the *order* in which coordinated treatments are executed. Therapeutic combinations and progressions are designed to optimize the impact of changes in a manner that would be more effective than if the order were otherwise arranged. In a catalytic sequence, for example, we might seek first to alter a patient's stuttering by direct behavioral modification procedures. This modification, if successfully achieved, would facilitate the use of cognitive methods to produce self-image changes in confidence, which, in turn, would foster the utility of interpersonal techniques to effect social skill improvement.

Synergistic therapy is conceived as a configuration of strategies and tactics in which each intervention technique is selected not only for its efficacy in resolving particular pathological difficulties but also for its contribution to the overall constellation of treatment procedures, of which it is but one.

CONCLUSION

The future of personology and psychopathology is both reassuring and substantial if efforts are directed to the task of building an integrated clinical science and profession.

REFERENCES

Allport, G. W. (1937). *Personality: A psychological interpretation.* New York: Henry Holt.

Bandura, A. (1977). *Social learning theory.* Englewood Cliffs, NJ: Prentice-Hall.

Benjamin, L. S. (1984). Principles of prediction using structural analysis of social behavior. In R. A. Zucker, J. Aronoff, & A. I. Rabin (Eds.), *Personality and the prediction of behavior.* New York: Academic Press.

Bowers, K. S. (1977). There's more to Iago than meets the eye: A clinical account of personal consistency. In D. Magnusson & S. Endler (Eds.), *Personality at the crossroads.* Hillsdale, NJ: Erlbaum.

Buss, A. J., & Plomin, R. (1975). *A temperament theory of personality development.* New York: Wiley.

Buss, A. J., & Plomin, R. (1984). *Temperament: Early developing personality traits.* Hillsdale, NJ: Erlbaum.

Buss, D. M. (1994). *The evolution of desire: Strategies of human mating.* New York: Basic Books.

Cantor, N., & Genero, N. (1986). Psychiatric diagnosis and natural categorization: A close analogy. In T. Millon & G. L. Klerman (Eds.), *Contemporary directions in psychopathology: Toward the DSM-IV* (pp. 233–256). New York: Guilford Press.

Cloninger, C. R. (1986). A unified biosocial theory of personality and its role in the development of anxiety states. *Psychiatric Developments, 3,* 167–226.

Cloninger, C. R. (1987). A systematic method for clinical description and classification of personality variants. *Archives of General Psychiatry, 44,* 573–588.

Cosmides, L., & Tooby, J. (1987). From evolution to behavior: Evolutionary psychology as the missing link. In J. Dupre (Ed.), *The latest on the best: Essays on evolution and optimality* (pp. 277–306). Cambridge, MA: MIT Press.

Ellis, A. (1946). The validity of personality questionnaires. *Psychological Bulletin, 43,* 385–440.

Eysenck, H. J. (1957). *The dynamics of anxiety and hysteria.* London: Routledge & Kegan Paul.

Eysenck, H. J. (1967). *The biological basis of personality.* Springfield, IL: Thomas.

Freud, S. (1895). Project for a scientific psychology. In *Standard edition of the complete psychological works of Sigmund Freud* (Vol. 1, pp. 281–397). London: Hogarth Press.

Freud, S. (1925). The instincts and their vicissitudes. In J. Strachey (Ed.), *The standard edition of the complete psychological works of Sigmund Freud* (Vol. 14, pp. 109–140). London: Hogarth Press. (Original work published 1915)

Gray, J. A. (Ed.). (1964). *Pavlov's typology.* New York: Pergamon Press.

Gray, J. A. (1973). Causal theories of personality and how to test them. In J. R. Royce (Ed.), *Multivariate analysis and psychological theory.* New York: Academic Press.

Hase, H. D., & Goldberg, L. R. (1967). Comparative validity of different strategies of constructing personality inventory scales. *Psychological Bulletin, 67,* 231–248.

Hempel, C. G. (1961). Introduction to problems of taxonomy. In J. Zubin (Ed.), *Field studies in the mental disorders.* New York: Grune & Stratton.

Kernberg, O. F. (1975). *Borderline conditions and pathological narcissism.* New York: Aronson.

Kiesler, D. J. (1986). The 1982 interpersonal circle: An analysis of *DSM-III* personality disorders. In T. Millon & G. L. Klerman (Eds.), *Contemporary directions in psychopathology.* New York: Guilford Press.

Kohut, H. (1971). *The analysis of self.* New York: International Universities Press.

Lewin, K. (1936). *Principles of topographical psychology.* New York: McGraw-Hill.

Loevinger, J. (1957). Objective tests as instruments of psychological theory. *Psychological Reports, 3,* 635–694.

Millon, T. (1969). *Modern psychopathology: A biosocial approach to maladaptive learning and functioning.* Philadelphia: Saunders. (Reprinted 1985 by Waveland Press, Prospect Heights, IL)

Millon, T. (1981). *Disorders of personality: DSM-III: Axis II.* New York: Wiley.

Millon, T. (1990). *Toward a new personology: An evolutionary model.* New York: Wiley.

Millon, T. (1997). *The Millon inventories: Clinical and personality assessment.* New York: Guilford Press.

Millon, T. (1999). *Personality-guided therapy.* New York: Wiley.

Millon, T. (2000). Toward a new model of integrative psychotherapy: Psychosynergy. *Journal of Psychotherapy Integration, 10*(1), 37–53.

Millon, T. (2003). Evolution: A generative source for conceptualizing the attributes of personality. In T. Millon & M. Lerner (Eds.), *Handbook of psychology: Personality and social psychology* (Vol. 5, pp. 3–30). Hoboken, NJ: Wiley.

Millon, T. (2004). *Masters of the mind: The story of mental illness from ancient times to the new millennium.* Hoboken, NJ: Wiley.

Millon, T. (with Davis, R. D.). (1996). *Disorders of personality: DSM-IV and beyond* (2nd ed.). New York: Wiley.

Millon, T., Millon, C., & Davis, R. (1997). *Millon Clinical Multiaxial Inventory-III (MCMI-III) manual* (2nd ed.). Minneapolis, MN: Pearson Assessments.

Murray, H. A. (Ed.). (1938). *Explorations in personality.* New York: Oxford University Press.

Quine, W. V. O. (1961). *From a logical point of view* (2nd ed.). New York: Harper & Row.

Rotter, J. B. (1954). *Social learning and clinical psychology.* Englewood Cliffs, NJ: Prentice-Hall.

Russell, J. A. (1980). A circumplex model of affect. *Journal of Personality and Social Psychology, 39,* 1161–1178.

Siever, L. J., & Davis, K. L. (1991). A psychobiological perspective on the personality disorders. *American Journal of Psychiatry, 148,* 1647–1658.

Symons, D. (1992). On the use and misuse of Darwinism in the study of human behavior. In J. Barkow, L. Cosmides, & J. Tooby (Eds.), *The adapted mind* (pp. 137–159). New York: Oxford University Press.

Tellegen, A. (1985). Structures of mood and personality and relevance to assessing anxiety with an emphasis on self-report. In A. H. Tuma & J. Maser (Eds.), *Anxiety and the anxiety disorders.* Hillsdale, NJ: Erlbaum.

Wiggins, J. S. (1982). Circumplex models of interpersonal behavior in clinical psychology. In P. Kendall & J. Butcher (Eds.), *Handbook of research methods in clinical psychology.* New York: Wiley.

Wilson, E. O. (1975). *Sociobiology: The new synthesis.* Cambridge, MA: Harvard University Press.

Wilson, E. O. (1978). *On human nature.* Cambridge, MA: Harvard University Press.

Zuckerman, M. (1991). *Psychobiology of personality.* Cambridge, England: Cambridge University Press.

Highlights of Theodore Millon's Career —————

Family

Ancestry: The paternal family history was composed of Talmudic scholars and Yeshiva teachers, notably eighteenth-century Rabbi Elijah Zalman, known in the Russian Pale as the Vilna Gaon, and Rabbi Judah Eliezer, who headed Padua and Milan (Italy) Yeshivas in the fifteenth century.

Parents: Abraham Millon (1900–1970) and Molly Gorkowitz (1902–1982), both modestly educated, lived on the ever-changing Polish, Lithuanian, and Russian border before, during, and after World War I.

They immigrated to the United States in the mid-1920s and married in New York City, where they resided for the next 40-plus years.

1928: "Teddy" (TM), as he was known throughout childhood, was born in Brooklyn, New York, on August 18, 1928. The number 8 was considered in the mysticism and numerical acrobatics of the Gematria of the medieval Jewish Cabbalah to be a lucky number; hence, he was seen by family and his ethnic community as a triply blessed child with a charmed future.

1952: TM married Renée Baratz shortly after her City College of New York (CCNY) graduation and had four children: Diane,

Ted at Age One

Ted and Renée Millon's Children, Circa 1990. From Left, Diane, Adrienne, Carrie, and Andrew

1955; Carrie, 1957; Andy 1959; and Adrienne, 1963; and eight grand-children (thus far), 1979 to 2003.

Early School Years

1934–1945:   TM entered Brooklyn's P.S. 177 in a first-grade class for children who spoke only Yiddish. He was taught algebra and geometry that year at home by his paternal grandfather and invited to attend a gifted program at New York City's Hunter College in third grade. He returned to fifth grade in Brooklyn to an excellent and kindly teacher, Martin Greenspan; a special friendship developed with fellow school artist, Maurice Sendak. His junior high school English teacher, David Oberman, was highly encouraging and stimulating, as was Lafayette High School math teacher, Albert Freilich. Friendly but competitive relationships emerged with fellow students Izzy Mandelbaum and Ed Murray, the latter a future university psychology colleague. Notable throughout this period was a preoccupation with theater and imitative singing (Bing Crosby, Perry Como, Danny Kaye), suggesting a possible career direction. That, as well as a serious future as an artist, was quickly dismissed by family as an inappropriate aspiration.

College and Graduate Education

1945–1949:   A carnival of majors ensued following admission to CCNY, each proving ephemeral. By chance and good fortune, TM was exposed in his last two years to philosophy, physics, and psychology courses; the latter became firmly and deeply embedded because of the appeal of an erudite and charismatic professor, Gardner Murphy.

1949–1950:   Summer psychometric fellowships were obtained at The Psychological Corporation to research the Differential Aptitude Tests. This corresponded with a one-year master's program at CCNY that included an assistantship, divided between sociology/anthropology and psychology, the latter with responsibilities to aid Daniel Lehrman, the ethologist, and Kurt Goldstein, the neurological theorist. An interview/questionnaire thesis on personality factors in mate selection also was completed. Notable during this period were occasional Sunday brunches at Margaret Mead's house with Gardner Murphy and Lawrence Frank, a leader of the Ethical Culture Society, as well as an abbreviated "creatively gifted analysis" with the psychoanalyst Ernst Kris.

1950–1953:   TM was inclined to spend a few years after his master's in artistic activities while living in Greenwich Village. The Korean War began that summer, however, and rather than serve as an army draftee, TM accepted a last-minute assistantship offered in the University of Connecticut's Social/Personality doctoral program. The UConn period was a mixed experience intellectually and personally. Excellent courses in social, statistics, and learning theory were interwoven with audited courses in Yale's Philosophy Department and in Harvard's Social Relations Department. A dissertation was completed in October 1953 with an experimental study into the perceptual behaviors of the so-called authoritarian personality.

Scheduled to enter the armed forces shortly thereafter, TM was surprisingly given a 4-F status and "freed" to go on his way. The search for an academic position was extensive but ended luckily with an assistant professorship in Lehigh University's Psychology Department, beginning the fall semester of 1954.

Academic Positions

1954–1970:   Lehigh's department had lost two members following the spring semester of 1954, a retiring social psychologist and a suddenly resigned clinical/personality professor. TM's not inconsiderable background in both subject areas fit the department's needs well, although he had a devil of a time preparing six new courses in his first year. Teaching was a highly gratifying activity, and TM undertook responsibility for a wide variety of psych and so-called "creative concepts" interdisciplinary courses.

1969–1977:   Approaching his 40s, TM began a search for more varied and challenging academic roles in the late 1960s. The opportunity that attracted him most was a chief psychologist position at the Neuropsychiatric Institute (NPI) of the University of Illinois (UI) Medical Center in Chicago. He also was given the opportunity to teach graduate seminars at the UI Circle campus and at the University of Chicago, beginning in 1972. With Mel Sabshin, psychiatry chair, TM led efforts to develop a doctorate in mental health degree and establish a School of Mental Health Sciences at the University's Medical Center Campus; neither innovative venture received sufficient administrative support to be implemented. TM did succeed, however, in establishing a required behavioral sciences course in the medical school curriculum, also editing a text, *Medical Behavioral Science,* in 1975 (W. B. Saunders), a book that soon became the standard for comparable courses at 80 other medical schools over the following decade. Relationships with numerous psychologists, psychiatrists, psychoanalysts, as well as neuroscientists and cultural anthropologists in the sophisticated academic environment of Chicago, were exceptionally rewarding—until biological psychiatry asserted its hegemony over all activities at NPI in 1976, leading TM to begin the exploration to move elsewhere. Health and family considerations pointed southward.

1977–2001:   It was thought that the clinical psychology director post that TM accepted at the University of Miami (UM) would slow his prior active pace

As a Young Professor, 1962

of professional activities—but not quite. Delightful colleagues and extra-ordinary students became a pleasure to mentor, many of the latter becoming notable scholar/researchers in their own right. In addition to the clinical program, an innovative doctorate in health psychology was soon developed with associates, one of the first two or three such programs in the nation.

1982–1994: Part-time visiting professorships were extended in 1982 to TM in the Psychiatry Department and Stanley Cobb Research Laboratories of Mass General Hospital at Harvard Medical School; one TM transferred to McLean Hospital in 1988. At Mass General, TM worked with Gerald Klerman, then head of the Cobb Laboratories; this led to a jointly edited book in 1986, *Contemporary Approaches to Psychopathology: Toward the* DSM-IV. At McLean, TM joined John Gunderson's *DSM-IV*-related New England Personality Disorders Group, as well as assuming partial responsibility for guiding international scholars.

1994-present: TM joined the Institute for Advanced Studies in Personology and Psychopathology (IASPP), enabling him to semiretire, write, and engage in research and teaching with diverse local graduate students and visiting international colleagues. TM has had the time to reflect leisurely and to tie together the threads of his past professional work.

Clinical Activities

1949–1952: Practica and clinical assistant, CCNY Psychoeducational Clinic; Norwich State Hospital, Connecticut.

1954–1956: Extern, Allentown State Hospital (ASH); Lehigh Valley Guidance Clinic, Pennsylvania.

1956–1963: Psychologist, Group Clinical Practice, Bethlehem, Pennsylvania.

1963–1970: Clinical psychologist, Lincoln Mental Health Center, Bethlehem, Pennsylvania.

1970–1977: Therapy supervisor, West Side VA Hospital; Illinois Mental Health Institutes, Chicago, Illinois.

1981–1997: Therapy/assessment supervisor, Psych Services Center, University of Miami, Coral Gables, Florida.

Administrative Responsibilities

1955–1970: Director, Lehigh University Graduate Clinical Program.

1955–1970: Chairperson, Board of Trustees, Allentown State Hospital, Allentown, Pennsylvania.

1957–1967: Director, Research Facilities, Allentown State Hospital, Allentown, Pennsylvania.

1963–1970: Chairperson, director, Psychology Internship/Psychiatry Residency Programs, Lincoln Mental Health Center.

1970–1977: Chief, Psychology Division/Research Director, Department of Psychiatry, University of Illinois Medical Center.

1977–1987: Director, Clinical Doctoral Program; Codirector, Doctoral Health Psychology Program, University of Miami.

1994-present: Dean and scientific director, Institute for Advanced Studies in Personology and Psychopathology, Coral Gables, Florida.

Professional Affiliations and Roles

1954-present: Member, American Psychological Association.

1956–1963:   Chairperson, Pennsylvania Community Civic League (state-sponsored association of agencies and volunteer groups fostering minority civil rights).

1957–1967:   Member, Pennsylvania State Welfare Board (state agency overseeing programs to assist the mentally ill).

1972–1981:   Member, Editorial Board, *Journal of Abnormal Psychology.*

1974–1980:   Member, American Psychiatric Association's Task Force on Nomenclature and Statistics (*DSM-III*).

With Ray Fowler (Executive Director Emeritus of the American Psychological Association) and Mel Sabshin (Medical Director Emeritus of the American Psychiatric Association) during Ted's *Festschrift Weekend,* Miami, Florida, October 2003

1978–1984:   Chairperson, Council of University Directors of Clinical Psychology.

1981–1985:   Member, Editorial Board, *Health Psychology* (Division 38 journal).

1983–2002:   Member, Editorial Board, *Psychotherapy and Private Practice.*

1984–1989:   American editor, *Psychology and Health: An International Journal.*

1985–1996:   Coeditor, *Journal of Personality Disorders.*

1985–2003:   Member, Editorial Board, *Journal of Personality Assessment.*

1986-present: President/member, Executive Board, International Society for the Study of Personality Disorders.

1988–1994:   Member, American Psychiatric Association's Task Force on Nomenclature and Statistics (*DSM-IV*), Axis II Work Group.

1989–1993:   Member, Institute of Medicine Committee, National Academy of Science.

Invited Lectureships

1958–2003:   Spoke/lectured at some 700-plus settings beyond university home base on diverse theoretical, assessment, and therapeutic topics, including more than 25 at APA annual meetings, some 40 or more at state and regional psychological associations, perhaps 50 university colloquia, about 150 clinical workshops, as well as 200 or more clinical seminars, including more than 20 international plenary lectureships. He participated in several professional circuits, such as the Cape Cod Summer Seminars and the annual Millon Conferences.

Research and Scholarly Ventures

1949–1950:   Designed interview and survey questionnaires at CCNY investigating attributes desirable in selecting potential marital partners.

1949–1951:   Psychometric development of the Differential Aptitude Tests at The Psychological Corporation.

1951–1957:   Executed experimental, social, and laboratory studies of trait characteristics attributed to the "authoritarian personality" at UConn and Lehigh U.

1955–1960:   Assessed the efficacy of new pharmacologic agents in several collaborative studies with Nathan Kline, MD, at ASH and Rockland (NY) State Hospitals: supported by Abbott Labs and Upjohn pharmaceutical grants.

1956–2001:   Mentored more than 400 graduate student theses and dissertations at Lehigh University, University of Illinois, University of Chicago, and University of Miami.

1957–1962:   Planned milieu therapy programs and community outreach projects at ASH; supported by NIMH grants.

1959–1969:   Observational and interview clinical studies of hospital patients to assess diagnostic taxonomies at ASH.

1971-present: Constructed separate self-report inventories assessing personality and covariant features of normal, psychiatric, adolescent, medical, preadolescent, college, and I/O populations; for example, to coordinate the interplay of Axis I syndromes and Axis II disorders; to appraise psychological correlates of medical disease complications, treatment, and outcome.

1985-present: Examined the logic and procedures for synthesizing diverse therapeutic orientations and techniques at UM and IASPP.

1987-present: Formulated an evolutionary model for deducing styles of adaptive and maladaptive psychological functioning at UM and IASPP.

1993-present: Built a scientific framework to coordinate the elements comprising clinical psychological research and practice at UM and IASPP.

Some Notable Publications

1967:   *Theories of psychopathology.* Philadelphia: Saunders.

1969:   *Modern psychopathology: A biosocial approach to maladaptive learning and functioning.* Philadelphia: Saunders.

1972:   *Research methods in psychopathology.* New York: Wiley.

1975:   *Medical behavioral science.* Philadelphia: Saunders.

1977:   *Millon Clinical Multiaxial Inventory,* manual (MCMI). Minneapolis: National Computer Systems.

1981:   *Disorders of personality: DSM-III: Axis II.* New York: Wiley.

1982:   *Handbook of clinical health psychology.* New York: Plenum.

1982:   *Millon Adolescent Personality Inventory,* manual (MAPI). Minneapolis: National Computer Systems.

1982:   *Millon Behavioral Health Inventory,* manual (MBHI). Minneapolis: National Computer Systems.

1983:   The *DSM-III:* An insider's perspective. *American Psychologist, 38,* 804–814.

1984:   On the renaissance of personality assessment and personality theory. *Journal of Personality Assessment, 48,* 450–466.

1985:   Refining personality assessments by combining MCMI high point profiles and MMPI codes, Part II: MMPI Code 27/72. *Journal of Personality Assessment, 49,* 5, 501–507.

1985:   Depression and personality. In E. Beckham & W. Leber (eds.). *Depression, treatment, assessment and research.* Homewood, IL: Dow Jones-Irwin.

1986:   *Contemporary directions in psychopathology: Toward the DSM-IV.* New York: Guilford Press.

1987:   On the prevalence and genesis of the borderline personality disorder: A social learning thesis. *Journal of Personality Disorders, 1,* 354–372.

1989:   New diagnostic efficiency statistics: Comparative sensitivity and predictive/prevalence ratio. *Journal of Personality Disorders, 3,* 162–168.

1990:   *Toward a new personology: An evolutionary model.* New York: Wiley.

1991:   Classification in psychopathology: Rationale, alternative & standards. *Journal of Abnormal Psychology, 100,* 245–261.

1991:   Normality: What may we learn from evolutionary theory? In D. Offer and M. Sabshin (eds.) *The diversity of normal behavior.* New York: Basic Books.

1993:   *Millon Adolescent Clinical Inventory,* manual (MACI). Minneapolis: National Computer Systems.

1993:   The five-factor model: Apt or misguided. *Psychological Inquiry, 4,* 104–110.

1993:   Personality disorders: Conceptual distinctions and classification issues. P. Costa and T. Widiger (eds.). *Personality disorders and the five-factor model of personality.* Washington: American Psychological Association Press.

1994:   *Millon Index of Personality Styles,* manual (MIPS). The Psychological Corporation: San Antonio, TX.

1995:   Development of the personality disorders. In D. Ciccetti and D. Cohen (eds.). *Developmental psychopathology.* New York: Wiley.

1996:   An evolutionary theory of personality disorder. In J. Clarkin & M. Lenzenwenger (eds.) *Major theories of personality disorder.* New York: Guilford.

1996:   *Disorders of personality: DSM-IV and beyond.* New York: Wiley.

1996:   *Personality and psychopathology: Building a clinical science* (selected papers). New York: Wiley.

1997:   *The Millon inventories: Clinical and personality assessment.* New York: Guilford.

1999:   *Personality-guided therapy.* New York: Wiley.

1999:   Reflections on psychosynergy: A model for integrating science, theory, classification, assessment and therapy. *Journal of Personality Assessment, 72,* 437–456.

1999:   *Oxford textbook of psychopathology.* New York: Oxford University Press.

2000:   *Personality disorders in modern life.* New York: John Wiley & Sons.

2000:   Reflections on the future of *DSM* Axis II. *Journal of Personality Disorders, 14,* 17–29.

2000:   Toward a new model of integrative psychotherapy: Psychosynergy. *Journal of Integrative Psychotherapy, 10,* 37–53.

2002: Assessment is not enough: The SPA should participate in constructing a comprehensive clinical science of personality. *Journal of Personality Assessment, 78,* 209–218.

2003: *Evolution: A generative source for conceptualizing personality attributes.* In T. Millon & M. Lerner (eds.), *Handbook of psychology, volume V: Personality and social psychology.* Hoboken, NJ: John Wiley & Sons.

2004: *Millon Pre-adolescent Clinical Inventory,* manual (M-PACI). Minneapolis: Pearson Assessment.

2004: *Masters of the Mind.* Hoboken, NJ: John Wiley & Sons.

2004: *Millon Index of Personality Styles: Revised,* manual (MIPS-Rev.) Minneapolis: Pearson Assessment.

Awards/Recognitions

Receiving a Doctor of Science Degree from Dean Hedwig Sloore at the Free University of Brussels, 1994

1994: Doctorate of Science (honorary), Free University of Brussels.

1997: Meritorious Career Award, International Society for the Study of Personality Disorders.

1998: Lifetime Achievement Award, Ontario/Canada Psychological Association.

1998: Distinguished Contributions Award, California Psychological Association.

1998: Lifetime Achievement Award, American Board of Assessment Psychology.

1998: Lifetime Achievement Award, Michigan Psychological Association.

1999: Lifetime Achievement Award, Texas Psychological Association.

1999: Distinguished Scientist Award, The Max Planck Institute of Psychiatry (Munich).

2000: Distinguished Contribution Award, Society for Personality Assessment.

2002: Medical library named "Theodore Millon Professional Library" at Allentown State Hospital, Pennsylvania.

2003: Conference room named "Theodore Millon Seminar Room" at University of Miami Psychology Building.

2003: Distinguished Professional Contributions Award, American Psychological Association.

Enjoying the Good Life in Coral Gables, Florida, 2003

Author Index

Subject Index

Diagnostic and Statistical Manual (DSM)
    (Continued)
    set theoretical approach (hierarchy in
        biological classification), 54–60, 68
    normality and, 232
    organization of mental disorders, 50–53
    organization of personality disorders, 26–27, 51
    proposals for revising, 123–125
    prototype model and, 63, 240–242 (*see also*
        Prototype diagnosis of personality)
    version in progress (*DSM-V*), 425–426
Dialectical behavior therapy (DBT), 301–304, 419,
    520
Diathesis-stress model, 148, 160
Differential diagnosis, 56–57
Differentiation-integration (systems theory),
    157–158, 159
Dilemmas, 519
Dimensional Assessment of Personality Pathology
    (DAPP), 107, 126
Dimensional/categorical systems, 126
Dimensional polarities. *See* Evolutionary-based
    model
Direct observation, 484, 491–492
Disease. *See* Medical diseases
Disintegration products, 191
Domain-focused psychotherapy, role of common
    factors. *See* Common factors approach
Domains of personality, Millon's, 479–483
    behavioral data/level of analysis, 480, 481
    biophysical data/level of analysis, 479, 481
    cognitive style, 481
    expressive acts, 480
    interpersonal conduct, 480–481
    intrapsychic data/level of analysis, 479, 481
    mood/temperament, 482
    morphological organization, 482
    object representations, 481
    phenomenological data/level of analysis,
        479–480, 481
    regulatory mechanisms, 482
    self-image, 481–482
Draw-A-Person (DAP), 318, 320
Dream interpretation, 75, 88–90
Drive theory, 192
"Dynamic" and "cognitive" (history and logical
    relations), 75–77
Dysfunctional personologic system, 520
Dyssomnias, 53
Dysthymic disorder (case study), 251–253

Early onset, course, and outcome in personality
    disorders, 32
Eating disorder, 251–253
Ecological accommodation/modification, 377
Ego defenses, 168
Ego strength, 166–167, 168, 169
Egosyntonic nature of early maladaptive schemas,
    467
Egotistical pattern, 283
Empathy, accurate, 433
Empirically Supported Therapy (EST) rules,
    420–421

Enhancing versus preserving (pleasure-pain), 380
Entropy and negentropy, 158
Epilepsis, 79
Evolution, 3–17
    artificial life, 10
    behavioral genetics, 3, 11–14
    brief history, 4–5
    evolutionary biology, 5–8
        evolution of sex, 7–8
        reigning paradigm, 5–6
        unit of selection, 6–7
    evolutionary ideas and modern psychology, 8–17
    evolutionary psychology, 3
        critiques, 16–17
        defined, 14–16
    genotype-phenotype relations, 9
    molecular genetics and evolution, 8–10
    natural selection, 3
Evolutionary-based model, 12–13
    borderline personality disorder, 295–296
    common factors approach and, 486–493
    dimensions of personality, 376–378
    domain of personality, 479–483
    future perspectives, 532–536
    normal personalities in, 373–378
    personality-guided psychotherapy, 147–148,
        482
    phases/stages and polarities:
        abstraction (thinking-feeling), 377, 381, 533,
            535–536
        adaptation (active-passive), 15–16, 202–203,
            205, 207–208, 376–377, 380, 533, 535
        existence (pleasure-pain), 203–207, 376, 377,
            380, 533, 534
        replication (other-self), 202–203, 205,
            209–211, 377, 380, 533, 535
    political personology, 202–220
    psychopathy, 282–283, 513
    psychosynergy, 147–148
    strategic versus tactical intervention approaches,
        482
    structuring a personologic theory, 533–534
    unified model, 147–148
Existence, aims of (pleasure-pain polarity):
    measuring personality, 376, 377
    motivational dimensions, 380
    personologic theory, 533, 534
    political psychology, 203–207
Expressive acts, 480
Extensional definition, 55
Extraversing versus introversing, 380

"Face of an Angel, The," 310–311
Facet traits, 109–110, 116
Familial and cultural transmission, 159
Five-factor model (FFM), 107, 257–267
    case study, 265–266
    cultural differences, 405–406
    DSM-IV categories and, 257, 258–262
    four-step alternative, 262–265
    NEO-PI-R (composition and diagnostic
        accuracy), 261
    psychopathy and, 281–282